JAMES DICKEY

A Literary Life

MERCER UNIVERSITY PRESS

Endowed by

TOM WATSON BROWN
and
THE WATSON-BROWN FOUNDATION, INC.

JAMES DICKEY

A Literary Life

Gordon Van Ness

MERCER UNIVERSITY PRESS
Macon, Georgia

MUP/ H1021

25 24 23 22   5 4 3 2 1

Books published by Mercer University Press are printed on acid-free paper
that meets the requirements of the American National Standard for
Information Sciences—Permanence of Paper for Printed Library Materials.

Printed and bound in CANADA.

This book is set in Adobe Caslon Pro.

Cover/jacket design by Burt&Burt.

ISBN 978-0-88146-826-7

Cataloging-in-Publication Data is available from the Library of Congress

This book is dedicated to my father and mother.

CONTENTS

ACKNOWLEDGMENTS

My family has accepted my commitment to James Dickey for almost four decades. I have neglected my older children, who no longer ask what I am writing or researching because they have known the answer for years. My younger children retaliated by hiding my Bic Fine Point Pilot pens and by using my yellow legal pads as sketchbooks. My wife, Dawn, encourages me to work in our English flower garden or to ride my ten-speed bicycle.

Clichés of acknowledgment rhetoric are sometimes accurate. This literary biography simply would not have been possible were it not for the generosity of James Dickey's family, friends, colleagues, acquaintances, and former students. They graciously shared memories, reminiscences, and experiences that provided me with the requisite clarity to engage the literary life of a complex writer. Dickey once wrote that no one would ever be able to reconstruct his life because it was more complicated than that of Lawrence of Arabia. Pat Conroy, who had been Dickey's student in the seventies and who himself became an acclaimed novelist, declared in his eulogy that "a whole city of men lived in that vivid, restless country behind James Dickey's transfixing eyes." Dickey himself wrote me on 29 November 1988, admitting, "As to your writing my biography, I would rather have you do it than anyone. But you will be horrified, I can tell you, by the amount of deception, cruelty, sadness, and general havoc I have caused to some of the people in the world. If you want to take this on, it is fine with me. What I have done, I have done. And there have been some good things, too, I like to think." Any biography of Dickey's life would likely be problematic, but these people helped me hold my ground.

No doubt André Maurois was correct in declaring that "the need to express oneself in writing springs from a maladjustment to life, or from an inner conflict, which the adolescent (or grown man) cannot resolve in action." I do not practice psychiatry, but informed statements about Dickey's psychological and emotional mindset can and should be made; they are appropriate if not mandatory. The maladjustment Maurois mentions may account for the compulsion to write, but not for the genius behind it. No one who ever talked to Jim Dickey about literature would be able to explain how the son of a ne'er-do-well lawyer who raised and fought gamecocks and a mother who was listed in the Atlanta social registry could write masterful poetry and best-selling fiction.

I am deeply indebted to the Dickey family, what Dickey himself called "those of the blood, and the heart's-blood," not only for actively supporting my research but also for their patience in answering my many questions. If a biographer's first duty is, as Dickey's literary executor Matthew J. Bruccoli once wrote, "to get things right," Christopher, Kevin, and Bronwen, Dickey's children; Deborah, his second wife; and Carol, his daughter-in-law, provided important information—not so much stories as closely shared moments and memories—that validated and enrichened my portrayal of James Dickey's literary life.

No amount of acknowledgment approaches my gratitude to the libraries and librarians who assisted me in my six-year effort to research, write, and edit this work. Kathy Shoemaker, reference coordinator of the Stuart A. Rose Manuscript, Archives and Rare Book Library of Emory University; as well as Heather Oswald, outreach archivist; and Carrie Hintz, head of Collection Services, provided me unlimited access to the massive holdings in the James Dickey Papers. Elizabeth Sudduth, director of the Irvin Department of Rare Books and Special Collections at the Ernest F. Hollings Library of the University of South Carolina, along with her assistants Matt Hodge and Adam Crosby, allowed me to examine whatever holdings I asked for and spent additional efforts providing me critical sources that invariably improved this literary biography. Brent Roberts, dean of the Greenwood Library of Longwood University, approved every request I made. Dana Owen, interlibrary loan specialist, was crucial to my acquiring copies of James Dickey's earliest reviews, and Jennifer Beach, research services librarian, facilitated my requests for additional searches. Tom Camden, head of Special Collections of Washington and Lee University, provided me copies of recently donated materials even as I was vetting the copyedited work, enabling me to more fully explore who Dickey was.

My greatest academic debt is to Don Greiner, who read and commented on individual chapters and who subsequently critiqued the entire manuscript. His infamous red pens only bettered my efforts by making salient observations, requiring me to provide additional explanation. Those pens also reduced the number of adverbs I used and suggested that I substitute more pronouns in lieu of proper names. In no small way, Don offered his own experiences with Dickey, whom he considered a close friend and colleague. In so doing, he too helped me "get it right." He has my utmost respect and gratitude.

Stephanie Sonnefeld Stinn not only shared memories about her two "power lunches" with Dickey, Don Greiner, and Ben Franklin, providing a viewpoint not apparent to older attendant faculty, but also poignantly detailed the final time she saw Dickey when he was frail and in failing health. Her perspective, in its gracious understanding and clarity, provided a real and abiding sense of who Dickey was to students. Julie Bloemeke, too, was indispensable, providing extensive details related to Dickey's final classes; she was there. Her notes testify to the seriousness with which Dickey undertook teaching literature. For his memorial service on the Green Horseshoe, she was asked by university administrative officials to read his well-anthologized poem "The Heaven of Animals." She did so with a profound and haunting reverence. The assembled crowd listened in perfect silence that served as tribute both to her effort and to Dickey himself.

Joyce Pair, who founded the *James Dickey Newsletter* and who died in 2015, published my scholarship on Dickey while I was still in the doctoral program at the University of South Carolina; she believed. Ken Autrey, a fellow student and classmate of mine at USC and a Dickey aficionado, shared his thoughts, experiences, and notes. The last time we were able to get together, he issued me an injunction as I was literally leaving the house: "Write that book." His words hovered over me every time I sat down at my desk.

The following are only some of the people who assisted me during the years I worked on Dickey: Jon Alter, Judy Baughman, John Boggs, Mrs. Earl Bradley, Craig Brandhorst, Ward Briggs, Ron Buchanan, Janet Lee Burnet, Keen Butterworth, David Cowart, Dan Dahlquist, Doug Dalton, Carol Fairman, Paula Feldman, Ben Franklin, George Geckle, Bari Goff, Tim Guthrie, Henry Hart, Herb Hartsook, David Havird, Mike James, Marian Janssen, Gary Kerley, Robert Kirschten, Gary Leising, James Mann, Marietta Mathews, Robert McIlwaine, Haywood Moxley, Joe Parris Jr., Jim Plath, Margaret Renkl, Meg Richards, Patrick Scott, Jes Simmons, Dave Smith, Randy Smith, Ernest Suarez, Mike Taylor, Nancy Lewis Tuten, Sue Brannon Walker, Annie Wright.

Finally, Marc Jolley, director of Mercer University Press, deserves my deepest gratitude for his deliberate willingness to publish *James Dickey: A Literary Life*. Both his graciousness and his professionalism demand my respect. That we share an intense interest in the French existential philosophers as well as literature only heightens my sense of his importance in today's publishing world. If Dickey's career is resurrected more than twenty years after his death, Marc's decision to publish this book will have been a large contributing factor.

I first encountered James Dickey in 1971 while attending Hampden-Sydney College in Virginia when I read his poems in a modern American poetry course. I was intrigued. Later, when the director of my master's thesis at the University of Richmond suggested that I consider Dickey's *The Zodiac* for a topic, my work was determined. My father and mother extravagantly supported their oldest son's obsession.

Dickey's life was indeed complicated, and I was never James Boswell to Dickey's Samuel Johnson, sensing that a measured distance provided objectivity. The whole truth about a writer can never be known, but his words endure, and they merit the highest attention.

PERMISSIONS

James Dickey's previously unpublished material courtesy of the heirs and estate of James Dickey and Raines & Raines.

The following libraries granted permission to publish from their holdings:

James Dickey Papers, Stuart A. Rose Manuscript, Archives, and Rare Book Library, Emory University, Atlanta, Georgia;

James Dickey Papers, Irvin Department of Rare Books and Special Collections, University of South Carolina Libraries, Columbia, South Carolina;

Matthew J. and Arlyn Bruccoli Collection of James Dickey, Irvin Department of Rare Books and Special Collections, University of South Carolina Libraries, Columbia, South Carolina;

Donald J. and Ellen Greiner Collection of James Dickey, Irvin Department of Rare Books and Special Collections, University of South Carolina Libraries, Columbia, South Carolina.

Ward Briggs Collection of James Dickey, Special Collections, Washington and Lee University, Lexington, Virginia.

"No one will ever be able to reconstruct my life. It is more complicated and more unknowable than that of Lawrence of Arabia."

Sorties

Who has told you what discoveries
There are, along the stressed blank
Of a median line? From it, nothing

Can finally fall. Like a spellbinder's pass
A tense placid principle continues

Over it, and when you follow you have the drift,

The balance of many compass needles
Verging to the pole.

"Basics"

"The thousand variations of one song."

Buckdancer's Choice

"Things go well here, though there is always a sense of pressure. But I was born for combat, for the struggle, and would be lost without it. He who ever strives upward, Goethe says: Ah! Him can we save!"

Letter to Gordon Van Ness

"But there are certainties that have been won from darkness, or that the darkness flung us. Chief among them is Location. In the unblocked on-come and crossfire of shining, the thriving needles, the far-storming and visible centers, sending fixedly and freely; in the frail raw sleeting of light, the incessant snowing of cross-stitched angles, the infinite spaces that so frightened Pascal, the turning mills of incandescent gas, the parabolas and planes of trajectory, you can understand without contradiction that there is a place which the universe cannot deny you. Toward where you are, the whole of it, alive with angles and exact, is pointing, and it will find you where you stand, and will—yet always with its wilderness arrogance—confirm you just as surely as it does the lion and the comet, and bear you out, and on."

"Cosmic Deliverance"

Heat makes this, heat makes any
Word: human lungs,
Human lips. Not like eternity, which, naked, every time
Will call on lightning
To say it all: No after
Or before. We try for that

And fail. Our voice
Fails, but for an instant
Is like the other; breath alone
That came as though humanly panting
From far back, in unspeakably beautiful

Empty space

And struck: at just this moment
Found the word "golden."

"Word"

The Dickey home at 166 West Wesley Road in Atlanta, Georgia.
Courtesy Joyce Pair

James Dickey's mother, Maibelle.
*Courtesy Stuart A. Rose Manuscript, Archives,
and Rare Book Library, Emory University*

Dickey's father, Eugene.
Courtesy Stuart A. Rose Manuscript, Archives,
and Rare Book Library, Emory University

James Dickey's high school senior portrait, 1941.
Courtesy Bronwen Dickey

James Dickey running the high hurdles
at North Fulton High School, 1940.
Courtesy Bronwen Dickey

James Dickey during high school football practice, 1941.
Courtesy Bronwen Dickey

James Dickey in his Army Air Force uniform, ca. 1945.
*Courtesy Stuart A. Rose Manuscript, Archives,
and Rare Book Library, Emory University*

Maxine Dickey, ca. 1940s.
*Courtesy Stuart A. Rose Manuscript, Archives,
and Rare Book Library, Emory University*

James Dickey and his family in Venice, Italy, 1962.
Courtesy Stuart A. Rose Manuscript, Archives,
and Rare Book Library, Emory University

James Dickey at Stonehenge near Salisbury,
Wiltshire, England, 1962.
Courtesy Stuart A. Rose Manuscript, Archives,
and Rare Book Library, Emory University

James Dickey playing guitar in Italy, 1962.
Courtesy Kevin Dickey

James Dickey reading in Italy, 1962.
Courtesy Kevin Dickey

James Dickey's family arriving in New York City from their travel
in Europe on his Guggenheim fellowship, 1962.
Courtesy Stuart A. Rose Manuscript, Archives,
and Rare Book Library, Emory University

James Dickey and his family driving
to Portland, Oregon, late 1962.
Courtesy Kevin Dickey

Christopher Dickey and his younger brother Kevin
by the swimming pool in the San Fernando Valley house
on Balboa Boulevard, 1965.
Courtesy Kevin Dickey

James Dickey lecturing at Reed College, 1963.
Courtesy Bronwen Dickey

James Dickey playing guitar while his son Christopher reads,
Portland, Oregon, 1964.
Courtesy Bronwen Dickey

James Dickey reading at the University of Texas
at El Paso, 12 May 1967.
Courtesy Jes Simmons

James Dickey talking with Eugene McCarthy,
Washington, DC, late 1960s.
Courtesy Kevin Dickey

James Dickey as Consultant in Poetry at the Library of Congress,
Leesburg, Virginia, late 1960s.
Courtesy Kevin Dickey

James Dickey on an archery range, late 1960s.
Courtesy Bronwen Dickey

Deborah Dickey, Joan Mondale, Rosalynn Carter, and James
Dickey in Washington, DC, 1977.
Courtesy Bronwen Dickey

James and Deborah Dickey meeting President José Lopéz
Portillo and his wife in Mexico, 1977.
Courtesy Bronwen Dickey

James Dickey, his son Christopher, and grandson J.B. "Tucky" Dickey, late 1970s/early1980s.
Courtesy Carol Dickey

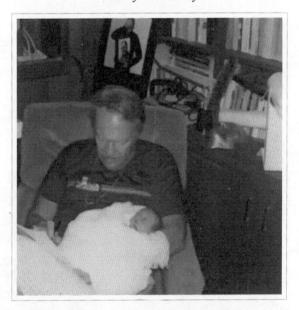

James Dickey, editing, with his daughter Bronwen, 1981.
Courtesy Bronwen Dickey

James Dickey with wife Deborah and daughter Bronwen.
Courtesy Bronwen Dickey

Dickey playing guitar at his home in Columbia,
South Carolina, mid-1980s.
Courtesy Bronwen Dickey

James Dickey outside his home in Columbia, South Carolina, 1987.
Courtesy Gordon Van Ness

William A. Bake and James Dickey at Oxford Bookstore on a
promotional tour for *Wayfarer*, October 1988.
Courtesy Joyce Pair

Lewis King with James Dickey in Atlanta following
the latter's speech to the South Atlantic Modern
Language Association, 14 November 1991.
Courtesy Joyce Pair

Al Braselton, James Dickey, and Joyce Pair at the Hyatt Regency
in Atlanta during the South Atlantic Modern Language
Association convention, November 1991.
Courtesy Joyce Pair

Don Greiner, James Dickey, and Ben Franklin at a "power lunch"
outside the Faculty House on the Green Horseshoe of the
University of South Carolina, 1993.
Courtesy Don Greiner

James Dickey visiting the grave of Lead Belly (Huddie Ledbetter) near Shreveport, Louisiana, where Dickey had received the John Williams Corrington Award for Literary Excellence, April 1993.

Courtesy David Havird

James Dickey's gravestone at All Saints Waccamaw Church
on Pawleys Island, South Carolina.
Courtesy Julie Bloemeke

JAMES DICKEY

A Literary Life

INTRODUCTION

In his October 1967 essay titled "The Difficulties of Being Major: The Poetry of Robert Lowell and James Dickey," published in *The Atlantic Monthly*, Peter Davison assessed the state of American poetry following World War II and declared that of all poets fifty years of age or under, only Robert Lowell and James Dickey could be considered "great." Today, however, while the literary reputation of Lowell remains firmly established, that of Dickey is almost nonexistent. Professors do not teach classes about him, and graduate students in literature rarely read his poems. Lowell, whose 1959 collection *Life Studies* finally enabled poets to escape the critical dicta of an entrenched modernism and establish their own poetic identities, has received significant scrutiny from critics such as Ian Hamilton, Paul Mariani, Jeffrey Meyers, and William J. Martz; their insightful biographies and scholarly studies have extended understanding of Lowell's life and his place in twentieth-century American poetry. Yet Dickey remains particularly problematic. Since his death in 1997, Henry Hart's thorough but misguided biography and Casey Clabough's critical examination of Dickey's novels remain the only book-length studies. Although Dickey's collected poems and correspondence as well as his class lectures and unfinished last poems have been published, no major critical appraisals have attempted to place his literary career in perspective, examine his changing "motions," or critique the development of his thematic concerns explicitly announced in *Into the Stone* in 1960. More importantly, Dickey's approach to poetry, specifically his use of personae and manipulation of form and language to reinforce dramatic effectiveness, still needs exploration. A half century later, Davison's statement remains true, but the question as to why Dickey's literary descent was so pronounced, so definitive, and so persistent demands explanation. As Ernest Suarez correctly noted, "The dramatic rise of Dickey's literary reputation in the sixties and his equally abrupt fall from critical grace after the early seventies is the most distinctive feature of his career. How is it possible, within less than ten years, for a writer to go from being hailed as the most important poet of his time to being virtually ignored in assessments of post-World War II poetic history?" (*James Dickey and the Politics of Canons* 1).

James Dickey was born in 1923 in Buckhead, Georgia, on Ground-hog's Day. A quiet, introspective child who played marbles, skated, and read pulp fiction, hiding his sensitivities and academic talents so as to appear "one of the boys," he grew into a callow teen interested in sports and girls. He discovered poetry during his combat service in the Pacific during World War II, avidly and unapologetically reading books between bombing missions, and writing to his parents, who had hoped he would become a businessman or an engineer, that his only interest was writing. During the fifties and sixties, he became a poet who, while raised in the South, transcended the limitations of any such regional label, winning the National Book Award and becoming the poet laureate of the United States. Crisscrossing the country, he barnstormed for poetry, reading to capacity audiences. In 1970 he published *Deliverance*, a best-selling fiction that became an award-winning motion picture the following year. Then his literary career faltered. He wrote large coffee-table books for general consumption, luxury editions that appealed to specialized audiences, and occasional poems, all designed to make money and all critical failures. None displayed the bold imagery and transcendence of his early works. His career seemingly disappeared.

Dickey was a study in contrasts, a complicated personality who once stated, "No one will ever be able to reconstruct my life. It is more complicated and more unknowable than that of Lawrence of Arabia" (*Sorties* 89). He exaggerated his football and track skills, enhanced his archery and tennis talents, misspoke about his hunting and canoeing adventures, and fabricated stories about his combat experiences in the 418th Night Fighter Squadron during World War II. Simply stated, he lied. He told close friends, fellow writers, and academic colleagues, for example, that he had been a successful Clemson halfback and would have played in the National Football League had not a physical injury precluded it. He wrote to James Wright on 3 October 1958 that he had finished Vanderbilt on a track scholarship and set a high-hurdles record for the South in 1947 at the Cotton Carnival Meet at Memphis. "I think the record is still standing," he stated, "though I am not sure" (*One Voice*, I 282–84). Neither statement was factual. Yet the truth is that the more Dickey deliberately created a myth about himself, the more readers and critics believed—and relished—the myth. He enlarged that myth, moreover, not only with the many masks he created for himself but also with the personae that readers equated with Dickey himself. Yet the public myth diverted attention from the private man and his literary work.

That is not to say, however, that Dickey lied to himself; he always knew where the lies stopped and truth began. He flew thirty-eight combat missions over thousands of miles of enemy territory and empty sea; he strafed, bombed, acted as bomber escort, and provided cover for landing forces and convoy attacks. He accrued 403 hours of flying time, 120 of which involved combat. Commissioned a lieutenant while overseas, he received four medals, including the Asiatic-Pacific Campaign Medal with seven battle stars, as well as two combat ribbons. Yet such an admirable war record was not enough in his mind, at least not for a poet. Despite being a flight navigator, he verbally promoted himself to a pilot who had flown a hundred missions and persuaded audiences to believe it. Once, he related the story of how he had frantically dodged a swarm of Japanese planes while in a dogfight over the Pacific and how his tail gunner had watched pieces of fuselage fly off as enemy gunfire raked the plane. He told his son Christopher he had been shot down over Borneo, bailed out over the ocean, and been miraculously rescued by a submarine (*Summer of Deliverance* 54). In the sixties and seventies, as he sought first to establish and then enhance his literary reputation and his role as poet, he continually embellished both the stories he told and the public perception of who he was, cultivating what John Updike in a 7 November 2004 letter to Don Greiner called his "aggressive flamboyance." He wore a white, ten-gallon hat and played six- and twelve-string guitars. He collected knives, wristwatches, voice recorders, and hunting bows. He built walls of books in every place he lived. At his house in Columbia, South Carolina, he kept a typewriter in every room. He drank heavily. Brilliant dialogue often degenerated into drunken performance. He sought notoriety. "That, in fact, is his problem," he knowingly wrote of himself in his 1969 essay "Barnstorming for Poetry," "the living-up-to it, the giving them what they want, or might be expected to feel entitled to from a poet aside from the poems themselves" (*Babel to Byzantium* 250). Among his papers at Emory University are notes Dickey made regarding the essay's composition. "The whole thing should turn," he declared, "on the poet's accepting and taking on an elaborate disguise (guitar, and so on): how he becomes this, how his 'ordinary personality' will not suit. And so the whole thing should be a kind of serio-comic charade typifying the poet's actual role in things," a statement that reflects both Dickey's love of masks and the deep insecurities that necessitated their use. Joyce Carol Oates recognized this complexity when she wrote in 1974, "Even more than Whitman, Dickey contains multitudes."

Once, after reading an interview in which he claimed to have run bootleg whiskey down from the Georgia hills in a souped-up automobile, I asked him why he had invented such a tale: "You never did anything like that." "It's all part of the creative process," Dickey said, looking me straight in the eyes. He believed, and believed absolutely, in what he termed "the creative possibilities of the lie." "I think lying, with luck sublimely, is what the creative man does," he had written in 1971. "Picasso once said something to the effect that art is a lie which makes us see the truth, or which makes truth better than it is. That is very much my feeling. When you see this, then you can act in your own way. And this is what the creative man does; this should be his sovereign privilege because the province of the poem is the poet's, and in it he is God" (*Self-Interviews* 32). Christopher Dickey later remembered, "My father came to believe that you could be a god, that you could, through poetry, through language, get in touch with experience and understanding of experience that you could not approach any other way. He really did think that poetry was the finest calling of a man or woman" ("Poems and Memories of James Dickey"). Dickey maintained this attitude throughout his life, admonishing his final class of students not to be constrained by facts: "Invent is the guts of it. 'To invent.' You can say as much as you like with stuff you know. But don't be confined to it. Don't think about honesty—honestly—don't think about telling the truth. Because poets are not trying to tell the truth.... They are trying to show God a few things he maybe didn't think of. It takes us to supply that." Yet Dickey did not limit his lying to his poems. He lied to interviewers, critics, other writers, friends, and family until one wondered whether he not so much knew them as imagined them. Pondering Dickey's complex life, Pat Conroy, the celebrated novelist who had been Dickey's student, speaking at the memorial service following Dickey's death, declared, "A whole city of men lived in that vivid, restless country behind James Dickey's transfixing eyes."

Even Christopher struggled to understand who his father was. In July 1996, as he attempted to overcome twenty years of estrangement, he and his father visited Litchfield, the elegant country club community on Pawleys Island, South Carolina, where Dickey had bought a home with monies earned by his novel *Deliverance*. They talked; Chris asked questions. "You're a journalist," Dickey said, "so the truth is important. Remember this, as if these were my last words. No matter what anybody said. Remember what I was—to you" (*Summer of Deliverance* 27). Dickey's reading tours only enhanced his larger-than-life persona such that the public

4

believed that the persona was synonymous with Dickey himself. "Long before *Deliverance*," Chris wrote in his memoir, "my father had begun to make himself up," concluding, "[h]e would not tolerate for a second the world as it was" (30). Indeed, Dickey agreed with Nietzsche: "No artist tolerates reality," which explains his statement that "one gets so *tired* of the truth. One wants to make another kind" (*Sorties* 103).

How does one explain the varied incidents in Dickey's life that suggest different selves? He had written his first wife, Maxine, in 1953 that he desired to create a new kind of poetry. "I have written some fair poems," he stated, "but no really good ones this summer. But, in each, I am nearer what I want: each one has more of the fast, athletic, imaginative, and muscular vigor that I want to identify as my particular kind of writing. I am learning how to do it" (*One Voice*, I 192–93). By 1970, middle-aged and successful, he had accomplished the muscular, virile poetry he had wanted, but it was no longer enough. *Deliverance* became a best seller, and the following year the movie, starring Burt Reynolds and Jon Voight, was released and nominated for an Academy Award as best picture of the year. Audiences wanted Dickey to live it; people wanted the show. *Playboy* magazine profiled Dickey in its May 1971 issue, and the title said it all. "The Stuff of Poetry," the headline read, is "a little guitar picking, fast-water canoeing, booze, archery and weight-lifting—if you happen to be James Dickey in search of deliverance." Yet no one knew the quiet, sensitive boy who believed that his own birth had depended on the death of his older brother Gene. No one knew the high school senior who, running in the 1940 North Georgia Interscholastic Conference, had gone all out and won the hurdles, despite hitting the final stick. With the tape around his neck, he had smashed into the spectators and bowled over a child who then lay on the grass, eyes crying and nose bleeding. "I went over to the little boy," so Dickey later claimed in his 1976 essay "Night Hurdling," "raised him up in my arms, wiped the blood from his nose, tried to comfort him, and kissed him." "In memory, now," he concluded, "that was the best moment I ever had out of sports" (*Night Hurdling* 184). No one knew how, even later, barnstorming for poetry in El Paso, Texas, in 1967, Dickey had sat down with his host Joe Simmons and, after playing the drums that belonged to Simmons's nine-year-old son Jes, had shown the little boy rudimentary guitar chords and taught him an old-time blues song. Missing his own sons, he gave the child a good-night kiss.

Following the death of his first wife, Maxine, in October 1976, Dickey had remarried in December. At fifty-eight years old and now with a five-year-old daughter, Bronwen, he had taught her in summer 1986 to swim in a neighbor's pool. No one knew how he and Bronwen would wake early and watch the sun rise above Lake Katharine at their home in Columbia. When it cleared the horizon, they would both shout together, "Fireball mail!" In their imaginative play, he and Bronwen had founded Whitewings Aviation. With Bronwen as president and Dickey as chief engineer and test pilot, they spent hours putting together various model airplanes on the kitchen table, planes made of a thick card stock, with names such as the Highwind, the Familiar, the Cirrus, the Elliptic, and the Dolphin, successfully test-flying them in the rolling spaces of the front yard. Dickey became, he said, an expert in glue. No one believed Dickey when in candid conversations and interviews, as he confronted his own mortality, he admitted that he had been a coward all his life.

Dickey himself seemed uncertain of what role he was playing. "I have self-dramatized myself out of myself, into something else. What was that other thing I have left?" (74), he wrote in *Sorties*, his 1971 collection of journals and essays. Crisscrossing the country in the sixties to promote poets and poetry, he thought to himself, "'Just be yourself.'... Ah, but *what* self? The self he has become on this trip bears little relation to the self he left at home in the mind of, say, his wife" (*Babel to Byzantium* 250). What he knew, however, was that the poem and the poet were inextricably linked. "I have never been able to dissociate the poem from the poet," he wrote in *Self-Interviews* (1970). "I really don't believe in [T. S.] Eliot's theory of autotelic art, in which the poem has nothing to do with the man who wrote it. I think that's the most absolute rubbish!" (24). In one of his early essays, "The Self as Agent," first published in 1968, Dickey elaborated on this interconnection. "Every poem written," he said, "—and particularly those which make use of a figure designated in the poem as 'I'— is both an exploration and an invention of identity" (*Sorties* 155). By connecting with each "self," Dickey asserted, the poet further understood who he was or who he might become; he created or discovered, in other words, his identity, driven by the need to "encompass and explore each of the separate, sometimes related, sometimes unrelated personalities that inhabit him, as they inhabit us all..., confront[ing] and dramatiz[ing] parts of himself that otherwise would not have surfaced" (161). Understanding Dickey's poetry therefore necessitates understanding Dickey himself.

Dickey's endeavors to promote poetry generally and himself specifically, frequently by also attacking fellow poets, resulted in ad hominem attacks by reviewers and critics who were more intent on criticizing

Dickey's personality than in examining his work. Condemning Dickey's self-promotion, they failed to admit their own agendas or the pervasiveness of such conduct in all professions. For example, Robert Bly's now infamous review, "The Collapse of James Dickey," published in the spring 1967 issue of *The Sixties*, labeled Dickey's *Buckdancer's Choice* (1965), which had won the National Book Award, "repulsive," and continued, "The subject of the poems is power, and the tone of the book is gloating—a gloating about power over others." He concluded by calling Dickey "a huge blubbery poet, pulling out Southern language in long strings, like taffy, a toady to the government, supporting all movements toward Empire, a sort of Georgia cracker Kipling." Dana Gioia, who admired Yvor Winters's formalism, similarly attacked Dickey's 1992 volume *Puella*, asserting that it was "an unqualified disaster," and accused Dickey of meaningless linguistic frivolity and strained effects that obscured the general sense of the poems. "It takes a certain genius to write this badly," Gioia sarcastically declared, and concluded, "The more one scrutinizes the language of *Puella*, the more it seems improvised and approximate, nothing but pure, old-fashioned sound and fury." Indeed, after the success of *Poems 1957–1967*, critics largely dismissed all Dickey's poetry, arguing that it lacked the brilliance of his "early motion." Typical of the early critical praise had been George Lensing's observation of the Whitmanesque affirmation in these poems, Dickey's ability to enter nature and participate in "a common vitality," a growing spirituality that enlarged his identity. During the intervening decades, however, Dickey not only lost or abandoned that afflatus, but also focused only on projects that promised money. His seeming inability to discover new poetic directions, at least partly owing to his increasing alcoholism, also led to poems written to order, assignment writing for Jimmy Carter ("The Strength of Fields") and about Vince Lombardi ("For the Death of Lombardi"), the Apollo moon mission ("Apollo"), and Justice William Douglas ("The Eagle's Mile"), none of which equaled his impressive early efforts. As R. S. Gwynn wrote in the winter 1994 issue of *The Sewanee Review*, "If a poet does not produce any work of unquestioned merit in a quarter of a century, no amount of spin control can save his reputation from a downward spiral" (154–56).

Gwynn's critical assessment discounted not only *The Eye-Beaters, Blood, Victory, Madness, Buckhead and Mercy* (1968), *The Zodiac* (1976), and *The Strength of Fields* (1979), volumes Dickey considered his "central motion," but also *Puella* (1982) and *The Eagle's Mile* (1990). Dickey had particularly hoped the latter two volumes would reestablish his literary ascendency. Critics, however, dismissed these works, favoring instead his early poetry despite Dickey's stated belief in and commitment to poetic experimentation. In an early notebook entry written in 1952, Dickey wrote, "To write (poetry) in ways that are difficult for you and alien to you is one of the major tools of exploration one can have. Cocteau: 'Learn what you can do well and then don't do it.' You can write any kind of poetry in any form. To assume the mask the poem requires" (Van Ness, *Striking In* 129). Almost twenty years later, critical of such poets as Richard Wilbur and William Stafford, he was still insisting on poetic experimentation as an inviolable principle, declaring, "One of the troubles of most of the poets of my generation, one of the reasons they seem unable to develop beyond a certain point, is that they don't *think* enough about what they are doing and about what they are trying to do, and about what they hope to do in the future." "That is the main trouble," he stated, "the sense of habitual dispatch. That is not only, in the end, tiresome, but can even come to seem a kind of poetic reflex" (*Sorties* 26, 45).

Even Christopher Dickey stated that *Poems 1957–1967* "defined the best my father could do" (*Summer of Deliverance* 148). Yet studies of *The Eye-Beaters* fail to critique the gapped lines and stanzaic form that distinguish these poems from his "early motion." No studies of *The Strength of Fields* examine either the volume's thematic concerns or the translations, what Dickey termed "Free-Flight Improvisations," that constitute more than half the poems. None have fully explored in *The Zodiac*, for example, the importance both of the poem's time frame and its structure as determined by the Zodiac poet's growth—his understanding of time and space or the nature and limitations of language and personal identity. None have analyzed a far larger and broader series of concerns, including references to the paintings of Wassily Kandinsky, the role of Martin Luther in European history, and the beliefs of Pythagoras. In *Puella*, critics have overlooked the volume's challenging techniques, for the images the persona conveys depict an emotional complex inherent in certain narrative points of time that increasingly seem timeless, that is to say mythical, presenting the simultaneous penetration of worlds—male and female, past and present, transcendent and physical. Finally, with *The Eagle's Mile*, the last volume Dickey published before his death, critics have failed to detail its thematic arrangement, a juxtaposition of two points of view, Platonic and Aristotelian, the ideal and the ephemeral.

The last time I saw James Dickey, he was in his Columbia home suffering from fibrosis of the lungs, which had developed independently from the liver problems that had earlier resulted in severe jaundice. Connected now to a respirator from which all the oxygen in the world did not seem enough to fill his embattled lungs, he was sitting in a corduroy-covered armchair, surrounded by towers of books, drawn from more than seventeen thousand on his home shelves, the personal library of a major American poet who never stopped reading and writing, a sort of kingdom of the mind. "I came to poetry," he had written in "The Poet Turns on Himself" in 1968, "with no particular qualifications. I had begun to suspect, however, that there is a poet—or a kind of poet—buried in every human being like Ariel in his tree, and that the people whom we are pleased to call poets are only those who have felt the need and contrived the means to release the spirit from its prison" (*Babel to Byzantium* 279). This idea of "breaking out," a sense of what is or could be possible, was important to Dickey and explains his need to continually explore in his poetry new forms, new uses, of language.

In *Sorties*, Dickey admitted, "I have been drunk, more or less, for about the last twenty-five years. Everything I remember is colored at least to some extent by alcohol" (84). This fact undoubtedly contributed to the decline critics perceived following the publication of *Deliverance*. So, too, did the financial windfall that resulted from the novel, which arguably undercut or distorted Dickey's desire to excel poetically, dissipating his creative and critical faculties. Unquestionably, he fabricated stories about himself, and his outlandish, even Rabelaisian, behavior distracted from his literary accomplishment and suggests complex emotional and psychological forces. Dickey understood this. "I can't imagine anyone going through such agony and terror," he wrote. "I am not what I seem to the world to be; a fine-looking fellow in the prime of life, big enough and strong enough to do almost anything he wants to do, a talented writer and the rest. No; I am a haunted artist like the others. I know what the monsters know, and shall know more, and more than any of them if I can survive myself for a little while longer" (*Sorties* 73). Yet, while Dickey's poetry must be viewed within the context of who he was, it is the work itself by which his place in American literature should be judged.

Dickey's artistic method involved invention generated by and from personal experiences from which he permitted his imagination to "create" a narrative or lyrical moment that might, but might not, correspond to what actually had occurred. He argued that any poem that arose from such fabrication also reinvented the truth and discovered some previously unknown aspect of his identity. His self was thereby enlarged. It was a process by which he was, in effect, continually bringing the world, and himself, into existential existence. As Dickey wrote in "The Self as Agent," "During the writing of the poem, the poet comes to feel that he is releasing into its proper field of response a portion of himself that he has never really understood" (157). In presenting a writer's life, professional biographers usually focus on the chronological development of events, a cause-and-effect linear approach that portrays how a writer became who he was. Henry Hart in *James Dickey: The World as a Lie* essentially presents a story by recounting the major and minor experiences that shaped, molded, and guided Dickey's life, beginning with Dickey's ancestors and his birth, early education, and adolescence, and then describing his combat as a navigator in the US Army Air Forces, his graduate school years, and his careers in advertising, teaching, and writing before his death in 1997. Hart, for example, discusses Dickey's experiences in World War II, quoting from the letters and poems the poet wrote during the conflict, in order to understand Dickey's viewpoint at those moments, and later depicting at the corresponding point in the chronology the later poems with commentary on how his ideas developed. The biographical dots are thereby connected linearly. Adolescent insecurities, contradictions, and jealousies, Hart shows, led to Dickey's flagrant exaggerations in adulthood. Hart's methodology, however, has throughout it an underlying pejorative thesis: Dickey lied not only in what he wrote but also in what he told others. The argument ignores both Dickey's commitment to allow the imagination to turn what William James termed "the cube of reality"—thereby making the world truer than the mere "truth" of facts—and the fact that "lying" is what a creative writer does.

By contrast, *James Dickey: A Literary Life* presents Dickey through the context of what he wrote—the poems, novels, and criticism that reveal who he essentially was and those principles that he valued. The linear presentation of the experiences that generated those works is not eschewed; indeed, it provides the general framework for this biography. However, the biography also centers itself on the varied aspects that constitute Dickey's life and career—his not only being a son, husband, and father but also an athlete, army air forces navigator, teacher, advertiser, critic, poet, novelist, bow hunter and canoeist, and the other personae—and how these "personalities" resulted from, while also shaping, his life experiences and his writings. In other words, this biography approaches Dickey's life through the magnifying lens of literature, whether in terms of Dickey's teaching it, reading it, promoting it, or producing it. It suggests that time within a literary-biographical sphere should not necessarily have to correspond only to the progress of a calendar. Dickey had many occupations, created masks both to enlarge his identity and protect his heightened sensitivities, wrote poems whose personae he encouraged readers to equate with himself, and mythologized his own life. This complexity necessitates the shape of this book, a development based not only on chronology (I have also provided readers with a comprehensive chronology) but also on his literary life, what he focused on as he moved from persona to persona.

This methodology is particularly appropriate given Dickey's abiding interest both in the mythological structuring of what he wrote and in the nature of time itself. That interest grew out of his service in the Pacific, where he first encountered indigenous peoples. Later he studied their cultural belief systems while at Vanderbilt University, reading extensively (and by his own admission randomly) among the shelves such mythologists and anthropologists as Joseph Campbell, Bronislaw Malinowski, and Paul Radin. The violence and brutality of the war itself had convinced him that modern society offered no sustaining beliefs, no redemptive ideals, by which life could be lived; indigenous tribes, whether of Australia, New Guinea, the Philippines, or the American West, suggested new possibilities by which to achieve closer connections to nature. Then, too, modernists such as Ezra Pound, T. S. Eliot, and William Carlos Williams had poetically explored and examined past civilizations, noting their important values and their historical heroes when compared to the present and to what Eliot termed its "hollow men." Pound, for example, had decried Western civilization in "Hugh Selwyn Mauberley" as "an old bitch gone in the teeth." Eliot, moreover, had questioned time itself, writing in "Burnt Norton," "Time past and time present / Are both perhaps present in time future, / And time future contained in time past. / If all time is eternally present, / All time is unredeemable." Myth and the simultaneity of all time became important ideas to Dickey.

As Dickey attempted to establish himself according to the New Criticism that defined and promoted these modernists, he embraced the idea of mythology and its rituals that attempted to reach beyond themselves to the transcendent. In his poetry, he initially re-presented biblical and classical stories, such as the Fall of Adam and Eve and the descent of Orpheus into Hades. Soon, however, he placed himself into such myths as the Resurrection ("Sleeping Out at Easter" and "The Vegetable King"), both based on his own personal experiences. "I was able to use a myth peculiar to me and at the same time make it something that could happen to anybody," Dickey wrote in *Self-Interviews*. "I was working both semi-consciously and quite consciously toward mythologizing my own factual experience. It's not that my experience lent itself more to mythology than anybody else's, but that my own life lent itself to being mythologized as *much* as anybody else's" (85).

Particularly influential among Dickey's readings at Vanderbilt was Campbell's *The Hero with a Thousand Faces*, which argued that all myths are a variation of the "Monomyth" and posits the belief that the hero is "the man or the woman who has been able to battle past his personal and historical limitations" (19) who undergoes a search distinguished by three distinct stages: "Departure, Initiation, and Return." Arnold van Gennep, an anthropologist whose *Rites of Passage* Dickey had also read, described these stages as "a separation from the world, a penetration to a source of power, and a life-enhancing return." In so doing, Campbell argued, that individual becomes "Master of the Two Worlds" and thereby achieves the "Freedom to Live." Myth, moreover, by definition suggests a space that defies time, that indeed is timeless, a transcendent place where the mythic hero in his larger awareness connects with universal or cosmological forces beyond the reach of ordinary men and women. The more Dickey read about myth, the more interested he became in time and timelessness. In 1964 he discovered J. B. Priestley's *Man and Time*, an extended essay in which Priestley explored in depth the various theories and beliefs about the nature of time. The book became among the most influential ones he ever read, particularly as Dickey aged. Priestley wrote, "My personal belief, then, is that our lives are not contained within passing time, a single track along which we hurry to oblivion. We exist in more than one dimension of Time....We are something better than creatures carried on that single time track to the slaughter-house. We have a larger portion of Time—and more and stranger adventures with it" (306). Dickey concurred. He had come to believe not only that chronological time led to loneliness and isolation as well as a diminishment of physical, mental, and creative capabilities, but also that there existed something greater and more enduring in what Priestley distinguished as Time. Priestley's view offered a movement from a one-sided ego to a larger, more broadly based Self, providing Dickey with the psychological/philosophical framework for his poetry.

This larger conception of Time, where past, present, and future exist simultaneously, expanded Dickey's sense of what poetry might also offer— the possibility of intimate inclusivity with the world itself, a vital and abiding connection with Otherness. In his poem "The Heaven of Animals," for example, the speaker imagines an afterlife for nature's predators and prey: "Having no souls, they have come, / Anyway, beyond their knowing. / Their instincts wholly bloom / And they rise. / ... / These hunt, as they have done, / But with claws and teeth grown perfect, / More deadly than they can believe." Their spring from tree limbs "May take years / In a sovereign floating of joy." The prey, in turn, have the reward of knowing "in glory what is above them, / And to feel no fear, / But acceptance, compliance." For Dickey, the cycle continues, transcending a linear chronology: "They tremble, they walk / Under the tree, / They fall, they are torn, / They rise, they walk again." Critics such as H. L. Weatherby had earlier noted Dickey's tendency to present poems in which the persona suspends reason and logic and enters a dreamlike state by which he assumes the consciousness of some Other—a dog, a fox, a deer. Such a state allows for an exchange of sensibilities before the speaker returns to his human condition, more conscious now of a fuller sense of being. Chronological time, however, must become temporarily suspended for any such exchange.

This complexity—Dickey's interest in time and timelessness as suggested by mythology and the various occupations, personae, and masks by which he presented himself—invites an analysis of his life through a methodology that avoids being strictly chronological but which is, instead, based on his literary life. The dynamics of change and development, a calendar-based chronology as it manifests itself in Dickey's career, do appear; however, situations, events, and writings are occasionally depicted as if they occurred simultaneously in order to remind readers of a previous point in Dickey's life or to permit them to anticipate what is to come. For example, Dickey's career as a critic, which began in the fifties as he wrote book reviews for the *Houston Post* and which lasted, in effect, until 1995, when he gave the commencement address at the University of South Carolina, is presented in chapter 9 so as to delineate how his criticism singularly evolved. Similarly, rather than spreading Dickey's teaching career over fifty years, I have condensed and centered it in chapter 11, detailing the content of the courses he taught at various colleges and universities as well as student responses to it. At the end of the chapter, I note that Dickey died three days later. His "death," however, does not actually occur until three chapters later, but what Dickey said during his last class and the circumstances under which he said it necessitate the reader having this juxtaposition. Such a methodology presents Dickey's life as one worked out in the imagination, as if liberated from time, a structuring that would have pleased Dickey.

CHAPTER 1

CHILDHOOD AND EARLY WRITINGS

James Lafayette Dickey entered the world on Friday, 2 February 1923, Groundhog Day, at Crawford Long Hospital in Atlanta. Later, quoting the Greek poet Archilochus in his classes, he would tell students, "The fox knows many things, but the groundhog knows one big thing." America was in transition. Fueled by excess nervous stimulation carried over from the Great War, the Roaring Twenties were already in full swing. The music was jazz, the dance was the Charleston, and the drink was gin. Discounting the future, the stock market was unconcernedly soaring. F. Scott Fitzgerald, whose celebration of youth in his 1920 novel *This Side of Paradise* had made him both an overnight celebrity and a spokesman for his generation, described the heady times in *The Crack-Up* (1945): "We felt like children in a great unexplored barn" (28), characterizing his generation as "a whole race going hedonistic, deciding on pleasure...living with the insouciance of grand ducs and the casualness of chorus girls" (15, 21). "The Jazz Age raced along under its own power," he wrote, "served by great filling stations full of money.... Even when you were broke you didn't worry about money, because it was in such profusion around you" (18, 21). If there was anything, however, upon which the major literary figures of the twenties could agree, and there was not much, it was that America was a mess.

In a 1922 volume titled *Civilization in the United States*, edited by Harold Stearns, thirty American writers from various professions surveyed the cultural landscape. Their effort, Stearns wrote in his introduction, was

> the deliberate and organized outgrowth of the common efforts of like-minded men and women to see the problem of modern American civilization as a whole....We wished to speak the truth about American civilization as we saw it, in order to do our share in making a real civilization possible—for I think with all of us there was a common assumption that a field cannot be ploughed until it has first been cleared of rocks, and that constructive criticism can hardly exist until there is something on which to construct. (iii–iv)

The writers unanimously concluded that American life was aesthetically barren, intellectually superficial, and stiflingly oppressive. Worship of technology and material wealth, Victorian morality, and the glorification of outmoded ideals, they argued, had caused the country to become a spiritual wasteland, making it impossible for art and intellect to flourish. Any objective observer, they declared, would have concurred. T. S. Eliot, whose volumes *Prufrock and Other Observations* (1917) and *The Wasteland* (1922) had exposed the cultural emptiness and ushered in modernism, had written, "After such knowledge, what forgiveness." In his ultimatum to fellow artists, Ezra Pound stated it more succinctly but just as conclusively: "Make it new." By the end of the decade, however, while Fitzgerald noted "the proper expression of horror as we look at our wasted youth," he would have also agreed that the decade produced a golden boom of creative energy, the richest decade in American publishing history, including works not only by Eliot, Pound, and Fitzgerald but also by Sinclair Lewis, Sherwood Anderson, William Faulkner, Ernest Hemingway, Gertrude Stein, Thomas Boyd, John Dos Passos, Willa Cather, Edith Wharton, Thomas Wolfe, E. A. Robinson, Robinson Jeffers, Robert Frost, Wallace Stevens, William Carlos Williams, Hilda Doolittle, and Amy Lowell.

Groundhog Day in 1923 seemed to promise nothing auspicious or even noteworthy. In its international and national coverage, the *Atlanta Journal* announced in its February 2nd headlines that German labor feared industrial collapse and that Congress had reached an agreement for funding British war debt. Women smokers, one story declared, were "suspected of having caused the heavy increase in loss by fires due to 'matches and smoking' in the United States." Locally, the newspaper noted that nine Atlantans had been injured in recent automobile accidents, that Atlanta school enrollment had increased by 14,000 pupils in the last two years, and that four men were seeking the position of city tax assessor. Nothing was said about whether or not the groundhog saw his shadow.

James Dickey was not a Southern poet like Sidney Lanier and Robert Penn Warren, writers whose poems were largely set in the South and which depicted regional concerns, but the South in which Dickey was born and raised influenced him and his writings. In his personal history *The South and the Southerner*, Ralph McGill observed,

> I had never really seen plantation country, save in passing, until after
> I came to Georgia in 1929. It was a bad time to see it. It was still
> struggling with the boll weevil plague which had come with the
> twenties. And it was soon to fall into the demoralization of land

and people which the depression of the thirties brought. A second cotton king died then. The cabins began to empty, their doors and shutters sagging. Looking back at it now, I knew that segregation began to die then, too. (157–58)

Within the years of Dickey's childhood, disparities of race and social class were so much a part of the culture, so much engrained in the region, that rarely would one hear them challenged. Indeed, those qualities for which the South felt praiseworthy—its strengths of character and personality, the comforting reach of church and family, the warmth of personal relationships, the fertility of the land, the beauty and yield of its woods and waters, the warmth of its winters—all these caused Southerners to remember the thirties and forties fondly. Certainly the Agrarians, centered as they were at Vanderbilt University, extolled these virtues in *I'll Take My Stand*, first published in 1930, and while they did not argue for a return to slavery, they did celebrate the patriarchal system that had reinforced that institution. Hardship abounded during these years, and the closer one got to the bottom of that social and economic ladder, the worse it got. Growing up, Dickey would have sensed and seen these disparities and, given his sensibilities, been affected by them.

Indeed, the South into which Jimmy Dickey was born and raised was, as John Egerton noted in *Speak Now Against the Day*, "a feudal land."

Its values were rooted in the land, in stability and permanence, in hierarchy and status, in caste and class and race. The highest virtues were honor and duty, loyalty and obedience. Every member of the society—man and woman, white and black—knew his or her place, and it was an unusual (not to say foolhardy) person who showed a flagrant disregard for the assigned boundaries and conventions. (19)

In 1932, two-thirds of Southerners lived on farms; malnutrition was rampant. Rural housing for all but the fortunate few was primitive—no running water or electricity, no appliances, no telephone, no insulation, no window screens, no paint. Clothing was inadequate. Shoes were a luxury, and coats and hats an extravagance. Food, Egerton asserts, was "a monotonous repetition of what little there was available: salt pork, lard, sorghum molasses, corn pone, biscuits, grits, white gravy, and a narrow selection of boiled vegetables—field peas, cabbage, sweet potatoes, greens" (21). Two major meals were considered fortunate; poor health was inevitable. While the region contained a quarter of the nation's population, it owned only a tenth of the wealth. Almost no one had money. In "A Folk Singer of the

Thirties" (1963), Dickey portrays a man during the Depression crucified on a boxcar by the railroad police, "an example for / The boys who would ride the freights / Looking for work, or for / Their American lives." As Egerton declared, "The big owners of industries, utilities, natural resources, and agricultural lands felt they had a perfect right to maximize their profits by whatever means necessary—to extract, exploit, use up, and throw away at will" (23). Laissez-faire capitalism, the greedy, all-or-nothing approach with no concern for consequences, caused nearly three and a half million more people to move out of the South than into it between 1900 and 1932, all searching for a better life. The irony is that in spite of these conditions, to say nothing of its defeat in the Civil War and the unfortunate consequences of Reconstruction, the South clung to the past. "The glorious Lost Cause," Egerton concludes, "had instilled a sense of pride and honor and moral superiority in many whites, but the hard truth was that the South in the 1930s was itself a lost cause, a downtrodden region hopelessly nursing wounds that were as much self-inflicted as administered from without" (24).

Then, too, the Ku Klux Klan had reemerged from the shadows to become a dominant social force, "one of the major news sources," McGill observed, "in politics, brutalities, murders and the activities of rascals. Atlanta was mecca for the faithful" (130), a hotbed during the twenties for thousands of white men, including a reported majority of the city's police force, who belonged to the secret society as proudly as to the Masons, Shriners, or Rotary. Anti-Negro and anti-Semitic, the group became virulent and menacing, openly promoting itself and controlling legislatures and state houses. At its height, the invisible empire of the Klan hosted an estimated membership of four million before declining during the Depression. Dickey undoubtedly knew of its activities, writing in his 1961 essay "Notes on the Decline of Outrage" on the racial and social changes occurring in the South: "To be a white Southerner in the mid-twentieth century is to realize the full bafflement and complexity of the human condition. It is not only to see parts of one's world fall irrevocably away, but to feel some of them, tenaciously remaining, take on an accusing cast that one would not have thought possible, and long-familiar situations assume a fathomless, symbolic, and threatening weight" (*Babel to Byzantium* 257). Dickey would later explore the power dynamic of slavery in "Slave Quarters" (1965), a poem which he intended "to strike right to the heart of the hypocrisy of slavery and show some of the pity and terror of it" (*Self-Interviews* 160).

Along with both his father, Eugene, an Atlanta lawyer, and his mother, Maibelle, as well as his older sister Maibelle, little Jimmy Dickey spent the first three years at his maternal grandmother's palatial, white-columned house at 1459 Peachtree Street, where the family "enjoyed all the benefits of a life made leisurely by wealth and servants" (Hart 3). Lena Burckhardt Huntley, or "Grossmutter" as she preferred to be called, had been born in Germany. Jimmy Dickey, playing in the nursery, learned some German from her. She frequently quoted a saying common in the vernacular—"*Es muss sein, es muss sein*" ("It must be, it must be"), which Dickey associated with the German poet and philosopher Friedrich Hölderlin and which he later used in conversation with both students and friends and in interviews and journal entries. If the gramophone was playing Beethoven or Mozart, she would demand quiet, announcing firmly, "Silence. There is music." She read Schiller and Goethe to the young boy, quoting her favorite lines. From Schiller, for example, she would repeatedly say, "Against ignorance even the gods have struggled in vain." From another favorite, Nietzsche, she would solemnly pronounce, "He who fights with monsters should be careful lest he thereby become a monster. And if thou gaze long into an abyss, the abyss will also gaze into thee." In her loving severity, she imparted to Dickey an affection for German culture, but he remembered with horror his grandmother's diabetes. Having grown fat, she had developed gangrene in her foot, and her leg had been amputated. Dickey's later writings reveal his fear of disease and dismemberment, including poems such as "Diabetes," "Mercy," "The Cancer Match," and "Madness," all published in 1969, and novels such as *Alnilam* (1987), whose protagonist, Frank Cahill, becomes blind from his own diabetes. Although Dickey himself did not suffer from the disease, he often claimed he did, largely owing to his need for attention. Don Greiner, Dickey's colleague at the University of South Carolina, remembers one evening during the seventies when, at a formal dinner party hosted at an elegant home, Dickey announced he was diabetic; the incident left guests initially shocked and then embarrassed.

Dickey's exposure to German in childhood facilitated his later interest in languages generally. In *Sorties*, he would challenge himself to "do something about the German language," admitting that Italian and Spanish were much easier to learn:

> What little I have been able to decipher of that curious language is enormously interesting. Though not a born linguist, I have a good

memory and can pick up a good deal of the language very quickly, though mechanically, in a short time. German is interesting to me because the manner in which words are combined, and the manner in which verb forms—that is to say, action words—are combined with other forms like adverbs and nouns, is extremely interesting and exciting.

"I have no doubt at all," he declared, "that something of this sort could be done in English, and it would have the effect of creating a very expressive new approach for poetry" (16). That rationale would lead Dickey to explore the possibilities inherent in other languages, including French, Spanish, Italian, and even Russian. It also anticipates Dickey's later "translations," or "free adaptations," his efforts in poems such as *The Zodiac* to get "the essence of the poetry over from one language to another, and not just a literal transcription" (Greiner, *James Dickey: Classes* 2).

In a *Washington Post* interview on 24 May 1987, Dickey discussed German culture. "I love to read dull books," he told the reporter. "I think it's because my heritage on my mother's side is German, and they run to that kind of thing. That's why they've produced so many philosophers, like Kant and Hegel. Especially them, but also Schopenhauer and Fichte and many others. To say nothing of the impenetrable Heidegger" (Trueheart F6). From boyhood Dickey was obsessed with Nietzsche's "ubermensch," the "higher man," whose enhanced physical and creative powers render him superior to others, a superman, or what Dickey in a 1979 essay would term "the energized man." Such an individual, Dickey wrote, possesses "vivid senses, a man alert to the nuances and meanings of his own experience, the man able to appreciate and evaluate his relationship between words in the right order—and the rightest order for words is in poems—the relation between words in the right order and his perceptions and his mental faculties in *their* right order" (Weigl, Hummer 164). Dickey's fictional heroes, Ed Gentry in *Deliverance* (1970), Joel Cahill in *Alnilam* (1987), and Muldrow in *To the White Sea* (1993), have their origin in the German culture inherent in Dickey's childhood.

"Grossmutter," however, was not the only deep and abiding memory Dickey retained into adulthood. Among early remembrances were stories of or anecdotes about other branches of the family—a woman on his mother's father's side, for example, a Swift, whom lore said had raised the Confederate flag after Atlanta had fallen to Yankee general William Tecumseh Sherman; she was spared hanging, the story went, only because she was a woman. On Jimmy's father's side, the Dickey forebears, few stories existed. James Lafayette Dickey, his father's brother for whom Jimmy was named, had made money in real estate as Atlanta began to grow. Supposedly the Governor's Mansion and the Atlanta Federal Penitentiary are on property he had owned. The earlier Dickeys were from the mountains of North Georgia, near Mineral Bluff, where the mountains of Georgia, North Carolina, and Tennessee come together. In Tennessee there is even a Dickey Mountain. Some Dickeys had been Union sympathizers. A great-uncle, for example, was named William Tecumseh Sherman Dickey. But Hannah and George Dickey, great-, great-grandparents of James Lafayette Dickey, were some of the very few slave owners in Fannin County and rumored to have raised slaves for sale.

With his Southern ancestry, Dickey would naturally have identified with his cultural heritage. In "The Confederate Line at Ogeechee Creek" (1997), one of the last poems he wrote before his death, the speaker addresses General Sherman. On Christmas Eve 1864, *Harper's Weekly* reported that Union forces under Sherman had crossed the river, passing through Millen on their advance to Savannah. In Dickey's re-creation of events, a retreating Rebel soldier imagines his compatriots regrouping: "Hawks / Hover like needles, trembling and trembling / Into certainty, all beaks and hooks / Set north. Tecumseh, not this time." The lines reflect Dickey's belief that all life involved warfare, whether against an opposing army, a rival football team, formalist literary critics, social norms, or even one's own creative or physical self, where habit and comfort on the one hand, and time or death on the other hand become the great enemy. Poetically, however, he became most obsessed with death—"that eternal process," he later wrote in "The Leap" (1964), "most obsessively wrong with the world." Many of Dickey's poems, particularly those written during what he termed his "early motion," centered on the brutality of military conflict, including "The Enclosure" (1959), "The Jewel" (1959), "The Performance" (1959), "Between Two Prisoners" (1960), "The Driver" (1963), "Drinking from a Helmet" (1963), and "The Firebombing" (1964). Indeed, Dickey divided *Into the Stone*, his first volume of poems, published in 1960, into explicitly labeled sections, including family, war, death, and love; these thematic concerns, the meanings of which become gradually enlarged and more inclusive as his literary career progressed, propelled his poetry. Occasionally, too, these thematic concerns merged. Poems, for example, sometimes involved both war and family, such as "Hunting Civil War Relics at Nimblewill Creek" (1961) and "Last Hours" (1994), where military conflict offers redemptive possibilities. Conflict, warfare, death and dying, the body against its own best self—these became the motifs that centered all Dickey's literary work.

Dickey had a whole collection of well-honed stories about family members, the characters who lived under his grandmother's roof, frequently telling listeners, "Both sides in my family are specialists in ne'er-do-wells and black sheep." Mr. Huntley, for example, Grossmutter's second husband, would get drunk and walk naked down the main stairs, playing a zither. Cousin Eugenia, according to family lore, would go to bed every night wearing a Kotex for fear a man would rape her in her sleep and she would otherwise not know it. Dickey was particularly fond of his uncle Tom Swift, the youngest of Grossmutter's five children and the only one who grew up to be, as many of the men in the family did, a drunk. "*Another alcoholic*," Dickey recalled, "of the most extreme and lovable kind." His recollection, years later, was as clear as it was intense, telling his son Christopher, "He was a heavyset fella who rather resembled Thomas Wolfe. Not that tall, but with a sort of heavy face, and a deep dimple in his chin. As a little boy, two and three and four, I became a great favorite of his, a great favorite. One day I was up in the upstairs hall, just rattling around the house, like children will do. And I passed by his door and it was open. He said, 'Come on in, Jimmy.'" When he had gotten halfway across the room, Dickey remembered, "a look of the most horrible fear—or some emotion—came over him. I had never seen anything like it on a human face. 'The cats, Jim. Get those cats out!' He scared the shit out of me. He was having the DTs" (*Summer of Deliverance* 34–35).

Little Jimmy's parents eventually bought a home on West Wesley Road, off Peachtree Street, with money inherited from the SSS Tonic Company, income from commercial real estate holdings, and securities investments. Grossmutter, irritated with her son Tom's alcoholic parties, built him an apartment over the garage, heated by a large potbellied stove. "He took right to it," Dickey told Christopher. "I heard later he'd have these huge carousers with all these reprobate friends—especially women— all these low women would come out. My poor grandmother would die to see that, I was told. And they would get drunk and Uncle Tom would rise and piss on the stove." As he related the story, Dickey would be bent over in laughter, short of breath, imagining the scene. "The steam!" Uncle Tom Swift was "a wastrel and a bum," Dickey told Christopher, who wrote that his father nevertheless loved him "and loved the sound of the phrase, too" (*Summer of Deliverance* 34–35).

Early short stories that Dickey projected but never completed were frequently full of characters loosely based on such family members. While teaching in 1950 at Rice Institute (now Rice University), Dickey purchased four bound ledgers, having heard that Thomas Wolfe wrote in such notebooks and hoping the method would facilitate his own creative efforts. He additionally used two ringed, loose-leaf notebooks, one blue and the other red. He intended in these separate notebooks or journals (he used the words interchangeably) to discuss his novels and short stories, to comment on books and essays that he read, and to record observations on specific events he felt significant. He also planned to keep notes for and drafts of his own poems and to analyze formally other poetic works. In practice, however, individual notebooks never achieved such specialized purposes and were never explicitly labeled according to purpose. While generally centered on a particular concern, each became a literary catchall in which Dickey continually briefed himself to determine his artistic mission, struggling to acquire a personal subject matter and a distinctive style. In these notebooks Dickey used family to develop and enhance his creative efforts.

"My whole childhood," an entry in his notebooks read, "rose crying to me." In one story he planned, titled "Shadows, Reeds," the unnamed protagonist, whose attitudes and sensibilities toward family and warfare resembled those of Dickey himself, is the illegitimate son of a Jewish New York broker, a figure based on Tom Swift, whom he identifies and describes as "a wastrel, 'peed on stove,'" then laid down among the slanting daisies." The protagonist, a veteran World War II commando with the British rangers, tells his father, whom he has approached for a job and who is uninterested in his son, of the raids in which he had participated: "I felt for once I had completely filled up my skin." "I would like to show," Dickey wrote in the following entry, "the sense of frustration the son has: that of many who have, in the violence of war, found a solidarity which is dispelled by the (old, familiar) civilian world returned to." The sentiment reflects that of Dickey in a letter postmarked 5 June 1945 and mailed from the Philippines where, as a member of the 418th Night Fighter Squadron, he was participating in daily sorties in support of combat operations. "No one but the men out here can realize the price our country is paying for its heritage," he wrote his father, adding, "I wish the people in the states, especially those who think they are 'doing their part' and feel they have performed a valiant feat when they buy an $18.75 war bond, could see these men out here." Of the fighting, which he described as "pretty stiff," he said, "It seems incredible that men should wish to behave this way to other men" (*One Voice*, I 88).

Dickey's notebooks also detail a planned novel titled "Done in a Thorn Tree." The work centered on the problem of communication. The idea originated from the 1944 novel *The Horse's Mouth*, written by Joyce Cary and produced as a film in 1958, which focused on an eccentric painter named Gulley Jimson, who is inspired to execute his largest work, "The Last Judgment." Dickey's protagonist, Sidney Leicester Etter IV, is "a man like the photographs of E. E. Cummings—wry, full of love, rascality + sanctity: a clown (a pathetic one) and a genius with no formal mode of expression." He is also wealthy, "something of a ne'er-do-well. He lounges around in the comforts of his class, but wants something better for it—A *good character*." The character wove together aspects of Tom Swift, described as a "snubbed member: humorous + shy," and Dickey's father, but more complex, artistic, strange—a man whom Dickey characterizes in his notebooks as "the 'queer' member of the family some like, some hate, one loves, the others mistrust or are made uneasy by." He is "perhaps partially insane," prone to curious actions, sending other family members bits of verse, fables, and the like, believing that "no one could understand anything unless he could talk to them." The projected novel also featured Eugenia, now named Jordenia, whom he describes as "sleeping with Kotex on. 'She will be undisturbed, you see,'" as well as "Aunt Jeannette," his mother's sister; Maibelle, Dickey's older sister; and Patsy, his younger brother Tom's wife. In the middle of the novel, Etter delivers a monologue showing "the kind of family, self-understanding, tradition, he would like to mould [*sic*]." "It is the only family I have," he thinks, "And I thought I spoke to them all, though one by one they left, all except Hermia, who sat, wringing her hands, as I lugged out all the metaphors about the sun I had ever concocted and turned them loose; then she left, too, and the moon came and fell directly onto the stringless piano, and stood, very priceless, exactly and perfectly in its polish." With few exceptions, Dickey never completed any of the fictions proposed in his notebooks. What is clear, however, is that he intentionally used family and friends as well as literary figures on which to base his characters, re-creating them to express emotional concerns and ideas reflected in his own childhood memories and experiences.

In 1926 the Dickeys moved to Buckhead, an enclave on the edge of Atlanta that was the home of many Atlanta professionals; the area was not annexed until 1952. The house at 166 West Wesley was a two-story brick

Georgian with a circular driveway in front and a wide side porch, elevated to the tree branches because of the property slope. A swinging bed, suspended by chains, hung from one end. For Chris, who "spent a lot of time in that house," the bed became "our pirate ship—spacecraft—stagecoach and, in the summer, a magical, frightening place to sleep" (*Summer of Deliverance* 36). Such adventures must surely have occurred with his father, who likely played on it as a child and who slept on it as a teenager. Wild strawberries grew on one side of the lot; on another side was a thick strand of bamboo. A towering fir tree rose in the front yard with branches so thick and low a child could hide beneath them. The yard sat on more than an acre with a separate garage at the back as well as a chicken coop where the father, Eugene, kept the gamecocks he pitted against competitors. In the garage Dickey's younger brother Tom held meetings of a Seckatary Hawkins club, for which Dickey was secretary. Dickey carved his initials on a wooden post. The official club name was "The Fair and Square Club," and the club slogan was "A quitter never wins, and a winner never quits." Based on a series of children's novels by Robert F. Schulkers, the fictional club, the smartest of whose members was Seckatary Hawkins, was regularly called upon to solve mysteries and keep the neighborhood safe.

Buckhead during Dickey's childhood was rural; no superhighways existed. In 1959, Lenox Square Shopping Mall would eliminate many of Buckhead's small businesses, rendering the town of Dickey's youth virtually unrecognizable. By the early sixties, the area was considered prestigious, less a geographic area than a group of young men who "once represented the best that privilege offered, a kind of monied hypermasculinity that strutted with the confidence of a time and place that viewed itself as manifestly special." However, the years following World War II still exhibited a sort of "Leave-It-to-Beaver" innocence, with sexually mandated gender roles but, in Buckhead, possessing more discretionary spending. It was, so to speak, its own nation-state, with specific rituals, manners, and rites of passage. Those rites included cars, girls, and football. Anne Rivers Siddons, whose novel *Peachtree Road* was set largely in Buckhead, declared of the Buckhead Boys,

> Theirs was a rigidly masculine world of money, privilege, grace, ritual, preening foolishness, high spirits, and low expectations. They were not groomed for their future roles as power brokers because it was taken for granted that they would slide as easily into them as their fathers had into their own earlier and simpler niches.... Insular, careless, totally and imperviously self-assured, chauvinistic in

the extreme, naïve and unsophisticated, arrogant, profoundly physical rather than introspective, largely unburdened by intellect, and almost laughably White, Anglo-Saxon Protestant, they were as cohesive as cousins and as stunningly insensitive as young royalty.

Yet, she added, "it was a world with hidden reefs and shoals that could, and did, wreck the unwary, the deviate, the maverick, the vulnerable or gentle or complicated or different ones" (10–11). Dickey's sense of entitlement was grounded in the family's affluence. The money inherited from the SSS Company, which sold tonic that supposedly cured ailments from dyspepsia to cancer and syphilis, allowed Dickey's mother, Maibelle, to provide for the family as if the Roaring Twenties had never ended. Dickey's aloofness, however, was countered and mitigated by his heightened emotional sensitivities and by a firm desire to appear simply as "one of the boys." Indeed, he was often embarrassed that the family had servants and by the fact that he was chauffeured to elementary school even as he enjoyed his privileged status by imploring his private nurse, Mamie Doster, to bring him books to read.

If Dickey believed his life was more complicated than that of Lawrence of Arabia, it should not be surprising; the crosscurrents that involved his personality and that resulted in his contradictory actions and attitudes throughout his life originated in the conflicting ideals of his father and mother, beliefs that spanned business, art, athletics, soldiering, and the outdoors. Fiercely competitive, Dickey attempted to excel in all fields, and whenever he failed, he frequently turned to self-aggrandizing fantasies and exaggerations to compensate. Efforts to please both parents necessarily satisfied neither, leaving him with feelings of inadequacy and guilt.

That Dickey's father, Eugene, hailed from Yankee sympathizers in North Georgia's mountainous Fannin County did not sit well with Maibelle Swift's family. Eugene had played football, run track, and studied law at Georgia Tech and Mercer College. Maibelle was the privileged daughter of Charles Swift, a captain in the Confederate army who amassed a small fortune after founding the Atlanta-based Swift Southern Specific company. She had attended Washington Seminary, a finishing school that served young women on the Atlanta social registry, and then Brenau College, where her interests centered on the arts, including writing, painting, and singing. After marrying Maibelle in 1910, Eugene acclimated himself to the Swift inherited wealth and devoted himself to the illegal sport of cockfighting. A lawyer by education, he was a cockfighter, gambler, and real estate investor by desire.

Dickey's attitude toward his father was at best ambivalent. He declared in *Self-Interviews* that "my father and I have always been close.... [H]e was always reading law books and records of famous cases to me.... And this gave me a liking for words that I might otherwise not have had" (26). Eugene Dickey had also introduced his son to verse, reciting the powerful rhythms of "Horatio at the Bridge" and "The Shooting of Dan McGrew," ballads whose forceful intensity caught the listener up and conveyed him to imagined situations. Their powerful attraction, which Dickey in a 1965 interview would suggest had led him to read Poe, enhanced his interest in and understanding of what he termed "the *conveying* power of the metric," although he found Poe "not especially appealing."

> It seemed to me that despite everything that I'd heard to the contrary, that the anapest or the dactyl, I guess, or whatever you call it depending on where you start counting, really is capable, if you vary it strategically, of a new kind of sound, or a kind of sound which is unusual because one thinks of it mainly as something connected with either Poe or 'The Shooting of Dan McGrew'; but this doesn't exhaust the possibilities of the anapest, and I began to experiment with it to see what could be said this way which would give this great, powerful, surging rhythm. (Baughman, *Voiced Connections* 14)

Yet Dickey's father, a dilettante lawyer and confirmed gambler, clearly did not understand his son's sensibilities, taking him to cockfights in which his own birds participated or to spectacles in which raccoons, chained to a log, fought off hounds—in short, Christopher Dickey later stated, "to just about anything else where blood and violence had money resting on them" (*Summer of Deliverance* 36). The violence that became a pervasive thematic concern in Dickey's poetry and fiction and which he himself personally viewed in World War II was anticipated by these animal blood sports to which his father exposed him. To young Jimmy Dickey, life at such moments was reduced to a predator/prey relationship; however intriguing to a young boy, he found such spectacle abhorrent.

"My father loved country people and country ways," Dickey once told me, "but the lesson I most learned from him was 'Go thou and do otherwise.'" In the 1987 interview, he remembered, "My father liked to go out into the country a lot. He hunted with a shotgun, and he would bring back rabbits and squirrels which we ate" (Baughman, *Voiced Connections* 247). As far as his legal profession was concerned, Eugene cared for neither salary nor success, earning him his son's lifelong scorn. To Christopher, Dickey confided, "He just drifted. And because he was like he was, it filled me with, as they used to say, a burning desire for consequence. Value. To attach significance to things. Because there was not anything to him that had any significance. Any" (*Summer of Deliverance* 37). In *Sorties*, his condemnation was more forceful and more direct: "I am appalled by the thinness of my father's experience. It has been monotonous, tiresome, and valueless because he has been essentially passive. And he has been monumentally and not creatively lazy.... I cannot imagine a more awful old age than that of the lazy man, of the passive man, who wished only 'to be let alone' to do his thing. The trouble with my old man is that he never had enough energy to have a thing" (68). His ambition was simply to be an expert in cockfighting, insisting on Jimmy's attendance at such events in order to overcome his son's fear of blood and carnage.

In a 1973 interview, Dickey recalled,

> my whole early life was conditioned by going with my father to the [cock] walks and with the various country people he had keep his chickens for him.... I remember saying to my father, "Dad, why do you fight chickens?" I know my mother was telling me—my mother was a kind of religious fanatic who suggested that this was a disreputable business my old man was engaged in. When I was no more than nine or ten years old, I went to my father and said, "Dad, why are you doing this here chicken fighting stuff when you could be providing your family a little better some other way than gambling on your chickens?" He said, "'Cause, I tell you, it's *inspiring*. Every man that ever lived would like to have the *guts* those chickens have." (Baughman, *Voiced Connections* 102)

Maibelle Dickey, however, was not "memorably religious at all, much less a fanatic," Chris Dickey remembered. "She was just another social Episcopalian. Maybe my father did not want to reflect on the idea that she found cockfighting and the people connected with it *socially* unacceptable. That was the relevant point." Dickey would surely have had his own father in mind when he asked, in his essay "The Energized Man," "Why are men content to go through life with so little recompense? Why will they not make just a *small* effort? Why must they be content to have, really, so little of themselves?" Against "the vast, sluggish forces of habit, mechanization, and mental torpor" (Weigl, Hummer 165), he believed the individual needed to act, for only by doing so could one be delivered from drift and inconsequence. As he wrote in his poem "Falling" (1967), in which a young stewardess is accidently swept from an airplane when an emergency door springs open, "*One cannot just fall just tumble screaming all that time one must* use / *It.*"

Maibelle Dickey, whose father had opposed her marriage to Eugene, was by all accounts caring and generous, "a deeply feeling, quiet, sort of retiring person," Dickey remembered, "who stayed alone in her thoughts most of the time, but humorous and sweet as she could be, and helpful. She was almost the ideal mother because she stayed out of the way" (Hart 8). Christopher remembered her as also being "funny, very cutting about other adults, and gloriously, playfully indulgent with children" (*Summer of Deliverance* 35). She retired each afternoon to the cool darkness of her bedroom, partly to escape her husband, whom everyone called "Pop," as well as other men around the house, including Old George, who tended the yard, and Wha-cha-know Joe, who raised and cared for the gamecocks. Often Maibelle would read Uncle Wiggly to her son. She suffered from a valve malfunction in her heart caused by rheumatic fever, frequently complaining of angina and of being fatigued, and using her afternoon "naps" to rest. On the wall, diagonally across from her bed, hung a framed photograph of a little boy in a sailor suit, Gene, who had died before Jimmy was born. When Dickey himself died sixty years later, that same photograph was hanging on his office wall at the University of South Carolina.

Gene, named after his father, was born on 14 September 1914; he had died suddenly of meningitis, or what was then called "brain fever," on 4 April 1921 at the age of six. Dickey wrote in *Self-Interviews* that he had gathered "by implication and hints of family relatives" that his mother, "an invalid with angina pectoris, would not have risked having another child had Gene lived." "I was the child," he declared, "who was born as a result of this situation. And I have always felt a sense of guilt that my birth depended on my brother's death" (89). Gene's death was recent enough for Jimmy Dickey to have heard, and remembered, comments made about the child.

Throughout his life, Dickey never escaped the attendant guilt that he owed his life to his brother's death and to his mother's subsequent willingness to risk another birth despite the perceived danger. Those facts hardened within him. That Maibelle later had another son, Tom, never mitigated or called into question what he believed. It was as if Dickey carried within himself the sense of an original sin that demanded expiation, the need for some heroic act that would return his brother to life and validate his own existence. Simply stated, he felt responsible, writing in a 1950s notebook, "Theme of mine. The search for the (ideal) brother and the turning inward to the self in search of him, finally. Narcissus, solipsism." Many of his early poems, including "The String" (1959), "The Other" (1959), "The Underground Stream" (1960), "In the Treehouse at Night" (1961), and "Armor" (1961–1962), allude to Gene. In "In the Treehouse at Night," for example, the speaker thinks, "Each nail in the house is now steadied / By my dead brother's huge, freckled hand. / Through the years, he has pointed his hammer / Up into these limbs, and told us / That we must ascend, and all lie here." In a poem such as "The Lifeguard," where the speaker fails to save a child from drowning, Gene's presence is evident. As the lifeguard repeatedly dives under the surface of the lake searching for the boy, he continually falls back, overcome by the changes in the faces of the children watching at his defeat: "As I move toward the center of the lake, / Which is also the center of the moon, / I am thinking of how I may be / The savior of one / Who has already died in my care." Finally, however, his failure becomes apparent: "I wash the black mud from my hands. / On a light given off by the grave, / I kneel in the quick of the moon / At the heart of a distant forest / And hold in my arms a child / Of water, water, water." Dickey's early poems largely depict afflatus, the possibilities inherent with the imagination, but "The Lifeguard" reveals its limits, the inability to transform or redeem the human condition or escape Aristotelian duality. Platonic idealism fails. The conflict between these two opposing philosophies would play itself out in Dickey's poetry throughout his literary career and resolve itself only in *The Eagle's Mile*, his last published volume before he died.

Dickey's first published poem, titled "Christmas Shopping, 1947," appeared in the winter 1947 issue of *Gadfly*, the literary magazine of Vanderbilt University, which he attended following World War II. However, at the age of five, he wrote "You and Yourself," a nonfiction piece on personal hygiene, specifically toothbrushing. Bound with string and eleven pages in length, the "book" featured a magazine picture of a child pasted on the cover. Inside, opposite his signature, Dickey posted a picture of Forhan's toothpaste, a woman, and a toothbrush; he also drew a calendar in order to track daily toothbrushing, perhaps conscious, as in advertising, of the consumer. Other cutout pictures include familiar domestic scenes, such as a child drinking orange juice from a straw, a mother pouring her little boy a glass of milk, various healthy foods, and two boys playing marbles as an adult watches the game. A year later, he penciled his autobiography, "The Life of James Dickey," a five-page fantasy of himself as a combat pilot filled with crayon drawings of airplanes. His introspection and his fantasies were ingrained from the beginning.

The vision of becoming a pilot remained an abiding dream of Jimmy Dickey's, partly owing to the rise of aviation during the twenties. In the early 1900s, the Wright brothers had begun testing airplanes at Kitty Hawk, North Carolina, and during Dickey's childhood, stunt pilots regularly displayed their acrobatic feats at county fairs. In 1923, the year Dickey was born, two army lieutenants flew across the United States in a Fokker monoplane. On 9 May 1926, Lt. Cmdr. Richard Byrd crossed over the North Pole, followed a year later by Charles Lindbergh's historic flight in *The Spirit of St. Louis* from Long Island to Paris. In a partnership he called "we," Lindbergh landed after flying thirty-three and a half hours solo over the Atlantic, spurred by a contest prize of $25,000. One hundred thousand Frenchmen greeted him, now a world hero. President Coolidge dispatched the USS *Memphis* to bring him home. Atlanta had quickly built an airport, as did other major cities, and by 1928, regular flights had commenced. The thrill and daring of aviation, of entering into the very air men and women breathe, quickly captured Jimmy Dickey's imagination. Taking off, as he later wrote in his posthumously published poem "For Jules Bacon" (2015), he would be "All the way down / The whole runway, slamming and slanting with runway-power, / Rising full into the unequal air." While Herman Melville's imagination had centered on the sea, Dickey, who would later write his master's thesis on that novelist and poet, coveted the air.

Jimmy idealized his mother, and his boyhood idols were everything his complacent, sedentary father was not. He was particularly enamored of body builders. Among the memorabilia his mother saved for him was a 1935 brochure from the York Bar Bell Company—"The Road to Super Strength." It promised that "you will be like the soldier buckling on his sword. Equipped for life—capable to meet every physical emergency." He added, "The world wants strong men today more than ever. Men of action, endurance, pop, punch and power. The type of man your heart aches to see you be" (*Summer of Deliverance* 38). Later Jimmy Dickey became a fan of Charles Atlas, whose "Dynamic Tension" fitness program, consisting of twelve lessons, supplemented by photographs of Atlas demonstrating the exercises, and one final perpetual lesson, was marketed for the "97-pound weakling." Indeed, Dickey's fascination with fitness remained with him throughout his life; even as a member of the 418th Night Fighter Squadron during World War II, when he was stationed in the Pacific, he would read the monthly copies of *Strength and Health* sent to him from home. During the long daylight hours before his nightly missions, he would lift weights, utilizing a regimen prescribed by Jules Bacon, Mr. America 1943, a ritual detailed in "For Jules Bacon." His pilot, Earl Bradley, remembered Dickey outside their tent, lifting weights in the hot sun of the Philippines, after which he would flex his muscles, watching himself in a mirror. "I went for bulk: for inches," the speaker in "For Jules Bacon" declares, "On the arm, on the thighs, on the pectorals and trapezius, / More everything / I didn't have, everything / I needed to raise on me / And above me." It was as if Dickey believed that through such sustained and systematic training, he could become not only bigger and stronger, but literally a new man whose renewal was in some sense redemptive, and he would have achieved this transformation solely by means of his own efforts. Such self-reliance was necessary, even if it necessitated invention. Dickey later declared in a 1990 interview with me,

> I'm essentially a coward, so therefore I flew with the night fighters in the Pacific, or in football I hit the guy especially hard because essentially I was afraid of him. I think you must turn these things to your favor.... I was a timid, Ernest Dowson type—a "days of wine and roses," decadent, late-romantic poet—so therefore I go for force and vigor. And it works. My assumed personality is working for me just as much as Lawrence's worked for him or Hemingway's worked for him.

That plan for systematic development—a step-by-step approach which Dickey would apply to his poetry during the fifties when, under the influence of modernism, he consciously endeavored to build or "construct" poems—first manifested itself during childhood in calculated efforts to improve his physique. Believing himself, as he wrote in "The Other" (1959), "a rack-ribbed child," he undertook a methodical regimen of self-improvement, chopping stumps or logs with a heavy ax and climbing a thick rope hand-over-hand that he had suspended from a tree, hoping

That the chicken-chested form I belabored

Might swell with the breast of a statue
From out of the worm-shattered bole,

While I talked all the time through my teeth
To another, unlike me, beside me:
To a brother or king-sized shadow
Who looked at me, burned, and believed me:
Who believed I would rise like Apollo

With armor-cast shoulders upon me.

A continual, concentrated effort, he believed, could change his body, weight-lifting repetitions that would result in a new physical definition of himself. It is the same attitude that Lewis Medlock exhibits in Dickey's *Deliverance*:

> Lewis wanted to be immortal. He had everything that life could give, and he couldn't make it work. And he couldn't bear to give it up or see age take it away from him, either, because in the meantime he might be able to find what it was he wanted, the thing that must be there, and that must be subject to his will. He was the kind of man who tries by any means—weight lifting, diet, exercise, self-help manuals from taxidermy to modern art—to hold on to his body and mind and improve them, to rise above time. (9)

At the conclusion of "For Jules Bacon," the speaker, now "glowing with health / And muscles and ego, / Alive and alert in the timelessness / Of take-off," rises in his newly empowered body: "I broke / Entirely from earth. This was it. This was the whole thing / We could do against death." To facilitate his physical development, Dickey also built a small sawdust pit in the backyard of the West Wesley house and equipped it with a high-jump bar. Not just bodybuilding, he recognized, but sports, too, could allow him "the body / That would save me from the war, the world- / Wreck I was in." Football and track provided additional means and new possibilities for renewal. "New thresholds, new anatomies" (113), he would later write in *Sorties* and lecture to his students, quoting Hart Crane. Simply stated, he wanted to be mythic; like his protagonist Lewis Medlock, he needed "to rise above time."

His interest in sports, however, also derived in large measure from its elevated status in American culture during the twenties and thirties. This was the age of idols and ballyhoo, and sports provided both—Jack Dempsey in boxing; Bill Tilden in tennis; the Four Horsemen of Notre Dame in football; the Sultan of Swat, Babe Ruth, in baseball; and Bobby Jones in golf. While both physical exercise and sports would enhance his physique, his interest also acknowledged his belief that all life was conflict, a recognition that mandated his need to win in direct competition. The psychological origins of this need lay in his older brother's premature death and Jimmy's subsequent guilt from his being alive, a fact that required atonement. Life necessitated proof of worthiness. Regardless, while culture surely provided motivation to excel, Dickey clearly wanted to exhibit the socially determined, male gender role that required physical strength, prowess, stamina, and courage.

In *Self-Interviews*, Dickey stated, "My main interest was in athletics in high school, and so I had very little time for poetry; it was just something to make me interest*ing*, and in the process, I got interest*ed*" (23–24). The statement is factual so far as it goes, but the truth is more complicated. Dickey valued the aesthetics of sports, the agility and gracefulness of the motion involved, just as much as, if not more than, the athleticism. Calling himself "an indifferent performer in the sports I liked best—football and track," he stated in his essay "Starting from Buckhead—A Home Address" (1983) that he was intrigued by "a dimension of movement, a kind of significance, in certain sports that I don't think was ever noticed by my more successful competitors." "The arc of a javelin," he wrote, "mattered more that the distance it traveled." In football, he declared, "I had rather see the receiver of a forward pass wait for the ball than see him catch it. There was something in the quality of expectation that made the receiver graceful, just for an instant or two, and that was what I enjoyed watching. No wonder I spent most of the time on the bench!" (*Night Hurdling* 185). What he gleaned while sitting there, however, was a set of aesthetic attitudes and responses. Yet Dickey's sensibilities, manifested both by his admission that the first poets in which he became interested were the romantics Byron and Shelley and by his need to be viewed as "one of the guys," required that he seem indifferent to academics, although as his older sister Maibelle noted, "He was born with a book in his hand" (Hart 7).

Their father respected books but was opposed to a son who wanted to write them. Eugene Dickey had career plans for his son, largely involving business and sports, boxing and baseball in particular. The idea of Jim Dickey writing poetry offended his traditional views of masculinity; society largely viewed poets as sycophants and outcasts. His mother, Maibelle, moreover, hoped Jim would reside in Atlanta and become a wealthy businessman like her father, Charles Swift. Dickey's later obsession with money, his demands for large reading fees and top dollar for his papers, owed to his desire to make writing as lucrative as any other profession. Awards, prizes, fellowships, honorary degrees, and publishing contracts— all these would render him, he believed, outwardly successful and justify himself, a son who read and wrote books.

During the twenties and thirties, there were pulp magazines, hundreds of them, which Jimmy Dickey would read one after another, lying on the swinging porch bed of his West Wesley home. They were usually restricted to a genre—love stories, western stories, sports stories, sci-fi stories, mystery-crime-detective stories—most of which cost a dime so that readers could afford them. Edgar Rice Burroughs, creator of Tarzan, was among his favorites, but it was not the Tarzan played by Elmo Lincoln, Gene Pollar, or Johnny Weismuller in the Hollywood movies. Rather, Dickey admired Lord Greystoke, raised by the Great Apes after his parents were killed in the African jungle—a lone man who could kill the strongest bull ape with only a knife and who could also, and just as importantly, teach himself to read using the primers left in his parents' abandoned cabin. This idea—that one man, alone, could improve and educate and in so doing transform himself—fired Jimmy Dickey's imagination and became an informing principle in his creative efforts.

Tarzan, however, was not the only Burroughs hero who came alive in Jimmy's imagination. John Carter of Mars, Carson of Venus, and David Innis at Earth's core all captivated him, but while these characters certainly excited the young Dickey, it was a place—Pellucidar—with which he was most intrigued. It was Earth's core, the place into which David Innis, a mining engineer, using his "iron mole," had burrowed, five hundred miles to the crust. In Burroughs's novels, Earth is a hollow shell, the internal surface of which is Pellucidar, accessible only through a polar opening that allows passage between the inner and outer worlds. Pellucidar's geography is peculiar due to the concave curvature which prevents any horizon; the higher it appears to be, the more it becomes lost in atmospheric haze and mist. The sun, a molten orb, is permanently suspended in the center of the sky. Time appears to stand still. Powerful, primitive men and enormous beasts roam the jungles and the plains. Pellucidar is a vast yet finite world, otherworldly but accessible and self-contained. That the hero is able not only to enter such a place but also to survive in it immediately interested a young Dickey, whose later poems also involved inner and outer worlds.

Such survival, however, anticipated another pulp hero of Dickey's childhood, Kenneth Robeson's Doc Savage, the Man of Bronze, who transformed himself through stubbornness of will and sheer discipline of self to be superior to everyone, a super-man. "This was a hero little Jimmy Dickey wanted to know all about," his son Christopher later remembered. "My father would tell me how Doc Savage managed to exercise every muscle in his body even as he was performing equations or practicing new languages in his head, and it was clear to me that Dad thought, 'Yeah, you could do that.' That *he* could. And that *I* could" (*Summer of Deliverance* 39). Doc Savage, whose real name is Clark Savage Jr., was a physician, surgeon, scientist, inventor, explorer, researcher, and even musician. Trained from birth, he possessed strength and endurance, a photographic memory, a mastery of martial arts, and a vast knowledge of the sciences. His oath was straightforward: "Let me strive every moment of my life to make myself better and better, to the best of my ability, that all may profit by it." Each month, Doc Savage in a new pulp novel commanded missions to destroy evildoers in exotic locales, trampling through Asian jungles to destroy gigantic, man-eating falcons, battling fabulously wealthy foes in an ancient Mayan kingdom, or plunging deep into Earth to counter the survivor of a lost civilization who killed with the touch of his finger.

In Robeson's *Land of Always Night*, for example, the March 1935 issue, one villain named Watches declares, "That bird Savage is a wizard! They say he knows all about electricity and chemistry and psychology and engineering and them things. They say he is a mental marvel. On top of that, he's supposed to be able to bend horseshoes in his hand.... He's what the newspapers call a big-time adventurer. He's supposed to travel around over the world, helping people out of trouble and punishing wrong-doers." In the October 1939 issue titled *The Stone Man*, Doc Savage and his intrepid little fighters battle white-haired supermen in a land beyond the mists; Savage, "whose movement always had method," Robeson wrote, is "feared by all who prey on the weak. He rights wrongs."

Jimmy Dickey's love of the mythic also drew him to such pulp fiction as *Dare-Devil Aces*, *Sky Bird*, *War Birds*, and *Flying Aces*, stories that involved dauntless combat pilots whose successful exploits against enemy aviators involve courage and skill. In a 21 August 1951 letter to his wife, Maxine, after he had been recalled for the Korea conflict, Jim Dickey related how, while stationed at Connally Air Force Base in Waco, Texas, he and a fellow squadron member "wandered around town and into a store that specializes in old pulp magazines. To our immense delight, the shelves were groaning with numbers of 'War Birds,' 'Doc Savage,' 'Flying Aces,' and 'The Secret Six,' which we remembered from our boyhoods. We bought a couple of them" (*One Voice*, I 176). Typical was the February

1935 issue of *War Birds*, which billed itself as "The Oldest Air War Magazine." It featured a novel by Frederick C. Painton titled "Daisy's Devil Aces," the description for which declared, "A grave in the sky is the reward for living when two cadets fly to join in doom's dirge with Daisy McCloud and his hell-binders." The issue also included Arthur Guy Empey's "O'Leary, Hell's Thunderbolt"; the byline read, "The devil's pack roars skyward, blasting and searing he who had the courage to lead a Spad stampede into Hell's hottest fire." In his youthful fancy, these adventurers became versions of an idealized self that Dickey envisioned. "What I *really* want to be—or become—a messiah," he wrote on loose-leaf page among his notebooks. "The only excuse for getting older," he would later tell his Verse Composition classes at the University of South Carolina, "is that you're getting better." While it is problematic whether Jimmy Dickey actually wanted to become a Doc Savage or Lord Greystoke, these characters constituted an ideal to which he would aspire, for behind the enhanced physical strength and intellect lay the image of Gene, his six-year-old brother, "*Dead before I was born*," as he wrote in "The String." That little blond-haired boy with the serious expression on his face demanded Jimmy's attention. "I cannot stay here with this!" he declared in "Lazarus to the Assembled," a poem written in the sixties but not published until 1992, "The sun comes into my mouth. / 'Bring out your dead,' I cry." Just as pulp fiction, with its heroes and adventurers, offered the gate to his image of himself, so too did physical activities and sports, with their culturally mandated venues of manhood, provide the key by which to enter a larger world.

Quiet, unassuming, dreaming of piloting planes and engaging in heroic activities, Jimmy Dickey in the second grade was a member of the "Make Yourself Do Right Club." He reveled in the playground activities of E. Rivers Grammar School, including dodgeball, football, baseball, running, and marble games, the last of which he fondly recalled in the reminiscences of Frank Cahill in *Alnilam*: "Though he loved quick movement and speed, they were not natural to him. The position of marbles in a ring and his careful drawing down on them, the flick of the taw from his thumb, the ringed explosion, the picking off of the last marble, were things he missed when he left grammar school; in fact, he would have liked to play now, were there any way to justify it" (81). Other sports interested Dickey as well, including skating, which, because it was inexpensive, captivated many children during the Depression. Buckhead's long winding streets proved ideal for such simple entertainment. "It was sort of like a skiing slope," he reminisced in a 1996 interview. "You could really get to flying. You could get hurt, too. You'd fall, and we didn't have all those knee pads" (Hart 28). Frank Cahill also possesses Dickey's love of roller skating:

> Skating: that was close: that was near running. Alone, he had skated the streets of south Atlanta, swinging from one leg to the other along many streets, through rich and poor neighborhoods, past communities, stores, unknown schools with their frazzled poplars and empty playgrounds and the brick chimneys of their power plants. He remembered once going with a strong wind, and a piece of wax paper that had blown beside him, a foot off the ground for a whole block, the fragile paper twisting at his side like an obsession, its crackling drowned out by the rolling of his feet. (81)

Cahill remembers one particular moment when he "was going so fast that he was swept into a really dangerous velocity," when he "was centering into a condition he needed," and when "he swung up from the heft of the earth and felt it fall away." When he "spun on himself as he knew how to do, low-positioned, contained, self-solid with whirling," he understands that

> there was something *in there* with him, something drawn into the most central of his spinning, from the outside world, from any-where and everywhere, as from an infinite and ever-present waiting, an enormous hovering without air and without anything of the me-chanical or the lawful, and he spun, as though enclosed in live stone, dangerous, containing all fragility, impregnable with speed, then wheeling slowly down, restoring the trees and mailboxes to their places. (82)

In his imagination, his senses heightened and his existence intensi-fied, Dickey's elementary school years, in retrospect, seemed a golden world. At E. Rivers, he met many of the Buckhead Boys who would make his childhood memorable, including Jack Emerson, a superior football player at E. Rivers who later starred at North Fulton and Clemson, as well as Richard Lamb, Bill Barnwell, Dick Harris, and Jack Coleman. When a heart attack killed his childhood hero, Jack Emerson, Dickey wrote Cole-man on 24 March 1971, expressing a longing for those golden days:

> [Our lives] will never be what they were when we were boys, and as I think back on those times I am filled with an enormous nostalgia for the decent fellows we were in those days, though God knows, as boys we were certainly not any angels. But I remember the long afternoons when we played football until we could hardly see the

ball in the air any longer, and the rest. That is not the worst way to grow up.... When the war came along, all those days went with them, and all we can do now is remember. (Hart 28)

Dickey would memorialize his friends in his October 1969 poem, "Looking for the Buckhead Boys":

> Some of the time, going home, I go
> Blind and can't find it.
> The house I lived in growing up and out
> The doors of high school is torn
> Down and cleared
> Away for further development, but that does not stop me.
> First in the heart
> Of my blind spot are
> The Buckhead Boys. If I can find them, even one,
> I'm home. And if I can find him catch him in or around
> Buckhead, I'll never die; it's likely my youth will walk
> Inside me like a king.

In 1936, when Dickey graduated from E. Rivers, he appeared a normal, happy-go-lucky boy who nevertheless kept his literary interests and class-consciousness to himself. Under his name, the school yearbook, *The Rivers Overflow*, read, "A good old scout, Everyone's happy when he's about." Dickey's report cards for grades 3, 4, and 5 reveal almost all As. Only in "Hardwork" and "Writing" did he earn Bs. In grade 6, his grades fell slightly, a balance of As and Bs over all four quarters of the academic year with a C– in English and a C+ in geography for the second quarter. A classmate, Virginia Kirkland, remembered Dickey as bright and handsome, a shy, quiet boy who rarely spoke in class. Teachers, she stated, recognized his literary abilities. After reading a story in class, one teacher said to Dickey, "You could have written that" (Hart 26). E. Rivers, Kirkland declared, was a potpourri of wealthy and poor students from different sections of Atlanta. It felt rural partly because children living in shacks in the Peachtree Creek neighborhood attended. Students from the country, moreover, were bused in and sat side-by-side in class with scions of families such as the Dickeys, whose son Jimmy would play dodgeball and marbles at recess while wearing fashionable knickers. What was not apparent, but which would appear more so in high school, was Dickey's intense desire to excel, to transcend the world as he knew it, because the world as he knew it was inadequate.

In 1939 the North Fulton High School football team had compiled twenty-two consecutive victories and won the North Georgia Interscholastic Conference Championship. Dickey had made the team the year before. "I can surely say," he later wrote in *Self-Interviews*, "that the high school experience is absolutely transformative in the case of boys. I think failure in athletics is one of the most terrible things that can happen to a person. I was sort of neutral in high school, poised between success and failure" (151). For Jim Dickey, that would not have been enough. His idealized sense of self, his heightened sensitivity to perceived challenges, and the belief that his father not only did not understand him but also considered him a failure all rendered his athletic performances on the gridiron and on the track field less than adequate. Indeed, these same attitudes would later result in Dickey's sullen or occasional belligerent words and actions, which baffled friends and colleagues to whom Dickey was always gracious and accommodating if not outright generous. "He was a big, powerful man," his son Chris stated, "and he would use that in situations where he thought he could intimidate other men physically. He was also belligerent dealing with other writers and sometimes with editors." Such moments were almost subconscious, self-protective responses to perceived threats or to the failure of others to acknowledge his perceived self-worth.

Although Dickey made the football team all four years of high school, most of the time was spent on the bench as a substitute quarterback or a second-string wingback, the equivalent today of a wide receiver and running back. A fellow player, John Jarrell, described Dickey as a satisfactory blocker and tackler at a time when players served on both offensive and defensive teams, but Dickey earned a reputation of being "self-conscious, thin-skinned, and literary" (Hart 37). Football, however, allowed him to claim an area where he, and not his younger brother, Tom, could excel, even if he were not the star he desired to be. Sibling rivalry had become inevitable since Tom's birth on 5 February 1925, two years after Jimmy's. Al Braselton, who befriended both men while working in Atlanta advertising during the fifties and sixties, later wrote in his unpublished memoir, "Jim was the apple of his mother's eye until Tom Swift Dickey was born. Tom soon took his mother's attention from his older brother and Jim, until then a fairly dutiful, sensitive child, got his first taste of competition. He lost. He never regained the number one child slot." Jimmy was quiet; Tom, by contrast, loud and boisterous, demanding attention by screaming for it.

As each grew, Tom's natural athletic abilities made him a star of playground activities. Jimmy vied for parental attention and praise but usually fell short. In high school and at Louisiana State University, Tom was the son whose athletic accomplishments in track made headline news. Baselton remembered, "Jim went out for everything Tom went out for in high school athletics and came in second best in the one that was most important to the Dickey brothers: track and field. Tom was delicate so Jim could beat him at the rougher sports like football." Tom's career reached its zenith in 1948 when he qualified for the Olympic tryouts, but a persistent injury hindered his performance. Dickey wrote James Wright on 6 September 1958, declaring, "I have been connected with sports all my life, as has my whole family (my brother just missed the 1948 Olympic team by about six inches, give or take)" (*One Voice*, I 280). Ironically, Jim Dickey himself possessed considerable talent in track.

Dickey impressed his high school track coach, Robert Lowrance, with his strength and agility. Lowrance recalled, "I squatted beside the hurdle and watched him barely clear the cross-piece and slap his forward foot as close to the hurdle as possible, then stride to the next one. Jim was 'doing it right.' His championships testify to that. Although slightly tall for the low hurdles, Jim was a strong, intelligent athlete, and he adapted his stride to a conquering length and pace" (Hart 38). While he achieved only a backup position on the football team, Dickey broke records on the track team. By April 1941, he had the fastest time (26.6 seconds) in the 220 low hurdles in the history of North Fulton High School. The 1940 team, on which Dickey ran, surpassed all previous teams, winning the North Fulton relay and almost all of its other meets. In his essay "James Dickey's Glory," which first appeared in the October 1976 issue of *Esquire*, he commemorated his highest achievement, his performance in the 1940 North Georgia Interscholastic Conference track meet. He had lost in the trial to a hurdler from New Canton because of a bad start; his opponent had set a new conference record. In the finals that night, however, Dickey sensed that he and the New Canton racer were even:

> The finish-line crowd was coming at us like a hurricane. I concentrated on staying low over the hurdles and made really good moves on the next three. I began to edge him by inches, and by the next two hurdles I thought that if I didn't hit the next two I'd make it. I said to myself, *don't* play it safe. Go low over the last stick, and then give it everything you've got up the final straight.

> But I did hit the last hurdle. I hit it with the inner ankle of my
> left foot, tearing the flesh to the bone, as I found out later, and the
> injury left a scar which I still have. However, my frenzied momen-
> tum was such that I won by a yard, careening wildly into the crowd
> after the tape broke around my neck. I smashed into the spectators
> and bowled over a little boy, hitting him straight into his nose with
> my knee. (*Night Hurdling* 184)

Crowded by spectators and well-wishers who surrounded him with congratulations, Dickey bent over the boy, whose nose was bleeding, and
kissed the child. Nosebleeds would later appear in entries in his notebooks
written during the fifties (where he characterized a nosebleed as "a fresh-
ening of the blood") and in *Alnilam*. Later, Dickey would often surprise
children of faculty with whom he stayed during his reading tours by kissing
them upon the head. Regardless of whether he had, in fact, injured a child
and then attempted to make him feel better, the story reveals, if only
through invention, not only Dicky's competitiveness, his head-down and
head-long rush for glory, but also his sensitivities, a kind of kinship, a
larger sense of family.

High school, like his years at E. Rivers, seemed in memory a magical
time for Dickey, a sense of which appears in his essay "Starting from Buckhead":

> Those are the main parts of this particularly odd Odyssey: how a
> decent enough and rather plodding young fellow from Buckhead
> ended up as a poet. And if I've left out the reading and studying and
> concentrated on the people, that's probably as it should be, for they
> are more important. And so if anybody asks you how Jim Dickey
> became a poet, starting from Buckhead, you can say that one day he
> got off the bench at North Fulton High School, but instead of go-
> ing into the football game, he got a red motorcycle belonging to Ed
> van Valkenberg and rode off into North Georgia. Tell whoever asks
> you, that Jim Dickey listened to a lot of jazz with Walter
> Armistead,...and that he published, in the end, some poems based
> on these things. (*Night Hurdling* 188)

Richard Lamb, with whom Dickey watched B-grade movies at the
Buckhead Theater on Saturdays as well as participated in sports at Dickey's
homemade backyard complex, and Bill Barnwell, who exuded a free-spirited love-of-life attitude that Dickey liked, were friends, part of the coterie
of boys that made Buckhead special. Barnwell loved poetry; he and Dickey

shared their favorite poems by Robert Frost and Edgar Allan Poe, particularly the former. For the young romantics, Frost became the "king of poets," though Dickey, in a 1974 interview with Don Greiner, later distinguished between "the man and his public image and what he actually did put down on the page" (Baughman, *Voiced Connections* 134). Dickey always celebrated what he termed Frost's "technical triumph," which he defined as "the creation of a particular kind of poetry-speaking voice," while criticizing Frost "the raconteur," who "certainly must have been one of the worst sons of bitches that ever lived" (134–35). "The Frost I like is the plain-speaking guy," Dickey stated, "who can in the most conversational way say things that you wouldn't have thought of in a million years" (138). Fifty years later, Barnwell could still recite lines from Dickey's favorite Frost poems (Hart 34), including "Acquainted with the Night" and "After Apple-Picking." Two of Dickey's favorite friends, Ed van Valkenburg and Walter Armistead, were members of the 1939 class of North Fulton High School. Both boys had taught Dickey to ride motorcycles, which he would drive to his father's old homestead in Mineral Bluff (*Night Hurdling* 186). Van Valkenburg, "an extraordinary person," would recite Rudyard Kipling and Robert Service while lifting weights with young Dickey. Armistead loved music, especially the drums; he and Dickey listened obsessively to records of Gene Krupa playing with the Benny Goodman Band. Dickey later recalled, "I never think of Blake's wonderful statement that 'exuberance is beauty' without thinking of Walter" (*Night Hurdling* 186). Armistead was killed in an airplane crash after being recalled for the Korean conflict.

As with family, Dickey incorporated his high school friends and classmates in the poems he later published; they provided poetic subject matter and reinforced aesthetic principles. Writing in an early notebook in 1952, he examined his poetry:

> There is a perfect and diamond clarity about the fact that my best and profoundest asset is my analytic refusal to be hoodwinked; my best quality is my facility for analysis. On this depends my best poetry, the best character-searching I do, the deepest convictions I have. This may depend at least in part on intuition (perhaps not), but most of it is contained in the stubborn "not-to-be-fooled" principle which I exercise even in looking at someone. There is that in me which cherishes, longs for, a sincere and self-negating (but *is* it that?) delusion, but my analytic faculty will forever prevent this while I am worth anything. A good delusion (while one is *aware*

that it is a delusion: Walter Armistead, etc.) is a pleasant diversion,
or an intense one, a sort of gentle and deep layering of the ghost of
one's youth, but the delusion must not be a *principle* of contemplation (except as an *exploratory* devise) or action, must never supplant.
(*Striking In* 78)

Dickey understood and valued the sustaining illusion that offered a truth
beyond mere facts. He also recognized from among the many imaginative
worlds he poetically visited the finite reality of where he finally stood.
Armistead reminded Dickey of the necessity of "a good delusion." In an
elegy titled simply "Walter Armistead," written in the fifties and published
in 1992, Dickey honored his music-loving friend, a fellow student at
North Fulton "whose admiration for the swing music of the early 40's gave
me my first notion of what genuine ecstasy might be" (*Night Hurdling*
186). Other friends and acquaintances were similarly instructive. Mary
Ann Robinson, a young woman Dickey remembered as pretty and quiet,
reminding him of his own vulnerabilities, became Jane MacNaughton, the
athletic tomboy on "the passionless playground" in "The Leap," who, as a
mother of four, later commits suicide. "The Shark's Parlor" (1965) re-
counts an ambitious fishing trip with Bill Barnwell, who remembered
Dickey as introspective and well mannered, not given to aggressive male
behavior, fighting, car racing, or drinking. Charlotte Sheram Holbrook, a
year ahead of Dickey at North Fulton and who was voted the "Most Original" girl in her class (just as Walter Armistead had been "Most Original"
the previous year), became Doris Holbrook in "Cherrylog Road" (1963).
Her clandestine sexual rendezvous with the speaker in the middle of a car
graveyard depicts the human need to live life fully, a desire to be "Drunk
on the wind in my mouth, / Wringing the handlebar for speed, / Wild to
be wreckage forever."

Dickey graduated from North Fulton High School in 1941, having
lettered in football and track in 1940 and 1941. His academic performance
was mediocre, failing courses in algebra and Latin; only his grades in English were acceptable. Generally he earned Cs, the reason perhaps why in
"The Last Will and Testament" section of the 1941 North Fulton yearbook, Dickey is listed as "just hop[ing] to leave." The yearbook photograph
shows a handsome young man with wavy blond hair brushed stylishly back
from his forehead. Unlike the other young men, he is smiling, as if he
knows a superior secret. His outward appearance and inner feelings reveal
a study in contrasts. Conventional in his efforts to appear as "one of the
boys," indifferent to academics while seriously involved in sports, playing

gender-specific male roles, Dickey also seemingly embraced Southern-specific rituals of manhood, courtship, and familial duty. Years later, he would romanticize his high school years, reminiscing about being a carefree and indulgent rebel, gunning his motorcycle through the North Georgia hills, shooting pool, and racing cars, at times even a dangerous character. Beneath the façade, however, behind the bravado, was a quiet, sensitive young man who hid his literary yearnings. His imaginative projection of self-mandated extraordinary efforts and accomplishments required, if necessary, repudiation of accepted norms and acknowledgment by others of who he essentially was.

Estranged from his father, who failed to understand his son's sensitivities, and overly close to his mother, who initially wished to protect him from lower-class influences and later from involvement in the Second World War, Dickey felt guilt over his resentment toward his parents, plagued by his belief that his birth depended on the death of Gene. He began, though he was likely unaware of it, a frenetic search for new values, knowledge, truth, an answer-to-it-all explanation of and justification for the intellectual journeys he would soon undertake and which would move him through the demesnes of religion, philosophy, anthropology, psychology, art, and music. Indeed, his poetry may be explained largely by the precarious position in which his early recognition of human frailty and mortality placed him. As Chris Dickey would later write, "He just could not bear to let those years, that life, that energy of the handsome track star slip away from him. He wanted to recover it all in his writing, his drinking, and in me" ("23 Years after My Father's Death: 'A Poet's Family Album'").

CHAPTER 2

SEPARATION

In a 1965 interview, James Dickey was asked when he began to write poetry. He had been intrigued in high school by Shelley's poem "The Cloud,"
one of whose lines reads, "I change, but I cannot die," and by Byron, who
"seemed to me to epitomize the man who both scorned women and was
sought out by them" (*Self-Interviews* 23). That portrayal led to his reading
John Drinkwater's biography, *The Pilgrim of Eternity, Byron—A Conflict*.
Dickey responded to the interviewer by stating, "I began, the nearest I can
remember, in writing long letters. The early 40s were great times to write
letters to girls from the people in the service, and I wrote long, romantic
letters to girls and out of those, somehow, developed a kind of rudimentary
poetry" (Baughman, *Voiced Connections* 12). If Byron's tempestuous behavior and outright rebellion against the entrenched aristocratic class into
which he was born interested Dickey, the young women he met and dated
unknowingly stirred his literary ambitions. They included Virginia Kirkland, Peggy Steward, Beverly Adams, and Angelique de Golian, whose
wealthy and cultured family served in Dickey's mind as a marked counterpoint to his own. While the Dickeys were financially well-off, his father's
background, illegal activities, and inherent laziness compromised any
sense of being upper class. De Golian became the basis for an early unpublished poem, "The Entrance into Jerusalem," written in the early fifties. In it, he compares her splendid home to the holy city and himself to
a supplicating Christ. While romance provided motivation for Dickey's
poetry, a practical justification for his interest, books and bombing missions finally determined him to become a writer, coalescing his literary
sensibilities and providing them with purpose and direction. "The war,"
he later declared, "did not really come completely to bear on me significantly, other than my personal participation in it, until the years after the
real war was over and this sort of Proustian memory thing takes over and
makes of it not what it was but what it was to you. That's when the poems
began to be written about various aspects of it" (248). Before he entered
that conflict, however, Dickey began to separate himself from the world as

he knew it, the safe confines of Buckhead, with its mandated rules of social conduct and parental expectations.

Following a year at Darlington School, a military preparatory academy in Rome, Georgia, which Dickey attended partly to improve his football skills and partly to enhance his otherwise lackluster academic credentials, he enrolled at Clemson A & M College in fall 1942, intending to become an engineer. His idols, Jack Emerson and Tom McIlwain, played football there. Dickey had not been happy at Darlington, later describing his athletic performance at the school as "dismal" (Hart 49), largely the result, he claimed, of hamstring problems. That his younger brother was already excelling on the high school track field rankled him; indeed, Tom would eventually appear on the May 1947 cover of *Southern Coach & Athlete* while he attended LSU. Outwardly Dickey was moody and distant at Darlington, though polite and quiet in class. His permanent record indicates that he enrolled in French II, physics, math, and English. Frank Rogers, a graduate of the University of North Carolina and a Victorian specialist and gifted teacher at Darlington, would watch Dickey trudge alone to his dormitory, the dining hall, or the classroom buildings. "He broke our hearts," Rogers remembered. "Nobody could get close to him." Under Rogers's tutelage, however, Dickey's grades improved, and he later admitted to the teacher's formative influence. "He was a lover of Browning," Dickey stated. "I don't think I've read any Browning since those days, or very little. Also, 'The Rubáiyát [of Omar Khayyám' by Edward Fitzgerald]. He would read it to us in class. And then I could get something from that" (49). Dickey even won his first literary prize at Darlington, the Society of Colonial Daughters' "Patriotic Essay Medal." Gradually his grades in English became As, while those in math, French, and science remained mediocre. Rogers and other faculty, including Headmaster Ernest Wright, who had attended William and Mary and then earned a master's degree from the University of Virginia, could not have been more surprised, and perplexed, therefore, when Dickey entered Clemson as an engineering major, a decision he made to appease his father.

The medal-winning submission was a one-page, single-spaced typed paper in which Dickey recalled a magazine article that featured an Italian immigrant who ran a small gas station and who daily put a dollar of his earnings into a cigar box to purchase defense bonds. Pointing to the American flag flying over the establishment, he says to a customer who has inquired about his practice, "Well, that flag, she done swell by me, now I'm gonna stick by her." Dickey uses the story to argue that if "this country would catch the spirit of this lowly, foreign born immigrant, we would be a whole lot nearer to winning the war." The essay, now among the Dickey papers at Emory University, then proceeds to suggest that Americans, "softened by twenty years of peace," are now going through "the toughening stage" and that "no price is too great for our precious heritage of freedom." Dickey effectively ends the essay with a series of rhetorical questions and declarative statements that increasingly build verbal momentum.

> What does a pleasure ride in the country mean beside freedom of speech? Who would prefer sugar in his coffee to freedom of thought and action? This liberty, this thing which enumerable brave men and women have sacrificed, fought, and died for, is a sacred trust. They conceived it, they built it, they preserved it, they passed it on to us. Shall we let the torch be extinguished which was kindled by the dreams, the sweat and blood of our ancestors?

As counterpoint to sentences that parallel clauses and phrases, Dickey concluded this overt patriotism with a simple sentence whose brevity deepens its forcefulness: "I say NO."

That Dickey's father wanted his son to become an engineer and his mother to prevent his going to war rendered Clemson a logical choice. Dickey himself still desired to play sports, and Clemson was a dominant school in the Southern Conference, even winning the Cotton Bowl in 1939. Yet the idea of his becoming a writer was deepening. He had read his first serious novel at age fourteen, W. Somerset Maugham's *Of Human Bondage*, which his sister, Maibelle, had checked out of the Yellow Lantern Lending Library. Dickey had discovered it lying around the house. He later told Chris, "I was outraged, because, in all the books I had read, the hero was so virtuous. Here was this novel about this crippled guy who had all these evil, lustful fantasies. I thought, 'Jesus, this guy is too much like me'" (*Summer of Deliverance* 45). Dickey convinced others, moreover, that his parents, whom he claimed were divorcing, had forced him to attend Darlington (Hart 50). In the 1942 Darlington yearbook, *Jabberwokk*, while Dickey stands in the last row, far right, with the football team, wearing jersey #83 and an old-fashioned skullcap helmet, only his name appears in lieu of a graduation photo in a special section titled "Seniors Without Pictures." A sense of Dickey's disdain for Darlington can be gleaned from an unpublished letter dated 25 May 1981 to President James P. McCallie, who had written Dickey soliciting alumni for financial support. "Let me make myself quite plain in his matter. Anything pertaining to Darlington

School, past, present or future, is thoroughly abhorrent to me. I was there one year, and a more disgusting combination of cant, hypocrisy, cruelty, class privilege and inanity I have never since encountered at any human institution." The letter concluded, "I hope this note will serve to get me forever off your mailing list. And if possible, please expunge me also from your rolls, if that is possible, as I wish I could do with the recollection of the place that I have."

That Clemson was a pragmatic choice did not alter the fact that Dickey disliked it almost immediately. Clemson president R. F. Poole had undoubtedly stirred Dickey's patriotism when, in August 1942, he had addressed the freshman class: "You are entering college at a time when practically the entire world is at war. Our nation will not perish if we prepare adequately for its defense" (Hart 61). While Dickey was completing his first semester at Darlington, Japan had attacked Pearl Harbor on 7 December 1941; Congress declared war the next day, and Germany and Italy subsequently entered the conflict against the United States. Like millions of young men, Dickey prepared to answer the call for America's defense. As he had written in the essay for the Society of Colonial Daughters, "If we are to defeat the Powers of Evil who threaten us, every man, woman and child must do his part, however small."

Having taken ROTC at both North Fulton High School and at Darlington, Dickey was not averse to military training, but Clemson's program was both rigorous and humiliating. In those years Clemson was an all-male institution with a strong military atmosphere. "Rats" had their hair shorn and were paddled for reasons as inane as failure to remember an upperclassman's name. As part of the hazing, rats hauled the arriving students' trunks from the parade ground to the barracks. In an 11 September 1942 letter to his parents, Dickey said,

> There are a lot of country hicks around here, but most of them are pretty nice fellows. I am working as hard as I can on everything I have to do, and I think I can make a success of most of my endeavors up here. We haven't started classes yet, but probably will within the next couple of days. This place is kind of tough to take for one who loves home as much as I do, but I'll get along o.k. I went out for football yesterday, and did pretty well considering it was my first day. I was one of the littlest ones on the team, so you can see what I'm up against. (*One Voice*, I 32)

Confronted by country hicks and huge football players, Dickey managed to survive the Darwinian environment where the fittest survive and dominate while the weaker lose and disappear.

Dickey's letters home strained to sound upbeat. He usually wrote his parents separately because they were so different in personality. "Dear Pop," he opened an early September 1942 missive, "After all those boys were so nice to me, we went to a pep meeting, and I stood there and sang the college songs with tears rolling down my face. It's a feeling impossible to describe; but I know that, win or lose, this is the only school for me.... Sometimes it gets pretty hard here, but I can stick it out all right. I'm taking Civil Engineering, and it's pretty tough. I passed my math exam, and now I don't have to come back next summer, if I pass all my subjects" (*One Voice*, I 33). He wrote his mother more frequently. "Dearest, dearest Mom," he began a letter postmarked 21 September,

> I'm doing pretty well in my books, except for a few things. I am working hard to become a successful engineer, though sometimes I wish I was just going to be a 'helluva' engineer at [Georgia] Tech, and drinking liquor and belonging to a fraternity and having dates all the time in my old home town.... Mom, I know you would be the last person in the world to say such a thing, but I feel that I have been such a disappointment to everyone. I wish sometimes I could just pass out of the picture, but then I think of my wonderful family, and that gives me strength to go on. (*One Voice*, I 34)

It is possible to argue that such sentimentality and homesickness reveal a manipulative desire for attention from his father and even oedipal feelings of attachment to his mother; at the very least, however, they suggest deep dissatisfaction with his present situation. Though football interested him (he played safety on defense and wingback and quarterback on offense), he never played well enough to be a consistent starter, informing his father in September 1942 that he had been demoted from the first to the third string for loafing: "That's one thing they won't stand for around here.... Every player on the team is but a means to an end, to win for the school" (*One Voice*, I 33). Years later, he would write several poems on football, including "For the Death of Vince Lombardi" (1971) and "In the Pocket" (1983), both of which use the sport as an analogy for the conflict inherent in life itself. In "In the Pocket," for example, which Dickey wrote after the poem was commissioned by the National Football League, a quarterback searches for his receiver before the offensive line protecting him completely collapses. He thinks, "Throw it hit him in the middle / Of his enemies hit him move scramble / Before death and the ground / Come up." Football becomes a trope for warfare.

While Dickey liked the problem-solving nature of engineering, the subject itself was difficult, and he struggled with math. The pressure to enlist, moreover, was intense. Major Farr addressed the cadets in early December 1942: "Clemson men, the time has come when we must think and act not as individuals or as separate states, but as a nation. Firm, constructive, hopeful Christian leadership is what the world needs now. We must stand ready to fight and die if necessary to uphold the ideals upon which our nation was founded. This is the only way by which German aggression and Japanese imperialism can be destroyed." The speech, published in the 3 December issue of *The Tiger*, the Clemson student newspaper, served only to increase the pressure to join the service. Dickey left the university the following day and enlisted, writing his parents in a letter postmarked 24 February 1943, "I'm feeling fine. Tell everyone hello for me and, since I'm in the army, watch the paper for news of a big Allied victory" (*One Voice*, I 37). As he had written in his childhood autobiography, he was going to be a pilot.

The Second World War became the most significant and formative event in Dickey's life. In *Self-Interviews*, he asserted, "There's a God-like feeling about fighting on our planet. It's useless to deny it; there is, or at least some of the time there is. You can never do anything in your life that will give you such a feeling of consequence and of performing a dangerous and essential part in a great cause as fighting in a world war. The greatness is not only in the ideological sense, but exists also because millions of people are involved in the event" (137–38). After the conflict had ended and his ensuing education at Vanderbilt had been completed in 1950, he began to feel in retrospect, particularly after reading Sir James George Frazer, Jane Ellen Harrison, and Joseph Campbell, that his experiences in the army air forces constituted a mythic adventure. He viewed himself as a hero because he had separated himself from the known world, entered a heightened one, and returned with an enhanced knowledge while others had died. Now safely in Atlanta, he had brought back in 1946 an understanding of men, the world, and the nature of power, a "treasure" denied to most civilians who lacked the physical involvement in combat that he had won. His sensitivity and aesthetic responses mandated a need to be different; consequently, he now sought to mythologize himself and his experiences in poems. He perceived the war not as it was, the objective facts of squadrons and engagements, troop movements and casualty numbers, but rather as it had been to him, its personal significance. Combat also brought an increased personal guilt caused by his inexplicable survival while friends had died. The brutality of war necessitated the need for a psychological unity that would establish life-enhancing, more humanly vital connections. Excitement and youthful expectation, however, and a decided willingness to embrace new situations principally characterized the early months of his enlistment. Though he couched his letters home from various training bases in language designed to reassure his worried parents, he viewed what awaited him with satisfaction. He was a young man on a new track.

That track began in late February 1943. Pvt. James L. Dickey was stationed at Miami Beach, Florida, part of the 548th Technical School Squadron. Records from the Headquarters of the Fourth Service Command indicate that Dickey formally requested his appointment in a letter dated 5 January 1943. His trigonometry professor at Clemson, W. Gilbert Miller, wrote him a letter of recommendation. "In what association I have had with him," Miller declared, "I have found him to be trustworthy, industrious, courteous, neat and above average in technical ability. His physical qualifications are excellent and as far as I know he is in good health. In my opinion he would be successful in any endeavor requiring coordination, stamina and courage." Major Henry Konigemark Jr. acknowledged receipt of Dickey's application and advised him that, because appointments as an aviation cadet were made only after receiving specific quotas and directives from the War Department, he could not indicate the approximate date of Dickey's assignment. America's involvement in the war was just beginning, however, and Dickey was inducted quickly. He wrote his parents on 24 February that the train ride to Miami Beach had been wonderful, that he had met a girl with whom he had had "a pretty good time," and that his food and present accommodations were "swell." The customary haircut made him look "like several varieties of hell." "Where I'm staying," he wrote, "is a 'military secret,' but you can take it from me, it is really a swell place." He was having "a wonderful time," he optimistically declared, at the same time keeping "'on the ball'" (*One Voice*, I 36–37). Less than a week after arriving in Miami Beach, Dickey was assigned to the 412th Training Group, Flight E-1, to begin the process of determining whether he could qualify as a pilot, navigator, or bombardier.

Dickey received standard training, writing his parents on 14 March 1943 that he marched every morning with his Enfield rifle and gas mask, crawling on his stomach, rising quickly, and then flinging himself, he said, "'bodaciously' to terra firma once more. Ditto in the afternoon." He wondered if he were infantry. In the afternoon he did the same thing. "It's all a lot of fun," he wrote, "but the constant drilling *is* a trifle monotonous" (*One Voice*, I 38–39). Two days later he informed his mother that he had not yet passed his physical because of high blood pressure caused by nervousness. "He wanted to be an officer," his son Chris later related, "he wanted to be a pilot, and he wanted it all so bad, it scared the hell out of him" (*Summer of Deliverance* 44). Certainly such failure would have challenged his outward confidence and inner sense of self-identity. "If I don't measure up they'll throw me out of the Cadets," he told his mother. "Nothing ever happens the way I want it to, anyway. I knew almost from the beginning I was no good and that something would happen to thwart my plans. It's always been that way, and it always will. I'll never even see an airplane" (*One Voice*, I 39). The protestation was partly a plea for sympathy or attention and partly a statement, perhaps impetuous, of despair. Such moments, when Dickey seemed poised between two opposing possibilities, would became a feature in his later poems, including "The Driver" (1963), "Walking the Fire Line" (1963), and "The Flash" (1968). In "The Driver," for example, a soldier at the end of the war swims down under water and sits in a rusted sunken half-track, seeming to move "in the depths with the movement / One sees a thing take through tears / Of joy, or terrible sorrow, / A thing which in quietness lies / Beyond both." As he becomes accustomed "to the burning stare / Of the wide-eyed dead after battle," he comes to see "the uneasy lyrical skin that lies / Between death and life, trembling always." A week later Dickey informed his mother that he had passed the physical, and, although his blood pressure remained above normal, "now every thing is fine again." He wished he had left Clemson and joined the army air forces sooner, he declared in his 25 March letter. "I am absolutely crazy about it, and feel as if I were doing something for the first time in my life. Lord, how I hated Clemson" (*One Voice*, I 40).

Dickey's orders were slow in coming, and he worried about the delay. All but twenty-five of the original 105 in his section had already left. "I hate to stay behind," he wrote his mother on 26 March, "when everyone else is moving forward" (*One Voice*, I 41). On 4 April, however, he was at High Point College in North Carolina, a small, co-ed, liberal arts school affiliated with the United Methodist Church near Greensboro and Winston Salem, where enlistees took college courses in physics and other disciplines, including English. He immediately liked the college, he informed his mother on 8 April 1943, because it had "plenty of girls (it's co-ed) good food, and the purest and cleanest air that I've seen anywhere." He threw himself into his studies, optimistic, even buoyant, over his chances for success, which in the army air forces meant "almost 100% attitude, and the way you go about things." "Some people," he asserted, "the army starts on the downward path, but with me it is doing more good that I can ever possibly tell you. When I come back to you, I'll be a much better Jim than when I left. And you can depend on it" (*One Voice*, I 42). Dickey wrote his father on 12 April that he was now a lieutenant in the College Training Detachment, the fourth-ranking officer for a group of more than 200. "Don't ask me how I did it," he stated, "I have changed so much since I left home I can hardly recognize myself" (*One Voice*, I 43). He was proud of the flight group under his charge, Flight A; his "boys" continually won dress parade. The cadets were divided into flight groups, or classes. New arrivals eventually worked themselves up from Flight A to the first class, where they began actual flying instruction. Dickey was in Flight D, the second class section, from which the "officers" were selected. The first class was due to graduate on 22 May, at which time he would move up to Flight E and commence initial flying practice; his graduation was set for 19 May. Since he had had "a taste of command," he wrote his mother in an unpublished letter on 13 April, "I'm forever spoiled for being in the ranks."

Dickey's letters while at High Point reveal two principal concerns—family and war. He quoted from Poe's "To My Mother" in his 3 May 1943 letter. Though he recognized that "you don't love poetry as I do," he thought these lines might be appropriate:

> Because I feel that, in the Heavens above,
>   The angels, whispering to one another,
> Can find, among their burning terms of love,
>   None so devotional as that of "Mother,"
> Therefore by that dear name I long have called you—
>   You who are more than mother unto me,
> And fill my heart of hearts—

"But the rest" he declared, "doesn't pertain to the subject" (*One Voice*, I 44). The remainder of the poem concerns itself with a mother's death. He wrote his father on 11 May that the fighting would likely last much longer but that the United States would eventually win. "It is impossible that any other country could have the training facilities that we have, and trained men will win the war, depend on it" (*One Voice*, I 45). Newspaper headlines the previous week reported that American troops had established the first breach in the German defenses in North Africa. Troops had captured Tunis and Bizerte in Tunisia, seizing fifty thousand prisoners. More than 2,500 sorties were flown on 7 May alone, and 1,250,000 pounds of bombs dropped. In the Pacific, American submarines had sunk six Japanese ships, including two destroyers, and a troop transport had been hit near New Guinea. Dickey intently followed these war bulletins, knowing that he would soon be a participant. He told his father that "the great news in Africa must have cheered Mom up considerably."

Behind these letters, however, full of unrelated accomplishments and unnecessary information, lay Dickey's real intention, which he had slowly been approaching. College physics, Tom's track success, girls Dickey had met or liked or to whom he wanted his mother to send a photograph of himself, a letter he had received from Jack Emerson who had broken his leg at the Parris Island Marine Base—such news, awkwardly linked or quickly conveyed, belied his principal concern. "I know I'll be commissioned as a pilot," he wrote his mother on 31 May 1943, "for something wonderful has happened. I know I am good for something. First, I can run. The coach here clocked me in ten flat yesterday.... But that is secondary. *I can write*. Always before I have had some doubts as to my ability, but not any more. The English teacher here says my themes are the best he's ever read" (*One Voice*, I 47). He included the rough draft of an essay on Bix Beiderbecke, the largely self-taught jazz cornetist, pianist, and composer of the twenties, that he had written for an English assignment. Titled "The Rebel Soul—1931" and included in his letter, the 1,000-word piece was not altogether successful, he admitted, but he felt the essay had some merit and was interesting "in a feverish, breathless, sort of way" (*One Voice*, I 48–50). The essay opens, "Most of us are cut from the same pattern, and, with minor variations, have practically the same intents and aims in life. But there are some, yes, many, who by the very nature of their own being, and by their particular talents, are destined to be singled out from the many and live brilliant but somehow strangely distorted and out-of-focus lives." He placed Beiderbecke with such figures as Napoleon, Alexander the Great, Beethoven, Byron, and Shelley as possessing the spark of greatness. "After they have gone," he asserted, "everything is not quite the same. Things have been altered." "The music was in him," Dickey wrote, "and he had to get it out. Get it out or perish. His music never satisfied him.

He was always striving, seeking new notes, combination of notes, chord sequences; many of which were not possible to render upon his instrument." Beiderbecke's attitudes reflected Dickey's own and help explain the poetic experimentation characteristic of Dickey's career. It explains why, in his early notebooks, he would quote Jean Cocteau and why in *Sorties* he would declare, "The longer I live, the longer and better the whole perspective of possibility becomes, and the more I see how necessary it is to *throw* one's self open to the least chance impulse or stimulus coming from anywhere" (53). "I want now to gear myself up to say what nobody could have thought of in a hundred million years," he stated. "I want to make a new reality; this one is not good enough. Words can change it all, if they come from the right direction and fall in the right ears" (56).

While at High Point, Dickey's facility with language became apparent not only to his instructors but also to his fellow cadets who enjoyed his "extemporaneous flights of fancy" (Hart 68) that served to cajole and entertain. Among the cadets Dickey knew were Frank Spain, Winston Smith, Joseph Dole, and Watson Smooth. Spain appears as a cadet in *Alnilam*, described as "a good boy" and "a real hard knocker" (237) who is high-up in the Alnilam conspiracy. One of Dickey's closest friends at High Point was Andrew Harbelis, to whom he confided his desire to become a writer and his intention to obtain a job in advertising, which he believed compatible with writing. Harbelis also appears in *Alnilam* as well as its unfinished sequel "Crux," which concerns the air war in the Pacific. "Harbelis," Chris Dickey later wrote, "is nothing but Intercept Officer Jim Dickey. Harbelis 'had washed out of flight training because his captain had decided he could not fly well enough for the time he had logged, and he had joined the eliminees. It did not bother him'" (*Summer of Deliverance* 48). Harbelis encouraged Dickey's literary ambitions, and Dickey, in turn, offered Harbelis lessons on appropriate running techniques in advance of their five-mile jogs across the North Carolina countryside.

On the day he received his first flight instruction, learning all the maneuvers and attempting an unsuccessful loop, Dickey wrote his father a prose description of a day's football practice at Clemson. He had used as a model, he said in his letter postmarked 8 June 1943, Remarque's *All Quiet on the Western Front* (1929) in order to provide a sense of simultaneity of action. He wanted to keep in mind "not a single day's performance but a composite of all the days we scrimmaged the varsity." The description was aimed at making the reader experience what he himself had, a situational immediacy that required or insisted upon participation, though he was "considerably disheartened" by the essay. In *Sorties* he later commented on Remarque's novel: "They [the critics] fault it for its lack of characterization. But what seems to me to be good about the book, as an account of warfare, is this very simplicity, and the fact that the author is not forever analyzing the characters and the inner relationships of the people in the story" (23). Titled simply "Practice at Clemson," the essay opens, "I go from my last class, which is Trig, to my room in the second barracks. I lie on the bed from three to three thirty, then get up reluctantly and start down toward the gym. I take my time about it, for I am in no particular hurry" (*One Voice*, I 50–53). The search for a radically new and simple style eventually led Dickey to experiment with language in his own novels and in various verse forms. Remarque's portrait of trench warfare achieves verisimilitude through concise yet versatile language that skillfully weaves together a series of episodes told by the protagonist in first person. He presents the events subjectively, not objectively, with selective observations filtered through the narrator's consciousness. Dickey later adopted this technique in his poetry by presenting objective settings and situations which then gradually yield to the speaker's subjective reinterpretation of them. Remarque also extolls the one great quality that the war produced in the combatants, the sense of comradeship and the affinity of those linked together in a gigantic undertaking, as if the millions of soldiers on the Western Front constituted a team of immense size. A football team differed only in number from that of an army; both desired to win.

June 1943 found Dickey in Nashville, Tennessee, for classification. He had barely passed his final check-ride in a little 65-horsepower Piper at High Point with a 72; 70 was failing. Only in taxiing on the ground, taking off, and holding in a traffic pattern had his grade been average. "He must have known then," Chris Dickey wrote, "it was going to be tough to make it as a pilot" (*Summer of Deliverance* 44). He did not relate his doubts to his parents and likely did not acknowledge them to himself. He wrote his mother on 23 June that the camp compared "favorably with most of our Georgia prison camps" and was "the most *in*efficiently run army camp I've ever seen.... No one does any work unless a stick of dynamite is placed under him" (*One Voice*, I 53–54). Selected as barracks lieutenant, or barracks chief, where, in exchange for his ensuring that the huts were clean and inspected, he was excused from KP and guard duty, he was not happy. His newly acquired free time was wasted because the squadron itself was on quarantine for two weeks, restricted to an area of about five acres. During the first week in Nashville, Dickey underwent a barrage of mental, physical, and psychological tests to determine his classification. Several of these gauged alertness, coordination, memory, reflexes, and manual dexterity. He attributed his success in these tests to his participation in sports and optimistically felt he would soon be classified as a pilot. He informed his father on 27 June, however, that "anything the army wants to do with me is o.k." (*One Voice*, I 54–55). Though he wanted to be a pilot, his desire to become a writer had become more important.

On 29 July 1943, Dickey, no. 14175259, was stationed at Maxwell Field in Alabama, preparing for basic flight training in Squadron H of Group V. While at Nashville, he had received his warrant as a flight officer and was now a pilot trainee. Further testing would determine his final classification. His grades were good, he informed his mother in an unpublished letter dated 7 August, and he was "really learning something." "This place is the first evidence I have seen of the Army Air Force really doing business." In an unpublished letter to his brother, Tom, dated the same day, he was both more emphatic, "Boy, they are really working the shit out of us," and more specific, informing him of the coursework, which included aerial navigation, Morse code, aircraft identification, math, physics, and military and physical training. Dickey's later interest in stars and in navigational location commenced during these weeks, eventually manifesting itself in his long poem *The Zodiac* and in his second novel, *Alnilam*. After he became poet-in-residence and professor of English at the University of South Carolina in 1968, he would use his sextants at his home on Lake Katharine to determine his exact position in the universe. In a 1983 essay "Play for Voices: Log of a Stationary Navigator," Dickey wrote, "I take the noon-position sight from the sun every day as a matter of homage to this particular locality. I want God to assure me, through the movements of the celestial bodies, that I really am here, at 34 degrees, no minutes and 2-tenths north and at 80 degrees, 57 minutes and 7-tenths west. This morning I was off about half a mile but I'll get it back tomorrow" (*Night Hurdling* 197). A man's position in time and space, his exact location, constituted a statement of self-identity and a confirmation of his existence.

As the months passed since Dickey's induction, the tone of his letters became increasingly more serious and responsible as he experienced different areas of the South and met people of various ethnicities and backgrounds, enlarging his perspective and further separating him from the safe provinciality he had known at home. "It's a funny thing," he wrote his mother on 23 August 1943, "but I've learned how to get along with all kinds of people. Jews, Greeks, Wops, all kinds." The routine at Maxwell Field stiffened, and while his correspondence was frequently light-hearted, a kind of casual banter, two cadets died of heat exhaustion during physical training on the obstacle course. Dickey badly cut his hand there. His mother had informed him that two of his friends had been killed while flying. Dickey responded simply, "Those things happen in the air, though, and no one is to blame. Don't worry about me, though. I'll probably get washed out before I ever solo!" (*One Voice*, I 56–57).

On 1 October 1943 Dickey was stationed in Camden, South Carolina, for his primary flight training. Letters home became sporadic. Most of his time was used to accrue the sixty-three hours of required flight time. Though the army was washing out many of the flyers, Dickey still believed his military career was "right on the beam" and that he would succeed, but if he did not, he wrote his mother on 8 October, "what the hell! I'm trying the hardest way, as my Yankee friends would say" (*One Voice*, I 57–58). Three weeks later, on 28 October, Dickey wrote his brother a long letter left-handed, detailing how he had "busted" his thumb in a crack-up. Flying solo for the first time, he had become so nervous that as he approached the landing, he cut the engine: "I was shaking so bad the plane was vibrating like Pop's '34 Ford on the road to What-cha-know Joe's. I was afraid the engine would fall out, so I cut the motor and came in" (*One Voice*, I 58–59). The plane bounced thirty feet in the air four times and one wing caught the dirt, causing the aircraft to spin in a circle. Dickey was thrown against the instrument panel. He did not mention the incident to either parent but wrote Tom, "When I got out I expected St. Peter to greet me at the Pearly Gates, but it was only the mechanics with a hose to clean the *shit* out of the cockpit" (*One Voice*, I 58–59). On 12 November, he informed his mother that he had failed his first check-ride, though he added he was learning quickly and, determined to show his parents that he would succeed, declared he had little doubt he would subsequently pass. If he washed out as a pilot, he stated, he could still qualify as a navigator or bombardier. All his roommates from Maxwell Field had washed out (Hart 72).

If Jim Dickey were to become a pilot, it would be here in these little two-seater Stearman biplanes repeatedly taking off and landing on dusty runways. He desperately wanted to succeed and to please his parents. His letter to Tom, however, has the voice of a Southern schoolboy brushing off the incident as unimportant. Yet behind the tone is also the sense of something more important. Before he ever saw combat, Jim Dickey was writing. As his son Chris would later remember, "Maybe it was when he was back at Darlington composing patriotic essays or maybe it was long before that, while he was lying on that swing bed in Atlanta, that Jim Dickey got it into his head that writing was what he really wanted to do, and a writer was what he wanted to be" (*Summer of Deliverance* 45).

In a 1970 poem titled "Camden Town—Army Air Corps Flight Training, 1943," Dickey described and then reimagined his experiences in the Stearman in which the army air forces trained pilots. The poem opens, "With this you trim it. Do it right and the thing'll fly / Itself. Now get up there and get those lazy- / eights down. A check-ride's coming at you / Next week." The aircraft is "holding the West by a needle," and the speaker realizes he is in "Death's baby machine, that led to the fighters and bombers, / But training, here in the lone purple, / For something else." He then understands what is now necessary:

> I pulled down my helmet-flaps and droned
> With flight-sleep. Near death
> My watch stopped. I knew it, for I felt the Cadet
> Barracks of Camden die like time, and "There's a war on"
> Die, and no one could groan from the dark of the bottom
> Bunk to his haggard instructor, I tried
> I tried to do what you said I tried tried
> No; never. No one ever lived to prove he thought he saw
> An aircraft with no pilot showing: I would have to become
> A legend, curled up out of sight with all the Western World
> Coming at me under the floor mat....

The poem exemplifies Dickey's re-creation of an actual incident to explore its inherent possibilities, no matter the seeming consequence or even silliness of that moment. "Things matter to me," he declared in *Sorties*, "big things, and little things. I feel for them in some manner, and so I remember them. My whole poetic work, pretty much, has been made of such memories" (21). Rendering those memories, however, necessitated a choice of how to convey what he termed "the poem's passion." "As Longinus points out," Dickey declared, "there's a razor's edge between sublimity and absurdity" (65). "I finally concluded, it's not a question of whether the poet is going to manipulate his language or not; he is. It's a question of the effectiveness and the expressive function of the manipulation and how well it comes across. That idea was the bursting of a dam for me. I could see infinite possibilities for expression in such a conception" (*Self-Interviews* 33). Reviewers, however, were not averse to criticizing some of Dickey's early poems as simply too unbelievable. Wendell Berry, for example, argued in the November 1964 issue of *Poetry* that the situations in these works often seemed staged, affected, and occasionally preposterous, citing "Springer Mountain" from *Helmets* (1964), in which the speaker, hunting deer, strips off his clothes and imagines himself becoming a buck, "a beast loving / With the whole god bone of his horns." Berry concludes that nothing mitigates "the inherent silliness and clumsiness.... I have no faith in it, no belief that anybody ever did any such thing" (130–31). Dickey remained undeterred. In what amounted to a figurative if not literal race to establish and confirm his poetic presence, he viewed critics and reviewers as opponents. "Camden Town" also reveals Dickey's tendency to mythologize himself. Influenced in the fifties by modernist dicta, he endeavored to establish his poetic presence by imitating that movement's use of mythology in poems such as "The Vegetable King" (1959), "Sleeping Out at Easter" (1960), and "Walking on Water" (1960). As his career advanced, however, he centered the mythology on himself. In *Self-Interviews*, he admitted that "In 'The Vegetable King,' I try to mythologize my family; this, I guess, is my answer to Eliot's use of the Osiris myth. It was one of the first poems in which I was able to use a myth in a way peculiar to me and at the same time make it something that could happen to anybody. I mention this poem to illustrate that I was working both semi-consciously and quite consciously toward my own factual experience." He concluded, "It's not that my experience lent itself more to mythology than anybody else's, but that my own life lent itself to being mythologized as *much* as anybody else's" (85). The speaker's awareness of and need for myth in "Camden Town"—"I would have to become / A legend"—suggests Dickey's own recognition of his mission and the deception necessary in communicating to others what happens in adventurous flight. The poem also contains what became the working title of *Alnilam*, which was originally called "Death's Baby Machine" or simply "The Machine," which "does not apply to any real machine, except perhaps the aircraft the boys are flying, and those they will fly later. The machine, however, that I am really referring to is the bureaucratic machine of the Air Force, and the social system that makes it possible and even mandatory. It is a thing which human beings must go through, be rejected by, or survive, but can never really escape from" (*Sorties* 42).

Dickey's first year in the army air forces had found him stationed in five camps. For someone who at North Fulton High School had devoted himself to football, track, and girls, he had nevertheless maintained and nourished an interest in literature. He read according to whim, but he read avidly, particularly as the months of duty passed and he requested volumes from his mother; to his inquiring mind, all books became a sort of literary loose fish. When he had finished reading them, they became a part of his psychological and emotional makeup that further distanced him from Buckhead and family. In letters home, Dickey's dissatisfaction with contemporary America would soon evidence itself, revealing his sense of being an outsider disturbed by and at odds with established norms but who nevertheless desired to help reshape America's conception of itself. Unlike Allen Ginsberg and Robert Lowell, for example, Dickey was never an overtly political writer, but in poems such as "A Folk Singer of the Thirties" (1963), "Coming Back to America" (1965), and "The Strength of Fields" (1977) and in essays such as "Notes on the Decline of Outrage" (1961) and "Upthrust and Its Men" (1983), he displayed dissatisfaction with the passivity and materialism of American culture. In "Coming Back to America," the speaker returns home from Europe to a city, apparently New York, which is bathed "in all-night squinting barbaric rays of violently unavoidable glory." Deciding to go swimming in the hotel pool, he passes "through ceiling after ceiling of sleeping salesmen and whores." The lifeguard's right leg is "slick and lacquered with scars," where "a five-car wreck / Of taxis" had knocked her unconscious and taken her kneecap. "Vulnerable, / Hurt in my country's murderous speed," she becomes a "claspable / Symbol the unforeseen on home ground." Dickey's essay "Notes on the Decline of Outrage" focused on the racial situation in America and more directly addresses social inequality:

> It is an even more terrible paradox that the very quality that has been obscured all the time—the Negro's ordinary, everyday humanness—is obscured even more thoroughly, now that he has become a symbol which concretizes the historical weariness of an entire people, pointing up, as nothing else in this country has ever done, the fearful consequences of systematic and heedless oppression for both the oppressed and the oppressor, who cannot continue to bear such a burden without becoming himself diminished, and in the end debased, by such secret and cruel ways that he is never really sure what is happening. (*Babel to Byzanyium* 258)

America, Dickey recognized, with its headlong, unquestioning embrace of capitalism and the attendant dehumanization of its people, necessarily needed to reshape its conception of itself.

Gradually those extensive readings while in the army air forces and at Vanderbilt University yielded a larger understanding of himself and of the nature of a life fully lived. "It seems to me," he later wrote in *Sorties*, "that I am the bearer of some kind of immortal message to humankind. What is this message? I don't know, but it exists" (54). The statement, while bombastic and designed to incite controversy, nevertheless reflected Dickey's sense of mission. As Chris Dickey has noted, "There must have been times when, drunk or dreaming, or writing or giving readings or fucking, he felt that he was getting close. You see that in the poems, if you read them all together" (*Summer of Deliverance* 33). It also masks the fears that were part of Dickey's personality and which he sought to hide or camouflage by bravado, self-promotion, and occasional belligerency. Beneath the spectacle lay feelings of inadequacy and failure, a lack of self-worth, and the need for attention. For the moment, however, he had only crossed a threshold; his new world yet lay unexplored. Yet Dickey's restlessness had enabled him to sense that possibilities lay with literature. In Camden, he was commissioned a navigator, not a pilot as he had always insisted he would be, but what had become more important to him, before he even entered combat, was that he was writing. Words had happened, and he was likely as surprised as anyone that they had happened to him. "I eased into poetry," he wrote in *Babel to Byzantium* (1968), "over the course of many years, by some such route. As a writer of poetry I began comparatively late, around my twenty-fourth year. I came to poetry with no particular qualifications" (279).

The poems had not yet come; Ariel had not yet emerged from the tree. It would take books and bombing missions for that finally to happen.

CHAPTER 3

OF BOOKS AND BOMBING MISSIONS

In his 1966 essay "The Poet Turns on Himself," Dickey related how early in his career he recognized "that words, once placed in a certain order, will stay where they have been put and say what one tells them to say." The problem arose in his not knowing what exactly he wanted them to say. "Very slowly," he stated, "I gravitated toward another idea which, like the other, has never left me: the belief in the inexhaustible fecundity of individual memory. When I examined my own memory, I found that certain images stood out in my mind and recurred to me at odd times, as if seeking something, perhaps some act of understanding from me" (*Babel to Byzantium* 280). The memories that emerged in the years leading up to, during, and immediately following World War II, which Dickey explored in what he termed his "early motion," centered largely on family and war as well as particular concerns inherent in these subjects—love and death. *Into the Stone* (1960), *Drowning with Others* (1962), and *Helmets* (1964) all reveal Dickey's effort to explore past memories that demanded confrontation and in so doing to discover aspects of what he termed "the I-figure," that personality whose "actions and meanings, and indeed his very being, are determined by the poet's rational or instinctive grasp of the dramatic possibilities in the scene or situation into which he has placed himself as one of the elements" (*Sorties* 156). Dickey's combat in the Pacific as a member of the 418th Night Fighter Squadron and the education he received while reading between missions, and afterwards while attending Vanderbilt University, not only determined that he become a poet but also provided the fertile memories that would largely become his subject matter. Indeed, Dickey would later tell his poetry classes of the moment in August 1945 when he decided to become a poet. Following the Japanese surrender, with his squadron stationed on Okinawa and the Third Fleet out in the harbor in Buckner Bay firing celebratory ammunition, he remembered lines by Trumbull Stickney that he had read in an anthology: "Thou art divine, thou livest,—as of old / Apollo springing naked to the light, / And all his island shivered into flowers." Doubtless the process was longer, more convoluted, but he had noted the moment in his notebooks during the fifties: "The chair above the bay at Okinawa...where I had my first look as a poet at the world." Certainly Flight Officer Jim Dickey believed that was the definitive moment, the still point in his turning world, where he determined who he would become.

1944 found Dickey at Buckingham Field in Fort Myers, Florida, for aerial gunnery school, instruction intended to last six weeks after which he would be sent to Boca Raton for a radar course. Buckingham Field, he informed his mother on 16 January, was "a typical G.I. army camp," but the theater, basketball court, and recreation hall rendered it, in his view, "not such a bad place." He claimed that within six months "there is a chance I will be a *first* lieutenant" but cautioned by quoting the Greek writer Pallas, "There's many a slip 'twixt the cup & the lip'" (*One Voice*, I 59–60). He wrote his brother, Tom, who was attending the Baylor School in Chattanooga, a detailed account of target practice; while B-26s and AT-6s towed targets, he shot at them from B-17s, an activity he found nerve-wracking. In "Crux," his unfinished fourth novel about the air war in the Pacific, Harbelis, the thinly disguised Intercept Officer Jim Dickey, fires at the target in three-second bursts and thinks:

> There was a fascination in it, in the rhythm, in the fact that he was doing what he was, and in the indifference of the long target, moving as though an escort, unswerving, unflinching. The training plane slowed and increased speed, and he was back into leads again: forward leads, overtaking leads, tracking leads. During one of the tracking runs he was amazed that he could actually see the bullets in the air: a blink, a hinted gold, but definitely copper-jackets, rim-touched between him and the target.

The reality of the training, however, was anything but literary. To learn the workings of machine guns, he spent hours blindfolded taking them apart and reassembling them. Instructors occasionally included extra parts as decoys.

Throughout his enlistment, Dickey had been purchasing war bonds, and in an unpublished 25 February 1944 missive to his mother, he requested that she cash in some of these and purchase books for him, including Hemingway's *The Sun Also Rises* (1926) and *A Farewell to Arms* (1929), Farrell's *Studs Lonigan* (1933), Joyce's *Ulysses* (American edition, 1934), and Van Tilburg Clark's *The Ox-Bow Incident* (1940). Also included were several collections of poems: Jesse Stuart's *Man with the Bull-*

Tongue Plow (1934), which was a volume of 703 sonnets and sonnet variations, the two-volume *Poetical Works* (1908) by James Thomson, and *Selected Poems* (1929) by Conrad Aiken. His request was the first of an increasingly common practice. Until the conclusion of the war, Dickey continued to ask his mother to order books for him. Some he requested that she keep for him safely at home; others she shipped to him at training camps and overseas. Earl Bradley, Dickey's pilot in the 418th Night Fighter Squadron to which Dickey was finally assigned, remembered him in an unpublished letter to Henry Hart as having "his nose forever in a book." As literature consumed more of Dickey's free time, he felt distanced from sports. He inquired in an unpublished 25 February letter to his brother, Tom, about the upcoming track season, even offering advice and reminiscing about his own track experiences. "Don't work too hard too early in the season or you'll pull a muscle like I did at Darlington. I was just your age, then." "It seems so long ago," he concluded and then added, "there is not much more to say." He wrote Tom again on 23 March 1944, cataloging their common friends and discussing what had happened to them in the year since he had left Atlanta. Among them was Warren Watson, who had joined the naval air corps and subsequently been killed. Watson, Dickey remembered, used to talk about his possible death. Now he was gone, he told Tom, and concluded simply, "That was too bad."

That Dickey was reading a novel as complicated as *Ulysses* indicated his literary seriousness. His embrace of Hemingway derives largely from the stoicism, cynicism, and hedonism of the latter's fictional characters, attitudes Dickey himself adopted during his service years. The Hemingway style, the simple and direct use of diction and sentence structure, was also reflected in Dickey's own writing efforts, including his nonfiction essay "Tacloban," which he wrote at Vanderbilt, and his last completed novel *To the White Sea*. Thomson's "The Seasons," the principal poem in his *Poetical Works*, consists of more than 5,500 lines in blank verse; cyclic in structure, it concerns nature and its impact on the sensations, imagination, intellect, and moral character of humankind. Its dominant theme is the search for knowledge and understanding of the harmony inherent in the confusing and often contradictory array of experiences presented by nature. In his own poems Dickey would also endeavor to discover the fundamental unity in natural occurrences. In his 1961 poem "In the Lupanar at Pompeii," for example, the speaker observes the shadowed remains of the couples who died from the suffocating ashes of Vesuvius as they endeavored, Dickey declared in *Self-Interviews*, "to give themselves completely,... a total act of the body, true passion" (116). As he surveys the scene, the speaker thinks, "We can never really tell / Whether nature condemns us or loves us / As we lie dying of breath." In Dickey's longest poem, *The Zodiac*, the protagonist, a drunken Dutch poet, is obsessed "with connecting and joining things that lay their meanings / Over billions of light years / eons of time—Ah, / Years of light: billions of them: they are pictures / Of some sort of meaning. He thinks the secret / Can be read." In Dickey's first known poetic effort, titled "Rain in Darkness" and written in blank verse, which he enclosed in an October 1944 letter to his mother, the speaker seeks nature's healing influences: "Pouring always / From dim heaven, O rain / Take not your love from us, we who need you" (*One Voice*, I 65–66). Dickey would have agreed with Thomson's characterization of nature in "Spring" as "this complex, stupendous scheme of things." Thomson's relevance, though less obvious in Dickey's fiction, also appears in *Alnilam*, where Dickey has Joel Cahill assume Thomson's cryptic initials, B. V. Additionally, Joel's disciples recite fragments of Thomson's verse.

On 12 March 1944 Dickey left Fort Myers for Boca Raton, Florida, to become part of what he later described as "some sort of secret program" (Hart 75). Radar had been successfully employed by the British night fighters in Africa, and the American air corps had initiated its first training program in the new technology a year and a half before Dickey arrived at Boca Raton. Considered so potentially advantageous to the war effort that the program was top-secret top secret, Dickey had only the haziest notion of what was involved. The technology must have reminded him of the futuristic weapons used by Doc Savage and the other pulp-fiction warriors he had read as an adolescent. He described the program in "Crux": "In cinderblock cubicles, on which a light sweat stood and in places ran, Harbelis and the others were hooded, and in as much dark as could be made, faced into a screen where, in perverse, unreliable, grass-like electricity, danced the secret, the green-ghostly wings that could not be believed, but must be; they were the enemy's." Like Harbelis, Dickey felt himself "far from earth in an invisible field that only he controlled, master, in total darkness, of the invisible hunt."

The mystique of radar was addictive. "It was like some weird miracle," Dickey recalled. "It seemed beyond science to turn some dials and to see something come up on the screen and represent its relationship to you and your aircraft" (Hart 75). He would later consider poetry itself to be the "secret program," one that could most offer up the hidden world. This specialized training, in effect, began his effort to turn his own experiences into myth, to enlarge his own adventure and render it "better than the truth." In an unpublished essay titled "The Poet and Memory," he declared, "The poet takes on faith that his experience is enough like that of other human beings to shed some light on them; and he also must believe that his personal individuality is unique enough to shed a light on common experience that could be shed only from his peculiar angle: that what he has to say is, because he *is*, unique, inimitable." Knowledge of radar, its secret powers, enabled Dickey to believe he had penetrated into a source of hidden strength—the warrior as mythic hero.

Radar school was difficult. Guards searched soldiers as they entered and exited the buildings, which were surrounded by barbed wire. Security considerations necessitated that soldiers not be allowed to have notes outside the sound-proof classrooms. During the day, cadets simulated night flying by blacking out the windows of their planes. They flew blind just as the blind Frank Cahill does in *Alnilam*. Because radar technology was in its infancy, the screen cadets depended upon to locate and track enemy aircraft was primitive and difficult to read. Dickey emphatically advised Tom in an unpublished 28 March letter not to enlist: "Boy, don't let anybody convince you that you should join the army. Go to college and get an education so you'll be good for something in later life." On 7 May 1944 Dickey's instructors awarded him a certificate for mastering all the equipment in a P-70's rear cockpit, and two weeks later officially classified him as an "Aircraft Observer, Radar Observer Night Fighter." The headquarters of the Army Air Force Eastern Technical Command temporarily appointed him a second lieutenant, or flight officer.

Flight Officer Jim Dickey spent the last six months of 1944 training at Hammer Field outside Fresno, California, "such a nice place," he wrote his parents in a letter postmarked 11 June, that "I could just stay here forever and not mind it. This is the best post in the army." The train ride had been "a wonderful trip out, a Pullman all the way" (*One Voice*, I 60). More importantly, he had met a tall, beautiful young woman named Gwen Leege, a student at Bryn Mawr who was returning home to San Francisco for summer break. Dickey had dated girls in Atlanta such as Peg Roney, whose father was a college professor, and impressed them by quoting lines from poems he had learned. Dickey remembered Roney in a 1987 interview as a young woman "rather elusive for me. She was an interesting, sort of witty, rather pretty girl in an unusual way.... But she never really cared much about me, which was too bad" (Baughman, *Voiced Connections* 248). Leege, however, could respond in kind to Dickey's quotations and include passages from German writers such as Goethe, Schiller, and Kant. She was as much taken by Dickey as he was by her. They talked about life, literature, and philosophy, and she invited him to visit her family's country estate in Marin County, just outside San Francisco. Dickey spent a week there, enjoying trips with Gwen to the city's Chinatown, zoo, aquarium, and nightclubs. He wrote his mother on 22 July 1944, "I am in love with Gwen, but I don't think anything will ever come of it." Gwen, he said, was inclined to be "snotty" when she did not receive everything she wanted, and she wanted "plenty" (Baughman, *One Voice* I, 62–63), a statement that reflected his class consciousness. In a 1987 interview, he declared that Gwen could not have survived "the scruffy life I lived as a student.... She was not made for the nitty-gritty of life, of getting in there and shoving with the rest" (*Voiced Connections* 251). Though they became informally engaged (he did not give her a ring), Dickey did not want a wife with such feelings of entitlement, telling his mother in the letter that love and marriage differed in much more than name: "I have an infinite capacity for one and absolutely none for the other." Gwen, however, played a large role in Dickey's literary development both during and immediately after the war. "We corresponded," he wrote in *Self-Interviews*,

> all the time I was overseas in the Pacific. She introduced me to some experimental writers and also to something for which I will always be grateful, the Gotham Book Mart in New York City. When I got back from the Pacific, I went to New York to see her, and we visited the Gotham Book Mart. There were all the books I had heard about all those years and had never seen copies of. I had some money and some mustering-out pay, so I bought a lot of them and began to read. I had a vague notion then that I might try to write a poem myself one day. (26–27)

"The euphoria faded as she got ready to go back to school," Chris said of his father, "but this rich, educated girl with her European background had made the idea of writing that much more important, that much more imperative" (*Summer of Deliverance* 49). In a 31 January 1995 letter, Leege (now Gwen Walti) reflected on her relationship with Dickey. "In my vivid memory," she declared, "our friendship remains extraordinary, cherished and timeless—a caring, loving, tumultuous Strum und Drang relationship in the tense years of war and postwar from 1942 to 1946. Jim was a dashing young US Army Aircorps officer (navigator), carrying out night missions in the treacherous Pacific area. I was an enthusiastic California student at

Bryn Mawr College, studying German and Spanish literature and philosophy. We met by miraculous chance." Late in his life, Dickey sought to reconnect and resume their correspondence. In a 26 December 1995 letter, he wrote her of his health, his literary efforts, and his family, and inquired news of her. "Send me some recent photographs," he said, "and long letters—at least one—like you used to write when I was in Fresno, or overseas. Fresno was a true high point for me: I was young. I had discovered poetry, I was going to a war, and I was in love. That's a combination that can't be beat; of that I'm sure: as they say, 'from experience'" (*One Voice*, II 497–98). As of this writing, no response from Walti has appeared.

With Gwen as his instructor, Dickey read a wide variety of novels, and he had his decided favorites. In a letter to his parents dated 16 August 1944, he commented on the article in *Life* which featured the leading novelists of the previous two decades. The list included Ernest Hemingway, Willa Cather, John Dos Passos, Sinclair Lewis, Thomas Wolfe, Ellen Glasgow, Theodore Dreiser, John Steinbeck, Kenneth Roberts, William Faulkner, and Marjorie Rawlings. The *Saturday Review of Literature* had recently celebrated its twentieth anniversary; in recognition, the editors had invited its contributors to choose the best novel and the best novelist to appear on the US publishing scene during those two decades. In an effort to show its readers just how difficult such a selection process was, *Life* presented a list compiled by Dr. Henry Seidel Canby, founder of the *Saturday Review* and its associate editor, of the one hundred outstanding books from 1924 through 1944, the most prolific period in American publishing history. Among the poetry volumes in Canby's grouping were Robinson Jeffers's *Roan Stallion*, A. E. Housman's *Collected Poems*, Stephen Spender's *Poems*, T. S. Eliot's *Four Quartets*, and Stuart's *Man with the Bull-Tongue Plow*. In order of importance, the *Saturday Review* had selected as the five best novels of the period Lewis's *Arrowsmith*, Hemingway's *A Farewell to Arms*, Dos Passos's *U.S.A.*, Steinbeck's *The Grapes of Wrath*, and Hemingway's *For Whom the Bell Tolls*, all novels, *Life* noted in the article, belonging to the realist school. Among novelists, Wolfe had been placed in fifth position, much to Dickey's disgust, behind "such *outstanding* (???) 'artistes' as Willa Cather, Ernest Hemingway and (the last straw) Sinclair (Arrowsmith) Lewis. What a laugh that is." Dickey declared that he was "reading enormously" while at Hammer Field, and kept "a gigantic array of ponderous books" in his room, asserting that when he finally got out of the army, he would attend a school where he could attain "a good education in letters, whether it be L.S.U., the University of

Virginia, Harvard, or Oxford. I am convinced that the only thing I will ever have any interest in as a career is authorship, or something akin to it." While he admitted that he had not displayed the abilities of John Keats, "I have shown an infinitesimal scrap of talent and originality in my writing" (*One Voice*, I 63–64), which was more, he asserted, than he had displayed in any other educational endeavor. Not surprisingly, Dickey's early poetic efforts were sentimental and derivative, as in "Rain in Darkness." Although he had committed himself to a literary career, he knew that the war first had to be won.

The routine at Hammer Field permitted Dickey to fly in a variety of aircraft, including P-70s, P-61s, Bearfighters, and Mosquitos. Practice missions were flown at night; during the day, he relaxed, read, and swam at the officers' pool. "If it were not so hot out here the climate would be wonderful," he wrote his mother, and he quoted from James Thomson's "City of Dreadful Night": "Drink, drink! Open your mouth! / This air is as rich as wine; / Flowing with balm from the sunny south, / And health from the western brine" (*One Voice*, I 62–63). Thomson had dedicated his gloomy and pessimistic poem to revealing "the bitter old and wrinkled truth / Stripped naked of all vesture that beguiles, / False dreams, false hopes, false masks and modes of truth." He had speculated in the poem that his most sympathetic reader would be "someone desolate, Fate-smitten, / Whose faith and hopes are dead, and who would die." Dickey was not that, but he was rapidly moving beyond both the false dreams of childhood, such as becoming a professional athlete, and the Southern provinciality of his parents.

Dickey's separation from home and his growing sense of independence, enhanced by his increasing belief in and commitment to literature, clearly strained relations with family members. Despite his attraction to Gwen Leege, he pursued relationships with other women, enjoying the status of an airman soon to be shipped overseas. Asked about these months, Earl Bradley, who would later become Dickey's pilot, remembered, "Jim loved Hammer Field. He was single and the California girls loved men in uniform, especially flying officers." A popular 1942 song, "He Wears a Pair of Silver Wings," sung by Dinah Shore, captured the romantic ambience: "Although some people say he's just a crazy guy / To me he means a million other things / For he's the one who taught this happy heart of mine to fly / He wears a pair of silver wings." Dickey's pursuits, however, soon became viewed as immoral by his father. In a letter postmarked 16 October 1944, Dickey responded, "I realize that you advise me according to your conception of my best interests, but you have such a vague knowledge of this particular situation that I cannot help but feel that you are totally unqualified to pass competent judgement upon it." "You seem to think," he proceeded to declare, "that in my reaching the age of 21 I have used my new-found 'freedom' for an orgiaic [*sic*] display of atheism and free love. Nothing could be further from the truth." The woman in question was Jane Kirksey, the daughter-in-law of the former commanding officer of Hammer Field, whom Dickey claimed had helped him publish a pastoral lyric in a little-known monthly for which he had been paid three dollars. He did not identify the magazine, and the poem, if it existed, has never been located. However, that he made the claim, which was intended to justify the profession of writing, was also part of his fledging effort to mythologize his life: that he was a *published* poet even during the war. Dickey cited "the rapid and constantly changing and interchanging of the (for want of a better term) scale of human values. While this sort of thing in most incidents is not condoned, it is recognized in life" (*One Voice*, I 64–65). Kirksey became the subject of an unpublished Dickey poem, "Jane Proctor's Love Song," which opens, "Yes. I was across / You I looked in the mirror and I was really / There though it could not be me / And I had been nowhere / Like it before." Dickey informed his mother that Kirksey was "quite a student of poetry (my first love in literature)," writing in a letter postmarked 20 October that "Jane, my (wife!!?? And I have been having quite a gay time." However, he cautioned his mother not to worry: "My theories are but theories at best. Better than to say I were an atheist, agnostic or what have you, were to confess, wearily, that I do not know!" (*One Voice*, I 65–66). Perhaps faith was the answer, he declared, but he had little. His roommate, Bob Davis, had died the previous night when his aircraft exploded on impact in the Sierra Mountains. As one critic has observed, "Such accidents proved that existence was precarious and precious, and God absent or inscrutable. Like the existentialists he would soon endorse, he felt that all life—and all women—should be passionately embraced rather than abjured by a worn-out ethical code" (Hart 82). In a 1971 essay titled "Complicity," Dickey would later write of women, "If she is not the secret of the universe, then there is none. To us she appears in the clandestine and burning center of the mind as the form we most deeply desire and must create or die" (*Night Hurdling* 217). James Thomson lay partly behind Dickey's new attitudes regarding life. "The City of Dreadful Night" opens with the speaker, a thorough pessimist suffering from melancholia and depression, searching vainly for meaning:

> I have searched the heights and depths, the scope
> Of all our universe, with desperate hope
> To find some solace for your wild unrest.
>
> And now at last authentic word I bring,
> Witnessed by every dead and living thing;
> Good tidings of great joy for you, for all:
> There is no God; no Fiend with names divine
> Made us and tortures us; if we must pine,
> It is to satiate no Being's gall.

Enclosed with the letter to his mother was his poem "Rain in Darkness." "The unknowing godfather of this unworthy piece," he wrote, "was Robert Bridge's 'London Snow,'" although his own inspiration derived from having "lain on the side porch listening to rain enough times to be fully aware of it's [*sic*] significance and meaning in the minds of most people." He referred to the poem as "an obviously amateurish bit of fancy" (*One Voice*, I 65–66).

In a 1987 interview Dickey commented on that poetic effort. "Robert Bridges is a strange one for me to have been influenced by," he stated, "even to the extent of trying to write an imitation of him. But I think what interested me in Bridges is that he was such a fanatic about prosody itself, about the mechanics of it. That's what appealed to me" (Baughman, *Voiced Connections* 250). Dickey believed then, "and to a certain extent still do," he stated, that "the poem can be engineered, can be put together like a machine" (250). Dickey's early poetic efforts reveal his avid reading of fin-de-siècle Victorians, but he was also reading modernists such as T. S. Eliot and French symbolists such as Paul Valéry. He had bought Eliot's *Four Quartets* while in California, but unlike Eliot, he continued to employ archaic diction, conventional meter, and predictable rhyme. Later, traveling in Europe in 1955 on a *Sewanee Review* Fellowship, Dickey hoped to visit Eliot, but miscommunication and Eliot's illness prevented their meeting. Eliot wrote Dickey on 9 March 1955, regretting the missed opportunity and expressing hope that "there will be some future occasion to meet on one side of the water or the other." The meeting never occurred, though Dickey courted other modernists, particularly Ezra Pound and William Carlos Williams. While Dickey embraced Eliot's use of myth, he never fully adopted other Eliot tenets, such as learned allusions and ironic juxtapositions. In a 6 July 1979 letter to John Simon, a controversial but well-respected literary, theater, and art critic, he was similarly harsh:

> But the whole notion of treating *The Four Quartets* as some sort of sacrosanct revelation of the Holy Mysteries of Religion is manifestly absurd. Like Auden, Eliot is a profoundly unreligious man, interested in the paradoxes and intellectual problematics of theology more than anything else; his pose of humbleness is frightfully false, as it is quite clear and the kind of snobbery that has always been his personal characteristic and stigma. The grave, owlish, pontificating tone is very enervating to me; the qualities I like are drive, purpose, and imaginative energy. (*One Voice*, II 217–18)

Eliot specifically and modernists generally became opponents Dickey felt he needed to confront; his intense competitiveness, derived from the rivalry with his brother, Tom, mandated it. As Al Braselton noted in his unfinished memoir, "If it had not been for Tom, Jim might have been one of those Byron-quoting kind of failed Southern talkers." Yet behind Dickey's desire to succeed, to out-rival Tom on the football field, on the track, or in his mother's eyes, was Gene, the older brother lost to death before Dickey was born. Dickey was addressing himself when, as the protagonist in "The Cancer Match" (1969), he declared, "Get 'em, O Self / Like a beloved son! One more time! Tonight we are going / Good better and better we are going / To win, and not only win but win / Big, win big." Gene was dead, Warren Watson was dead, Bob Davis was dead. To justify his own survival, Dickey needed to become larger than life, a self-made myth, to rise above time, as he would later write of Lewis Medlock in *Deliverance*. His participation in physical combat, however, was imminent, and he first needed a pilot so he could rise in air.

In a 1996 interview, the year before he died, Dickey discussed how he met his pilot, Earl Bradley: "All the new pilots and all the new intercept officers, or radio observers [gathered] in one big room, and we went around from one group to another, talking to each other. You'd team up. I fell in with a kind of stocky guy.... I was convinced, just by talking to him, that he would be quite a good pilot to team up with. And I was never sorry, because I flew with him all through combat" (Hart 78).

On 22 November 1944 Dickey arrived home for a fourteen-day leave before departure overseas; the visit apparently went smoothly with no evidence of recent tensions regarding his relationships with women. Back at Hammer Field, he wrote his mother in an unpublished letter dated 9

December that everything had been "absolutely perfect," and he sought to reassure her of his safety: "I have the most careful pilot in the U.S. Air Force today, and I can hold up my end o.k. too." With his father he was more circumspect, not mentioning the trip home, dwelling instead on his preparations for deployment. A final letter from the States, addressed to both parents on 25 December, noted that this Christmas was "quite a bit different from my other twenty" and requested that they purchase for him the collected poems of Wilfred Owen and Siegfried Sassoon's *The Old Huntsman*. He also asked that they obtain the collected poems of Roy Campbell, the first volume of which was not published until 1949 (English edition). He was reading anthologized poems from Campbell's earlier volumes, such as *The Flaming Terrapin* and *Adamastor*, published in 1924 and 1930, respectively. All the books, he stated, were "for post-war consumption," and added parenthetically, "purely recreational." His parents would be pleased to know, he declared, that he had purchased "a good many technical and engineering books for overseas study" (*One Voice*, I 66–67). As he prepared for combat, he noted that everyone at Hammer Field was excited about the German drive detailed in the news, but now that it had been stopped, everything was quiet. Beginning on 16 December, a major German counteroffensive, led by Field Marshall Karl von Rundstedt, had punched a forty-five-mile breach in the southern flank of the American First Army, cutting deeply into Belgium and Luxembourg. A record assault by Allied planes and troops had halted the German army by Christmas Day.

Given his imminent deployment, Dickey immersed himself in war poetry. Wilfred Owen's *Collected Poems* contained a sharpness of observation and an unrelenting truthfulness that Dickey liked. The preface, however, spoke directly to Dickey's immediate concerns:

> This book is not about heroes. English poetry is not yet fit to speak of them.
> Nor is it about deeds, or lands, nor anything about glory, honour, might, majesty, dominion, or power, except war.
> Above all I am not concerned with Poetry.
> My subject is War, and the pity of War.
> The Poetry is in the pity.
> Yet these elegies are to this generation in no sense consolatory. They may be to the next. All a poet can do today is warn. That is why the true poets must be truthful.

War fired Owen's imagination; the subject possessed his letters and best poetry. He concerned himself with its savagery and futility, with "super-human inhumanities" and "comrades that went under," as he wrote in "Spring Offensive," and with the landscape of death, its familiar pervasiveness. Apparent in the poems, too, is Owen's sense of the gulf separating the combat soldier and the civilian at home, a gulf that Dickey would feel and about which he would angrily write his parents. Like Owen, Dickey came to feel, perhaps through his reading of Hemingway, less hostility toward enemy soldiers than to those who were either profiting from the conflict or who considered themselves patriotic participants simply because they had bought a war bond.

Sassoon's *The Old Huntsman*, though not as realistic in its depiction of war, portrays the poet's own changing attitudes toward the conflict—from his view, as he wrote in "Absolution," that "war has made us wise, / And, fighting for our freedom, we are free," to the knowledge, as he declares in "A Letter Home," that "everywhere men bang and blunder, Sweat and swear and worship Chance, / Creep and blink through common thunder. / Rifles crack and bullets flick, / Sing and hum like hornet-swarm. / Bones are smashed and buried quick." Dedicated to Thomas Hardy, the volume reflects Sassoon's shift from seeing war as a chivalric ideal to his impression, directly uttered in his best poem, that war is nakedly savage and dehumanizing. The title poem concludes in part with the old huntsman examining his past:

> So I've loved
> My life; and when the good years are gone down,
> Discover what I've lost.
> I never broke
> Out of my blundering self into the world,
> But let it all go past me, like a man
> Half-asleep in a land that's full of wars.

Dickey determined not to permit his life to pass without confronting, and engaging, its possibilities.

Dickey's early war poems, published in the late fifties and early sixties, derived from specific experiences in the Pacific, the memories of which demanded interpretation or understanding. Unlike the British World War I poets he was reading, however, his poems were less an attack on or censure of war than an effort to comprehend their personal meanings to

Dickey himself. By contrast, unpublished poems written earlier, especially during the war itself, were superficial and derivative, overtly generic and occasionally bizarre, as in a fragment titled "Prelude to Combat," when the speaker stares at the propellers and wings of his plane and sees "The whirled, light rinsing blades / Shift the shades of rotting men. / Upon the tapered way, the curve-ended shell /Which lifts us and our sharp-voiced pebbles of destruction / Dance young carrion spectres of Teuton dead." Among Dickey's published war poems were "The Enclosure" (1959), "The Jewel" (1959), "The Performance" (1959), "The Wedding," (1960), "Between Two Prisoners" (1960), "A View of Fujiyama after the War" (1960), "The Island" (1960), "The Driver" (1963), "Horses and Prisoners" (1963), and "Drinking from a Helmet" (1963). In "The Jewel," for example, the speaker, "doubled strangely in time," walks toward his aircraft in preparation for his night mission and in "the faceted lights of a cabin, / There, like the meaning of war, he sees / A strong, poor diamond of light." The moment yields questions: "Truly, do I live? Or shall I die, at last / Of waiting? Why should the fear grow loud / With the years, of being the first to give in / To the matched, priceless glow of the engines?" The allure of power, the richness of its detachment, leaves him "*alone, in late night.*" His frequently anthologized poem "The Performance" centers on the beheading by the Japanese of Dickey's fellow pilot Donald Armstrong, a man he asserted in *Self-Interviews* was "probably my best friend in the squadron" (92) whose P-61 crashed while returning from convoy cover. Armstrong died in the crash, but Dickey in the poem mythologizes his friend, renders him larger than life.

While in the service, Dickey frequently quoted poets such as Poe, Campbell, Ernest Dowson, Hart Crane, and Alexander Bergman, believing their lines best expressed his own thoughts. His readings then and in the coming months were eclectic. In *Self-Interviews*, he wrote, "When I first began to write, I was very much influenced, stylistically, by other poets.... I read a lot of modern poets and decided that my contemporaries were much greater than the poets of the past" (27). "Ernest Dowson appealed to me," he stated in a 1987 interview, "the same way he appeals to any young person. He's got that certain melancholia.... It's funny that a minor 1890s versifier could have been such a phrase-maker such as everybody and his brother could have picked up on. 'Gone with the wind' comes from Ernest Dowson. 'Wine and women and song' and 'days of wine and roses' comes from him." Roy Campbell's poetry, however, differed from that of Dowson's; its dramatic visual power attracted Dickey. The plane

Dickey and his pilot, Earl Bradley, flew was named *The Flaming Terrapin* after Campbell's poetic volume: "But when the winds have ceased their ghostly speech / And the long waves roll moaning from the beach, / The Flaming Terrapin that towed the Ark / Rears up his hump of thunder on the dark." "I liked his energy and his satirical bite," Dickey declared. "As clumsy as he is, he had a lot of masculine vigor that I liked. I think anybody's taste could be judged by the good-bad poets that he liked or the bad-good poets. He was mine" (*Voiced Connections* 249). In his 6 February letter to his parents, he requested that they purchase any of Campbell's poetry for him, specifically identifying such volumes as *Adamastor* (1930), *Flowering Reeds* (1933), and *The Georgiad* (1931) as well as *The Flaming Terrapin* (1924). He had been reading Louis Untermeyer's anthology, *Modern American and British Poetry*, originally published in 1919. The compilation included biographical summaries and verse selections from 131 American and British poets, among them Conrad Aiken, Ernest Dowson, Siegfried Sassoon, W. J. Turner, Richard Aldington, and Wilfred Owen, all of whose books he eventually asked his mother to purchase. In the preface, Untermeyer declared, "Most of the poets represented in these pages have found a fresh and vigorous material in a world of honest and often harsh reality. They respond to the spirit of their times; not only have their views changed, their vision has been widened to include things unknown to the poet of yesterday. They have learned to distinguish real beauty from mere prettiness; to wring loveliness out of squalor; to find wonder in neglected places" (21). Campbell himself called *The Flaming Terrapin* "a symbolic vision of the salvation of civilization," an interpretation fitting his attitude that man could overcome the beasts of this world, real and political, with perseverance and strength. The poem, what Campbell called "a lyre of savage thunder," ends with a central vision of man as a mythic creature seeking the limits of his potential: "I am that ancient hunter of the plains / That raked the shaggy flitches of the Bison: / Pass, world: I am the dreamer that remains, / The man, clear-cut against the last horizon!"

Dickey imagined himself as "that ancient hunter," a "dreamer" standing "clear-cut against the last horizon," and throughout his life he sought to project that image to his parents, to audiences, to friends and acquaintances, and to journalists and other writers. That personality, however, masked insecurities and fears, a sense of incompleteness and a fundamental vulnerability, even as it conveyed a vital need for a life well lived. He feared failure. He needed attention, the sense of abiding accomplishment. He would later write his mother that he thought it funny Tom worried about running the 100-yard dash a tenth of a second faster when he had seen airplanes flying 500 miles per hour crash into one another, "guys all shot to hell, and guts hanging out and japs lying rotten in the sun" (*One Voice*, I 88–89). That need to embrace a life of consequence, the life of what he termed an "energized man," became a raison d'etre, and he remained emphatic as to its necessity. "My purpose as a poet," he wrote, "insofar as other people are concerned, is to liberate into the depths, not surfaces" (*Sorties* 72). "The world, the human mind," he asserted, "is dying of subtlety. What it needs is force" (85), "savage delight" (97), "poetry of murderous drives" (97). While his father's passivity if not laziness revealed the necessity for such an attitude, the war mandated it.

When Dickey next wrote home on 27 January 1945, he was in Hollandia, Dutch New Guinea. He had initially arrived at Finschhafen twelve days earlier after a long voyage on a troop transport that was "one hell of a trip" (*One Voice*, I 67). The army air forces had prepared him for that trip with inoculations against smallpox, tetanus, yellow fever, cholera, plague, and influenza; Dickey himself had prepared by reading the British war poets, whose works confirmed his belief in the horror, futility, and dehumanization of combat. He had then packed his gear, including goggles, gloves, helmet, microphone, flashlight, flyer's bag, and flying glasses, into his duffel bag and boarded the USS *General A. E. Anderson* for embarkation, a vessel more than six hundred feet long and built to carry more than ten thousand troops. On the final afternoon of 1944, the ship eased out of San Francisco Bay, passed slowly under the Golden Gate Bridge, and began its long slow course across the Pacific, zigzagging to avoid Japanese submarines. Dickey would later reimagine the momentous journey as a mythical descent into an infernal and chaotic underworld; in reality, the trip was tedious, cramped, and oppressively monotonous. Soldiers slept in close quarters, their bunks sagging down on those below; even moving around on deck was difficult. They ate two meals a day standing up and showered only every other day. When the transport crossed the equator, the heat became stifling. Dickey generally kept to himself, reading Thomas Hardy and Robinson Jeffers; both poets depicted the world as a Darwinian battlefield governed by chance and instinct, an attitude that complemented his own gloominess now that he had actually entered the Pacific theater. After the *Anderson* passed Hawaii, Dickey would stand on deck, fascinated, to watch flying fish leap from the sea and glide airborne almost a hundred yards; he would never forget the image. In "Crux," unfinished at his death, he had endeavored to describe the beauty and inscrutability of the scene:

> They broke; there just enough. Now he would add one thing to them, each time they rose. One thing. They flattened into their pattern, the sun catching everywhere on it, one speck to a fish. Or it could be a contest of some kind: not to get somewhere first but to go farthest, stay, hold out for most time in the air? Was the same one always in front? Yes, it must be, it must be that way, Harbelis thought. Why not? Joel had said that you fly in the stuff you breathe. He would have got the parallel quicker than I did, Harbelis was sure. Thousands of fish not made, really, for flying, but they did it. They fly like we do, who are not made for it either?

The image transfixed him.

As he was to do in each of his three published novels, *Deliverance*, *Alnilam*, and *To the White Sea*, Dickey used a specific image either to open the fiction or to center the narrative. Those images might come from anywhere, but they always generated what he termed in "The Flash" (1966) as "your long-awaited, / Blinding, blood brotherly / Beyond-speech answer." "Something far off," the poem opens, "buried deep and free / In the country   can always strike you dead / Center of the brain. There is never anything / It could be   but you go dazzled / Dazzled   and all the air in that / Direction swarms." The consequence of modernism's early influence, images became for Dickey a source of meaning. In an essay originally delivered as the 1979 Ezra Pound lecture, administered by the University of Idaho, Dickey articulated those aspects of Pound's work that he discerned as instrumental to his own poetry, declaring,

> Pound's wish was always for more insight, more understanding, more consequentiality: in a word, more *life* for us. What he wanted for each of us, and for all human culture, was highly relevant personal experience: the guarantee of this within ourselves and our culture's guarantee that such experience should be ours. A sense of the consequentiality of things, actions, men, ideas and civilizations is what we most want, and what we most sorely need. (*Night Hurdling* 44–45)

The harbor at Hollandia, as Dickey's pilot, Earl Bradley, remembered, was "gorgeous, surrounded by vine-covered cliffs topped by mahogany trees." The troop replacements, however, remained on the transport for a week. An early poem, "The Baggage King," written in the fifties and unpublished until its inclusion in *The Whole Motion* (1992), details the confusion of disembarkation: "We came from the rusted freighter / With the thousand bags, duffel, / Kit-bags, B-4's, A-3's, / Barracks-bags, hand-bags, / Kits, 'personal bags,' musette bags, / Parachutes, kith and kin, / And were left, there, / The recruits, / The never-failing replacements." The speaker, however, cannot find among the mountain of baggage his own belongings: "My bag, my flying gear, my books, / And so would not leave." Finally, he resigns himself to the chaos: "I sat in trashy triumph at the top, / Knowing my own equipment, my own link / With the past was buried beneath me, or lost," recognizing that at least he was "commanding the beach / Where life and death had striven, but safe / At the top of the heap." Here, then, is Dickey looking back at his twenty-two-year-old self, a "replacement" not only for older airmen but also for his older brother, Gene, and who, because of his position, is paradoxically both "command-ing the beach" and vulnerable to enemy fire. He is utterly alone "in the dark / Where no lights came through / From the water, and nothing yet struck," a recognition that in the fifties, while a survivor and ambitious, he was not yet "at the top."

Dickey and his fellow combatants were shuttled among transit camps before being assigned as replacements for the 418th, a squadron encamped in a forward area of the Philippines and which Dickey, in a 6 February 1945 letter to his parents, described as "the hottest in the war. This outfit has more victories than all the others in the Pacific put together" (*One Voice*, I 69). The Allies had recently captured Leyte, and Dickey and the other replacements were flown to Tacloban, one of its principal airstrips. On the way, they stopped at Peleliu, a small, beautiful island with pristine, snow-white sand. The island, Bradley recalled, "was the scene of the first or at least early use of flamethrowers. The Japs were holed up in caves in what was known as Bloody Nose Ridge. Most of the Japs got fried." "You never saw such carnage in your life," Dickey himself remembered. "I sure didn't know in my wildest dreams it would be like this. Wreckage all over the place was the first thing you saw. American planes that had ditched in the water or crashed on the beach. Japanese aircraft. Landing ships that had had direct hits on them blown in half. There wasn't [*sic*] any dead people around. I guess they had been gotten off in the last few days. But there was blood all over everything. Or rust." "Or rust," he repeated. "Rust" (*Summer of Deliverance* 50), as if the image even years later remained too direct, too glaring or demanding. The memory never diminished. Dickey related in a 5 August 1996 interview that "it was very traumatic. That was the first time I knew I was really in a war. Boy, it looked like a war. It looked like every set you ever saw for a war in the movies except much worse. There were all kinds of planes on the beach that had bellied in.... You could look at them and there was blood all over the cockpit." The Japanese were attempting to reoccupy the airfield or at least to disrupt American operations by bombing it.

Tacloban was Dickey's formal entrance into the Second World War. The devastation, the ongoing efforts of the Japanese to recapture the area, and the brutality of the fighting, all against a background of natural, even pristine beauty affected Dickey's sensitivities and challenged the quiet complacency of his Atlanta childhood. Not surprisingly, he would write about this initiation; in his mind, his mythic adventure was literally underway. On 29 June 1946, after the war had concluded and Dickey was enrolled at Vanderbilt University, he sent his mother a two-page composition titled "Tacloban" that he had written for his English class, Literature and Composition, a course for which he eventually earned a B. The accompanying letter is lost. In the prose piece he remembered the devastation, recalling too the moment he realized that Donald Armstrong, a fellow airman, had become his best friend in the squadron:

> We were very crowded in the C-47. Armstrong and I were half-sitting, half-lying on barracks bags, parachutes and other equipment which members of our replacement squadron shipment had brought with them from New Guinea. We had been riding in that fashion all the way from Peleliu, the last fueling stop between New Guinea and Leyte. We were all so fagged out it didn't create much of an impression on anyone when the co-pilot opened the compartment door and told us we had arrived.

The essay then proceeds to describe the aftermath of the battle in which Americans captured the landing field: the wrecked P-38s covered with blood that the speaker pretends is rust, a soldier stationed at an antiaircraft emplacement who is seriously reading a comic book and whose skin is bright yellow from atabrine, the P-61s "looking ungainly and sinister, like tarantulas," with black paint scaling from the fuselage in long patches, the blasted palm trees, the lapping of waves "gentle and insistent" on the beach. When the speaker and Armstrong return to the transport to view the invasion-littered beach, Dickey concludes, "He [Armstrong] looked out toward the ships, and I watched him, thinking that he was the best friend I had, and while we were sitting there it started to rain, softly at first and then more fiercely until we could not see the ocean any longer. But we sat quietly and did not speak." In its simplicity of statement and directness of observation, the prose reflects the influence of Remarque and Heming-way. As Earl Bradley stated in a 13 January 1998 letter, "Jim perhaps saw each of these rather innocuous experiences as seeds from which grew great stories." For Dickey, such transformation was not lying; rather, he was turning factual events into personal myth. Tacloban had been the site of General MacArthur's well-publicized return to the Philippines after his retreat to Australia. The airstrip, in Dickey's imagination, became a rite of initiation, the reason why he wrote one of his first themes at Vanderbilt on his experience there.

. From Tacloban, Dickey and the other crews flew to Mindoro, just south of Luzon. Looking out the plane's window, he saw Manila burning. In the following weeks, as Japanese soldiers butchered, tortured, and raped Filipino civilians, the Allies bombed the capital of the Philippines, fighting from building to building to rout the enemy. Dickey did not participate in that combat, finally landing in the town of San Jose on Mindoro on the evening of 6 February, where he and the other replacements helped set up camp on a small hill overlooking a Catholic cemetery. "We are really in the big time now" (*One Voice*, I 69), he wrote his parents. The 418th Night Fighter Squadron was in the process of being turned from a defensive unit charged with convoy cover and the protection of Allied bases from Japa-nese aircraft to an offensive unit that bombed and strafed enemy positions. "I was not at all averse to that," Dickey related in an interview on 5 August 1996. "I was a good navigator and taking on long-range missions, I was not averse to that at all. In fact, I wanted to do that. I took every mission I could find, with Bradley or with anybody else." Dickey was part of ten new crews providing relief for the squadron. One of those going home was Maj. Carroll C. Smith, the commanding officer who had won the Silver Star by destroying four Japanese aircraft in one night. He was replaced by Capt. William B. Sellers, under whom the 418th's role changed and who himself flew the first P-61 intruder mission, a twelve-hour flight to For-mosa. Long-range missions subsequently involved flights not only to For-mosa but also to the Japanese home islands and to China, including Shanghai.

The P-61 Black Widow, designed by Northrup Aircraft specifically for night combat, was highly prized for its maneuverability, its reliable per-formance at altitudes above thirty-five thousand feet, and its state-of-the-art radar interception equipment. Equipped with 20-mm cannon and four

.50-calibre machine guns, the aircraft culminated several years of focused efforts by Northrup to build a masterful night fighter plane. To become an offensive aircraft, the P-61 had two thousand-pound bombs attached to its wings and two three-hundred-gallon belly tanks in order to bomb Japanese airstrips, bridges, hangers, and munition factories. The tanks contained either napalm or phosphorus. "We were just getting set up to do napalm work," Bradley related, "and Jim and I dropped the only ones that our squadron dropped." In one of his most anthologized poems, "The Firebombing" (1964), Dickey imagined the effects of an "anti-morale raid" on the unsuspecting Japanese civilians below when "the roofs will connect / Their flames, and make a town burning with all / American fire." "I didn't have the insight," Bradley declared, "to really see what was taking place in philosophical terms.... Jim had more time to and from our targets to reflect on the overall meaning of the whole thing. And that seemed to be his bent more than mine." In a 14 April 1997 letter, Bradley elaborated, "I always maintained a detached state of mind when we did things like this, but Jim, as I believe do most creative people, placed himself, mentally, into the scene." He added, "I honestly believe that Jim imagined what it must have been like to have been on the boats or in those houses when they were attacked. It probably made a better poet out of him but what we now have is the products of his vast imagination rather than reality."

On 7 February Dickey flew his first mission, logging in one hour and ten minutes of combat time. Though he claimed in an August 1996 interview that he and a pilot named Carl Cedrick covered MacArthur's landing in southern Manila, Harold Whittern, whose responsibility involved flight assignments for new crews, stated that Dickey's first mission was for the purpose of orientation, not combat cover (Hart 87). Dickey wrote his parents in a published letter postmarked 10 February 1945 that the squadron had "got this place pretty well cleared out. At first the Nips were a little rough, but now it is getting tame." He added, "These Japs are really fanatical. Some of the things they do you wouldn't believe" (*One Voice*, I 70). By mid-February, the "rookies," as the *History of the 418th Night Fighter Squadron* observes, had assumed local patrols and convoy cover. Japanese aircraft, however, had "already vacated" the area, and flights over Manila "were reduced to drab routine," though American and Japanese artillery fire was frequently observed by night fighter patrols. Shortly thereafter, the squadron suffered its first tragedy among the new replacements. Two crewmen were killed when their plane hit an oil truck on the runway.

The significance of these bombings never left Dickey's imagination. In his last published novel, *To the White Sea*, he dramatizes a briefing for a firebombing raid on Tokyo. The commander addresses the air crews: "'We're going to bring it to him,' the Colonel said with satisfaction. 'A lot more than usual.'"

> "Fire," he said again. "We're going to put him *in* it. That's saying, friends, that we're going to put fire around him, *all* around him. We're going to put it over him and underneath him. We're going to bring it down on him and on *to* him. We're going to put it in his eyes and up his asshole, in his wife's twat, and in his baby's diaper. We're going to put it in his pockets, where he can't get rid of it. White phosphorus, that'll hold on! We're going to put it in his dreams. Whatever heaven he's hoping for, we're fixing to make a hell of it." (1–2)

When the more than three hundred planes attack, Muldrow experiences what the colonel has promised:

> Then all at once I felt my back warm up, a heavy slash of heat, and I turned around toward the docks. Up and down where I had been was on fire, with the deep orange of napalm and also the blue-white of phosphorus, which is not so much like any fire you'd know, but was more like the end of a blowtorch, all spread out and shooting up curlicues and wriggles of itself like tracers that had gone crazy, and were meant to. (43–44)

In a letter to his brother, Tom, postmarked 2 March 1945, Dickey complained about the long hours between night missions. "It gets pretty boring around here in the daytime. It is hot as hell, and we all lay [*sic*] around and try to sleep without much success" (*One Voice*, I 71). To pass the time, Dickey had pounded a ring out of a Dutch silver dollar, which he enclosed to Tom; later, he portrayed such endeavors in "The Wedding," the efforts of airmen "so full of the thoughts of their wives / That the scratched, tired, beaten-out shining / Was more / Humanly constant / Than they. Years later, I go feeling / All of them turn into heroes." What haunts the speaker, however, are "the moon-glowing, center-bound rings / We made good before the dark missions, / Softly pounding our handful of money, / ... given safely to children, / Or nothing, / Or to the sea, / The human silver, essential to hope in the islands, / Now never worn by woman in its life." In addition to suggesting the efforts of airmen to combat the tedium, the poem portrays the rituals used to sustain oneself, an interest readily revealed in works such as "The String" (1959), "Springer Mountain" (1962), and "Approaching Prayer" (1964). Dickey and the other airmen frequently played softball and volleyball or simply sat and talked or drove to the beach to swim. They also watched movies. "Some of them," Dickey remembered, "were fairly current. I remember *Meet Me in St. Louis* with Judy Garland. *The Picture of Dorian Gray*, the Oscar Wilde story with George Sanders and Lauren Hatfield. Angela Lansbury was in that.... And also *Laura*." Additionally, he watched *They All Kissed the Bride*, the 1942 comedy from Columbia Pictures directed by Alexander Hall and starring Joan Crawford and Melvyn Douglas, as well as *The Keys to the Kingdom*, a 1944 film directed by John Stahl and starring Gregory Peck, Thomas Mitchell, and Vincent Price. Boxing and other sports newsreels were also favored recreation. The squadron, moreover, possessed a record player and three records, Dickey told his mother in a letter postmarked 24 March 1945, all by Spike Jones, the musician and bandleader who specialized in satirical arrangements of popular songs. He would later ask her to send him records, which he donated to the Special Service Unit, writing in a 20 September letter that "Take It, Jackson," performed by Vaughn Monroe and His Orchestra in an album titled *Hawaiian Sunset*, had arrived cracked but "still plays fine" (*One Voice*, I 94). Other music, however, he asked that she keep safely for him at home, including Debussy's *Clair de Lune* as well as Leybach's *5th Nocturne* and Beethoven's *Air for G String*. He also requested the sheet music for *Clair de Lune*, declaring, "God, how I love Debussy!!!!" (77).

Dickey, not surprisingly, frequently availed himself of the squadron library, reading paperbacks of what were called armed service's editions, including works by James Stevens and Mason Goodrich. The latter's 1941 novel *Delilah* concerned the World War I navy and revolves around a fictive American destroyer, the USS *Delilah*, and her crew in and around the Philippines from 1916 to 1917. In particular, the novel centered on the relationship between officers and enlisted men and the strict stratification of naval personnel, a thematic concern whose relevance becomes apparent when Dickey's son Chris later asked his father directly why he had washed out: "The officer business, it was not for me. I didn't want to command anybody. I, first of all, didn't want to be commanded. The standards were just not right for me. I didn't like it" (*Summer of Deliverance* 45). Stevens, the Irish poet and novelist, published critically acclaimed retellings of Irish myths and fairy tales. Weight lifting was also important to Dickey, who exercised using old engine parts and emulating the regimen prescribed by

Jules Bacon, Mr. America 1943. Later he would describe his efforts to improve his physique in his posthumously published poem "For Jules Bacon," collected in *Death, and the Day's Light* (2015). The speaker decides to enhance his body: "I was looking / To loot, Jules, to rob the dead / Metals, and come up / With a self. All these had mass. All could have become / Part of a new human body / Made from the old. You could take these in / And make yourself out / Of them, as you have not / Yet been." In effect, the least important detail or image of an action or activity became important to Dickey, who focused and transformed it. "There is no doubt that Jim elaborated and even embellished some the facts," Earl Bradley related in a 21 June 1994 letter, "but heroic poetry has always done that.... I wonder what would happen if one wrote about the many boring days of the war when the planes were held on the ground, although there are stories there also—how does one occupy himself far from home in living conditions akin to squalor. And Jim with his nose forever in a book." "Random sets of events do not necessarily fulfill the need for literary completeness," Bradley asserted. "They are neutral. The poet or author has to supplement, something like completing a jig-saw puzzle. I might add, a dynamic jig-saw puzzle whose final form is a function of the creativity of the author or poet." For Dickey, revealing identity necessitated mixing fact and myth.

Dickey's poems projected a heightened view of reality, driven by his intense competitiveness and his need to be heroic, to exaggerate and change the world and his place in it. In a 10 February 1945 letter to his father, he wrote that the squadron had finally managed to clear the island of Japanese. He was in line, he claimed, to receive the Air Medal "in about 85 more hours combat flying and [I] hope to get the Distinguished Flying Cross and maybe a few more medals before I get back." He also stated that he was grappling with calculus and differential equations, which he had been studying when he left Clemson. "Pretty tough stuff," he declared, "but a technical education is the best future there is and I aim to get one" (*One Voice* I, 70), a statement designed to placate or reassure his father but one decidedly untrue. He had no interest in becoming an engineer. In an unpublished letter to his mother the same day, he uncharacteristically detailed the danger all airmen faced, asserting that no one would "think the Japs are easy if he had ever seen a Jap dive his 'Tojo' fighter into a fully loaded ammunition boat," an act, however, he himself had not witnessed, though the squadron had experienced such destruction the previous Christmas on Mindoro when a suicide bomber hit the landing ship dock just as it beached. All the equipment and a few men were lost. "The Japs have a funeral service for the pilot," he continued, "at which he is *present* before his flight, and he takes off dressed in his ceremonial robes. The only one we found had his feet, or what was left of them, shackled to the rudder controls. Also, there has never been a B-29 shot down over Japan. They were all rammed. The Japs have a *school* for it." Many such assertions were either exaggerations or invented, efforts to mythologize his experiences and thereby heighten his sense of self. At the same time, he complained that "things are a little dull now; we are on the prowl every night, but nobody has gotten a Nip in two weeks. We are hoping to move over to China so the squadron can get more action." "To tell the truth," he admitted, "I am having quite a fine time here."

The contradictions in the letter speak to the conflicting attitudes and emotions within Dickey himself. Partly he sought to reassure his mother, whom he idealized, but partly he reacted to an increasing need to glamorize himself, a man engaged in a heroic adventure or journey. "You can never do anything in your life," he wrote in *Self-Interviews*, "that will give you such a feeling of consequence and of performing a dangerous and essential part in a great cause as fighting in a world war" (37–38). Earl Bradley agreed. "Jim is absolutely right," he wrote in a 21 June 1994 letter, "there is no more maturing experience than fighting in a war. Most people, even if they had been shot at one time in their entire life, would never forget the incident. Multiply that by some large number and one can imagine the psychological effects." Dickey demanded of himself a life of consequence. Literal truth did not matter, which is why in his frequently anthologized poem "The Performance," he mythologized his best friend Donald Armstrong, showing his aircraft "staggering oddly off into the sun" and then having the speaker move "some way to one side" so that "his body might pass through the sun," a clearly mythic image. Finally, Dickey imparts to Armstrong's execution by the Japanese swordsman a significance his tragic and meaningless death did not otherwise possess: "The stand on his hands, / Perfect, with his feet together, / His head down, evenly breathing, / As the sun poured up from the sea." Armstrong then kneels down "in kingly, round-shouldered attendance,/ ... / Beside his hacked, glittering grave, having done / All things in this life that he could." Later critics failed to understand that while "The Performance" ostensibly centers on Armstrong, its real focus is Dickey himself, the poet who must reimagine Armstrong's execution to render a reality far better and far different from the truth of facts, a lie that "makes truth better than it is" (*Self-Interviews* 32). As his son Christopher admitted, "Armstrong should have—they *all* should have—died so well, my father thought. And now they had" (*Summer of Deliverance* 53).

Dickey's awareness of his own survival opened his sensibilities to the external world. In *Sorties* he asserted,

> The longer I live, the longer and better the whole perspective of possibility becomes, and the more I see how necessary it is to *throw* one's self open to the least chance impulse or stimulus coming from anywhere. Who knows where that "anywhere" comes from or is.... No wonder Whitman is the poet who opened up America for us: he was open to *all* kinds of possibilities. A man sawing a plank was a great man to Whitman and imminently worth watching and learning from. (53)

That openness explains Dickey's choice of unusual subjects and perspectives, as, for example, in "The Sheep Child" (1966), about which he would write, "I don't know what other defects or virtues the poem might have, but I think it can hardly be faulted from the standpoint of originality of perspective" (*Self-Interviews* 165). Part of the poem is related by a farm boy years later of the proscriptive effect of the myth on boys' sexual urges and part by the sheep child itself, speaking from the bottle of alcohol in the museum. Dave Smith, commenting on Dickey's poetry, later observed,

> Well, that was Dickey, wasn't it—the poem as an entrance to the unmade, a wiggle into interior experience as the idiom of exterior expression. Let us say one exploration may be altogether simple. Play. Gaming. The pursuit of excitement in competition. Dickey kept writerly journals in which, as in his interviews, he liked to observe his working self, his subjects and potentials. One often finds him asking, "What can be done with this?" It is the query of a working man, a man in whom the spirit of creation swells. The answer, often silent but never absent, is to make a better self. ("Afterword" 86)

Dickey's service in the army air forces and his actions in the Pacific theater permanently altered his life and determined his career. In works published from the late forties until the year before his death, Dickey reinterpreted his combat experiences, frequently centering on a specific image that conveyed personal significance, including poems such as "Amputee Ward" (1948), "Whittern and the Kite" (1949), "The Confrontation of the Hero" (1955), "The Work of Art" (1957), "The Performance" (1959), "The Enclosure" (1959), "The Jewel" (1959), "Between Two

Prisoners" (1960), "A View of Fujiyama after the War" (1960), "Mindoro, 1944" (1960), "The Driver" (1963), "Horses and Prisoners" (1963), "Drinking from a Helmet" (1963), "The Courtship" (1963), "The Fire-bombing" (1964), "Victory" (1968), "Patience: In the Mill" (1992), "The Contest" (1996), "The Mission" (1996), "The Valley" (1996), and "The Coral Flight" (1996).

"The Enclosure" exemplifies his use of ordinary, seemingly inconsequential events whose persistent memory requires imaginative exploration as if they sought subjectively determined or imposed meanings. Based on "an actual circumstance," he asserted in *Self-Interviews*, the poem depicts "the inaccessibility I've always deemed an important part of the man-woman relationship: the idealization of women" (91). The speaker, riding in a truck to the airplane in which he will fly his nightly missions, passes a GI hospital and leans over the tailgate and sides of the vehicle to glimpse the few nurses who tend the wounded: "I thought I could see / Through the dark and the heart-pulsing wire / Their dungarees float to the floor / And their light-worthy hair shake down / In curls and remarkable shapes / That the heads of men cannot grow." He imagines the "women stand deep in a ring / Of light, and whisper in panic unto us / To deliver them out / Of the circle of impotence." "There was a small contingency of nurses," Earl Bradley recalled, "not too far from the little village of Santa Fe." Because the squadron had its own doctor, however, the airmen consequently had no need to visit the medical compound; the nurses remained an illusion, an enrichment of fantasy, what Dickey would later term, quoting the poet Paul Claudel, "the promise that cannot be kept" (*Night Hurdling* 217). "Mindoro, 1944," originally titled "Poem from an Old War," also recalls a specific image. The poem centers on "six boys [who] have slung a coffin by the ropes / Above the dog-eye-colored land / And town of San José." The narrator understands, as he "picks up everything and loves," that "*sun falls, man falls together. / Light rises from earth alone.*" In the midst of death, the speaker recognizes, is love. "Drinking from a Helmet" stems from an incident that occurred on Okinawa: "We were fighting on Coral Ridge and the graves registration people were about two hundred yards in the rear laying out a cemetery that the fellows fighting up on the ridge would soon be occupying. This was one of the weirdest sights I ever saw" (*Self-Interviews* 123–24). The physical involvement of the speaker in combat, his proximity to death, initiates a larger awareness: "I kept trembling forward through something / Just born in me." He places a nearby helmet on his head and knows "I have inherited one of the dead," recognizing in the image of the soldier's "blond brother," likely Dickey's older brother, Gene, his own connection to both the living and the dead. Throughout his career, his major thematic concerns, love and death, on the one hand, and family and war, on the other hand, mingled in his poems.

Dickey's increasing independence from what he viewed as outdated parental values and his growing commitment to a literary profession became more apparent during spring 1945 in his letters home. In a missive to his mother postmarked 2 April, he denigrated what he labeled "the pursuit of the ordinary (home, wife, children)," which he declared "leaves me quite cold, if not horrifying me outright." Though he qualified the indictment, telling her that "you have always had the most wonderful ideas concerning marriage, especially my own," he defiantly added,

> The trouble with the majority of people is, they don't want fiercely enough to accomplish things. The average Joe wants security and some poor woman as defeated as he, to tell him that he is wonderful and all the rest of the post-marital baloney that is the stock-in-trade of wives. Men marry when they are sick of struggling with the world and acknowledge defeat. They want a hole to crawl home to every night, and love paid for by countless bills, rents and endless trivialities. (*One Voice*, I 74–76)

Dickey appeared at the time obsessed with the subject of marriage, writing again on 7 May 1945, in what he termed "my monthly tirade against the joys of wedded bliss": "Guys who get married are afraid, and more than that they are moral cowards. Tired of the struggle and weary of self-consolation at failure they are willing to accept the burden of a wife to have someone to tell them how wonderful they are." He added, "That is not for me, now or ever. If I ever form any lasting attachment for a woman, it must be someone who would not only live with me openly sans ceremony, but insist on it." "Either I am constructed differently from the ordinary run of human drudges or I have been reading too many books by Ernest Hemingway. Maybe a little of both" (82), he concluded. His rebellion against standard social constructs was no less strident in a letter to his father postmarked 5 June. While he praised the American war effort and its heroic attempts to counter totalitarianism despite "the price our country is paying for its heritage," he nevertheless attacked the "Hollywood patriates" and their misrepresentation of war. "A combat report can tell of a life, a hundred, a thousand lives lost, but cannot show the individual deaths, some quick, and some infinitely slow and painful," he declared. "And for every one some person's [*sic*] will bear a life of grief." "Most of the people in the States," he concluded, "are not fit to shake the hand of any of the men on Iwo, Leyte, or any of the rest of these Pacific deathtraps" (*One Voice*, I 87–88).

In Fresno, California, Dickey had ordered a long list of books from a local bookstore. While in the Philippines awaiting their arrival, he read Shakespeare and Louis Untermeyer's *Modern Poetry Anthology*. He worried about the volumes he had at home, asking his mother in a 10 March 1945 letter not to let "Maibelle or anybody else fool around with my books. I dread having anything happen to them. *Please* keep them in a safe place" (*One Voice*, I 72). His belief in poetry which the reader could believe and in which he could participate stems from these months when he was reading extensively amid the destruction of war, his life now almost exclusively centered on books and bombing missions.

Proclamations on marriage to his mother were frequently accompanied by poems or poetic fragments, as in his 2 April letter, in which he declared, "I have no other interest (as a profession) than writing. If there were more money in poetry I should quite naturally turn to it, but I fear I am not the genius that Shelley was." He included a short unrhymed cadence on clouds, blatantly sentimental and romantic, that he had written that day: "Now hanging marble, wind-chiseled / Now piling, shapeless / Swiftly flowing / Lit with the laughter of suns / Shifting— / Always the silent radiant tumult / Above our leaded wings." In the same missive he enclosed a sonnet on death "since almost every other poet has had a try at it" (*One Voice*, I 74–76). The sonnet is Elizabethan in rhyme scheme, but as with a Petrarchan sonnet, it shifts focus at the conclusion of the second quatrain. The poem depicts the traditional idea of the suddenness and randomness of death but also suggests that death is probably more surprised than are those whom it chooses. Another poem appeared in Dickey's 29 May letter to his mother. He asked her to copy and send him two poems by Ernest Dowson, "Breton Afternoon" and "Impenitentia Ultima." "I really like Ernest Dowson," he announced, and then sent her an untitled work he had penciled:

I having found in you more than dreams
. more sunlight than pride or wine
kindles in the heart, now sanction,
before diaphanous memories bequeath us
to nothingness effete—

the sun, sinking
the slow radiance
fading
dissolving the lean shadow—
all glorious things
in utter loveliness stand
held in an instant fleeting to darkness.
(*One Voice*, I 85–86)

Dowson's sentimental melancholy as well as his gift for memorable phrases appealed to Dickey. In *Self-Interviews*, he asserted that "the poetry I wrote before *Into the Stone* was influenced stylistically not so much by individual writers as by an amalgam of writers: something called, in capital letters, MODERN POETRY" (46), by which he meant, initially, poets such as George Barker and Stephen Spender and, later, Eliot and Pound. However, Dowson's idealization of purity and his fin-de-siècle romanticism affected Dickey's own vulnerabilities. "Dedication, To Ernest Dowson," a Shakespearean sonnet, appears in an unpublished pamphlet of poems titled "Poetical Remains" that Dickey wrote in the Philippines and that one critic correctly described as "little more than juvenilia. Awash with sentimental pining and sententious philosophizing, the poems are interesting mainly for the light they throw on Dickey's emotional state during the war: his homesickness, his sorrow over lost loves, his disillusionment with the military, his morbid cynicism about life, and his interest in 'easeful Death' and other forms of oblivion" (Hart 96).

Handwritten in a Jewel filler-tablet notebook with narrow-ruled lines, "Poetical Remains" consists of twenty-two poems. Under the title, in distinctively florid cursive, is the poet's name—James L. Dickey—a quite conscious statement of identity. In addition to "November Rainlight," which he had previously enclosed to his mother, the poems include meditations on nostalgia, early autumn, and time, as well as a work titled "Lines Inscribed to an Unknown Pioneer Buried Atop Vinings Mountain." Dickey as a child would have known about this mountain, which rises significantly from the surrounding terrain, although actually at a slightly below-the-average elevation for the region. Myth relates that in 1864, Union general William Sherman got his initial look at the church spires of Atlanta from the summit of Vinings Mountain. A meditation on the land and the inevitability of death, the poem addresses the grave of the pioneer: "Surely you have seen these things / Before Death with patient fingers shoved gently and tottered you / Into the earth. Surely you have been filled / By great visions, kindled and yet softened by such scenes as these." Several of the poems center on aspects related to war, including short poems "Take-Off," "Landing," "Advice to New Crews," "Howitzer," and "Prelude to Combat." None of the poems reveal his later interest in myth or in startling images that open the world in surprising new ways; rather, they reveal in structure, tone, and diction the clear influence of nineteenth-century Romantic and Victorian poets.

Though he was reading poetry extensively during the spring and early summer, Dickey was also involved with works ranging into other disciplines. On 30 June he sent his mother a remarkable request for more than four dozen books. The list included Sigmund Freud's *A General Introduction to Psychoanalysis*; *The Standard Book of British and American Verse*, edited by Nella Henney; W. J. Durant's *The Story of Philosophy*; *Invitation to Learning*, edited by Mark Van Doren, Allen Tate, and Huntington Cairns; S. E. Frost's *Basic Teachings of the Great Philosophers*; Jack Randall Crawford's *What to Read in English Literature*; *American Harvest*, edited by Tate and John Peale Bishop; Philip Goepp's *Great Works of Music*; Clement Wood's *The Complete Rhyming Dictionary*; *The Cambridge History of American Literature*, edited by Van Doren et al.; Bullfinch's *Mythology*; Fred Millet's *Contemporary American Authors*; Whitney Jennings Oates and Eugene O'Neill's *The Complete Greek Drama*; Bernard Guerney's *A Treasury of Russian Literature*; Barney Ross's *Fundamentals of Boxing*; Darwin's *Origin of Species* and *Descent of Man*; and Conrad Aiken's *Modern American Poets*. Among the specific poets and works Dickey requested were W. H. Auden's *Poems, On This Island*, and *Another Time*; C. Day Lewis's *Collected Poems*; Trumbull Stickney's *Poems*; Malcolm Cowley's *Blue Juniata*; Kenneth Patchen's *Cloth of the Tempest, First Will and Testament*, and *Before the Brave*; W. J. Turner's *In Time Like Glass, New Poems, The Dark Fire*, and *Pursuit of Psyche*; Richard Aldington's *War and Love* and *A Fool i' the Forest*; Richard Church's *Mood without Measure* and *Twelve Noon*; Richard Hughes's *Confessio Juvenis*; Dylan Thomas's *The World I Breathe*; Robert Penn Warren's *Selected Poems*; R. P. Blackmur's

The Second World; Alex Comfort's *Elegies*; Sean Jennett's *Always Adam*; Randall Jarrell's *Blood for a Stranger*, and "anything by Selden Rodman" (*One Voice*, I 90–93). The only novels included in the list were Aldous Huxley's *Antic Hay* and *Point Counterpoint* and Eric Knight's *This Above All*. Soon, however, he requested that his mother send him Faulkner's *The Marble Faun*, *As I Lay Dying*, *The Sound and the Fury*, and *Salmagundi*. The sheer number and breadth of the request indicated a final commitment to literature, not simply escapism or the passing of time.

To be sure, Dickey had long periods of inactivity, for the rainy season often grounded most aircraft. The weather also compounded the risks involved when crews were flying. Landing in a rainstorm, for example, he reported to his father on 28 May 1945 that the C-47 plane had skidded off the runway at 90 miles per hour and ended in a ditch. Though no one was killed, Dickey "pretty well smashed" his left hand while others were "cut up pretty bad." The incident may have provided the basis for an unpublished poem titled "Two Hands, One Broken," which opens, "By separation made complete, / One figure lies in shadow, one / In the sun of a window. / Time is feeling with essential energy / The broken member." To sharpen his navigational skills, he was studying two hours each day: "This night fighting is really a precision business and you can always learn something more." He informed his father on 26 May that the squadron had begun extended missions, flying long routes over Japan and China. "Once in a while," he stated, "we lose a plane or two, but not too many" (*One Voice*, I 85). A week later, two air technicians, Andrew Cobb and David Markowitz, were killed by the accidental discharge of a 20-mm cannon mounted on the aircraft on which they were working. Dickey, who had volunteered to replace Philip Porter in March as the squadron historian, wrote, "The effect of this happening on the personnel of the 418th cannot be described. T/Sgt. Cobb was one of the most reliable crew chiefs on the line and greatly beloved by all who knew him. Cpl. Markowitz, though a recent addition to the Squadron, had already established himself as a technician, as well as an exceedingly fine man" (Dickey, *History of the 418th Night Fighter Squadron* 99).

Dickey's prose in the unpublished typescript of squadron history, while largely maintaining a straightforward and factual focus on combat missions, the arrival of replacements, awards bestowed, and veterans returning stateside, nevertheless often displays a fluidity that establishes mood and conveys a personal connection to the events it relates. In May, for example, he noted the opening of the officers' club. Earl Bradley, in a

21 June 1994 letter, remembered it wistfully: "The thatched roof club we built out of bomb crates; cutting each other's hair; lieing [*sic*] about our exploits with the opposite sex; getting to know even the smallest details of each others' lives." Rather than situate the club in the midst of other duties or activities, however important, Dickey portrayed the event more immediately and in far more noteworthy detail:

> Fortified by several gallons of green Manila whiskey, brandy, rum, and miscellaneous mixtures of doubtful origin, the gallants of the 418th held sway in what was afterwards called the most royal celebration in the history of the Squadron. Ignoring (not quite successfully) the myriad flapping bugs clustered about each light, the officers in no uncertain terms proclaimed the superiority of the night fighters to the rest of the air force and that of the 418th to the rest of the night fighters. (99)

The language is descriptive and slightly old-fashioned. By contrast, however, his earlier entry in March regarding the deaths of Donald Armstrong and James Lally is direct and sparse, as if Dickey were unable to process what he termed "a most unexpected and tragic occurrence." The two airmen had been returning from night cover for a convoy making its way to Panay, an island about one hundred and thirty miles southeast of their base. Relieved by the day fighters, Armstrong had decided to buzz the Japanese airstrip on Panay. Their plane crashed in a high-speed stall; Armstrong was killed and Lally, badly injured. The entry concludes, "There has been no further news to date" (89). When the Allies landed on Panay, Lally, who had been captured and taken to a nearly schoolhouse, was beheaded by his captors. Dickey re-created Lally's imprisonment in "Between Two Prisoners." While "The Performance" mythologizes Armstrong, "Between Two Prisoners" assumes the perspective of the guard who was "hanged / A year later, to the day, / In a closed horse stall in Manila. / No one knows what language he spoke / As his face changed into all colors." In *Self-Interviews*, Dickey declared that both men had survived the crash only to be executed, writing, "Almost every word of 'The Performance' is true, except that the interpretation of the facts is my own" (92). Dickey believed Armstrong his best friend, likely because the latter was off-beat and free-spirited, a pilot about whom other air crews were "a bit chary" (91) because he "was always doing crazy things" (92). In re-creating Armstrong's death, Dickey confirmed his belief in the transcendence of the imagination. As he later wrote in a 14 December 1988 letter to Gore

Vidal, "I make no distinction between fact, fiction, history, reminiscence and fantasy, for the imagination inhabits them all" (Bruccoli, Baughman 455).

In June 1945, in preparation for the invasion of Japan, the 418th received new aircraft and routinely flew extended missions carrying bombs and extra tanks. On 1 July the squadron participated in the initial landings on Borneo, flying convoy cover and bombing enemy positions in the Battle of Balikpapan. The battle, the concluding stage of Operation Obie, saw the Australian 7th Division make an amphibious landing following heavy bombardment and shelling by Australian and United States air and naval forces. Sorties were additionally flown over Canton and Hong Kong, which provided "invaluable experience to the participants for our future night intruder missions" (Dickey, *History of the 418th Night Fighter Squadron* 109). That same month the squadron departed Subic Bay in the Philippines and landed on Naha, Okinawa, establishing base camp twelve miles from the beach. "The first night on Okinawa was a nightmare," Earl Bradley remembered.

> At the south end of the island, near Naha, the fighting was still going on and the Japs were being pushed into the sea. We did not take the north end of the island until much later and the Japanese were sneaking through the American lines to what they considered refuge.... There were several Japanese bodies laying around, some of them had been run over many times by our trucks. One fellow set up a tent and discovered that a body had been blended with the mud and was part of the floor.

Dickey wrote in the squadron history, "The area assigned to us proved to be in the middle of one of the largest battlefields of the war. Everywhere were helmets, canteens, rifles, gas masks and Japs in various stages of decomposition." The bodies were "discretely buried and ceased to stink as much." The squadron, however, remained on high alert, expecting a Japanese attack. One night the area erupted into a "shooting gallery" as security officials and guards believed the camp was being infiltrated. "Every bush and shadow in the area were ruthlessly perforated with carbine and .45 fire from the 418th and Chemical Company in the next area" (109), Dickey recorded, though no Japanese bodies were discovered the next morning. In a 1987 interview, Dickey recalled the confusion: "It was just absolute chaos, absolutely. There was a place up in back of our area which was all coral caves and where the Marines and infantry had just gone and scoured through those with flame throwers. There were Japanese guys sitting up there in what must have been a machine-gun emplacement just incinerated. Just black" (Baughman, *Voiced Connections* 252). To add to the pervasive squalor, a strong storm ravaged the island, uprooting most of the tents and creating more confusion.

By the end of July, all crews of the 418th had flown missions over Japan, bombing and strafing targets over Kyushu, attacking Tomitaka, Tsuiki, Fukuoka, Kumamoto, and Kanoya. On one mission over Honshu, an eighteen-hundred-mile round trip, Dickey's aircraft did not have enough fuel after landing for the plane to be parked. He related in a 5 August 1996 interview, "We all figured that we would die over there. Nobody figured we would survive. We hated the Japanese so much.... I would have done anything against the Japanese. If there were any creatures on earth that I would want to drop an atomic bomb on, it would have been them. And I still would. I've never gotten over it." Bradley felt similarly, recalling in a 4 February 1997 interview, "I expected to die over there with the impending invasion. We all hated the Japs." On 7 August 1945, the United States dropped the atomic bomb on Hiroshima, one of four cities previously spared intensive bombing in order to gauge the damage following the explosion. "We thought it was just some sort of extra powerful type of dynamite. We didn't know. Everybody was mystified by it," he remembered. When photographs of the damage were released, "we were all flabbergasted and dumbfounded that nobody knew what to think." Three days later, another atomic bomb was dropped on Nagasaki, and Japan surrendered. "You should have seen the celebration here," Dickey wrote his mother on 16 August, "when the Jap peace note was recieved [*sic*]. Everybody went absolutely wild." In the squadron history, he wrote:

> On the night of 14 August the 418th was torn away from "Two Girls and a Sailor" by a most unprecedented demonstration of fire from practically every gun on the island. At first everyone ran for cover, thinking the Nips were making final Kamikaze charges to all installations on Okinawa. Soon, however, rumors spread across the island that the Japs had sued for peace. Everyone became violently excited with every news report on the radio or with liquor laid away against VJ Day. As each outfit heard a fresh rumor, there were new outbursts of hilarity and fireworks until there was a greater display of ack ack in the sky than there had been for any Nip bomb raid. The celebration came to a sudden halt when the island commander

ordered a red alert as a safety precaution against wild shooting and
falling flak. (114)

In late September Dickey wrote his father, "I really didn't think I had
much chance of getting back. You can't imagine how this work tells on
you, unless you've done it. Then, all of a sudden the war is over and now
it looks like I'll be in the land of the living for awhile yet despite the Japs.
To say I was stunned by the news of the peace is putting it mildly. It seems
15 or 20 years ago that I played my last game of football. You just forget
about those things that's all" (*One Voice*, I 96–97). Dickey would have
agreed with James Jones, who wrote in *Whistle*, his 1978 novel about
World War II, "In our profession, we pretty much lived by superstition.
We had to. When all of knowledge and of past experience has been utilized, the outcome of a firefight, or a defense or an attack, depended largely
on luck. Awe of and reverence for the inexplicable, that heart of a dedicated gambler's obsession, was the only religion that fit our case." Muldrow
in *To the White* Sea expresses similar feelings when a train fortuitously
passes by, thus enabling him to elude Japanese pursuit: "Luck or not, I
wouldn't tell you," he thinks, as he attempts to escape Japanese detection
and capture, "but I believe in luck, which sometimes you can push and
sometimes just comes, even when it doesn't have to" (124). Dickey had,
with luck, survived, but friends from Atlanta and fellow airmen and combat personnel had not.

He later reimagined the Allied celebration in his 1968 poem
"Victory," which opens:

> By September 3rd I had made my bundle
> Of boards and a bag of nails. America, I was high
> On Okinawa, with the fleet lying on its back
> Under me, whispering "I can't help it"
> and all ships firing up fire
> Fighting liquids   sucking seawater, hoses climbing and coloring
> The air, for Victory.

As he would throughout his career, he then transformed the event to
explore its personal significance. Declaring that "I was ready to sail / The
island toward life / After death," the speaker "reached for a bottle" and
soon believes himself a savior: "What could I do but make the graveyards
soar." At the poem's conclusion, with a newly tattooed serpent coiling
around his body, he prepares to return to the States: "The snake shone on

me complete   escaping / Forever surviving   crushing   going home / To
the bowels of the living, / His master, and the new prince of peace." The
alcohol-induced dream releases his confusion as he struggles to comprehend the end of the war and his own survival. "With my skin running out
of the world / Wide sun," his return to the living is diminished by the
inscrutable human cost of the conflict.

By November 1945, Dickey and other airmen of the 418th were living in the former kamikaze pilots' barracks at Atsugi Field in Tokyo. He
wrote his father, "My orders are in to go home on combat fatigue. I didn't
want to bother anybody at home with it before, but I am pretty well shot
as far as nerves go. That last part of the war, June, July and August was
carried on at a terrific rate. Now that the merry-go-round has slowed down
it sure leaves you with a funny feeling" (*One Voice*, I 97–98). He had been
promoted to second lieutenant in May. Officers enjoyed private rooms,
and each had a valet. Japanese cooks, under American supervision, prepared watercress salads and other fresh foods. He informed his brother,
Tom, on 15 November that before the war ended, "I was down to about
165 lb. [from around 200] from nerves and Spam every meal, but we are
eating pretty well now and I guess I weigh about 175 or 180. I am too lazy
to really find out" (*One Voice*, I 99–100). New crews now did most of the
flying, although Dickey and the older air crews flew enough to earn
monthly flight pay. He visited Tokyo, where he walked around the em-
peror's palace, as well as Atsugi and Yokohama. Crews watched movies
every night. "All I do is lay [*sic*] around and read," he wrote his mother on
8 November, "and fool around Tokyo" (*One Voice*, I 98–99). He wrote
again a week later. "I sure am glad the war's over," he declared. "I can't get
over not getting killed. This squadron was just like those in the movies
where everybody sits around wondering who's going to get it next. We had
the most impossible missions you ever saw. At briefing it would have been
funny, had it not been so serious, when we were told our targets" (*One
Voice*, I 99–100). He had a jeep at his command, which he used to visit
Mount Fujiyama, the subject of a later poem, "A View from Mount Fujiyama after the War." The speaker quietly watches as "snow streams from
the mountaintop / And all other mountains are nothing," and he wonders,
"Can he know that to live at the heart / Of his saved, shaken life, is to
stand / Overcome by the enemy's peace."

Dickey returned to America on a troop ship, the USS *Sea Devil*, early
in 1946. His separation qualification record states that his formal discharge

from the Army of the United States occurred on 1 March 1946 at Fort McPherson, Georgia. The summary of his military occupations reads:

radar observer for the 418th Night Fighter Squadron on Okinawa. Flew long range strafing and bombing missions. Acted as bomber escort on night missions and provided cover for landing forces and convoy attacks. Tracked and bombed seaborne and land targets by means of synchronized radar methods, using designated radar bombing equipment. Operated and performed first echelon maintenance on radio and radar sets and equipment. Completed 38 combat missions. Total Flying time 403 hours, of which 120 were combat hours.

Dickey's journey to war had begun on New Year's Eve; his return to civilian life had followed almost exactly one year later when the USS *Sea Devil* brought him home to the States. That the ending would, in this fashion, effect a circular pattern became the archetypal plot that held Dickey's imagination the remainder of his life. The idea of a quest, with its separation from the world, penetration to a source of power, and life-enhancing return, now "master of two worlds," as Joseph Campbell described it in *The Hero with a Thousand Faces*, yielding him a secret knowledge, appealed to Dickey's need for myth.

His need to reconstruct or reinvent experiences, to explore the poetic possibilities he believed inherent in them, owed initially to early feelings of inadequacy. Subsequent insecurities, such as his fear of failure, led to an intense competitiveness. A quiet, sensitive boy eventually believed it necessary to become larger than life. The war purged the superficial values of his Atlanta childhood, rendering him acutely conscious of human frailty and the transitory nature of existence and convincing him finally of the subversive nature of literature and the ultimate redemptive possibilities of imagination. He insisted on an invented world of his own creation. Indeed, it was imperative, given the death of his older brother and the brutality of combat, that he discover a means to live more fully and to offer that possibility to others, to render reality better than it is. What was needed, he wrote Andrew Lytle on 20 June 1954, was "the dedication of the artist and the sacramental quality of his imagination. And courage, determination, and imaginative joy" (*One Voice*, I 216–17). He wrote Donald Hall in an unpublished letter dated 10 February 1963, more certain then of his mission and the course he needed to pursue, stating, "It's good to do new things, as you are doing, but it is also good to remember that a writer has one main stream running through him and a lot of tributaries that feed into it (also a lot of sumps and stagnant water), and that the work has force and truth only in that current, as it must flow." Though Dickey's work would offer many perspectives and indeed styles, and though he himself would display many personalities during his career, his was always one voice, direct and forceful, committed, precisely because he recognized that "one main stream" and flowed with it.

CHAPTER 4

VANDERBILT

Dickey was officially enrolled in Vanderbilt University in Nashville, Tennessee, for the summer quarter of 1946. In a letter postmarked 26 May 1945, while he was still stationed in the Philippines, he had written his mother regarding his college plans. If Harvard did not admit him, he wanted admission either to Princeton, University of Virginia, University of Mississippi, University of Florida, University of Southern California, University of Maryland, or Vanderbilt. "Nothing definite," he declared, "I'd prefer not too large a school, and rather quiet. I want to relax after being under tension so long" (*One Voice*, I 84). He had returned from Japan and, following minor surgery for the removal of a cyst, was mustered out at Fort McPherson in Atlanta. He renewed acquaintances, visited high school friends, and received veterans' benefits from what was referred to as the 52-20 club, a provision of the Servicemen's Readjustment Act of 1944, also known as the GI Bill. Simply with his signature, a veteran received twenty dollars each week for a year while he pursued employment or a higher education. Dickey also visited Gwen Leege in New York City, where she introduced him to the Gotham Book Mart. Though he had not heard of the establishment, the bookstore was an institution. One recent source claims it was "responsible for sponsoring Joyce, for publishing Lawrence, helping with Kenneth Patchen's hospital bills, lending money to Edmund Wilson, employing Tennessee Williams, and even unclogging Marianne Moore's kitchen drain on one memorable occasion" (Sante).

During the war, male students at Vanderbilt had enlisted by the hundreds, leaving dormitories and fraternity houses abnormally quiet. The largest exodus occurred during the 1942–43 school year, completely shutting down such male clubs as the Owl Club, the Ace Club, and Calumet. The following year women on campus outnumbered men by two to one. Not only were students volunteering but also faculty as well. Among faculty who joined the service were mathematics professor John Dyer-Bennet, psychology professor Meredith Crawford, and history professor Henry Lee Swint. Even the registrar, Robert Cunningham, left. Hardest hit, however, was the athletics department, where Roy Sanders, head football coach; Paul "Bear" Bryant, assistant football coach; and Norman Cooper, head basketball coach all left the university to serve. By December 1944, however, the military had the manpower it required, and training programs on campuses such as Vanderbilt started to be phased out. In January 1945, students began returning to Kissam and McTyeire Halls, the men's and women's dorm, respectively. That fall, six hundred first-year students enrolled at Vanderbilt, a class so large that the university built temporary housing. "Fraternity and sorority rush was back in full swing," as one historian noted. "Men's organizations like the Owl Club were back on campus. Even head football coach Red Sanders came back from the war" (Carey 198–202). "Vanderbilt is a school," Dickey later wrote,

> where you can't be interested in literature without being made aware of the Vanderbilt literary tradition and the great days of the late twenties, the days of the Fugitives and *The Fugitive* magazine and of the manifestoes, such as *I'll Take My Stand*, and of the illustrious literary and political heritage of Vanderbilt and the people who made it so, men like Donald Davidson, who was the only one there when I was there, and Robert Penn Warren, Allen Tate, Andrew Lytle, William Yandell Elliott, and the other people who were associated with the group. I began to read around a great deal in their work. (*Self-Interviews* 33)

The Fugitives, owing to their outcast status, their sentimentalism for the Old South, and their trenchant opposition to the commercialism of the New South, had taken a defiant stance in favor of Southern agrarianism and antebellum Southern values. When Dickey entered Vanderbilt in 1946, however, the campus had undertaken a postwar expansion; construction equipment seemed everywhere, and the identity of the university as an agrarian stronghold must have appeared outdated. Harvie Branscomb, who had left Duke Divinity School in 1946 to become Vanderbilt's chancellor, believed the campus undersized and dilapidated. In his memoir *Gone with the Ivy*, a biography of Vanderbilt, Paul Conkin wrote that the university was "surrounded by privately owned, deteriorating property and thus was increasingly isolated on its meager acreage," adding that it was "an impossibly provincial campus, with half the students from Nashville, two-thirds from Tennessee." Three of the university's professional schools—law, religion, and engineering—had "woefully inadequate facilities," and the School of Social Work had no permanent facilities at all.

Faculty salaries were low; fringe benefits, few. Four fundraising campaigns in eight years yielded diminishing returns. Unrestricted gifts for 1946–1947 totaled only $8,000. Conkin concluded, "Vanderbilt was no longer a pacesetter for the South, for it had almost no impact on the South" (444).

Vanderbilt's literary tradition, however diminished, and its embrace of Southern ideals nevertheless attracted Dickey. The university was a staid, even placid, contrast to the combat savagery he had witnessed in the Pacific both as a participant and in his imagination, a refuge that appealed to his Romantic sensitivities and his commitment to literature. Calhoun Winton, a fellow student, whose friendship with Dickey lasted their entire lives and who later was Dickey's faculty colleague and department chair for three years at the University of South Carolina, remembered that Vanderbilt was a "somewhat dingy collection of redbrick buildings, crowded helter-skelter into a hillside in residential Nashville. Summers were hot and humid, and in the winter black coal dust poured from nearby chimneys and smokestacks." "Though the oaks and hackberry trees provided some green relief," he remembered, "it was not a prepossessing place. We went there for an education; that was why Dickey joined hundreds of other veterans in the long registration lines" (Kirschten 69). Along with Duke, Chapel Hill, University of Virginia, and Tulane, Vanderbilt was considered a top-tier university in the region, offering as good an education as that of Yale, Bryn Mawr, and Princeton at a substantially lower cost. "The combination of a high-quality education and a bargain price," Winton declared, "made Vanderbilt attractive before the war to that brilliant galaxy of writers and thinkers who styled themselves the Fugitives" (69).

While Dickey's own feelings of being an outcast, a man self-consciously separated from the mainstream, were mirrored by the Fugitives generally, specific members of the group influenced his poetics. John Crowe Ransom's poems and New Criticism, for example, provided standards for his early poems, though later Dickey would renounce Ransom's rigid style. When Ransom left Nashville for Ohio, becoming editor of the *Kenyon Review*, he published some of Dickey's early poems, including "Awaiting the Swimmer" (1959), "The Change" (1961), and "In the Lupanar at Pompeii" (1961). Allen Tate, who had joined the Fugitive group while a student around 1921, was instrumental in securing a Sewanee Fellowship for Dickey, enabling him to travel around Europe and write poetry in the early fifties. Indeed, writing Monroe Spears on 1 April 1954, Dickey declared, "I am very glad, indeed, to hear what Allen Tate has to say about my work, and feel rather as I imagine I would if D. H. Lawrence leaned down from his pedestal and said to me, very strictly, 'Young man, you are not dead. You are one of the live ones'" (Bruccoli, Baughman 59). Tate's own poems, moreover, as one critic has noted, "encouraged Dickey to explore rituals of redemption in a highly wrought, rhetorical style" (Hart 123). Robert Penn Warren became one of Dickey's closest friends later in life; both shared an interest in nature's savage beauty. Additionally, Warren encouraged Dickey toward looser, more open poetic forms, a style which later characterized Dickey's "central motion." Andrew Lytle would soon become Dickey's mentor, engaging in an extensive correspondence that enabled Dickey to formulate an initial poetics centered on myth and symbol.

Dickey's interest in the Fugitives, however, had as much to do with their ideas as with the literary tradition they embodied. Bright and ambitious, deeply competitive, recently released from the armed services, and determined to make up for lost time, he desired nothing more than to immerse himself in the arts. Having decided in spring 1947 not to practice with the football team, Dickey instead chose to run the hurdles for the track team, but after two unsatisfactory seasons, he abandoned that sport as well. Though fraternities and sororities once again dominated the social life, he ignored them, seeking instead a literary subculture. "Dickey had built an impressive library collection of his own," Winton remembered, "emphasizing poetry and literary criticism." Simply put, he lived among his books. Once, when Dickey and Winton were in the Vanderbilt bookstore, where Winton was buying a copy of Wallace Stevens's *The Man with the Blue Guitar* on Dickey's recommendation, Dickey grabbed the book from Winton's hand and read from the title poem, accenting the reading to emphasize his point: "Things as they are / Are *changed* upon the blue guitar" (Kirschten 70). For Stevens, art and the imagination remade "things."

While the tension between industrialism and the largely agrarian culture of the South no longer dominated discussions at Vanderbilt, the issue remained, and Dickey, whose own family roots almost mandated his involvement, concerned himself with regional identity even as his larger thematic concerns transcended it. "I read an awful lot," he wrote in *Self-Interviews*, "mainly of the writings of the Fugitives. I read *I'll Take My Stand*, which is still very powerful, because after all, I'm a Southerner too, and the problem pertained to me as it pertained to any other Southerner, or indeed any citizen of the Western world" (34). He also read W. J. Cash's *The Mind of the South*, "which I thought was very good" (34). However, of all the Fugitive writings, Dickey believed the best was Donald Davidson's *The Attack on Leviathan*. Davidson's essay in *I'll Take My Stand*, titled "A Mirror for Artists," would have immediately interested Dickey, who had already committed himself to a literary profession. Davidson emphatically argued that industrialism was antithetical to the humanities generally and the artist specifically. "The making of an industrialized society," he asserted, "will extinguish the meaning of the arts, as humanity has known them in the past, by changing the conditions of life that have given art a meaning" (Donaldson et al. 29). "The artist, who is in spirit dissociated from the industrial's scheme of society but forced to live under it, magnifies his dissociation into a special privilege and becomes a noble exile" (32). A noble exile is exactly how Dickey viewed himself.

In *The Attack on Leviathan*, Davidson confronted what he believed to be the evils of industrialism, defending regionalism by celebrating what he termed the "diversity of America." "Davidson pointed out," Dickey relates, "that you belong to a specific time and place where you can see the same things and a certain number of the same human beings everyday. He says this is far from chauvinistic. This is the way human beings were meant to live. This is the way they can root down into a place and develop their own way of life in harmony with the environment. For Davidson, cultural pluralism is all-important" (*Self-Interviews* 81). "Regionalism," Davidson declared, "may be described as a retreat from the artistic leviathanism of the machine age, symbolized by the dominance of New York during the nineteen-twenties" (*The Attack on Leviathan* 81). It constituted "the natural condition of the arts among a people united in a general culture and living under a Federal government, but divided by the process of pioneering and settlement into cultural areas that could not be forced into any narrow pattern of national art" (95). For Dickey, as he later wrote, "differences give richness and variety to life and offset the terrible monotony that we're drifting toward in Americanizing the whole world" (*Self-Interviews* 35). Not surprisingly then, Dickey rarely ventured to New York during his career except to meet publishers or to attend gatherings of the American Academy of Arts and Letters, into which he would later be inducted in May 1988. This attitude also partly explains his later interest in translations, his use of literatures from such countries as France, Spain, Italy, and Russia.

In fall 1980, while teaching in the Honors College of the University of South Carolina, Dickey taught the Fugitive poets as part of his American Poetry course. Citing Davidson in his lecture notes as "the most violent and vociferous and insistent proponent of Southern agrarian self-sufficiency," he recommended that students also read his poetry, "some of which is very powerful," including such poems as "On a Replica of the Parthenon" and "Sanctuary," both of which he declared involve the theme of flight and pursuit. "As a scholar and as a polemicist and as a literary critic," Dickey asserted, Davidson was "very nearly first rate." "He really understands country people and country ways better than any of the other Fugitives; he is more at home among them, and his feeling for Southern place and landscape, as such, is better than theirs. He is obsessed with the Civil War, and the lost cause, and as time passes his preoccupation with that period seems a little quaint." In his notes Dickey was no less straightforward, critically astute, and deeply opinionated regarding John Crowe Ransom, a minister's son who was "withdrawn, quiet, reserved, ironically intelligent, compassionate, rueful and intelligently and ironically helpless." He possessed, Dickey asserted, "a kind of assumed archaic and pedantic, oblique method of presentation," and with such poems as "Janet Waking" and "Antique Harvesters," Dickey noted Ransom's "odd combination of Elizabethanism, scholarly words, and elaborate courtly phrases from Southern elocution and religion." Regarding Allen Tate, Dickey was more effusive and complimentary, largely because in Tate's main theme, "the loss of meaning in the modern world, and what is left when religion dies, custom is forsaken, greed and self-seeking take over, when centerless, spaceless organization takes over, when, to disprove his own existence, the mind must feed on itself in a condition of paranoid intellectual claustrophobia." Discussing such poems as "Shadow and Shack," "Aeneas at Washington," and "The Wolves," as well as Tate's essay "Narcissus as Narcissus," he concluded that Tate's literary techniques largely derived from Latin, T. S. Eliot, and his friend Hart Crane, and acknowledged Tate's "high merit as an introspective literary critic."

Despite Dickey's later statement in *Self-Interviews* that upon entering Vanderbilt he was "still undecided about what I wanted to do" (29), he had clearly committed to a literary career even if he did not believe he would be successful. "I went through college gradually building up a belief in myself as a writer. I really don't think I was markedly original at all, but I thought I might write some kind of solid, intellectually respectable and, with luck, interesting poems" (29). The Calumet Club at Vanderbilt had been founded in 1906 "to strengthen the literary spirit of the university," according to a statement in the 1950 edition of *The Commodore*, the university yearbook. By the forties, however, the focus of literary activity with respect to publication was *Gadfly*, the quarterly literary magazine. As its name suggests, the magazine stood firmly outside of the Vanderbilt social mainstream. *Gadfly* published four of Dickey's poems, including "Christmas Shopping, 1947" (Winter 1947), "Sea Island" (Spring 1948), "King Crab and Fiddler" (Spring 1948), and "Whittern and the Kite" (Summer 1949). These poems, later collected in *Veteran Birth* (1978), reveal the interests and observations of an airman returned from combat who feels displaced in the civilian world. Around him are scenes of American materialism and the warfare that Dickey believed inherent in all life. "These are the poems of a returned airman," he wrote in the preface,

> one who has been through the Inferno and the Purgatoria, but not the Paradiso—there was none—of the Second World War. They are the writings of a veteran desperately behind the position he should have been in: behind because of the war and the convulsions of history. But in the South Pacific he had caught intimations of a new kind of life, different from the college football field from which he had come, and from suburbia. Words had happened, although clumsily, to the returned veteran, wandering about the campus of Vanderbilt in a filthy flight jacket.

These poems, the first published by Dickey, reveal his interest in dramatic structure enhanced by unique, even startling, imagery.

Also apparent, specifically in "King Crab and Fiddler," is Dickey's interest in nature and the violence inherent in it. The poem depicts the brutality of these creatures, who pursue survival with naturalistic determination: "Collusive crab and rampant snake defeat / All enterprise, enisled and spectre-blind, / And mythic shapes embroil / The quick." Despite the opaque diction and rhetorical devices that anticipate his adoption of modernist techniques, "King Crab and Fiddler" also reveals Dickey's belief in what Robert Penn Warren termed "impure poetry," or as Dickey wrote in his class notes, poetry "of drive, guts, reality—whatever that is—instead of sweet sounds and vague sentiments." What attracted Dickey to Warren was "his power, his haunting nightmare quality, his gripping seriousness.... His concern with large, inescapable, unanswerable questions, the true dilemma of being human." Such an attitude would invariably have interested Dickey, whose passive father mandated the need for a virile, energized life in a world preoccupied with comfort and safety. Among Warren's poems that Dickey recommended were "Bearded Trees" and "Prairie Harvest."

Having officially entered Vanderbilt for the summer 1946 quarter, Dickey enrolled in four courses: College Algebra, Composition and Literature, Introduction to Social Science, and Elementary Spanish. After a mediocre performance in high school, he earned two As and two Bs in his college studies since returning from combat. His teacher in his first quarter of Composition and Literature was William Hunter, a visiting assistant professor from the University of Georgia. "He was a very fine teacher," Dickey recalled in *Self-Interviews*, "I could see that, even though I had never had an English class of any distinction before" (29). One-third of the course was devoted to the study of literary masterpieces, the remainder to the composition of expository essays. Hunter permitted Dickey to write whatever and however he wished after reading Dickey's first assignment. While other students, most just out of high school, composed themes on such topics as "What the American Flag Means to Me" and "My First Day on the Campus of Vanderbilt," Dickey wrote on the invasion of Okinawa. Hunter's favorable reaction and his relaxation of formal class requirements were, Dickey declared, "marvelously encouraging to me" (29). Subsequently he wrote a sonnet sequence, a critical article, and a surrealistic play as well as his essay on Donald Armstrong. He also wrote poems influenced by Kenneth Patchen and George Barker. Patchen's diction, "that sort of apocalyptic vagueness, that visionary quality" (27), interested Dickey, as did the rhetorical devices of Barker, who provided Dickey with "a sense of style" (28). In a 1987 interview with me, Dickey recalled his early Vanderbilt experience.

> I took that course [Composition and Literature] and I began to read a lot. I had been reading as much as I could overseas but I read more and more and began to write a lot, to experiment in various different kinds of things. I really didn't know what I wanted to do. I thought if I read enough I would become a fairly good critic. I hadn't thought really about trying to write creatively. But the more teachers I had, the more they told me that that was what I should do— to write things. I didn't think I could really write poetry because I thought it was both too technical and really too far above me. But I thought maybe if I wrote anything I could write short stories, maybe, or maybe eventually a novel. I was much taken with the short story as a form and I read a lot of them. I read more short stories than I did anything, even poetry. Although I liked poetry the best, I didn't feel that I had the wherewithal. I felt that poetry was something that you had to have been doing from an early age,

maybe almost infancy, like playing a musical instrument. But I knew that some prose writers like Conrad, for example, had not published anything until they were in their 40's, so I figured that might possibly augur well for me. I didn't know that Wallace Stevens hadn't published a book until he was 46 or thereabouts.

As Dickey struggled to discern a literary direction, his academic coursework in other fields, often undertaken by chance or whim, assisted his search for a style and subject matter that would center his poetic efforts. Courses in philosophy, art, anthropology, and astronomy all widened his understanding of the world. Dickey enrolled in General Astronomy as a prerequisite to Observational Astronomy ("Theory and Use of Astronomical Instruments"), enhanced by a course in algebra and plane trigonometry. "In 1948," Cal Winton declared, "astronomy was only a one-man division within the Department of Physics and Astronomy, but Carl Seyfert was an extraordinary teacher." "Under Seyfert's direction," he stated, "[Dickey] gazed through the night skies at those strange constellations which had once been only navigational aids for him" (Kirschten 72). Through Seyfert, Dickey wrote, "I got a feeling of intimacy with the cosmos," declaring that Seyfert would fondly cite E. A. Robinson's line, "The earth is a hell of a place, but the universe is a fine thing" (*Self-Interviews* 36–37). Dickey's interest in and knowledge of the stars led to his later taking correspondence courses in the use of sextants as well as to his sixty-one-page poem, *The Zodiac*, which depicts the efforts of a dying Dutch poet to write the ultimate poem that connects him to the universe. "I have always wanted to energize," Dickey told an interviewer in 1972, "what little I remember about the stars and galaxies onto poetry." That was difficult to do, he continued, because "the universe is so vast, and how do you tie something as big as the universe—the Milky Way, the solar system—into something that's so small and intimate as human life on earth?" (Baughman, *Voiced Connections* 90).

At Vanderbilt, Dickey also enrolled in a variety of art courses, including Introduction to Art, Modern and Contemporary Art, and Renaissance Art; he earned As in all of them. His interest in art was lifelong. His son Christopher remembered, "My father was very interested in painting, and as we grew up he loved to leaf through art books—particularly modern art—asking us what we thought of Picasso or Kandinsky or whoever. He was also fascinated by modern architecture: Louis Sullivan, Frank Lloyd Wright, Le Corbusier, Mies Van De Roke—those generations." Occasionally, specific artists would appear in Dickey's poems, as in *The Zodiac*, when the drunken Dutch poet finds himself in a room where "in the half-light one of Kandinsky's paintings / Squeezes art's blood out of wallpaper." Wassily Kandinsky, the twentieth-century Russian painter and art theorist, developed abstract art following a long period of development and maturation; central to his art was what he termed "inner necessity," a devotion to inner beauty, fervor of spirit, and spiritual desire. Carol Dickey, Chris Dickey's wife, remembers a conversation that Dickey had with her mother, Madeline Salvatore, who in her late fifties had returned to school to earn a master's degree in art history. Once, while Carol and Chris were at Dickey's home in Columbia, South Carolina, she had called to say hello, and Dickey had asked to speak to her mother. He was curious about Marsden Hartley's *Portrait of a German Officer*. Hartley, an American modernist painter, poet, and essayist who had befriended Kandinsky in 1913, had died in 1943. His work reflected a combination of abstractionism and German expressionism, fueled by his personal brand of mysticism. Dickey questioned her about that movement in American art—Arthur Dove and others. Dove, an early American modernist often considered the first American abstract painter, used a wide range of media, sometimes in unconventional combinations. He also experimented with techniques, combining paints such as hand-mixed oil and tempera. Dickey identified with artists who rejected the conventional. Indeed, experimentalism characterized his poetry throughout his career. "I am full of ideas," he wrote in *Self-Interviews*, "about what might be done, and I ought to be pushing out the levels of what I have already done" (26).

Dickey was also interested in music as well as painting. In fall 1947 he enrolled in Materials of Music, another humanities course for which he earned an A, and as with painting, he remained intrigued by it throughout his career. He wrote his mother on 14 April 1947, for example, informing her that he had just finished studying and was listening to the Philadelphia Philharmonic playing Shostakovich's *6th Symphony*, "which seems to me to be pretty good" (*One Voice*, I 100). Music opened one up to life, which led to new experiences, new understandings. "It is a matter of what Henry James called 'accessibility to experience,'" Dickey wrote in *Self-Interviews*. "I imagine I was born with some kind of extra sensitivity to things. But that is hard to determine. I sometimes think that sensitivity, so called, is partly a capacity to be hurt by things, and partly intelligence both natural and cultivated" (20). Nowhere is Dickey's "accessibility to experience" more apparent than in *Sorties*, where he comments on what he has read or is currently reading. Biographies, essays, collected poems, movie reviews,

scholarly studies, novels, autobiographies, literary journals, popular magazines, art books, philosophy books, pre-Socratic writings, translations, diaries, anthropological studies, mythologies—all intrigued him "The longer
I live," he wrote, "the longer and better the whole perspective of possibility
becomes, and the more I see how necessary it is to *throw* one's self open to
the least chance impulse or stimulus coming from anywhere" (*Sorties* 53).

Dickey's extensive reading and his dedication to writing while at Vanderbilt did not mitigate his romantic interests, one of whom was Margarite
McEachern, with whom he talked poetry, including such writers as
Frederic Garcia Lorca and Arthur Rimbaud. Years later, Dickey wrote to
her in an unpublished 21 January 1969 letter, "You represent for me the
sad, intelligent last gasp of adolescence, in this case after a long war. Which
is to say that in a sense you were indispensable to me and you remain so
wherever you are." Another interest was Louise Brown, a dental receptionist, who motivated him to take notes for short stories he planned to write
(Hart 132). However, the woman who elicited his most romantic feelings
was Anne Locke, for whom he composed a series of poems. Locke, an
English major and philosophy minor at the University of Tennessee, was
then pursuing a master's degree at Vanderbilt. They had met in the library
on a December afternoon in 1946 and soon found themselves talking literature. Dickey eventually gave her books by Frederic Prokosch, Robinson
Jeffers, George Barker, and James Joyce, all writers who reflected his own
interests. The unpublished first poem he wrote her, "Poem for Anne in
the Twelfth Month," reflected not only the ardor of his interest but also
the opaqueness of his poetic diction: "Our place arises between blood-
pulses / Where the dove and the skeleton intertwined / Grow from the
clock's face and lock the hands of love."

Dickey's academic talents, as well as his formidable memory, drew
the attention of Vanderbilt's English department. Betty Spears, who was
teaching a section of English 101, the required freshman composition and
literature course, had assigned her first paper on Edward Donahue's story
"Head by Scopas." She believed Dickey's essay too capable for a first-year
student to have written it. Her husband, however, the eighteenth-century
scholar Monroe Spears, identified several errors, nevertheless acknowledging it "an essay of superior quality" (Kirschten 72). She recommended
Dickey enroll in his literature survey course the following quarter, which
Dickey did. Spears encouraged him to attempt different verse forms. "The
Gadfly poems," Cal Winton later remarked, "show him doing just that"
(72). About Spears, Dickey wrote in *Self-Interviews*, "He was the finest

critical literary intellect that I had encountered up to the time I was in college...his mind was like a laser beam. The fact that a man of this enormous critical acuteness could devote himself to literature instead of engineering, medicine or something sanctioned by the scientific orthodoxy in this country, was inspiring to me" (30). Dickey would credit Spears with helping him write poetry less apocalyptic than his previous efforts and of introducing notions of measure, form, and wit.

In April 1981 Dickey wrote "To Posterity," an emotional tribute to Spears, who became a lifelong advocate of his work and who remained a "continuing presence in everything my mind conceives." Calling Spears "my first real teacher," "incomparably the best," he declared, "In the parlance of the football field, it was Monroe Spears who threw the key block for me: who opened up the whole field upon which all kinds of running were possible. I would wish for every writer to have such an angelic blocker ahead of him, but there is only one Monroe." Inspired by Spears, he attempted heroic couplets in which Alexander Pope had excelled, but realized that his inclination and strength lay in the visionary qualities of romantic poets such as Blake and Coleridge, in afflatus, and in expansiveness. As he wrote in *Sorties*, "I don't like the locked-in quality of formalist verse.... [T]he human imagination is wide—very wide indeed. I want, mainly, the kind of poetry that opens out, instead of closing down" (8, 9). Spears attempted to temper his pupil's romantic excess, in particular the apocalyptic imagery and opaque diction Dickey had adapted from George Barker and the metaphysicals, hoping that the intellectual precision of eighteenth-century poets such as Pope would enhance Dickey's already formidable ability to reshape the truth in his writings. Spears recognized the difficulty of what Dickey was endeavoring to do—to understand personally "the exotic and beautiful Pacific islands filled with violence, brutality, and sudden death" (751–52).

In effect, Spears became a surrogate father, teaching him how the imagined world might become better reflected from reality through a honed diction. Once, while examining some of Dickey's poems, Spears asked his student why he had not rendered the narrative more dramatic. Dickey replied, "Because it didn't happen that way," to which his mentor supposedly said, "Well, what difference does that make? It would be so much better if you did it that way." "I could see it immediately," Dickey later wrote. "So I did it that way, and that's when I began to swing, though it was surely a very small motion in the beginning" (*Self-Interviews* 33). The poet, he realized, was going to manipulate his language; the question then became simply whether the manipulation was effective given its expressive function: "I think I really began to develop as a poet, at least according to my own particular way of looking at things, when I saw the creative possibilities of the lie" (32). Liberating his student from the idea that only fact is truth, Spears enabled Dickey to assume the mantle of a secondary creator.

In 1947, as he had the previous year, Dickey enrolled in summer session; classes included Introduction to Reflective Thinking, taught by Eugene Bugg, whom he liked and admired; Plane Trigonometry, which he failed and upon retaking in the fall semester earned an A; and the remaining two parts of Survey of English Literature, achieving an A in both classes. Among the essays written for the last of these courses was an analysis of the eighteenth-century poet William Collins titled "The Fitful Gleam," which opens, "It has been suggested that William Collins was, in a sense, a failure as a poet because the temper of the age in which he lived never permitted his natural poetic instincts to come to terms with the man within which they resided." The paper, which received an A, is the kind of essay Dickey would eventually require of his own students—a personal encounter with the poet and his work, scholarly and critically insightful but also one that critiqued the writer individually, as when Dickey concluded, "We can deplore Collins' affectations and his weaknesses, but we can also enjoy the delicacy and calm spirit of some of the finest fragments of pastoral poetry ever written in English." Another essay centered on Stephen Spender, who later was writer-in-residence at South Carolina while Dickey was on sabbatical. Titled "Deaths and Evasions," it opens, "Stephen Spender, in a rather curious remark to have been made by a modern poetry writer, writes: 'In poetry one is wrestling with a god.'"

> The subjugation of the "god" and his display within a framework of words and images is the poet's only concern throughout the engagement; if the artisan's perseverance, integrity and his skill of arranging mirrors are equal to the occasion the caged "god" will appear as a strangely familiar aspect of the onlooker's own experience, and the latter's sensitivity to present as future parallels of the same basic reality will correspondingly be heightened. If, however, the poet is not really a poet at all, but merely a popular sentimentilizer [sic], his subject will invariably defeat him. The cage may be erected, to be sure, but it will contain only the familiar back-yard dog or cat, thoroughly tame, and in no need of subjugation, much less of display.

Dickey discerned in Spender's work both the true poet as well as a writer whom he would later describe as "suspect," the writer whose lines, stanzas, themes, and whole poems

> seem to be sheer effrontery to his sense of what the truth of these subjects must be or could possibly be: that seem to have been invented to satisfy the rules of some complicated but learnable (for many have learned) game which keeps changing from generation to generation, but which always, whether it means to or not, brings into being a truly remarkable amount of utter humbug, absolutely and uselessly far-fetched and complex manipulation of language. (*The Suspect in Poetry* 9)

As Dickey's criticism would later frequently do, his judgment on Spender both praised and damned: "He simply does not have the floodlight-like capacity for illuminating the plexus of a situation or a state of mind which characterizes the work of a Lawrence Durrell or a Dylan Thomas. His integrity is unquestionable, however, and most of his poetry is much more than adequate. These are significant compensations." Responding to the essay, which earned an A, the professor wrote, "You might have commented on the language & meter of the poems in more detail, but this is a fine critical essay as it stands."

In fall 1948, Dickey began his senior year by again enrolling in a wide spectrum of courses. In addition to art, his studies included History of Philosophy, Modern Drama and Theater, General Astronomy, General Anthropology, Cultural Anthropology, and Comprehensive Course in English Literature. He would earn all As. General Anthropology, taught by Charles Brown, was a survey concerned with the biological and cultural history of mankind and the present racial, linguistic, and cultural distribution of peoples. Cultural Anthropology was a comparative study of human societies and basic problems common to human groups throughout the world. According to the Vanderbilt catalog, Emilio Willems, a visiting professor in sociology, taught the course and required a research paper on primitive ritual. Dickey chose the Murngin tribe, a people living in Arnhem Land, an almost uninhabited region of northern Australia between the Gulf of Carpentaria and the Indian Ocean. The Murngin are a variant group blending features of the white and black races. The fundamental basis of their society resides in an elaborate kinship system in which everyone is related to everyone else. The various tribal clans claim local territories given them by their totems. Each clan has multiple totems and a sacred water hole where the high totems, the totemic ancestors, the ancestral dead, and the totemic spirits of the unborn all live. Every member of the clan is born from the water hole and returns to it at death to live with the mythological ancestors. The Murngin's sense of a larger group unity, their communion with the dead, and their ritualistic use of water influenced his early published poems. "The Signs" (1959), "The Game" (1959), and "The Underground Stream" (1960) all possess elements present in their culture.

Commenting on Cultural Anthropology, Dickey related in a 1987 interview with me:

> That was a good course but mainly what I remember from it is what I read myself. When I was a junior, I was given a stack permit. I just went back there and read. I remember I read through a whole row of anthropology books. I read Malinowski, Radin, Robert Louie, Clark Wissler on the American Indians, Franz Boas, W. H. R. Rivers, Freud. I read everything that was on that row. Radcliffe-Brown, I read the Cambridge anthropologists, the mythologists. I read Cornford. I read Jane Harrison. *Themis* was wonderful! Fascinating! I didn't have to read systematically, but I read because I thought this would give me some kind of long-standing basis for the mythological interpretation of things.

These concerns reveal themselves in an unpublished poem Dickey gave Cal Winton shortly before 1949. "The Earth Drum" depicts in obscure language an anthropoid with "unsubtle, shagged and plexus-dweller / Brow" as he surreptitiously watches with carnal longing a blond-haired creature whom he desires to "anoint with semen" and who "curvets the void / Bequeathed by the latest girl his hands misplace." Dickey's interest in and understanding of ritual and myth would explicitly appear in *Deliverance*, which he characterized as "a sort of semi-conscious employment of the rites de passage—the three steps [of the journey of the mythic hero] which involves a withdrawal from the world, a penetration to the source of power, and a life-enhancing return." "All of that," he declared in his 1987 interview, "was of great importance to me and of great use."

Malinowski, Radcliffe-Brown, and Rivers imparted to Dickey an understanding of the mythologizing of totem animals; Jung yielded him a sense of the collective unconscious. Dickey also read James Frazer's *The Golden Bough*, Stanley Edgar Hyman's *The Tangled Bank*, and Joseph Campbell's *The Hero with a Thousand Faces*. His frequently anthologized poem "The Vegetable King" (1959) owes its origins to Frazer's study of Near Eastern fertility rituals. "The living victim was dismembered," Dickey relates in *Self-Interviews*, "thrown into a river or lake, and was supposed to be gathered together and resurrected when the crops came up in the spring." He used the same situation in "Sleeping Out at Easter" (1960). "I took an ordinary householder in the spring of the year," he wrote, and "had him sleep in the backyard and dream that he was the one who was dismembered, thrown into the water, and gathered together again. What if he then came back into the house and realized that this hadn't happened to him except in a dream? But how could he be sure? Maybe when he returned he really *was* the resurrected Vegetable King and the whole spring *had* been brought by him!" (*Self-Interviews* 90).

"The mythological interpretation of things" was also enhanced by Dickey's History of Philosophy course. He filled his Vanderbilt notebooks with entries detailing the polytheistic views of early Greek philosophers, noting in one entry that Greek culture exhibited "little distinction between animate & inanimate objects. Man was at home in the world of Nature— much of Christian thought is opposite this." In subsequent writings, he endeavored to show the human need to reconnect with the natural world. "The Owl King" (1961–1962), "A Dog Sleeping on My Feet" (1962), "Springer Mountain" (1962), and "Fox Blood" (1964), for example, all depict the unspoken human need to reunite with nature. Ed Gentry's climb up the sheer cliff in *Deliverance* provides a compelling example of the deep and abiding power inherent in nature and man's effort to connect with it. As Gentry maneuvers against "a surface as smooth as monument stone," the immense rock "seemed to spring a crack under one finger of my right hand; I thought surely I had split the stone myself. I thrust in other fingers and hung and, as I did, I got the other hand over, feeling for a continuation of the crack; it was there. I had both hands in the cliff to the palms, and strength from the stone flowed into me" (165). At the conclusion of *To the White Sea*, the narrator Muldrow, having perfected the art of camouflage, eludes his Japanese pursuers by finally entering into the frozen world around him: "I was sure I was gone. But the cold and the snow came back. The wind mixed the flakes, and I knew I had it. I was in it, and part of it. I matched it all" (275).

Dickey also studied Orphic mystery cults, learning that ancient Greek philosophers believed nature was instilled with "anima," or spirit, and that a corresponding sympathy existed between human and natural spirits. "Orpheus before Hades" (1959), one of his earliest published poems, portrayed this unity. "All of life comes in in a breath," the speaker thinks, "My eyes turn green with the silence / Of the thing that shall move from the hillside." These animistic perspectives informed much of Dickey's future nature writing; they anticipate his environmentalism. Even in *The Eagle's Mile*, he remained fixated by the ancient Greek belief that the world was composed of four basic elements—earth, air, water, and fire—and he composed a series of poems, titled "Immortals," that celebrated this pre-Socratic theory best exemplified by the philosopher Lucretius in his study *De Rerum Natura*. Other Greek philosophers interested him as well, including Anaxagoras, who believed that a spiritual mind, what he termed "nous," set the elements in motion. Titles of his later collections of poems, *The Early Motion* (1981) and *The Central Motion* (1983) as well as *The Whole Motion* (1992), reflect this idea, as if Dickey as a secondary creator or prime mover was setting into motion his own Creation.

History of Philosophy proved an influential course in Dickey's Vanderbilt education, so much so that he minored in philosophy. B. A. G. Fuller's *History of Greek Philosophy* was a course text, and Dickey additionally read Bertrand Russell's *A History of Western Philosophy*, Plato's *Republic*, and *Phaedo*, and Aristotle's *Physics* and *Metaphysics*. These texts formed the basis of his philosophic study between 1946 and 1950, ideas which appear again later in the fifties when he read Kenneth Burke's *A Grammar of Motives* closely, making extensive notations in his early notebooks on those sections that discuss Plato and Aristotle and the principles of motion and inaction, actuality and potentiality, and form and end. In one notebook entry, he contemplated a poem titled "Prayer Becoming": "See Fuller on Plato, Plato, *Radin*, Jung, theoretical anthropologists" (*Striking In* 37). In another entry, he used his knowledge of Greek mythology to critique Burke: "Burke is more a categorizer and characterizer, a parer and fitter, a kind of academic Procrustes, than anything else. He solves most of his problems by seizing on a particular phase of a philosophy, emphasizing it according to his needs, and slanting it to fit" (93).

Indeed, philosophy so intrigued Dickey, intertwining as it does with mythology and anthropology, that his philosophy notebook provides a thorough outline of Western thinking so as to encompass and understand its organic development. Starting with the Greek philosophers, including Pythagoras, Heraclitus, Plotinus, Parmenides, Empedocles, Plato, Anaxagoras, Socrates, and Aristotle, the outline provides a fascinating view of his effort to arrive at a weltanschauung, or world view, eventually listing Augustine, Philo Judaeus, Duns Scotus, William of Occam, Bacon,

Bruno, Hobbes, Descartes, Spinoza, Leibnitz, Locke, Berkeley, Hume, and Kant. The extensive handwritten notes detail the pre-Socratic philosophers, frequently contrasting their thoughts with those of later Christian thinkers, as, for example, in an entry stating,

> Religion was extroverted rather than introverted—Religion was anthropomorphic but not anthropocentric—Immortality played a minor role—also ancient Hebrew rel. Emphasis on here & now—living a rich & fruitful life. Influenced by mystery, religions. Orphic cult emphasized dualism of soul & body, taking flesh & blood of sacred but denial of pleasures, reincarnation—influenced Pythagoreans, Plato & Socrates. Religion entwined with morality and the dichotomy of Greek and Christian ethics.

"The pre-Socratic philosophers," he would later write in *Sorties*,

> have always fascinated me enormously. What must it have been like to be a thinker in those days, when men really *did* have the illusion that the whole composition of the universe could be reduced to one or two elements: when men really did think that they could find the answer: *the* answer, the only one... Human thought was reduced to a few essential laws, and the rest was brilliant speculation. But *what* speculation! It was a time when science and poetry were marvelously wedded, and we shall not see its like again. (32)

In particular, Kant's treatise on aesthetics, *The Critique of Judgment*, offered a transcendental view of the mind, the idea that, as Dickey wrote in his notebook, "we cannot know thing-in-itself—the phenomenal world is one of our own making." That recognition would lead Dickey in his early poems to depict what H. L. Weatherby in 1966 called "the way of exchange," in which the speaker attempts to become Other. Focusing on "A Dog Sleeping on My Feet," whereby the creativity of the narrator depends upon his exchanging identity with the animal, Weatherby, in what constituted the first substantive essay on Dickey's aesthetics, noted, "For the exchange to become possible the opposites, the man and the dog, must die to each other. The dog must give up his immediate perception to the man and the man must give up his power of reflection, his power to fix and see, to the dog, so that in the giving and the taking, the mutual surrender, a new and otherwise impossible point of view can be created." This heightened perspective, the knowledge of a deeper world achieved through a shared participation, once more permits Dickey's persona, what he terms his "I-figure," to lose his self-identity and to become indistinguishable from the whole of nature, from its life and death drama. Dickey intends to portray, Weatherby concluded, "the perfect union of man and his opposite, the *me* and the *not me*" (Kirschten 22). To be successful, however, the exchange required that the speaker eventually return to *his* life, now energized and now, as Joseph Campbell described, "Master of the Two Worlds."

Dickey's recognition that the universe can only be subjectively expressed, that despite the poet's attempt to merge imaginatively with the phenomenal, he remains outside it, manifested itself in his poetic effort to unify Platonic and Aristotelian philosophy. Plato's theory of knowledge derives from his belief that in the universe Ideas or Forms are real and immutable; by contrast, the physical world possesses a relative reality that remains constantly in flux. Arguing in the *Republic* that only the ultimate truth, the knowledge of the Good, gives "their truth to the objects of knowledge and the power of knowing to the knower," Plato declares that a concrete reality partakes of a Form, which is the Ideal, but does not embody it. Dickey, on the other hand, reveled in the physical things of this world, declaring in his essay "The Wild Heart" "how much there *is*, really *is*, upon earth: how wild, inexplicable, marvelous and endless creation is" (*Night Hurdling* 215). Though adopting early in his career the Platonic concept of Form, Dickey clearly qualified his desire for a union or exchange with some ideal Other by embracing material reality in all its manifestations, asserting that "God is so much *more* than God" (*Self-Interviews* 78). Throughout his poetic career, he struggled to reconcile these opposing philosophies, needing to believe in the continuity of the former and the rich variety of the latter. Works such as "The Scarred Girl" (1963), "The Flash" (1966), and "Two Women" (1987) exhibit this effort. Though he was not religious, he understood that the physical world intimately reveals "God"; things are not mere shadows of the Ideal but, as Aristotle says in his *Physics*, "everything which is generated is generated from a subject and a *form*" (Book A, 190b 20). Yet Dickey's acknowledgment of this Aristotelean attitude, the idea that form possesses no separate existence but remains immanent in nature, did not mitigate his desire for some transcendental Other. He searched for an Ideal that provided some emotional or psychological guarantee of continuity.

That need for continuity was temporarily assuaged when Dickey married Maxine Webster Syerson on 4 November 1948 above a feed store in Rossville, Georgia. There were no witnesses. Rossville, just across the state border from Chattanooga, was the principal "Gretna Green" for residents of East Tennessee. Marriage mills were "big business" partly because Georgia had recently passed a premarital blood-test law. Facilities were hastily set up to provide testing to assure survival of the "marriage business," which was thriving now that World War II was over. Dickey did not want to wait. Though the idea of domestic responsibilities repelled him, his belief in the ideal of marriage as well as his latent conservatism, reinforced by his childhood upbringing, drew him toward the stability it offered. As he later wrote in his essay "Complicity," "If [Woman] is not the secret of the universe, then there is none," declaring her "the promise that we men make to ourselves hour after hour every day of our lives" (*Night Hurdling* 217). He had known Maxine only briefly, having been introduced to her by his math instructor. Maxine had previously married Joseph Watts on 1 July 1944 when she was only seventeen. Watts was a navy pilot stationed near Pensacola, a fact that would have rankled Dickey; following the war, Watts became a small-town jeweler and gift shop owner. The marriage, however, soon faltered. When Dickey met Maxine, she was living with her mother in a hotel apartment in downtown Nashville and worked as a reservation receptionist for American Airlines. Occasionally she would fly routes as a stewardess. Dickey had moved from Kissam Hall to a single apartment newly constructed by Vanderbilt and, intent on maintaining his grades, had bought himself a typewriter to facilitate his composition. Calhoun Winton remembered Maxine fondly, stating, "My earliest remembrance of her is in her airline blue uniform. She was a young woman of great beauty and considerable wit, but not much formal education—nothing beyond a convent high school" (Kirschten 74). Dickey's mother, Maibelle, liked Maxine immediately, glad that her son had married at all but also impressed by her practicality. She gave her new daughter-in-law a multifaceted diamond ring. Gwen Leege's broad learning may have intimidated Dickey as much as it attracted her to him, but Maxine's common-sense approach to domestic life and responsibilities, as well as her dependability and determination to help her husband succeed, rendered her a perfect wife. Practical and friendly, she supplemented her modest salary by working part time at a country music station. Later, in *Self-Interviews*, Dickey asserted, "The most fortunate event of my whole life was my marriage. Without my wife Maxine's encouragement, help, and care of the details that enabled the family to survive, I would never have been able to do what I did." "I can write an awfully long time," he declared, "But I wouldn't have been able to do as much work if I had thought that my writing was a self-indulgence that neither myself, my family, nor my economic situation could afford. Maxine created an atmosphere and also a feeling in me that any time I was able to spend on my work was well-spent. That was all I needed" (39–40). Dickey's poem "Awaiting the Swimmer" (1959) celebrates Maxine, idealizing her innate power: "What can I perform, to come near her? / How hope to bear up, when she gives me / The fear-killing moves of her body?" Maxine also became the basis for Ed Gentry's wife in *Deliverance*. Together Dickey and Maxine moved into an off-campus apartment. "I discovered one thing immediately about Maxine," Dickey related in a 20 March 1987 interview, "She could cope like nobody else on earth" (Van Ness).

Dickey graduated magna cum laude on 5 June 1949. Out of a class of 446, he ranked fourteenth with a 2.67 average out of a possible 3.00. He was Phi Beta Kappa and frequently walked around campus with his honorary key hanging from his belt. According to his Vanderbilt transcript, Dickey entered the graduate school four days later, enrolling in two classes for the summer quarter: Seminar in Romantic Prose and Poetry, taught by Claude Finney; and Contemporary Philosophy, directed by Eugene Bugg. He earned As in both courses. The following academic year Dickey enrolled in five classes: The Nineteenth Century; Seminar, 1660–1800; Seminar in American Literature; Aesthetics; and Milton and His Age. Monroe Spears taught the Seminar, 1660–1800 course. Winton was also enrolled in Spears's class and remembered that Spears early on had admonished the students, "By the end of the term I would expect you graduate students to be able to distinguish the couplets of John Dryden from those of Alexander Pope, without reference to their content" (Kirschten 75). Spears demanded a close attention to the poetic line, an approach Dickey would embrace in his own teaching. Richmond Croom Beatty taught the Seminar in American Literature, a yearlong course that chronologically surveyed major American writers—Irving, Poe, Hawthorne, Melville, Whitman, and others—using a standard anthology he himself had coedited, *American Literature in Tradition*. Somber and introspective, Beatty would frequently sit almost immobile behind his desk, offering commentary. Dickey, however, appreciated his considerable learning and requested that Beatty direct his master's thesis.

That thesis, titled "Symbols and Images in the Shorter Poems of Herman Melville," totals ninety-three pages and consists of an introduction, five chapters, and an appendix. Dickey attempted to derive Melville's attitude toward life through an analysis of his symbology, admitting, however, that while justification exists for even the most extreme praise of Melville's better lines, "It is a sad fact that Melville never wrote a poem which is good all the way through" (3–4). Declaring that Melville's principal symbols are essentially revealed throughout his *Collected Poems* (1947), Dickey then states, "If, as Alfred Kazin asserts, art is 'perfected communication,' then surely the central concern in literary discourse *is* discourse, communication, and not *what* is communicated. Ideas are the material of which poetry is made. They are not poetry" (16). His intent was to comprehend Melville's poems by interpreting the pattern or system of images, metaphors, and symbols, thus implying that a critical examination of the construct allowed one to understand not only the philosophical ideas that constitute their foundations but also the artist himself.

"My suggestion," the thesis concluded, "is that Melville's 'tragic sense of life' results from his inability to discern clearly man's guides and bases for action." He continued, "*From* Melville's Deity man must save himself by an identification with a humanist ideal" (56, 64). Melville feared "not only that a knowledge of the springs of human action was inaccessible to him, but that the springs themselves had no existence, that the whiteness of neutrality and apathy not only *overlay* the workings of the cosmos, but *underlay* them as well" (67). The thesis anticipates Dickey's poetic interest in identity, the relationship of the individual to the larger world, and the need to discern purpose, motivation, and direction. His exploration of Melville's poems, while academic and occasionally disjointed, suggests in its approach and conclusion an outgrowth of Dickey's anthropology readings—the search for meaning. To a degree, Melville's writings were literature of affinity and recognition. Having rejected orthodox Christianity and confronted the brutality of war, Dickey necessarily concluded that design lay elsewhere. He discovered in these readings that ritual and myth, imposed on one's own experiences, offered liberating poetic possibilities against the dark conclusions that Melville reached and with which Dickey found himself in agreement.

In spring 1950, as he completed his master's thesis, life must surely have seemed full of possibility to Dickey. Happily married to a woman intent on her husband's happiness, immersed in literature, he regularly visited Zibart's Book Store, two or three miles downtown, long the focus of Nashville bibliophiles whose regular advertisements in *Gadfly* read, "Come in and browse." Dickey did. The Dickeys, moreover, had an automobile, an old white Ford, which provided transportation in warm weather to the Willow Plunge swimming pool in Franklin and to the Gerst Brewery for bock beer. Perhaps best of all, *The Sewanee Review* had accepted his poem,

"A Shark at the Window" (1951), for publication. Finally, classes ended, Dickey submitted his thesis, which was approved, and he accepted a teaching job at Rice University in Texas. The future seemed set. He graduated on 25 June 1950.

Within a year he would be back in uniform.

CHAPTER 5

IN MEDIAS RES

As Dickey and Maxine prepared to move to Houston, Dickey's optimism regarding the future was tempered partly by the fact that his salary at Rice Institute would be meager, approximately $3,000 a year with no monies during the summer, and partly because at Rice he would be viewed neither as a reputable scholar nor as an accomplished poet. At Vanderbilt, he had at least established himself as a thoughtful, even insightful student and as a talented writer. Aggressively competitive, fiercely at odds with the status quo, and deeply conscious that America largely ignored or distrusted poets, the very profession he pursued, Dickey determined to meet whatever challenges he encountered and react accordingly; life was warfare. In fall 1950, however, he could not have known the tumultuous literary, political, and social forces in the middle of which he was moving. For all intents and purposes, the fifties would be a decade of reconnaissance for Dickey, sorties flown and initiatives undertaken to discover what was possible in unfriendly skies.

In fall 1950, when Dickey began teaching at Rice, modernism still dominated the literary air. Attempting to establish himself as a poet, he extensively used notebooks to discover a subject matter and style while writing poems he hoped literary quarterlies would publish. As he did so, Dickey found himself confronting the formidable presence of T. S. Eliot and other modernists, including Ezra Pound and William Carlos Williams. Delmore Schwartz had argued the year before that "it might be desirable to have no literary dictators" ("The Literary Dictatorship" 137), and Edmund Wilson would soon observe in his journal that Eliot seemed "an obsolete kind of American" (127). *Time* magazine, however, which had viewed *The Waste Land* as a hoax in its 3 March 1923 issue, labeling it "a new kind of literature...whose only obvious fault is that no one can understand it" ("Shantif" 12), enthroned Eliot on its 6 March 1950 cover, acknowledging his "Olympian judgments" and declaring, "Mr. Eliot is secure and honored in his high place as one of the foremost men of English letters." Pound and Williams, moreover, had both issued major collections which had seemed to consolidate their work; yet the publication of *The Pisan Cantos* (1948) and *Paterson* (1946–1951) demonstrably revealed that modernists could extend themselves into unexplored areas. In doing so, they reaffirmed such critical dicta as tightly structured lyrics, learned allusions, witty figures of speech, and verbal ambiguity. Dickey therefore understood that poetry continued to be judged by its adherence to New Critical principles. Because these elder poets had successfully achieved a literary hegemony, he determined to court them, praising their work and assuring them of his shared sensibilities, while he simultaneously wrote poems that stressed, at least initially, artistic impersonality and a poetics grounded in irony and linguistic construction. This effort involved subjugating his natural inclinations toward sensuous, if energetic, romantic verse as well as toward narrative in an endeavor to become more widely published. Winning the war had now become a question of poetics.

Indeed, poetics constituted the front lines of the literary war currently being waged. Delmore Schwartz had been only twenty-seven years old when his essay, "The Isolation of Modern Poetry," appeared in the spring 1941 issue of *Kenyon Review*. He had published his first work, *In Dreams Begin Responsibilities*, in 1939 and, almost overnight, had achieved critical attention and a reputation for precocious brilliance. His essay openly asserted that American poets had become fundamentally isolated from their own culture, separated "from the whole life of society" (211) and invisible to it. Industrialization as well as the daily activities that derive from it, Schwartz believed, had effectively exiled cultivated men and women whose poetry, sensibility, and imagination now became irrelevant. The sentiment did not go unshared. Randall Jarrell, for example, in his 1951 essay, "The Obscurity of the Modern Poet," published in the January–February issue of *Partisan Review*, reinforced this indictment of American society, stating, "Any American poet under a certain age, a fairly advanced age...has inherited a situation in which no one looks at him and in which, consequently, everyone complains that he is invisible" (70). Because the culture had lost its old hierarchy of values wherein art and artists might flourish, Jarrell argued, the poet had become "a condemned man" (71).

Concern about the arts deepened shortly thereafter when a university survey reported that 60 percent of Americans in 1954 had read no book that year except the Bible. Weldon Kees, in a 31 July 1954 letter to his friend Anton Myrer, an aspiring novelist, captured the contemporary despair: "Maybe someday they will find a name for this period, and it won't be the Age of Anxiety, either. The Age of Flying Apart, perhaps, or the

Age of the Asps. Meanwhile a lot of pretty fair people get badly banged up.—You know all this without me telling you, though" (Knoll 182). Even in 1960, Paul Goodman continued to argue similarly. In his personal and sociological attack on American culture, *Growing Up Absurd*, he asserted, "We live increasingly...in a system in which little direct attention is paid to the object, the function, the program, the task, the need; but immense attention to the role, procedure, prestige, and profit" (xiii). America, he said, had become a missing community, a "canned culture" (241) that avoided risk and self-exposure and that consequently had lost group solidarity and group variety on the one hand and individual excellence on the other hand. What had resulted was a social and political system whose mores were a "death to the spirit" (241). In the forties and fifties generally, artists agreed that American society, with its organized and highly urbanized, free-enterprise system, had become indifferent and even hostile to the imaginative sensibility.

Schwartz, however, had taken the matter further, suggesting in his essay that by viewing art as a superfluous amusement or decoration, American society treated the modern poet as a bohemian who ignored conventional behavior in pursuit of mere personal pleasure. That public attitude contributed to artistic sentiment (at times, a decided conviction) that writers had lost almost all cultural support and resources and that consequently they had "no connection with or allegiance to anything else" ("The Isolation" 215) except Beauty. This condition, however, only enhanced the isolation. Not only was the modern poet alienated from society in his total commitment to "the practice of Art and the works of art which already exist" (216), but he had also become estranged from his family. He was "a stranger, an alien, an outsider [...who] finds himself without a father or mother, or he is separated from them by opposition between his values as an artist and their values as respectable members of modern society" (216). Schwartz, by no means the oldest of this generation of American poets, believed this latter separation involving family derived from the larger prevailing social forces. Though Schwartz did not elaborate on this observation, he clearly intended to suggest that, denied approbation from family, poets initially attempted to overcome the inconsistencies they discerned in their culture through a poetry primarily intellectual rather than emotional or subjective. By their efforts, they hoped to redeem both themselves and the public through works that denied them their individuality but adhered to accepted modernist practices that supposedly assured success. They failed to recognize, however, that American family life had been largely sculpted by the society they were seeking to transform and that became increasingly conformist and politically paranoid as the fifties progressed. It was a script that assured disaster.

The ambivalence that these poets felt in their attitudes toward Eliot paralleled the uncertainties and tensions of Americans generally during the fifties, a decade that glittered on the surface with prosperity and leisure but which also contained McCarthyism, the Cold War, and the development of the hydrogen bomb. Indeed, far from being a decade, as the 16 October 1972 issue of *Newsweek* nostalgically regaled in its cover story, "when hip was hep, good was boss and everything nice was copacetic," the Eisenhower years were more accurately "tired, dull, cautious, and anxious" (Miller and Nowak 7). The latter characterization belies the images of Hula Hoops, Davy Crockett coonskins, and tail-finned Cadillacs as well as the music of Little Richard, Chuck Berry, and the Platters and helps to explain why American artists viewed themselves as isolated from society. Poets felt alienated because Americans themselves felt alienated, cut off from those sources that had previously contributed to a confident, prosperous, and self-assertive national psyche. Despite popular misconceptions, the fifties were not monolithic; they changed in character as the decade proceeded. However, though interest in cultural activities increased, artistic license remained limited not only because the modernist tradition still generally prevailed but also because the decade stressed the status quo. Conformity was the password—one got ahead by going along—and poets generally felt their imagination and originality at odds with the national temperament dictated by events at home and abroad.

Following the end of the Second World War and lasting approximately until 1953, Americans reacted to Communism and the Cold War first by suppressing all liberal attitudes or tendencies as well as all dissent and then by demanding compliance. President Truman set the tone of these years in March 1947 when he issued Executive Order 9835, which mandated a loyalty review program intended to achieve "maximum protection" for the United States against "infiltration of disloyal persons into the ranks of its employees." Some 6.6 million individuals were investigated between the initiation of the program and December 1952. Though not a single espionage case emerged, about 500 people were dismissed from employment for "questionable loyalty" (26). States, cities, and counties quickly adopted their own loyalty programs as a wave of conservative hysteria reinforced the public's absolute need for security and for the preservation of established order. External events only contributed to this mentality. A coup established a Communist government in Czechoslovakia, the Soviets blockaded Berlin and detonated their first nuclear weapon, China became Communist, and fighting erupted in Korea, where American armed forces were committed against North Korean and Chinese Communists in a war that Americans believed was undertaken to stop Soviet expansionism but which was fought to a frustrating stalemate. When a jury found Alger Hiss guilty of perjury on 23 January 1950, Americans became convinced that a web of Communists had infiltrated their government. Though Hiss could not be tried for espionage because the statute of limitations had expired, his conviction for lying under oath set the stage for Sen. Joseph McCarthy's witch hunt and accelerated the massive outpouring of anti-Soviet propaganda, including essays with titles such as "Commie Citizen?" (*Newsweek*, 14 April 1947), "Communists Penetrate Wall Street" (*Commercial and Financial Chronicle*, 6 November 1947), and "Reds Are After Your Child" (*American Magazine*, July 1948) and books such as Hamilton Fish's *The Red Plotters* and Richard Hirsch's *The Soviet Spies*. Hollywood, never far behind, produced movie thrillers with titles such as *I Married a Communist*, *The Red Menace*, and *The Red Danube*. The paranoia that these works stirred not only allowed McCarthy to pursue his vitriolic rhetoric and tactics, thereby causing teachers, educators, and entertainers to be dismissed, textbooks to be censored, and libraries to be closed, but also moved Americans to unite themselves under a national faith that broached no dissent. The world was now seen as involved in a dualistic struggle where the noncritical, conservative values that united Americans confronted a monopolistic Communist ideology intent on domination. To assure continuation of the American way of life, the public did not exempt artists from its demand for conformity.

Lacking a doctorate degree, Dickey taught three lower-level English courses at the rank of instructor, including English 100–Composition, and Study of Fundamental Literary Forms, a class required of all freshmen, according to the Rice *General Announcements*, "to give students the command of written English." A secondary purpose was "to examine the chief types of prose and poetry, as a foundation for further courses in literature or for private reading." Dickey also taught English 200–Outlines of the History of English Literature and English 220–Composition and Expression. The former was, in effect, a survey course of readings by major authors covering the various literary periods; the latter, a writing course primarily for science-engineering students that centered on letters, reports, and argumentation involving the study and discussion of selected prose readings. Not surprisingly, Dickey spent long hours grading essays and other assignments from large numbers of students, academic requirements that, while necessary, nevertheless irritated him. Not only did he already feel behind where he believed his career should be as a consequence of World War II, but he also considered low-level courses to uninterested students a distraction. He wanted to write poetry, and he wanted to make money. Materialism during the fifties brought out an ever-increasing volume of fast automobiles, bombs, bazookas, bubble gum, televisions, and crying dolls, a spending excess that encouraged waste, inequality, and environmental misuse. Artists, comparing the financial precariousness of their profession several years previously, now enjoyed a measure of success as teachers in colleges and universities. Literary prizes had increased in number, and monetary awards were larger. However, though no longer quite social outcasts, poets found prosperity a mixed blessing, having consequently to spend much of their time teaching composition or literature rather than writing the poetry that had initially earned them their teaching positions. The resulting struggle to produce art only heightened their disillusionment when the public first treated them as outcasts and then "rewarded" them by promoting their talents with academic positions that failed to provide them the time necessary to write. Not surprisingly, therefore, Dickey wrote Maxine in spring 1951 and noted the vacuous actions of those around him, seeing only "the star of the West decline. There is not much in or to us (the Western powers) anymore, except a tremendous power of production[;] the rest has been consumed by greed and the kind of desperate and fanatical dogmatism that Americans have" (*One Voice* I, 159).

Nevertheless, he endeavored to effectively utilize the creative time he did have by extensive use of his notebooks, four bound ledgers and two ringed, loose-leaf binders, in which he not only detailed ideas for his fiction and poetry but also explored the literary techniques he thought interesting. The ledgers reveal a concentrated effort to maneuver through the teaching and, shortly, military demands made on him. As he wrote me in a 24 January 1990 letter, "You can see how hard it was for me to articulate anything, but you can also see how hard I tried, and how I did not fool myself about what I was doing" (*One Voice*, II 466). He extensively scheduled his days, a practice he used throughout his career and that permitted him to explore the novels, short stories, poems, and criticism he planned to write as well as the reading and exercise necessary to promote and enhance his writing. The notebooks, in short, show the remarkable efforts

Dickey undertook to prepare himself for the profession of authorship. One entry notes literary journals he ordered, including the summer and fall issues of *Kenyon* and the fall issues of *Poetry, Sewanee,* and *Hudson*; in the same entry, he also ordered George Barker's *Janus* and Henry Green's *Loving.* Other entries cited what he termed "type figures," images and unusual phrases from his reading or his imagination that he considered emotionally arresting or surprising, such as "*drink* the *passage,*" "pitch of brightness," "rotting rust," "we hauled in the net of our routes," "tree *threw* a *moment* of shade," and "pitch of brightness." Kings and kingship, warfare and violence, and ritual and myth are all informing concepts in stories and poems Dickey contemplated, though he despaired at ever satisfying what he thought literature ought to be. "My life is a perpetual proof," he wrote in a notebook entry, "proving nothing" (*Striking In* 52). He worked diligently on a poem titled "The Red Garden," concluding, "The rhythmic structure of the lines...is not good; the method by which it got composed is not good. Instead of letting the lines fall more or less as they will, try to *feel* and *hear* what you want, *what will do,* what the thing needs, *must have,* both in each line and in the overall stanza. Let your ear forge the thing all of a piece" (55). He believed that, to a certain extent, a poem could be constructed or built. Under the influence of modernism, he detailed a "sketch" for what he termed "the building of the rational poem" (114), and he distinguished between two types of poems—poetry of "form" and of "release." Critics insisted upon the former but Dickey preferred the latter. "To write 'out of' the brute and animal nature of reality," he declared, "to deal with essences, entelechies [Rilke, (Graham), Roethke] *as if I were* a stone, frond, tiger, kiss. There is too much clever, 'judged' poetry, 'judged and rendered' verse. I would like a poetry which proceeds naturally (or *is*) from the situation or encounter, which is the *essence* of its make-up, its being, which is the situation as it utters itself through me." He then elaborated, "In poetry, you have to let yourself feel *in behind* what you are trying to do. You must allow the original experience, or an invented one, perhaps more original, to begin to word itself, darkly or blindingly, and to see itself in the words" (118). Because critics would oppose such efforts, Dickey contemplated using a pseudonym, "Virgil Shawker," to write these "word-led" poems, while using his own name to continue in "the forms."

Dickey recognized that he needed to be a modernist but his interests and sensibilities lay elsewhere. "Tomorrow I begin to go earnestly into poetry instead of fooling around," he asserted in a ledger. "I would like to know and use 'the forms' before discarding them" (113). As "a good forebear," he cited Ern Malley, the invented persona of two Australian poets, Donald Stuart and James Macauley. Stuart and Macauley intended to debunk modern poetry; they composed sixteen poems during the course of an afternoon and, posing as Malley's sister Ethel, sent them to Max Harris, editor of *Angry Penguins*. Believing their story that Malley had died at age twenty-six of Graves' disease, Harris put out a special issue of his journal as well as a first edition of Malley's extant poems titled *The Darkening Ecliptic*. Dickey used one line from the book's epigraph in *Alnilam* and attributed it to Joel Cahill: "Do not speak of secret matters in a field full of little hills." Stuart and Macauley finally exposed the hoax. Dickey had become aware of the controversy during World War II. Throughout his life, he remained intrigued by the idea of a hoaxer; his exaggerations and misrepresentations partly derived from his emotional vulnerabilities and the need for psychological defenses, but partly they also owe to what he considered an extension of the creative act, as if he were playing a game just to discern what was possible. Initially, however, his interest centered on poetics. With respect to Ern Malley, Dickey wrote in his notebooks, "The hoaxer revealed some of the depths of the kind of poetic construction I would like to do: philosophy, politics, and frivolity of the (mere) technics of poetry. To a mind which cultivates words and images, the poem will seem to leap into them, as an animal creates his own shape in the net that confines him. The net is nothing without the beast, but perhaps it would be better were he free" (113).

While at Rice, Dickey also undertook a novel titled *The Casting*. The title, derived from Sir Walter Baldwin Spencer and Francis James Gillen's anthropological study *The Native Tribes of Central Australia*, published in 1938, suggests that the unfinished work centered on the initiation into manhood. Although the plot remains unclear, important characters and scenes anticipate *Alnilam*, published in 1987 but begun in the fifties. Julian Glass, the protagonist of *The Casting*, resembles Joel Cahill in *Alnilam*; both are estranged from their fathers, and both seek to control others. Julian reflected Dickey's interest in role-playing and hoaxes, noting in *Striking In* the intent to "work into the thing Julian's (as mine) fondness for masks: the consequent tension between 'putting the mask over' and the anxiety of its success thus" (42). An entry concerning an old man suffering "cancer in the center of his forehead 'like a diadem'" anticipates Frank Cahill, Joel's diabetic father, and the shuttling gold sparks he sees in his blindness. Dickey also planned a crucial scene involving a sudden nosebleed, which foreshadows the one involving Frank Cahill and Hannah Pelham.

Another entry projects a short story that seems to allude directly to the central character in *Alnilam*—a young airman who believes his entire career has been a preparation to confront himself "in the center of the flame of a burning aircraft." Although he had not yet conceived the narrative for *Alnilam*, Dickey had discovered aspects of it. He gradually seemed to lose interest in *The Casting*, however, and became increasingly preoccupied with poems and with another novel, *The Entrance to the Honeycomb*, which he did finish and which was submitted to Lee Barker, an editor at Doubleday.

Dickey's paltry salary continued to rankle because it was necessary for him to appear financially successful. "Teaching English from a rigid syllabus to bored freshmen," his son Chris recalled, "seemed too high a price to pay when the pay he was receiving was so abysmally low" (*Summer of Deliverance* 71). To provide additional monies, Dickey wrote reviews for the *Houston Post*. Although he doubted he could become a poet at almost thirty years of age, he thought it possible to establish himself either as a respectable critic or a short story writer. He wrote eleven such reviews, largely centering on fiction by William Humphrey, Jean Stafford, Herbert Gold, Peter Taylor, and John Hawkes, as well as Dylan Thomas's play *Under Milk Wood* and Conrad Aiken's *Collected Poems*. These early assessments reveal the attitudes he would later develop and more emphatically argue in *The Suspect in Poetry* and *Babel to Byzantium*, the need for believable writing that involves the reader personally. For example, while initially declaring that Humphrey's *The Last Husband and Other Stories* is "very nearly a model of its kind," Dickey then focuses on his primary complaint: "Humphrey does not seem to be sufficiently involved in, committed to, his material, seems rarely to look on it as anything other than material. He is a little too studiedly casual, detached, demanding of his prose only a small part of what it should give, setting up his effects carefully and then leaving the room and turning the light down to the right intensity" (7). Similarly, he observes Jean Stafford's *Children Are Bored on Sunday* and declares, "Reading the book, one feels a dreadful suspicion arise at one of the lower levels of the mind: A notion that the stories are stories only, that their potential life has been arranged away, that they are often skillful to the point of parody, and that Miss Stafford has succeeded in making dummies do some of the things real people have been known to do" (7), a sharp condemnation despite the belief that "Stafford is one of the really gifted writers of her generation...superbly intelligent, sharply observant and extremely well-trained." Conrad Aiken's *Collected Poems* also received this mixture of praise and damnation. He praises ("He is one of the few living writers able to produce lines the reader can run his ear over without flinching; the Donne-Hopkins strain seems never to have touched him") while also questioning Aiken's decision to include poems that are "hopelessly barren": "A Collected Poems is generally taken to be a kind of monument. The poet says to the book, 'Go and do what you can for me, as you can.' But who else but Wordsworth could have set down and wished to preserve so many lines? And let his publisher charge ten and a half dollars for the book containing them?" (5). Dickey's reviews also reflect his effort to canvas widely, including French writers Jean Giono and Marcel Ayme as well as *Bottegre Oscure*, the literary journal published and edited in Rome by Marguerite Caetani from 1948 through 1960. The journal published poetry and fiction in five languages (Italian, French, and English and, in alternate issues, German and Spanish). "There is really no other magazine anywhere like Bottegre Oscure," he wrote. "Talk about cultural pluralism!" (7). Dickey's own poem, "The Shark at the Window," which *The Sewanee Review* had accepted while he was at Vanderbilt, appeared in the April–June 1951 issue. Another poem, "Of Holy War," appeared that fall in *Poetry*, his first in that review. These publications, he later asserted, "sustained me during the trauma of being recalled into the service. I had hoped never to be in another plane again. It was a dreadful time for me, as it was for many others" (*Self-Interviews* 41).

"Of Holy War" and "The Anniversary," the latter of which *Poetry* would publish in June 1953, reveal the extent to which Dickey was adhering to modernist principles to achieve critical acceptance. "Of Holy War" uses obscure language to juxtapose the holy war at Acre, where Christians fought during the Crusades, and the modern holy war at Caen, the city in Normandy that served as a primary target during the Allied invasion in World War II. The sparse, allusive form typifies the poetry he wrote in the late forties and early fifties.

> O sire, I dreamed
> You danced with greaves
> Afire (it seemed)
> In Caen gave on
> A peregrine:
> Penumbrally seen.

That phoenix watched.
Rood and gate
Embered and percht
His spreaded weight.
Sire, flee this shadow.
I grass his meadow.

As with "The Earth Drum," "Of Holy War" utilizes inflated language and obscure allusions, including references to John Bunyon's *The Holy War* and possibly to Yeats. Its publication in *Poetry* reflects the New Critical emphasis on crafted, concise form. Except for lines two and four in the second stanza, Dickey utilized four syllables and three stresses per line. The parenthetical interjection in line three forces a strong end rhyme. The poem deferred to the modernist demand for intellectual verse at once impersonal and objective, a poet in conscious control of his craft, promoting a standard advocated by Eliot in his essays and by influential texts such as Brooks and Warren's *Understanding Poetry*, which Dickey had read.

"The Anniversary," whose title alludes to Donne's sonnet, further reveals the aesthetic norms Dickey was attempting to imitate, specifically Eliot's embrace of the metaphysicals. While Donne's narrator argues that all things after a year lie closer to their demise except the love shared with his lady, Dickey's speaker provides an ironic reversal. After detailing a pleasant sexual experience that "coined a stitch / To lure the river / An inch from sight," a union whose alchemy culminates in "two golds together / That else would've been / No hue to the scene," he then depicts the experience going awry. As the speaker plays a guitar, symbolic of the lover's body, the imagery alters to reflect not only the metaphysical interest in rough verse and strained imagery but also the psychology behind the emotion of love: "The hell of the ear, / I splay the guitar, / Bleeding my faces." The poem's images, including that of metallurgy, sewing, guitar playing, and bookmaking, parallel Donne's penchant for extremes. Almost a decade would pass before Dickey's early motion, with its predilection for narrative and strong anapestic rhythms, would emerge.

A month after Dickey received his master's degree from Vanderbilt, seventy thousand troops from North Korea breached the 38th parallel and invaded South Korea, quickly capturing the capital of Seoul. General MacArthur, Dickey's former commander, assumed charge of the United Nations troops preparing to counter the aggression. On 15 September 1951, marines landed at Inchon, recaptured Seoul, and pushed northward. Two months later, two hundred thousand Chinese troops positioned them-selves at the border to block MacArthur's advance. MacArthur responded by advocating the invasion of China even if it initiated another world war, a brinksmanship that led to President Truman relieving him of command. The United States, however, remained supportive of South Korea, and Dickey, who had voluntarily signed up for the active reserves at the con-clusion of World War II, now found himself once more preparing to enter a major conflict.

In January 1951, following his first semester of teaching at Rice, Dickey received notice from Major General Thomas to begin a twenty-one-month term of duty from 10 March until 9 December 1952. If he had felt his career slow in developing as a consequence of the Second World War, Dickey must have despaired at this new deployment. "He loved to tell me over dinner," Chris Dickey recalled, "how much Mozart had done at my age" (*Summer of Deliverance* 69). Dickey's daughter, Bronwen, also remembered her father's preoccupation with time, the terrible realization that time, if not used effectively, becomes lost. "I remember us talking a lot about relativity and different theories of time. He loved those lines from Eliot's 'Four Quartets' ('Burnt Norton'): 'Time present and time past / Are both perhaps present in time future / And time future contained in time past. / If all time is eternally present / All time is unredeemable.'" These conversations, Bronwen declared, invariably led to discussions of the work of P. D. Ouspensky, Albert Einstein, and Niels Bohr as well as J. B. Priest-ley, whose *Midnight on the Desert* dealt with various theories of time and its relationship to math, physics, and astronomy and which was one of Dickey's favorite books. "He discussed time a great deal," Bronwen re-called. "I don't remember Dad having one specific philosophy of time. He was more excited by the many possibilities that various physicists and mathematicians had proposed over the years." Dickey's interest in the pos-sibilities of time, Chris stated, was "the centerpiece of our conversation." "Dad was especially fascinated with the precognitive power of dreams," he declared. "I think that eventually dovetailed into his belief or hope that the dream world was a taste of eternity[,] a foreshadowing of heaven." This idea overlapped with Dickey's interest in reincarnation and Nietzsche's idea of the Eternal Return. For Dickey, time lost could not be recovered. That abiding belief explains both his penchant for schedules and for the determination to accomplish as much as possible. Maxine, he concluded, would have to handle day-to-day affairs of their marriage.

The air force ordered Dickey to report to Maxwell Air Force Base in Montgomery, Alabama, for "reindoctrination," after which he was instructed to travel to McGuire Air Force Base in Trenton, New Jersey, as a "radar observer on fly status." He was assigned the temporary rank of 1st Lt. on 23 January 1952. He wrote Maxine from Maxwell on 19 March 1951, emphatic in his conviction that the military could offer him nothing as a career: "I have decided on one thing: that no matter what the air force offers me, no matter how little I can earn 'on the outside,' or no matter *what*, I will not (or *could* not) make a career out of this life." Such a life, he declared, "is essentially a surrender: a surrender to the 'good deal,' a surrender to an indolent, unthinking life, a surrender to expediency, a surrender to the officers' club, and a surrender *of* all I most want to do" (*One Voice* I, 156). Dickey disliked the temporary job in Maxwell's Records Processing Department, though he befriended Albert Murray, a young African American writer on leave from the English department and ROTC at Tuskegee Institute. Murray recalled,

> I spoke to him because I was surprised and pleased to find another Air Force Lieutenant reading the sort of literary publications I saw on his desk...*Kenyon, Paris Review, Southern Review*, stuff like Ransom, Blackmur, Eliot, Pound,...Randall Jarrell.... He in turn was also surprised and pleased to find another officer type who not only had literary interests but was also in personal contact with some of the New York people. (Hart 161)

Their friendly conversations initiated a decades-long literary friendship. The leisurely demands on Dickey's time allowed him hours of extensive reading, including Kenneth Burke's *A Grammar of Motives*, which Dickey thoroughly analyzed in his ledger, as well as Kafka's diaries and various literary quarterlies. He wrote Maxine on 4 April that Burke was "really a very clever man; not profound or really very complex, but alert and active. We are still good friends. But his excessive reliance on terminology irritates me at times" (*One Voice* I, 157).

Dickey was next ordered to Keesler Air Force Base near Biloxi, Mississippi, for a twenty-four-day refresher course in night fighter radar observation and navigation. His correspondence to Maxine, who was now pregnant with their first child and living with her mother in Nashville, reveals his loneliness. In a 4 April 1951 letter, he declared, "I love you and want and need you so very much.... Do you seriously think, did it ever really *occur* to you, that I would leave you behind. It would be unthinkably hard on *me* if I had to do without you even for a little while" (157–58). He also continued his criticism of those around him, including his roommates, who expressed curiosity about his many books. "When I explained amusedly and a little tiredly why I lugged the books around[,] there was only bemused and incredulous shakings of head," he informed Maxine. "They are not bad fellows, really. That is the trouble. No one wishes harm; each wishes his own life happily mediocre."

> No one has any aspirations, one way or the other. They care a little bit about what becomes of them, but not much; they are mostly interested in THE NEW BUICK, or something *really* important, like "Do you know what Arthur Godfrey said last Tuesday! How does he *get away* with that stuff on the radio? He practically came right out and said it..." and so on and so on, as the line in the PX gets longer (or shorter) and the day gets hotter (or Hotter) and everything collapses in a huge mire of inconsequence. (160–61)

If others were content with a life of inconsequence, Dickey would have none of it. "The human animal," he declared, "in the main, will never change in that respect; we must be saved, as Gide says, 'by the few'" (161). He concluded that the mass of mankind needed deliverance.

Dickey's military responsibilities at Keesler Air Force Base included learning about recent developments in radar interception and navigation. Recalled servicemen hoped to earn a job as instructor. Reading Gide, however, and then seeking to translate aviation manuals proved a challenge. The "Syllabus of Instruction" was eleven pages long, highly structured, technical, and complex. Dickey's notes for the course were detailed: "*Dipole* type antenna is cut to wave length—*Wave length is determined by frequency*—Higher frequency the smaller (the wave length) (or parabola laws, Inversely proportional." Another entry read, "Condenser charges as long as positive signal of A.C. comes in: this is positive half of cycle—when negative half of A.C. cycle comes in the top half ceases functioning & bottom half functions—When current is cut off, condenser wants to discharge: it can't to the left so it goes through resistor—this prevents return to zero." Such entries typify the technical complexity that Dickey was confronting. To prepare for the instructor course, he took a study habits inventory, earning 102 points out of a possible 144; a score of better than 100 indicated a good student. He rated himself low in such categories as "I select important points, then write them in my own words" and "I review material with others" and high in "I have a definite time for study" and "I make occasions to use the thing I have learned."

Despite, or perhaps because of, what he called "the boring Air Force business," Dickey managed to read constantly, including John Berryman's *The Dispossessed* (1948), Stephen Spender's *World within World* (1951), and Jose Ortega y Gasset's *The Revolt of the Masses* (English translation 1932), as well as work by Richard Aldington, Allen Tate, Robert Penn Warren, Richard Wilbur, John Graham, Dylan Thomas, and William Carlos Williams. He claimed frequently to read during his "flying time": "What it amounts to is that I get up in the nose of a B-25 and read for three or four hours, scarcely noticing where I am, occasionally looking out the bombardier's compartment at something relatively uninteresting sliding past on the flat and green ground, and then back to whatever it is that I am reading" (*One Voice*, I 160). Not unlike F. Scott Fitzgerald's teaching his wife, Zelda, a college of one, Dickey undertook to increase Maxine's education. He wrote her on 4 May 1951, "Darling, don't think I am going to be 'ashamed' of you if you don't read things I am interested in. I don't want you to listen to music and read and look at pictures as a favor of any kind to *me*, but to open up the areas of response in *yourself* that are by all odds the best part of you" (162). Later that month, he wrote, "For the first two and a half years of our marriage you have made wonderful progress in many directions. Best of all, you have been truly moved by at least one poem ('The River-Merchant's Wife' [by Ezra Pound]) and by many paintings, and for the right reasons, I think. The rest is simply learning, 'feeling,' analyzing, insisting upon getting things into some kind of significant relationship to yourself and love" (165–66). At times, however, his attitude seemed condescending, as when he wrote Maxine, who was reading Saint-John Perse in translation from a Selden Rodman anthology: "My poor child *will* pick those things *so* far over her curly little head" (170).

Dickey's intensive reading influenced his own creative efforts. In his 4 August letter to Maxine, he wrote:

> I am reading a good deal and getting ready to write another poem. The last one is 48 lines long, and I am going to try to work up a long poem (about a hundred lines) in a fixed stanzaic pattern more or less as discipline, an exercise. I am, like Milton, narrowing down the subject matter slowly, prior to choosing a subject. I'll let you know about it when I actually begin. I have read Bertrand Russell on Hegel (for the third or fourth time), Russell on Schopenhauer, Neitzche, Antisthenes ("I had rather go mad than experience

pleasure!"), Aristipus [*sic*], the Medieval Schoolmen and John Dewey. In the new Kenyon I have just finished a long, rambling essay by Paul Goodman called "Avant-guard Writing: 1900–1950" ("Avant-guard" means advance guard, i.e. experimental) which has some interesting insights and a good many misconceptions, all concocted in a restless, impatient style which is rather intriguing, at least to me, after the usual dryness of the literary quarterlies. (168)

He had submitted his latest poem, "Perseus," to *Hudson Review*; other works, he claimed, were being considered by *Kenyon Review*, *Furioso*, and *Accent*. "Perseus," whose reference to myth and use of both alliteration and assonance reflect the modernist emphasis on craft, opens, "Andromeda my cloudy shield / Has shored. To cypher ease / I pluck it bold from groaning doves, / Buckle and stare." Other projected poems included "The Warrior's Birth" and "For a Ballet" (he also considered "Figure for a Ballet" as a title). Dickey had high expectations for "The Red Garden," though he later expressed disappointment with the poem, which concerned a king who had been murdered or allowed to die and which he variously subtitled "a baroque dialogue" or "a rococo dialogue." He wanted the communication between the personae, a court jongleur and a princess, to be complicated, he wrote in his notes, reflecting the diction of Hart Crane and W. S. Graham, "an intense, witty, language-borne, amusing, and tragic interplay." The Jongleur makes "the obviously 'strong' speeches, she the 'pretty' ones; the object here is to make the apparently pretty ones say more, and more strongly, than the other, and to make the 'strong' ones sound somehow decadent and 'aesthetic.'" Additional notes state that as the Princess listens to the song of the Jongleur, to "a twangling of light razors in the shade," she becomes "the chaste constellation of his notes." In what is perhaps the earliest statement of Dickey's interest in "exchange," he observed, "When a thing becomes us, we are no longer separated from it by anything, the thing is then said to be absent." Only fragmentary drafts of "The Red Garden" exist, but they reveal his modernist leanings even as he was endeavoring to move beyond them.

In a May 1951 letter to Maxine, Dickey also expressed high hopes for "The Litter Bearers," which he had submitted to *Hudson Review*, a poem on which he had extensively worked and in which he was doing "my own kind of playing around with Hopkins and sprung rhythm" (*One Voice*, 165). Like Hopkins, he wanted to know what language could deliver and consequently explored the varied possibilities of the verse line, an effect that was both technical and imaginative in nature. He believed a poem could be constructed, but he also desired to explore, even bring into being, some unrealized aspect of himself. He would later observe:

> The poet is aware, more than he is aware of anything else, of the expressive possibilities of his use of himself: that agent in the poem whom he calls "I." He feels a strange feeling and a new set of restrictions when he realizes he can call into play—can energize—any aspect of himself he wishes to, even if he doesn't yet know what it is to be: any self that the poem calls for.... His personality is fluid and becomes what is poetically profitable for it to become in a specific poem in which it comes to exist. (*Sorties* 160)

If Dickey's personal actions later became outrageous or destructive, his poetry, as he would write of Gerard Manley Hopkins, always sought "the pushing of vision, the pushing of poetic devices beyond themselves, to a point one degree farther than the *reductio ad absurdum*, one degree higher than the ludicrous, which is in some cases the degree of sublimity" (*Babel to Byzantium* 239). Seeking a personal subject matter and style, he moved from depicting traditional myths and archetypal situations to centering himself *within* a myth, desirous of creating a new dimension for poetry and, dissatisfied with who he was, a larger sense of self.

In his notes Dickey indicated that he wanted "The Litter Bearers" to consist of three formal stanzas, the "fore and aft" of which would center on the explicit "cause" of the litter bearers, while the blank-verse middle section, twenty lines of Rilkean evocation, would offer up "the vision of the wood, the jungle, *as it appears and feels*" and which would "plunge them into the jungle with little but the most tangled reference to their plight." The section opened:

> Stashed sea's fall in venom, victim, arterial tree
> Broadening the waters O of exile, sucked thirst,
> Raft, seabranch and salt, flows round the tongue of us
> In drying hairs. Each hacked frond springs an angel from
> The heel, who struggles round the brow in mold and curse
> And green. Hanghammer wave caught down in vine.

The litter bearers themselves, he wrote, "might represent those who sweetly bears [*sic*] a life to its more understandable doom." The "wound" that necessitated the litter bearers was "self-knowledge and the general and generally human characteristics" that they inexplicably understand as good. "I don't want the poem to be about the jungle,.... [N]o pretty excuse poem, a la Merrill.... '[O]ne can but toy with imagery' indeed." *Hudson Review* declined the poem.

Having fulfilled the requirement for the Technical Instructor course, Dickey received his USAF Air Training Command certificate on 24 July 1951. By the end of August he had logged about forty-six hours in C-47 and B-25 aircraft in Keesler's 338th Technical Training Wing. Orders to travel to James Connally AFB in Waco, Texas, arrived on 7 August. "I plan to leave Monday," he wrote Maxine, "so you can still write once or twice more, if you would like. You had better like!" (*One Voice* I, 170). He informed her that, in anticipation of the birth of their first child, he had been working on a new forty-line poem titled "The Son," which he completed and sent to her the following week. In inflated language and obscure images, the poem centered on what he termed "the parricidal vision from the loin" and included references to "ritual coming-of-age ceremonials, which should indicate the taking of the father's place by the son" (172). Still following modernist dicta, Dickey's poems remained highly crafted, dense with allusions and formal diction. His son Christopher was born on 31 August, his birth reflected in another poem, "Utterance I" (1953), which was published in *Soundings: Writings from the Rice Institute*, Dickey's first publication in a book. However, the tone now is softer, the imagery less abstract. The speaker, in attending the child's birth, dwells on the eternal cycle of nature and his son's new place in it: "Enter and enter into my breath / Forever dying out of each new sound / That he may your peace, my praise / Breed and outleap." *Poetry*, in its June 1953 issue, published "The Child in Armor," another poem centering on Chris, in which Dickey better commands the diction and images. As in "Utterance I," the poem depicts the relationship between father and son within a mythic framework:

> Somewhere a hound barks, and suddenly the window
> Is green with moss, the sun is out,
> The helm is opening. He lifts now
> A sword with no will but his own,
> And I sit here in the light, gazing not at his visor
> But at my ancient son, with nothing but his armament renewed.

As the fifties progressed, Dickey, needing to be published, consciously embraced myth and mythical imagery, gradually abandoning the obscure and inflated language, in such poems as "Orpheus before Hades" (1959), "The Vegetable King" (1959), "Lazarus to the Assembled" (1960), "Sleeping Out at Easter" (1960), "Walking on Water" (1960), "Adam in Winter" (1962), and "The Rib" (1962), and adopting a more focused narrative. What is clear in examining these poems is that while he initially used classical and biblical stories necessary to satisfy standards for critical acceptance, he quickly centered himself in the myth for reasons that owe less to modernism and more to psychological needs. He understood, as he declared in a notebook entry, that "to be a great writer, it is necessary to go strongly and break things" (*Striking In* I, 56). "A poet begins as an imitator almost invariably (how else is he to begin?). It is only gradually that he builds away from this" (65). As his poems moved from imitating and reflecting modernist tenets, poems of "form" that openly revealed the writer as craftsman, to works in which he realized aspects of his own personality by giving himself over to the poetic situation, a transition that occurred slowly during the mid- to late fifties, Dickey understood the sense of abandon necessary to create a distinctly unique poetry. "Poetry is yourself," he wrote in his notebooks, "your personality, whatever things peculiar to you as a human being, smashed, forced, and bled through whatever poetical techniques you have mastered. Enough of the technique should stick to the utterance to make it say itself most effectively, but not enough to allow the utterance's individual quality and its essential humanity to be destroyed" (53).

Dickey's decision to center himself in his own poetry paralleled the autobiographical underpinnings of the fiction he was writing. Journal entries suggest that he began working on a short story, "The Eye of the Fire," in 1952 after he had been assigned to Connally Air Force Base. Other titles Dickey considered included "The Fire Music" and "Up from Tacloban." The story involves a group of airmen in World War II, their relationships among themselves, and their response to loss. The narrative weaves together figures Dickey knew as a member of the 418th NFS and events that occurred within the squadron—the loss of Armstrong and Lally, the construction of an officers' club, and the efforts of crew members to lessen boredom through activities such as pounding out rings from Filipino coins. The fiction was published posthumously in the May/June 2001 issue of *The Oxford American*. Though he conceived numerous stories with what one critic called "Southern abandon" (Hart 170), he completed almost none of them. Dickey, however, extensively plotted out these stories, not only detailing the characters and specific scenes but also plans to bring them together in a collection titled *Sennacherib and Other Stories*. He projected at least nine stories for the volume, including "The Eye of the Fire" and "Sennacherib." The title story depicts a waitress who, having just completed her shift, talks to a rich woman about a history professor who left his wife every weekend for a month to visit her, saying his wife could not provide him the satisfaction he needed. Her rendezvous with the professor occur at a tourist courtyard called the Assyrian Kings in the "palace" of Sennacherib. After he leaves one night, he is killed in an automobile accident which she comes upon, seeing in the ambulance "a wound under [the] man's ear, shining in my lights" (*Striking In* 122). "You Pleasure Seekers," she tells "Mrs. Wingham," the newest customer, "are mostly good women, and by God I want you to know I for one appreciate it."

Other stories, though highly reimagined, nevertheless have autobiographical origins. "The Hawk" depicts "the man who kept Pop's chickens for a while and pulled out his automatic and fired at the hawk. He has 'done time': this somehow known to children (two little boys), but forgotten by stages as they ride on horse: crystallized by moment of firing" (*Striking In* 122). "Where Lies This Stone Delivered?" derived from Dickey's sister, Maibelle, who had an abortion: "Her furious screaming that she will not be able to perpetuate herself, that her image has been marred: idiot child passes over into real grief at funeral" (123). Another story, whose working titles included "Reeds, Shadows" and "Through the Loft," concerned his uncle, Tom Swift and his Jewish paternity. "The Porpoise" involves a father and his fifteen-year-old son on their first fishing trip together; neither knows the other well. When the father throws a catfish the son has caught toward the stern of the rowboat, the fin accidentally sticks in the boy's leg: "He starts up unbelievingly and in horror (thinks Father does not love him): sways in boat. At same time a huge porpoise surfaces with a rolling motion not five yards from the boat, his blow-hole visible" (121). "The Spring Garden" centers more obviously on Dickey's service years. A young recalled soldier stationed in North Florida visits New Orleans because he has always wanted to see it. While there, he meets a poor girl bedazzled by the glittering costumes they see at the Cabildo and has an affair with her without her knowing he is married. Two months later he ships to the coast and, passing through the city, calls her on impulse: "He somehow really cares for her; it has nothing to do with his wife and child. 'I just felt awfully sorry for your wife.' His sense of loss" (122).

Always ambitious, Dickey conceived a tetralogy. One novel focused on old people in Florida, another on an aging historian, another on the historian's effort to resurrect Assyrian civilization in his imagination, and another on the aftermath of World War II. None were completed or even undertaken, though he did finish *The Entrance to the Honeycomb* in 1953, his 151-page novel in which he explored the need to enlarge his life by re-creating aspects of it. As the narrative unfolds, the protagonist, Dickey's alter ego Julian Glass, a high school quarterback who realizes that "achievement is a form of coercion" (1), progressively exposes his emotional sensitivities and physical insecurities. The novel's epigraph, "I, said the sparrow," from the nursery rhyme "The Life and Burial of Poor Cock Robin," suggests that Dickey intended the archetypal story to reflect the ritual sacrifice of a king figure. It also expressed his feelings about the failure to meet his father's expectations. Eugene Dickey neither expected nor wanted a poet for a son. Julian's search for acceptance and for a sense of self-esteem results in his admiration of Jack Herlong, a teammate and later backfield coach of the Antler High School football team and "an exponent of deceptive ball-handling" (29) whose strength, agility, and convictions, so removed from his own seclusion and intellectual talents, Julian admires:

> I bought a set of barbells, and exercised with them three days a week. The rest of the time I wandered about the public parks of the city, or took long drives in the country, to small towns where I was certain no one knew me, and sat in their drug stores and restaurants talking with whomever I chanced to meet. At times, I read, but I was careful not to become bookish, remembering that my friend Jack Herlong had deliberately failed English #100 twice, with an enviable air of distinction. (23)

To Julian, Herlong represents an ideal, and he divides his life on the basis of their friendship: "Jack was one of the reasons that there was a definable past for me. With one or two exceptions, little of my life save what I associated with him seemed to be worth remembering, though the rest was always there to be remembered. Jack was himself: I had never attempted to determine what I meant by this, but the words occurred to me each time I saw him" (39–40). Dickey wrote Maxine on or about 12 August 1953 from Atlanta, where, in order to save money, he spent the summer writing at his parents' home while Maxine and Chris stayed with her mother in Nashville: "The book is finished, except for the closing three pages, which I will do tomorrow" (*One Voice* I, 195). *Honeycomb* was submitted to Lee Barker, an editor at Doubleday. Likely begun as "The Casting," the manuscript was not accepted, and Dickey later claimed that he withdrew it because the publisher wanted revisions. The nature of these edits is not known, but the sado-erotic material would have been problematic for a conventional publishing house in the fifties. That Dickey refused to alter the typescript reflects his defiance of social and literary standards, a determined opposition to the status quo and a willingness to chart his own course according to self-determined principles. The novel concludes with a newly energized Julian:

> Now the trees were filling with darkness, as evening moved to exert its influences. One flat space of lawn lay between me and the street. I swung my arms, believing myself without effort into the image, which, though hitherto despairing and inconstant as smoke, had pulled my mind futilely into shape toward it for five years: the trim and powerful figure running slyly and contemptuously over a green field slashed violently with chalk, leaping upward now, inviolably, springing the dangerous, flaunting right arm forward into the dazzling lights, his back straightening like a bow into the surfing sound, as of many urgent voices, to display the floating, long release upon the air.
>
> I walked on, hurrying a little, eager to open the house for Sara's inspection, to ask Jack to serve as best man, hearing in the red light the voices of the crowd, of Jack, and of one another, fading gently as I passed before them, taking their praise, untouched, stronger than water, and as happy as a stone. (150–51)

Dickey discussed the Doubleday impasse with Willard and Margaret Thorpe in a 26 December 1953 letter:

> Doubleday and I corresponded vigorously about the book, but ended looking at each other like two stags (deer) must look into (or for) each others' eyes when their horns are locked and they are tired of fighting. There's just no way to *laugh* in such a situation, with neither of you satisfied or willing to back down. So I withdrew the book in favor of another I'm about half-way through the first draft of; it is immensely and excitingly better than the old *Honeycomb*, which I am saving to rob a few of its good passages, for use in later stuff. (*One Voice*, I 197–98)

Dickey did not endeavor to publish the manuscript elsewhere, but aspects of the novel, including scenes depicting sadism and voyeurism, were incorporated into *Alnilam* as well as in poems such as "Cherrylog Road," "The Fiend," and "May Day Sermon." He did, however, endeavor to rework "The Entrance to the Honeycomb." An undated and mostly un-numbered draft of a novel-in-progress whose principal character is Julian Glass exists among Dickey's papers at Emory University and may be the novel that he wrote about to Andrew Lytle in spring 1954. "As you say," he declared on 23 March, "I am probably writing novels too fast. I wrote and threw one away, which was only realized in one or two pages. After that, I had the feeling that I had better explore a bit, and not spend time 'perfecting my mistakes.' I think I have the makings of a fairly good book now, one which will justify all the attention I can give it" (200).

Dickey's interest in male camaraderie, first depicted in "The Entrance to the Honeycomb," would appear throughout his later fiction. While he frequently centered his novels on men generally isolated from, if not out-right ostracized by, society, elements of "homo-fascination" evidence themselves in both *Deliverance* (Ed Gentry/Lewis Medlock) and *Alnilam* (Joel Cahill/the Alnilam conspirators). Only Muldrow in *To the White Sea* seems outside of all male influence. These relationships involve a band of brothers, not manly love or overt homosexuality, an unspoken celebration of male physique and sensibility. As early as high school, Dickey was ob-sessed with developing his body, an ideal re-creation of himself that, in turn, led to a general interest in or fascination with manhood. His son Chris remembered, "There is a line of poetry—an image...about Leonidas and his men at Thermopylae combing out each other's 'long Botticellian hair' before the battle. He often cited that scene when he dreamed about making a movie about that battle." Earl Bradley, Dickey's pilot in the 418th NFS, recalled the hours Dickey spent working out in front of their tent with discarded war material that he used as weights and barbells, after which Dickey would flex his hardened muscles in front of a mirror and shave off any chest hair, acts which he later depicted in his poem "For Jules Bacon."

Simply stated, Dickey was at war in the fifties with the puritanism reigning in America. Arguably beginning with his relationship with Jane Kirksey and the poem that derived from it, "Jane Proctor's Love Song," that rebellion manifested itself in increasingly violent scenes of sadism. In "The Entrance to the Honeycomb," Julian's father strips, binds, and beats his daughter Ann "increasingly hard" (21) to keep her "in line" (91), and Taz Lighthorn whips Laverne Coachman as Julian watches. In *Deliverance* one of the mountain men sodomizes Bobby Trippe, and in *Alnilam* Frank Cahill beats Hannah Pelham at her request. By the seventies and eighties, such physical violence in fiction was commonplace, and publishers no longer felt constrained in their editorial decisions.

Despite, or perhaps because of, his dislike of constraints, whether military or civilian, Dickey heavily structured his available time. Following the completion of his air force duties in the morning, he spent the afternoon hours from noon until 6:00 P.M. writing fiction and poetry. Time was even prescribed for the creation of what he termed his "image bank." After exercise and dinner with the family, he allotted additional hours for analyzing poems, novels, and stories; reading philosophy; and outlining prosody books. He went to bed at 11:00 P.M. In December 1951 Dickey's military commitments changed, and he spent fewer hours instructing radio operation and more hours actually flying both day and night. For his service, the air force promoted him to first lieutenant on 23 January 1952. As summer approached, his hours in instruction in the B-25K training aircraft further lessened, and graduating radar observers left Texas for Korea, Japan, and Alaska. Dickey's last few months at Connally were spent in the scheduling department planning training flights. In Korea, MacArthur's replacement, General Ridgeway, achieved peace; armistice negotiations began on 10 July 1951, though final agreement was not reached until 5 March 1953. Dickey left Connally, his records indicate, on 7 August 1952. He received a mustering-out payment of $200. At six feet three inches in height and weighing 198 pounds, he was in superb physical shape.

CHAPTER 6

EUROPE

Dickey's recall to the air force, though irksome, had not been, in fact, burdensome, for he managed enough free time to read extensively and to write poems that, if he considered them good enough, he submitted to literary journals. The idea of returning to Rice, however, oppressed him, partly because of the meager salary and partly because, lacking a doctorate, he stood little chance of professional advancement or of teaching advanced courses. He wrote Maxine in a letter dated 26 July 1953 that "I sorta dread getting back to grading those god-damned freshman themes (My First Day at The Rice Institute or My Biggest Thrill: Playing for the Championship of the Texas Class Double 'E,' Triple 'A' Baseball League) [*sic*] If they can't do any better for us than that, we should try looking around a bit" (*One Voice*, I 192–93).

Dickey read and wrote extensively while at his parents' home. "The thing here I really enjoy is being with *all these books*," he wrote Maxine on 20 July. "Every night, when I finish up the novel for the day, I go over the shelves picking out the ones I want to look at, and then retire to the porch and browse until I get too sleepy to hold out any longer" (*One Voice*, I 190–91). He read F. Scott Fitzgerald's *The Last Tycoon*, Jack Dunphy's *Friends and Vague Lovers*, Jean-Paul Sartre's *The Age of Reason*, and E. M. Forster's *Howards End*, about which he declared, "It is really very good indeed. You must read it. He is a beautiful writer, and his asides and generalizations as [*sic*] better than Proust's" (*One Voice*, I 189). In an August letter, Dickey discussed additional books, including Christopher Isherwood's *Lions and Shadows*, Philip Toynbee's *The Barricades*, Wrey Gardiner's *The Dark Thorn*, D. S. Savage's *The Withered Branch*, and George Barker's *Janus*. He liked Gardiner's autobiographical novel, written, he declared, "in the extreme 'expressionistic' style of Henry Miller" and which he had read previously. "It's a little pretentious," Dickey observed, "but you do get a pretty fair notion of what the modern writer is like." Savage's critical essays led Dickey to conclude that "none of the modern figures are any good. Joyce is no good, Yeats is no good, Hemingway is no good, Virginia Woolf and

Aldous Huxley are less than no good. The trouble with all these unsatisfactory people is that they have no consistent philosophy, or, as Savage puts it: 'no center of opinion or belief from which to project their visions.'" Partly, such declarations were just showing off his extensive reading, but Dickey also had clear favorites. About Barker, he was more upbeat:

> *Janus*, by that fire-boy Barker, is completely formless, absurd, nit-witted, and really beautiful in places. God, what an imagination. You get the feeling that Barker, when he sits down to write, (Or maybe he's that way all the time: *I* can't tell) is drunker on words than the worst drunk is on whiskey: sometimes he sees visions, sometimes the words don't hold up. But even his misses are good, and it is very hard to find anything of his with nothing at all good in it. (*One Voice*, I 196–97)

Though he claimed to be lonely without Maxine and his son, the letters suggest that Dickey was genuinely enjoying himself; he played tennis, went swimming, and attended movies, including *The Story of Three Loves*, starring Kirk Douglas. He also lifted weights, continuing to physically train his body. "I have been exercising a whole lot," he informed Maxine on 26 July, "and I really look rather good, if you want to know. Even better, I think, than last summer, when I thought I had 'reached my peak'" (*One Voice*, I 192). Mostly, he wrote. "Write, write, write! All day, every day," he said in his 10 July missive. "But the thing is getting done" (*One Voice*, I 188). He had written a poem titled "The Urchins" that he thought very good and that he intended to submit to *Partisan Review*. It is unclear, however, that he ever did so; the poem was never published. As with almost all those Dickey wrote in the late forties and early fifties, the poem's dramatic situation, centered on economic disparity, remains allusive, and the imagery vague, including references to "their king," "a beast's presence," and "the blond knight," all of which provide "The Urchins" with archetypal overtones within a modern setting:

> Men, buildings, a few plants, you watch
> Breathlessly at morning, and look
> Blindingly up the pale and dancing waters
> For the urchins descending into their cries

Out of the dark, unlaboring, between
Embedded stars and lightening of bones
Into the trembling stone of light.

Before such significance, the speaker declares, "the precious liquor of a dream / Coagulates and shines, until you kneel / And scream, one hand about the smooth and knowing rock, / The other dead, from fear of flowers." What Dickey most desired, however, was to send a "really superior" group of a half dozen poems to *Poetry*. "It is now my ambition," he wrote, "to be the 'headliner' on the *Poetry* cover" (*One Voice*, I 191).

The Dickeys moved back into Rice's university apartments on Mount Vernon Street in August. By the end of 1953, Dickey recognized that he had no future at Rice; the department chair, Dr. Alan McKillop, had reiterated the university policy of terminating contracts of professors who lacked doctorates. Dickey had published a few poems and reviews, nothing substantive, and he did not possess a PhD. "He didn't *mind* my writing," Dickey later wrote, "but he didn't want me around unless I became a reputable scholar. The fact that I had been through two wars, had tried desperately to get educated, and was trying my best to develop as a writer under almost overwhelmingly adverse conditions concerned him not at all" (*Self-Interviews* 42). Indeed, Dickey's long reading lists and detailed journal notes suggest his personal education was more extensive than most doctoral programs. After meeting with McKillop, Dickey wrote Willard Thorp, a visiting professor from Princeton who also disliked Rice.

> I told him that there was not much chance of my ever taking a degree, as I have not yet learned how to support my family on ninety dollars a month; he had no further comment than that I should get a Fulbright. The general import of the conversation seemed to be, "We don't care *what* you do, but *we* certainly can't be expected to keep you, improperly qualified as you are." Against which I kept silently and redly thinking, though I never said, "Asking me to teach freshmen English is like asking Rembrandt to draw Dick Tracy." (*One Voice*, I 198)

McKillop's entrenched attitude riled him, further revealing that he was not "the man in the gray flannel suit," the title of Sloan Wilson's 1955 novel about a businessman who got ahead by going along. War had become a permanent condition of Dickey's consciousness.

He also commiserated with Lester Mansfield, a disgruntled colleague raised in France who cultivated Dickey's knowledge of existentialism. Because Dickey had felt the need to camouflage his sensitivity and to fight against social standards of morality and success, existentialism's imperative, to force into existence what is most human, most "real," became compelling. Not surprisingly, he consequently embraced existential philosophers, such as Jean-Paul Sartre and Albert Camus, whose attitudes regarding freedom and the human condition resembled his own. Mansfield had introduced existentialism to Dickey while at Rice, presenting a lecture on 11 October 1954 which was subsequently published in the October 1954 issue of *The Rice Institute Pamphlet*. In his presentation, Mansfield argued that the French philosophical movement derived from a particular moment in history—World War II—and a particular experience—Sartre's work with the French Resistance—and suggested that because the freedom to act remains unconditional, the human self is always a possibility:

> At any moment we can choose to be something else. Since human liberty is always intact, human character is never a reality, but merely a possibility. The only reality is human action. The key to our behavior is not to be found in the past but in the future, for whatever we do, the character we seek to found is always in some future to our project to found it. This is why Sartre says of his own characters that each one "after having done anything whatsoever, can do anything whatsoever." (Hart 174)

Dickey immediately embraced this conception because it suggested a continuous state of Becoming. In his 1968 essay "The Self as Agent," he evoked similar ideas regarding his poetic persona: "The personality that the I-figure has therein may never recur, and the external poet, the writing poet, is under no obligation to make him do so. Likewise the *author's* personality as it changes from poem to poem is not itself assignable to any single poem. A certain Protean quality is one of the poet's most valuable assets" (*Self-Interviews* 156). The stories and exaggerations Dickey told, as well as the personae he assumed in his poems, were variations of his own voice, all designed to create himself and, in existential terms, to Be.

In January 1954, as editor of *The Sewanee Review*, Monroe Spears invited his former student to submit some poems for the fellowship his journal sponsored; Dickey hoped this would clarify his employment situation and enable him to leave Rice on his own terms. In his statement of project he detailed an ambitious proposal, a poem several thousand lines in length, two poems of about three hundred lines each as exercises, as well as about twenty lyrics he had occasionally drafted in different forms. Regarding the long poem, he wrote, "I intend it to make extensive use of devices adapted from both cinema and 'still' photography, and from painting, and that it will include a good many narrative passages, and will cut back and forth in time from place to place, threading together historical events and certain personal associations in a manner which I hope will produce something of a 'timeless' perspective." He continued, "I intend it to deal in some fashion with a theme from athletics, with one from crime, with the Air War in the Pacific, and with the child's world of fable." He mailed the poems to Spears and explained, "The money would make it possible for me to complete work on a great number of poems now only floating around...and on my second novel (some Texas people are interested in the first one, now completed), which I have about half the notes for" (Hart 176). On 29 March, Spears informed Dickey that he had won, and Allen Tate and Andrew Lytle, both *Sewanee* judges, sent congratulations. To Lytle, Dickey wrote on 3 April that he was overwhelmed:

> Allen Tate writes (Spears tells me): "Dickey seems to me to be one of the most original young poets I have read since the war." All the good fortune is a pretty terrible burden on the vanity of one who has not, until now, had much contact with people whose opinion on literary matters he respects. With luck I may, though, assimilate it in a valuable way toward a productive self-confidence, instead of, as now, feeling as though I have been given momentarily a marvelous kind of dream-strength with which to set the cloud-capp'd palaces and towers of the earth in a shrewder and more releasing light, but suspecting all the time that the strength will be rescinded, and I, waking, shall see that I have done or earned nothing. (*One Voice*, I 202)

In the coming weeks, Lytle became the father figure Dickey had always wanted, a relationship foreshadowed by the deference with which he closed his letter: "I'd like to try to stand up, here, and say without embarrassing either of us that I thank you from the strength of all the accumulated silences I have lived under and tried to articulate, for your part in giving me the opportunity that the fellowship allows: to pick up all this crippled shrillness of words and throw it with both hands toward the light, where the thing can truly be made" (203–204). From April until the

Dickeys left for Europe in August, Lytle maintained a steady correspondence; in doing so, he provided Dickey the means by which to articulate his own view of the nature of art and the role of the artist. On 17 April 1954, as he prepared to leave Houston, he wrote Lytle:

> Your letters have set me thinking along new lines, trying to define the artist for myself. I have never run much to generalizations, as I expect you have already surmised; my mind is mostly images and not propositions, and I can only hope that the images can have some of the value of propositions, but from their own angle. I heard once that Michelangelo, when asked how he cut stone, said that the form (of a woman, maybe) was already in the block of stone, and that all he had to do was liberate it. This is a real parable, I think, and not just of a certain theory of organic form, either. The artist (stone-cutter) is setting up something to stand against time, often quite literally (wind, rain, seasonal change, even animals). He is performing a kind of synthetic miracle, which is yet natural (the woman *is* originally in the stone). The result is both him and itself, and resides at that place where these two entities meet and enrich each other, and finally only the enrichment itself is left, for contemplation. If any human work ought to be able to stand up to time, and not only stand, either, but stand *significantly*, it is an endeavor of this order. (204)

Dickey confided to Lytle the details of the novel on which he was working, an early draft of what years later became *Alnilam*, and the problem of how "to show a middle-aged fellow, a mildly truculent, inconsequentially mistrustful man, for a few days at a Primary Training Base of the Air Force, during the early part of the last war. His son has been killed a couple of weeks earlier" (206). Dickey, however, had not yet worked out the details of the plot. "I simply wanted to wind up and sling the thread into the labyrinth as far as I could, and then follow it in, in hopes that it had gone around some of the right corners. I don't want to limit the material, but to try to open it up, to find a way into it. I would question the Minotaur himself, if I thought he could tell me anything. And stay in there with him, too" (206).

Whatever artistic triumphs a writer might have, Dickey asserted to Lytle on 26 April, come only "from having given failure a chance at us; there are no meaningful victories when there has been no chance of defeat" (208). He recognized his principal challenge regarding his fiction was effecting a coherent wholeness, a seamless exploration of character and plot.

"The problem of unification of any work I do," he wrote, "has always been the chief one. I am weak in what Coleridge called the 'architectonic' faculty; I fear in his book I would be a poet of fancy rather than of the imagination, and yet perhaps not wholly, either. But it is easy to impose form on words; that is, *some* form. What is hard is to arrive at that coincidence of individuality and necessity: to make the form absolutely part of an utterance which is uniquely yours" (208). Lytle even seemed willing to critique Dickey's own poetic efforts. When, for example, he stated that "The Angel of the Maze" lacked a dramatic focus, Dickey conceded the point. "There is always the problem of *means*," he wrote, "and of the employment of what one hopefully takes for possible means: the problem of selection." Lytle's letters, offering encouragement and objective criticism, released Dickey's literary aspirations, confirming that he had chosen the right profession despite his father's objections and his mother's concerns, and giving him a concrete reason to believe that he might be successful as an artist. Lytle's erudition and literary reputation provided his protégé with what he had previously lacked—validation of his self-worth. For the first time an established writer was engaging Dickey in extended written exchanges on literary subjects he deemed of the highest importance.

In late April Dickey undertook the packing up of his apartment in Houston, an effort which resembled a Robinson Crusoe-like salvage operation. He then drove Maxine and Chris to Nashville to stay with her mother while he moved into his parents' house on 166 W. Wesley. Lytle planned on visiting an Atlanta friend, Whittier Wright, before attending a literary conference. When he inquired whether he and Dickey might finally meet, Dickey insisted Lytle stay with him rather than at a hotel. "In thinking of you," he wrote, "I believe that you are the man who paints a true vision of the earth under the eyelids of the new dead, then sets the lids on fire, so that their sight is a flaming in the eyes of sleep, and the earth is burned down in the still brain in a defining cloud, and that because of this the dead have a new way to watch for time, and a new way to lie quiet, in sharpness and anticipation and understanding." Such soaring rhetoric, almost apocalyptic in its effusiveness, reveals the rarified air in which Dickey now felt he was flying. It also displays how "that fire-boy" George Barker influenced not only the imagery in Dickey's early poems but also the inflated language of his correspondence.

Dickey's meeting with Lytle on 12 June 1954 was everything he had anticipated. The two writers spent the entire day discussing literature and exchanging manuscripts. When Dickey finally returned Lytle to the airport for his scheduled flight, both men remained deeply affected by their hours together. Dickey wrote Maxine on 17 June, stating, "We stood there a moment and said a few things to each other, quietly, and then he reached out and took my hand and put his arm around my neck, the way fathers sometimes do with grown men" (215). By contrast, Eugene Dickey's own relationship with his son remained strained. Lytle wrote him a day later not only to thank him for his hospitality but also to hopefully alleviate the indifference or disdain Eugene felt toward the literary career his son had charted. "He's already a fine poet, a gentle sensibility, and a man," Lytle declared. He continued, "He's going to make literary history, if he has luck.... Generally neglect, misunderstanding and small change is the joy the world gives to its artists." Exhilarated but exhausted by Lytle's presence, Dickey returned home from the airport and slept for sixteen hours. He wrote Lytle on 20 June and unabashedly praised him: "You are the greatest man I have ever known, and the only great one." "The fact that we were once together for a few hours," he stated, "would itself justify my life, but for the fact that I may do something to bear out the trust and confidence you have in me. This possibility takes me up like the hero his enchanted weapon" (217). Lytle's visit rekindled Dickey's conception of himself as a larger-than-life figure who through perseverance and tireless effort, in an odyssey that is nothing less than mythic, overcomes personal trials. In this energized vision, Lytle became a guiding spirit whose understanding and counsel resembled protective amulets against parental neglect and social pressure. When his father told Dickey that Lytle's note had centered on important concerns in a manner he himself had not previously considered, Dickey felt vindicated.

During the summer Dickey had been steadfastly preparing for the family's extended stay in Europe, a trip that his son Chris would later characterize as a watershed event. "Afterward," Chris wrote, "we would measure every event in our family's life as 'before we went to Europe' and 'after we went to Europe.' As little as I was, I had this sense that our trip had changed everything. In the minds of my parents I believe it had" (*Summer of Deliverance* 71). If his Pacific combat had determined Dickey to be a poet, his European travels—the artists he met and with whom he conversed and the places he visited and poetically depicted—filtered and focused the kind of poet he would be. On 4 August 1954, Dickey and his family boarded the *Queen Elizabeth*. Crossing the Atlantic seemed to Maxine the beginning of a better life; she had wanted to be married to a great man. Now her second husband seemed to fulfill that wish. She wrote her mother, "I feel we are in the big league now and Jim is holding his own" (Hart 182). A poem he wrote, "*Invitatión au Voyage*," conveys Dickey's tangible sense of an enlarging world:

> Rest on the bright decks,
> Along the others, all of them seeming your family.
> [...]
> Your head is suddenly luminous,
> And all there is
> Trembles to you, through the circling
> And weaving gulls, in and out
> Of the great wild shape on the sea.

Dickey was in high spirits when the liner docked on 9 August, feeling not unlike the nineteenth-century British Romantic poets, such as Wordsworth and Byron, whose European travels had resulted in poems that addressed personal or universal truths, or the twentieth-century American expatriate writers, including Hemingway and Fitzgerald, who had left home for a less restrictive life and whose work sought to portray a younger, restless generation. Before the embarkation, Dickey had visited his Vanderbilt friend Cal Winton in Princeton, New Jersey; the family stayed a week. One night they dined with Allen Tate and his wife, the novelist Caroline Gordon. While Chris slept in Tate's study, they talked until 2:00 A.M. The following evening, the Dickeys returned for more conviviality and literary discussion. Gordon, who had spent the previous year in Italy with her husband, graciously provided Dickey with addresses of hotels and restaurants in Florence and Rome. Recognizing that Dickey would need employment upon his return, Tate offered to secure a job for him at the University of Minnesota.

Despite the trip's auspicious beginning, Dickey became sick in Cambridge while visiting David Dowler, a former student at Rice. He described the illness as "a kind of dysentery which seems to go with the British weather" (*One Voice*, I 223). After his health improved, he met the scholar Arthur Mizener, a professor of English at Cornell University who in 1951 had published a biography of Fitzgerald titled *The Far Side of Paradise*. He described Mizener as "an attractive, open-going, assured sort of fellow, very professional and hearty, like a successful doctor" (223). Dickey reflected on where he was and how he came to be there. "It is a good thing to be here in England," he wrote Lytle on 15 August, "looking up every now and then at the hills reflected in the mirror behind me, seeming, as they do, to exist patiently, in a knowledge without sharpness or rebellion, under a small mist like the shaken powder of fatigue. It is good especially as I remember you, the real bulwark, the foundation stone whereon every house I enter rides steadily in light" (223). London, with all its aristocratic traditions and ceremonies, attracted Dickey, but he told Lytle in a 26 August letter that the city was not only giving itself over to American commercialism but also losing the power of its ceremonies, the rituals that mystically conveyed the relationship among the king, the land, and the British people. He knew Lytle, as a Southern Agrarian, would identify with the indictment. Lytle's essay in *I'll Take My Stand*, titled "The Hind Tit," which Dickey had read at Vanderbilt, argued against the loss of identity that monied culture had brought the South. Lytle had opened his essay with a direct challenge:

> They tell us—and we are ready to believe—that collectively we are possessed of enormous wealth and that this in itself is compensation for whatever has been lost. But when we, as individuals, set out to find and enjoy this wealth, it becomes elusive and its goods escape us. We then reflect, no matter how great it may be collectively, if individually we do not profit by it, we have lost by the exchange. (Davidson et al. 201)

Regarding the British people, Dickey concluded, "They don't realize what they are giving up" (*One Voice*, I 224).

Allen Tate had encouraged Dickey while in England to visit Stephen Spender, who edited the magazine *Encounter* and whose poetry and prose Dickey had read and admired since initially encountering his work during World War II. However, he found Spender personally distant and "vague about everything," though "a very nice fellow, in a sort of misty, homosexual way" (224). They spent several afternoons discussing the British literary scene and the possibility of Spender publishing some of Dickey's poems, including "The Angel in the Maze." Spender eventually rejected the poems, citing their obscurity and the need for dramatic focus, a snub that immediately rankled Dickey and which he never forgot, writing Lytle on 14 November, "I have had rejections before, plenty of them, but somehow the memory of that professional shrinking violet condescending to me, talking about 'compression' and 'why don't you read Auden' wrung me about as disagreeably as anything can" (234). Dickey's entrenched sense of competition precluded his acknowledging the aptness of Spender's assessment. "I thought then, in a rush, that if this was 'literature,' if this was the sort your work has to go through to reach publication, then he and the ones like him can have it." He added, "I was raised, almost from the time I could stand, in the fiercest strain of competition: on basketball courts, in boxing rings, on fields, on tracks. Times like this bring all that back. But Spender is receding in my mind, and I hope will eventually be out of sight. To hell with him" (234). Even after they were colleagues for one term at the University of South Carolina, Dickey never again considered Spender worthy of literary respect, writing Alan Keele, a professor in the honors program at Brigham Young University, in a letter dated 27 June 1989, that Spender was "hopeless" (Bruccoli, Baughman 469). Spender became, in Dickey's poetry lexicon, "suspect," the trait of a writer whose false demeanor suggests manipulation. Rather than projecting a basic emotional honesty, Spender's pose resembled that of a propagandist or advertiser.

Dickey's efforts to actively court his literary elders began with T. S. Eliot, whom he hoped to meet while in London. Circumstances, however, did not permit it. First Dickey became ill, though upon renewed health he immediately began immersing himself in the sights of England. Then Eliot became sick. Dickey continued his travels and, in January, wrote Eliot from Italy that he hoped they would finally meet upon his return to London. Eliot, however, having fallen ill again, wrote on 9 March 1955 that he would be in New York. Dickey subsequently returned to America, crossing the Atlantic as Eliot simultaneously returned to England. They never met, although while abroad Dickey listened to Albert Camus lecture and talked to Pablo Picasso, Richard Wilbur, and Peter Viereck. It is possible to argue, as Henry Hart does, that Dickey simply avoided Eliot, awed and intimidated by the latter's literary stature. If so, he would not have been the only poet to be so; John Berryman and Winfield Townley Scott, among others of their generation, felt similarly. However, with Ezra Pound, himself a literary giant and a notorious one as well, Dickey showed no reticence and established an immediate rapport when they met in June 1955.

England proved more expensive than Dickey had anticipated. Having purchased a British car, he set out for Dover, abandoning previous plans to visit Ireland, where his mother's ancestors had lived, and hoping now to find less expensive accommodations. He would later remember the trip in his 1958 poem "Dover: Believing in Kings," in which the speaker, having arrived with his family, falls asleep and dreams he is a king's son. When his father is murdered, the son slays the betrayer and assumes his father's throne. Upon waking, however, the speaker cannot decide who he is: "I thought of him who would tell / To himself, gotten-up in his candle-cast bones: / Every man, every man / Not a king. It is I":

> Yet who is *he*? Whom does he face, in reflection?
> The stained-glass king,
> Or the child, grown tall, who cried to earth and air,
> To books and water: the sun and fire and father
> And nothingness to come and crown him, here?

The poem reveals what would become a familiar aspect of Dickey's early poems—the question of identity and the use of dreams or reverie and the absence of reason to achieve sustaining connections with some Other. At such heightened moments, the poet's response to the immediate physical world around him becomes temporarily enhanced by the unconscious or irrational part of his mind, though this elevated state of consciousness cannot be maintained.

On 2 September 1954 the Dickeys boarded a ferry for Dunkirk, spent the night in the small French town of Arras, and headed for Paris the following morning to visit Lester Mansfield, his colleague from Rice to whom Dickey would later dedicate his 1970 volume of poems *The Eye-Beaters, Blood, Victory, Madness, Buckhead and Mercy*. As they had done in London, the Dickeys visited the requisite tourist sites, including the Eiffel Tower, Montmartre, the Arc de Triomphe, the Champs Elysées, and the Luxembourg Gardens as well as museums, zoo, cafés, and restaurants. Mansfield also introduced Dickey to the city's many bookstores. In a 1965 interview, when asked to identify those writers who had influenced him, Dickey singled out his sojourn in Paris:

> The poets who have interested me in my fashion from the time I really started publishing books were foreign-language poets, mainly the French: Jules Supervielle, Pierre Reverdy, André Frénaud, René Guy Cadou, and other writers of the contemporary French scene. Now these are not names that are known much by people here, but they were wonderful to me. I discovered them when I used to sit in cafes in France in 1954, and, as you know, in those days you could walk into a French book store with five dollars and walk out with as many poetry books—or any kind of books—as you could carry. (Baughman, *Voiced Connections* 20)

He wrote Lytle that French writers enabled him to see "what the imagination is capable of, at its full stretch" (*One Voice*, I 227); later, he told James Wright that Mansfield "knows more about modern French literature than anybody in the world" (*One Voice*, II 97).

For a week they shuttled about, ending up at Cap d'Antibes, where Fitzgerald had set the opening of *Tender Is the Night*. Tourist season was ending, and in Villa Galidou, Dickey informed Lytle, "We found just what we need: a big house with a tremendous yard full of red flowers, cactus, lizards, and little birds, with a great yawning silence surrounding it, which I hope to fill with poems" (*One Voice*, I 226). In London he had managed to write "a good war poem" (225) titled "The Lemon Tree" and another he had dedicated to Lytle, "The Farm," "about your land inundated by TVA [Tennessee Valley Authority]" (225), but he admitted that his work, as always, went slowly. *The Sewanee Review* had published "The Ground of Killing" in its autumn 1954 issue, a poem that centers on the predator/prey relationship in nature in which man himself participates. Dickey realized, he told Lytle on 25 September, that

> my own work has got to discover more surely its own laws and disciplines. I want to study a good deal here. And write. And write. I want to do some experiments in syntax and diction, toward developing the sense of immediacy in poetry, the controlled spontaneity that I am convinced my writing should have: a form like that of fountain water, wherein the shape is secured by the substance (poem) falling and arcing freely, and is maintained thereby. (227–28)

He wrote Monroe Spears three days later describing the villa and its "great yard": "At night a light-house beam crosses us, and the shadows start and reel, never completely under control. There is going to be all the time on earth to work, and I should get a great deal done" (229).

Dickey did indeed "get a great deal done," writing dozens of poems in the seclusion of Villa Galidou as well as elsewhere in Italy, working toward a poetry that satisfied him by experimenting with imagery, meter, and stanza form. "What if images, insights, metaphors, evaluations, nightmarish narratives," he later reflected, "all of originality and true insight, were put into—or *brought* into—the self-generating on-go that seems to have existed before any poem and to continue after any actual poem ends? What if these things were tried? What then might be done? What might become?" Dickey was working toward poems that displayed what he termed "a night-rhythm, something felt in pulse, not word" and that was "dictated by the blood, by the nerves' hunger for unassailable rhythmic authority" (Preface, *The Early Motion* vii–viii). Anapestic meter, he believed, which he had first encountered in the poetry of Tennyson, Swinburne, Poe, Kipling, and Robert Service, offered an instinctive rhythm that, while crafted, nevertheless suggested the elemental rather than the intellectual complexity of modernists.

Dickey was also experimenting with verse forms. In his early notebooks, he had extensively studied the structure of certain well-known poems, in particular Thomas Hardy's "The Convergence of the Twain" and "Channel Firing," both of which displayed previously unseen stanza forms. "One of Hardy's greatest assets," he wrote, "is that he perfectly seriously believes the platitudes he builds his poems on, believes them structurally, and *believes* them." He added, "The study of *attitude* in poetry is important. Why has this been neglected? It is the necessary prologue to all technical devices, is what calls them into play, or even *into* being" (*Striking In* 62, 63). He declared,

> It seems to me that, in effect, most (good) poetry is saying not "This is the way it is" but "this is the way it *can be* regarded, seen," or "it is possible to regard, see, it this way, and I choose to do so." Poetry is in this sense a pure construct built out of associations both personal and literary and techniques partly personal but mostly literary, an imaginative construct to satisfy both of insight and desire for form, mutually moving, completing, and calling forth to view. (63)

Dickey undertook his own creative forms in such poems as "The Underground Stream," written in semi-couplets, as well as "On the Hill Below the Lighthouse," which consisted of a simple rhyming quatrain followed by a refrain, the refrain lines themselves serving as a summation or coda. *Poetry* published the latter poem in its July 1959 issue; the *New Yorker*, the former in its 21 May 1960 issue. Both poems, however, resulted from dozens of earlier unpublished efforts completed immediately after his European travel but which Dickey decided lacked the requisite qualities he was seeking, including "Against History," "The Bay of Naples," "Church Candles in Crete," "Europe," "Praiano Lights," "The Rampart at Antibes," "To Gweno, With a Guitar," and "Umbria." In "Europe," Dickey seemed to suggest that, like Michelangelo seeking the form hidden in the stone, he was discovering, among the events and experiences of his travels, the

hidden aesthetic form. Subtitled "Villa Borghese, Rome," the poem's unusual stanzas reflect the artist at his work and his emerging creation.

> Feeling is the movement of the soul
> Toward where it can use its hands:
> Toward light,
> Where life can be carried from within
> Through marble, emerging in beasts and fauns
> And children, of mothers of stone:
> Most precious folk of a silence:
> *Things made in the look of their spirit.*

> One comes among them, the least
> Of many men, who reckoningly have looked
> Down into stone
> As into the ray of dust, between the trees
> Holding the sun, and seen these figures smiling
> Timelessly, whose lips now smile with them,
> Bringing speech, and never a word.
> *The dead may but sing, in their spirit.*

The poem concludes with Dickey himself seeming to offer up a poetic
imperative:

> Stand living, then, and deliver
> What the dead alone can receive,
> Whose eye is fixed
> Amazingly on Form: whose look
> Includes your body's shape
> As it should be. The dead this ground
> Have made, that the live heart leap. Come
> *From the stone, and risk the spirit.*

Visiting Europe, immersed in the history all around him, and meeting fellow artists excited Dickey. He wrote Lytle on 14 November 1954, "The
more I read of the European writers, the prouder I am to be of the same
calling." The war had enabled him to see clearly that

> most of the things I had been told about human life were false: were
> constructions, rationalizations only, and would not stand up under
> any kind of forceful reality. But then I had not taken cognizance of

the artist's way, the search for the hidden anatomy. Proust found a part of it, and James did,...and the Spaniard Lorca, and Valery. The better you understand life, the more you feel *clearly*, the more you begin to see the value of it (but perhaps it take [*sic*] value from this seeing and feeling more, and in a more prominent order, even of spontaneity). (*One Voice*, I 234)

In this creative frenzy, Dickey completed "The Sprinter's Mother," which *Shenandoah* published in its spring 1955 issue, a poem which, he told Lytle, "rounds out the design" (235) he had begun with "The Angel of the Maze": "to write about the effects of death in different family relationships" (235). He also informed Lytle that he was working on another poem whose "possibilities are so great that I feel like farming them out to Shakespeare and Dante" (235–36). That poem, "The Confrontation of the Hero," was published in the summer 1955 issue of *The Sewanee Review*.

Not surprisingly, Dickey embraced the artistic community in Provence. He told Lytle that he had met Picasso several times in Vallauris, a nearby mountain town, and he lived close to renowned writer Nikos Kazantzakis, who had been a runner-up for the Nobel Prize. In Antibes Dickey had set himself the task of learning French well enough to read the poets he already knew in translation. By November he had done well enough to write Bill Pratt, his close friend from his graduate days at Vanderbilt, "You *must*, Bill, learn French.... There is so much in it that the first look is breathtaking, and the substantive ones slaying, except for the fact that you are being recreated all the time" (Bruccoli, Baughman 84). Among the French writers he specifically identified in his 28 January 1955 letter were René Char, Paul Éluard, Henri Pichette, Antonin Artaud, Pierre-Jean Jouve, and Michel Leiris.

The Dickeys found the increasingly unbearable cold overwhelming. Maxine and Chris became sick; Dickey struggled with the coal- and wood-burning furnace to keep the family warm. In January he decided to search for a more hospitable climate, driving along the Italian Riviera through Genoa, Pisa, and Florence. Heartened by the warm sunny weather of Florence, they located a modern pension, indulging themselves in the local cuisine. They also went sightseeing, visiting the famous cathedral, the Duomo; the church of Santa Croce, which held the tombs of Galileo and Michelangelo; and the Uffizi Gallery, where Dickey was particularly affected by Michelangelo's *David* and Cellini's *Perseus*. He visited the statue of David every Sunday, writing Lytle, "Sweet mother of the Muses, what a form! *There* is heroic statuary! He has the...look that, somehow, fits the hero, a face somewhere between an unconcerned woman's and a gilded and lazy god's, a torso like a young bull, full of balance and cruelty" (Hart 189). Such sculptures appealed to his mythic imagination, obsession with the male body, and the heroic role he envisioned for himself. He was struggling with a poem about Perseus and the Medusa which he intended, as he wrote Lytle, as "a kind of personal farewell to the war, and the use of myth." "For a long time," he declared, "I wanted to work at the intersection of the classic myths and everyday life: to try and discover in what ways the ageless patterns contained in the myths are played out, most of the time unknown to the players, among the real things and situations of life" (*One Voice*, I 238). Dickey was also working on another ambitious poem, "The Vision of the Sprinter." Neither poem was ever published, largely because, though the dramatic situation in each was clearer than in earlier efforts, the lines had become clotted with "tangential things" that "swirled in, until the whole thing was a whipped snarl of lines and meanings" (238), the focus frequently on sound, not sense. Dickey, however, still felt this was the best writing he had ever done.

Searching for warmer weather, he drove his family south to Naples on 11 April, where they stayed for a week in a pension facing the sea before continuing to Rome. He intended to remain in the Holy City until mid-May. While in Rome, the Dickeys toured the Forum, the Coliseum, St. Peter's Square, and the city's many museums. Additionally, they took side trips to Capri and Pompeii, the ancient Roman city destroyed by the eruption of Mt. Vesuvius around 79 A.D. While in Pompeii, Dickey visited the Lupanar, the Roman whorehouse buried by cinders and ash and where some patrons had been buried in medias res. In his poem "In the Lupanar at Pompeii," published by *Kenyon Review* in its autumn 1961 issue, Dickey sought to depict "the hopeful attitude we all have toward passion, not only sexual passion, but passionate experience. We don't want to live and die as zombies" (*Self-Interviews* 116). "I sit down in one of the rooms," the speaker declares, "Where it happened again and again. / I could be in prison, or dead," and he concludes, "We never can really tell / Whether nature condemns us or loves us."

The Dickeys stayed in Rome for three weeks during which he met the poet Richard Wilbur. While he liked Wilbur personally, Dickey always had reservations regarding what he considered the latter's mechanical verse that never attempted anything new. In a 1959 review of Wilbur's *Advice to a Prophet*, Dickey wrote, "I have never liked Richard Wilbur for the reasons reviewers have generally given: his lightness, grace, wit, the assuredness of his technique, and his delight in making complexities sound natural, amusing, and easy." He admitted, however, that "the thing that should eventually make him the truly important poet that he deserves to be...is the quietly joyful sense of celebration and praise out of which Wilbur writes" (*Babel to Byzantium* 170–71). Dickey also made the acquaintance of Wilbur's close friend, the poet William Jay Smith, whose book *Poems 1947–1957* he also reviewed, declaring, "The poems show, again, how much of the dramatic the lyric attitude can hold, if managed by a very talented poet, one who is privileged to bring instruction out of delight, a lasting pleasure into the ear, and the things he knows and loves each into its proper place where it has always been, and where it would never have been, had not the right eye seen, the right voice said" (*Babel to Byzantium* 74–75). Smith thanked him for the review, to which Dickey responded in a 3 October 1958 letter, "I tried to do you what service I could by saying exactly what I thought (and think) about your work.... There are so many good things there that I am sorry I didn't have more time to expound, or to quote things" (*One Voice*, I 281).

Dickey received a letter in Rome from Lytle regarding the possibility of a teaching position at the University of Florida. He would have to teach introductory freshman and sophomore courses, but he could also team teach an upper-level creative writing class with Lytle. He accepted the position, though the salary was only marginally better than what he had earned at Rice, writing Hooper Wise in a letter dated 22 April 1955 that he had come "very quickly to recognize the importance of the English teacher's function, not so much in the forming (in the sense of restriction to a preconceived pattern), but in the releasing, through discipline, of the student's mind to its own potentialities. Teaching is my chosen profession," Dickey wrote. "I believe in it, and I believe in my own powers to contribute something of permanent value, to human beings, through its exercise" (*One Voice*, I 239).

Dickey and his family left Rome in mid-May, driving through the Italian countryside in the spring warmth and stopping in Venice for a week, where he met the poet Peter Viereck before continuing to Cortina, Salzburg, and Innsbruck. On 26 May they finally arrived in Zurich. He hoped to find his former girlfriend Gwen Leege, but failed to do so. Later, he would write a poem, "To Gweno, With a Guitar," in which the persona imagines sending her a guitar as a gift: "You would be larger, now, and loving more / All nimble sounds of the ear, / All winds and strings of the same light on the earth." They arrived in Paris on 1 June after driving through Lucerne, Interlaken, and Bern. "Paris is jumping," he wrote Bill Pratt on 11 June, "and we are jumping with it" (Bruccoli, Baughman 87), hoping to enjoy the last few weeks of Europe as much as he could, "trying to wing the best punches our poor few dollars on the Sewanee's money will buy for us" (88). He admitted being glad that soon he could quit "this suit-case living" but felt elated that he had seen so much, read so much, and written so much: "Venice, Rome, Provence, Paris, Florence, all living and taking the colors of the mind, and giving back their own. Ah, I won't go on. Some day we'll do all this. Again! Again!" (88). On 17 June the family sailed from France on the SS *United States*, arriving in New York Harbor on 21 June as the ship steamed past the Statue of Liberty.

Dickey's European travels—the iconic sites he visited, the art he viewed, the writers with whom he talked, the many books he read—not only deepened his commitment to and belief in a literary life but also enlarged his cultural perspectives. Europe had provided him with a wide view of Western civilization. Returning to America, he no longer detailed in his notebooks and journals short stories and novels he would never write. Rather, he sought to systematize a poetic vision and bring poems to publishable completion. Writers such as James, Pound, Eliot, and Joyce provided him with the requisite mythic underpinnings by which to pursue his future endeavors, and the French surrealists, whom he had begun translating, offered a new sense of imagery by which to present the world. As he wrote Bill Pratt, "It is fine when you can read a little French (which, after all, is all I can do), and you can go into a book-store and pick up a surrealist poet (between covers, that is) who tells you that he would like to have a peninsula that dances like a fire, or an exiled tree that invents a kingdom" (Bruccoli, Baughman 88). Europe, in other words, had given Dickey the clear sense of the artists who could discover, or deliver, the figure in the block of stone.

CHAPTER 7

OF MODERNISTS, PEN WOMEN,
AND ADVERTISERS

Dickey returned from Europe excited by French symbolism and intent on using mythology to explore his own identity, ideas that set him apart from modernists who insisted upon artistic craftsmanship and required the poet to be detached and impersonal. Having chosen a literary profession, he more than anything else wanted his poems in print; without publication, they meant nothing. Because writers want to make money, he determined to ingratiate himself with successful artists from whom he might learn and who might assist him in placing his work in journals, magazines, and reviews. Although he failed to meet Eliot on either side of the Atlantic, he jumped at the opportunity to talk to Ezra Pound when Bill Pratt, who was researching Eliot, Pound, and Henry James for his Vanderbilt dissertation, arranged a visit.

Financially strapped, Pound had agreed in September 1939 to broadcast for Radio Rome's nightly "American Hour," targeting the Jews, the British, the gold standard, the gun manufacturers, and Franklin Roosevelt. A committed fascist sympathizer, he urged America not to enter the war. At the end of 1941, Germany and Italy had declared war on the United States after months of strained relations. Pound continued to broadcast. In its April 1942 issue, *Poetry* disowned him in an essay titled "The End of Ezra Pound," written by Eunice Tiejens, a member of the advisory board, who wrote, "The time has come to put a formal end to the countenancing of Ezra Pound. For a number of years, at the beginning of the magazine, he was associated with *Poetry*, and the association was valuable on both sides." "Then," she declared, "he quarreled with us, as he has quarreled with everybody, yet continued to use the magazine as an outlet for the publication of his *Cantos* and other poems. Now, so far as we and the rest of the English-speaking world of letters are concerned, he has written *finis* to his long career as inspired *enfant terrible*" (Kenner 38). In May Pound was arrested by the United States Army in northern Italy and interned in the Disciplinary Training Center at Pisa. When his health declined, he was transferred to the medical compound of the center where the eleven Pisan Cantos were written with writing materials supplied by the army and a packing-case given him surreptitiously by an African American prisoner for use as a table.

In November Pound was flown to Washington to stand trial for treason, a charge for which he had been indicted in 1943. Found mentally unfit, he was committed in February 1946 to St. Elizabeths Hospital, where he would remain for twelve years. Occasional periodical publication of the new Cantos occurred until all eleven appeared in book form in 1948. Serious controversy erupted, however, when the work was selected for the first Bollingen Prize for Poetry as being the best book of verse by an American-born or American-naturalized person published in 1948. The committee making the recommendation to the Bollingen Foundation consisted of the Fellows of the Library of Congress in American Letters, at that time Conrad Aiken, W. H. Auden, Louise Bogan, T. S. Eliot, Paul Green, Robert Lowell, Katherine Anne Porter, Karl Shapiro, Theodore Spenser, Allen Tate, Willard Thorpe, and Robert Penn Warren. In its statement accompanying the prize, the committee declared, "The Fellows are aware that objections may be made to awarding a prize to a man situated as is Mr. Pound. In their view, however, the possibility of such objection did not alter the responsibility assumed by the jury of selection." Further, "To permit other considerations than that of poetic achievement to sway the decision would destroy the significance of the award and would in principle deny the validity of that objective perception of value on which any civilized society must rest." The outcry, however, was immediate and intense, and the controversy soon spread to the newspapers and to Congress. The Library decided to cancel all awards, including those in music and art as well as in literature, and the selection of future Bollingen prize winners was entrusted to Yale University.

In 1948 America was in no mood to sanction, much less reward, nonconformity. The world was now viewed as involved in a dualistic struggle where the noncritical conservative values that united Americans confronted a monopolistic ideology intent on domination. Communism seemed to be encroaching everywhere. To assure continuation of the American way of life, the public did not exempt artists from its demand for conformity. Dickey found himself obligated to maintain the literary criteria for success even as he determined to discover and promote poetry that revealed "a new, intimate, and vital perspective on his own life as a human being" (*The Suspect in Poetry* 9).

In conversation Pound usually discoursed about his literary friends in Europe, most of whom were now either in his past or deceased, including D. H. Lawrence, Ford Madox Ford, James Joyce, and Ernest Hemingway, as well as his political and economic themes to save Western Civilization from Jews and Negroes. Deferential during their meeting, Dickey largely sat on the lawn, listening. "He was no more crazy than I am," he later recalled. "He was like an older American person, like maybe your grandfather or a slightly eccentric uncle, who would say things like: 'My son, you're not going to get this in the history books, but whatever happens, this is the truth of it'" (Hart 194). Pound asked about his European trip, and Dickey related what he had done and the fellowship that had made it possible. They also talked about French writers. Pound liked Jean Cocteau but admitted he no longer kept up with the French literary scene.

In late August Dickey initiated a correspondence with Pound that would last three years. The first letter, dated 29 August 1955, demonstrates his desire to endear himself, informing Pound that he would "like very much to hear from you" and thanking the poet for providing "a new orientation toward America." Though he did not specify the nature of this change, he implied that in "the vast, lucid (but withal bewildering, despite everything) tangle of highways and super-highways" through which he had driven from New York, he had seen the misdirection of American values. His missive displayed a continental sensibility, with Dickey suggesting the country's cultural bankruptcy and lamenting that after his European travels, "American life has us by the throat again." When he declared that "poetry has come again to have the attributes of a personal weapon rather than those of artisanship" (*One Voice*, I 240), Dickey was clearly *acting* like a modernist. His guise was successful; Pound responded within the week.

The subsequent correspondence reveals an increasingly familiar tone. Dickey, for example, addressed Pound as "Cher Maitre" or "Uncle," and even signed his letter of 30 September 1955 as "Yr O'bt Sv't," mimicking Pound's odd style. In his letter dated 15 August 1956, he praised Pound's recent Cantos, saying, "They are mighty good. But you sure don't need me to tell you that" (*One Voice*, I 256). He also related that he and his wife, Maxine, had knit him a sweater which he should receive in a few days. "It is good and strong," he wrote, "and should keep the *Cantos* warm this winter, and thereafter" (255). Such conscious flattery continued. Writing the following June, he declared that the image of the water bug and its shadow in *Rock-Drill* was the best single image in all the *Cantos*. He asked Pound to recommend books on monetary reform: "I know nothing about money except that it is hard to come by" (256–57). To show that he shared Pound's poetic sensibilities and predilections, Dickey declared in his 20 February 1956 letter that he had written an omnibus review that "gets in some good licks against a man by the name of [Randall] Jarrell, whose work has been to some extent influential, in a bad and sentimental way, here for the last few years. He should read [Basil] Bunting, and either change or kill himself" (242). He also hoped Pound would want to read a poem of his, "The Swimmer," which would appear in the spring 1957 issue of *Partisan Review.* Another poem, "The Father's Body," which would be published in the December 1956 issue of *Poetry,* would result in Dickey's abrupt departure from the University of Florida following its reading to, and the subsequent protest by, the American Pen Women's Society. "All accusations refuted," he wrote Pound on 15 August, "but that of being the bohemian type" (255–56). It is unclear whether Pound ever read the poems. Dickey did not send a copy of either, but in mentioning the situation and his alienation from the university, he hoped Pound would sympathize, viewing him as a confrère. Pound did, responding on 6 June, "If Pen Women mean P.E.N. club wimmen / you have been ditched by one dirty jew gang to be taken up by another / be prudent and don't mention my name till the bastards have actually printed you /."

In his 1983 essay "The Water-Bug's Mittens," Dickey acknowledged his debt to Pound: "Pound's presence is so pervasive that a contemporary poet cannot put down a single word, cannot hear, even far off or far back in his head, a cadence, a rhythm, without the suspicion that Pound has either suggested it or is in the process of causing him to accept or reject it" (*Night Hurdling* 30). Pound's primary influence on his poetry, Dickey asserted, was his perception of the world's beauty, that is, of "the *qualities* of its beauty" (31), and his insistence on the validity of the perception, its "wording or *voicing*" (31). He labeled Pound "the inspired image-maker" (33) whose presentation of an observable or imaginable part of reality could be said in "the tone of a thing *meant,* which is also the tone...of a delivered truth" (41). "Pound's wish," Dickey wrote,

> was always for more insight, more understanding, more consequentiality: in a word, more *life* for us. What he wanted for each of us, and for all human culture, was highly relevant personal experience: the guarantee of this within ourselves and our culture's guarantee that such experience should be ours. A sense of the consequentiality

of things, actions, men, ideas and civilizations is what we most want, and what we most sorely lack. (*Night Hurdling* 44–45)

It was through Pound, he stated in a later essay, that he became centered on "the necessary and infinitely valuable personal nature that is evoked" ("LIGHTNINGS" 11). Such statements suggest, ironically enough, that his courtship of modernism generally and Pound specifically led to Dickey's discovery of his own voice. At the very least the process was occurring during their correspondence.

At about the same time he ended his correspondence with Pound, Dickey wrote William Carlos Williams, describing his letter in summer 1957 as a "cry of homage": "I hope it dins in your ears with at least as much force as the others coming in over the brain-waves of poets every day." He thanked Williams for "a lifetime of devotion to the language I love, and for bringing to it the resources of a beautiful and responsible human being." He then praised Williams's poetry, singling out its "hardness" and "vividness." "This is understanding life and experience," he wrote, "because the feelings themselves *are* the understanding, if you can get them into words" (*One Voice*, I 259). When Williams responded by seeming to criticize Dickey's sentimentality in describing experiences with his son Christopher, Dickey explained in a letter dated 22 November 1957 that because he was now working in advertising, which he described as "a terrible, well-paid life" (263), he had little time to write and read; consequently, he had a personal relationship to poetry, having recovered the feeling of its personal worth. "I have pretty much become dissatisfied with the things of mine I see appear from time to time," he wrote. "I am casting about, destroying fifteen or twenty lines for every one I keep, in an attempt to get only the essential down" (262).

Dickey never discussed literary theory with Pound; their correspondence, for example, never addressed the latter's insistence on presenting "the thing itself" or in defining the image as a psychological or emotional complex necessary to convey that thing. Moreover, Dickey did not offer any sense of his own poetics. Unlike his letters to Pound, however, which centered on concerns largely unliterary, Dickey's correspondence with Williams, while deferential and flattering, began to reveal the outlines of a poetry grounded in private experience and past memories. In his 22 November letter, he asserted the dangers of becoming what he termed "a 'literary career boy,'" whereby one lost "the essential, the *personal* meaning of writing: that is, the sense that poetry has something to do with the movement of your life, and comes out of it." Williams's poems, he claimed, with which "I have been familiar...for as long as I have known about poetry," possessed "concreteness" and a sense of "letting the world have its own say, instead of serving as 'material' for a 'work of art.'" Dickey then added, "It seems to me that all the poetry I care anything about has this quality, which is at once impersonal and yet so deeply personal that one cannot imagine the world seen any other way" (*One Voice*, I 262). The statement must have baffled Williams. Yet even as he attempted to defer to modernist tenets, Dickey clearly desired to push the poet, the essential complex of his experiences and memories, into the forefront of the poem. As he later wrote in an unpublished essay titled "Under the Social Surface,"

> I think it is perfectly true to say that one may learn to know oneself, and in intimate and wonderful ways, by seeking out in memory certain moments in which one seemed to be living as vigorously and as *naturally* as possible: those moments that seem to be—that *are*— most firmly attached to one's own nature, for whose living and whose remembrance one seems to have been made, moments to which one can cling, and around which one can recompose oneself.

Only by withdrawing into one's self, into one's solitude, he declared, can the poet then enter what he labeled "the kingdom of the Other," all that is Not-Me, as existentialists argued, in order to learn from it. Dickey would later complain of Williams's lack of personal vision, which brought all his poetry "to the same dead level of commonplaceness: commonplaceness of fact and commonplaceness of apprehension of the fact" (*Night Hurdling* 34).

In an unpublished essay likely written in the sixties when Dickey was, in his own words, "barnstorming for poetry," he elaborated not only upon the rich complex of poet, memory, and imagination that produces, with luck, a poem but also upon the relationship between the poet and the images that spring from his unconscious associational process that is the creative act, what Rilke called "translating the endless song welling up out of silence":

> It is for this that the poet writes: to take his own life to the end, into the depths, into the philosopher's stone of himself, and see what the meanings are. If they are valuable to others, he is happy, for he is usually a compassionate person with a good deal of outgoingness towards others. After all, you can't go deeply into yourself without coming, also, on all of mankind, in one form, in one symbol or

another. And to understand mankind from within yourself is to sympathize with it: and profoundly. But it isn't toward an eventual sympathy that the poet goes, though he is glad of it when he discovers it. It is out of the same kind of fascination with which Narcissus watched his own image in the pool. He wanted to *know* what the image meant: what the image was: what *he* was. And somewhere amongst what he has been is the answer. Amongst the images of what he has done and been—everything, *everything* he has done and been!—amongst those, as his personality, his mind, and the mysterious, individual processes of his imagination and his unconscious have acted on them, furnishing him with a perpetual flux of recurring, changing associations, images, pictures and potential meanings, all of which, with the help of his great instrument, his great key to existence: language, lie under his hand to explore, to put together and take apart, to worry with, to articulate, to mull over, to enjoy, to fear, and to understand.

The unpublished essay, titled "The Poet and Imagination," was the second of two such introductions, following "The Poet and Memory," intended to precede and anticipate readings of his poems, such as the one at the New York Poetry Center at the 92nd Street Y, where, in November 1966, he read "Power and Light," "Encounter in the Cage Country," "The Sheep Child," and "May Day Sermon." If Pound and Williams sought to be detached, even scientific, in their analysis—craftsmen who constructed the world through poetic devices that readers must intellectually engage—Dickey, by contrast, endeavored to involve those readers emotionally if not instinctively, confronting them with as much presentational immediacy as possible at the heart of their being. "For out of two things," Dickey affirmed in "The Poet and Memory," "the basic likenesses between us...and the precious *individual* contributions we bring with us, poetry is made. In the land where those two things interpenetrate, poetry lies." He then declared, "The poet takes on faith that his experience is enough like that of other human beings to shed some light on them; and he must also believe that his personal individuality is unique enough to shed a light on common experience that could be shed from his peculiar angle: that what he has to say is, because he *is*, unique, inimitable." The declaration suggests Dickey's acute belief in the psychological connection between the individual and the whole of humanity, a connection explored by Carl Jung, whose works Dickey had read at Vanderbilt and that had influenced poems on which he was even then working, including "Prayer Becoming" (*Striking In* 37).

His daughter, Bronwen, later remembered, "I only have distinct memories of a few of the books he actually carried around. The Viking Portable Jung was one that was with him all the time."

A poem became a statement of personal identity for Dickey, intimate and essential, borne out of imagination and a search for meaning that might deliver to him his own life and connect him in a humanly vital way to others. "What a poet is after," Dickey wrote, "is not *a* meaning, but *the* meaning.... I think that it is, at bottom, this devotion to his own personal truth that drives the poet, that drives any creative artist to go on, on and on, searching, maneuvering words, failing again and again and again, sometimes almost succeeding, then failing more, trying again," all in an effort to discover, or perhaps recover, who he is or was in the continual process of change his life undergoes in memory and imagination. What he least wanted, Dickey argued, was the truth of mere fact, a stance that in effect elevated the poet to secondary creator. "We take God's universe and make it over our way," he told his last class of students on 14 January 1997. "The difference lies in the slant that we individually put on it and that *only* we can put on it" (Greiner, *James Dickey: Classes* 282). Dickey envisioned the poet himself as central to creation, whose words extended and enlarged who he was, reshaping the world and revealing its essential divinity. It was a romantic poetic whose origins lay in sensibilities his father had denigrated, attitudes that became an emotional seismograph, registering slights and criticisms but also seeing the world re-created in a more meaningful and empathetic way. These same sensibilities were enhanced by a deep and precocious imagination and an incisive intelligence. Poetry was not only a profession; it was a mission, a calling with divine intimations. Personal insecurities would frequently cause him to believe he was a coward, but his conviction that poets were secondary creators, taking "God's universe and mak[ing] it over our way," would not permit him to follow the status quo; creativity mandated he challenge it.

Initially Dickey found teaching at the University of Florida genial. His class load was light, teaching one lower-level class and assisting Lytle with his creative writing seminar, which met in the evenings. He wrote Bill Pratt on 11 June 1955, stating, "It is a huge high-schoolish University I am in, and a little forbidding, with its kindly old gentlemen running the English department and asking me if I have read Walter Pater, and if I thought Edna Millay and Emily Dickinson were representative modern poets." "The salary is pretty good," he admitted, "and they tell me that 'we don't insist on you writers working summers,' which naturally pleases me a good deal" (Bruccoli, Baughman 90). Although he initially believed the situation was satisfactory, if not comfortable, for the present, he soon became disgruntled again at grading dozens of composition papers. Believing himself, correctly, near a poetic breakthrough, he chafed at lowly and repetitive duties; poetry demanded and deserved more time, offered more that was humanly consequential. He wrote Pratt again on 6 September: "I think the hardest thing to get, in writing (especially in poetry is this true), is a feeling of inspired honesty, of an honesty beyond honesty, of a cracked kind of honesty that turns out to be more necessary that [sic] our other kinds, and more whole. The truth, or a truth, is very hard to find, especially one that is bound up in the language peculiar to oneself. Yet that is the hunt we are committed to" (91). As the academic year progressed, however, Dickey realized that the very organizational structure of the university itself precluded a remedy to what was increasingly a sense of confinement.

In 1935 the University of Florida had reorganized itself. All freshmen and sophomores were placed in one college, the University College, which administered the work of the lower division, including the preprofessional work of the upper division schools and colleges as well as the core program of general education required of all students. According to the 1956 University of Florida catalog, the comprehensive courses that made up the core program included political science, physical science, freshman English, logic, mathematics, the humanities, and biology. Freshman Composition, known as C-3, consisted of reading, speaking, and writing and involved three components—writing lab, classroom, and lecture. Dickey despised this byzantine structure, whose complex hierarchy relegated him to teaching basic writing to basic students in a restrictive environment that precluded both creative pedagogy and imaginative discussion. Despite being Lytle's assistant, Dickey felt himself no better off than he had been at Rice.

In April 1956 Dickey stunned both Lytle and his departmental colleagues by abruptly leaving Gainesville, a stack of ungraded bluebooks piled on his office desk. He would later explain that his decision to leave owed to a poetry reading and discussion he had been asked to give by a local group of elderly female writers, the Pen Women.

> I had begun to get some notion of the kind of poem I wanted to write. I wanted to do something about sensual experience that had not yet been done. So I wrote a poem called "The Father's Body" about a child's recognition of the physical differences between himself and his father. As a result of writing the poem and reading it at

the insistence of a group of ladies at the University of Florida, I got
into a certain amount of trouble which I resolved by simply walking
out. I told Andrew Lytle that I had no further interest in teaching
at the University of Florida—which indeed I did not, and I haven't
seen him to this day—and I told the authorities there I had no intention of apologizing for my supposed transgression. (*Self-Interviews* 43)

What upset members of the Pen Women was not the poem itself, which
was innocuous and likely too obscure to be understood, but rather the ob-
scenities Dickey used in commenting on the poem, strong language that
offended accepted values of social propriety. The women formally complained to the president of the university, Wayne Reitz. Like many Southern schools, the University of Florida welcomed neither blacks nor homo-
sexuals, and liberals were considered suspect as possibly Communist; a
poet who deliberately incited such protest would have been viewed suspi-
ciously. Dickey had no qualms, however, challenging established attitudes;
he viewed himself at war with social norms.

Jacob Wise, chair of the English department to whom Reitz had expressed dismay, prepared to sue Dickey for breach of contract, but Lytle
interceded even as he admonished Dickey:

> The whole matter is in how a thing is done. The thing to have done
> was for you to have gone to Wise, instead of Maxine and me. You
> had the same case, except it had more authority with you. All you
> had to do was say exactly what Maxine said, but you could have said
> it before the fact, and all the difference is in that. You had a false
> premise. Neither Wise nor the university was vindictive towards
> you, but they could have become so by your behavior. Wise is a just
> man, and he acted justly, although his first impulse was to sue you,
> because you didn't do him the courtesy of coming to tell him.

Lytle's letter angered Dickey, who believed he had acted on principle, not
pretentious posturing. He had taken a job at the prestigious ad firm of
McCann Erickson, temporarily staying at the New York Western Hotel
before moving to the Hotel Winslow on 55th and Madison. He complained to Maxine, who remained in Florida, in a letter dated 20 April
1956: "Get the reference to *my* making a show of the thing." "He believes
himself sincere and honest," he wrote, "brave and true, and all that. But it
was all *talk*. When the time comes to act, he shrivels up with fear and is
worse than any file-clerk worried about getting fired" (*One Voice*, I 249).

Lytle had advised him to "accept and respect the egos of people you deal with, and that takes a sharp measure of thinking about," adding that such action "always requires the conventions and forms, which make it possible." Dickey, however, would have none of it, writing Maxine that Lytle needed to "'learn to live in the world,[']," rather than that of 'artistic creation'" (246).

Dickey's inadequate salary, according to his standards for success, undoubtedly contributed to his decision to leave Gainesville. He admitted as much to friends, writing William Jay Smith on 11 March 1956, "There is nothing here for me but the genteel poverty of a University teacher, and the possibility, in twenty years, of its being a little more genteel. 'Here lies one whose name was writ on fifty-seven thousand freshmen papers.' So we're thinking about chucking it, and trying to get into something where they'll give a man a salary he can ride, where the world is pushy, crass, and rich, and poets are eaten up with the disease of money" (243). In relating the incident three years later to James Wright, he declared, "I feel I have gained a kind of revenge over my self-righteous tormentors, however, for I now earn more than the whole English Department at the U. of Florida, and can snap my fingers (really snap them: you know: good and loud) at the money troubles that used to drive me off my nut" (273). However, his conviction that academe was burying his talents and that society, smug in its conservative values, would continue to view poets as bohemian outcasts validated his departure. He simply walked away. The existential writers he had been reading, including Kierkegaard, Sartre, and Camus, had accurately presented the plight of the individual in society and the consequent need to exhibit, in the words of another existentialist, Paul Tillich, the courage to be. As Tillich wrote in his 1952 book of that title, the courage to be is "self-affirmative 'in-spite-of,' that is in spite of that which tends to prevent the self from affirming itself" (32). For Dickey that meant the rejection of accepted behavior norms when necessary to pursue personal values. Leaving Gainesville and going to New York was a declaration of independence, an act of existential self-affirmation. Kierkegaard had stated the dilemma in *The Sickness unto Death*, which Dickey had carefully read. Defining the self as "a relation which relates itself to its own self" (269), Kierkegaard argued that spiritual death stems from not embracing one's own self. His inability to become himself leads him into what Kierkegaard called despair, an argument that, though presented within the context of Christianity, nevertheless reflected Dickey's predicament:

A despairing man wants despairingly to be himself. But if he despairingly wants to be himself, he will not want to get rid of himself. Yes, so it seems; but if one inspects more closely, one perceives that after all the contradiction is the same. That self which he despairingly wills to be is a self which he is not (for to will to be that self which one truly is, is indeed the opposite of despair); what he really wills is to tear his self away from the Power which constituted it. But notwithstanding all the despair, this he is unable to do, notwithstanding all the efforts of despair; that Power is the stronger, and it compels him to be the self he does not will to be. To be *self* as he wills to be would be his delight..., but to be compelled to be *self* as he does not will to be is his torment, that he cannot get rid of himself. (281–82)

"I went to New York," Dickey later wrote, "to become a businessman of whatever kind it's possible to become at the age of thirty-three" (*Self-Interviews* 43). He told Maxine, "How right I shall have been, when spring comes!" (*One Voice*, I 247).

As spring did come to New York, he increasingly believed his decision to have been right. Initially his parents continued to forward him money, but the company offered him $8,600, more than twice what he had earned teaching at the University of Florida, and he soon found himself fully involved in the advertising trade, writing copy and participating in production. He wrote Lytle, endeavoring to make amends, but to Maxine he quipped, "I'm glad I don't have to depend on getting along with him, for my livelihood! He comes somewhere near being the biggest fake I've ever known" (*One Voice*, I 249). As he better understood the business mentality, and as his superiors at McCann Erickson complimented his efforts, Dickey believed he had permanently separately himself from academe. His new vocation required only variations in perspective, a change in how to present America.

The work itself, composing ads first for magazines and then for radio and television, offered him the larger salary he needed, but the pressure of meeting deadlines caused headaches and reduced the time available to write poetry. Lytle had cautioned him about the dangers, declaring it "a dangerous job for poets.... I'm told it is fast, compettitive [*sic*], and brutal." Dickey remained ambivalent. On the one hand, he was learning, as he observed, to consider products from a "commercial standpoint, or from a design standpoint, as to what would be effective in the design," a perspective that had poetic implications. On the other hand, New York's imposing

skyline and executive lifestyle were far removed from the Southern provinciality of his childhood in Atlanta and his teaching sojourns in Houston
and Gainesville, and he felt alienated. The job offered no true glory. "I had
no illusions," he later stated, "about being full of integrity as far as the
advertising business was concerned; I was in it for the money, to make a
living. The integrity came at night, on weekends, at sales meetings, on
holidays, or whenever I could get to write my 'own thing'" (*Sorties* 19; *Self-
Interviews* 44). After endeavoring to please copy chiefs and assistant creative directors all day, he returned in the evenings to his room at the Winslow Hotel, wrote Maxine, and worked on poems, in particular a long, ambitious effort titled "The First Morning of Cancer." The poem depicts the
visionary flights of a man who has developed brain cancer; the subsequent
chemical changes cause him to identify with Christ:

> In his light, inside the light
> Of the first morning, he stood by the stone, and could hear,
> Beyond, the death from the nearest of flesh,
> In its basket of hands, nailing one
> To another, and deadly, self,
> Up and down and crossing from within.

Through such vicarious participation Dickey achieved the heroic stature
of self he wanted, the illusion temporarily satisfying basic psychological
needs. The poem was published in the May 1957 issue of *Poetry*. "After I
had been trying to please different people—copy chiefs and assistant creative directors—all day, it was exciting to be able to sit down in front of a
type writer and write something I wanted to," he later declared in *Self-
Interviews*. "No words could explain how exciting this was: when I could
do it in my own way! I was selling my soul to the devil all day and trying
to buy it back at night" (44).

His three-month business training and the nightly efforts to write did
not, however, mandate a monkish retreat from the world. He spent time
in Greenwich Village with literary bohemians and artists and attended
parties given by Oscar Williams, whose anthologies he had read in the
Pacific. He boasted to Maxine that he had read some of his own poems at
one of Williams's parties and that the host was now trumpeting him as his
own "discovery." At another party, Dickey claimed that Edwin Honig,
whose poetry book *The Moral Circus* he had unfavorably reviewed in a recent issue of *The Sewanee Review*, verbally sniped at him. When Dickey

challenged Honig's "half-hidden nastiness," the latter left and "everybody went back to having a good time" (*One Voice*, I 254). Dickey also renewed his acquaintance with Richard Wilbur and dined with Criterion Books editor Sidney Phillips, who expressed interest in publishing a book of Dickey's poems.

The review of Honig's book, while attracting attention from New York literati, also revealed that Dickey had now firmly established an aesthetic of poetic principles on which he would stand and with which he would be identified throughout his career. Titled "Some of All of It," the review had appeared in the April–June 1956 issue of *Sewanee Review* and also critiqued other new poetry collections, including David Ignatow's *The Gentle Weight Lifter*, Kenneth Burke's *Book of Moments*, Howard Nemerov's *The Salt Garden*, and Randall Jarrell's *Selected Poems*. It specifically accused Honig of being distanced from his own life and experiences and of slavish adherence to current literary practices. The craftsmanship had produced poems that were dutifully neat, tidy, and workmanly but in which "very little is brought to life at an intense, sustained, and individualized level." The poems lacked believability because they seemed to strive for statements that were merely clever. Dickey believed that Honig, while seeking to explore "the nightmare mythology of modern life," had settled instead for the principle of surprise. Rather than struggling "to find the Way," Dickey concluded, Honig had been "content to follow the Ways" (*The Suspect in Poetry* 10). In later essays, such as "The Suspect in Poetry" (1960) and "Metaphor as Pure Adventure" (1968), he would similarly chastise poets whose work lacked presentational immediacy and which was not grounded in the reality of the physical world. Poetry was about "being" and "becoming," both important ideas to existentialists. It was illusion that revealed truth. As he wrote in his review, "What matters is that there be some real response to poems, some passionate and private feeling about them: that for certain people there would be certain poems that speak directly to them as they believe God would. And it is hard to believe most of the poems we read in this light" (10).

By late summer McCann Erickson had transferred Dickey to Atlanta. With the assistance of his brother, Tom, who then worked in real estate, Maxine found a house in Buckhead, only a few blocks from her husband's childhood home at 166 W. Wesley. Dickey's mother provided financial help with the down payment, and Maxine's mother arrived from Nashville to assist with the move from Gainesville. Before long, Maxine had their house at 2930 Westminster Circle running efficiently. In fall 1956 Dickey worked to supply copy to dozens of independent Coca-Cola bottlers across the United States. Overwhelmed by the demand to create so many separate ads, he experienced an almost tangible ennui. The title of his first poetry collection, *Into the Stone* (1960), suggests his petrified sensibilities during this time, the burial vault into which American business in general and McCann's offices at 836 West Peachtree Street in particular had locked him. While the money had saved his life, it had not made his life worth saving. Later he ascribed his boredom to Ed Gentry, the narrator in his 1970 novel *Deliverance*. As vice president of an advertising agency, Gentry experiences "the old mortal, helpless time-terrified human feeling": "The feeling of the inconsequence of whatever I would do, of anything I would pick up or think about or turn to see" (18).

With neighbors and office colleagues, Dickey attempted to avoid the lassitude by taking up canoeing, archery, and tennis and by hunting with bow and arrows and with blowgun. Such new sports were both escapist and energizing, but as with Dickey's war experiences, they soon became woven with exaggerated stories that he conveyed to others. It was as if he were deliberately re-creating himself to reflect what Stanley Edgar Hyman had observed in his 1949 review of Arnold van Gennep's *The Rites of Passage* in the summer issue of *Kenyon Review*: "'Myth' is the new intellectual fashion, and...there is more than one way to skin a myth" (455–75). He exaggerated his respectable archery skills, for example, proudly boasting he had won a state tournament, and he often recounted exploits in the deep woods of hunting for boar, fox, deer, and bear. Modernism may have facilitated his interest in myth and rites of passage, but such concerns also addressed deeper issues of personal identity. Using elements of mythology in his own poems and then extending this creativity through "lies" he offered to others were merely different aspects of his imagination, what he would term in his poem "Buckdancer's Choice" as "The thousand variations of one song." Throughout his life Dickey needed to demonstrate uniqueness and superiority. Everything he did he viewed as a personal challenge, approaching each new task competitively as if by it alone could he prove himself.

Dickey's eclectic reading during the Pacific war and, later, his formal education at Vanderbilt (he read Hyman's review, for example, while there), his travels in Europe, and his dialogue and communication with other writers now coalesced in a surge of poetic creativity and literary correspondence. From 1956 until the publication of *Into the Stone* four years later, Dickey published more than twenty-five poems, including "Dover:

Believing in Kings," which won the Union League Civic and Arts Foundation Award sponsored by *Poetry*, and reviewed more than five dozen books and anthologies in journals such as *The Sewanee Review* and *Poetry*. In addition, he wrote other artists, including John Berryman, Donald Hall, and James Wright, because such interaction alleviated the estrangement advertising induced and allowed him to remain connected to art. His correspondence during these years is significant because it demonstrates not only how thoroughly he identified himself with certain poetic principles, as in the Honig review, but also how he would counter any real or perceived challenge with an entrenched directness. To validate and enhance his argument, he would exaggerate his experiences, as when he wrote Berryman a flattering letter requesting information for a planned essay on the work of neglected poet Bhain Campbell, one of Berryman's closest friends, who had died from cancer, stating that he first discovered Campbell when he bought his book at a department store counter after he was "in the Air Force for the second time, and just back from Korea" (*One Voice*, I 258). He sought to ingratiate himself by citing Campbell's belief that a critic should "read all the books of criticism, rebore the blocks, and get ready to run steadily fo [*sic*] five years." He then declared, "The attitude struck me as very much like my own" (258). Later he praised Berryman's poem *Homage to Mistress Bradstreet* in a review, asserting that Berryman himself, "although not a natural poet, although anything but natural sounding, is sometimes very nearly a great poet" because his linguistic manipulations are erected and maintained "through sheer will and guts" (*Babel to Byzantium* 198–99). Berryman seemed a poet willing to follow those artistic principles that Dickey in his 8 July 1957 letter termed "the best of a man" (*One Voice*, I 258).

As he attempted to write and arrange enough poems to submit a book manuscript to Sidney Phillips and Criterion Books, Dickey struggled with his time-consuming business regimen. Donald Hall offered his critical expertise. Hall had already established himself both as editor of *Paris Review* and as a poet. In their steady correspondence, Dickey discussed other artists, arguing for poets such as Theodore Roethke, Richard Eberhart, and Geoffrey Hill and against Richard Wilbur, W. S. Merwin, and Anthony Hecht, whose work constituted a "well-meaning, mannered management of nothing. They ought to call this 'the garden school,' since it is almost devoid of anything but prettified description, impeccably presented, and absolutely empty of any human life at all" (*One Voice*, I 260). They also examined the state of poetry generally. "I want a poetry," Dickey advocated, that "illuminates my experience. I want a poetry that gives me some of my life, over again; that restores something to me, or creates a need for more life, more feeling; something that gets me closer to the world: that gets me *inside* the world, in a new way, or in a way older than the world" (260). As their correspondence continued and journals regularly began accepting Dickey's poetry, he became more encouraged, more self-confident, more assertive.

While Andrew Lytle had reawakened Dickey's artistic ambitions and provided him with the respectful acknowledgment of an established literary figure, the correspondence with James Wright offered him the genuine friendship of a published poet based on mutual affection and common values. Although Wright had initially written to voice anger over Dickey's review of a recent anthology, *The New Poets of England and America (I)*, in which Dickey complained about the work of Wright and Philip Booth (in the review, entitled "In the Presence of Anthologies," he described Wright as "ploddingly 'sincere'"), the two men soon became close. Lengthy letters provided extended discussion on their composition methods, poetic philosophies, pasts, present health, and families. Wright arranged for them to read together at a program sponsored by Robert Bly at New York University. Flushed with excitement following the reading, Dickey declared, "Write soon, holy being that you are, and tell me how to live." Wright also attempted to secure Dickey a teaching position when he eventually quit his job in advertising.

McCann's numbing routine and excessive demands for ad copy chafed Dickey, who felt himself in harness. He transposed this attitude into his poetics, declaring, "I don't like the locked-in quality of formalist verse. The only reason for writing verse of this sort is to attempt to come at an effect of inevitability. There are lots of other kinds of inevitability than this, and the best of these do not have the sense of claustrophobia that formalist verse has" (*Sorties* 8–9). He corresponded with Pound and Williams partly because, like the former with his confinement at St. Elizabeths and the latter due to his vocation as a practitioner of medicine, he felt himself similarly restricted by business. Advertising requirements, however, also mandated that he organize his writing schedule in such a way as to benefit his poetry. The more formal obligations imprisoned him, the more Dickey structured his time and wrote poems. Structure, the "form" of the day, liberated his talents. His complaints about business to Wright, Hall, and others and his subsequent assertions that he wished to return to teaching always diminished when money made its presence felt.

If Dickey occasionally felt chained, the chains were golden, and becaus~ the American public defined success financially, he was secretly pleased. By the spring of 1958, however, he had mostly finished *Into the Stone* and had undertaken the search for a publisher.

He had not, however, freed himself completely from feelings of inadequacy and failure. He told Wright on 26 July, "I don't write much, but it is labored-at forever; I don't like to turn loose of anything that doesn't come as close to satisfying me as I can get. And yet, of all the stuff I've brought out, *none* is good. Since I've been publishing since 1951, this is almost ten years of very hard labor for nothing." What was needed, he declared, was "a poetry that *gives us life*: some act of the imagination: the live imagination as it leaps instinctively toward its inevitable (and perhaps God-ordained) forms: some that restores our sense of continuity with tragic life, or joyous life, or dying life" (*One Voice*, I 270–71). To attain that prescription, Dickey struggled against the monied allure of business as well as the formalist principles that still commanded respect, the rising confessional and Beat movements, and a public generally indifferent or even hostile to poets. Although he had gained some financial success and a degree of recognition, he had not yet achieved the stature he had wished for since childhood. Alternately angry and frustrated, he provoked confrontation in reviews and letters designed to assert his uniqueness among other writers and to establish the legitimacy of his poetic ideas. For example, in his review of Allen Ginsberg's *Kaddish*, he baldly asserted that the poems seemed

> a convenient prototype of all such writing: a strewn, mishmash prose consisting mainly of assertions that its author is possessed, is often if not always in "holy ecstasy," and so on. But the writing belies all such claims quite heartlessly; there is nothing holy about it in any sense that I can understand, and its obsession is evidenced only by its efforts to be so. Confession is not enough, and neither is the assumption that the truth of one's existence will emerge if only one can keep talking long enough in a whipped-up state of excitement. It takes more than this to make poetry. It just does. (*The Suspect in Poetry* 19)

In October 1959 Dickey left McCann Erickson for another agency, Liller, Neal, a move that allowed him additional creativity in developing ads, but more importantly, also provided him more time to write poems. He had won a *Sewanee Review* Fellowship and the Union League Civic and Arts Foundation Prize, and in January he would receive the Longview Foundation Award from *The Sewanee Review* for his poem "The Vegetable King" and the Vachel Lindsay Prize for eight poems published in the July issue of *Poetry*. Yet he continued to feel victimized by the advertising business and placed high expectations that his first manuscript would bring him artistic recognition. Insecure, he did not think he was making progress. Wright had recently received his doctorate from the University of Washington, and Wesleyan had accepted his book *Saint Judas*. "If I can just hang on and write a few more poems like Dover," Dickey wrote Wright, "(or perhaps *un*like Dover), and if the book comes out, I will for the first time in my life really *believe* I have some chance against the personal difficulties that have plagued me, perhaps forever" (*One Voice*, I 277). With utter honesty, he admitted, "Despite the air of assurance in literary matters, I am really a pathetically unsure, groping person" (277). Possible publishers for *Into the Stone*, he claimed, included Macmillan, Scribner's, Doubleday, Grove, and Wesleyan, and though he disliked Scribner's three-in-one Poets of Today format, Dickey accepted its offer. He informed Ted Weiss that his second book, *Drowning with Others*, was almost finished and Wright that he would "get the whole thing up out of the new style." The next book, he stated in his 9 September 1959 letter, offered "a new approach, a new world constantly coming up out of the old one": "I have a distinct feeling that the poet, as though he were Picasso or somebody, should constantly be trying new things. Cocteau's advice to poets is really the best that can be given, I think: 'Find out what you can do well, and then don't do it'" (305).

Despite the acceptance of his first book, Dickey did not now consider himself noteworthy. In a 27 November 1959 letter to Wright, following their reading with Bly at NYU, he bemoaned his return to "travelling, seeing clients, and the rest of the time-consuming clap-trap of business life." A few months later he would quit advertising altogether and undertake his extended mission to encounter a new world. "I am *convinced*," he wrote Wright early in their correspondence, "that, even in the face of all that has been done, poetry is capable of as yet unheard-of flights, depths, and motions that, to contemplate, would put you in the presence of God" (*One Voice*, I 271).

CHAPTER 8

BARNSTORMING FOR POETRY

Scribner's published *Into the Stone* on 23 August 1960 when Dickey was thirty-seven years old. Though Frost and Stevens were also both "older" when their first books were published, Dickey nevertheless believed it "late in the day to be publishing a first book of poems" (*Self-Interviews* 83). He had reservations about the Poets of Today format, which brought together three different poets, informing William Jay Smith on 3 October 1958, "I don't under any conditions want to dive headforemost into that wretched, handsome 'Package' format that Scribners keeps grinding out" (*One Voice*, I 281). By June 1959, however, he had changed his mind. He wrote James Wright that while he had hoped for his own book, "free and clear," his editor John Hall Wheelock had convinced him that the three-decker format had its own advantages as well. Along with Dickey, *Poets of Today VII* included Paris Leary and Jon Swan. Wheelock, he added, "has been so understanding of my peculiar and unclear problems that I am more than happy to let him do the book" (304). Those problems centered on an overly long manuscript that included poems about which he was either wavering or doubtful and an arrangement into seemingly arbitrary sections. Among the poems that concerned Dickey were "Dover: Believing in Kings," "The First Morning of Cancer," and "The Red Bow." Wheelock omitted all three, thereby rendering the manuscript an acceptable length. While "Dover" would be published in *Drowning with Others*, the latter two remained uncollected until 1996, when Dickey included them in *Striking In*, his edited early notebooks. Wheelock also helped to finalize the arrangement of the poems in each section of *Into the Stone*, which Dickey later acknowledged was important. "I had no notion that that would be of advantage," he stated. "But it was, because they did group into three or four broad categories" (*Self-Interviews* 84).

Scholars have focused little critical attention on *Into the Stone* largely because, after omitting one-third of its poems from *Poems 1957–1967*, Dickey overlooked the volume completely when he compiled *The Early Motion* (1981), the collection which depicts the first phase of his professional writing career. In his final volume, *The Whole Motion: Collected Poems, 1945–1992*, he included some, though not all, of *Into the Stone*—fifteen of the original twenty-four poems. Though such exclusion owed partly to Wesleyan University Press's concern over size, and hence cost, of the book (*Puella* was similarly truncated), more than marketing was at issue in the tendency to downplay *Into the Stone*. Rather, omissions resulted from Dickey's deliberate efforts now to distance himself from almost any poem that owed a heavy debt to modernist tenets, works that included "The Signs," "The Call," and "Orpheus before Hades."

While his subsequent volumes, *Drowning with Others* (1962) and *Helmets* (1964), exhibit a stronger poetic control of form and meter as well as of imagery and theme, *Into the Stone* clearly suggests Dickey's emerging voice, his emphasis on direct experience and the complex of emotional and physical responses that act as ritual to invite a transcendent communion, particularly with the dead. The volume identifies, even proclaims, his thematic concerns: family, war, death and dying, and love. Dickey kept the divisional scheme for his next two collections as well, though he eliminated the section titles. The subject of each of the sections also broadened in scope. While the third part of *Into the Stone*, for example, confronts the demise of immediate family members and friends, death in this third section of *Drowning with Others* focuses on the surrender of consciousness to a dreamlike state or magical moment in which rational faculties are suspended. The poems in the third section of *Helmets* subsequently assume varied and unique perspectives, the "death" of one's immediate self, as it were, such as that of an unspecified being, a bum, a snake, and a sleeping child. Death imagery, including graves, candles, prayers, and coffins, links these poems into a coherent whole. *Into the Stone*, moreover, contains rich, daring language, such as "blaze of tears" and "utter, unseasonable glory," that approaches overstatement but which also, as James Wright noted in his review, "transfigure the most elemental facts of the universe and...embody the transfiguration in an unforgettable phrase" (Kirschten 29–30), as when Dickey depicts the moon as a "huge ruined stone in the sky" ("Near Darien"), sunlight as a "great, ragged angel" ("The Game"), and moonlight on grass as "a weightless frosted rain" ("The Sprinter's Sleep"). The strong narrative element fuses the chronology of events with their imaginative transformation, achieving what Dickey meant in *Babel to Byzantium* when he declared the necessity to show "'what happens' in its pure, inexplicable, purposeless instancy and intensity: in its meaning-beyond-meaning" (104).

Critical reviews of *Into the Stone* were sparse but generally positive. Writing in the December 1961 issue of *Poetry*, Wright praised Dickey for his "creative tenderness," declaring that the poems embodied a "confrontation of some of the most difficult and important experiences that a human being can have," experiences brought forth by "an unpredictably joyous imagination" (178–80). Gene Baro in the 30 October 1960 issue of *The New York Herald Tribune Book Review* labeled the poems as "metaphysical dramas" (10), and John Thompson in the winter 1960–1961 issue of *Hudson Review* found the poet "very imaginative, even fanciful" (623). Reviewers generally thought *Into the Stone* the best of the three books included in *Poets of Today VII*, surpassing Paris Leary's *Views of the Oxford Colleges* and Jon Swan's *Journeys and Returns*, and noting the anapestic meter that presented the intense personal experiences, what one critic termed "poetry in staccato, three beat lines." Dickey had deferred to the modernist emphasis on form but only as a means to metamorphose and magnify "a portion of himself that he has never really understood" (*Sorties* 156, 157). Form, whether traditional or newly created, did not function to reveal only the poet's craftsmanship but rather to release identity and concentrate both meaning and a sense of inevitability.

Reflecting Dickey's reading of Freud while at Vanderbilt, the poems in *Into the Stone* depict the binary conflict between Eros, the life force, and Thanatos, the death force, which Dickey viewed as the basis of existence. As with other Romantics, he celebrated the imagination, believing in its ability to redeem existence by recapturing a sense of life's essential mystery. The poet, therefore, emulates the Creator, and the poem becomes a necessary illusion that momentarily sustains a new creation. Following such modernists as Eliot and Pound, he utilized fertility myths to dramatize the creative and destructive cycles of life, the difference being that he now centered himself in those myths, whether classical ("The Vegetable King") or biblical ("Sleeping Out at Easter").

In "The Vegetable King," for example, Dickey imagines an ordinary homeowner who awakens one spring morning, having slept in his backyard, and dreamed, as in Near Eastern fertility myths, that he has been dismembered, his body parts thrown into water and gathered together again. Entering the house, he realizes that he has had the dream, but he cannot be completely certain that he is not the Vegetable King, whose death and rebirth have brought back the spring flowers and crops, or that the cycle will not repeat itself the following year. He

Begin[s] to believe a dream
I never once have had,
Of being part of the acclaimed rebirth
Of the ruined, calm world in spring,
When the drowned god and the dreamed-of sun

Unite, to bring the red, the blue,
The common yellow flower out of earth
Of the tended and untended garden.

Similarly, "Sleeping Out at Easter" depicts the rebirth of a man who, after sleeping overnight in his backyard with his child, becomes another person "through the twin influences of the Easter ritual and of nature itself" (*Self-Interviews* 86). In so doing he grasps "the source of all song at the root." Written in his business office over a three-week period, the poem initially displayed complicated lines full of rhetorical effects, but Dickey soon realized that such an approach precluded presentational immediacy. The lines eventually became more direct ("All dark is now no more. / This forest is drawing a light") and exhibited the marked rhythmical effect that he wanted, an almost hypnotic beat that evokes a primal response ("My child, mouth open, still sleeping, / Hears the song in the egg of a bird").

Other poems in *Into the Stone* that present the dichotomy between life and death involve Dickey's dead brother, Eugene, including "The Signs," "The Underground Stream," and "The String." In "The String," for example, the narrator admits, "I cannot bring my brother to myself. / I do not have his memory in my life, / Yet he is in my mind and on my hands." Such survivor's guilt also appears in war poems such as "The Jewel," where the speaker asks, "Truly, do I live? Or shall I die, at last, / Of waiting?," and in "The Performance," where Dickey only digs meaningless foxholes after his best friend Donald Armstrong "knelt down in himself / Beside his hacked, glittering grave, having done / All things in this life that he could." Moreover, the conflict in *Into the Stone* between death and a new life transformed by a mythical passage frequently involves a fundamentally unheroic but sensitive speaker who nevertheless sees, as in "The Game," "the sun strongly divide / Into light and death," or as in "The Call," when "the breath falls out of my voice, / And yet the singing keeps on." He may have been, as in "The Other," a "rack-ribbed child" with a "chicken-chested form," but "in utter, unreasonable glory," he has labored, believing "I would rise like Apollo / With armor-cast shoulders upon me." Consequently, he now finds himself "telling nothing but how I made / By hand, a creature to keep me dying / Years longer." Through these rites of passage, Dickey's friends, fellow soldiers, and athletes struggle heroically to redeem themselves and realize their imagined ideals; by depicting their efforts, however, Dickey reimagines his own.

By the time *Into the Stone* was published, he had completed enough poems for *Drowning with Others* and had started assembling poems for *Helmets*. While Maxine typed the new manuscript, Dickey planned to approach Harcourt Brace, Houghton Mifflin, Wesleyan, and Farrar Straus. His poems were now frequently appearing in the *New Yorker*, including "The Underground Stream," "Trees and Cattle," "A Birth," "Autumn," "Listening to Foxhounds," and "The Magus," and he had signed a "first-reading" contract with the magazine in November 1959 that featured a bonus and $1.90 a line. His reviews were also appearing in *Sewanee Review*, the eminent Southern journal, which may have led Louis Rubin to invite him in November 1960 to Hollins College to read poems and debate aesthetics with Randall Jarrell, whose critical acumen Dickey had always admired. Rubin had also commissioned Dickey to write an essay for a book on Southern culture. That essay, "Notes on the Decline of Outrage," spoke for the white Southerner whose attitudes regarding the dismantling of the antebellum racial order combined sadness, anger, confusion, and relief. Characteristically, Dickey described his exchange with Jarrell as a competition, telling James Wright on 20 November 1960, "We agreed on almost nothing (and I *mean* nothing!) and we cut and slashed and parried with deliberate and desperate urgency." He continued, "We went at it hotly: the sound of a crowd cheering for the home team to score in the last quarter, or the sound of a good, knowledgeable and enthusiastic crowd at a jazz festival, when one of the musicians (for some reason I think of tenor sax players) goes from technical virtuosity into inspiration, or art. It was a great experience for me. God knows what I said, but I certainly said it, I am sure" (*One Voice*, I 359).

Shortly before the publication of *Into the Stone*, Robert Bly had invited Dickey to participate in a new series of poetry readings he was arranging for New York University. He planned to join Wright, Dickey, and possibly the British poet Geoffrey Hill, who was replacing Donald Hall at the University of Michigan for the 1959–60 academic year. Hill eventually declined the invitation. The New York venue pleased Dickey, but the reading and the subsequent drinking and camaraderie left him elated. He told Wright in a 27 November 1959 missive: "There is still this dead-sure certainty: nothing I could ever write would do justice to the feeling of ab-solute *rightness* I had about everything we did in New York. Hart Crane and Lorca were leaning from the windows saying 'Yes! Yes! That's it! Go on and say it! Go on and do it! It's all right! It's all right! You're home, now!' And we were." However, he had now returned, he declared, to "the time-consuming clap-trap of business life," what he termed "another one of the Histories of Hell." Yet he added, "One of the most terrible and frightening things about being in such a situation as we were in in New York is that you are permitted, just for a few hours, for a day or two at most, to see how things, how human life *could* be. Perhaps it is a taste of Heaven, or perhaps everyday reality is simply Hell itself; I don't know." He shared Wright's conviction, he declared, that they would all get to-gether again, laugh, joke, drink, and read poems, and he concluded, "Time is running out on this letter, though. I must eat, I must sleep, I must die, I must rise again. But I do so thinking mostly of you and Bly, and the reasons that I must rise" (*One Voice*, I 312–13).

Though his attitudes toward Bly and Wright would change, Dickey clearly believed his participation in the New York reading had altered his personal landscape. It was unlike anything he had previously experienced. He felt beknighted. Artists had achieved notable victories within Ameri-can culture in the previous twenty years; the number of poetry prizes, awards, grants, and honors, for example, had increased, such that five ma-jor prizes now existed. Whereas only the Pulitzer had distinguished a poet earlier, awards now also included the National Book Award for Poetry, the Bollingen Prize, the Fellowship of the Academy of American Poets, and designation as the United States Poet Laureate. That success owed in no small measure to the popularity of Dylan Thomas's visits to America be-tween 1949 and 1953, when he read to public gatherings from his own works as well as from other major British poets. His readings, moreover, had been anticipated by those of Robert Frost, who called such tours "barding around." In so doing, Frost and Thomas literally made artists visible to Americans. Their readings gave poets a human face, and writers soon began to read or lecture at colleges, universities, and conferences. John Berryman, for example, undertook a lecture tour of India under the auspices of the US Information Service in summer 1958, and Frost was sent to the USSR in 1962. Moreover, far from the obscurity or opaqueness the public found when encountering the works of Eliot and Pound in print, Thomas's poems produced an excitement, even an intense admira-tion, when experienced aurally. They communicated a sense that whatever explicit meanings a poem might outwardly display, a deeper and truer truth also lay within. If a modernist poem seemed in print like a crossword puzzle whose concealed meanings had to be intellectually interpolated as an academic exercise, Thomas's poems were vital, offering concrete and intensely personal meanings and emotions. They held within them a living voice.

Authorship had effectively become a profession; poets gave readings and taught creative writing, composition, and literature at colleges and universities. Consequently, however, less time existed for writers themselves to write, and there was less pressure financially to publish. Moreover, the complacency with which America asked its poets to *be* poets resulted in the absence of any strong, new movements. Though the San Francisco poets, under the guidance of Kenneth Rexroth and Allen Ginsberg, were certainly making their presence felt, their influence was not pervasive nor were they accepted even within the literary arena. In "The Present State of Poetry," for example, a lecture delivered at the Library of Congress in 1958, Delmore Schwartz had accused these writers of self-promotion, calling them the "San Francisco howlers," artists who advertise themselves as self-styled "super-Bohemians" and who "scream against the conformity which prevails in society and in literary circles" (26). He labeled them "imaginary rebels" because the violent nonconformity that constituted the substance of their work was a condition which they already possessed and which necessitated no true insurrection since it was readily available to anyone who wished to attain it. However, he lamented the ease into which American poets and poetry had become mired in conformity, wistfully acknowledging the radical transformation that modernism had earlier provoked, and declaring, "What was once a battlefield has become a peaceful public park on a pleasant Sunday afternoon" (26). Even Eliot himself, alluding in *East Coker* to earlier times, had seemed to signal in 1943 that while modernism had expended itself, a new poetic direction had not yet emerged:

> That was a way of putting it—not very satisfactory:
> A periphrastic study in a worn-out poetical fashion,
> Leaving one still with the intolerable wrestle
> With words and meanings. The poetry does not matter.
> It was not (to start again) what one had expected.
> What was to be the value of the long looked forward to,
> Long hoped for calm, the autumnal serenity

Of the wisdom of age? Had they deceived us
Or deceived themselves, the quiet-voiced elders,
. Bequeathing us merely a receipt for defeat?

No new, redemptive poetics, Eliot appeared to be saying, had arisen as an antidote for this "receipt for defeat."

Schwartz's poor assessment of poetry appeared brightened by the 1957 publication of an anthology titled *New Poets of England and America*, edited by Donald Hall, Robert Pack, and Louis Simpson, which centered on poets under age forty. The anthology offered an introduction by Robert Frost and presented works by writers who, by and large, would soon establish themselves as the new generation, including Robert Bly, Anthony Hecht, John Hollander, William Meredith, Adrienne Rich, and others. Dickey was not included. Frost's invocation, however, which readers might reasonably have assumed would herald a new direction or offer some new literary manifesto, did neither. Indeed, it is not clear from his introduction whether Frost even read any of the poems. He never mentions by name a single poet contained in the collection, commenting instead only on the general quality of the poets and poems in the anthology. "Maturity will come," he wrote. "We mature. But the point is that it is at best irrelevant." He added that readers, not the anthologized poets, stood on trial, for they would have to decide "without critical instruction the differences between the poets who wrote because they thought it would be a good idea to write and those who couldn't help writing out of a strong weakness for the muse, as for an elopement with her" (11). The lack of any direct statements regarding shared themes, use of poetic forms, or innovative techniques indicated to critics the problems that artists following Eliot, Pound, Williams, Stevens, and others were generally having in their efforts to establish themselves. Reviewing this important anthology in the spring 1958 issue of *Sewanee Review*, despite his not having published a book himself, Dickey observed,

> The fault of most of this poetry...is that one simply doesn't *believe* it. One longs in vain for some standard by which to measure the capacity of works of art to reach us "where we live"; to be able to say something definitive about the mysterious enlightening conjunction between the good poem and the inner life of the beholder, without which poetry is an exercise differing from any other linguistic usage only in format. (297–98)

On 26 July 1958, he wrote Wright similar sentiments. "What we must have," he asserted, "is a poetry that *gives us life*: some act of the imagination: the live imagination" (*One Voice*, I 270). He would later admit to Donald Hall in a 15 July 1961 letter, "Believe me, the fifties were a bad time for poetry; if our generation can't do better then let some other folks, even (other than beatniks), who can give the Word a little life blood instead of using it as a beribboned bar, take the ball and run with it for a while" (*One Voice* I, 363). F. W. Dupee, reviewing the book that summer in *Partisan Review*, declared, "The presiding muse here is unassertive, intelligent, charming, voluble, company-conscious—the perfect guest" (457). Schwartz himself discerned in the new anthology what he termed a "tameness and restrained calm" ("The Present State" 28), which he attributed to the international situation and the existence of totalitarian police states that threatened the American way of life. Yet unlike Frost he gleaned a common thematic concern—the objects and events of ordinary personal experience, including sexuality, treated in a matter-of-fact way and lacking in self-consciousness. Such personal events had heretofore been outside the realm of poetic treatment. As the fifties ended, therefore, substantive changes had begun to emerge even if their presence was not yet clear, and Dylan Thomas's wildly successful readings seemed to crystallize and even herald a tangible new direction.

These readings brought Thomas money and popularity, both central concerns to Dickey, who determined to achieve likewise. Throughout the sixties he undertook extensive and hectic poetry readings, exhaustive tours of one-night stands at colleges and universities across the country. Typical was his barnstorming tour beginning in fall 1964. He first traveled to Dartmouth in mid-October, the event hosted by Richard Eberhart, the poet-in-residence, where Dickey read his poems and entertained students with folk tunes from his guitar. He next performed at the Young Men's Hebrew Association (YMHA) in New York on 25 October and then flew west for the Ohio poetry circuit, where he shuttled to a new town almost every day, a candidate stumping for poetry. He read at Cleveland State and Oberlin College on 29 October and Kenyon College the following day. On 1 November he performed at both Kent State and Fern College, Ohio University on 2 November, Denison University and Ohio Wesleyan on 3 November, Miami University on 4 November, Wabash College on 5 November, Earlham College on 6 November, and Antioch University on 7 November. Following his tour of the Midwest, Dickey traveled to the University of Rochester on 9 November and then flew to UCLA for a reading on 20 November. While no two campuses were alike, the routines largely remained the same—dining, drinking, reading poetry, and then rushing to his next destination—all of which he described in his 1965 essay, "Barnstorming for Poetry," published in the *New York Times Book Review*. Recognizing that "he is not Robert Frost or Dylan Thomas," Dickey was nevertheless surprised at both the size and enthusiasm of his audiences. While he eventually believed such responses were "excessive and even manic," he found "these small, repeated tastes of local notoriety definitely agreeable" (*Babel to Byzantium* 249–50). What concerned him most, however, was the question of who he was supposed to be, or become, during the events, the expectation that at the readings themselves as well as at the inevitable parties that followed, he must do "something idiosyncratic that people are expecting and that, much more dangerous to psychological stability, he expects of himself" (250). To that end, he occasionally played a few songs on a guitar he had acquired but which he had not played for years. When he performed, he wrote, "the image of his great predecessor, the only predecessor, Dylan Thomas, blazed up humiliatingly in the front of his mind" (251), so that later he drank twice as much as he should, waved his arms wildly, and said anything that came into his head, insulting someone whose name he could not remember. He recognized that "all roleplaying is shameful beside the feeling...that his words are being received almost as things [that] have the quality of gifts" (252), but what exalted the poet, he believed, was the show itself, the performance. Alcohol enhanced the roleplaying. "It is not only poetry that is involved," he declared in his essay, "it is the poet as well" (250), such that he needed to drink both before and following the reading. The alcohol, his son Chris remembered, gave his father "a divine sense of license, and, hell, Dylan Thomas drank. It's what poets do" (*Summer of Deliverance* 122). Although Frost did not drink, the statement reflected the public perception of poets.

Just as Dickey sought to create in his poems a world "realer-than-real," he also endeavored in his barnstorming tours to fashion a "fictional self," an identity that was "better than truth." His aesthetic, in other words, paralleled his personal sense of identity, grounding who he was in the poetics he espoused, thus blurring the distinction between poet and poem. "Perhaps in the end," he wrote in *Night Hurdling*,

> the whole possibility of words being able to contain one's identity is illusory; opinions, yes; identity, maybe. Perhaps the whole question of identity itself is illusory. But one must work with such misconceptions for whatever hint of insight—the making of a truth—

they may contain: that fragment of existence which could not be
seen in any other way and may with great good luck, as in the best
poetry, be better than the truth. (xi)

Scorning the intellectual elitism of modernists, Dickey now transfigured
his public self into a more representational one—an athlete, a combat veteran, a businessman, a sportsman—who was now compelling audiences to
respond directly and emotionally to ordinary experiences, a poet speaking
to the common man, going from campus to campus reading his poems.
Though he had taught at several colleges and universities (including the
University of Florida), won prestigious awards, including a Guggenheim
Fellowship, and published three volumes of poetry by 1965, Dickey presented himself as "usual and ordinary," an identity that was just as crafted
as the fictional self he portrayed in his poems.

While it is unclear whether Dickey as a child witnessed or attended
the barnstorming events during the twenties and thirties where stunt pilots
performed tricks either individually or in groups called flying circuses, he
would certainly have been aware of this form of entertainment and the
enhanced stature of the performers, which seemed founded on bravado,
with one-upmanship as a major incentive. Moreover, he thought of himself as a flyer, *the* pilot. Despite reservations, however, he took unabashed
pleasure in the spotlight that audiences shone on him. It promoted his
reputation as a poet. Indeed, Dickey's experience in advertising had resulted in a clear sense of how to sell and merchandise a product, regardless
of whether that product was Coca-Cola, Lays Potato Chips, or Delta Airlines, all accounts on which he worked. Advertising allowed him an intimate understanding of business means and consumer interests. The poet
needed to sell himself. While Dickey frequently complained about the
crass mediocrity of American capitalism, he also acknowledged how it had
enhanced his poetry career. "It is time for me to pay a debt to the advertising industry," he wrote in *Sorties*, "even if only in my mind. It is important that I was in advertising, and it is also important that I was in it
for as long as I was" (19). Both from a commercial and a design standpoint,
he said, advertising offered new creative perspectives, adding, "It is foolish
to say that these things are not important; they are *very* important" (19).

While Allen Ginsberg and Robert Bly attracted the counterculture
and the anti-war movement, Dickey's readings from 1963 through the remainder of the decade projected a strong assertion of independence, a determined effort not to be caught up in any movement but rather to

maintain, as he later wrote, "the poet's sensibility and of his freedom to select his own subject matter by virtue of what moves him as a human being" (*Self-Interviews* 72). Although most of his contemporaries were writing topical poems that addressed social and political issues, including Allen Ginsberg's "Howl" (1956), Lawrence Ferlinghetti's "I Am Waiting" (1958), and Robert Lowell's "July in Washington" (1964), Dickey was exploring metrical possibilities and searching for ways to write about "war, about love and sex, about athletics, about being a Southerner, about hunting and flying and canoeing, about the flight of birds and the movement of animals and the feeling of swimming in the presence of fish" (*Babel to Byzantium* 281–82). He was also doing so in a way that offered presentational immediacy, bringing these worlds directly to the audiences and allowing them to experience the creative mysteries of existence. Looking to stand apart from other poets, Dickey criticized formalists such as Yvor Winters, writing, "One can't help being struck by the poverty of Winters's emotional makeup," adding that he found his poems "lifeless and life-destroying," full of "enforced sterility" (185). He also attacked Ginsberg, arguing that his poems reveal only "unrelated associations, wish-fulfillment fantasies, and self-righteous maudlin-ness" (53–54).

Dickey's insistence that poetry not only results in self-actualization but also opens the poet and reader to an intimacy with nature occurred as the environmental movement was establishing itself as a legitimate scientific, political, and moral force. In 1962 Rachel Carson published *Silent Spring*, which linked pesticide use to the destruction of animal species (between 1950 and 1962, the amount of DDT found in human tissue had tripled). The following year Congress passed the Clean Air Act; the Water Quality Act passed in 1965. The Endangered Species Act in 1966 authorized the protection of domestic fish and wildlife. The first list of these species included the national symbol, the American bald eagle. Paul Ehrlich's *The Population Bomb*, published in 1968, argued that the world's environmental problems were caused by human overpopulation. That same year the Wild and Scenic Rivers Act provided a system by which rivers were identified and placed on a protected list. This legislation, along with the increasing involvement of the Sierra Club, which had committed itself to the protection of the planet, occurred during Dickey's literary ascendency. As his critical acclaim and popularity increased, so too did American interest in the environment.

Dickey's early volumes revealed his participation in and concern for the natural world. Though not programmatic, he nevertheless wrote poems that centered on nature and that revealed a reverence for and affinity with it, among them "Listening to Foxhounds" (1960), "The Movement of Fish" (1961), "The Owl King" (1961–1962), "Springer Mountain" (1962), "Deer Among Cattle" (1965), "For the Last Wolverine" (1966), and "Pine" (1969). In addition, *Deliverance* cannot be fully understood without comprehending Dickey's belief in nature's redemptive powers. Its plot results from the flooding of the Cahulawassee River to build a hydroelectric dam. "There has never been in the history of the world," Dickey wrote in *Sorties*, "and never will be anyone whom the wilderness fascinates as much as it does me…. Most of my poems about woods and lakes and rivers and so on depend on my *not* knowing these things very well, so that they remain strange to me: that is, so that they remain in at least some sense *visions*" (39–40). His daughter, Bronwen, remembers his interest in nature, the wonder it inspired, and his despair at its loss. "He loved learning about and being around animals," she said, "We went to the zoo more weekends than I can count. And we watched a *lot* of Jacques Cousteau documentaries, a lot of *Wild Kingdom*. He was also a fan of *Nature Scene*, which ran on South Carolina Educational Television for many years and bought several of those multi-volume sets of nature/wildlife books from Time-Life." She continued, "The strongest memories I have are of him discussing the horror of extinction, pollution, deforestation, etc. when we were watching nature documentaries together. In the early '90s, we went to see a forgettable Sean Connery/Lorraine Bracco film called *Medicine Man*, which ends with a broad swath of the Amazon forest being clearcut, and I remember him being deeply upset by that." Dickey's environmentalism, swelling from his empathetic sensibilities and heightened by the environmental movement during the sixties, was echoed in virtually everything he wrote.

During his years in advertising, Dickey's unapologetic and determined loyalty to and promotion of poetry made him what Neal Bowers termed "a double agent" (56). Not only did he secretly bring poetry books into business meetings, but he also surreptitiously worked on drafts of poems he was writing behind the closed door of his office. "I hated office work," he later confessed, "a kind of genteel hell of absolute inconsequence, and every day I used to take a book of poems with me just to touch, every now and then, or as a reminder of the world where I lived most as I wished to." He continued,

And I remember also the very distinct sense of danger I felt when carrying the book through the acres of desks where typists typed five carbons of the Tony Bennett Record Promotion: the distinct and delicious sense of subversiveness and danger in carrying a book or the manuscript of a new poem as if it were a bomb, here in this place that had no need of it, that would be embarrassed and nonplussed by it, that would finally destroy it by its enormous weight of organized indifference. (*Night Hurdling* 352)

Dickey was effectively waging a private war. "I was in it for the money," he admitted, "to make a living" (*Self-Interviews* 44). Maxine had given birth to their second son, Kevin Webster, on 18 August 1958. In America, money defined success, and Dickey was deeply conscious of the deprivation he felt his family had suffered while he taught at Rice and the University of Florida, having seen, as he wrote Wright on 23 July 1958, "my poor family do without everything except the basic essentials" (*One Voice*, I 268). He determined never to have that happen again. After informing Wright on 6 September that his new son was "making fine progress toward becoming recognizably human," he declared, "I have just got an immense raise at the legendary (legendary in the same sense as Hell is), 'The Office.' I would be embarrassed to tell you what I make, it is so unfair. But I have been so poor so long, I still have trouble believing that I am not so, still" (280).

The attention that Dickey received at poetry readings was not happenstance nor was it discouraged. Rather, it was actively embraced by a poet who took barnstorming on the road and eagerly welcomed the subsequent recognition and even adulation. He publicized himself, taking unabashed delight in the spotlight, which prompted many in academe to label him egotistical or narcissistic. That Dickey promoted his own reputation cannot be denied; the level of his visibility underscores such accusations. Yet the extent of his advocacy for poetry itself is perfectly illustrated in a 1982 advertisement by the International Paper Company titled "How to Enjoy Poetry," a two-page broadside which appeared in a variety of national magazines and later as both an offprint available for use in schools and as a poster suitable for framing. In it, Dickey offers guidance to readers as to how to approach poetry so as to bring pleasure and meaning to life, written in Dickey's characteristic voice that blends both vigor and plainspokenness: "When you read, don't let the poet write down to you; read up to him. Reach for him from your gut out, and the heart and muscles will come into it, too."

Dickey had become convinced, as he wrote in his 1966 essay "The Poet Turns on Himself," that "there is a poet—or a kind of poet—buried in every human being like Ariel in his tree, and that the people whom we are pleased to call poets are only those who have felt the need and contrived the means to release the spirit from its prison" (*Babel to Byzantium* 279). He determined to assist that escape, suggesting that poetry need not be overly complex, focusing only on the abstract and cerebral. His remarks in the ad were intended to destroy any preconception that poetry was exclusive or obscure. He urged readers to connect with the immediate world: "A handful of gravel is a good place to start. So is an ice cube—what more mysterious and beautiful *interior* of something has there ever been." His objective was to encourage readers to try their own hand at poetry: "Bypass all classrooms, all textbooks, courses, examinations, and libraries and go straight to the things that make your own existence exist: to your body and nerves and blood and muscles." He challenged readers to enter the world and participate in it. Poetry opened Possibility. As he later observed in *Sorties*, "I wish the poem to be a large, intense and *complete* experience," one that required the reader's involvement. "I want my poem to *devour* the reader," he insisted, "so that he cannot possibly put it down as he reads it, or forget about it when he finishes" (48).

While his barnstorming tours promoted Dickey specifically and poetry generally, they also deliberately advanced the idea of a particular kind of poet, a visionary engaged in a mystical quest for wholeness, a search fundamentally spiritual in nature. That search involved the assumption of various perspectives, lower as well as higher animal forms, for example, but the objective remained the same—to achieve a heightened perception of a coherent universe where life remained purposeful. Never a traditional Christian, Dickey infused his poems with primitivistic and animistic elements, all largely presented within a personal context to create a world sanctioned by the poet himself. His readings while a student at Vanderbilt of anthropologists and mythologists had revealed belief systems far more alive and vital than that of contemporary America, societies in which primitive tribes felt literally connected with their environment rather than utilizing it for material gain. They explain a poem such as "Springer Mountain," where the speaker enters into the natural world, into "the kingdom of life and death, into the eternal cycle of predatory animal and those hunted by the predators" (*Self-Interviews* 126). As Dickey asserted in *Self-Interviews*,

What I want more than anything else is to have a feeling of wholeness. Specialization has produced some extremely important things,
like penicillin and heart transplants. But I don't know how much
they compensate for the loss of a sense of intimacy with the natural
process. I think you would be very hard-put, for example, to find a
more harmonious relationship to an environment than the American Indians had. We can't return to a primitive society; surely this
is obvious. But there is a property of the mind which, if encouraged,
could have this personally animistic relationship to things. (68)

Barnstorming allowed Dickey to nurture in his audiences that "property of
mind" that would bridge the divisions between the self and Other and that,
if successful, enabled a harmonious relationship with nature through a
more inclusive self.

For Dickey, loss of self-identity denoted death. Theodore Roethke,
the poet whom he claimed to admire most, had depicted a mystical journey
seeking a symbolic union with the sub- and preconscious mind, one that
subsumed everything and which abandoned individual identities. Dickey,
by contrast, offered what Howard Nemerov in his 1963 review of *Drowning with Others* called "the language of a willed mysticism" (Weigl, Hummer 13). By committing himself entirely to his invention, Dickey brought
his audiences into the experience. By "*giving* himself to his invention,
which, with luck, is also his vision" (*Self-Interviews* 91), he hoped to render
the fiction real, creating a shared experience by which both he and his audience could momentarily participate in an exchange with some Other.
Poets who merely contrive language he labeled suspect; they bring into
being "a truly remarkable amount of utter humbug" that has no relation to
ordinary experience and which "degrad[es] it by offering experience as a
series of unbelievable contrivances, none of which has the power of bringing forth a genuine response" (*The Suspect in Poetry* 9). Barnstorming
across the country in the sixties, Dickey challenged both the function of
poetry and the raison d'etre of the poet himself. He subscribed to the idea
that the poet was a kind of shaman, a spiritual leader whose elevated position in primitive society sought to reveal the divine through ritual magic
and incantations. Such early specialized language had evolved into poetry;
language, in effect, was magical. Yet he noted in his 1960 essay "Toward
a Solitary Joy," "The battles of art are silent, bloodless, and usually result
in defeat more total than any others. This is especially true of poetry, where
the writer has virtually no audience at all, and puts in his hours, almost
always after work, in dogged misery, determined to realize himself and to

communicate even if there is no one to communicate with" (*The Suspect in Poetry* 118). Barnstorming, with luck, enabled him to communicate with others by "moving and speaking among his kind" (*Babel to Byzantium* 256) while also setting himself apart from other poets, centering the performance on himself by reading poems largely from his own experiences and by exaggerating his behavior at the readings themselves.

Self-centeredness was hardly unique to Dickey. Writers as different as Whitman, Clemons, Hemingway, Ginsberg, Bly, and Mailer all engaged in such self-advertising, attempting to distinguish themselves and secure recognition in literary history. His reading tours allowed audiences to conflate his poems with events in Dickey's own life. Indeed, in interviews, essays, and reviews he exaggerated those experiences such that biographical interpretations of his poetry and prose fiction seemed not only possible but also warranted, as when he wrote in a journal entry in *Sorties*, "I am Lewis" (9), referring to a character in *Deliverance*. Critics consequently felt themselves justified in assessing Dickey's work within the context of the image he presented.

Hoping to create more time to write, Dickey left the advertising firm of Liller, Neal after a year and moved to Burke Dowling Adams in Atlanta, where he became creative director in charge of the copy and art departments as well as campaigns for principal accounts, including Delta Airlines. To relieve the stress from advertising, he joined an archery club in November, the Cherokee Bowmen, and participated in hunting and canoeing excursions with friends and associates when circumstances permitted, rarely, however, killing any boar, deer, fox, or grouse but almost always enabling him to enter nature and providing him with poetic material. "Springer Mountain" and "Approaching Prayer," for example, owe largely to these expeditions. Both poems were published in *Helmets* and celebrate the hunt. In the latter, Dickey writes of a man like himself who discovers "the head of a boar / I once helped to kill with two arrows." Like a shaman, the speaker puts on his father's sweater and gamecock spurs as well as the boar's head over his own so that he understands both predator and prey on the one hand and dead father and living son on the other hand. Though he would boast in his letters to Wright and others of his kills, in the poem his sympathy lies with the boar, knowing now "that reason was dead enough / For something important to be: / That, if not heard, / It may have been somehow said."

As he had done at Liller, Neal, Dickey devoted considerable time at Burke Dowling Adams to his poetry, discontented with the numbing routines and excessive demands of business and determined to use office hours to complete *Drowning with Others*. "Dover: Believing in Kings," while not included in *Into the Stone*, had been published in the August 1958 issue of *Poetry*. The editor, Henry Rago, informed Dickey that the poem had won its Union League Civic and Arts Foundation Prize, which Dickey incorrectly claimed had previously been awarded to Robert Frost and Dylan Thomas. Recent winners, however, had included Robinson Jeffers, Robert Penn Warren, and Robert Duncan. As with his salary, Dickey exaggerated. In March 1961 he sent a first draft of the new collection to Donald Hall at Wesleyan for evaluation. When Hall responded favorably on 30 March, he confidently submitted the manuscript for formal acceptance. In April he applied to the Guggenheim Foundation for a fellowship, requesting $11,600 to travel to France and Italy, writing in his application that because his first book had benefitted from the artistic influences of those countries, he believed his next book would as well. John Hall Wheelock wrote a letter of recommendation. The Guggenheim judges, who had no way to know that the book was already almost finished, awarded him a $5,000 fellowship. Wesleyan, however, rejected *Drowning with Others* in late May because, as Hall explained, some board members did not feel it was as good as they had expected. John Hollander and Richard Wilbur, formalist poets who might reasonably have been expected to look unfavorably on the manuscript, had supported it; Norman Pearson expressed reservations. Hall subsequently urged a bewildered Dickey to add new poems and resubmit the manuscript. Acceptance was also hindered by the fact that Wesleyan's publication policy limited the press to publishing only two poetry books a year, one of which had been Wright's third collection, *Amenities of Stone*. When Wright unexpectedly withdrew his collection, however, Wesleyan accepted *Drowning with Others* "enthusiastically and without dissent." On 7 September, Dickey thanked Hall. In an unpublished letter among his papers at Emory University, he noted the January publication date, and reflecting the Cold War tensions, he added, "if we are not all hydrogen dust by that time. Even if we are, my dust will be grateful to you for your long championship of the book and of my writing generally. I can't really tell you how much I owe you; it should be a kind of feeling that can communicate itself by some metaphysical means through the air between Georgia and Michigan; I hope you can sense it, for the air is full of it. It is my answer to the H-bomb."

As he had with Wheelock, Dickey relied on Hall for editorial suggestions regarding not only poetic content but also the arrangement of the poems, writing on 14 September 1961,

> I *depend* on you to get the book into the best shape possible. My arrangement was only provisional at best; my only method was to try to keep the animal and hunting poems together, the war poems, and the family poems, but it is a loose, rather arbitrary arrangement, and I give you complete *carte blanche* to arrange the poems as you and the other editors (but mostly you) see fit. (*One Voice*, I 365)

Hall even decided to conclude the volume with "In the Mountain Tent" rather than "The Hospital Window," which became the last poem in the third section focusing on death and dying. When three of the poems in the collection, "Between Two Prisoners," "Listening to Foxhounds," and "Walking on Water," were included in *Best Poems of 1960*, edited by Lionel Stevens, Dickey enthusiastically wrote others with news of the honor. Literature was competition. As with his aerial barnstorming counterparts, his personality mandated one-upmanship, exaggerating his athletic feats, business salary, reading fees, and poetic submissions and acceptances. His son Chris reflected, "My father was fiercely and almost randomly competitive. The ferocity was worse when he got older, and worse still when he drank, but it was always there" (*Summer of Deliverance* 114).

In July 1961 Dickey quit Burke Dowling Adams, though Glen Verrill, who also worked for the ad company, claims Dickey was fired for taking a one-week unauthorized vacation and for lackadaisical work habits (Hart 262–63). In letters to Hall and Wright, Dickey suggested that the decision to leave had been his: "I have done it at last. Five minutes ago I quit my job as 'Atlanta's fastest-rising young businessman' (a term used by my present agency to its own purposes)," he wrote Wright on 10 July. "I will probably be around Atlanta until the end of next winter, doing odd jobs and trying my best to live on my wits, until we leave on the Fellowship next March. But the main thing is that I am *out*. I am OUT, thank God!" He added, "I simply could not do it any longer, and now the break has come, 'everything I look upon is blest.' I feel like overhauling the poetic engine, grinding the valves, re-boring the block, and getting set to run like hell on the poetic road to Glory (or elsewhere) for the rest of my life, God willing!" (*One Voice*, I 360). Maxine supported her husband's decision to leave, though his parents demurred, believing that to leave a lucrative enterprise in which he had at least distinguished himself to write poetry in

Europe was reckless and irresponsible. He now had a wife and two sons to support. As Chris later wrote, "A steady income, my schooling—the whole predictable package of middle-class life in Atlanta was jettisoned. And my mother was as anxious to get back to Europe as any of us. She was married to a genius, she knew, and others were beginning to recognize him as a genius—but not enough others. There were too many gray affable men in Atlanta. There were too many garden clubs. He was straining to get away from this life now" (*Summer of Deliverance* 105–106).

Before Dickey's employment was terminated, he composed a poem for Joe Parris, a fellow copywriter who listened sympathetically to Dickey's struggles while at the agency. Later he wrote Parris, admitting in an unpublished 4 December 1973 letter, "I learned my craft among fellow workers in advertising, such as yourself, And [*sic*] I remember my time with you, particularly, as being productive, friendly, and valuable." The poem, titled "Parade" and with the epigraph "for Joe F. Parris," presents Dickey as a returning combat veteran, celebrated and celebrating, in a welcome-home parade, who suddenly sees himself in a detached state of being and realizes that events were orchestrated while "madmen played gold music in my ears." Never published, "Parade" reveals both the isolation Dickey felt from civilians and his dislike of American capitalism. Ironically, though he despised the monied culture and the loss of moral and aesthetic values it entailed, he used its financial criterion as a measure of his own success.

It was a valorous music poured upon us
In that bright morning, and it was as though
The whole dour earth were moved by those sweet sounds
That played around our bodies and in motion
Conceived in us a love, but not of loving.
We might have been alone upon the sun.

We were then pierced by pride that was entrancing
And stood there, made of sweat and steel and polish,
Each with his latest thoughts wounding,
A being is a being. The white music
Caught us in its clouds of sound and swirled us skyward.
We were aware of nothing but our fires.

Then suddenly I lived beyond my breathing,

Dissolved the mists of music, saw beside me
Myself in such a stance, in various guises,
The eternal soldier; and the ground was stirring
Beneath my feet, and cities falling down
And madmen played gold music in my ears.

Dickey signed up for unemployment and, as if to appear "a starving poet," falsely claimed he gave guitar lessons and moonlighted in Atlanta coffeehouses to make ends meet. Maxine, however, kept strict finances, and Dickey's mother sent regular checks to her son, who was also receiving dividend checks for his SSS Tonic stock. He supplemented his income during the months before his Guggenheim, whose monies did not begin until 1 February 1962, by directing a poetry workshop in Atlanta, an offering in the adult education classes of Emory University. Fond of the class, he wrote "To Guy Landrum, Beginning to Write at Sixty," which celebrated his genteel, eccentric student's late start as a poet, a situation he felt he shared.

Even to himself he cannot say
Except with not one word,
How he hears there is no more light
Than this, nor any word

More anywhere: how he is drunk
On hope, and why he calls himself mad.

Published in the May 1960 issue of *Atlantic Monthly*, the poem reveals Dickey's belief that the poetic effort to make the truth, not merely to tell it, is noteworthy even if unsuccessful. The poet, he stated in his last major interview before his death, "tries to make, to state things so powerfully and memorably and imaginatively, that you, after you have encountered what he says, can never view the thing in any other way. He has given you an enhancement of your own ability to perceive and respond and experience by his words" (Greiner, "Making the Truth" 18).

Donald Hall informed Dickey in July 1961 that he had selected two poems, "The Performance" and "Hunting Civil War Relics at Nimblewill Creek," for his edited collection *Contemporary American Poetry*, which Penguin published the following year. Dickey himself later claimed that he knew at the time that "['The Performance'] was on another level.... It had a different color, a different sound, a different approach" (Greiner, "Making the Truth" 7). In October he went on a two-week tour through Virginia and North Carolina, reading from his poems at Washington and Lee College, University of Virginia, and other smaller schools. Barnstorming events also took him farther from Atlanta, including one at Miami of Ohio. He informed Hall that he was amenable to teaching again if he received "the right offer." "Already," he declared, "seven or eight have written me." He added, "Right now I'm just waiting until all he bids are in." The barnstorming, he said, made enough money "to keep us alive for a couple of months, but will need to read some more before we leave. I am supposed to be pretty good, or so everybody tells me, though I like to think that it's the poems that are good and not just the reading" (*One Voice*, I 367). He invited Robert Bly to spend Thanksgiving in Atlanta, arranging a cocktail party, introducing him to friends, and showing him his childhood home at West Wesley. At the party Bly captured everyone's attention with a dramatic reading of Neruda's famous poem "Walking Around," in which the poet longs for an escape from his numbing domestic and financial situation. The poem opens, "It happens that I am tired of being a man," and continues, "I do not want to go on being a root in the dark, / hesitating, stretched out, shivering with dreams, / downwards, in the wet tripe of the earth, / soaking it up and thinking, eating every day." Working in advertising, Dickey himself had felt a similar lassitude. Not to be outperformed by his guest, he recited from memory an extended passage from André Gide's *Journal*, which had long been an important book to him. He had written Maxine in 1951 while at Keesler Air Force Base complaining about the complacency and ignorance of the men around him. "The human animal," he wrote, "in the main, will never change in that respect; we must be saved, as Gide says, 'by the few'" (*One Voice*, I 161). Dickey considered himself "one of the few."

Preparing for their return to Europe, Dickey first drove to Charlottesville, Virginia, where he lectured on Hart Crane at the Rushton Seminars with R. W. B. Lewis, whose 1955 critical study *The American Adam* had postulated a character archetype in American fiction through the nineteenth century, and who later became a professor of English at Yale University and the Pulitzer Prize-winning biographer of Edith Wharton. Lewis, whom Dickey admired, would socialize with his friend in the coming years at meetings of the National Institute of Arts and Letters and would attend Dickey's birthday symposiums at the University of South Carolina. In his unpublished essay titled "Hart Crane and the Peripheral in Poetry," Dickey commented on what he termed "the extraordinary hold that Crane has on generation after generation of American writers," adding, "He has come to be not a writer of verse, a poet, but something of a culture hero, even a martyr, an archetypal figure of the American poet, complete with misunderstanding, neglect, the agony leading to an early death, and uncontrollable genius; as such he seems to gather upon himself the whole attitude of our culture towards poets, and to show the terrible workings and consequences in his life and fate." In New York the Dickeys stayed at the Bristol Hotel, visiting the Wintons and Wheelocks. He also introduced the poet E. E. Cummings at the Poetry Center, about whom he had written in 1959, "Cummings is a daringly original poet, with more virility and more sheer, uncompromising talent than any other American writer," declaring "all of Cummings's skill, so special to himself that we cannot imagine anyone else making use of it, has gone to establish and consecrate the *moment*: the event which is taking place *now*: the thing which will never be repeated in quite the same way, and which, quite likely, would ordinarily not even be noticed as it happens" (*Babel to Byzantium* 100–106). Cummings died later that year in New York. Dickey also got together with James Merrill with whom he hoped to reunite in Athens, Greece, where Merrill did his writing. Though friends, Dickey faulted Merrill's poetry, labeling it graceful, attractive, and accomplished but which "just as surely stopped short of real significance, real engagement" (97–100).

On 13 February 1962 the Dickeys boarded the SS *France*, watching the New York skyline recede as the ship embarked for Southampton, England. Two days later Wesleyan published *Drowning with Others*. Though the collection did not garner a single award, it was nominated for both the National Book Award and the Pulitzer Prize, a remarkable accomplishment for a poet who had published only one previous volume. Lewis Untermeyer, whose anthologies had played a large role in introducing Dickey to poetry while he served in the Pacific, wrote in his letter to the Pulitzer Prize committee,

> This, a thoroughly "seasoned" book, is far and away above most of the books of poetry published during the year. It is as imaginative and it is ingenious; it is penetrating without being pretentious; it is, as Robert Frost mentioned that poetry should be, both playful and profound. Technically Dickey owes little, if anything, to anyone. Scorning intellectual obfuscation, his thoughts are cleanly shaped and clearly communicated. He is not only one of the best of the so-

called younger poets but unquestionably the best of the Wesleyan crop. (Hart 285)

Reviews were positive. Critics noted Dickey's images, a spiritual approach to the world that sees, as one reviewer noted, "the infinite in the infinitesimal, the Godness in man and things" (Francis D6). R. W. Flint, in the spring issue of *Partisan Review*, noted the "pious ecstasy" in the poems: "I am struck dumb by Dickey's deep-Dixie spiritual approach," adding that in poems such as "Dover," "Dickey's conversational iambic ground-tone, which can be monotonous or transparent according to whether he has anything or not to say, deepens to a fairly rugged and, at the close, powerful incantation" (292–93). Critics compared the poems with those of Theodore Roethke and Dylan Thomas. John Simon in the *Hudson Review* praised Dickey as "a major talent" (466–67), and in November Dickey learned that the English poet and publisher Michael Hamburger had recommended that Longmans publish the book. Dickey wrote Donald Hall on 31 July 1962 from Paris: "Some fellow tells me I am a (or maybe *the*) leader of something called 'the new mysticism,' which is certainly new to me; I don't even know what the old mysticism is" (*One Voice*, I 370).

Drowning with Others presents the poet's mystical search for identity, a larger sense of self by or through which he might more fully enter and participate in existence. In poems such as "A Dog Sleeping on My Feet," "In the Lupanar at Pompeii," "Hunting Civil War Relics at Nimblewill Creek," and "In the Mountain Tent," the poet, as had Whitman, is engaged in enlarging himself; as different as these dramatic situations are, the speaker in each poem necessarily desires to leave who he is and become some Other—a dog, a Civil War soldier, a lost brother. In "In the Tree House at Night," for example, he sleeps in a tree house with his brother, remembering however another brother, now dead: "My green, graceful bones fill the air / With sleeping birds. Alone, alone / And with them I move gently. / I move at the heart of the world." "Listening to Foxhounds" depicts the speaker as he sits by a fire with other hunters, listening to and imaginatively participating with the hounds who are chasing a red fox: "Who runs with the fox / Must sit here like his own image, / Giving nothing of himself / To the sensitive flames, / With no human joy rising up / Coming out of his face to be seen." H. L. Weatherby would later describe these early poems as an "exchange" by which the speaker attempts "a composite vision" such that "a new and otherwise impossible point of view can be created" (Weigl, Hummer 21, 22). The poems deliberately rejected the cerebral, packed claustrophobia of Eliot, who was still the commanding presence on the American literary scene. Confessional poets, moreover, such as Robert Lowell, Allen Ginsberg, and Anne Sexton, wanted only to tell the reader about an experience, thereby closing the world, centering it only on the artist. "I want, mainly, the kind of poetry that opens out," he stated in *Sorties*, "instead of closing down" (9).

"One must be able to distinguish real perception and literary sophistry," he asserted. "I read in Conrad Aiken's *Ushant* that everyone is floating upward 'towards that vast, that outspread sheet of illuminated music, which is the world.' Now who on God's earth has ever experienced the world—that is, the *world*—as a 'sheet of illuminated music'? That is what I refer to as the literary syndrome: saying something fine, but very untrue to experience" (8). If the locked-in quality of modernist verse was false to experience, so was poetry that centered on only the poet or that distorted reality by description that was essentially false. In *Drowning with Others*, however, Dickey was largely successful in universalizing private experiences and emotions in narratives that convincingly grounded mysticism in fact.

Five days after leaving New York, the Dickeys arrived in England, crossing the channel the following day to Le Havre, France, before making their way to Paris and the beginning of their European adventure. The following months would enable Dickey to achieve new heights of literary and financial success. "My family and I have been everywhere and done everything," he wrote Wright from Paris on 31 July 1962, "a wild, soaring release from the endless nightmare of business, with its 'inexorable sadness of pencils'" (*One Voice*, I 369). One month later he wrote Donald Hall from London, "I have a great, bursting sense of the untried *possibilities* of language, and think continually of people unleashing tremendous reservoirs of human energy, faith, love, and human accomplishment out of places in themselves which have been waiting, and are waiting, for something like the truth of poetry" (*One Voice*, I 372).

CHAPTER 9

THE POET AS CRITIC

In a letter to James Wright on 6 September 1958, Dickey wrote, "When I examine my own reasons for writing, I am generally brought back to the assumption that a few incidents (usually concerning my family) have been of extreme importance to me, and in fact seem to contain and carry the meaning of a part of my life. I write verse in order to understand these times and states, and to perpetuate them. I write criticism almost by accident" (*One Voice* I, 278). Wright had written to voice anger over Dickey's review of a recent anthology, *The New Poets of England and America*, in which he had complained about the works of Wright and other poets, including Kingsley Amis, Anthony Hecht, and Richard Wilbur. "It is easy to like them," Dickey had declared, "but difficult to care about them. Most of these are occasional poets; most have been schooled or have learned to pick up pretty nearly any scene or object from memory and make acceptable poetic currency of it" (*The Suspect in Poetry* 42). The two men, however, had subsequently become close friends, exchanging frequent and detailed correspondence. In the letter, Dickey then discussed his criticism: "Though writing poetry myself, I have sort of overflowed into making judgments on the work of others, which I am always somewhat reluctant to do. Once undertaken, however, such a task *must* not be faked. If it is, it is valueless. Whatever 'influence' my critical writings may have will perhaps be traceable to the fact that I insist on poetry's meaning something to *me*: *really* meaning something" (*One Voice*, I 278). His criticism, in other words, "spilled over" from his poetic efforts to understand previous experiences whose memory demanded attention. Because of the convulsions of history and his consequent combat service, he believed himself "desperately behind the position he should have been in" ("Preface"), as he wrote in *Veteran Birth* (1978), his specialty volume of poems written while a student at Vanderbilt and published in *Gadfly*, the university's literary magazine. Indeed, Dickey once thought he would become a critic, not a poet. "I didn't think I could ever be really a writer, a creative writer, much less a poet—the highest calling among them," he later recalled, "but I thought I might be a book reviewer or a book columnist or something like that, eventually on some small-town newspaper.... I was way late in the game" (Greiner, "Making the Truth" 6–7). His reviews, first in the *Houston Post* and then in such literary journals and magazines as *The Sewanee Review*, *Hudson Review*, *New York Times Book Review*, *Virginia Quarterly Review*, and *Poetry*, were at least partly an effort to jumpstart a professional career in criticism.

"Any collection of writings," Dickey wrote in 1983, "is an assertion of identity" (*Night Hurdling* ix), yet scholars largely failed to examine his criticism. Dickey characterized his poetry by referring to its "motion," and critics generally agree that consistent methods of treatment, emphasis on metrical rhythm or structure, and use of particular subjects enabled him to group previously published volumes into collections such as *The Early Motion: Drowning with Others and Helmets* (1981) and *The Central Motion: Poems, 1968–1979* (1983). Later volumes, such as *Puella* (1982) and *The Eagle's Mile* (1990), which presumably constituted his late motion, were included in *The Whole Motion: Collected Poems, 1945–1992* (1992). By continually experimenting with language over his literary career, Dickey sought to distinguish and consciously explore his personality, an existential effort to understand his identity. Yet his literary criticism, because it had carried over from his poetry, also reveals its own pattern of development, a "motion" that derived from the poet's changing perception of himself and his poetic mission. Like his poetry, his criticism "is both an exploration and an invention of identity" (*Sorties* 155). His belief that he was "way late in the game" and that the profession of authorship consequently remained beyond his natural talents explains in part the tentativeness and hesitancy reflected in his initial book reviews. Though he lacked scholarly gravitas and felt conflicted about critiquing other writers, his sense of competition mandated that he confront prevailing literary opinions.

Because he was a new presence on the literary scene, Dickey used his early critical writings to survey and characterize poets and poetry he viewed as influencing American society. In doing so, however, *The Suspect in Poetry* (1964) and *Babel to Byzantium* (1968) established a poetic philosophy to which he would adhere for the remainder of his life, a comprehensive presentation that advocated for poems whose presentational immediacy emotionally involved the reader and enlarged the poet's identity. *The Suspect in Poetry*, published by Robert Bly's Sixties Press, consists of twenty-four of Dickey's previously published book reviews; three short commentaries that serve to group and categorize poets, some of whom are the focus of these reviews; and two long essay-reviews of *New Poets of England and America* and *The New American Poetry: 1945–1960*, respectively. *The Suspect in Poetry* opens with a critical declaration:

> This air of falseness, of the Suspect in poetry, is one cause of the fatal and much-deplored rift between poet and audience in our time. Very subtly, the feeling of basic honesty...has evaporated from our poetry; there is no longer a sense of communion involved: that communion upon which all communication in the arts depends. "The poets lie too much" has grown from a still small voice into a thundering accusation, though it has been with us at least since Plato. (10–11)

Dickey then opened fire on the major literary camps, determined to engage all poetic approaches that did not offer a new and vital perspective on life:

> The poet must evoke a world that is realer than real: his work must result in an intensification of qualities...that we have all observed and lived, but the poet has observed and lived most deeply of all. This world is so real that the experienced world is transfigured and intensified, through the poem into itself, a deeper itself, a more characteristic itself. If a man can make words do this, he is a poet. Only men who can do this are poets. (76)

Against the formalism of the Yvor Winters approach, represented by Ellen Kay, Dickey declared, "In the end one reads this kind of writing only as another more serious-minded and semi-codified form of jargon verse; in any meaningful sense it is subjectless, all 'strategy' and no passion" (15). Allen Ginsberg's *Howl*, which presented Beat attitudes, was only "the skin of Rimbaud's *Une Saison en Enfer* thrown over the conventional maunderings of one type of American adolescent, who has discovered that machine civilization has no interest in his having read Blake" (16–17). An anthology such as Donald Allen's *The New American Poetry*, which featured Beat writers such as Ginsberg and Jack Kerouac, offered "an enormous amount of fairly low-grade whale-fat" (51). The Beat guru Kenneth Patchen had produced "a genuinely impassable mountain of tiresome, obvious, self-important, sprawling, sentimental, witless, preachy, tasteless, useless poems and books" (59). Charles Olson, one of American poetry's elder statesmen, and his theory of "projective" or "open" verse provided simply "creative irresponsibility with the semblance of a rationale which may be defended in heated and cloudy terms by its supposed practitioners" (29). Confessionals such as Anne Sexton, Robert Lowell, and W. D. Snodgrass, moreover, gave rise to "a new kind of orthodoxy as tedious as the garden-and-picture gallery school of the forties and fifties," which amounted to "very little more than a kind of terribly serious and determinedly outspoken soap-opera" (35). Dickey even labeled the Lamont Prize, which he himself had won, as "surely the most infallible badge of accepted-and-forgotten mediocrity our culture can bestow," admonishing readers also to examine the Yale Series of Younger Poets "if you feel in the mood for a sad, unbelieving laugh" (26). Such verbal attacks centered attention on himself.

Yet Dickey frequently tempered this condemnation of other poets, often concluding a harsh review with a qualifying compliment that damned with faint praise, as with his statements regarding Olson's *Maximus*. After noting that the poem is inept and the theory behind it flawed, he observes that Olson "has managed to write a few modestly interesting sections of a long, unsuccessful poem which must have been the labor of years, and these are worth reading" (31). Thom Gunn's poetry "has not the slightest power to touch you (or to touch me, perhaps I should say), or to make you feel that the situation with which it is dealing has any importance whatever," yet Dickey then describes Gunn as "a fashionable, rote versifier of some skill and intelligence" (20). Harold Witt's poetry "displays a good deal of verbal busyness, an air of brilliant slap-dash improvisation, and very little real feeling of consequence," but Dickey concluded with, "Nevertheless, he has an enviable store of energy, and obviously he loves the language. He may yet go through a thousand changes, and one of them may be the right one" (32). Such hesitancy, or caution, suggests that Dickey felt uncomfortable rendering definitive pronouncements, as if he were aware that he lacked the requisite qualifications to do so. However, he also believed the role of critic demanded honest and thorough circumspection, a recognition of its seriousness of purpose. In a journal entry, he critiqued contemporary poetic criticism: "Far too much is made of far too little. The critic is attempting to be more ingenious and talented than the poem, and stands on his head to be original: that is, to *invent* an originality for the poems that can come to them only through him" (*Sorties* 6). Dickey's tendency, then, was to give credit where it was due but always to point out suspect poetry. The attacks this early in his career, however, also suggested his insecurities as a poet.

Recognizing how few "born poets" there are (he identified only writers such as Orpheus, Rimbaud, and Dylan Thomas), Dickey focused in *The Suspect in Poetry* on what he labeled the poets of the Second Birth who, lacking at birth "the complete instrument in their hands," must therefore strive to acquire it, "brought on slowly if at all by years of the hardest kind of work, much luck, much self-doubt, many false starts, and the difficult and ultimately moral habit of trying each poem, each line, each word, against the shifting but constant standards of inner necessity." Each works to become "master of a superior secret" (55). The statement described himself. That secret, Dickey asserted, dwelt "in the development of personality, with its unique weight of experience and memory, as a writing instrument, and in the ability to give literary influence a new dimension which has the quality of this personality as informing principle." He cites W. S. Graham, Theodore Roethke, and John Berryman as examples. "The belief in the value of one's personality," he argued, "has all but disappeared from our verse. Yet the inexhaustible vitality and importance of writing are there, and nowhere else. Berryman and Roethke show us this, as do Robert Penn Warren, Lawrence Durrell, Edwin Muir, and Richard Eberhart." Dickey then concluded with a direct challenge: "Let the poets of my generation ask as much of themselves" (57). Later, however, he indicated that his contemporaries had generally failed. "One of the troubles of most of the poets of my generation," he wrote in a journal entry, "one of the reasons they seem unable to develop beyond a certain point, is that they don't *think* enough about what they are doing and about what they are trying to do, and about what they hope to do in the future. One can learn a lesson from Hart Crane in this regard. He theorizes endlessly, and, though a good many of his theories are rather silly ones, the great poems could not have been written without them" (*Sorties* 26). Poetry demanded continual exploration.

"Toward a Solitary Joy," the short essay that concludes *The Suspect in Poetry*, attacked American commercialism, celebrated the "hardscrabble labor of writing poems" (118), and justified the role of the literary critic as he "takes up again the hard and frequently bitter business of discrimination, which is not the wildness but the practicality of hope" (120). What emerges is the clear sense of Dickey's dislike of his country's materialism and its deadening effects.

> To read even a dreadful poet like Tennessee Williams after watching an evening of give-away programs and "true-life dramas" on television, or looking with half-persuaded and fascinating disgust at the rest of the comfortable and deadening "Consumer's Paradise" around us, where every means is used to persuade us that life, American life, consists, doesn't it, of the radiant happiness of the clean, pretty, harmless and helpful things we buy, and of the nice, fun-

loving people that we ourselves should (no; *must*) want to be: to read even Williams, or Allen Ginsberg, is to have one's eyes fill with tears. (120)

Such a statement reflects Dickey's continued social criticism evidenced earlier in his war correspondence and in poems such as "Christmas Shopping, 1947" and "Coming Home to America"; it also serves as an implicit manifesto justifying the role of the critic, which mandates that he search out the Suspect in poetry "who, like the Devil, is always with us." "Let us be doubly ruthless," Dickey admonished, "and deny him whenever he may arise, offering us a synthetic apple" (120). The admonition served to justify what *The Suspect in Poetry* attempted to do.

Babel to Byzantium, published four years later, after Dickey had not only won the National Book Award for *Buckdancer's Choice* (1965) but also been named consultant in poetry to the Library of Congress (today called poet laureate), expanded his examination of contemporary poets and poetry by reprinting many of the reviews in the earlier volume and presenting additional ones written in the fifties and sixties. Along with critiques of sixty-seven individual poets and a brief essay on anthologies, he included a second section that discussed five specific poems he believed important: Christopher Smart's "A Song to David," Matthew Arnold's "Dover Beach," Gerald Manley Hopkins's "The Wreck of the *Deutschland*," Francis Thompson's "The Hound of Heaven," and William Carlos Williams's "The Yachts." The essays had all appeared two years earlier as introductions in *Master Poems of the English Language*, edited by Oscar Williams. The three essays in the final section of *Babel to Byzantium*, "Barnstorming for Poetry," "Notes on the Decline of Outrage," and "The Poet Turns on Himself," were similarly recycled from previous appearances either in anthologies or newspapers. The fact that the book contained relatively little new material suggests that Dickey now felt he needed to move beyond criticism that outwardly examined the poems and poets around him and, instead, to center more specifically on himself, an investigation of his own identity. The reuse of previous essays also manifested the business approach he was now bringing to the profession of writing in an effort to "sell" himself.

The final essay in the volume, "The Poet Turns on Himself," anticipates the self-preoccupation that characterizes *Self-Interviews* and *Sorties*, his middle criticism, published in 1970 and 1971, respectively, following the critical and financial success of his first novel, *Deliverance* (1970).

Dickey's contention that the poet's inner life is intimately connected with his poems, that memories are "potential raw material for the kind of poetry I wanted to write" (280), and that his previous poems revealed "a strange, incantatory sound, a simplicity that was direct without being thin, and a sense of imagined urgency" (284) centers the criticism in and on himself— *his* poetry and *his* poetic beliefs. These qualities led, he declared, to his conception of the "open" poem, one whose presentational immediacy causes the reader to forego literary judgment and involve himself in the dramatic situation. The essay, then, became Dickey's first sustained critical effort to understand his own identity and to put into practice his belief that personality is, or should be, the poem's informing principle. However, this tendency toward egotism, which identifies the middle criticism and reflects the "central motion" of his poetry, is the quality reviewers and critics such as Margaret Wimsatt, John Norton, and David Kalstone later attacked, failing to see it not as a critical guideline for Dickey but as evidence of his narcissism.

Critical response to *The Suspect in Poetry* was mixed. Kenneth Fields in *Southern Review* and Robert Watson in *Poetry* both faulted the brevity of Dickey's reviews, the latter asserting that most of the reviews were "too short to be effective," though he added that "where he does take space to explain his position he can be very good" (332–33). The anonymous critic in *Prairie Schooner*, however, was more direct: "Reviews should not be published in book form" ("Bookmarks" 176). Reviews of *Babel to Byzantium* were more numerous and more positive. Phoebe Adams in *Atlantic Monthly*, for example, praised Dickey as "versatile, learned, and sympathetic" (114), and Thomas Lask in the *New York Times* argued that *Babel to Byzantium* "is not a book that will be superseded because it deals with all that is 'necessary' and 'inevitable' in the writing and reading of poetry" (M45), a sentiment echoed by Ralph Mills in the *Chicago Sun Times*, who praised the book as a "brilliant and nearly complete chronicle of our poetry from the mid-1950's to the present" (4). Paul Carroll, whose work had been included in Donald Allen's *The New American Poetry*, argued in *Chicago Review* that *Babel to Byzantium* was the "sanest, most invigorating and most fun to read since Randall Jarrell's *Poetry and the Age*" (82–87). Detractors, however, included Howard Kaye, who in the *New Republic* declared that Dickey's attempt at "bodily experience" was "wrong about as often as it is right" and labeled the book "superior entertainment" (28–29). The unnamed reviewer in *American Literature* explicitly condemned the book: "For the most part the comments are amateurish chatter" (436).

With the publication of *Self-Interviews* and *Sorties*, Dickey's earlier reticence either to comment directly on himself and his poetry or to condemn suspect poets disappeared. In *Self-Interviews* he centers on his own poetic origins and the genesis of many of his poems to the extent that the volume is more closely autobiography than criticism. Nevertheless, the discussion of how he discovered poetry, what he feels about it, and where and when he wrote it establishes particular critical ideas essential to Dickey, including his belief that art and the artist are inextricably connected. Other concepts readily appear: art as creative illusion (32); the need for presentational immediacy in the poem (47); the "fabric of memory" as "the only kind of wholeness we have" (57); instinct as a principle of action (58); the imperative to constantly experiment, believing that the poet must court the ridiculous in order to achieve the sublime (64–65); and the conservation of passion within a poem, or what he terms "emotional expressionism" (64), so that energy always seems latent within the poem. What distinguishes *Self-Interviews* and renders it important in Dickey's criticism is its obvious correlation to his earlier statements that the poet needs to explore his identity. Dickey was effectively applying a declared poetic principle to himself, not engaging in a rambling celebration of his ego.

Sorties continued Dickey's dichotomy of poetic voices, separating them into "those who generalize and those who describe states of being" (55), terming these "the meditative poet and the poet of action" (95), the principal difference being that the former possesses "imaginative power but no human power" (90). Unlike his early criticism, he castigated, with little or no qualification, such poets as Robert Bly, Anne Sexton, Ann Stevenson, Adrienne Rich, John Berryman, Sylvia Plath, Donald Hall, Tom Clark, Donald Barthelme, Kathleen Raine, and W. S. Merwin. However, because his comments occur in journal entries, which inherently lack sustained or systematic discussion, the criticism comes indirectly. Although certain principles or preferences appear, Dickey's poetic posture seems not so much philosophically explained as his critical resentment against other artists appears vented. For example, he groups Sexton, Stevenson, and Rich, declaring that they are "desperately afraid of being caught out; of being rhetorical or bombastic" (53). Berryman is "a timid little academic who stays drunk all the time" (52). Plath's poetry emerges from an "hysterical intelligence" (69), while Barthelme's work resembles "cute trash" (88). Merwin writes "a poetry of interchangeable parts" (107). Not surprisingly, reviewers such as Margaret Wimsatt, John Norton, and David Kalstone were hostile to what they considered a self-chartered ego trip.

Wimsatt, for example, objected to the lack of profundity in *Self-Interviews*, declaring that Dickey's reflections failed to explore the emotional, psychological, or philosophical depths suggested by the poems themselves; Dickey, she asserted, was primarily speaking or writing "hogwash" (502). Norton called the autobiographical information "drippings from the poet's mundane existence" (10), and Kalstone labeled *Sorties* "little more than swashbuckling costume drama," declaring that Dickey's literary dissatisfactions, rather than exposing contemporary poetry, sounded as if he were "jockeying for position" (6). The indictment was at least partially true. As the title suggests, the book is more than self-examination or aggrandizement. Although he had won the National Book Award in 1966 and been appointed as consultant to the Library of Congress, Dickey's mission, while focused on examining his identity, was also offensive. He believed himself under attack by liberals for his failure to condemn the Vietnam conflict, particularly by Robert Bly, whose essay "The Collapse of James Dickey" had appeared in the spring 1967 issue of *The Sixties*.

By 1963 Dickey's friendship with Bly, which had initially been respectful, now manifested signs of strain. Bly's influence on the American literary scene was not insignificant, and while Dickey supported the former's efforts to promote poetry, he had begun to distrust Bly's motives, more and more of which appeared designed to attract followers to his interest in, and use of, "deep" or "underground" imagery, the projection of the visual image to access deeper levels of feeling or consciousness, often in the form of sudden epiphanies or revelations of insight, which Bly termed "psychic leaps." As such, Bly was becoming a competitor, not a confrère. In Dickey's view, Bly had already seduced both Wright and Donald Hall, diluting their poetry and seeming intent on altering Dickey's poetics to advance his own theories. When Hall expressed concern over the deterioration of the relationship, Dickey responded in an unpublished letter, "I am fond of Bob; very fond. But this is not to say that I agree with him when I don't, or encourage him to meddle with other—and better—men's poems. He must learn to go his own way, and not ask for disciples."

A general consensus was that by the mid- to late sixties Dickey and Robert Lowell stood alone on Parnassus. Peter Davison, the director of the Atlantic Monthly Press, spoke for many when he wrote, "Of all major poets of fifty or under, there are only two who could yet be thought in the running to pass Mr. Auden's test [for major poets]: Robert Lowell and James Dickey" ("The Difficulty of Being Major" 116–21). Bly, however, thought differently, and in his review of *Buckdancer's Choice* (1965), he issued an ad hominem attack prompted by Dickey's refusal to oppose the Vietnam war. Citing what Bly considered the abrupt decline of Dickey's work, he asserted that Dickey merely "takes his life and laminates poetry onto it" (Kirschten 33–38). Dickey himself expressed indifference and subsequently concluded he no longer cared about Bly. He never published an attack, though in conversations and interviews he disparaged Bly's work. Clearly, though, his strident statements in *Sorties* suggest that he viewed himself as under attack. Aggression was his defense.

The remainder of *Sorties* consists of a series of essays, the last of which, "One Voice," centers on emotionally honest and life-enhancing poetry and is the only effort not recycled. Its title connotes a sense of isolation and feeling of estrangement. In the essay he described true imaginative poetry metaphorically. When a poem opens to the world's possibilities, he wrote, the experience resembles that of wearing the earphones of an old crystal radio set. From the static of the void periodically comes "a voice that speaks clearly through it, and says something remarkable, something never before heard—or overheard—in human time" (*Sorties* 226). While the crystal remains the touchstone, the void momentarily pulls back, and the speaker discovers a new voice intimately connected with the things of this world. In other essays he suggests that such poets as E. A. Robinson and Theodore Roethke constitute separate voices within Byzantium, a critical development from his earlier distinction between born poets and those of the Second Birth. In these examinations, he explores the nature of their distinctive voices. However, since the Robinson essay was a previously published review of Louis Coxe's biography, and that of Roethke a similar examination of Allan Seager's profile, their critical discussion is limited. Dickey describes Robinson, for example, as "the poet of secret lives" (212) and Roethke as "a poet of pure being" (220). Rather than broadly attempting to survey the contemporary literary scene, Dickey now sought to discover the nature of true poetic voices, including his own, by determining under what conditions or circumstances the crystal might become a touchstone. Indicative of this new critical tendency are other essays in the volume, particularly "The Self as Agent," in which he becomes more centered, more strident, and more analytical.

Dickey contends in "The Self as Agent" that while writing a poem, "the poet comes to feel that he is releasing into its proper field of response a portion of himself that he has never really understood" (157). However, because the persona is forged more by linguistic requirements than by any literary event upon which the poem is based, the likelihood that the "figure" is synonymous with the poet constitutes "a misreading of the possibilities of poetic composition" (156). The essay, originally written for *The Great Ideas Today 1968*, partly constituted a response to Bly's essay, which based its ad hominem attack on the supposition that no difference exists between the persona and poet. Dickey argued that in attempting to locate the truth, the poet creates an identity aligned with the poem's dramatic possibilities, a persona who may be part of himself but who acts independently of the poet. Within the poem's fabrication, the "I-figure" moves. As he receives reality, both from the poet and that which the persona discovers, "so his being, his memorability, and his *effect* increase, and his place in his only world is more nearly assured" (162). By this means, Dickey argued, the poet discovers himself. Critics in the sixties, however, failed to comprehend this distinction. Using Dickey's own critical commentary, as in "The Poet Turns on Himself," where he asserted, "What I have always striven for is to find some way to incarnate my best moments—those which in memory are most persistent" (292), they equated Dickey with his poetic personae.

Dickey's concern with his own identity, his self, appears in other essays in *Sorties*, such as "The Son, the Cave, and the Burning Bush," "Metaphor as Pure Adventure," and "Spinning the Crystal Ball." Each begins with Dickey as an informing presence on the American literary scene. He comments in the first essay as a middle-aged poet on an anthology of new writers titled *The Young American Poets*. In the others, he lectures as consultant to the Library of Congress on, respectively, the poet's search for metaphors of discovery and the present movements in, and future course of, contemporary poetry. Unlike his critical stance in "The Suspect in Poetry" or his reviews of other poets, however, Dickey here clearly makes himself the critical center. For example, in "The Son, the Cave, and the Burning Bush," he considers the prospect that young poets might fulfill the redemptive potential of poetry, declaring, "For a middle-aged poet like myself this promise takes on a particularly acute anguish of hope" (166). The concern is with his own emotional reaction. When he then adds, "The aging process almost always brings to the poet the secret conviction that he has settled for too little, that he has paid too much attention to the 'limitations' that his contemporaries have assured him he has, as well as to literary tradition and the past" (166), the lack of first-person point of view never mitigates the sense that Dickey is referring to himself, particularly when one remembers his preoccupation in *Sorties* with aging and death and with his stated concern for the "forms" of poetry.

"Metaphor as Pure Adventure" and "Spinning the Crystal Ball" also place Dickey's self at the center of the criticism. The former opens by establishing the poet's inward exploration: "The longer I continue to write, the more it seems to me that the most exciting thing about poetry is its sense of imminent and practical discovery" (172). The essay presents what he conceives poetry to be, what he favors or opposes, and how he believes the mind operates in relating items. When he asserts that the poem is "a kind of action in which, if the poet can participate *enough*, other people cannot help participating as well" (173), he not only offers his own understanding of poetic effect but establishes his self as essential to the process. "Spinning the Crystal Ball" more explicitly advances that involvement, stating that his lecture "will be partly about what I think will happen in American poetry and what I hope *will* happen" (189). At the conclusion he expands the perspective to include everyone: "That is what we want: to be gathered together once more, to be able to enter in, to participate in experience, to possess our lives" (204). Such an extension, however, proceeds outwardly from Dickey himself, for he then asserts, "I think that the new poetry will be a poetry of the dazzlingly simple statement" (204). This poetry, if attained, will reveal a new, intimate aspect of self, one more vital and enhanced than any currently known. It will share in the forces and processes that govern the universe. "We have one self that is conditioned, all right," Dickey asserts, "but there is another self that...connects most readily with the flow of rivers and the light coming from the sun; it is in this second (or first) and infinitely older being that we can be transfigured by eyes and recreated by flesh" (204). His criticism exposes this possibility; the poetry, he hopes, will actualize it. As consultant to the Library of Congress, he was both spokesman and seer.

Dickey's early criticism placed other poets into perspective on the basis of their poetry, a perspective determined only by the absolute honesty of their writing. As he received offers to become poetry editor of various journals, including the *Paris Review*, he increasingly defended the realm of art in general and poetry in particular from voices that would compromise Byzantium and threaten to render it into linguistic babel. In doing so, he presented himself as a kind of guardian spirit intent that synthetic apples not cast poetry into confusion. His middle criticism, by contrast, positioned him as the literary center, projecting the attitudes he believed correct on matters poetic but also political, cultural, and even personal. It was a role at once broader and more egocentric, motivated partly by the need to defend himself and partly, as Joyce Carol Oates observed, by the belief that "the unrestrained and un-imagined Self must be related syntactically to the external world in order to achieve meaning" ("Out of Stone into Flesh" 100). Although Oates limited the restless concern with self to his poetry, he clearly also used his literary criticism to explore his identity.

This emphasis on exploring his self continued in Dickey's late criticism, where he offered, as he wrote in the introduction to *Night Hurdling* (1983), the threads of his identity: "There are a good many threads here, all out of the same body. I don't have much of an idea as to where they lead, or if they weave themselves into a fabric, but they are the threads that have come, and the air of the book is the air through which I have followed them" (ix). The volume is a collection of poems, essays, conversations, commencement addresses, and afterwords. "The Water-Bug's Mittens: Ezra Pound: What We Can Use" and "The G.I. Can of Beets, The Fox in the Wave, and The Hammers Over Open Ground," in particular, constitute his most detailed scrutiny of his own poetry as a means not only of examining himself but also of determining new directions for his own poetry. As he writes in "The Water-Bug's Mittens," "I sought to clarify my own feelings about Pound's work, and to ascertain and evaluate the aspects of it which might implement the poetry I would presumably write" (29). While this late criticism, however, objectively explored other poets, it did so not to defend himself, as in *Sorties*, but to provide the critical means by which to understand what poetic possibilities remained for him. By examining other artists, he was, by extension, still searching for his own identity, investigations of self to discover the anatomy of a new poetry.

In *Sorties* Dickey had indicated at the conclusion of "The Poet Turns on Himself" the need to move away from the narrative poetry of his early work. What eventually resulted were the poems of his central motion, including *The Eye-Beaters, Blood, Victory, Madness, Buckhead and Mercy* (1968), *The Zodiac* (1976), and *The Strength of Fields* (1979). In *Night Hurdling* the essays set out by design to identify qualities that have distinguished other writers, qualities that subsequently became categorical imperatives for Dickey's own writings. These traits derived from a widely diverse group of artists, not all of whom were poets: the "inquisitive vitality" of W. N. P. Barbellion, the "radiant metaphysical terror" of Robert Penn Warren, the lyricism of F. Scott Fitzgerald, the complete absorption of Jack London in the world he evokes, the total commitment to "his own powers of invention" of Vachel Lindsay, and the "images of velocity" of Joe Simmons. Even infrared light receives his attention in "Visions in the Invisible Dimension," a meditation on the part of light "most penetrating,

mysterious, and dark-seeing" (80). Taken together, these qualities constitute aspects of Dickey's self because they are, he believed, traits he discerned in his own poetry and which he wanted to advance in a new poetic
direction.

The four Ezra Pounds that Dickey discusses in "The Water-Bug's
Mittens" reflect qualities that Dickey long valued—"the Pound of ideas,
discoveries, and rediscoveries" (31); Pound the "inspired image-maker, the
answer to his own Platonic dream-image of the ideal Imagist poet" (33);
"the culture-plundering..., complex-associational" riddler (35); and the
poet committed to "the cross-fertilization of languages, cultures, [and]
writers" (38). Admitting that the third Pound is, unfortunately, the most
recalled by others, Dickey expresses a profound interest in the last figure,
whose translations have opened for him "new writers, new lines, new
sources of imaginative joy, new access to the stealing of the fundamental
Promethean fire, the living flame of poetic insight: the true spark, no matter in what language, what place or writer or work" (38). Pound's love for
all that he believed excellent in the world, while often resulting in heavy-
handed assertions, also provided what for Dickey was most important—
"startling, isolated shocks of possibility: conjunctions of words that opened
up my own rather unbookish but very word-sensitive mentality to what I
might come upon in my own memory and set forth with a corresponding
imaginative forthrightness" (42). Citing Pound's desire for a highly relevant, individualized experience, guaranteed by ourselves and our culture,
Dickey concluded, "A sense of the consequentiality of things, actions,
men, ideas and civilizations is what we most want, and what we most
sorely lack. Pound was on the right side of the question" (45). The statement immediately evokes an earlier assertion in *The Suspect in Poetry*: "Almost all poetry contains elements that are suspect, having no relation to
what readers believe in as 'reality,' and even in a sense degrading it by offering experience as a series of unbelievable contrivances, none of which
has the power of bringing forth a genuine response" (10). Dickey argued a
similar thought in *Sorties*, praising the young poets then speaking because
their poetic voices sought immediacy and consequence: "Such clearness
and passion as theirs has not been heard in a long time, in our land and in
our language" (170). Dickey's exploration of Pound not only reaffirmed
his consistent advocacy of those traits or attitudes that rendered poetry
believable and incredibly relevant or redemptive but also resulted in his
interest in translation. Second languages offered "a kind of magic" (38), he
wrote, with new writers, new insights, and new metaphors. Consequently,

he ventured into poems that constituted a form of linguistic cross-pollen-
ization that he explicitly stated were never mere copies or translations but
rather altogether new works; in later volumes he grouped these in sections
titled "Free-Flight Improvisations from the unEnglish" and "Double-
tongue: Collaborations and Rewrites."

Dickey's interest in translation first became apparent during late fall
and early winter of 1954 when, during his travels in Europe as part of his
Sewanee Review Fellowship, he undertook the study of French. He had
enrolled in Elementary and Intermediate Spanish as an undergraduate at
Vanderbilt during 1946 and 1947, courses for which he earned As and Bs.
In Paris Dickey's French was insufficient to converse with writers or to
read their works. To improve his command of the language and its literature, he bought dozens of books at the city's many bookstores, including
Max Jacob's *Le Cornet à dés*, Léon-Paul Fargue's *Déjeuners de soleil* and
Déjeuners de lune, and Oskar Milosz's *Ars Magna* as well as volumes by Luc
Bérimont, Maurice Blanchard, and Malcolm de Chazal. He read as much
as he could with dictionary in hand. At Cap d'Antibes, however, he set
himself the task of learning French well enough to appreciate the local
poets he already knew in translation. By November, he seemed to have
learned the language. His interest in languages, therefore, was initially
practical; having sailed to England, he was traveling principally through
France and Italy. However, he believed that French artists, with their emphasis on surreal imagism, might enhance his own poetic efforts. He had
not yet determined to engage formally in translation, but that would
change. Realizing that foreign poets offered a larger sense of what language made possible, he quickly immersed himself in the original works
not only of French poets but also of Spanish and Italian.

In 1958 Bly sent Dickey a copy of the most recent issue of *The Fifties*,
the literary magazine which he edited. Bly was openly rebelling against the
entrenched New Critical orthodoxy that seemed both immovable and in-
tractable, arguing instead for a surrealist free verse, an archetypal and
mythic poetry that explored the unconscious mind and that he discerned
in the literature of other countries. His magazine was full of translations,
including a recent rendering of a poem by Georg Trakl that had impressed
James Wright. Wright had subsequently requested that Bly send Dickey a
copy, including two dollars for him to do so, only to discover that Bly had
independently already done just that. Bly found Dickey receptive to his
attitude, for the latter was himself unhappy with the then-contemporary
literary scene. Dickey was already using hallucinatory imagery in his

poetry. Poems such as "The Shark at the Window" (1951) and "The Child in Armor" (1953) clearly reveal this tendency, though the archetypal images of sun and sea in "The Beholders" (1962), for example, lacked what Bly considered "rebellion and contrast." They were, instead, too pastoral, and he suggested Dickey "cut out everything but the images" (Hart 229). While Dickey disagreed with Bly's assessment, arguing instead that the latter's poetic aesthetic was merely a revision of Pound's imagism, Bly did convince him that translating foreign poets would invigorate Dickey's own creative efforts, creating new ways to see reality. In the summer of 1959, Dickey translated the French poets Yves Bonnefoy and Lucien Becker, and he continued such efforts in the months following in order to enhance and embolden his own poetry. In a letter dated 30 June 1962, while he was in Venice traveling through Europe on a Guggenheim Fellowship, he sent Bly a series of French and Italian translations from the originals which, as with his earlier efforts, were sensitively and solidly written. Poets included André Frénaud, Salvatore Quasimodo, and Giuseppe Ungaretti. He hoped Bly would publish this large group in his now updated magazine, *The Sixties*, stating, "Let me know what you think of these while I am in Zurich.... If your letter misses me there it will be a long time catching me, for we are doing some hard travelling from then on out. And could you pay for the other poems now (and any of these you want to print?)?" (*Crux* 188). Bly, however, published none of the poems.

Dickey recognized in Pound his own need for startlingly new ways of seeing reality, approaches that revealed the world's inexplicable wonder and essential mystery and that imparted intimacy and consequence. Language that yielded such highly personal response, however creatively manipulated, became important, as did Pound's insistence on direct presentation of images, or what Dickey termed "the wording or *voicing* of the perception" (31), believing that images, to be most effective, must not only derive from unusual perspectives but also, and more importantly, be just or appropriate. Images center the late motion of his poetry and explain his intense interest in discovering the right literary setting or context for a particular image, at once simple yet extraordinary, as of fish in a flock waiting to swerve. Their poem and sea await his creation, Dickey asserted in "LIGHTNINGS or *Visuals*," first published in 1992 in *South Atlantic Review* and then reproduced from its manuscript form in the *James Dickey Newsletter*, but the image, its "word-radiance" (9), held him, a "personal *possession*" (12) until the exact words arrived.

The essays in *Night Hurdling*, the self-proclaimed and self-proclaiming threads of his identity, also continue his exploration of the nature and intent of poetry. "The G.I. Can of Beets, The Fox in the Wave, and The Hammers Over Open Ground," for example, distinguishes two kinds of poets and opens the possibility, in the title's third image, of where his open poetry might lie, a new realm within Byzantium. The "Commentary-on-Life" party, Dickey asserted, attempts to present what happened to someone or the condition of that happening by using words unobtrusively, like a clear pane of glass, while the "Magic-Language examplars [*sic*]" permitted words to illuminate one another, shimmering off the external world, which acts only as a kind of backdrop to the linguistic interplay. The former group, which includes Homer, Frost, Masters, Larkin, and Jarrell, believed in words "as agents which illuminate events and situations that are part of an already given continuum" (131). They were, in fact, literalists. On the other side were such poets as Hopkins, Hart Crane, Berryman, Mallarmé, and Valery, writers who generated "the proliferation and dance of words themselves, among themselves" (131), for whatever meanings they may evoke. While Dickey experimented with this magical side of language, specifically in *Puella* (1982), he confided that he belonged to the group that depicts the human condition.

His interest in translation, particularly Pound's *Cathay* poems, brought Dickey hope that with such a surrealist approach, where the mind is given its absolute freedom of expression within the linguistic confines of the poet's own formal restrictions, "new thresholds, new anatomies" (133) might open. Against the image of a literalist, Jarrell's "G.I. can of beets," and that of a magician, Dylan Thomas's "fox in the wave," Dickey posited another, offered in a line from Michael Hamburger's translation of Paul Celan, "the hammers / will swing over open ground," a creative re-creation of the literal wording, "the hammers will swing free." In his essay Dickey began a critical search for this new poetic ground where images are imaginatively delivered and built upon but held within the poet's imposed limits, which for he would not so much involve meter, rhyme, or any such traditional poetic conventions but rather "the right kind of seeming arbitrariness" (138), the language having the sense of possessing the world.

If these images constituted correlatives to the kinds of poetry he discerned, other images served to relate the development of Dickey's criticism—the synthetic apple, the old crystal radio set, and the flock of fish. In "LIGHTNINGS or *Visuals*," his last published critical essay before he died, Dickey declared, "Certain images burn as with immortal light. These are ours, and ours alone. The most valuable thing a poet can give another person is this sense of personal *possession*, ownership. Nothing can interfere with it; everything is possible" (12). Yet as critic, he also offered the reader aspects of his self—in the synthetic apple that represented his fear of poetry's betrayal by suspect writers, in the old crystal radio set that suggested his need for momentary stays against the void's confusion, and in the flock of fish waiting to swerve, which held within it his belief in the miraculous possibilities of language to impart to others the poet's own imagination and simultaneously to open the world to them. The development of Dickey's criticism, then, its motion, reveals the progressive discovery of his personality, of the writer as a man, by establishing those values he believed imperative in this world and in his poems.

CHAPTER 10

ANGELS NINE, OR
"THE LORD IN THE AIR"

In correspondence and conversations, Dickey was not averse to relating, even exaggerating, his World War II military experiences as a navigator in the 418th Night Fighter Squadron. The aircraft in which he flew, nicknamed the Black Widow and introduced into the Pacific theater during summer 1944, had a range of 1,350 miles, a maximum speed of 360 miles per hour, and a ceiling of six miles in altitude. It was not uncommon in such encounters for Dickey to use military slang, including the term "angels," which described a pilot's altitude in thousands of feet. When he felt his career was "flying high," he would declare that he was at "angels nine," nine thousand feet, an elevation that would not have challenged the P-61 but which indicated a sense of his literary success. From 1964 to 1972, Dickey's career was undoubtedly at "angels nine." Magazines were paying high fees for his poems. *Drowning with Others* and *Helmets* were nominated for prizes, and *Buckdancer's Choice* would win the National Book Award. His criticism, particularly *Babel to Byzantium*, was selling well. He would win the Melville Cane Award from the Poetry Society of America, a National Institute of Arts and Letters Award, and the poetry consultantship at the Library of Congress, recognition that boosted sales of *Buckdancer's Choice* from 1,810 to 3,752 in the four months following his acceptance speech for the National Book Award. In his 27 December 1965 letter to Lewis Mumford regarding the position of consultant in poetry, Dickey wrote, "I accept it, if I may, in the name and spirit of the American poets of my generation" (*One Voice*, I 425). His first novel, *Deliverance*, published in 1970, would become a critical and financial success and be turned into a major motion picture two years later, earning three Academy Award and five Golden Globe nominations, achievements which only elevated his literary altitude. The European travels he undertook on his Guggenheim Fellowship—the sights he experienced and the poems that transformed them—made possible Dickey's unprecedented rise in acclaim.

On 18 February 1962, five days after leaving New York, the luxury liner SS *France* docked in Southampton, England. A day later, the Dickeys disembarked in Le Havre, France, and proceeded to Paris, a city Dickey still considered a vital artistic center. He spent considerable time at Le Pont Traversé, the bookstore favored by his friend Lester Mansfield and owned by Marcel Béalu, who knew most of the local writers and who provided Dickey not only with the latest news regarding his favorite older poets but also with information about emerging younger artists. Béalu, himself a poet, had introduced Dickey to the work of René Char, René Menard, Louis Emié, and Lucien Becker, the last of whom Dickey considered, as he wrote James Wright on 6 September 1958, "the best young poet writing in French today" (*One Voice*, I 278). Dickey admired Becker's use of the quatrain form as well as "the unemphasized, poignant, simple diction, and the continued emphasis on futility." "Though many poets have written about futility," he noted, "and the occasional ecstasies of love and love-making, I know of no poet anywhere who does this with such divine simplicity and naturalness as he does" (*Sorties* 15). Dickey would later publish a translation of Becker's poem "Heads," which he included in *The Eagle's Mile* (1990) in a section titled "Double-tongue: Collaborations and Rewrites." French involvement in Algeria, however, had resulted in frequent terrorist bombings and murders. Gendarmes carried machine guns beneath their capes at the Eiffel Tower, and Paris generally did not seem safe. He decided to leave, purchasing a Volkswagen bus for $2,500 and driving south to Antibes.

Yet Antibes, too, had changed. "There we found nothing but the shuttered windows of Galidou," Chris Dickey recalled. "Nobody was home. Monsieur Aldon had closed his bookshop and moved on. The waiters at Le Glacier said they remembered us, but didn't really seem to. The wind blew cold gray waves across the bay at La Garoupe. 'You cannot go back,' my father said as we drove along the corniche toward Italy" (*Summer of Deliverance* 107). Continuing his search for inexpensive accommodations favorable for his writing, Dickey traveled to Aix-en-Provence and Cannes before leaving France for the Italian coast and finally heading inland on 28 February for Florence. Their former pension was under new manag ement, but Dickey tracked down the previous owner, Signora Carmaratta, at her present location. The cold, wet weather improved, as did Chris and Kevin's health; both had had bad colds. Dickey visited the Uffizi Gallery as well as the other museums, churches, and public squares that had so captivated him during his previous stay. He was again mesmerized by the statue of Perseus and Medusa and by Michelangelo's *Guiliano dei Medici* and Botticelli's *The Birth of Venus*. His fascination with sculpture, which reveals itself in his early notebooks and in poems such as "The Angel of the Maze," also accounts for his frequent analogy that a poem, like a statue within its block of marble, must be made to reveal itself. When he returned to teaching, he would announce the goal for which his students must strive: "Discovery. Everything is in that. Everything is that," he said to his final class before he died. "We have to fight for it. We have to fight through to it. We have to cut the angel out of the marble, out of the rock, the form of the angel. Michelangelo used to say the angel is already in the stone, all I got to do is chip the rock from around it and set it free. Well, the shape is already in there. It takes a lot of chipping to get the angel to stand up, much less to fly" (*Summer of Deliverance* 268). The extensive work necessary to free the angel and give him flight elevated the poet. "Flaubert says somewhere that the life of a poet is a hell of a life, it is a dog's life, but it is also the only one worth living," he told his students. "You suffer more. You also live so much more. You live so much more intensely and so much more vitally." Poets were "secondary creators," and though the world did not esteem them much, their efforts were inspired, redemptive, and messianic.

During their stay in Florence, "my father discovered and rediscovered this world of Florentine history and art," Chris Dickey remembered, "with the enthusiasm of a child—no, more than that—with the enthusiasm of the man remembering the child" (107). In the tiny jewelry shops along the Ponte Vecchio, he searched for agate beads among the semiprecious stones for use as marbles, the childhood game he had played during the Depression and for which he had fond memories. With its stalls of leather vendors, the Straw Market became a maze through which he veered to arrive at the bronze boar, whose magic nose he rubbed and wished on. "We'd work our way to the chilled, cavernous halls of the Uffizi," Chris wrote. "My father's excitement was something you could feel in the air around him when he'd look at some of the paintings" (107). He told Chris to touch Botticelli's *The Birth of Venus*: "And when I had, he put his own large hand gently, as gently as humanly possible, against the surface of the paint, just to know that it was there, and that he was there" (108). He beheld the painting in wonder. For Dickey, all art was redemptive, an attempt to reach the divine. As a teacher, his course on modern poetry was not a literary survey in the usual sense of a chronological study of selected poets who represented "the tradition," but rather a systematic analysis of the nature of the artistic impulse and the conditions under which it thrives, beginning with the prehistoric cave paintings he admired in Lascaux, France, and in Altamira, Spain. The origin of the creative impulse, he asserted in his lectures, lay in man's religious nature, which flourished even amid his brutal and terrifying life, his living like an animal in the depths of caves. Botticelli's painting, he believed, likely created in the mid-1480s, was simply a more recent effort to move beyond the human condition.

By mid-March the Dickeys had arrived in Rome after visits to Siena, Perugia, Assisi, Gubbio, and Lausanne, renting a quiet pension for two weeks just across the Tiber from the Piazza del Popolo and the Borghese Gardens. "Everyone had seen *La Dolce Vita*," Chris Dickey recalled, "and everyone visiting Rome thought he could live that way someday—if he wasn't living that way already." *Cleopatra* was being filmed at Cinecittà Studios in Rome. "The romance between costars Elizabeth Taylor and Richard Burton was the scandal of the moment. Roman decadence, Hollywood glamour, all of it seemed right at hand and wonderfully accessible," Chris recalled, "and my parents were having a lot of fun" (*Summer of Deliverance* 109). At a bar called Bricktop's, they saw Taylor and Burton slip into the shadows of a rear table. At the Roman zoo, the family lined up behind Martin Landau and struck up a conversation. In an unpublished letter on 22 March 1962 to his sister-in-law Pat Dickey, Dickey wrote, "I have dreamed of this place for such a long time, sitting in dreary offices where a kind of terrible dust, as deadly as silica, settles on every thing and everybody, that I have been walking about in a kind of trance ever since I have set foot on this holy soil." Although he eschewed the Church and considered himself an atheist, he remained fascinated by the rituals of Catholicism. The family visited the Vatican Museum, viewed the pope's private chapel, and attended the consecration of a new cardinal. Dickey also toured the Roman Forum, delighting to stand at the supposed spot where Caesar was stabbed. "Gradually," he wrote his sister-in-law, "I am working back into a sense of reality, and it is a reality far more beautiful and life-giving than any dream." He informed her that he was learning Italian, which he had not done during his previous visit, and attempting some translations, enclosing a short poem by Salvatore Quasimodo, the 1959 Nobel Prize winner: "Each stands alone at the heart of the world / Pierced by a single ray of sunlight. / Almost at once it is evening." The poem provided a basis for Dickey's "In the Treehouse at Night":

To sing, must I feel the world's light?
My green, graceful bones fill the air
With sleeping birds. Alone, alone
And with them I move gently.
I move at the heart of the world.

The Dickeys left Rome for Naples and Sorrento and on 6 April arrived at the small fishing village of Positano, which Richard Wilbur had recommended on their previous European trip. Despite their original plan to travel to the tip of Italy and take a ferry to Sicily, where the cost of living was cheaper than on the mainland, Dickey became enchanted with the town's provincial life—the old women in dark skirts, the lights from well-kept houses, the fishing boats with men tending nets, and the ancient roads. He signed a lease for several months on a small house at 13 Via Boscariello that overlooked the Mediterranean, hiring the owner's daughter as a full-time cook, maid, and babysitter.

After two months of travel, Positano became the center for Dickey's creative efforts; it provided him with the stability he needed to write. As Chris recalled, "We were only there for seventy-five days in all. But even a couple of years later we would have the impression that we'd lived in Positano—really lived there—for the better part of a year" (*Summer of Deliverance* 111). In an unpublished letter to his parents dated 23 May 1962, Dickey wrote, "The good weather has really set in at last: day after day of half-warm, half-cool sunlight, and the big blue of the sea framed in the window of our little house, constantly changing colors. In the morning when you wake up it practically climbs through the window and gets into bed with you." In the weeks that followed, poems poured forth, including almost all those in *Helmets* and such unpublished efforts as "Goodbye at an Office Party," "The Rampart at Antibes," "Umbria," "Europe," "The Bay of Naples," "Praiano Lights," "Net, Drying," "Hand-line Fisherman," and "Church Candles in Crete." "Jim Dickey in Positano had the energy of a man who might die tomorrow, or never," Chris wrote, "and he was writing with a sense of absolute certainty" (116). All reflect his early motion with its emphasis on narrative, the italicized stanzaic line, and the use of anapestic meter. The *New Yorker* was regularly publishing his poems, and *Virginia Quarterly* had awarded him the Balch Prize for "Springer Mountain," a recognition which he exaggerated to his parents as "one of the biggest literary prizes."

When not writing, Dickey sunbathed, swam in the open waters of the Mediterranean, hardened his body with isometric exercises, jogged up the hundreds of steps leading from the beach, picnicked with his family, and explored the surrounding countryside. "My father was building his body every day," Chris later wrote, "he was always trying new techniques" (*Summer of Deliverance* 114). Though later he became fat, slow, and even slovenly, at Positano he resembled his fictional character Lewis Medlock in *Deliverance*, about whom Dickey would soon write: "He was the kind of man who tries by any means—weight lifting, diet, exercise, self-help manuals from taxidermy to modern art—to hold onto his body and mind and improve them, to rise above time" (9). One day, relaxing in a little boat with Chris, he observed Casey Deiss, an American in his twenties with long dark hair and a beard, whose appearance anticipated that of the hippies, climbing the seven-hundred-foot rock face of the cliff around Fornillo Beach on which Positano was situated without using ropes or pitons. "As my father and I lay back in the fishing boat and watched Casey climb," Chris later remembered, "Dad must have felt a twinge of jealousy.... Casey, high above us there on the rock face, a younger man scaling the cliff as my father himself would never have dared to do, must have given my father pause" (114). The image of Deiss clinging to the cliff crystallized the conception of his protagonist Ed Gentry. Thirty-eight-years old with a wife and two young sons, a combat survivor, Dickey had begun to recognize his own mortality, the insistent pressure of time, in a way different from what he had experienced during World War II, where death was everywhere, violent, and most likely sudden. Always competitive yet afraid of failure, believing himself a coward, and desperate for praise yet unable to achieve the high expectations he set for himself, he now viewed the encroachment of age and the debilitation of time as threats, concerns that would dominate the central motion of his poetry. In Positano he wrote "The Ice Skin," which the *New Yorker* would publish on 28 December 1963. In the poem, he presented these concerns in the image of a tree encased in winter ice whose branch breaks when "a cannon goes off / Somewhere inside the still trunk." As the speaker watches his young son, he senses the cold weight of his own years, feels himself

> Stooping more, but the same,
> Not knowing whether
> I will break before I can feel,

Before I can give up my powers,
Or whether the ice light
In my eyes will ever snap off
Before I die. I am still,
And my son, doing what he was taught,
Listening hard for buried cannon,
Stands also, calm as glass.

Dickey never stopped worrying that his talents would decline or that he would fail to find the elevated status to which he aspired. His increasing use of alcohol was in part an effort to stimulate his creativity and soothe his fears. In 1971 he wrote in his journals, "The most awful thing about middle age is that you are simply a body with nothing particular to recommend it.... [A] middle-aged man—or woman—is nondescriptness itself. There is only a body waiting to fill a grave" (*Sorties* 47). In his 1976 essay "The Energized Man," he remained similarly emphatic: "The main feeling I have as I live longer and longer is a sense of purposelessness, of drift, of just getting along from day to day, of using those faculties which we must use in order to earn a living, or in order to experience a few of the well-known physical pleasures so dear to the human heart" (Weigl, Hummer 163). Because time, as he wrote in *The Zodiac*, is "the thing that eats," he believed it imperative, in a world that offered unexpected encounters, to experience great, constantly surprising joy and to feel the exhilaration of a life lived passionately, to "move at the heart of the world." Watching Casey Deiss climb the towering rock cliff at Positano using only his bare hands, Dickey felt time pressing against him as surely as the tides he swam in each day. Yet in the sight of Deiss climbing, he also gleaned the central image for *Deliverance*, which he originally titled "The Deliverer" and which would launch him to the national literary prominence he most wanted.

The outpouring of poems at Positano resulted in part because Dickey had received a job offer from Reed College in Oregon, telling his father in an unpublished 9 June letter that it is "a place everybody is always trying to get a job teaching at; it is supposed to be pretty nearly ideal from every point of view, and the money is the best I have ever been offered in teaching by nearly double." The prospect of freedom from financial worries following his return from Europe helped to release his creativity. The position required that he teach a creative writing class one semester and a modern poetry course the next; no tedious composition or general education literature class was required. Because Donald Justice had agreed to teach the fall 1962 class, Dickey could continue his Guggenheim travels. Reed president Richard Sullivan offered him $3,750 for the following spring and $8,000 for the 1963–1964 academic year with the rank of assistant professor and poet-in-residence. For the present, however, Dickey did worry about money. Maxine and Chris had become sick, and Kevin suffered a mysterious infection that defied treatment by the local doctor. Though his parents continued to forward additional monies, medical bills pinched Maxine's family budget, and Dickey pressed Robert Bly about payment for translations he had submitted. Bly's elitist attitudes toward the *New Yorker* as a magazine that pandered to the American public irritated Dickey, who believed that its acceptance of his poems at a time when the family needed income deserved recognition. Bly countered that Dickey should remain purely above materialism.

In July the Dickeys finally left Positano for Zurich, where they stayed with Gwen Leege Walti and her husband. "We had a fine time in Zurich with Gwen," Dickey wrote his parents in an unpublished letter dated 14 July 1962. Gwen was "aging very gracefully," he stated, "but she is dreadfully nervous and seems rather unhappy, with all her gardeners and other menials milling around and her stiff, formal rich husband who makes such an exquisite effort to be nice to her scroungy-looking friends." Two weeks later they drove to Paris, where Dickey hoped to meet John Ashbery. The latter's poetry lacked the concreteness of detail that Dickey had begun to incorporate, but Ashbery shared his interest in contemporary French poets, particularly Pierre Reverdy. The meeting, however, never occurred because Dickey traveled to England instead; there he met Patrick Bowles, an editor for *Paris Review*, a magazine he hoped would promote Bly's translations and perhaps his own. He also spent several days with Geoffrey Hill, writing Donald Hall on 27 August 1962,

> Geoffrey kept telling me, and almost from the first, about how we "sat there, hating each other's guts," and then in the next breath saying, or mumbling inaudibly, "But...now...for God's sake...can't you stay another day." Well, we did stay another day, and disagreed violently, and agreed even *more* violently (and when Geoffrey agrees with anyone, the sun comes out all over England, a thing which, as you know, it rarely does). He showed me some new stuff he has done which is *wonderful* (by which I mean incredible, stupendous, Ezekiel-saw-the-wheel-in-the-air stuff, and I mean, as the Bible says, in the *middle* of the air. But it's like her early stuff, as I was

exstatically [*sic*] careful to point out to him (as I am to you, and triumphantly).) (*One Voice*, I 373)

He informed Hill that his third book, tentatively titled *Springer Mountain*, was almost finished; many of the poems were slated for publication in the *New Yorker*, but he needed to complete two long poems, including "Drinking from a Helmet." Hall would later convince Dickey to change the title to *Helmets*. "I want to pass out of the first phase and on to something totally different, as yet only hinted at," Dickey wrote. "And then...God knows what. But I have a great, bursting sense of the untried *possibilities* of language" (372). "As I get more bogged down in the technicalities of poetic statement, and in the *ways* of saying things," he admitted, "I still harbor a kind of delighted notion of poetry as *saying*, a divine communication" (372). Finally, on 6 September, Dickey and his family departed Southampton for home.

In early January 1963, the Dickeys headed to the West Coast, driving through New Mexico and Arizona before turning north at Bakersfield, California, toward Portland, Oregon, and Reed College. They settled in a house rented from a political science professor on sabbatical, which Dickey in his correspondence variously referred to either as "a rambling old barn" or "this half-haunted old hotel of a place." The nonconformist atmosphere at Reed, which sanctioned no athletic teams, outlawed sororities and fraternities, deemphasized grades, and favored small classes, delighted Dickey, who decided to teach courses in both modern poetry and verse composition, a practice he adapted for the remainder of his teaching career. With his students and colleagues, he assumed poses, such as that of a Southern redneck (the first black students had enrolled at the University of Mississippi the previous October, and twenty thousand federal troops had been dispatched to quell the subsequent riots), an expert archer, a daredevil combat pilot, and a proficient guitarist who played at local coffeehouses and gave lessons. Exercising what Joel Cahill, the protagonist in his 1987 novel *Alnilam* calls "continuing invention," he believed that such falsehoods stimulated the creative and imaginative faculties and raised his perceptive consciousness.

Dickey wrote Wright on 10 January 1963, informing him that the family had "just pulled into Portland, loaded down with guitars, manuscripts, broken toys and archery equipment, and are setting up housekeeping." He wrote Donald Hall the same day, declaring his interest in doing a reading with him, "for it would give us a long-deserved chance to get together and solve the State of Things, in Poetry and Life" (*One Voice*, I 377, 378). He loved the nonconformity at Reed and was pleasantly surprised by his students' writing abilities. The growing social and sexual freedoms of the sixties, without the drugs and violence, were everywhere, and he relished the drinking and flirtation with female students. "My father was living a life that wasn't about us," Chris later recalled, "and that threatened us as a family because it threatened my mother's whole sense of what the family was and who she was." Unable to control her husband's behavior, Maxine became "hard, that kind of hard you are when your life comes apart...and you just sort of shrug to yourself and say less and less to anyone and take another drink" (*Summer of Deliverance* 126).

The publication of *Helmets* in February 1964, and the laudatory reviews it received, convinced Dickey to press Willard Lockwood, the director of Wesleyan Press, for a bonus; he threatened to leave Wesleyan unless the press advanced him $500 for his next poetry book. Lockwood responded by declaring that he could front only half that amount and assuring Dickey that he would continue to promote and disseminate his books energetically. Loyalty and publicity mattered to Dickey, but he wanted the money only a large commercial publisher could command. He therefore approached Ken McCormick at Doubleday, who expressed interest in his next collection but who would make no commitments without seeing a manuscript. Temporarily, Dickey decided to remain with Wesleyan, writing Hall on 11 May,

> do let me hear what you think of [the manuscript] as soon as you can. I gather that time is of the essence, since the Wesleyan board meets in June and must then OK the book for it to be brought out in February. If it isn't brought out in February I will move to another house, for I must push on, and can't hang fire over the details of getting things published and waiting out publishers' lists. I have too many things I want to write, and the shadow is (very lightly as yet, thank God) beginning to fall. (*One Voice*, I 400)

He settled his immediate employment plans by accepting the offer of San Fernando Valley State to teach from fall 1964 until the end of 1965 as well as that of the University of Wisconsin in Madison for its winter 1966 semester. When he left Portland on 10 June for San Francisco, Dickey did so with regret and anticipation, making a farewell speech and giving a valedictory poetry reading. He had genuinely enjoyed Reed and his first writer-in-residence position, but *Helmets* had been selected as a finalist for the National Book Award, and he believed greater opportunities lay in the future.

In *Helmets*, Dickey revisited familiar subjects with new understandings. Structured thematically around previous concerns of family, war, death, and love, the book was an effort, he declared, "to deepen some of the themes announced in *Into the Stone*, but mainly in *Drowning with Others*." He added, "I thought that the best way for me to move was not toward a number of other lyric poems about the subjects I wanted to deal with, but rather toward an attempt, in William James's great phrase, to turn 'the cube of reality,' to show the same action from different sides as seen or imagined by one person" (*Self-Interviews* 123–24). In effect, *Helmets* celebrates the imagination, liberating Dickey from perspectives that narrow and restrict the world. Pat Conroy, who became one of Dickey's students at the University of South Carolina, would later write, "In the world according to Dickey, the only limitations to art were the blindfolds and restraints we would choose to hobble our own free-folding imaginations" (Greiner, *James Dickey: Classes* xv). In the *New York Times Book Review*, X. J. Kennedy cited the "relentless intelligence" (5) of the central consciousness, and Denis Donoghue, in his essay for *Hudson Review*, noted Dickey's use of "images of survival" that offer the continual possibility of "rising to local occasions, American occasions of insight" (267–77). Louis Martz spoke for many reviewers when in the December issue of *Yale Review* he lauded the format of the poems, declaring that they "tend to open with a taste of actual world around us and then move on into a transcendent vision" (289).

Critics generally agreed that the new poems broke through artificial enclosures to enhance specific objects and places—chenille bedspreads, kudzu, quarries, horse farms—with a rich immediacy that invites personal participation. Family, for example, now includes horses, fish, deer, and even imaginary animals, and war has become an individual conflict against all that debilitates, including an invasion of kudzu, a rattlesnake bite, or a facial deformity caused by a traffic accident. Despite its redemptive vision, however, *Helmets* did not receive the National Book Award, which was won by Theodore Roethke's *The Far Field*.

While his family stayed the summer with his mother-in-law in Florida, Dickey again lived with his parents in Atlanta, hoping to work on *Deliverance* and finalize the manuscript of *Buckdancer's Choice* for Wesleyan. These separations, initially to save money, soon became problematic, highlighting marital difficulties and Dickey's desire for less restriction of his activities. Donald Hall wanted to postpone publication, believing that too many titles on the market would curtail sales of the new book. Sales for *Drowning with Others* had topped two thousand copies, and not only had Bly published *The Suspect in Poetry* in 1964 but Monica Mosely Pincus had also printed a limited collectors' edition of *Two Poems of the Air* for Centicore Press, which Dickey had dedicated to the students of Reed College. Dickey, however, disagreed with such restriction and pressed for an early release date, writing Hall on 21 May 1964, "Nothing could matter to me less than the deliberate hoarding and juggling with poems, the strategic employment of them in the interests of my 'career.' That has no fascination for me." He continued, "We're not in the gold market, after all, but are trying to get something said. And if it's said it should be heard" (*One Voice*, I 401). Poems for Dickey were no good unless they were published. Hall also did not think as highly of the new poems as he had of those in *Drowning with Others* and wanted extensive revisions. Eventually, however, accommodation was reached, and Dickey wrote Hall on 1 June: "I know how honest you are in all things, and am just damned glad to have honesty and integrity of that kind working for me" (403). Indeed, Dickey had asked Hall to become his literary executor.

At the end of August 1964, Dickey moved his family to Northridge to begin the academic year at San Fernando Valley State College, a recently built school whose enrollment had mushroomed almost 750 percent in its first decade and whose generous state funding had allowed it to invite such prominent artists as André Malraux, Anaïs Nin, and Derek Walcott to lecture. He had made little progress during the summer in furthering the plot of *Deliverance*, writing Hall on 26 September 1964,

> I spent most of the evenings playing the guitar in some dark dive in Atlanta where I was known, for some reason I could never fathom, only as 'Clem'.... I also almost got killed again in a canoeing accident in North Georgia on the greatest river in the world, the Chatooga [*sic*] (not the Chattahoochee or the Chattanooga), swam a good bit, read some things I'd always wanted to read, and geared up for the next struggle, which was (and is) California. (*One Voice*, I 409)

With new building construction and an expanded library, the college, Dickey wrote Stanley Burnshaw on 6 February 1965, seemed "a kind of multiversity" (*One Voice*, I 410). The family lived on 8950 Balboa Boulevard, just across the street from a large discount mart, in a cedar-sided bungalow that Chris remembers as "slightly sad." "The yard was spotty and dry, front and back," he wrote, "the cinderblock wall on one side was unpainted, and the wooden fence on the other was splintering; and there would have been nothing to recommend the place at all if it had not had a pool. But it did, and the pool was where we lived" (*Summer of Deliverance* 129). Here Dickey wrote "The Night Pool," published in the spring 1965 issue of *Virginia Quarterly Review*. Throughout his life he always felt a special connection to water; he loved rivers, lakes, and oceans, and he loved swimming in pools. Chris relates a recurring dream his father had which always made him happy: "In it several friends would be sitting around a swimming pool and talking. There was nothing special about the pool itself. Nobody walked on water. And he never told me who the friends were.... But what he took away from the dream was a sense of contentment, of being at ease with himself and the world, as if he had gotten a preview of heaven. He called that place 'the happy swimming pool'" (128). "Dad never mentioned any specifics as to the denizens of the HSP [Happy Swimming Pool]," his daughter, Bronwen, recalled,

> other than there were lots of "pretty girls." One could draw any number of less-than-flattering conclusions about that (and those conclusions would be more than fair), but when I think about that dream—and how much it revealed about Dad's emotional life—I feel so sad for him. A recurring dream of being accepted and wanted and desired, of visiting a place where everyone is happy to see you, and then waking up and feeling that you could never attain that in your actual life? God, that's just devastating.

Dickey and Maxine often swam in their backyard pool in the evenings. The poem imaginatively presents one such night, with elements of the ritual and myth through which he was viewing his life:

> There is this other element, it being late
> Enough, and in it I lift her, and can carry
> Her over any threshold in the world.

Later he would poetically revisit the same setting in "False Youth: Spring: The Olympian," published in 1982, in which the persona, now older and overweight, races his son's junior-high algebra teacher, an Olympic medalist, on a homemade obstacle course laid out around the pool, lumbering

>   down the fast lane,
> Freeswaying, superhuman with rubberized home-stretch,
>   The four hundred meters from Tokyo
>   To Balboa Boulevard.

What mattered to Dickey, and for his personae, was the competition, the body against others and against its own best self.

The dark ranch house on Balboa Boulevard was also the setting for Dickey's "The Lord in the Air," published in the 19 October 1968 issue of the *New Yorker*. Chris had been killing time by the backyard pool when he started blowing on a crow call he happened to have; inexplicably, seemingly out of nowhere, a dozen or more birds appeared, drawn by the sound. They eventually dissipated, their curiosity apparently appeased. In the poem, Chris delivers with his wood whistle "a tone never struck in the egg in the million years / Of their voice." Immediately the birds respond:

>   The whole sky laughs with crows   they creak
> And croak with hilarity black winged belly-laughs they tell
>   Each other the great joke of flight sound living
> Deep in the sun and waiting...

>   Surely like new
> Power over birds and beasts: something that has come in
>   From all over come out but not for betrayal, or to call
> Up death or desire, but only to give give what was never.

Now presented in a radical new style that uses gapped lines and a truncated narrative, the mystical connection—the same surprising union that occurs in Dickey's "Encounters in the Cage Country," published in the 28 August 1966 issue of *Atlantic Monthly*—is less about his son, though the event actually occurred, than Dickey's desire to attain a heightened perspective of reality, a man larger than life who has discovered a superior secret. He needed to center the air, holding at "angels nine" a world beyond simple facts.

Meanwhile, notable poets were extending their compliments regarding his poetry. Randall Jarrell, for example, wrote Dickey on 23 April 1965, expressing admiration for "Fence Wire," which had been published in the 24 February 1962 issue of the *New Yorker* and collected in *Helmets*, declaring, "You seem to me a real poet, your poems come out of life and not literature and the best are a wonderful surprise, both natural and strange. When before too long I have an anthology of modern poetry I want to ask you about letting me have a number of yours." Dickey, however, was still unable to make progress on *Deliverance*, which owed partly to his extensive reading tours. Beginning on 2 February 1964 at the Poetry Center in New York, he traveled the Midwest Poetry Circuit, reading at almost twenty colleges and universities in an effort to increase his income, enhance his popularity, and advocate for what he believed poetry should be and do.

When the 1964–1965 academic year at San Fernando Valley State opened, Dickey determined to undertake a more decided assault on his unfinished novel. Details of the narrative, however, remained elusive, though he would later claim that within five minutes of the initial idea for the novel, he knew the entire plot. Soon after classes started, he cancelled them to begin another barnstorming tour, traveling first to Dartmouth in mid-October, where Richard Eberhart, the poet-in-residence, hosted him. Dickey then read at the YMHA in New York on 25 October before flying west for the Ohio Poetry Circuit. After a whistle-stop tour of the Midwest, he flew to the University of Rochester on 9 November and to UCLA on 20 November. San Fernando Valley apparently overlooked his absenteeism. At the conclusion of his teaching the spring 1965 term, he returned to Atlanta to continue work on what was still titled "The Deliverer" while his family remained at Northridge, an arrangement that ostensibly would provide time to complete another draft of the novel as well as improve their finances. He had finished *Buckdancer's Choice* and then undertaken another extensive reading tour in February, traveling initially to Beloit College with subsequent readings at Miami University, DePauw, the University of California at San Diego, and Stanford, concluding at Pitzer College on 26 April. Because he defined success financially and worried about his earnings, he accepted an offer by the University of Wisconsin at Milwaukee to teach a poetry seminar from 21 June until 16 July, writing Maxine, "It is pleasant here, everyone is very appreciative of having me here, and all in all I would do it anytime for $500 a week." Separated from her, he was "very lonely," and in a long letter to Chris, who was undergoing teenage anxieties and behaviors, he admonished,

> Under the great stars at night, and against the Enemy, which is Time, Death, Separation, we cannot afford to spend too much time in irritation with those we are in the human condision [*sic*] most closely and essentially with. The essential, the great, the best Team

is you, me, Kevin and your mother. Let us spend more time living as though our every day with each other were the last. Then we will have a more adequate idea of what a human family means, and the basis on which it rests. (*One Voice*, I 420)

During the fall 1965 semester Dickey once against barnstormed for poetry in the midst of his teaching duties. From 22 October until 7 November, he read at more than a dozen colleges. His attention, however, soon focused on publicity when *Buckdancer's Choice* won the National Book Award (which included a $1,000 prize) against strong competition: Elizabeth Bishop's *Questions of Travel*, Richard Eberhart's *Selected Poems: 1930–1965*, Irving Feldman's *The Pripet Marshes*, Randall Jarrell's *The Lost World*, and Louis Simpson's *Selected Poems*. Ben Belitt, Phyllis McGinley, and Elder Olson had judged the award. Journalists quickly sought out Dickey in an effort to learn more about him. Dickey himself was elated. He had experimented with what he labeled his "block format," stretching poetic lines until they resembled prose and then splitting them into word clusters surrounded by spaces that acted like punctuation to resemble the way the mind thinks or to imitate short linguistic bursts. Reviews were overwhelmingly favorable, Bly's ad hominem assault notwithstanding. Citing the volume's "expanded narrative" as well as Dickey's use of a "gap-device," Joseph Bennett in the *New York Times Book Review* asserted that *Buckdancer's Choice* revealed "a lensing of the totality of being" (10), and Charles Monaghan in *Commonweal* declared it "the finest volume of poetry published in the sixties and the best since Lowell's *Life Studies*" (120).

In his acceptance speech Dickey commented on the poetic approach to the world in which memory and imagination conjoin to transfigure reality:

> What comes through to me continually as I go on writing poetry is the infinite renewability of the individual human life, both as it is lived and enhanced by the poetry that one knows and reads, and as it is relived in memory.... And each time one dips into that increasingly full reservoir, one notices that everything that comes from it brings to the surface not only itself, but an implicit meaning. To discover that, to invent that, to transmute it into language, is the beginning of things for the poet, and the end as well.... [P]oetry, through its own means, moves toward an affirmation of this kind, taking on faith that what meaning *is* can sometimes be *said*, and that the very saying has the peculiar grace of being able to raise one's random perception of a blade of grass bending in the air to a kind

of *nth* power of fragile significance. It is this that we have, in the end, against the "silence of the infinite spaces." We don't have it forever, but for a while we do have it; and it is, because we are human beings, and because this is our condition, magnificently enough. (*Night Hurdling* 109–11)

The encroachment of middle age, while sharpening the awareness of his mortality, only heightened his sense that poetry was redemptive. He had always been a man at war with Time.

Dickey taught the spring semester at the University of Wisconsin at Madison; because their marriage had become dysfunctional, Maxine and the children stayed in California. "Here I am," he wrote Maxine on 30 January 1966, "having set up my little kingdom in Room 410 of the Claridge Apartment Hotel, with typewriter, manuscripts, guitar—with my clothes hung up properly (you'll be glad to hear), stacks of paper to write on, envelopes bought, the situation at school wonderful, the town good, and a fine two months coming up" (*One Voice*, I 426). Despite the apparent optimism, however, he felt beleaguered, pursued by Time and the diminishment it brings, and he wanted an enhanced sense of being alive. Shortly after assuming his teaching duties at Madison, he invited Robin Jarecki to live with him.

Robin Jarecki was a twenty-eight-year-old student at UCLA enrolled in evening classes and working full time at an advertising agency and part time as a waitress. Sensitive, possessing humor and an abiding love of literature and language, she had first met Dickey in 1962 when he was traveling on his Guggenheim Fellowship. Standing in line at an American Express office in Italy to cash a check, Dickey was immediately taken by her beauty when she asked him about Ezra Pound. When she stated that she was from Southern California, he replied that he had only one fan in that area. After the *New Yorker* published "Slave Quarters" in its 14 August 1965 issue, Jarecki wrote Dickey in care of the magazine. Recalling their brief meeting in Rome, which she assumed he would not remember, she declared, "Quite frankly at the time I was totally unfamiliar with your writings...and, more than likely at this moment you have considerably more than one fan...non-the-less [*sic*], I wanted you to know that you have another name to add to the list of readers who rank you high among the score of contemporary poets." Since she lived in nearby Los Angeles, Dickey telephoned, and they met for lunch. Soon he was visiting her house to discuss books or she was accompanying him to the archery range. Something of a bohemian, she had traveled to Mexico and Europe and was saving money for another trip to Italy; when Dickey asked her to live with him in Madison, her free spirit agreed to his offer.

If Maxine's practicality and willingness to assume daily routines yielded Dickey the time necessary to write uninterruptedly, Robin Jarecki inspired him. His passion for her caused him to consider divorcing Maxine and marrying Jarecki. Her beauty, intelligence, and love of life engaged him, and he beheld her as an ideal. "What matters," he later wrote, "is that Robin and I tried to make some kind of life. We tried to make something with the tools that we were allowed, and they were pitiful indeed. But we tried, and for a while, we did. A very little while indeed, but that is what life tells us we must be content with. Why should this be? It must be. It must be" (*Sorties* 71). When Robin suddenly began to lose feeling in her hands and feet and to suffer constant chills, he became worried and urged her to return to California for medical treatment. Her debilitation, however, continued, and she died on 29 April 1967 at the age of thirty of Guillain-Barré syndrome, a disease that causes inflammation of the peripheral nerves surrounding the brain and spinal cord and that results in severe weakness or paralysis. Only 5 percent of patients die. Her family eventually believed that her death resulted from overextending herself.

Jarecki's death grieved Dickey, who channeled his anguish into poetry. In "The Indian Maiden," he tried to capture, as he wrote in his notes, "knowledge of the body, through love and help." The poem opens, "Where can I reach your blood, / And do you good? Where will it best go / All over you?" "Will 'The Indian Maiden' ever be written?," he asked himself in a journal note. "I don't know. Maybe there is too much there; maybe too much. I am terribly, terribly afraid." In the following entry, he added, "There is an element of play, and fun, and improvisation, and escape. No one can tell me that this is not important. This, Robin Jarecki and I had. We were like children who had discovered sex and literature together, I at the age of forty-three, she at twenty-nine. I think of this as true glory, at least for me. It was doomed, but not doomed in the way that it ultimately *was* doomed" (70). The manuscript of the poem remains lost.

In "Exchanges," published in the 6 July 1970 issue of the *Harvard Advocate*, Dickey again mourned Robin's absence, attempting to commune with her by interspersing lines from the nineteenth-century poet Trumbull Stickney with her memories. The persona recalls playing ballads for her on a cliff overlooking a Pacific oil slick and the Los Angeles smog:

...we sang and prayed for purity, scattered everywhere

> Among the stones
> Of other worlds and asked the moon to stay off us
> As far as it always had, and especially far
> From L.A.

The effort fails, however, and the speaker remains emotionally wounded: "It is I / Howling like a dog for the moon, for Zuma Point no matter what / The eye-damage   howling to bring her back note / By note." Personal resurrection, too, fails:

> Nothing for me
> Was solved. I wandered the beach
> Mumbling to a dead poet
> In the key of A, looking for the rainbow
> Of oil, and the doomed
> Among the fish.

Dickey links his discovery of poetry and her loss with the launch of a Saturn V rocket—"Apollo springing naked to the light"—but he does not name Jarecki. The poem addresses an important philosophical dilemma that Dickey never completely resolved: Platonic idealism and Aristotelian duality. Fixity, permanence, and ideality, so necessary to his romantic sensibilities, are fundamentally undercut by entropy, flux, and materialism; even the pretense that a recognizable dream is achievable remains defeated, and no challenge seems possible. Devastated, the poet can only address the world, saying simply, *"Let us speak softly of living."*

"My mother certainly got word of some of my father's affairs," Chris remembered, "which were none too discreet. He once got a letter from Allen Seager's daughter describing him as a 'real ass man' when we were in Oregon. That was a major melt down. In LA, I learned later, some of the time he spent on the archery range was spent with Robin." Maxine may not have known specifically about Robin Jarecki, but she knew about many of the other women, and they affected her and her children. Her marriage to Dickey continued to falter.

As Dickey prepared to begin his new duties in Washington, DC, as consultant in poetry to the Library of Congress in 1966, Paul Brooke, editor in chief at Houghton Mifflin, urged him to finish *Deliverance* so as to capitalize on the recent publicity and his growing popularity. Brooke wanted the manuscript by the end of the summer in order to complete the final editorial review in early fall; the novel would then be published in spring 1967. Dickey argued against the schedule; his contract stipulated 31 December 1967 as the deadline for the final draft. The duties and requirements of his new post as well as his desire to undertake high-profile assignments precluded substantive work on the novel. A sense of how marketable Dickey had become is suggested by Willard Lockwood's letter dated 12 July 1968, in which he declared, "We now have our year-end tabulations of sales, and I can't resist dropping you a quick note. All four of your books are within the top ten, of all books on our list, sold during the last year. The four combined have sold something over 10,000 copies (whereas the top ten including your four, combined, sold 27,748)."

In summer 1966 Dickey once again drove his family across the Unites States, leaving California and settling in Leesburg, Virginia, just outside Washington, to begin his duties as poetry consultant. They lived in Loudoun County, which his son Chris described as "rough, luxurious hills full of rednecks and Southern gentlemen, long-distance commuters living in cracker-box houses and Yankee millionaires hunting foxes across vast estates" (*Summer of Deliverance* 145). Residing at 47 North King Street, Dickey believed he had once more returned to his Southern roots. The grand antebellum house exuded a stately gentility. Rumored to be haunted and, according to local legend, the place where Robert E. Lee had withdrawn following the second Battle of Manassas, the domicile was situated thirty-five miles from the capital. Dickey immediately assumed his new duties at the Library of Congress, determined not to present the staid formality that characterized the position. His schedule demanded constant meetings, appointments, and travel. Responding to a query on 11 November 1966 about his writing for children, he apologized to Lily Poritz Miller, associate editor for the Junior Book Division of McGraw-Hill, for his tardiness, stating, "I have been enormously and confusingly busy...and have had no time to write anyone but those to whom the government obligates me to write" (*One Voice*, I 432). By the spring of 1967 Dickey's reading fee had increased several hundred dollars, and magazines paid substantial fees for his poems. The *Saturday Evening Post*, for example, paid $1,000 on 23 November 1966 for "Dark Ones." Two weeks later the *New Yorker* renewed his first-reading arrangement, offering him a signing bonus of $400 and increasing by 25 percent the magazine's rate of $2.30 per line. He began to think that poetry, after all, could at least ease his persistent worries about finances.

Dickey's travels for winter and spring 1967 outpaced even his busy schedule the previous fall. From October to November, he was again on a reading tour that began at Harvard, extending west to Washington University in St. Louis, south to Foxcroft Academy in Middleburg, Virginia, and north to York University in Canada. He was also hosting poetry readings at Coolidge Auditorium in Washington, DC, as part of his duties for the Library of Congress. On 22 January 1966 he had met at Whittall Pavilion with previous consultants, including Conrad Aiken, Babette Deutsch, Richard Eberhart, Howard Nemerov, Stephen Spender, Louis Untermeyer, and Reed Wittemore. The discussion centered on Spender's suggestion to have two poets read at each presentation, one British and one American, with the possibility of having foreign poets as well. Untermeyer had liked the concept, stating, "The idea of anything like combat, like controversy, the two points of view of what poetry is today in this particular maelstrom—or femaelstrom—the whole idea of making this thing alive and exciting, and it brings up the idea—then you *Could* have two people in one evening." Dickey, however, demurred.

> I think it's a good idea to emphasize the poetry rather than the poet. But, there's a question in mind as to how to best do this. It seems to me that programs like these that we're talking about, had best be spent in trying to give the audience, the individual person in the audience, the experience of poems. And presenting one or more points of view, setting two people of opposite schools in public controversy with each other, seems to me to diminish the emotion of this entirely. You get arguments about theories, you get excessively theoretical, and it seems to me that the poetry is bound to be diminished in importance, as the personalities of the people debating with each other become more and more important.

Eventually, however, Dickey acquiesced and paired readings occurred throughout 1967 and 1968, including Josephine Miles and Elder Olson on 25 March. He even offered suggested pairings in order of preference, a list that brought together Ben Belitt and Louise Bogan, May Sarton and Malcolm Brinnin, and May Swenson and Richard Howard.

During a reading tour in spring 1967 for which he visited, among other schools, Texas Christian University, Dickey met J. Edgar Simmons, who taught at the University of Texas at El Paso and who would shortly publish *Driving to Biloxi* with LSU Press. Simmons was also marketing his manuscript *Osiris at the Roller Derby* while simultaneously working on a verse novel sequel. Simmons had read "Cherrylog Road" when it first appeared in the 12 October 1963 issue of the *New Yorker*, writing Dickey an enthusiastic letter claiming to know the actual place where events in the poem had occurred. Dickey was flattered by the praise but more intrigued because, as he wrote in an unpublished letter dated 31 May 1964, "there is some kind of feeling of an interesting personality in it." Subsequent correspondence confirmed his intuition, writing again on 14 November, "You've got more energy and imagination than anyone I've run across in years." He pledged to assist Simmons in publishing his poems, recommending them to *Sewanee Review*, and in obtaining a teaching position at Yale. Simmons sent Dickey not only poems to critique but also newspaper clippings and letters of all descriptions, what Dickey termed in a 16 February 1965 letter as "the floods of your fine fury." Simmons arranged to bring Dickey to campus for a reading as well as to receive a key to the city while staying at his home. Dickey would later write of their conversations in his essay "Devastation in the Arroyo," discussions which lasted over three days

> in which all kinds of things poured out: war experiences, his notion of alcohol as a divine form of human fuel, sex, extreme violence, delirium tremens as "a kind of glory," a fascination with music—he was a drummer, semi-professional—and above all endless frenetic pages about poetic technique. He believed in "discontinuous bursts of verbal energy," and claimed to see this in some experiments I had been doing. He sent me the manuscript of his book, *Driving to Biloxi*, in which clusters of words were similarly spaced, or as he said, "spark-gapped."

Dickey's split-line technique, reflected in such poems as "The Fiend," "The Shark's Parlor," "Dust," and "Slave Quarters," all of which appeared in *Helmets*, suggests that he saw in Simmons's poetic experimentation a kindred spirit, allowing him to say of Simmons, when comparing him to Robert Lowell and his confessional circle, "Simmons is larger than they, freer and more reckless, open-ended in form, metrically experimental, full of guts, willing to be wrong" (*Night Hurdling* 77, 79).

Simmons's "discontinuous bursts of verbal energy," such that clusters of words are "spark-gapped," resembled Dickey's split-line technique and his block format, which identify his "central motion," his effort, as he states in the preface to *The Central Motion: Poems, 1968–1979*, "at writing a different kind of poem from the anecdotal narratives of the previous books and lead forward from them toward further, perhaps more extreme, changes" (v). The change in subject matter and method underscore Dickey's insistence on poetic experimentation. "Falling," "Slave Quarters," and "The Firebombing" all depict the split line in which Dickey attempted to "reproduce as near as I could the real way of the mind as it associates verbally." "The mind doesn't seem to work in a straight line," he wrote, "but associates in bursts of words, in jumps" (*Self-Interviews* 184), the gaps acting as a kind of punctuation. Dickey and Simmons appeared to be working along parallel paths in expanding the poetic line and then grouping the word clusters. Dickey complimented Simmons's poem "Reminiscences at the Roller Derby," which *Poetry Northwest* had published in its autumn 1966 issue, telling Simmons in a 6 January 1967 letter, "The 'gap' technique is really well employed here; I like the way you use it a lot. It makes me feel that the thing was worth my doing in the first place, if it can have such a good influence as this."

Dickey also presented to the Library of Congress a list of suggested novelists for readings at the Coolidge Auditorium, including those he preferred—Walker Percy, Saul Bellow, Katherine Anne Porter, Elizabeth Hardwick, John Updike, Reynolds Price, Peter Taylor, and Ralph Ellison. On 13 November 1967, he hosted John Updike and Peter Taylor. In his opening remarks, Dickey told the audience attending the program in American literature, "I am tempted to call it an 'exchange' rather than a joint reading, for I hope that we can encourage an exchange of views between our participants." Taylor read his unpublished short story "The Elect"; Updike followed with "Harv Is Plowing Now" from his collection *The Music School*. Discussion then centered on the methods and procedures of contemporary fiction. Updike declared, "Everyone who writes is trying to find a way of writing, of what his language is to be and what sort of form he is to find. But everybody aspires to write that story that has the complete control that can make it an essay or a poem and it still be a story." Dickey responded:

> This is the kind of attack that surely interests me very much because it seems to me that some of the methods of modern poetry are among the foremost kinds of things that modern fiction is doing— the kind of juxtaposition of a love story and archeology of this sort. That's kind of the method of poetry. This abrupt transition of this sort is something that we expect more of poetry than we do of prose fiction. Or did until the last few years.

He added, "I will say that you're coming closer to poetry and I'm sorta going toward prose." Dickey's recent poems were becoming less lyrical, more prosaic, while early drafts of *Deliverance* show the poetic prose for which Updike distinguished himself. The cross-fertilization of styles reflected Dickey's need to experiment and constituted one reason for his friendship with Updike.

Dickey had also participated in judging that year's National Book Awards and then flown to New York to meet W. H. Auden and Howard Nemerov, his fellow judges, to take part in the award ceremonies in Philharmonic Hall. In accepting the prize for *Nights and Days*, James Merrill not only acknowledged Dickey's critical acumen but also expressed gratitude for Dickey's faith in his work. Dickey was himself then celebrated at a party given by Wesleyan on 25 April for the publication of *Poems, 1957–1967*, a collection of his first four books as well as almost two dozen new poems. Sales of the new book had been brisk; Wesleyan sold 5,153 copies by the beginning of September 1967. He gave a reading of his own poems for the Library of Congress on 6 May 1968, including "Chenille," "May Day Sermon," "The Eye-Beaters," "The Lord in the Air," and "Victory."

Among the new poems was "Falling," which had originally appeared in the 11 February issue of the *New Yorker*, generating more mail than any other poem poetry editor Howard Moss had published. Based on two 1962 articles in the *New York Times*, it concerned Françoise de Morière, a young and emotionally troubled amateur painter and stewardess for Allegheny Airlines, who had been sucked from an airplane on a flight from Washington to Providence when the rear emergency door had suddenly sprung open. Describing her fall in lines that stretched from margin to margin and which were broken by spaces that clustered the words, Dickey presented a rhapsodic, slow-motion descent that mythologized the stewardess into a birdlike goddess who unites with the earth. Several months later Dickey received a seventeen-page, handwritten letter from Andrew Sherwood, one of de Molière's closest friends. Sherwood had become emotionally overwhelmed after first reading the poem. "I am extraordinarily moved by your vision of what might have been," he wrote. Sherwood had his mother send one of de Molière's paintings to Dickey, which he framed and hung in his office and later in his living room after he became poet-in-residence at the University of South Carolina.

With Dickey overseeing arrangements, the poetry office bustled with activity. The report for the 1966–1967 fiscal year noted numerous acquisitions, including a series of taped readings by Randall Jarrell. In addition, it listed 18,383 typed documents; 1,997 reference telephone calls; 731 visitors; and 23 separate performances in Coolidge Auditorium (Hart 369). His extensive reading tours had also enhanced the visibility of the office and increased his earnings. On 2 November 1966, Lewis Mumford extended an invitation for Dickey to serve a second term. Technically on vacation during summer 1967, he nevertheless handled correspondence and attended meetings related to the consultantship. On 9 August he had dinner with Eugene McCarthy, who admired his poetry and frequently quoted it. McCarthy himself wrote and published verse. Although Dickey considered it amateurish, the two men became close. It was a curious friendship, however. McCarthy distrusted an imagination that centered on violence, so tangibly present in poems such as "The Firebombing" and "The Sheep Child," and Dickey had reservations about a political idealism that perceived a world divorced of real human motivations. Dickey, finally, was a romantic for whom passion and sensitivity mattered and who sometimes courted chaos; McCarthy, by contrast, was a classicist who believed in reason and an acceptance of human limitations. Their dichotomy reflected the larger contradictions inherent in the decade itself.

While John F. Kennedy's inauguration in 1960 as president of the United States had seemed to signal a new, youth-centered progressivism in a decade that would see the passage of the Civil Rights Act, his assassination three years later heralded, instead, an increasing social fragmentation, punctuated by the killings of Robert Kennedy, Malcolm X, and Martin Luther King and the malicious wounding of George Wallace. North Vietnam's Tet Offensive and the subsequent My Lai massacre revealed how deeply American morality had become compromised by the Vietnam conflict. Racial riots, campus protests, and the efforts of women to assure themselves equality further splintered the country, creating what the novelist Anne Rivers Siddons termed "a psychedelic breakdown." Against the mantra of Timothy Leary to "turn on, tune in, drop out," with its stress on peace and love, came the equally strident cry of Malcolm X—"Burn, Baby! Burn!"—that followed the Watts riots. As Eugene McCarthy's anti-war message attracted more and more followers, Lyndon Johnson withdrew from the 1968 presidential campaign. Dickey attempted to assist McCarthy's own efforts. In the end, however, George McGovern became the Democratic nominee, Richard Nixon became president, and the breakdown continued. Throughout the decade, the common denominators were violence and estrangement.

Dickey's poetic attempts to enlarge his identity by enabling "creative lies" to explore dramatic situations led critics to increasingly confuse Dickey himself with his personae. He elaborated in a later essay, "LIGHTNING, or *Visuals*,"

> I am preoccupied with what C. Day Lewis calls, in his fine phrase, "the visual word." If someone asks me, as people are prone to ask writers, if such and such a poem or incident in a novel or movie was "based on actual experience," I never know what to answer. To those who have questions of this sort, "actual experience" refers to occurrences in which the individual in question has been either an onlooker or a participant—usually, they hope, a participant—and they do not understand or perhaps are not capable of understanding that "experience" is by no means limited to either onlooking or participating, but contains everything a mind, a human sensorium, has ever had impinge on it: not only "facts" but dreams, fantasies, anecdotes, movies, jokes, photographs, fever-visions, even whatever may come from racial memory. (4)

"The Firebombing," "May Day Sermon," and "Slave Quarters" all depict the violence and social divisions deeply entrenched in the decade, and reviewers, most particularly Robert Bly, believing Dickey himself to be the persona, now argued, for example, that he had evolved from a poet writing sensitive mythical poems about nature to an insensitive brute deriving pleasure from a sadistic relish in power over others. "The Firebombing," these critics argued, presented Dickey's delight in a detached, God-like power to kill innocent civilians in what he termed "an anti-morale raid"; "May Day Sermon" depicted a father's brutal abuse of his daughter in an effort to teach her about sin; and "Slave Quarters" provided ample evidence of Dickey's entrenched Southern racism, for his persona accepts the Southern treatment of slaves. As one critic has noted, "Bly's broadside typecast Dickey in the literary establishment for decades" (Hart 346). A note among Dickey's papers describing his poetic intent for "May Day Sermon" shows the distance between what critics perceived and what Dickey intended. The poem, he noted, was to be "about love, sin, overthrow and escape: I guess, a kind of ghost story in which the principals are not a knight and lady, or a demon lover and a lady, but a motorcycle mechanic and a red-headed country girl." Later he wrote Barbara and Jim Reiss, informing them on 27 February 1969, "Various readers and critics have made various things of the poem, but it really is a very simple one. It is just a retelling of a local folk myth" (*One Voice*, I 450). His literary mission, flying at "angels nine," was encountering stiff and sustained headwinds that were both social and political, opposition whose strength he initially failed to gauge. Though his attitudes toward Vietnam, the Old South, and the women's movement were deeply ambivalent and never as simplistic as Bly and other critics suggested, Dickey's intense competitiveness necessitated that he garner his supporters and keep the throttle pushed forward as he confronted what he termed the New York literary establishment. He also undertook his most ambitious poetry-reading tour yet.

At the request of the Department of State, he agreed to act as a poetic ambassador to New Zealand, Australia, and Japan, flying to New Zealand on 5 March 1968, where he lectured and read poems at Wellington and Auckland before traveling to Sydney. There he met Craig Powell and Bruce Beaver, both poets with whom he developed a friendship. He wrote Beaver on 1 October 1968, thanking him for their evening together. "I have regarded Australia if not quite a second home, then as something like the great Good Place to which I would return if *I* were very good." He asked Beaver to tell everyone who was there, "with the surf pounding and the sun shining on the water all the way back to America, that I remember, and the memory is pure radium" (*One Voice*, I 444). Always needing to re-create himself, he also related how, as an American serviceman in the Pacific during World War II, he had married a young woman from Adelaide, whose death shortly thereafter only increased his special feelings for Australia. Dickey next flew to Adelaide and on 10 March formally addressed a weeklong literary festival attended by 750 writers from all over the world. After subsequent readings to numerous schools and other organizations, he visited Japan for a final week of appearances before returning to the United States on 23 March.

While in Japan, Dickey's schedule called for appearances at the American Cultural Center in Shin-Osaka on 18 March, conferences with professors and graduate students in Kyoto the next day, and readings and discussions at the Tokyo American Cultural Center on 20 March. During these events Dickey avoided reading poems that depicted the war. In Tokyo, however, several Japanese listeners brought up the subject and asked him to read a few war poems. Dickey obliged, and questions followed. In his answers, he expressed his pleasure at the Japanese attentiveness to his poetry. When a Japanese listener fluent in English asked if the poems in *Helmets*, which he believed celebrated war, death, and violence, were consistent with the definition of art, Dickey responded calmly that a poet had the right to address any subject. Another woman asked if Dickey knew that the firebombings of Tokyo, in which she presumed he had participated, had killed more civilians than the rest of the war, including the atomic bombs dropped on Hiroshima and Nagasaki, and Dickey shrugged his shoulders. He had no intention of debating actions he believed legitimate during war or of informing the woman he had never firebombed Tokyo.

Rather than rest, he immediately undertook a frenzied reading tour before leaving on 13 April for London, where he discussed contemporary poetry with M. L. Rosenthal, David Davie, and A. Alvarez at an American Embassy conference and read his poetry with George MacBeth on the BBC. When he returned on 1 May to read at Princeton, he was in high spirits, partly because while there he met his friend Ted Weiss, who had published some of Dickey's early poems in *Quarterly Review of Literature*, and partly because such intense activity always accentuated Dickey's feelings of self-worth. The following day he attended a party at the Gotham Book Mart organized by Farrar, Straus and Giroux to cerebrate publication of *Babel to Byzantium*. The book was generally well received, though some reviewers faulted Dickey's conservative tastes in criticizing poets such as Allen Ginsberg, Charles Olson, and Anne Sexton.

Shortly after he completed his second term at the Library of Congress, he accepted a project proposed by James and Barbara Reiss to comment on his life and writings in an oral biography. On 6 June 1968, the Reisses drove to Leesburg to tape-record Dickey's reflections. Because he was in the process of vacating his office at the Library of Congress and preparing to move to Columbia, where he had accepted a job offer as writer-in-residence at the University of South Carolina, Dickey had only planned to talk for a day or two, but as he reminisced, he warmed to the proceedings and eventually became enthusiastic, agreeing to speak for a full five days. He wanted the book, which was tentatively titled "Listening to James Dickey: The Poet in Mid-Career," but which became *Self-Interviews*, to ignite controversy. Such debate, he knew, would also promote sales. He hoped, too, that the book would result in fundamentally changed perceptions about poetry. Following the extensive interviews, Dickey continued to respond to specific queries from the Reisses, answering their questions about *Helmets* and *Buckdancer's Choice* and about "The Step-Son," a poem on which he was then working. "Let me know how else I can implement the book. And *do* let me know what the market prospects are," he wrote on 20 February 1969, adding, "I have no doubt at all that it will appear in many, many places, and be enthusiastically reviewed and attacked when it comes out as a book" (*One Voice*, I 451). *Self-Interviews* sold well considering that it centered on a poet's career. By 30 October 1970, 4,395 copies had sold; by January 1971, the total had reached 8,500.

Dickey gave the commencement address at the University of South Carolina on 1 June 1968 in preparation of assuming teaching duties that coming January. Although the antebellum house in Leesburg had offered him a sense of the South, he was now literally in the place, as he later wrote in retrospect, where he felt himself home. Attuned to navigation since his Pacific combat, he valued Columbia's symbolic position, "the way it balances Appalachia and the Atlantic...the deer of the mountains and those of the sea...: that is my balance, and it is right for me: the starry place between the antlers" (*The Starry Place between the Antlers* 11, 14). Outside a brick ranch house situated on Lake Katharine, he used his sextant and other navigational equipment to calculate each day his exact position under the stars. Always, it was 34 degrees, 00.2 north and 80 degrees, 58.5 west.

Teaching two courses each Tuesday and Thursday, Modern Poetry (which he called An Experience of Poetry by Americans) and Verse Composition, Dickey finally committed himself to completing *Deliverance*. On 22 September 1969, he told his literary agent, Theron Raines, that he had finished a fifty-page section of the penultimate draft. In December he sent Houghton Mifflin another ninety-four pages of revised manuscript (Hart 402). More progress would have been achieved had not Dickey characteristically accepted two new offers. *Life* magazine asked him to write a poem about Apollo 7, the first manned Apollo spacecraft. On the morning of 11 October, he watched in awe its explosive liftoff, the booster and capsule separating from the scaffolding and arcing into the cold void of space. As if finding the experience beyond his poetic capabilities, he composed three pages of prose describing his encounter with the astronauts in their living quarters. *Life* reduced Dickey's story to several paragraphs and ran them with photographs in its 1 November 1968 issue; the heading read "A Poet Witnesses a Bold Mission." His later poem celebrating the voyage of Apollo 8 astronauts Lovell, Borman, and Anders around the moon, "For the First Manned Moon Orbit," appeared in the 10 January 1969 issue.

A second proposal arrived in early November 1968 when Dave Boss, the creative director of NFL Properties, asked Dickey to write a small book of poems about football. Dickey eventually declined but did accept a more modest proposal to write a poem on football for the special issue of *Life* commemorating the NFL's fiftieth anniversary. What resulted was "In the Pocket." "It is suppose [*sic*] to be a kind of rapid fire stream of action interior monologue," he wrote Boss on 16 March 1969,

> about the sense impressions and thoughts on an NFL—or indeed, any—T formation quarterback as he tries to find his receiver before the opposing linesmen break through to him. It seems to me that there are other considerations in such a mental state than merely the pattern of play: these are thoughts that link up not only with the play book but about man, fate, destiny, life, death, and probably a lot of other things too. I didn't want to state all these but try to imply them. (*One Voice*, I 454)

Although Boss liked the poem, later critics viewed Dickey's topical efforts as a falling off from his early work, the prelude to a more pronounced deterioration during the seventies.

As he continued work on *Deliverance*, Dickey was also completing his next collection of poems, tentatively titled "The Eye-Beaters, The Stepson, Victory, Madness, Blood, and Eden," and attempting to leave Wesleyan for a larger publisher that would better promote his books. While he believed that any new poetry book would compete in the marketplace, whether it competed successfully or not depended on publicity and the money spent on it. Much of Dickey's own "self-promotion," his boastfulness and self-aggrandizement, owed to his firm conviction, derived from his years in advertising, that such activity enhanced sales. The marketplace was another theater of war, and one entered it with as many advantages as one could. Among the larger publishing houses he considered were Doubleday; Atheneum; Farrar, Straus and Giroux; and Houghton Mifflin. He aggressively negotiated with Willard Lockwood, demanding—and receiving—an advance of $1,500 for his next two books, an amount three times larger than any advance he had previously received. Lockwood conceded that Dickey's sales, thirty-five thousand books during the sixties, merited the money. However, on 9 October 1968, Ken McCormick at Doubleday offered him $25,000 for his next two works, and when neither Farrar, Straus and Giroux nor Houghton Mifflin matched the offer, he left Wesleyan for Doubleday.

In *The Eye-Beaters, Blood, Victory, Madness, Buckhead and Mercy*, Dickey decisively entered into his "central motion," abandoning his compact, myth-laden poems in favor of a more expansive, less restrictive form. The new poems, including "Diabetes," "Mercy," "The Cancer Match,"

"Venom," and "Blood," suggest a larger self-awareness; less centered on personal identity, they exhibit a preoccupation with aging, disease, and death, the individual against unstoppable forces. Against the affirmation and afflatus of "Seeking the Chosen," for example, published in the 25 November 1965 issue of the *Times Literary Supplement*, where the persona realizes that "I still could achieve it, still rise," he now posited the doubt and uncertainty of "The Cancer Match," where the speaker understands,

> I don't have all the time
> In the world, but I have all night.
> I have space for me and my house,
> And I have cancer and whiskey.

Dickey's concern with disease may have stemmed from a physician's misdiagnosis of symptoms related to diabetes, but he had long been conscious of such progressive disabilities.

Although this central motion typographically opens itself through long lines gapped with words and phrases that physically invite a shared participation, it offers no sense of closure, of ideas and attitudes being definitively decided. Dickey's principal thematic concerns of family, war, death, and love remain, but they broaden to reveal a social consciousness. His sense of affirmation, his innate belief in imaginative possibilities, becomes more tenuous and strained than in previous volumes. At times, it cannot even be discerned, as if he has given himself over to Aristotelian attitudes of flux and finitude. Platonic ideality is abandoned. The titles of his early collections reflected his knowledge of advertising, his marketing of the best poem in each volume in order to "promote" the entire volume. However, *The Eye-Beaters, Blood, Victory, Madness, Buckhead and Mercy* offers as a title a series of poems that, while reflecting the long, extended lines of the poems themselves, also suggests indecision or even confusion, though it might be argued that the title poems, instead, offer variations on a theme. Despite its important position in Dickey's canon, however, the volume received scant critical attention. Early commentary was unfavorable, largely because reviewers perceived the poetic technique as prosaic. Robert Shaw, for example, in his July 1971 review in *Poetry*, believed *The Eye-Beaters* full of "long-winded loquacious poems, springing from a milieu of tall tales, yarns, leisurely long-summer-evening-front-porch stories" (230). His review, titled simply "Poets in Midstream," argued that Dickey insistently talked *to* the reader rather than engaging him imaginatively. The gap-stopped lines build tension in a poem like "Madness," but in "The Eye-Beaters" the spacing technique seems only "chronic stutter." Benjamin DeMott, in his 28 March 1970 review in the *Saturday Review*, called the collection "death-obsessed, dense with assault and pain." While Dickey physically endeavors to grasp the world, DeMott declared, the poems seem "a contrivance for one particular aptitude" (26) that lacks form and becomes directionless. Herbert Leibowitz, in his 8 November 1970 review in the *New York Times Book Review*, reflected the views of many readers when, citing "Looking for the Buckhead Boys," "Living There," and "Mercy" as examples, he asserted that Dickey was floundering in a "poetic backwater" and that a hysteria resembling "a childish petulance" pervades the poems. They offer few answers to what Leibowitz sees as "self-mistrust and backsliding" (22). Even the title, he asserted, suggests a debate about the future course of Dickey's art.

In middle age, Dickey worried about aging generally and his health specifically. He wrote in his journal, "I must let youth go, and liquor with it. To me liquor is youth, since I don't have the right, slight number of years anymore; but I must find something better." He counseled himself: "If I slowed my life down, and lived more like an ordinary person, I might live a very long time and that is supposed to be the desired object of all human life. But it is not. The main thing is to ride the flood tide. Only a few get the chance to do this and one year of it is worth a thousand years of mediocrity" (Sorties 73, 75). Entries in Sorties, published the same year as The Eye-Beaters, reflect this abiding sense of concern. The first entry states, "You cannot feel your blood run. You can feel the pulse, but not what the pulse does: not what the pulse is" (3), and becomes more pointed: "The sadness of middle age is unfathomable; there is no bottom to it. Everything you do is sad" (55). As the decade progressed, so did his despair, deepened not only by declining health, thinning hair, and the loss of physical abilities, but also by the death of his parents and his wife, Maxine. "Doctors only tell me to do that which I cannot possibly do. My only hope is to gamble on their knowing nothing whatever about what they are telling me," he wrote. "How can I possibly hurt in so many places at the same time" (75). He was drinking excessively, beginning in the morning and continuing throughout the day. Partly, the alcohol fueled his imagination; partly, it alleviated fears and insecurities. To distract himself from himself, he pursued navigational interests—exploring his position in the universe with sextant, chronometer, circular slide rule, artificial horizon, and other mathematical and celestial

instruments—as well as playing guitar, ordering tapes of Ron Brentano
and Ry Cooder to which he could practice. To satisfy his desire to possess
and be the best, he bought a twelve-string custom guitar from Roy Noble
of Custom Guitars in California. He also purchased a painting by Anthony Rossiter entitled Storm Struck Corn, which was "the kind of picture I would try to paint if I had any talent as a painter, which I emphatically do not" (One Voice, I 466).

His literary pursuits were becoming more varied as well—some critics would say less demanding. Although he had scaled back his readings
while increasing his fee to $2,000, he was pushing forward not only with
Deliverance and The Eye-Beaters but also with another critical book,
which would become Sorties. In addition, he agreed to a request by Encyclopedia Britannica to document on film his life and writing and to
assist in organizing the cast, even asking Robert Lowell to participate.
"It might have some good effects," he wrote Lowell on 15 October 1969,
"for the benefit of the Generations to Come" (One Voice, I 482). The
movie was Lord, Let Me Die But Not Die Out, the title derived from
the last line of his 1966 poem "The Last Wolverine." Dickey was also
tangentially involved in another 16-mm film based on his poem "May
Day Sermon."

As 1969 ended, he had achieved unimagined success, but his extensive barnstorming tours, teaching duties, and varied literary and film projects all combined with both his heavy drinking and his need to become
an ever-larger success to undercut his energy and imaginative sensitivities. With each critical and financial accomplishment, he was driven to
win even more awards and to earn even more money. It was as if no
victory could win the war Dickey was waging within himself. Joseph
Campbell, in discussing the mythic hero after his miraculous passage and
subsequent return, observed:

> The battlefield is symbolic of the field of life, where every crea-
> ture lives on the death of another. A realization of the inevita-
> ble guilt of life may so sicken the heart that...one may refuse to
> go on with it. On the other hand,...one may invent a false, fi-
> nally unjustified, image of oneself as an exceptionable phenom-
> enon in the world, not as guilty as others are, but justified in
> one's inevitable sinning because one represents the good. (The
> Hero with a Thousand Faces 238)

While Dickey's letters to James Wright and others claim that suicide was an old foe against which he constantly fought, he never considered such an act for himself, despite the self-destruction of other poets he knew, including John Berryman and Randall Jarrell. Nor does his correspondence indicate any "guilt" toward those with whom he "battled," writers such as Lowell and Bly, or editors such as Lockwood. The letters, moreover, show no remorse for his condemnation of critics and reviewers he felt foisted suspect poetry on the American public. Indeed, what is most noticeable in the correspondence from the sixties is Dickey's sense of his own rightness, a belief that he served the highest cause—POETRY. Occasionally, he was contrite for his actions, as when he wrote Anne Sexton on 17 February 1966 to apologize for a late-night telephone call in which he insisted she profess her love for him: "It was one of those things that those I like the best are privileged to have visited upon them when I get lonely and drunk enough.... I *am* sorry" (*One Voice*, I 428).

According to Campbell, the true goal of myth, and of the mythic hero, is the "reconciliation of individual consciousness with the universal will," a unity achieved through "a realization of the true relationship of the passing phenomena of time to the imperishable life that lives and dies in all" (238). Dickey clearly had a sense of time passing and of the effects of that passage, even reflecting back in his 17 December 1969 missive to Philip Rahv to thank him for a kindness delivered "years ago." *Self-Interviews* and *Sorties*, moreover, constituted a reexamination of where he had been and where he should go. Yet such an intimate recollection did not arrive for another twenty-five years, when in falling health he presented that realization in letters and in his poetry, particularly *The Eagle's Mile*. Only then did he seem to understand this harmony. Indeed, though he returned to the South in 1968 as writer-in-residence at the University of South Carolina, a position which he held until his death in 1997, his adventure was only starting. His best seller, *Deliverance*, and the subsequent widespread public recognition, enhanced by television appearances, gained him such notoriety that Jimmy Carter asked him to participate in his 1976 presidential inauguration, where Dickey read "The Strength of Fields." Other trials awaited, however, including the critical failures of *The Strength of Fields* (1976) and *The Zodiac* (1979) and the death of Maxine.

In the unparalleled glamour following the publication of *Deliverance*, Dickey soared beyond anything he might have imagined when, as a six-year-old boy, he had composed a five-page autobiography, "The Life of James Dickey," characterizing himself as a combat pilot and illustrating the book with crayoned pictures of airplanes. Reflecting on the novel's publication, Matthew Bruccoli, a colleague at the University of South Carolina who become Dickey's close friend and literary executor, stated, "It was a very good and a very bad experience for Jim. It gave him an enlarged readership, but with the money he made from it, he began living too well and stopped working as hard as he had. I'm not saying he was corrupted, but the spur wasn't there anymore." Popular and critical interest in *Deliverance*, for which Dickey received a $5,000 advance, increased when *Atlantic Monthly* in its February 1970 issue printed an excerpt of the novel entitled "Two Days in September." Houghton Mifflin published the book in March with a first printing of fifty thousand, a high number for an author whose previous books were either collections of poetry or critical books about poetry, the largest printing of which had been 7,500 copies. By 21 July, *Deliverance* had sold 67,000 hardback copies and become a best seller. The paperback, published by Dell, was released in April 1971. By its eighth printing in June 1973, sales had reached 1,800,000 copies. Dickey seemed baffled by the response. Despite acclaim for the novel, he considered himself primarily a poet, but the financial windfall overwhelmed him. "All this is very strange," he wrote on 13 April 1970, to Jonathan Williams, a poet and founder of the Jargon Society, a small press specializing in poetry, art, photography, and fine printing, "to someone who is use [*sic*] to counting his literary earnings at the rate of fifty cents a line, doled out on that basis from *Kenyon Review*" (Bruccoli, Baughman 327). He reiterated the same point to Willie Morris, an editor at *Harper's*, in an unpublished letter dated 20 May: "All this is kind of strange to me, though very gratifying, as you may imagine." Dickey earned approximately $20,000 in paperback rights and $17,500 from the Literary Guild rights in 1970. The following year royalties totaled $45,000 (Hart 455).

The success of *Deliverance* changed Dickey's literary reputation, making him one of the country's best-known writers, but the fame arrived at a price; in gaining such heights, he lost his poetic bearings. He even appears to have been aware of the danger, writing Ken McCormick, his editor at Doubleday, in an unpublished letter dated 8 April 1970: "I *do* want you to know that I am battling hard to keep our book [*The Eye-Beaters, Blood, Victory, Madness, Buckhead and Mercy*] from being swamped by the attention paid to *Deliverance*, just as I have always fought to keep poetry itself from being ignored in the attention paid to the novel, generally." He expressed the same sentiment the following month to Donald Hall, who worried that Dickey would now abandon his poetry. In an unpublished letter dated 22 May, he thanked Hall for

> the things you say about *Deliverance*, and about the poetry. No; have no fear, I will not "go down for (on) poetry." Poetry is the center and the basis of everything I do, whether this is criticism, novel-writing, or even writing the advertising copy I used to do. So, if and when poetry goes for me, so will everything else, so far as the written word is concerned. So I will hang on to that before everything else.

Dickey's letters, however, clearly indicate that he became increasingly caught up by and involved in the publicity and fanfare, interviews and television appearances, surrounding both the publication of the novel and the subsequent filming of the movie, for which he wrote the script and in which he played a small part.

Dickey had worked on the novel throughout 1969, attempting to revise diction he considered too poetic for the narrator, Ed Gentry, the vice president of an advertising agency. In a 1976 interview he reflected on this concern with language:

> *Deliverance* was originally written in a very heavily charged prose, somewhat reminiscent of James Agee. But it was too juicy. It distracted from the narrative thrust, which is the main thing that the story has going for it. So I spent two or three drafts taking that quality out. I wanted a kind of unobtrusively remarkable observation that wouldn't call attention to itself. That's why I made the narrator an art director. He's a guy who *would* see things like this; a writer would perform all kinds of cakewalks to be brilliant stylistically, which would have interfered with the narrative drive of the story. (Ashley 77)

Jacques de Spoelberch, Dickey's editor at Houghton Mifflin, pressed for the revision of certain scenes. His efforts enhanced the novel's tight, at moments lyrical, flow, though reviewers nevertheless questioned the language. Evan S. Connell, for example, who reviewed *Deliverance* in the 22 March 1970 *New York Times Book Review*, noted that "it is just barely possible to accept the voice of a domesticated American businessman narrating such a horror story," adding, "the story is told in the past tense, yet it is full of absolutely remembered dialogue." Despite this reservation, however, Connell began the front-page review with unmitigated praise: "*Deliverance* is James Dickey's first novel and it is bad news for the competition" (1, 23). Reviews in *Newsweek*, *Time*, and *Life* were similarly good. Yet critics generally failed, as happened with Melville's *Moby-Dick*, to regard the novel as critically significant, largely discerning instead an adventure story. Benjamin DeMott, for example, in the 28 March 1970 issue of the *Saturday Review*, was typical when he dismissed the book as "entertaining, shoot'em-up mindlessness" and an "emptily rhetorical horse-opera played in canoes" (25–26, 38). Only later did critics properly understand the novel's mythic underpinnings and its significance in the development of American literature.

Dickey's reading of anthropologists and mythologists while at Vanderbilt provided him with the mythology that underlies *Deliverance*. In a 1949 issue of *Kenyon Review*, he had read Stanley Edgar Hymen's discussion of several books involving ritual and myth, including Joseph Campbell's *The Hero with a Thousand Faces*, in which Hymen quotes van Gennep's "Rites of Passage" as depicting "a separation from the world, a penetration to a source of power, and a life-enhancing return." The review provided Dickey with the narrative framework of his novel. Over a three-day canoe trip in the wilderness, the protagonist achieves an intimate connection with nature and returns home not with a golden fleece or a beautiful princess but rather with a treasure more intangible and more transcendent. "And so it ended," Gentry thinks, "except in my mind, which changed the events more deeply into what they were, into what they meant to me alone." He understands now what only he possesses: "The river underlies, in one way or another, everything I do" (*Deliverance* 274, 275–76).

As he exchanged a series of letters with Spoelberch discussing revision, Dickey inexplicably worried that some harm would befall either the manuscript or himself. On 5 August 1969, for example, he wrote a seventeen-page unpublished missive detailing proposed alterations throughout the typescript. "I have completed working on the book," he declared, "as you will see when I give you the manuscript in Boston next week. This letter is in the nature of a safety device in the unlikely event that something happens to the manuscript on the airplane or somewhere between here and Boston." The next day he wrote a shorter letter with additional changes he wished to make, asserting that "this is a precaution: it has to do with the unlikely eventuality that I, my wife, my family, vanish without a trace—or, maybe more to the point—without a trace of the manuscript." Later he would express a similar concern regarding *The Zodiac*, when in 1973 he instructed Stewart Richardson, his editor at Doubleday, not only about revisions he wanted to include but also about how the book-length poem should be marketed if anything should happen to him. It is unclear why Dickey felt threatened. Certainly, he courted the attention, but he was always conscious of chance and luck.

That insecurity owed to the increased economic and political instability during the late sixties and early seventies, including coups in Syria, Uganda, Chile, and Ethiopia; terrorism, moreover, was increasing around the world. Palestinians belonging to the terrorist group Black September organization kidnapped and murdered eleven Israeli athletes at the 1972 Olympic Games. Groups in Europe, such as the Red Brigade and the Baader-Meinhof Gang, were responsible for a spate of bombings, kidnappings, and murders. Weather Underground and the Symbionese Liberation Army were operating in the United States. Gwen Leege Walti, writing Dickey on 19 September 1970, expressed concern for her safety as she prepared to fly from Zurich to New York: "Should something happen on my trip tomorrow, know that you, Golden Boy, have been a wondrous, important part of my life for which I am grateful. I wish you and Maxine continued good fortune; don't get snowed under with golden cadillacs. I hope you can have that spacious modern house, & the mink coat etc you dreamed of giving Maxine."

In the 8 April 1970 letter to Ken McCormick, Dickey declared that he was selling as many copies of *The Eye-Beaters* as he was of *Deliverance* and that he hoped sales would soon top ten thousand copies, helped by his readings at Young Harris College on 2 April and Oklahoma State University on 4 April. Although sales of the poetry collection did reach the hoped-for number in late May, *The Eye-Beaters* could never attain the novel's popular success. Dickey also informed McCormick that sales of *Deliverance* were approaching one hundred thousand, an inflated figure since Houghton Mifflin's initial printing on 23 March had totaled fifty thousand. The exaggeration resulted partly from his competitiveness, his need to be best at everything he attempted. *Deliverance* was competing against Erich Segal's *Love Story*, Mario Puzo's *The Godfather*, and John Fowles's *The French Lieutenant's Woman*. The boasting, however, was also partly an effort to overcome feelings of inadequacy by projecting a confident superiority. In other words, the best defense was a good offense. He always needed his voice to be the loudest, the most acknowledged, and because literary success was defined by sales, he misled others to promote himself. The novel never reached number one on the *New York Times* bestseller list; in early June, sales slackened after *Deliverance* reached number three.

Dickey's competitiveness led to friction with John Boorman, whom Warner Brothers had hired to direct the movie version of the novel. Initially, the company wanted Roman Polanski, whom Dickey considered a mood director lacking the ability to project action well. He also worried about the recent murder of Polanski's wife, Sharon Tate. Dickey preferred Sam Peckinpah, whose recent film, *The Wild Bunch*, he admired for its treatment of violence within a civilized setting. The doomed gunslingers resembled the doomed adventurers in *Deliverance*. Peckinpah, an ex-Marine whose specialty was Westerns, had proven himself adept in depicting dangerous men in dangerous situations. He and Dickey met in London. "We talked almost the whole day long," Dickey later told his son Chris, "and I really thought he was going to be good. He had everything down in his head just like he wanted it." Peckinpah had said that what they both wanted, he in movies and Dickey in poetry, was "to create images people cannot forget." "My father thought that was so right that more than a quarter-century later," Chris wrote, "he could even remember where and when Peckinpah said it, in the late afternoon standing there in Regent's Street saying goodbye" (*Summer of Deliverance* 164). The selection of Boorman, however, excited Dickey. Boorman's film, *Hell in the Pacific*, had portrayed a single Japanese soldier and a lone American fighter isolated on a Philippine island where they engage in combat to the death. The movie reminded him of his own experiences in the Pacific during World War II, which *Deliverance* indirectly re-created, and imparted to the action a philosophical, even existential dimension that reduced life to its essential elements.

Dickey had written the screenplay, disregarding sample scripts Warner Brothers had sent, including that for *Clockwork Orange*. He used as examples, instead, treatments written by James Agee. Warner Brothers approved the script on 20 August, but Boorman immediately proposed alterations that substantially changed the novel's opening and closing scenes and revised the dialogue. At the center of the disagreement was the question of who controlled the script, which is to say, what the film's emphasis would be. To enhance the action, Boorman wanted to place the four suburbanites on the river as quickly as possible; by contrast, Dickey insisted on preserving the novel's mythical structure, the circular movement that would effectively render *Deliverance* a contemporary representation of the *Odyssey*. He believed "the hero with a thousand faces" to be, he wrote Boorman on 18 January 1971, "the most powerful theme in all of literature, all of mythology" (*One Voice*, II 118). Despite attempts at reconciliation,

Dickey concluded that Boorman lacked artistic vision, and Boorman believed Dickey was cinematically shortsighted and would remain intrusive; as a consequence, Boorman assumed complete control of the screenplay. Dickey, who had been informed in December that John Calley of Warner Brothers would accept a script only by the director, nevertheless insisted that he alone receive screenwriting credit. While Boorman later claimed that "in fact, I wrote the script; it wasn't he who actually drafted it" (Hart 475), the Credit Arbitration Committee determined in Dickey's favor. Dickey's efforts to influence the selection of actors and musicians, however, were ineffectual. Not only was Jon Voight selected to play Ed Gentry despite Dickey's attempt to use a cast with no star, but Dickey was also unable to fulfill a promise to Mike Russo and Ron Brentano that they would play the music for "Dueling Banjoes." Final defeat came when Boorman asked Dickey to leave Clayton, Georgia, where the movie was being shot, because he was interfering too much with the director and the actors.

That he viewed himself constantly at war is evidenced by an unpublished letter dated 9 October 1970 to Christopher Sinclair-Stevenson of Hamish Hamilton, his British publisher, who had informed him that sales of *Deliverance* were going "extremely well." While obviously pleased, Dickey remained concerned about the critical reception of *The Eye-Beaters*, pleading, "For God's sake, *do* get Vernon Scannell or Dennis Enright or somebody over there who *likes* my poetry to review the poetry book when it comes out. A lot of people over there apparently dislike my verse rather violently, and we'll need something to redress the balance!"

In the fifties and sixties, Dickey had struggled to win in a literary field dominated first by modernists and then by Beats and confessionals. He had gained the advantage, risen, and commanded the artistic skies, but such distinction only required that he achieve greater success. It also made him more visibly a target. As he wrote in "The Cancer Match," first published in the June 1969 issue of *Poetry* and included in *The Eye-Beaters*:

> Tonight we are going
> Good better and better we are going
> To win, and not only win but win
> Big, win big.

For Dickey, each "win" had to be bigger than the last.

With his psychological need for increasing recognition, he actively began to solicit honorary degrees. When Austin Briggs at Hamilton College in New York asked him to contribute to a volume honoring its alumnus Ezra Pound in order to fund a lectureship in Pound's name, Dickey declined in an unpublished letter dated 17 August 1970, citing commitments regarding *Deliverance*. He added, "Although I myself would probably not be able to take the Pound Lectureship were it offered to me, I would like for you to count me in as far as making recommendations for it is concerned." In correspondence dated 2 November, he then informed Briggs, "I have held off accepting honorary degrees, but I would surely accept one from Ezra Pound's old college.... I am kind of touchy about this subject. I have turned down a good many degrees from schools that did not seem to me to have the proper literary associations yours does." As Wesleyan College in Georgia and College of Charleston in South Carolina did, Hamilton agreed to Dickey's request; a year later, Moravian College also gave him an honorary degree. Dickey continued to invite such honors throughout the seventies and into the eighties, often making it a condition for a reading or an address. When Pitzer College, for example, asked him to speak at the tenth-anniversary commencement in 1975, he responded to its president, Robert Atwell, on 11 September 1972: "But I would also like the guarantee of an honorary degree." During the summer 1981 he pressured James Kilroy, chair of the English department at Vanderbilt University: "I cannot for the life of me understand why Vanderbilt, my old university, has not seen fit to confer an honorary degree on me. Though I realize this may sound fatuous, it is a matter of some concern to me. I have six others, but in all the time since the first one Vanderbilt did not come forward." Kilroy responded simply that Vanderbilt traditionally did not confer honorary degrees. Typical of Dickey's correspondence regarding speaking fees and commencement addresses is an unpublished letter dated 15 January 1975 to David Larrabee, director of New Hampshire Technical Institute, who had written and invited him to participate in commencement exercises: "My fee for such events is $3500 plus all first-class expenses. I know this is high, and it is deliberately so, not because I am particularly mercenary, but because these days, time is of much more importance to me than money, and it takes a good deal of money to justify my expenditure of time and energy in doing such things." Dickey then added, "Also, should I participate in your exercises, I would like to receive an honorary degree from your institution." By 1993, he had acquired more than a dozen doctorates, though not one from New Hampshire Technical Institute.

Dickey's drinking progressively worsened. During the fifties he drank largely for pleasure. "My father thought alcohol was about joy," Chris remembered.

> He didn't like the taste very much, he'd say, he just liked the way it made him feel. And it did seem to me there were a lot of good times made better—more joyful—by the beer, by the whiskey, by the gin he was knocking back. He'd have drunk in any case, but there was no reason not to in America in the 1950s. Highballs and dry martinis lubricated every gathering, starting with the three-martini lunch. (*Summer of Deliverance* 101)

Now, however, he often appeared completely intoxicated during poetry readings or while teaching his classes at the University of South Carolina. His wife, Maxine, had also begun drinking heavily, as if in resolution to the question of her leaving the marriage. Her husband behaved outrageously, openly conducting extramarital affairs with, among others, Amy Burk, a single mother acting in Brendan Behan's *Borstal Boy* of Broadway whom he had met at an *Esquire* party; Mary Cantwell, the managing editor at *Mademoiselle*; Rosemary Danielle, who had taken his poetry writing workshop; and Paula Goff, a former student who became his secretary. As she increased her drinking, Maxine gained weight, which increased her health problems and eventually led to her death in 1976. Dickey at times admitted his own problem with alcohol, declaring baldly in *Sorties*, "I have been drunk, more or less, for about the last twenty-five years. Everything I remember is colored to some extent by alcohol" (84). Soliciting submissions as poetry editor to *Esquire*, he wrote John Berryman on 20 July 1971 in an unpublished letter: "We *should* get together, because, as they say on the pro football games on Sunday afternoon, the clock is running. I know all about the alcohol situation, though my own condition is further complicated by diabetes," a statement that was not true. Shared physical debilities or poetic sensibilities generated such confession and created a genuine need within Dickey for camaraderie and kinship.

Yet efforts to establish such kinship were sometimes feigned, letters that flattered the recipient to convey a sympathetic sensibility and secure a favorable impression, as he had done with Ezra Pound and Wallace Stevens, or to create a sympathy for or interest in himself, as had happened with James Wright. Exaggerated stories and demands for honorary doctorates as well as correspondence that endeavored to manipulate confirm an uncertain, emotionally insecure poet seeking to bolster his literary reputation, assuage his ego, and create a self-identity. The actions suggest, too, a writer who has lost his artistic bearings and is searching not so much for poetic transcendence as for navigational landmarks. Personal setbacks and literary turbulence had endangered his success, and he struggled to regain control by searching for others who had experienced difficulty.

This affinity extended to writers other than Berryman, including James Wright and Stanley Burnshaw. In an unpublished letter to Wright dated 13 September 1971, Dickey eagerly agreed to introduce his friend at a New York reading of his poetry, stating, "There is no other American poet that I would prefer to introduce, and that's the truth," and alluded to the "very moving phone call" they recently shared. Wright had written him earlier to praise the publication of *The Eye-Beaters*, and Dickey had responded on 16 March 1970, thanking Wright for his "wonderful, life-giving letters":

> I am *so* happy that you like the new book, for it is really not very much like any of the others.... It seems to me that the great lesson of Picasso is that he never allowed himself to be trapped in a single style, as so many of our young and not-so-young American poets have done.... You have convinced me that I have made at least part of the right move, though while I was writing the book I was quite prepared to have critics say that this book was "disappointing," that it "represented a regression," and so on. As I say, I was quite ready for that. I hoped that there would be a few people who were not mystified but interested in what I was attempting to do. But *your* letter! All I can say is thanks, and with great humbleness. (*One Voice*, II 62)

Berryman's suicide on 7 January 1972 stunned Dickey, and though he had once called Berryman "a poet so preoccupied with poetic effects as to be totally in their thrall" (*Babel to Byzantium* 198), he nevertheless felt the loss. Robert Lowell had recently suffered another manic-depressive breakdown (he would die five years later); when Ezra Pound died in a Venice hospital on 1 November, Dickey was almost overwhelmed, conscious as he was of Pound's influence on his own poetry and of their meeting and correspondence during the fifties. Commenting on Pound's death, he told *The State* newspaper in Columbia, South Carolina: "Pound was a monolith, a great writer" who "did more for the human imagination, did more for the cause of imaginative delight and personal power, than anyone of our time" (A1). Later, in his 1982 essay titled "The Water-Bug's

Mittens: Ezra Pound: What We Can Use," he detailed Pound's importance. Pound's love for all he believed excellent in the world, while often resulting in heavy-handed assertions that proselytized, also provided what for Dickey was most important—"startling, isolated shocks of possibility: conjunctions of words that opened up my own rather unbookish but very word-sensitive mentality to what I might come upon in my own memory and set forth with a corresponding imaginative forthrightness" (*Night Hurdling* 29–46).

In the early seventies, with his career seeming to stall and his health to decline, Dickey genuinely sought shared sensitivities. If his personal behavior appeared callous and self-destructive, it was a measure of how off-course his mission had become, his voice muffled by circumstances that increasingly appeared to frustrate and overwhelm him, causing him to act erratically. Arguably the best objective correlative for the faltering state of both Dickey's career and his literary status was the Apollo 11 moon landing, for which *Life* magazine had commissioned him to write a poem. It had previously asked him to write about Apollo 7 and Apollo 8, the first manned mission to orbit the moon. The magazine published "The Moon Ground" on 4 July 1969. Dickey had reminisced about the Apollo 7 launch in *Sorties*, expressing confusion and regret over a moment he had failed to experience:

> I think with terrible sadness of the evening spent with the astronauts a couple of nights before Walter Schiarra's lift-off. I was drunk out of my mind, and could not focus on anything that happened, but simply sit in a corner in a drunken stupor.... And yet if I had been cold sober what would I have done? Would I have been an eager-eyed middle-aged fellow, terribly receptive to all their personalities, and so on? No, if I had it to do again, I would be a drunken poet among the astronauts. (55–56)

"Apollo," Dickey's poem in response to the moon landing, is less about the awe-inspiring launch where, as Chris described in his memoir, spectators felt the powerful sound almost overwhelm them, "a noise as deep as space that hammered our ears, heads, bodies, until some people fell on their knees and others, shielding their eyes, looked as if they saw God Almighty rising from the swamplands of Eastern Florida" (*Summer of Deliverance* 159), than it is a meditation on the human spirit to explore. "You and your computers," the poem reads, "have brought out / The silence of mountains the animal / Eye has not seen since the earth split." Despite his injunction to himself and to his students—"Don't tell 'em, show 'em"—Dickey was unable to elevate the moment above the prosaic. "We were here," Chris stated, "because James Dickey was a god," but "the fantastic experience, the writing of verse, in the service of journalism, in the service of fame, was becoming a kind of routine" (152, 159).

Dickey was fond of quoting Jean Cocteau, the French writer, visual artist, and filmmaker whose versatility caused him to experiment continually in almost every artistic medium: "Learn what you can do and then don't do it." Throughout his career, Dickey justified his poetic experimentation in letters and interviews. That he divided his poetry into different "motions" shows his commitment, as Pound declared, to "make it new." Yet the poems Dickey was now writing after *Buckdancer's Choice*, while revealing a new poetic, failed to impress critics, who considered them bloated and self-centered. His Rabelaisian and at times self-destructive behavior, fueled by alcohol, offended his audiences. Having raised the profile of poets and poetry generally and himself specifically as he explored and enlarged his identity during the late fifties and early sixties, he no longer seemed in control of himself or his poetry by the late sixties and early seventies. He might as well have been talking to himself when, at the end of "The Moon Ground," he wrote, "We stare into the moon / dust, the earth-blazing ground. We laugh, with the beautiful craze / Of static. We bend, we pick up stones."

CHAPTER 11

THE POET AS TEACHER

James Dickey would frequently stress to his students the importance of discovery. Getting older, he insisted, mandated that one also got better: "The only *raison d'etre* for being middle-aged or old is the possession of an absolute mastery of *something*. Otherwise the aging process is a ridiculous spectacle" (*Sorties* 47). Learning, therefore, was of paramount concern. Ill and confined to a wheelchair, he directly stated this attitude in his 1995 commencement address at the University of South Carolina, titled "The Weather of the Valley." He told graduating seniors, their friends and families, faculty and administrators, as well as alumni: "I have always believed that teaching is the second greatest occupation that the human mind and energy can undertake...the *most* important...is learning" (1). Certainly he himself never stopped learning. His personal library was the working collection of a major American author who was continually reading, discussing, and writing. Often he would sit in his living room in a big easy chair surrounded by a castle of approximately a thousand volumes in towers more than four feet high. Seventeen thousand additional books crowded shelves on the other side of the room and continued into the hallway, all part of a personal library a half century in the making. When Dickey would enter his classroom, usually dressed in blue jeans and a cotton knit turtleneck, he would be lugging an obviously heavy suitcase whose contents he would then spill onto the desk and carefully arrange—books, some two dozen of them, a rich collection of prosody, criticism, anthropology, philosophy, nonfiction, and poetry by diverse writers such as J. B. Priestley, Herbert Read, André Malraux, Stanley Edgar Hyman, Joseph Campbell, Henry Miller, Virgil, Milton, Lucretius, Dante, and others. All looked well read because they were all well worn.

"When I first began to teach full-time," Dickey wrote in the introduction to *From the Green Horseshoe*, his collection of the best poems by his students, "I never had any doubt—and I have never had any since—that the things that had proved helpful for me as a poet—that I had learned through much frustration and a few right moves—would prove helpful to others embarked on the same path." Over the course of a teaching career that spanned almost fifty years, he endeavored to achieve what he termed "the teaching poet's primary function": "to galvanize the associative energies of the individual student, to make him aware of the memory-process, to encourage him to use these with spontaneity and without fear, and secondarily to awaken him to the creative possibilities that reside within the nature of Form itself" (ix). Pat Conroy, who himself became a noted author, audited Dickey's two classes in fall 1971, driving two and a half hours from Beaufort to Columbia twice a week to sit in Dickey's courses in the Welsh Humanities Building. "When he entered a room," Conroy wrote, "James Dickey took possession of it, mastered its corners and shadows, adjusted the spotlight to himself, and then drew the class into himself" (Greiner, *James Dickey: Classes* xiv). Dickey taught at nine colleges and universities over his life, beginning at Rice Institute in 1950 and ending with his death at the University of South Carolina in 1997, where he had joined the faculty in 1968 as First Carolina Professor and poet-in-residence. Wherever he taught, students responded enthusiastically. He lectured without referring to his notes and oftentimes interspersed his comments with witty or profane observations. Conroy recalled,

> I found Dickey a mesmerizing, fully engaged teacher, an enchanter who could enter into the depths and reveries of any poem and bring back its ores and fluids and essences dripping from his hands, eager to share the wonders he had discovered.... No one loved to drift into waters where human beings had never been before or were not meant to go, but that is exactly what he required of his classes with every poem we read together. In his classes, we were fully expected to give ourselves up to poetry with a completeness that was sacred in nature. (xiv)

After Rice, Dickey taught at the University of Florida during the1955–56 academic year. His course load included introductory freshman and sophomore classes as well as an upper-level creative writing course with Andrew Lytle. Dickey's syllabus for his C-32 course, the general education literature class, provides a sense of the values he promoted. It listed the following lectures: "Why Literature?," "The Enjoyment of the Short Story," "Speaking Clearly and Accurately," "The Novel, a Reflection of Life," "Some Great Novels," "How to Read Novels," "Drama in the Movies," "The Realm of Poetry," "The Language of Poetry," and "The Kinds of Poetry." While the outline covers the customary three genres, it also suggests that Dickey's approach centers not only on showing students how to read and interpret the literature but also how literature itself should assume a personal meaning or significance in their lives. It was an attitude or philosophy on which he firmly stood for the remainder of his life. His advertising broadside, "How to Enjoy Poetry," for example, published by the International Paper Company in 1982, reflects the same commitment as that of his lectures regarding the significance of individual response. After asking what poetry is and declaring it not a school subject on which students must take exams, he stated his premise: "The first thing about poetry is that it comes to you from outside you, in books or in words, but that for it to live, something from within you must come to it and meet it and complete it. Your response with your own mind and body and memory and emotions gives the poem its ability to work its magic." He continued, "Poetry makes possible the deepest kind of personal possession of the world." The following year he reiterated the personal identification necessary to glean the world's "intensified particularity." In his essay "The Wild Heart," he insisted

> how wild, inexplicable, marvelous and endless creation is, and in what vivid and self-discovering ways the mind can, if it wishes, come upon each of its parts, for the imagination is nothing more or less than the perception—or the personal creation—of individual meaning out of the essentially meaningless chaos.... It is making our kind of peace with the world, and in the end, if we are honest enough we will be perceptive enough, and will then conceive what will quite literally be the truth. (*Night Hurdling* 215)

Throughout his formal teaching career, whether with regard to the interpretation of other poets or to the creation of their own poems, Dickey urged students to trust their own perspectives in interacting with the world.

Beginning with his appointment to Reed College in 1963, Dickey taught two courses each semester, one in Modern Poetry and another in Verse Composition. ("We don't live long enough to become poets," he told his students as to why he had thus titled the class.) In the fall semester of Verse Composition, he required students to engage specific poetic forms, one each week, including the sonnet, villanelle, lyric, and ballad, as well as poems that utilized epigrammatic couplets, blank verse, and satire. "It is best," he maintained, "for all serious poets to work with these forms even if they don't continue to use them beyond the time spent in class, for such discipline, even if imposed from outside, must be passed through before any sort of valuable 'free'—or organic—form can be reached, and rightly seen is part of the poet's self-exploration, as he undertakes to discover the as-yet undiscovered, the many selves within the one" (*From the Green Horseshoe* ix). In the spring, students wrote a poem in free verse, revising it weekly for the remainder of the semester, supplemented by class discussion and Dickey's commentary and driven by their own imaginations and curiosity.

When Dickey was not writing poetry, he devoted considerable energy to writing about it, which was another form of teaching. His early notebooks, letters, essays, and reviews discuss poetic theory, specific poems, and artistic technique as well as individual poets, both past and contemporary as well as American and foreign. The commentary that comprised his class lectures at the University of South Carolina dates from the 1971–72 academic year, soon after he assumed full-time residence at the University of South Carolina following his official appointment the previous year. These were years of triumph, when he was at "angels nine," just after winning in 1966 the National Book Award for *Buckdancer's Choice*, his two-term appointment in 1966 to 1968 to what today is the poet laureate, and the unprecedented fame he garnered in 1970 as the author of *Deliverance*. He treated his professorship seriously, faithfully teaching two Tuesday/Thursday courses each semester, except for an occasional leave or sabbatical, and keeping office hours afterwards. He was routinely assigned English 600/601 (Verse Composition), the creative workshop, as well as English 760 (Contemporary British and American Poetry Since 1900), a graduate-level survey. In academic year 1978–79, the university reconfigured the survey into English 760 (American Poetry Since 1900) and English 761 (Survey of Twentieth-Century British and American Poetry). Following this curricular change, his standard teaching assignment was English 761 and the seminar in verse composition, the latter of which required "consent of instructor." On occasion, undergraduates were granted permission to enroll. The former was an open-enrollment survey that Dickey often, though not always, designed such that one term centered on American poets, the other on contemporary British poets. The lectures were originally researched and delivered for the one-semester English 760, but the sheer number and variety of the assigned poets suggest that Dickey assumed many students would commit to the survey for both semesters. During his tenure at the University of South Carolina, Dickey also taught American Poetry, SCCC 150, at the request of Bill Mould, the dean of the esteemed honors college. While Dickey preferred graduate students, what mattered most was teaching.

When Dickey arrived in Columbia, South Carolina, in 1968, the Cold War remained deeply entrenched in the nation's psyche, facilitating the country's sense of superiority and entitlement. Hemingway had died in 1961; Faulkner, '62; Frost, '63; and Eliot in '65—all writers who had become cultural heroes. Americans needed to declare emphatically to the Soviet Union, "Our writers are better than yours." Dickey had seemed to burst onto the literary scene immediately, first as a National Book Award winner and poetry consultant to the Library of Congress and then as the author of a best-selling novel, and the public had responded, as if to say, "Here is one of our replacements for Frost and Faulkner and Eliot." Even as early as 1967, critics acknowledged Dickey's literary stature. In the October issue of *Atlantic Monthly*, for example, Peter Davison had written, "James Dickey began publishing poetry in 1957; and in an explosive ten years his work has developed in remarkable ways both technically and imaginatively" (119). He concluded the essay, titled "The Difficulties of Being Major," "If American poetry needs a champion for the new generation, Dickey's power and ambition may supply the need. His archetypal concerns are universal to all languages and will no doubt carry over into translation; his sense of urgency is overwhelming; his volume, his range, his technique, his process of maturing"—all these attributes, Davison declared, qualified him as being a major poet (121).

The University of South Carolina felt it had achieved a coup when it successfully brought Dickey onto its faculty. His best friend while a graduate student at Vanderbilt, Calhoun Winton, then a member and later chair of the English department at USC, had invited Dickey to campus after his second term at the Library of Congress ended. Dickey had assumed that he would likely return to California; his family liked it there. Always alert for the best possible situation, however, he was interested in what South Carolina might offer since, as a matter of general knowledge, the state was depressed economically. "As far as I knew," he later wrote, "South Carolina was soybeans, illiteracy, and maybe even pellagra and hookworm," adding, "my chief mental image of it was a dilapidated outhouse and a rusty '34 Ford with the number 13 painted on it, both covered by kudzu" (*Night Hurdling* 20). When Dickey asked university president Tom Jones what incentives might cause him to wish to live in South Carolina, the latter had responded, "Flowers and birds." "Talk on" (21), Dickey had supposedly said. He subsequently came to Columbia and in

January 1969 taught his first courses. Broad-shouldered and six foot three, he became the most recognizable face on campus.

Dickey's class lectures in English 761, while discussing major and minor poets he considered significant, more pointedly centered on the creative impulse, which he believed lay in man's religious nature and which manifested itself in a fascination with the objects and animals he worshipped, particularly the latter's strength, speed, or skill. Cave drawings frequently accentuated specific features, such as the horns of a buffalo. He viewed this characteristic as early evidence of the human need not simply to imitate but to create, which he called "man's delight in tinkering and playing with things." Man, then, was a defective, even inferior, animal; when he boasted, he pictured himself by referencing the animal world, a tendency that stressed both the child within as a source of genius and the Jungian urge to tap into the collective memory. Listening to Dickey talk, not a lecture, really, but rather as if communicating some secret knowledge, students felt connected more intimately to the world outside themselves. In a letter dated 6 August 1959, he told James Wright, "I was a good teacher...not because I was especially conscientious, but because I loved what I was doing" (*One Voice*, I 273). Conroy remembered how, in the four months he took classes, Dickey changed everything he thought he knew about writing and art:

> He spoke of the egregiousness of the craft of writing, the boldness required by it, the helium lift and cry of storm as the language broke in currents around us. Be afraid of nothing, he would say. Listen to what is real and essential inside yourself. Make yourself ready to embrace the spirit of the unknown and the unknowable. Drive yourself to the limits. Let nothing get in your way. Be open to all things, fully alive, the poet with arms outstretched, ready for anything the world or God would fling your way in the bright abundance of our supple language. (Greiner, *James Dickey: Classes* xv)

For Dickey, the poet was nothing less than a secondary Creator, the profession of writing poetry a religious endeavor because the poet *created* the truth.

Survey of Twentieth-Century British and American Poetry was not a survey despite the catalog description. "If I truly had my way," he informed his students on the first day of class, "it would not be called 'Modern American Poetry' (or 20th-Century American Poetry), but something like 'An Experience of Some Poems By Americans.'" He was particularly interested, he wrote in his lecture notes, in what he termed "a kind of inspired superficiality, which would cover many figures and poems not normally *read* in a course, or indeed at all." He conceived of the semester as "a long continual ramble in poetry, with lots of commentary by me and by you." In his early years at USC, he used *The Modern Poets*, edited by John Malcolm Brinnin, for major poets, and *New Poets of England and America*, edited by Donald Hall, a small paperback, for lesser and contemporary figures. Later, he adopted Richard Ellman's *Norton Anthology of Modern Poetry* as his required text.

During the second class meeting, Dickey began extensive remarks on prehistory. He cited Eric Hoffer's *The Devil and the Dragon*, Henry Miller's *The Colossus of Maroussi*, Jacquita Hawkes's *The World of the Past*, and Herbert Read's *Icon and Idea* and commented on the innate expressive function of the mind by referencing André Malroux's *Man's Fate* and *The Voices of Silence*. He stressed, in particular, Malroux's discussion of the Altamira bison, the idea that the painting is not the bison, not even expressly similar to the bison in its proportions: "The cave bison is *more* bison than the real bison, because the mind has insisted overly on the aspects of the real bison, which exaggerate the *feelings* that the bison produces in a human mind: his great bulk, the forward thrust of his chest, much larger in proportion than the chest of the real bison, his charge exaggerated to be more charge-like than would be the case of the bison out on the open plain," adding, "*these* legs are pure fury and power!" Comments on Stanley Edgar Hyman's *The Promised Land*—"Look at a people's money, it has been said ambiguously, if you want to learn what they worship"—led to Dickey's discussion of the nature of the hero, what he termed "the real hero, the hero of whole peoples, of what we would call the folk hero of past cultures, and the spurious folk heroes that we have." His lecture notes then transitioned to Joseph Campbell's *The Hero with a Thousand Faces* and the idea that all myths are in reality one myth, the monomyth, and its three stages—separation from the world, penetration to a source of power, and life-enhancing return. Ritual, he insisted, became codified to form a myth, and he concluded the class by circling back to cave art and the idea of "words-as-things."

Because their focus that semester was modern poetry, the culmination of a long historical process that needed to be understood, Dickey then discussed the classical world of Greece and Rome. Citing W. H. Auden's *The Portable Greek Reader*, he noted the simplicity and "firstness" of the poetry and Homer's ability to describe a thing or an event in language that fixed onto that thing or event and that avoided cliché. No one had previously described the Aegean, he declared, as "the wine-dark sea"; no one had described Achilles as "swift-footed" simply because he was fast. There was, he insisted, the freedom of classical poets to be obvious, a literary period that he called "the lost Eden of simplicity." Discussion subsequently centered on epic poetry generally and the nature of translation. Noting that Pound was against literal translation, against "laying out a poem in English," Dickey argued for Pound's approach based on intuition, that is, on the spirit behind the passage, a distinction Dickey adhered to in his own efforts to translate other poets.

The Roman world, he continued, though separated only by a few hundred years and very little distance geographically, was nevertheless immensely distant from that of Greece. The Greek mind, he insisted, wanted to know the world; the Roman thought it already did. The former was open-minded, spiritual, and adventurous; the latter, by contrast, was derivative and imitative. Consequently, Virgil's *Aeneid*, unlike Homer's *Odyssey*, was merely official art, a commissioned work. Writing it, Dickey argued, Virgil was fulfilling a religious and political duty in which the theme of Rome's glorious future overrode all other concerns. Decorum was his daily concern, such that Virgil insisted on the nobility of his hero at all times. There was none of Homer's beautiful images, such as the "far-shadowing spear." Where Dickey did celebrate Roman writers was in his commentary on Lucretius, whose *De reum natura* (*On the Nature of Things*) attempted to dispel shibboleth and illusion, arguing that truth was in nature as it is, not in how men think it is or want it to be. The book, he suggested, attempted to say everything like an epic poet but in a philosophical way, a prescientific scientific view of things that portrayed a mysterious vision of nature as an enormous living body pulsating with energy, with atoms that do not explain how it works but which nevertheless reveal a world "in all its self-sufficiency." Never a Christian, Dickey sympathized with Lucretius's effort to gird himself in the volcanic chaos of things where peace, the acceptance of death, prevailed because it was the truth of things of which he was a part.

In this pedagogical fashion, extensive commentary and analysis enlarged by and supported with additional readings, Dickey discussed the history of artistic creativity, subsequently moving to Dante and the change to the human psyche owing to Christianity, its impact on the Western mind, and the subsequent creation of a vast mythology and symbology from the Old and New Testaments that affected writers such as Chaucer and Milton. "What concerns us here," Dickey emphasized to students,

> is Milton's heroic effort to hang on to the crumbling mythology of Christianity. When you open *Paradise Lost* and find Milton saying that by his poem on the fall of man and his expulsion from the garden, which he calls "this great Argument," he "may assert Eternal Providence, and justify the ways of God to men," he has already given the game away. That is, the crumbling of the Christian-symbology game, as it goes with the break-up of the central church following Luther in 1517, and the advance of scientific investigation and experimentation which provided facts, more and more of them, that were against the most deeply rooted assertions of the church.

While his lecture notes cited Milton's "heroic effort," they stress that Goethe became the transitional figure in any discussion of the imagination; his Faust, so unwilling to be satisfied, typified a major theme in Western civilization—the questing, striving neurotic who will not limit himself on what he can do, on what is possible for himself to achieve. "His characteristic and almost overwhelmingly Goethian statement," Dickey asserted, "his national anthem, as it were, is 'he who ever strives upward: him can we save.' *Faust* is a lifelong work, written over a period of 50 years. It is a kind of historical phantasmagoria, and centers around the search for knowledge, and the consequences and costs—especially the psychological costs, and dangers—of its attainment." He contended, "Goethe gave us the central metaphor of our civilization. Faust wanted the light, unknown but not necessarily unknowable, a light different from the light that Dante saw when he looked up into the sky." "With Goethe," Dickey continued, "we mark a change in the whole mentality of the human race. The quest of Faust for all knowledge is the quest we have all undertaken. We have splintered into a race of specialists. With Goethe, the Renaissance ideal of all-inclusiveness vanished forever." Goethe was two hundred years after Milton, he reminded the class, and by the late eighteenth and early nineteenth century, the central problem had come out of the surrounding atmosphere of the culture and into the human mind itself—"the psychological questionings, and its *own* efforts to make sense of things. The eyes of men were turning inward, not upon the contemplation of some heroic image or belief but on the reflection of themselves." Dickey stressed that myth, now no longer an embodiment of cultural ideals, was becoming a cracked and individual mirror. Faust, in other words, became the first of the introspective and tormented geniuses of literature.

Dickey insisted that the loss of mythology was discernible in such poets as Lawrence Durrell and Robinson Jeffers and in T. S. Eliot's recourse to religion late in his career. He cited, for example, the conclusion of Jeffers's "Night," whose ending suggests the absence of faith that had previously sustained mankind: "Have men's minds changed, / Or the rock hidden in the deep of the waters of the soul / Broken the surface? A few centuries / Gone by, was none dared not to people / The darkness beyond the stars with harps and habitations. / But now, dear is the truth. Life is grown sweeter and lonelier, / And death is no evil." Yet Dickey argued that while a dilemma for twentieth-century writers, this torment also presented possibility. He saw Walt Whitman as the groundbreaker in this regard; his ability to see potential in even the smallest things rendered him the poet "who opened up America for us" (*Sorties* 53). Myth, morever, Dickey argued, had not been abandoned; rather, it had undergone a special kind of change. The giants of modernism had made their own myth in highly individualized ways. Citing Eliot and James Joyce as examples, he suggested that myth was now employed as a technique, not a belief, to be utilized in the construction of a work. *The Wasteland* used fertility and Christian mythology as well as the anthropological, sociological, and historical. Pound's mythology in the *Cantos* was based on economics, history, and historical personages. Yeats utilized Celtic mythology and, later, astronomical systems in his philosophical work *A Vision*.

Symbolism, however, came from the poet himself—his attitudes, emotions, psychology—whatever would serve him. All modern poetry, Dickey emphasized, derived both from the sixteenth- and seventeenth-century metaphysicals and from French symbolism, noting that Eliot's famous line comparing evening to "a patient etherized upon a table" constituted a radically different way of looking at what had previously been a romanticized view of evening. The school of John Donne, Dickey noted, including George Herbert, Robert Crenshaw, and others, turned the mind loose to play with itself, to make a game of what it would, to make a heaven of hell or a hell of heaven, believing that no limit existed to the associations the mind might make. Some comparisons were far-fetched and silly, possessing an outlandishness and straining for effect; some, profound and unique. Nevertheless, a new approach to sensibility had come into play, he told his students, and the game aspect of writing poetry, reinforced by wit, had begun to assume a strong importance. Noting works such as Frank

Kermode's *The Metaphysical Poets*, Joan Bennett's *Four Metaphysical Poets*, and A. Alvarez's *The School of Donne*, Dickey stressed the need of these poets to experiment—on language itself and on its expressive possibilities—through analogies from the technical and scientific spheres that were concerned specifically with paradox. "This free-ranging associationalism has come to be the primary quality of the modern poetry-creating mind," he asserted, and led directly to Eliot's "patient etherized upon a table."

French symbolism, too, initially only a literary undercurrent before establishing itself as a movement, assisted in this transition. Using Arthur Symons's *The Symbolist Movement in Literature* and Peter Quinnell's *Baudelaire and the Symbolists* as references, Dickey argued that these poets, including Baudelaire and Mallarmé, believed that things corresponded to other things in the world in a private, secret way. He believed that Edgar Allan Poe "threw a key block" for symbolists when he suggested that the poet was a soothsayer who alone could read that system of correspondences. Citing Edmund Wilson's *Axel's Castle*, Dickey also noted the circuitous route of influence from Mallarmé back into English and asserted that Yeats was an Irish symbolist. Poets, Dickey argued, deciphered correspondences. He called Baudelaire the great poet of the city, not a Wordsworth of pastures or Byron of the Alps, who explored the terrors of his own mind. Because to name was to destroy and to suggest was to create, these poets cultivated mystery or indefiniteness as, for example, Mallarmé's description of sunset: "victoriously fled the beautiful suicide." Similarly, Hart Crane, who identified with Rimbaud, described noon in New York City: "Down wall, from girder into street noon leaks, / A rip-tooth of the city's acetylene." Poetry was also to be evocative, not descriptive, and Baudelaire added to this what Dickey termed "the torment without God, which is the torment of the mind which feels guilt and yet has no overseeing force to condemn the guilt," that is, a guilt without morals. This guilt became a fixture in the modern sensibility and hence in modern poetry.

From these two main streams of expression, Dickey concluded, come all of modern poetry in one way or another:

> From the metaphysicals, the daring and associational freedom, the outlandishness, the capacity to make any kind of poem out of any kind of material, to make new amalgamations of meaning, to use all kinds of terminology—scientific, sociological, historical, religious, any kind—and from symbolism the analogy of poetry to music in creating an indefinite but troubling and disturbing effect by suggestion rather than by statement, the doctrine that to the private

sensibility all things are symbols in a self-contained subjective system of thought and response, the emphasis on connotation rather than denotation, the desire to make an associational penumbra or nimbus or kind of glowing halo around the object—in short, a kind of inspired indefiniteness, and a wish to make each reader his own *poet*, through the agency of the poem he is reading: all these came in from symbolism.

Throughout Dickey's extended discussion of creativity and the historical imagination leading up to the twentieth century, his central contention was that modernists now felt it necessary to become their own myth-makers. With all things calling to or corresponding with each other, the poem was to become a construct with a preconceived idea that would be its effect on the reader. As if to validate his point, he noted Yeats's emphasis on magic and unknown modes of being, Robinson Jeffers's inhumanism, Tom Gunn's focus on counterculture, Robert Penn Warren's historical mysticism, and Auden's interpretation of the death of culture and the subsequent feeling of dread and metaphysical angst. At the end of class, Dickey finally informed his students that the following week, "I will meet you in a garden in Amherst, Massachusetts, about 130 years ago."

Always beginning modern American poetry with Emily Dickinson, Dickey then chose poets who interested him or whose work underscored points he wanted to make; if needed, however, he would adjust assignments on the basis of class discussion. Following the background lectures during the fall 1979 semester, for example, the syllabus scheduled readings from almost three dozen poets, including Emily Dickinson, Edgar Lee Masters, E. A. Robinson, Robert Frost, Carl Sandburg, Wallace Stevens, Anthony Hecht, Vachel Lindsey, Marianne Moore, Elizabeth Bishop, E. E. Cummings, Hart Crane, William Carlos Williams, Edna St. Vincent Millay, Robinson Jeffers, John Crowe Ransom, Wendell Berry, Allen Tate, Archibald McLeish, Robert Penn Warren, Richard Eberhart, Theodore Roethke, Karl Shapiro, Delmore Schwartz, Randall Jarrell, Robert Lowell, John Berryman, Sylvia Plath, Anne Sexton, Adrienne Rich, Howard Nemerov, Reed Whittemore, Dave Smith, Richard Wilbur, and James Wright. British poets included Thomas Hardy, A. E. Housman, D. H. Lawrence, Gerard Manley Hopkins, W. B. Yeats, Louis MacNeice, Edwin Muir, Dylan Thomas, Keith Douglas, Alun Lewis, Wilfred Owen, W. H. Auden, Edith Sitwell, Geoffrey Hill, Robert Graves, Lawrence Durrell, Kathleen Raine, Ernest Dowson, David Gascoyne, and Lionel Johnson. Michael Taylor, who was enrolled in the course in fall 1983, remembered, "As the class moved from the early- to the mid-twentieth century, he seemed to know them all personally." David Havird, who attended Dickey's classes from 1972 through 1974, agreed: "He would talk about these poets as if he knew them and tell us these anecdotes." Integral to Dickey's class commentary were stories about specific poets. Jim Mann recalls Dickey relating a visit he had had with T. S. Eliot, who said he thought the Civil War could have made for an American *Iliad*. "What a tragedy it was for *your* country," Eliot had supposedly said, to which Dickey responded to the class, "Listen to him, Mr. Eliot from St. Louis." Dickey, however, never met Eliot. The story was another example of his creating his own myth, not "lying." He also told students he had informed Allen Tate, who had come for a reading in March 1973, that he had threatened Robert Bly with a lawsuit over what he perceived as slander: "The kind of stuff you're saying about me is actionable. I don't know whether you have the kind of money for legal expenses, but I do." Here, however, Dickey had essentially written as much to Bly in a letter dated 8 February 1971 (*One Voice*, I 123). Dickey also related a story about running into the British poet David Gascoyne in Soho, London, "a very nice fellow, a little bewildered," Dickey declared, with whom he discussed surrealism. "We're too levelheaded in England," Gascoyne reportedly said. "They disorder things better in France," claiming, however, that he had the most irrational line in English—"an arrow with lips of cheese—which was better even than Charles Madge."

Dickey frequently added to the readings two poets he had read while serving in the Pacific and who had contributed to his decision to become a poet, Frederick Tuckerman and Trumbull Stickney. Tuckerman, he suggested, anticipated E. A. Robinson in his preoccupation with failure and silence and unlived lives and whose ability to depict emblematically the passage of time, as in his line from "The Cricket," "Like yon escaping color in the tree," reflected Dickey's own preoccupation with death. Stickney, he told students, was "the muse of memory," who, like Tuckerman, was not a great poet but some of whose lines brought the term greatness to mind, as when he wrote, upon learning of the brain tumor that would end his life at an early age, "The green and climbing eyesight of a cat / Crawled near my mind's poor birds." In interviews and addresses, Dickey related how a passage by Stickney had determined him to become a poet. Stationed on Okinawa at the end of WWII, which he called "a place of bloody and terrible stone," he had read a line by Stickney referring to someone whose eyes were "somewhat more than blue." "Stickney was essentially a pagan," he told his USC commencement audience in 1995:

> Though super-civilized, educated beyond almost any of his genera-
> tion, his gods were the Greek gods of light and sea, of the salt and
> the air and the sun, of the body and the imagination. I remember
> standing on a hill overlooking Buckner Bay just after the War ended.
> The military graveyard there had just been completed, and symmet-
> rical crosses stretched nearly out of sight, almost to the ocean. Stick-
> ney had a sonnet which ended with the lines "Thou art divine, thou
> livest,—as of old Apollo springing naked to the light, / And all his
> island shivered into flowers."...I looked at the graves and I thought of
> Stickney's lines, and instantaneously believed that if the right wind
> were to blow the graves would turn to flowers; would shiver into
> flowers. (*The Weather of the Valley* 4–5)

Dickey would later incorporate lines from Stickney into his own poem "Exchanges," which he read at Harvard in 1970 as part of his Phi Beta Kappa address. For Dickey, words ordinary in themselves assumed a special color in Stickney.

The final course grade was determined by four papers. Two centered on established, older poets who were in most cases deceased. In those essays students could utilize any materials, both primary and secondary, that they wished. The other two papers focused on comparatively recent poets, most of whom were still living and whose reputations were still being established. Little commentary on them would be available. "Your individual assessments," Dickey emphasized, "are of greatest value here." There was no exam. The papers were not critical assessments per se but rather what Dickey would term "a personal encounter" with a writer's work. He was not a demandingly strict grader. As he read each paper, he would correct spelling and grammatical or syntactical errors; he objected to split infinitives, for example, and preferred the Oxford comma. Oftentimes he would briefly comment on a particular observation that the student had made, such as "Good," "Yes," and "True," often adding an exclamation point for emphasis. Other remarks were more focused, as when a student remarked on John Berryman's convoluted syntax. "Yes; and of a very special and curious kind," Dickey wrote. When that student then declared that Berryman, in presenting his protagonist Henry had provided readers with a model character, Dickey responded in the margin: "Heavens! One aspect of *this* you *surely* don't mean! Henry (or Berryman) is not *my* model!"

Dickey could also be humorous in his comments. When a student, for example, declared that encountering Sylvia Plath's poetry was akin to contemplating one's initial sexual experience, asking whether it were possible to lose one's virginity and not know it, Dickey wrote, "Might be difficult!" Another student quoted a section of Allen Tate's "Ode to the Confederate Dead," stating that the complete modern man seeks understanding of a tradition rather than one who blindly follows an idealistic cause. Dickey responded, "Ah, Mr. Eliot. *Do* have another beer." A paper centered on John Hollander found Dickey wishing that the student had talked more about the poet's vision of the City, but nevertheless suggested that the student send it to Hollander at Yale University: "He'd like that." Another student whose essay explored W. S. Merwin's work received an A on the paper; Dickey wrote on the front page: "Quite interesting, though Merwin is tedious to me, a kind of poetry of interchangeable parts; no sense of necessity.—But your paper is good; better than the subject." Haywood Moxley, who enrolled in Dickey's Modern Poetry course in fall 1984, remembered his essay on Yeats: "I recall his marginalia being very encouraging but also very critical of some convoluted sentences. I was desperately trying to sound profound back then, the way I thought he sounded. I was proud that Dickey thought my interpretations were original and meaningful, but I was also impressed that he challenged sloppy thinking and writing." Dickey's second wife, Deborah, recalled: "I remember very clearly his reading the papers. He sat in the library in the couch facing the front door. Many times he wanted to share his comments with me. He really got into it."

In reading and responding to student papers, Dickey never advocated for a particular critical approach. Although educated at Vanderbilt, a university associated with the then-prevailing New Criticism, he wanted students to determine their own critical stance. Articulated in the twenties to explain and promote modernism, New Criticism dominated literary discourse until the sixties, arguing that any work of art was a self-contained whole to be experienced and explained without any reference to or information from the artist's biography, historical or cultural context, or even intention. Meaning was only derived from a poem, for example, from the words on the page. Prominent New Critics included Allen Tate, Robert Penn Warren, and John Crowe Ransom, the very poets associated with Vanderbilt or the Fugitives, writers who had, in turn, influenced Dickey's thinking about the theory and practice of poetry. Dickey's intent, however, was to steer students toward the poetry, not the criticism. As his colleague

Don Greiner noted, "Of the thousands of books in his personal library, the ones that were certain to generate scornful dismissal were those written by critics who believe their commentary on the poetry is as enduring as the poems that initiated the comments" (*James Dickey: Classes* xxviii). It was always clear, however, which critics he detested and which he recommended. In his class on Robert Bridges, he mentioned both Yvor Winters and Randall Jarrell in the same lecture. Of the former, he stated, "I hated him and he hated me...he's an excessively bad critic of some importance." Of the latter, he was more explicit: "Randall Jarrell is the finest literary critic of my time" (xxviii).

The paramount importance in any class meeting was the poets and their art. Moxley recalled, "He taught writers I barely knew (James Agee, e.g.) and made me fall in love with them. He covered the giants, too, like Eliot and Dickinson, and taught us to appreciate their greatness. One never felt any resentment from Dickey. He never belittled a writer, but ingeniously built each one into a force worthy of close study. He pulled no punches, though, would note writers' weaknesses, but he always led us to their strengths." Throughout his career, Dickey's classroom methodology remained consistent. He normally began with an overview of the life of the poet under discussion; biographical and historical context were important to him. He would then read key poems for analysis and commentary, pausing on specific lines that revealed important aspects about that poet and that served to comment on the poet's attitudes, before concluding with recommendations for secondary books to consult and assimilate. The course was never designed to be an exercise in close readings of great poems or to provide guidance on such matters as research and the development of persuasive, clear argument. The sessions, moreover, were never formally constructed presentations. He rarely prepared in advance, relying on memory rather than a systematic planning, research, and review of assigned material. Students, however, were mesmerized. Such spontaneity frequently led to spirited class discussions as well as an occasional factual error. For example, Dickey told his class that Trumbull Stickney had died at the age of twenty-eight when, in fact, he lived until the age of thirty. As Greiner observed regarding Dickey's classes, "Full of asides, witticisms, and afterthoughts, they suggest not the pontification of a scholar at an academic conference but the confident learning of a practicing poet who happens to enjoy being in the classroom" (*James Dickey: Classes* xxvii).

An unusual feature of Dickey's teaching style was his original use of language to characterize a specific writer. As Greiner has noted, "Dickey's skills at making surprising connections in class and at reading the poems as extensions of the lives of the poets led inevitably to pithy one-liners and memorable asides" (xxx). Regarding E. A. Robinson, for example, Dickey observed, "He's probably the most *prolific* tight-lipped poet that ever lived" (92). Conrad Aiken was "always talking about lovers standing in a garden" (210). On Archibald MacLeish, Dickey declared, "I don't know exactly what to think about MacLeish" (236), while Emily Dickinson, he concluded, was "a nun of poetry." The effect of these summations not only enabled students to hold all of a poet in a phrase but also to suggest the importance of language itself, its possibilities to teach and inform and delight. Another unusual aspect of his classes was the unexpected juxtapositions in his reading assignments that brought together two writers, suggesting to startled students that literature should not, or need not, be studied chronologically. To encourage them to view poetry and poets in the largest possible context, he would yoke together the poet whose readings had been assigned for that day with another writer. It was not problematic, for example, as his long lecture notes on Emily Dickinson reveal, to interject a short comment on Kingsley Amis, a British writer better known for his novels than his poetry. Poetry, in other words, was not a roll call of the dead but a living tradition. Dickey's lectures also invariably moved outside poetry and art itself to other disciplines. When discussing Dylan Thomas, for example, whom he considered one of the most original users of the English language, Dickey nonchalantly referenced William James, the late nineteenth- and early twentieth-century philosopher and psychologist. No matter the poet, the prevailing tone of his classes was always joy—in art, in language, and in the writers themselves. "He is one of the best writers who ever lived," Pat Conroy declared. "I thought it then, when I sat through two classes without ever speaking a word, spellbound by the joy the man took in teaching, and I think it now. He was shot through with words; they spilled out of him, and he would have had it no other way" (xv).

The fall semester of Dickey's Seminar in Verse Composition course centered on Form generally and the various forms specifically. "Poetry is a matter of luck," he told his final class of students in spring 1997.

> You can't teach it. You can point it out when it occurs, but you can't teach it. Verse, however, you can teach. Verse comes in a number of received forms which you can teach and can learn. That is what we deal with. This is a class in verse...hoping to become poetry. With luck. The luck comes not from me. I don't know where it

comes from...from God. As Valéry says, the French poet, God gives a poet one line. He has to work like hell for the rest of them. It is a matter of finding what goes with something that did come to you out of left field or from the blue. As Plato's *To ontōs on*—a world of perfect forms.

"So, the first semester," he emphasized, "is a course in forms." It dealt with the formal aspects of composition and verse. George Redman remembered the first class meeting when he enrolled in fall 1976. Sitting at his desk, Dickey began,

> "Notice the title of this course," he said. "It ain't POETRY. You can't teach anybody POETRY." He had a precise sense of timing, in the sense of the best comedians, preachers, teachers, and story-tellers. He paused until he felt the message had sunk in. "But you sure as hell can teach verse composition," he said, and slammed his huge ham of a hand onto the desk, palm flat. He rolled his tongue about his cheeks as if adjusting false teeth. He leaned from the desk, excited, his eyes young and intelligent and alive. "You sure as hell can teach verse. That's why, when I ask you to rhyme, or put so many feet in a line, to construct a couplet—a verse—you'd best damned sure know your basics and demonstrate control of your craft. There's no excuse for sloppy work. No excuse." (12)

Reflecting on the course, Redman declared, "His classes demanded production, a steady effort at both process and product.... From that first day forward, a misspelling, a forced or untrue rhyme, any grammatical error, infinitesimal or egregious, would set off a complete replay of the 'know your basics' speech" (12).

Yet Dickey's approach with his students was always positive. He stressed the word "connect"—"the connection between what someone has put down, and *you*. Not you in a classroom, but *you*, anywhere." He declared, "Poetry, like love, has to do with intimacy." Their classroom focus, he said, involved "the bringing of *your* experience into the poem and so completing it, insofar as the poem and *you* are concerned." The emphasis for Dickey then was always on the poet: "He puts the world together *his way*, by means of the word. He puts it together out of what he has experienced," but experience, he stressed, is "*every*thing that has ever found a place in his memory," which includes facts, dreams, conjectures, fantasies, reading, movies, hearsay, stories, and gossip. "To the poet," he told students, "all sources are good, whether empirically verifiable or not. His interest is not in *telling* the truth but making it. He wants to impose his vision on the material that has come to him from, well, anywhere." For an example, Dickey would frequently cite "The Shark's Parlor," stressing that he never did any of the things described in his poem: "I just made it up." "The important thing to remember, though, is not the genesis of the work in the poet's mind—that is important only to him—the important thing is the poetic experience that the poem results in, in you." Noting Jeffers's poem "November Surf," he declared: "Your ocean, that Jeffers' poem calls up, may in reality not be much—or anything—like the real ocean that Jeffers saw. *Nevertheless*, it is your ocean, according to the images you have now. And that, for you, is where the poem happens." The poet and the reader, in other words, were inextricably linked. He added, "And nothing can be more important than this: the keeping-alive of the individual human sensibility. In this case, the keeping-alive of it by means of words. Words which call up a response in a person—you, me—and ask him to lay part of his life on the line, that is, the line or maybe the lines, of the poem." The poem and the individual sensibility, Dickey concluded,

> with its own accumulated memories and likes and dislikes, with its god-given—or I would say, angelic—capacity to respond with, as Henry James called it, its "accessibility to experience": these two things are not only in a personal and creative responsibility to each other, they are factors which enrich and deepen a person's experience and being *in* the world: vitally, intelligently, and bodily.

"The overall intention," Dickey explained in his lecture notes, "is that of a refining of instruments. Poetry is not gush, but an exquisitely refined instrument for communication-in-depth." "It is also a speculative instrument," he wrote, "and deals with and utilizes contingency and possibility." Therefore, he stressed the flexibility of class sessions, adding that although "the game plan" centered on progression, the slow and continual improvement of student sensibilities and capabilities, one question remained: "What is to be communicated by the very instrument that poetry is. This has to do with the personal psychology of the poet, as well as the individual psychologies of anyone who ever encounters his poems under any circumstances, or in any language." Course texts intended to facilitate that communication included Karl Shapiro and Robert Beum's *Prosody Handbook*, Lewis Turco's *Book of Forms*, and John Hollander's *Rhyme's Reason*. Dickey recommended as well *The Creative Process*, edited by Brewster Ghiselin, and Philip Dacey and David Jauss's *Strong Measures: Contemporary American Poetry in Traditional Forms.*

The early weeks of English 600 involved Dickey's efforts to reassure students and to engage them in the process, labeling inhibition as "one of the most pernicious besetting difficulties of young writers" and discussing what he termed "the tools of the trade." "What to the ordinary writer is a chisel, in the poet's case must be like a scalpel: much finer, much sharper, wielded with much more skill." He stressed, therefore, a continual recourse to "the elements of human language, centering on the English language: the syntactical and grammatical and general formal part, the codified part of verbal usage." Lean on the rules, he advised: "Rules are there; they change but as they change they are codified, and you can learn the changes." He believed mass media had disseminated bad usage. If students had a freshman text that codified the rules, they should retrieve it. Good writing denoted good grammar. Gary Kerley, who audited the course in fall 1976, recalled an amusing anecdote when the semester was ending. As Dickey walked by, he rubbed Kerley's head, and Kerley, "the elements of human language" now firmly codified, shouted to the laughter of other students, "I can write!"

To involve them in the creative process, Dickey initially asked students to concentrate on "Things," to psychoanalyze fire, for example, or to investigate the poetic qualities of special relationships. Citing Harold Pinter, he encouraged the class to enter into the interplay between buildings and the psychology of those people who lived and worked in them. The point of such exercises, he wrote in his lecture notes, was to "begin with the human perpetual organism and organization itself: with the five senses, with the brain and nerves, the neuro-vascular system." He quoted Mallarmé: "To be really man or nature when thinking, one must think with all one's body," and then modulated into Burnshaw's *The Seamless Web*:

> My approach, then, is "physiological," yet it issues from a vantage point different from Vico's where he said that all words originated in the eyes, the arms, and the other organs from which they were grown into analogies. My concern is rather with the type of creature-mind developed by the human organism in its long movement through time out of the evolutionary shocks which gave birth to what we have named self-consciousness. (1–2)

Burnshaw believed that human beings were intricately connected with the Earth's rotation and orbit. The body reflected the "circadian rhythms" in pulse rate, urine volume, and body temperature, all of which, Burnshaw stated, "are in phase with the time of his maximal physical activity. As the circadian cycle progresses, his body's condition changes" (2). Because instinct, involuntary receptivity, and the deliberate act of attention are linked, Dickey noted the importance of what Burnshaw termed "seizure," which used to be called inspiration. "It begins as dictation, with the poet listening to something that speaks to him: he listens and sees the words. They command his attention. They break through and into his awareness; they will not be ignored. They are using him as their recorder" (48). "The material mater, the mother material," he told his classes. "It's in the whole mind, as distinct from the conscious mind. The whole mind, and it's also in the body. I teach this semester what I call 'Creature Poetry.' Poetry written with the whole sentient organism. Mind, body, guts, blood flow, breath, everything that enables you to be a living being, we have as a resource." Dickey's first assignment, therefore, was for students to attempt to combine two things: "your concentration on an object or action or scene—preferably an object, either natural or man-made—and your simultaneous attempt to experience the object '*in*voluntarily': that is to say, to let the thing come over to you, to let *it give* you what to say about itself."

Following these discussions, Dickey introduced specific forms, beginning initially with epigrammatic and satiric couplets followed, first, by lines that were four or five beats in length and then by poems that displayed more complex rhyming. Eventually students were assigned the ballad, quatrain, lyric, blank verse, sonnet, villanelle, and sestina. Occasionally he would also teach haiku and terza rima. Multiple examples of each form were always distributed and discussed. For heroic couplets, for example, Dickey provided samples from Roy Campbell, John Dryden, Alexander Pope, and Christopher Smart; samples depicting four or five beats a line included works by Robert Lowell, E. A. Robinson, John Masefield, Andrew Marvell, Ben Jonson, and W. B. Yeats. For the villanelle, Dickey shared W. H. Auden's "If I Could Tell You," William Empson's "Villanelle," Dylan Thomas's "Do Not Go Gentle Into That Good Night," Theodore Roethke's "The Waking," William Bell's "Such Lovely Clouds Are Making from the Dead," and Eric Barker's "In Easy Dark."

Students frequently followed Dickey into English 601, in which they wrote one poem throughout the semester, continually revising or re-creating it by exploring the different ways it might be presented. As he informed his class, "Last semester we were concerned with form rather than subject-matter: were concerned with *what to do with it*. But where do you *get* it? Where does it come from?" The first assignment, from which everything else would develop, was for students to write three pages of invention: a dream, an image- or event-association, and a word- or verbal-association. Students labeled each example because, Dickey admitted to his students, these writings often overlapped: "I want to know where you started. Where you will finish, God alone can tell. And perhaps not *He*, either!" On the basis of one of these, students would begin to create their poem. Dickey posited the following considerations for poetic composition:

1. Invent: dream, associate, remember, seize things from (in) the mind *in any way.*
2. Scrutinize: what I call open scrutiny, vivid scrutiny, receptive scrutiny, of either subject or words themselves, *any* passage, *any* idea—concept of *sparking.*
3. This with a view toward ascertaining *possibilities*; and *further* sparkings of association: "new thresholds, new anatomies."
4. Assessment of options; evaluation of options, *whole* trains of thought or single fragments.
5. Choice, based either on intellectual or emotional intuitive factors, or both.
6. Extensions, development of theme. Technical and formalistic means of such extension and development. Assessment of what material might subsequently come in.
7. Conclusions: assess possibilities for conclusion coming naturally out of treatment of theme according to the six preceding steps. Or repudiation of *any* conclusion, if desired.

During the first class meeting, he sought to clarify the difference between verse and poetry, on the one hand, and between verse and prose, on the other hand, arguing that, unlike prose, verse had a self-imposed consistent structure of stresses. Poets, too, employed heavy meter, including Poe, Kipling, Robert Service, and Tennyson. Distinguishing poetry therefore became more difficult, and Dickey suggested it be defined as "an original insight arrived at by means of memorable language." "I sometimes think," however, he wrote in *Sorties,*

> that the best definition of poetic creativity that I know of is the title of the book by the French writer [Noël Mathieu] who calls himself Pierre Emmanuel, which means in English, *Poetry, Reason on Fire.* And if that's not what his title means exactly, it's what it *ought* to

mean. It seems to me that a kind of heightening of the reasoning faculty, the inducement or occurrence of a state in which the *reason* jumps back and forth making fortuitous and perhaps, under those conditions, inevitable connections, is what really happens when one is on one of those higher wave lengths of the imagination that produces genuinely new metaphors. (26–27)

Dickey also recognized the need to deliberately assault what he termed "the main barrier that exists for young poets: inhibition." To that end he added, "I want to get as much Romantic or 'let-go' feeling as I can into those of you who are classical in persuasion."

In the classes that followed, he discussed sources young poets might use to assist the creative process, quoting Thoreau to stress the difficulty involved: "The road to satisfaction leads through a long series of disgusts." The Greeks, he told his students, declared that memory was the mother of the Muse but, he then added, "it's not the only mother." Inspiration was "buried in musculature, the cardiovascular system." He specifically advised students to use the *American Heritage* dictionary, believing it the best; yet he also praised both the *Oxford English Dictionary*, which he called a "microscope where you can isolate yourself with the words themselves," and the *Harcourt Brace Handbook*. Dickey often cited examples from his own experience as support, as when he recalled an editor commenting on a section of *Alnilam*: "My editor referred to one section of my novel, which I thought scarcely divine, as illiterate." Also admonishing his students to use *Roget's Thesaurus*, he added, "I've found a word or two out of there myself, although I wouldn't admit to which."

As students worked on their first prose writing, the depiction of a dream, he talked at length about the dream experience, quoting the French writer Gérard de Nerval: "The dream is a second life." "Yes," Dickey would respond, "but of *maximum* intensity," and he then related a previous night's dream, one "in which I'd stare at everything." As he had the previous semester, he urged students to read Burnshaw's *The Seamless Web*, whose central premise was that poetry is not written by the mind alone. Instead, Burnshaw discussed what he termed "creature poetry," which also involved instinct and spontaneity. "In the end," Dickey later wrote regarding Burnshaw's study,

the reader, especially if he is a poet or aspires to be, thinks not about the book but about himself and his resources, about what the universe has given him to funnel into his words: the words waiting in his own biorhythms, the Circadian cycles, the tides and the sun and moon, in cosmic rays and forces beyond all of these, unascertainable but always incoming. One goes back through the book compulsively, then, re-assimilating everything, including the notes, *all* notes. Circadian cycle? Mystical, in essence. Instinct? Also. Birds? Perhaps the greatest mystics, with their celestial navigation, their homing capacities. Fish? Bees? All mystics. We? As well, in infinite complication and fascination. But also, by means of our language, with an opportunity to use all these things in a way that is ours alone. ("The Total Act" ix–x)

Burnshaw's idea of opening up words that were convincingly tied to the whole of creation required a form of contemplation that was, in an entirely new sense, religious.

Dreams, for Dickey, became one means by which to connect to that cosmic realm. "If we could speak our dreams," he told the class, "we would be dictating continuous poetry." As such, they are a primary resource to tap into the subconscious, "bottomless inexhaustible, endless." He agreed with Joseph Campbell's belief that dreams were a form of communication with ourselves in a unique, metaphoric language, what Montague Allman termed "moving metaphors," that contained our feelings about a situation, the past and present feelings related to these feelings, and our ways of coping with them. They provide direct access to key emotional issues. "The language of dreams is a personal one," he wrote in his lecture notes, "filled with meaning derived from our own unique experiences over a lifetime. There are a number of symbols that have a universal quality (fire, water, for example), but the real reward of dream work comes when we begin to learn our own personal dream language." In his spring 1996 class, he provided students with his own example of a prose description of one of his dreams:

On some steps that go down into an unlimited void, I am standing upright, with my hands on the hilt of a steel sword. My body is run-through by a bundle of invisible lines which are tied to the corners of the kind of open building I am in, and also run through the center of the sun. Without their wounding me I walk along holding all those threads going through me, and it seems as though my flesh comes to life more and more, in contact with these threads that are like the lines of perspective in a drawing.

If I trace around me a circle with the point of my sword, the threads which are nourishing me could be cut. I do this, and I end up inside something like a column of the building, or a place like a cistern or well. I wait for years, until it occurs to me to start bashing and banging with my sword, and I do, and cut down the walls, with great laps of sparks and deafening sound. I wake up covered with sweat. End of dream.

In spring 1997 he related a repetitive dream he periodically experienced. "I have a dream, a most terrible dream of pursuit," he said. "Of being pursued by something unspeakably terrible. I am always moving against a terrible wind, which doesn't bother my pursuer at all. But I have to grab the grass, try to inch forward, and something is just gaining on me with leaps and bounds. It's terrible. Some sort of guilt I guess. If I were a post-Freudian I'm sure I would have to admit to it." Dickey agreed with Rosalind Cartwright, he told the class, that dreams provided direct access to the key emotional issues in a dreamer's life, though he did not then suggest what issues his dream suggested.

In addition to dreams of the Happy Swimming Pool, his second wife Deborah Dodson Dickey recalled, he would often dream of roller skating, an activity he cherished as a child in and around Buckhead. West Wesley, Dickey told her, had "a perfect curve there." In that dream, he felt complete freedom, an exhilaration which he depicted in a scene from his novel *Alnilam*. His discussion of dreams also involved commentary regarding time, and Dickey mingled personal memories and coincidences with books students should read, including J. B. Priestley's *Midnight on the Desert*, Edwin Abbott's *Flatland*, J. W. Dunne's *An Experiment with Time*, Anna Balakian's *Surrealism: The Road to the Absolute*, and David Gascoyne's *A Short History of Surrealism*. Dickey's daughter, Bronwen, recalls a dream her father had after Maxine died about a girl with long black hair on a stage. Shortly thereafter he had met Deborah Dodson, who had recently performed in *Time and the Conways*, a play by Priestley, one of Dickey's favorite writers. Later, while *Deliverance* was being filmed, he was introduced to a film editor, Tom Priestley, whose father was J. B. Priestly. Throughout his life Dickey believed in the dream life and Jungian synchronicity.

Like dreams, images were also important to Dickey, and he stressed them in his Verse Composition course. "As a poet I am not only interested in how images arise in the individual mind out of words, and the ways in which these may be said, but how, conversely, images result in words, connect with them, call them into being, organize them into poems and other pieces of writing that have what we call the poetic quality"

("LIGHTNING, or *Visuals*" 6). The words "flock" and "swerve" intrigued him as did the phrases "align the bow" and "the lead buffalo." His emphasis, Dickey insisted, was on "the necessary and infinitely valuable personal nature of the image that is evoked, from whatever source" (11). Defining the image, focusing it to achieve clarity, becomes mandatory in the poetic search. "All poetry is in it," he declared. One of the most beautiful similes he knew occurred in two lines from Tennyson's notebooks: "As those that lie on happy shores and see / Thro' the near blossom slip the distant sail." "What would not be possible to focus," he asserted, "—the near and far together, equally defined—by a telescope or field glasses is perfectly clear to the inner perspective" (12). The mind's inner eye possesses a lensing quality that clarifies the image for the poet. From evocative images, say, the flower close to one's face, each petal and vein distinct, and through it, miles away, a moving sail, white and curved, not urgent but moving, and sharp in outline, may come a memorable poem, what Dickey termed "a kind of tapestry of inner light" (12).

Also believing, as did Herbert Read, that "art retreats before the intellect" and that a dream was arranged by symbolic intention, Dickey wanted his students "to find a way to get the underground stream of connectivity to show itself to light." He stated, "We need to find that entity Mr. Eliot calls the objective correlative." As students worked on their presentation of a dream as well as two rewrites, designed, as Dryden declared, "to move the sleeping images toward the light," Dickey discussed what aspiring poets should read. He frequently added asides that revealed personal preferences. When he recommended students read "*all* poetry written in English," citing W. H. Auden's five-volume *Poets of the English Language*, he noted that Auden considered Shakespeare's *Anthony and Cleopatra* as the most poetic play, but that he himself credited that distinction to *Macbeth*. Moreover, he told the class, they should read foreign language poems; books on or about poetic technique (including Brewster Ghiselin's *The Creative Handbook*; Babette Deutsch's *Poetry Handbook*, *Princeton Encyclopedia of Poetry and Poetics*, edited by Alex Preminger; John Hall Wheelock's *What Is Poetry*; and Paul Valéry's *The Art of Poetry*); interviews with poets (especially those in *Paris Review*) as well as their diaries, journals (he noted those of Hawthorne, Emerson, and Thoreau), and letters (Keats's correspondence was quite good); criticism (he especially liked that of Randall Jarrell); works on American culture, particularly Dwight Morris's *The Territory Ahead* and Seymour Crimms's *Views of a Short-Sighted Cannoneer*; fiction (because some writers such as Faulkner, Updike, Melville, and

Proust were especially poetic); movies and film scripts (Dickey favored James Agee's script of *The African Queen* ("Actually, the aesthetic quality of the script is far better than the movie," citing the line "the first faint splintering of rain" as an example); books on linguistics ("even dull books," he said); philosophy, including Bertrand Russell's *History of Western Philosophy*, and works by Nietzsche, Schopenhauer, Henri Bergson, William James, and Jacques Maritain; literary scholarship on poetry; books that evaluate critical taste, such as those of Stanley Edgar Hyman; mythology, including texts by Carl Jung, Joseph Campbell, and Robert Graves; material on music and painting; works on creativity, such as Arthur Koestler's *The Art of Creation*; anthropology, including studies by Franz Boas and others; books on style; cultural historians such as Lewis Mumford; books on science, such as those by Loren Eisley, Lewis Thomas, and Jacob Bronowski; essayists, especially those by naturalists, including John McPhee, Edward Abbey, Joseph Wood Krutch, and Edward Hoagland; and biographies. The list of recommended readings always overwhelmed students and left them convinced that Dickey had read almost everything.

In the classes that followed, Dickey discussed his seven rules for poetic composition, directing students to:

1. Invent, however primitive or absurd the material or dramatic situation;
2. Scrutinize either the subject or a passage with the central imperative that one remain open to further associations;
3. Assess the possibilities one has offered himself, remembering Hart Crane's dictum: "New thresholds! New anatomies!"
4. Assess one's options, which is usually a matter of intuition;
5. Choose based on intellectual or emotional (or both) factors;
6. Explore, extend, develop the theme; and
7. Develop the material from one point to a conclusion of some kind—think beginning, middle, end—because a poem is "a sequence of thought."

His litany then continued of writers and works he felt students should read, including the essays of J. B. Priestley, George P. Eliot, Leslie Fiedler, Stanley Edgar Hyman, John Burrows, Stephen Spender, W. H. Auden, William Hazlett, Alexander Smith, Arthur Koestler, and Aldous Huxley. His comments and asides were frequently humorous, such as his view of adverbs: "I pride myself on the use of adverbs. I defer to no man on this. I

am the very king.... Everybody knows it, especially because I tell them."
He freely offered what he had learned: "When a poet approaches an excellent poem, he thinks: 1) I must write it, but can't; 2) I can't write it; 3) The writer writes it." For homework, he assigned his own essay, "The G. I. Can of Beats, The Fox in the Wave, and The Hammers Over Open Ground," which discussed linguistic approaches to poetry and which he had delivered at the 1982 convention of the South Atlantic Modern Language Association. He continually stressed the imagination, citing Mallarmé's line on sunset, "Victoriously fled the beautiful suicide" and Hart Crane's "the seal's wide spindrift gaze toward paradise," which Dickey stressed was not factual but imaginary and linguistically oriented. The trouble with American poets, he declared, was that they succeeded early and kept polishing the same jewel; Richard Wilbur was an example: "Wilbur has written the same poem since he was 21." He wrote in *Sorties*, "I do not wish to say anything in poetry *neatly*. That is the main trouble with Dick Wilbur's poetry: the sense of habitual dispatch" (45). He added, "One of the good things about Robert Lowell is that he *did* change." The irony, however, is that by doing so so radically, both Lowell and Dickey lost their literary stature. "The problem of creative writing," he continued, "is essentially one of concentration, a focusing of attention in a special way that provides an openness to experience." This involved a spiritual state where "you forget you have a body. You feel the *necessity* to write poetry." He cited two types of concentration: 1) the immediate (Auden, Mozart) and 2) the plodding (Spender, Beethoven). Aiding in this effort, he asserted, was the use of notebooks, but he also emphasized the importance of inspiration, faith in oneself, and what he termed "the music a poem will assume."

Students who enrolled in Verse Composition appreciated what they believed Dickey had given them. Their course evaluations led to his being named Teacher of the Year by the English department for 1987–1988. Mike James, for example, who first met Dickey at the South Carolina Governor's School for the Arts in 1988, was impressed that Dickey had worked in business but entered teaching "because he thought he brought something unique—the idea that one should allow any and all ideas to come forward." If one is a poet, Dickey told James, he just has ideas. Prizes and awards come later, if at all. "There's only one reason to write anything, though," Dickey stated, "and that's to make it as good as you can make it." Michael Taylor, who spent a semester working on a poem titled "Into the Cave," declared,

He included my cave poem in *From the Green Horseshoe*, and I went on to write about caves and cavers around the world, publishing accounts in dozens of popular magazines, four books, and several documentary films and television programs.... I've taught graduate and undergraduate sections of creative nonfiction for over 30 years, and I still find delight in spotting a passion in students—any passion—whatsoever—and sharing with them good books and articles on that subject, which, thanks to Mr. Dickey, I somehow seem to know.

Margaret Renkl, whose creative thesis, "Small Comforts," Dickey directed, recalled how she had telephoned him at home one evening to say that she had finally discovered the one-syllable word needed in a particular passage. Dickey had immediately answered and, upon hearing that she had discovered the word neither of them had been able to discover in conference earlier that afternoon, exclaimed, "You got it! "He was always an absolute gentleman," she stated. "He believed in me." Dickey, while reading the draft of a poem David Havird had shown him, paused at the wording in one line, and quietly repeated it aloud. "The prodigious son," he said again. "That's perfectly beautiful." Havird enrolled in every Dickey course and became a poet himself, believing that Dickey excelled at drawing attention to wording that impressed him.

Dan Dahlquist, who enrolled in Dickey's creative writing classes during the 1981–1982 academic year and who also became a poet himself, remembers Dickey's parting words to him: "Quoting a German poet, he said, 'Businessmen have the look of sheep being led to slaughter. But you shall know your brother by the pure flash of his eye.'" "Dickey's insights were brilliant," Dahlquist declared.

Jim Dickey came at poetry from the *inside*. He was a fine novelist and critic, but he *lived* poetry.... His teaching style was warm and filled with humor—occasionally raucous humor. Much of his effectiveness lay in his ability to *perform* poetry to an audience. He had an actor's skill in playing his operatives, knowing when to understate moments of high drama. His warm southern accent could be spellbinding—and what is poetry if not a kind of spell?... To my mind Jim struck a fair balance between necessary truth ("You've got to be rough on the stuff," he told me once after class, "or it doesn't do anybody any good.") and praise that could sometimes be effusive.

Dahlquist continued, "James Dickey gave me, and countless other students, permission to be poets. He made me feel that being a poet was not only okay, it was the highest, finest thing I could hope to do with my life." "Yes. James Dickey was a barnstormer for poetry," Dahlquist concluded, "But he acknowledged that poetry is not for everyone. Without that flash of the eye, I can hear him say, we are, well, like the others."

Dickey's friend and colleague at USC, Don Greiner, requested Dickey visit his advanced honors college seminar, which concentrated on Pound, Frost, Stevens, Dickey, and Plath, asking him ahead of time to focus on his war poems, particularly "The Firebombing." "For that reason," Greiner remembered, "Jim wore his flight jacket and brought one of his instruments of navigation. I think he also brought his combat hat. I'll fall back on the cliché and say that his comments about the war and his war poems mesmerized the students. After the class, and after I had hurried to my graduate seminar, he walked with some of the students to one of the many campus coffee shops to continue the conversation. He was generous with them."

On 20 February 1996, Dickey announced that he would be awarding a prize—the "lead buffalo" belt buckle—to the best student poem in his English 601 course. The back of the belt buckle read: "A large male bison can stand as high as 6 ft at the shoulders and reach a massive weight of 7 ton [sic]. With its heavily muscled neck and matted forelock hairs, the bison's forehead has been known to stop bullets." Two weeks before the end of the semester, he began the process of elimination. "One by one he went over the poems," Julie Bloemeke recalled. "He would spend the entire class on one student and the next class he would present another student, praising what was strong in each poem, undoubtedly with asides." To her surprise, the award finally went to her. "Understand it was not because he felt my poem 'Transfusion' was a finished poem, but rather the poem that had most realized itself. I was utterly gobsmacked at the time of course. And over the years—especially when I had a lull in writing—it has been the lead buffalo that I have held in my palm, reminding me that if JD believed in my work, then I needed to do the same as well."

Deborah Dickey stated that while her husband was in Seattle for surgery to repair a hiatal hernia, Dickey had been given a Native American moniker by a member of the Sioux tribe: "Buffalo Who Grows." Perhaps it was not surprising then that Dickey should refer to the belt buckle as being the *lead* buffalo. Perhaps he meant to distinguish its metal composition, lead as opposed to brass or silver, but it is more likely, given his delight in language, that he intended to suggest the position of the bison at the front of the herd, that buffalo that would have surpassed all others and determined where, in the limitless horizon before it, it would go. In his mind it would have recalled the Altamira cave bison. Nor was it surprising that Dickey would offer the buckle up as an award to a student, one who with great good luck and perseverance would eventually write poetry rather than verse.

At the conclusion of his 14 January 1997 class, Dickey told his students, who were gathered around the table of his home on Lelia's Court,

> With my current physical shape, this will undoubtedly be my last class. Forever. So, that doesn't put any strain on anybody, on me or anybody else, but if I should have to terminate, or if some outside force should terminate me, and they assign you to another teacher, go ahead and do what he or she has you do. I will turn the class over to another poet to do it his way or her way. I don't think that's gonna happen. But what we start here, I would like you to continue on your own, regardless of the course, or what the person teaching the course, would have you do. When we start this process, I want you to continue with it. When we get started, I want you to fight this thing through. Fight the thing through that we start with your own unconscious and your own dreams and see where it comes out. That's the excitement and fun of it. Deep discovery. Deep adventure. It's the most dangerous game, and the best. Flaubert says somewhere, that the life of a poet is a hell of a life. It's a dog's life. But it's the only one worth living. You suffer more. Over things that don't bother other people. But you also live so much more. You live so much more intensely, and so much more vitally, and with so much more of a sense of meaning, of consequentiality, of things mattering, instead of nothing mattering.

"This," he concluded, "is the beginning place."
That Sunday night, 19 January, Dickey died.

CHAPTER 12

"WHERE THE SUN IS DOWN
ON HIM ALONE"

The publication of *Deliverance* put Dickey at the apogee of literary and financial success, but the fame he acquired and the monies he accrued undercut his intensive work ethic, one that created poems whereby, as Laurence Lieberman wrote in his review of *Poems 1957–1967*, "opposed worlds can meet and unite" (513–20). Even before the novel, however, Dickey's domestic life had become dysfunctional. Chris Dickey recalls the parties almost every Sunday while his father was teaching at Reed College in 1963. "Bacon and eggs and Ramos gin fizzes at eleven in the morning for a handful of students and favored faculty members," he later wrote. "It was good to be drunk. It was fun. And it was great to be living this kind of life in this kind of place. And Jim Dickey was starting to write the best poems of his career. And starting to work, seriously now, on *Deliverance*. What could be wrong with that? But we all knew something was wrong. And we even knew the drinking was part of it. The alcohol kept flowing just the same" (*Summer of Deliverance* 123–24). Financially comfortable after *Deliverance* in the success American culture provided him, Dickey became less focused on his writing and more acclimated to a lifestyle that justified and facilitated drinking and promiscuity. Indeed, he believed the public expected such behavior. Becoming a celebrated poet and novelist, moreover, rather than an engineer or businessman preferred by his parents, confirmed in his mind the elevated status he had yearned for as an adolescent when he read *Doc Savage* and other pulp magazines and novels. Not surprisingly, then, he declared in *Sorties*, "It seems to me that I am the bearer of some kind of immortal message to humankind" (54). His success also solidified a series of emotional and psychological contradictions which Dickey never finally resolved: his sense of being born only to mitigate the death of the "other brother"; his unwillingness in elementary school to be considered privileged when his parents were relatively affluent; his realization that he would never be a revered sports star, whether in high school or at Clemson, and that his brother Tom was indeed such a star; and his "washing out" of pilot training in the army air forces, having to settle for navigator when he had always imagined himself a pilot. The disparity between Dickey's idealized self and his actual identity created inner tensions that necessitated his creative stories and exaggerations. His war record, for example, exemplary in itself, nevertheless required that he present himself as a daring pilot who flew "over 100 missions against the Japanese" as well as a quarterback who played for Clemson and who was good enough to play in the NFL had not injury precluded it. He was creating himself as a hero, though he never came to believe, as some contend, the self-made myths about himself. They remained illusions he projected, not delusions that fractured his psyche.

Social drinking in the fifties yielded to extensive periods of intoxication in the sixties, seventies, and eighties; he needed the alcohol to calm his nerves, free his inhibitions, or sustain his creative impulses. With his faculties dulled by alcohol and his literary commitment weakened by wealth, the work he completed after *Deliverance* was largely dismissed by reviewers. Because Dickey had earlier clearly identified himself with his persona in an effort to distinguish himself from other poets, these critics not only quickly attacked the new poems but also Dickey himself. The transformation in his public persona perplexed his family. "At some readings," Chris remembered,

> James Dickey was triumphant, and the audience was on its feet. At some he was a spectacle of slurred words and awkward silences— and still he got a standing ovation. And I got used to that, more or less. But when he read the poems about himself and about us, I couldn't get over the idea that something was missing. My father was a better man, I thought, a braver man, more wise and loving and even more mystical than he would let on in public. His poet persona puzzled and angered and disappointed me. This half-drunk world he invented at the readings was less mysterious and exciting than the world as it was—or had been—his world, our world, the world that he had given us. (*Summer of Deliverance* 133)

After the family moved to Columbia, however, he recognized that his father did not believe the invented stories himself. What he said and what he did, Chris wrote, was "for the sake of the poem.... It was all a game. It served his needs, he said" (134, 135).

For Dickey a poem was always spiritual, much like prayer. It constituted an effort to connect with and enter a larger, more mysterious realm, enhancing one's self, bringing it into a deeper awareness of identity and its relationship to physical reality. As such, his writing was synonymous with the Romantic ideal, essentially a search for transcendence; facts were secondary, if not irrelevant. The imagination, he contended, must not be restricted and, given a poem's intent, no subject precluded. As he wrote in *Sorties*, "Anyone who courts sublimity has to run the risk of looking ridiculous" (53). Consequently, poems that dealt with past memories or present loved ones need not adhere too closely, if at all, to factual truth, a belief that explains why Donald Armstrong in "The Performance" died in his plane crash, not by a Japanese executor's sword; why Dickey needed only a few steps to reach out and grab his six-year-old son near a busy highway in California, not sprint at college-football speed to prevent Kevin in "The Bee" from running into murderous traffic; and why in "The Cancer Match" and "Diabetes," his persona suffers from diseases Dickey himself never had.

In the Preface to *The Central Motion: Poems, 1968–1979*, which includes *The Eye-Beaters*, *The Zodiac*, and *The Strength of Fields*, Dickey reaffirmed his commitment to poetic experimentation: "The three books here may show—do show, I feel—a change of subject matter and method, and, together with some failures of taste and understanding, make up my attempts at writing a different kind of poem from the anecdotal narratives of the previous books and lead forward from them toward further, perhaps more extreme, changes" (v). Each volume in the collection attempted a different approach or format. When specifically asked in 1996 about *The Zodiac*, for example, Dickey responded: "It's a failure as a poem, so everybody is overjoyed to tell me. But I would almost rather have written that than anything else. It takes more chances. It's an impossible thing to bring off. That's the kind of thing I like to try, to try to do the impossible. It's got some things in it that I wouldn't have missed; I surely wouldn't" (Greiner, "Making the Truth" 14). All three volumes, however, were critical failures. In mid-career, Dickey seemingly assumed that the transcendent exchanges clearly notable in his early poems had become impossible in life; Platonic idealism yielded to Aristotelian duality. As Christopher Morris wrote, each Dickey poem failed to present a sustaining image as it attempted "a new assault on the insoluble" (35). Chris Dickey later observed, "There is no glossing over the fact that for many years, as my father tried to write through a fog of alcohol, some of his oeuvre suffered" ("Foreword" xi).

The decline in Dickey's creativity owed to a variety of factors. In addition to alcohol and the absence of financial worries, the seventies brought an increasing sense of physical debilitation and human mortality, evidenced in part by entries in his journals. Moreover, the negative reviews of *The Zodiac* and *The Strength of Fields* owed partly to the fact that the enormous success of *Deliverance* contributed to the public's perception of Dickey as a novelist. In his 1979 essay "The Energized Man," he continued to anguish over the effects of aging as well as the decline of his poetic abilities:

> We somehow lead ourselves to believe that the moments of youth—ah, youth, indeed!—were those times when our faculties responded and we loved and hated violently, spent sleepless nights, conceived great projects, and lived in a world of purpose which could not have existed without us. We persuade ourselves that, yes, it was nice, but it was a long time ago, and we should turn to other things: things like...well, comfort. (Weigl, Hummer163)

He had lost the Platonic ideal to which his poetry had previously aspired and was, in fact, now waging a war against time.

Yet Dickey's abrupt fall from critical grace, following the dramatic rise of his literary reputation in the sixties, also owed to larger cultural and literary forces. The anti-war movement and the women's movement specifically and the liberalization of social values generally created an intellectual climate antithetical to the perceived values inherent in such poems as "The Firebombing," "May Day Sermon," "The Fiend," and "Slave Quarters," where combat was seemingly celebrated, women sexualized, and African Americans trivialized. The underlying political and social agendas of critics resulted in a too-simple dismissal of Dickey's work. As Ernest Suarez correctly noted, "His willingness to explore fundamental impulses from a variety of perspectives has generated a body of work that today's academy cannot accommodate" (157). Dickey was conscious of the political dynamic, though he failed to effectively counter it. While interviewed by William Buckley in 1971 on *Firing Line*, for example, he discussed what he termed "the moral put-down" that then existed: "In my own field, that of poetry, I have seen review after review saying that such-and-such a poet doesn't take the correct stand on Vietnam. He may be against the war in Vietnam, but he is not against it in exactly the *same way* that I am against it. Therefore, his is really a failure of morality, and his verse stinks" (*Night Hurdling* 150). That Dickey had actually encouraged reviewers, critics, readers, and audiences to view the poem's protagonist as synonymous with himself left him exposed to critical and personal attacks of which Bly's was only the earliest and most notable. As the seventies and eighties proceeded, he found himself increasingly ignored, even relegated to a regional poet. Later reflecting, Dickey must have felt his career to be irrecoverable. As he wrote in "Gila Bend" (1987),

> This silver-stone heat
> No man can cross; no man could get
> To his feet, even to rise face-out
> Full-force from the grave, where the sun is down on him
> Alone, harder than resurrection
> Is úp.

Dickey's father died on 12 March 1974. Although he had asserted in *Self-Interviews* that "my father and I have always been very close" (26), his attitude was better characterized by his statement in *Sorties*: "I am appalled by the thinness of my father's experience. It has been monotonous, tiresome, and valueless because he has been essentially, passive [*sic*]" (68). He had imagined his father's death in poems such as "The Hospital Window" and "Approaching Prayer," in which Eugene Dickey assumes an elevated or messianic stature, but his reaction now was muted. As he lay dying, Eugene requested that Dickey play on his guitar the Baptist hymn "Just a Closer Walk with Thee," which Dickey had learned as a child. By the time he finished the second chorus, Eugene had died. Chris Dickey remembers that "barely a ripple had passed through the family. Or, at least, none that I could feel. My father had built such a screen of contempt around his own father that he barely talked about him in life and seemed to forget about him in death. No reason he ever gave me could tell me why.... He was no more missed than a piece of furniture that had been moved to storage" (*Summer of Deliverance* 209). Dickey's relationship with his father, complex when he was a child, had become one of adult indifference with the coming of literary and financial success. Yet his response to his father's death, more reserved than indifferent—he kissed Eugene on the head and left the hospital with the mother of an Atlanta friend, Ashley Walker, who talked to him about her diabetic blindness—lay as much in his fundamental paralysis when confronting death as in any view of his father as a weak-willed tyrant.

Dickey's financial success continued. In 1974 Hollywood producers Malcolm Stuart and Charles Fries offered him $40,000 to write a screenplay for NBC based on Jack London's *Call of the Wild*, the last film version of which had been made in the thirties. London's novel portrayed the conflict between the wilderness and civilization that *Deliverance* had featured; like London, moreover, Dickey romanticized nature while admitting its stark brutality. However, his initial effort resulted in a script NBC executives considered too unpolished; Stuart wrote a five-page letter on 20 December requesting revisions. Two months later Dickey submitted his revisions, informing Stuart that he considered the script complete and advising him to begin production. The television adaption, which aired on 19 May 1976, straightforwardly depicted London's characters and ideas and revealed little imaginative creation. With Maxine and Christopher, Dickey flew to California to watch the "premier," an advance screening. Christopher, now twenty-three and married with a four-year-old son, remembered afterward, "I don't think any of us knew what to say. Even as a TV movie it was mediocre. But there was no way to tell that to Jim Dickey" (*Summer of Deliverance* 209). Dickey reveled in the new attention; in his letters his voice exuded confidence. He wrote Stanley Burnshaw on 26 April 1976, for example, describing *Call of the Wild* as a "television spectacular" (Bruccoli, Baughman 384). He wrote Burnshaw again on 24 September 1981, noting another project about the Yukon and the Klondike gold rush. Jerome Hellman, the producer, Dickey wrote, "is very prestigious and rich; at least he is rich *now*, and although wealth and affluence come and go very quickly in Hollywood, at this time he has or can get as much money as he wants to spend on any project he comes up with" (417). Hollywood money reinforced Dickey's sense of success.

Monies kept coming his way, though it was also clear that critical success was not forthcoming. During fall 1974, Dickey involved himself in the promotion of *Jericho: The South Beheld*, a coffee-table book so large (sixteen and one-half by thirteen inches) and so heavy (seven pounds) that he later claimed if one did not own a coffee table, the book would serve that purpose. Chris described this time:

> Jim Dickey was more famous than ever. But there were so many works in progress, and only the worst of them seemed to get done. We had entered the era of James Dickey coffee-table books, lavishly illustrated overpriced tomes published by the same company that did *The Progressive Farmer* and *Southern Living* magazines. They were marketed by junk mail like trinkets from the Franklin Mint.

The first was *Jericho: The South Beheld*, with tempera illustrations that were Southern sentimental knockoffs of Andrew Wyeth, and the books got worse after that.

The booze and bluster were carrying over into everything my father wrote, everything he did. The obsessions of the poetry—the whole voice of it—changed. Ecstasy and creation gave way to masturbation and menstruation. (*Summer of Deliverance* 198)

Over the previous two years, Dickey had worked intermittently on *Jericho*, a collaborative effort with Hubert Shuptrine, whose 101 watercolor paintings accompanied, though not necessarily followed, the imaginative journey Dickey's prose depicts in the book's 168 pages. As with his poetry and fiction, Dickey's plot was both picaresque and mythic, bestowing his imagination with "pure spirit" in its creative journey and asking his readers "to hover, to swoop, to enter into the veer of the land and rivers, to zigzag over the landscape of people, to live in the trembling of the Web of custom and family." Like the mythic Dedalus in James Joyce's *Portrait of the Artist as a Young Man*, who counsels his soul to soar above the restraints of nationality, language, and religion, it is also clear that Dickey's vision, the series of epiphanies he presents, is voiced in a more popularly accessible medium and therefore directed at a more profitable marketplace.

Oxmoor House, the publisher, extensively promoted the book, announcing that its printing required twenty-eight carloads (one million pounds) of paper and thirty-one miles of cloth. Critics quickly pounced on what they perceived as Dickey's commercialism. Eli Evans's review in the *New York Times Book Review* typified the criticism when he wrote on 9 February 1975 that "the poet decided to give himself over to the Alabama Chamber of Commerce" (4–5). Other critics suggested that Dickey failed to utilize the principal source of what had been his poetic power, specifically, his own artistic control of the transcendent experience. In the introduction to *Jericho*, he had asked the reader to become a "beholder," someone who can "enter into objects and people and places with the sense of these things entering into him." While this approach succeeded in an early poem entitled "The Beholders," published in the 1 December 1962 issue of the *New Yorker*, by fusing the personae with their surroundings, the implication in *Jericho* is that Dickey himself cannot impart the needed energy or transcendence, particularly when he asks the reader to provide the imaginative vision requisite for such a fusion of inner and outer states: "You, reader, must open up until you reach the point...of sensing your locality pour into you simultaneously through every sense." Dickey additionally eliminated, it was claimed, the need for the creative lie, the means by which he had previously provided transcendence and thereby given the reader, for example, a sheep-child ("The Sheep Child"), two young lovers in a mist around their wrecked motorcycle ("May Day Sermon"), a stewardess who lives only as she prepares to die ("Falling"), and blind children who attempt to see the origins of the race ("The Eye-Beaters"). In *Jericho*, Dickey took additional stories and simply asked readers to view them in a heightened manner, an approach that reviewers argued merely accommodated the readership of *Southern Living*. That, however, was precisely Dickey's intent. He had always understood that poetry, or poetic prose, might release a new or insufficiently realized part of women and men, might free them or render them more inclusive. In publishing a coffee-table book, he was merely targeting a wider, less scholarly audience, an advertising strategy that coincidentally would also earn him more money.

Initially, Oxmoor had ordered a printing of 5,000 copies, but because *Southern Living* had undertaken a lavish advertising campaign, 20,000 copies had been ordered by 8 December 1973. The publisher then revised its plans again, ordering a first printing of 150,000 copies and setting up a $100,000 two-month book promotion tour for both Dickey and Shuptrine that featured television, radio, and press interviews as well as autograph sessions. Stops included Birmingham, Alabama; Houston; New Orleans; Dallas; Atlanta; Columbia, South Carolina; Charlotte, North Carolina; Greenville, South Carolina; Richmond, Virginia; and Nashville, Tennessee. To guarantee the widest possible market, the two artists were also booked for appearances on the *Today Show*, Johnny Carson's *Tonight Show*, and the *Merv Griffin Show*. Dickey cancelled all his October classes to accommodate the tour without consulting William Nolte, who chaired the English department and who subsequently placed him on unpaid leave. In October 1974 *Jericho* sold 100,000 copies at a list price of forty dollars. In an unpublished letter dated 31 November, Dickey inquired whether the book might not be worthy of a review in the *New York Times*, asking, "Should not this huge sales volume entitle *Jericho* to a place on your best-seller list?" The book continued to sell after 1 January 1975, when the price rose to sixty dollars a copy. Dickey had received a $25,000 advance. Because his royalty agreement stipulated one dollar per copy, he garnered approximately $150,000 from sales after earning back the advance.

After concluding the promotional tour, Dickey seemed to withdraw into his self-made "cave of making," the room in his home by Lake Katharine where he wrote, determined to complete the most ambitious project he had ever attempted, *The Zodiac*. Totaling sixty-two pages when published in 1976 and divided into twelve sections, the single poem was the effort, he later declared, by which his poetic reputation would rise or fall (Francis Skipp 1–10). In its sprawling format and split-line technique, it resembled such previous efforts as "Falling" and "May Day Sermon," yet his use of a translated text that he then re-creates, his gradual merging of perspectives, and the transformation of a traditional Christian myth into a personal and universal mythology that comments on the nature of art and the artist all render *The Zodiac* unique. At its heart *The Zodiac* is a quest for the single redeeming poem that unites the poet with the constellations, with the star-beasts of "God's scrambled zoo." Discussing the poem in the preface to *The Central Motion*, Dickey stated:

> I sought to deal with risks, and take them, and to have my spokes-man exemplify the conviction that the poet must go all-out for his vision, his angle, as it presents itself *at that moment*. A good deal of *The Zodiac* is the self-hypnotized yammering and assertiveness of a drunk, but a drunk who would not be able to achieve his occasion-ally clear and perhaps deep focus on matters of concern to him un-less he had had his inhibitions broken down—or through—by the dangerous means he employs, for he insists on nothing less than a personal connection between an exalted and/or intoxicated state, the starry universe, the condition he calls Time, and words. Taking off from Hendrik Marsman's respectable and ambitious poem and re-inventing almost everything in it, I tried to present a number of states of mind in which the cosmos changes moment to moment in a single consciousness, from a display of miracles to a delusional nightmare—the horrors of delirium tremens—and then back, all changes being parts of its encounter with that hugely mortal beast, the universe, and the smaller, mega-billion-miled Forms, the ani-mals that comprise some of it, in their stark, hinting, and timorous patterns. (v–vi)

Marsman's poem, "De Dierenriem," translated from the Dutch by A. J. Barnouw as "The Zodiac," was published in the spring 1949 issue of *The Sewanee Review* while Dickey was attending Vanderbilt. Reprinted the following year in Barnouw's anthology, *Coming After: An Anthology from the Low Countries*, the translation served as the narrative basis for Dickey's longer effort. In a 1979 interview Dickey described the poem as a "subli-mated narrative" and asserted that its subject was "the kind of half-mad, half-drunken afflatus that gets into a poet, or a certain kind of poet, when he believes that he can write the ultimate poem" (Baughman, *Voiced Connections* 173–86). To find it, the drunken poet must glean from the external world the vision necessary to make his words "lie for glory," a vision that effaces the boundaries between the poet's inner world and the outer world of natural phenomena and that requires the Zodiac poet to rise above the pain of his personal and creative failures. A resurrection must occur, and appropriately *The Zodiac* spans a three-day period. Because the Zodiac poet only intermittently escapes his alcoholism, he pleads, "Oh, God you rocky landscape give me, Give / Me drop by drop / desert water at least." The redemptive vision comes: "A face-up flash. Triangular eyesight," but he cannot pen the universe

> That poetry has never really found
> Undecipherable as God's bad, Heavenly sketches,
> Involving fortress and flower, vine and wine and bone,
>
> And shall vibrate through the western world
> So long as the hand can hold its island
> Of blazing paper, and bleed for its images:
> Make what it can of what is:
>
> So long as the spirit hurls on space
> The star-beasts of intellect and madness.

Although he achieves the connection he desires, the poet ironically fails in the final object of his quest; he cannot write the ultimate poem: "The virgin sheet becomes / More and more his, more and more another mistake." The myth he writes recedes even as he grasps it; truth, Dickey insists, resides in flux and is unescapably subjective. Because he believed controversy and excitement about a forthcoming publication would increase sales, he claimed the poem would rival Eliot's *The Wasteland* as a major cultural work.

Reviewers were unimpressed. Turner Cassity considered the resemblance to Barnouw's translation too close, declaring Dickey's re-creation a "compromise" of what the poet obviously intended as "his artistic testament with the hint of plagiarism" (177–93), and Thomas Lask simply termed the poem a failure, noting "its clotted lines and convoluted ideas" and berating Dickey for trying to make his verse "virile" (19). Robert Penn Warren, Dickey's close friend, cited a vaguely defined structural principle in the opening half of the work and "some sort of structural blockage" in the concluding two sections, adding, however, that the bold imagery as well as varied rhythms "redeems all" (8). Although later critics were less condemnatory, labeling the work a flawed masterpiece, they frequently misread it. Dave Smith, for example, argued that the poem occurs over a single day (349–58), and Francis Skipp asserted that its divisions relate to the zodiac itself (1–10).

Although *The Zodiac* was discussed as serious poetry, critics noted Dickey's interest in a specialized market. The poem's working manuscript was sectioned and bound in special-edition volumes; these Bruccoli Clark collectors' editions were then sold by private subscription at $400 apiece. Other specialty volumes in the seventies, including *The Owl King* (Red Angel Press, 1977), *The Enemy from Eden* (Lord Jim Press, 1978), *In Pursuit of the Grey Soul* (Bruccoli Clark Press, 1978), *Head-Deep in Strange Sounds* (Palaemon Press, 1979), and *Scion* (Deerfield Press, 1980), only seemed to confirm Dickey's decline, as did the publication in 1977 of another coffee-table book, *God's Images*. Amid the disdain, Dickey himself became defensive, writing Dave Smith on 17 November 1980 that *The Zodiac* "of course is a failure; there is no way that any poem which attempts to be a projection of booziness and confusion is ever going to be the kind of hand-fitted-together sort of 'success' that, say, *The Waste Land* is" (*One Voice*, II 311).

Like the poem's protagonist, Dickey had returned to his native land following his service in World War II; that Marsman himself died during the conflict only heightened the emotional appeal. Moreover, Dickey's return to the South in 1968, his use of sextants to locate himself among the stars, and his alcoholic self-destructiveness (while on sabbatical in September 1975, he crashed his 1968 Jaguar into a utility pole after leaving one of his favorite bars) all contributed to his interest in Marsman's poem. Because *The Zodiac* centers on poetic inspiration and divine communication, however, critical efforts occasionally portrayed the work as overtly confessional. Henry Hart, for example, asserted, "Dickey transformed Marsman's hero into an image of his own drunken, garrulous self, careening between sublimity and bathos" (551). Yet the statement fails to consider Dickey's abhorrence of self-dramatized poetry; his interest in translation, or what he occasionally termed "double-tongue"; and his belief that the poem is a fiction in which the persona "is correspondingly conditioned far more by the demands of the poem as a formal linguistic structure than by those of the literal incident upon which it may be based" (*Sorties* 155). His art, however, did imitate his life. Drinking continued to mitigate his creativity.

During his trip to Hollywood in August 1974 to work on *Call of the Wild*, Dickey had proposed to Charles Fries another movie idea. Conscious of the proclivity in both himself and his recently deceased father toward cowardice, he imagined a character's difficult but, finally, triumphant struggle to overcome his fear. The proposed movie would dramatize the struggle of a man discovering his own heroism. The epigraph Dickey eventually selected for the screenplay derived from Berryman: "A man can live his whole life in this society, and never know whether he is a coward or not." The outline for the new film, originally entitled "Crownfire" and later "Gene Bullard," introduced Sheriff Bullard, whose first name reflected that of Dickey's father, as a former athlete who shuns violence and checks for parking violations while driving a meter-maid vehicle for the small North Carolina town of Ellijay, the town Dickey used in his 1962 poem "On the Coosawattee." Supported by a tough young woman, Beth Culclasure, whose last name resembles the maiden name of Paula Culclasure Goff, with whom he was having an affair, he confronts an assortment of local criminals, including Joby, the son of deeply religious Baptist parents who were killed in an automobile wreck when he was eighteen; Makens, a sadist who has committed several bizarre sex crimes; Leon, a comically moronic ex-convict; and Jimbo, a forty-five-year-old escaped convict whose name reflects Dickey's own. Fries was interested, and Dickey undertook writing another script.

In Hollywood again in March 1976 after a rough cut of *Call of the Wild* had been completed, Dickey once more endeavored to generate interest in "Gene Bullard," which had floundered at several film companies. He delivered an emotionally charged summary of the script that so mesmerized Gary MacElwaine, an executive at Warner Brothers, that he consented to produce it. Dickey's Hollywood agent, Robert Littman, arranged for his client to receive $40,000 for the first draft of the screenplay, $20,000 for revisions, $35,000 for another draft if Warner Brothers decided to produce the movie, and a $30,000 bonus in addition to royalties if Dickey received sole screen credit. On 25 May Littman informed Dickey that he had also formalized a deal with Columbia Pictures for another proposed film, "The Spell." In the prospectus Dickey characterized the plot as an examination of "the interaction between politics and religion, especially as it evidences itself in the South." The story featured a character much like Joel Cahill in *Alnilam*, Joshua Daniels, minister of a small rural

congregation who is "a spell-binder, that is, he can cast the spell over people, over his congregations, and over just about anybody he chooses to cast
it upon." In the synopsis he further characterized Daniels: "He does not
talk about sin, but of salvation, and his version of salvation includes the
element of joy: joy in nature, joy in sex, joy even in drink, but essentially
joy in existence." Daniels, who boards in the house of Hannah Crewes, a
widow, desires to unify everyone under a single idea; his obsession spills
over into despotic politics ("Prospectus for film *The Spell*" and "Synopsis
for projected Movie to be called *The Spell*").

By autumn, however, Dickey had become frustrated with the continual changes demanded by Warner Brothers for each draft he submitted,
not only refusing to make any more revisions but also demanding the final
payment stipulated by his contract. In stern, straightforward language, he
wrote Fries in an unpublished letter dated 1 October:

> I put a whole summer's work into the revisions you suggested. If
> that is not the fulfillment of a contract to write a screenplay, I do
> not know where to find it. And still no forthcoming of the required
> payment. Now I am absolutely dumbfounded at the request to make
> additional changes without the slightest indication of the monies
> for work I have spent a deal in doing.... I am bewildered by all of
> this, but I can categorically guarantee that I will not touch the script
> of *Gene Bullard* again until I have received payment for the first
> draft. I'd as soon drop the whole project rather than proceed on this
> basis.

Both "Gene Bullard" and "The Spell" languished, despite efforts by Fries,
and Dickey abandoned the projects, frustrated with Hollywood's procedures even as he remained attracted to the financial incentives.

In mid-October 1976 Maxine Dickey suffered a hemorrhage of the
blood vessels surrounding her esophagus, the bleeding caused by damage
from years of drinking. She lost half her blood. Despite being stabilized by
doctors and kept in intensive care, she hemorrhaged again and died on 27
October. Later Dickey would describe her initial collapse to his son Chris.
"She *exploded* in my *arms*," he said, imitating her voice and pretending to
throw up blood, "Buckets of it." Then amid tears of drunken grief, he declared, "Thirty years I was married to that woman. THIRTY YEARS.
And I killed her" (*Summer of Deliverance* 203). In the days immediately
following her death, Dickey attempted to assuage his grief and guilt

through poetry, writing an untitled and incomplete poem that Jim Mann, a former student, happened to see and transcribe while at their house.

> She died in October. She must descend
> First, somewhere vague and cold, spirit and seal,
> Her gift descend, and all that warm heart fail
> Somewhere. Imagination one's one friend
> Cannot see there. Both of us at the end.
> Nouns, verbs do not exist for what I feel.

The effort at consolation failed. Without Maxine's support and managerial skills, Dickey floundered. Dedicated to her husband's career, she had provided stability by organizing schedules, directing activities, entertaining literary figures, and raising children. In short, she had enabled Dickey not only to have a literary career but also a successful one. For her gravestone, he chose two lines from "Damelus' 'Song to Diaphenia'" by sixteenth-century English poet Henry Constable—"I do love thee as each flower / Love's the sunne's life-giving power"—a tribute that acknowledged his dependency. In the weeks following her burial, he appeared rootless and apathetic, often drinking excessively to assuage his grief. He told the *National Observer* on 4 December, "I've thought about my death a lot. Once I thought I wanted to die by violence—get killed by a grizzly, maybe. But now I think I'd prefer to die by water, by drowning not with others but alone. Just slip beneath it all" (24). Asked if he believed in an afterlife, he simply responded, "No. I saw Maxine lying there, and it could have just been a dead dog in the road" (24). He blamed his own actions for the alcoholism that had killed her.

Her death would forever haunt Dickey. In the January 1987 issue of *Southern Magazine*, he eulogized Maxine in a poem titled "Tomb Stone," addressing her in death as she lay buried in the churchyard of All Saints Waccamaw Episcopal Church on Pawleys Island: "I must ask you, though, not to fall / Any farther, / and to forgive me / For coming here, as I keep doing / For a while in a vertical body / That breathes the rectangular solitude / Risen over you.... / [F]or I understand / Now, that deep enough / In death, the earth becomes / Absolute earth. Hold all there is: hold on / And forgive." On 30 December, however, two months after her death, at the courthouse in Columbia, South Carolina, Dickey married Deborah Dodson, a twenty-five-year-old graduate student who had enrolled that fall semester in his Verse Composition course. As they climbed the courthouse steps, Deborah said, "This is the last chance to back out," to which he replied, "I ain't gonna take it, and you ain't gonna get it" (Ashley 28, 30). Dickey informed surprised friends and family as well as the press that Deborah had restored him, and temporarily he gave up drinking. Her presence in what he called "the new life" emotionally elevated him, heightening his sensitivity to the physical world and quickening his intuitive responses. As soon would become apparent, she also revealed to him previously unseen creative possibilities and guided him in directions that had remained undiscovered or unexplored. Deborah's youth and sensibilities energized him, making his 1982 poetry collection, *Puella*, possible. In many ways she became his muse, a mythical deliverer whose physical appearance, Dickey told friends, reminded him of Robin Jarecki. In a 1982 interview Dickey remarked on Deborah's effect on *Puella*, which was inspired, he asserted, "by the mystery of her existence, of her radiation, her mysterious radiation." He wanted the public, he declared, to perceive him not as simply an image of vitality or strength but as one possessing "above all a passionate and involved male tenderness" (Baughman, *Voiced Connections* 187–92). After the book's publication, he would write Deborah a poem that similarly identifies her with nature. Playfully titled "Tee-Row's Love-Letter #2," it opens,

> In clouds
>
> my loved girl in soft fleeces, in large fashionable wings,
> with deep eyes and gentle, generous lips, perfectly weightless,
> forming out of pure soft cloud, for nothing but luxurious, decadent,
> love-making.

Other sections of the unpublished work center Deborah elsewhere in nature—"On Islands" and "At Night"—and reveal a previously unseen poetic format.

In the commencement address Dickey delivered in December 1995 at the University of South Carolina, he commented on his marriages and specifically on Deborah's influence: "I married, and thirty years after that my wife died. I married again, to a young woman who loved the poetry of John Donne and showed me that I had never read it in depth before. I came especially to like some lines of his about waking up with someone you love. You can be sure that the love-relation is a true one when there is no apprehension present, no fear in it; fear of betrayal, of being lied to, fear that the other person will cease to love you, fear of anything" (*The Weather of the Valley* 6). Then he read those lines from Donne's "The Good Morrow":

And now good morrow to our waking souls,
Which watch not one another out of fear;
For love, all love of other sights controls,
And makes one little room, an everywhere.

Yet Dickey's relationship with his new wife was deeply troubled. Her later addiction to drugs and her various arrests became media news, and rumors of her physical and verbal abuse also circulated. In interviews, Dickey frequently deflected questions about separation and divorce. Reynolds Price, in a tribute to Dickey following the latter's death, called the poet's situation "tragic" (31). Because of the turbulence, Chris and Kevin Dickey retreated from almost all contact with their father.

Dickey was not by nature inclined to involve himself in politics. During the Vietnam conflict, he had assiduously avoided participating in popular protests—unlike, for example, Robert Lowell and Robert Bly—nor did he issue any tracts, make any statements, or write any topical poems in support of or in opposition to the war. Although opponents labeled him conservative, for Dickey poetry was all that mattered. He did, however, cultivate his relationship with Jimmy Carter during Carter's campaign for the presidency. They had met during the Atlanta premier of *Deliverance*, and Carter later invited Dickey to become Georgia's poet laureate, an honor Dickey declined because he was living in South Carolina. In an unpublished letter dated 4 August 1976, he reintroduced himself and delivered an inspirational message that promoted agrarian values and idealism:

The clue to our national and international salvation lies not in a futile yearning for a nebulous "unity," but in an emphasis on diversity, or the right—and eventual glory, given the right government—of differences. The South is not the East and the East is not the Pacific Northwest, nor is any one of these Alaska or Hawaii. What we should seek, as a political organ, is a reaffirmation of the principal differences, both local and individual.... I would like very much, Jimmy, to see an emphasis, under your Presidency, on the diversity of peoples that we have in this country, and a fertile cross-fertilization of different kinds of groups, mores, fashions, and all of the diversity that gives richness to life.

Carter responded with a note thanking Dickey for his comments on diversity. In subsequent letters over the next few months, Dickey offered Carter advice on his campaign and on the televised debates.

The correspondence eventually led to Carter's request that Dickey write an inaugural poem. Dickey responded with "The Strength of Fields," which he read at the inaugural concert on 19 January 1977. He later told the *Christian Science Monitor* that, as in *Deliverance*, he had based the poem on vVan Gennep's "Rites of Passage." After winning the election, Carter returned to his hometown of Plains, Georgia. "I cast Jimmy Carter in his withdrawal from Washington and his return to his roots, his hometown, in the role of a mythical hero, and that is always the same. It doesn't make any difference if it's Theseus or Perseus or any one else" (Loercher 19). Carter's victory over Gerald Ford, though narrow, seemed to promise a new beginning, a new hope, for a nation that had surrendered to cynicism and despair following Vietnam and Watergate. Nixon's resignation had symbolized the final defeat. Carter's humility, his sense of moral wholeness, appeared to many Americans a national deliverance that began with the organization of a five-day People's Inaugural celebration. Six hundred Iowa farmers and their families, 106 Minnesota square dancers, twenty-six Crow Indians and their families, and an assemblage of Irish musicians, bluegrass groups, country singers, Hollywood celebrities, and Georgia working folk joined one million other Americans in Washington to herald the new day promised by Carter. "How to penetrate and find the source," Dickey's speaker asks in "The Strength of Fields," "Of the power you always had." The poem's quiet, dignified, and uplifting conclusion seemed appropriate when Dickey read it at the Folger Theatre.

> Lord, let me shake
> With purpose. Wild hope can always spring
> From tended strength. Everything is in that.
> That and nothing but kindness. More kindness, dear Lord
> Of the renewing green. That is where it all has to start:
> With the simplest things. More kindness will do nothing less
> Than save every sleeping one
> And night-walking one
>
> Of us.
> My life belongs to the world. I will do what I can.

Dickey's presence, however, was not without controversy, for the perceived racist and sexist attitudes his personae portrayed appeared at odds with the tone of the inauguration. Denise Levertov publicly attacked Dickey's attitudes, including his support of American involvement in Southeast Asia. Yet many felt the poem epitomized the country's yearning and concurred with Dickey's belief that "we can all be saved / By a secret blooming."

Shortly after the inauguration, Carter asked Dickey to represent the United States at a ceremony opening the Franklin and Jefferson exhibit at Mexico City's National Museum of Anthropology. Honored, Dickey agreed, and flew with Deborah to begin his ambassadorial duties on 14 April, attending receptions, discussing *Deliverance*, lecturing on modern poetry, conferring with dignitaries, and sightseeing. Before an audience that included Mexico's president, José López Portillo, he celebrated the spirit of friendship and cultural cooperation between the two neighboring countries. He also met with Octavio Paz, whose acquaintance he had first made as poetry consultant and whom he believed to be not only Mexico's finest poet but also deserving of the Nobel Prize for Literature. Later he would re-create some of Paz's poetry, including "Mexican Valley," which he included with other translations as part of *The Strength of Fields* and published in a specialty edition in 1979 titled *Head-Deep in Strange Sounds*.

By translation Dickey clearly meant the transposing of a poem written in another language, French or Spanish or even Chinese, for example, into English as closely or exactly as possible so that the new poem presented a copy or replica of the original. Such a methodology, however, was anathema to Dickey, who viewed it as derivative and unoriginal. His theory regarding collaboration is perhaps best detailed in the transcription of his lectures while poet-in-residence at the University of South Carolina. In these lecture notes, he pointed to Ezra Pound and his effort to "intuit" a text, attempting to achieve "the spirit of the original" rather than a literal translation: "He takes what he wants from people who are lifetime scholars in one field, such as, say, Japanese poetry, Chinese poetry. But he himself doesn't stay in that position long enough to consolidate anything. He prefers to work by intuition, so that his translations, especially the translations from the Chinese, have set the model for what every other translator, or at least every other translator who is a poet, has tried to do since that time" (Greiner, *James Dickey: Classes* 165). Pound's translations, properly speaking, were "free adaptations" (166), Dickey declared, an attempt to get "the essence of the poetry over from one language to another, and not just a literal transcription" (2). Pound, he argued, was a great believer in trying to "intuit" the poem and maybe taking some liberties and sometimes a great deal of liberties with the text in order to get an original poem in English that he intuits is the equivalent of the original, that is, it carries something mysterious about it that Pound calls "the spirit of the original" rather than the letter. What is it the Bible says, the letter killeth but the spirit giveth life? It's *that* kind of approach to translation which is most prevalent now. (2)

Head-Deep in Strange Sounds: Free-Flight Improvisations from the Un-English included a group of fifteen poems that are renderings or readings of works by Po Chü-yi, Alfred Jarry, Eugenio Montale, Vicente Aleixandre, Octavio Paz, and others. Reviewers and later critics ignored these poems, perhaps unaware that Dickey was working from translations and lacking the requisite knowledge of Chinese, French, Italian, and Spanish, which would have enabled them to understand the nature of his practices. Typical was the comment by Ronald Baughman, who observed that in these improvisations, Dickey's voice merges with that of other poets. Calling these efforts "noteworthy," he nevertheless asserted that the poems in the first section of *The Strength of Fields* were "more significant" (*Understanding James Dickey* 130). Baughman's observation that Dickey's voice "merges" with that of the original poets echoed a primary complaint by critics regarding *The Zodiac*, who argued that Dickey's voice became indistinguishable from that of the drunken Dutch poet whose story he endeavors to relate.

Following his return from Mexico, Dickey continued to send Carter political advice, and in a long letter dated 16 July 1979, he analyzed the latter's energy speech. Carter had addressed a nation crippled by the oil crisis and confronted with a severe shortage. Dickey's analysis disparaged Carter's rhetorical strategies and urged him to uplift the country by gathering up its "great resources of intellectual and spiritual power...a kind of hidden treasure: enormous, full of power and light and certainty and even a fierce and renewing kind of joy: above all, a sense of *going-toward* rather than *escaping-from*. It is a great deal better to lead people toward a goal, a kind of just city, a 'city of the sun,' than it is to attempt to intimidate a nation of sluggards and timorous wastrels into action for its own good" (*One Voice* II, 219). Dickey, in effect, seemed to be instructing Carter, outlining how to achieve that promise if Carter would, as E. M. Forster had written, "only connect," a phrase Dickey had used as an epigraph in his 1967 poem "Power and Light."

Attracted by the spotlight of national politics, Dickey continued his correspondence with and pledges of support for the Carters, including sending Christmas cards. The Carters, in turn, invited the Dickeys in January 1980 to participate in a White House reception honoring American poets. Louise Glück, Simon Ortiz, David Ignatow, Theodore Weiss, Philip Levine, Maxine Kumin, Stanley Kunitz, and Richard Eberhart attended. So, too, did James Wright, physically diminished by a debilitating cancer that would within four months bring about his death. After Wright had greeted him and explained his medical condition, Dickey suddenly grew angry and left, bewildering Wright and angering his wife, Anne, who never forgave Dickey for what she termed, in a 28 June 2005 letter to me, as "his mischief and what I think of as misbehavior." Dickey's own health problems, a malfunctioning esophagus that would soon require major surgery, and his shocked recognition of what he told David Wagoner, in a 21 April 1980 letter, of Wright's "hoarse, diminished and obviously dying ghost" (Hart 584) turned sadness and grief into anger at life's processes and physical limitations. Unlike Theodore Roethke, who understood, as he wrote in the title poem of his last poetry collection, *The Far Field*, "the pure serene of memory in one man,— / A ripple widening from a single stone / Winding around the waters of the world," Dickey never truly accommodated himself to time and its diminishment.

Carter's campaign never contacted Dickey during the 1980 reelection efforts. Undeterred, Dickey proffered his counsel, writing Carter a week before the election, "Since I haven't heard from Jody Powell, and since time is getting short, I thought I had better send you what thoughts I have on the points you might want to emphasize in your debate with Reagan." He urged Carter to have a simple, widely applicable metaphor that would catch up the public and describe his position, suggesting the image of driving defensively. Americans, however, had wearied of Carter's liberal humanitarian ideals and his inability to solve the Iranian hostage crisis. In rhetoric that Dickey must surely have admired, Ronald Reagan projected himself as a mythmaker, a leader who could energize the country and lead it to the "city of the sun." His victory at the polls largely signaled an end to Dickey's participation in politics; his correspondence with Carter noticeably diminished following Carter's defeat.

Dickey continued to work on his projects during the late seventies, including *God's Images,* a new coffee-table book, and several screenplays, one of which, "The Sentence," involved a professor at a Southern university coping with an arrest and incarceration and which was based on his 1975 crash into a utility pole. "The Breath" was a dramatic presentation of a hunt for one man by another. Quentin Dodson, the protagonist, whose last name parallels Deborah's maiden name, resembles Julian Glass, the main character in *The Casting,* Dickey's unpublished first novel, in his voyeurism and perversity, and in some ways anticipates Muldrow in his last novel, *To the White Sea,* in his inability to understand reality. "The Buzzer," another proposed screenplay, explored life as a competitive game. The single-page prospectus presents an unnamed protagonist, an outstanding basketball star, sensitive and withdrawn and idealistic, who leads his team to the championship game but who then surrenders the chance to win because he is disgusted by the mob-like vulgarity of the sport. His final action, throwing the ball down and walking off the court, repudiates the profession he represents.

Reviews of *God's Images,* published in 1977, were mixed, and later critics compared it unfavorably to *Jericho.* Less ambitious in size, though not in artistic intent, it contains fifty-three prose poems that not so much reinterpret as represent particular biblical texts from individual perspectives. Etchings by Marvin Hayes accompany Dickey's interior imagery. Oxmoor House, anticipating controversy from the book's unusual perspectives, established an advisory board of biblical scholars, both Jewish and Christian, to assure that the portrayals were faithful to scriptural materials. GraceAnne DeCandido, reviewing the book for *Library Journal,* considered Dickey's text "oddly secular," stating that it lacked "palpable spirituality" because emphasis shifts from God to the figures that present the biblical story, characters moreover who are "predominantly masculine." Noting the absence of Judith, Esther, and Mary Magdalene from the portrayals and declaring that Ruth and Mary are only "shadow and symbol," DeCandido believed *God's Images* narrowed the Bible to "the worldly visions of two men" (154). Her review, however, ignored Dickey's own statement in the book's forward:

> To an artist such as Marvin Hayes, or to a poet, such as I hold myself to be, these images have unfolded in us by means of the arts we practice. These are *our* images of *God's Images....* Hayes and I do not wish to supersede or in any way substitute our interpretations of the Bible for yours. These are crucial to you, and therefore vital and

living. We should like to think, though, we may be able to give an additional dimension to your own inner Bible and enrich your personal kingdom of God, there where it lies forever...within you.

Failing to allow Dickey the choice of his material, DeCandido nevertheless reflected a problem that Dickey's personal projection of male bravado caused him. His career suffered because, in depicting himself with masculine boisterousness, he opened himself to charges of political incorrectness, a problem he would recognize and attempt to counter in *Puella*.

In their critical study Richard Calhoun and Robert Hill viewed *God's Images* as more academic than *Jericho* because within Dickey's text lie the voices of Milton and Blake as well as the translators of the King James Bible, not simply certain past and present Southern poets. While the book lacks any unifying theme, they argued that Dickey reworked the images in his own poetic idiom and that in attempting to recover the common, unrecognized culture of his readers, he actualized the biblical images that "lie buried and live in us" (107–108). The book, therefore, was more than a mere commercial enterprise. Jane Martin-Bowers, however, considered the book a decided retreat from Dickey's previous efforts. Dickey, she argued, believing that his interpretation of readers' personal images would engender a heightened understanding of each biblical story, had relied not on his own creativity but on preexisting text. Consequently, the fusion of the readers' own state with the larger Kingdom of God lay with the audience, not the poet. In other words, he had avoided his creative responsibilities (Weigl, Hummer143–51).

Despite the negative reviews his work was now regularly receiving, Dickey endeavored to broaden his artistic capabilities with his first children's book, *Tucky the Hunter*, published in 1978 and named for and written about his grandson, James Tuckerman Dickey. In his notebooks from the fifties, he had cited the need to explore creatively, to cast a wide artistic net. In good children's poetry, words and illustrations, taken together, constitute an integrated, complex work, with each aspect complementing the other, so that the book's format and layout are, finally, a coherent aesthetic, psychological, and intellectual presentation. However, while the pastel sketches of Marie Angel in *Tucky the Hunter* delicately cohere with Dickey's text rather than confront it, the plot itself is simplistic and the protagonist's adventure mostly static. Reviews were again largely negative, offering no substantive analysis and often revealing only the most general knowledge of Dickey's poetic themes. The poem celebrates the imagination of Dickey's grandson, what John Logue in his review called "his oneness with the animal kingdom and his popgun" (68), but the anonymous critic for *Kirkus Review*, comparing the book to other works by noted authors of children's literature, including Maurice Sendak and M. M. Milne, labeled the verses "forgettable" (917). With Dickey's poems appearing less and less frequently in prestigious magazines and journals, reviewers were now greeting his books with indifference or hostility.

God's Images had recently received an auspicious reception at the American Booksellers Association Convention in San Francisco, news that heartened Dickey. Sales were brisk, although they never approached that of *Jericho*, and were quickened when the book was nominated on 10 April 1978 for the Carey-Thomas Award, which *Jericho* had won for the most significant publishing event in 1974. In many ways the book constituted an act of atonement. In the foreword, he had honored Maxine: "She was all her life a devoted dweller in the Bible, and now, through the flowering tomb, she resides among the superhuman reality of God's images. God bless you, my good girl, bride of the first night, and now in the first light." The statement was an exaggeration. According to Chris Dickey, Maxine was "a moderate, social church-goer." Dickey was never a Christian; for him, the universe and its creative forces were God. Yet he liked the rituals of the church and the stories, language, and images of the Bible. When Deborah asked for a formal wedding at St. Joseph's, a Roman Catholic Church in Columbia, he acquiesced. Matthew Bruccoli, his colleague at the university and eventually his literary executor, was the best man.

Dickey continued to stay busy. On sabbatical for the 1978 winter and spring terms, he undertook numerous readings in Washington State; taught classes at George Mason University in Fairfax, Virginia, for John Gardner, who was ailing; and on 6 March 1978 attended a Library of Congress reunion with twelve former poetry consultants. Daniel Boorstin, the current librarian, as well as Howard Nemerov, Elizabeth Bishop, Stanley Kunitz, Daniel Hoffman, and Stephen Spender convened to discuss past problems and offer possible solutions. Dickey bemoaned the absence of poetry on cassette and video and spoke about the program of taped readings he had initiated. Later the poets read to an audience of more than one thousand people for two-and-a-half hours.

Dickey's mother, Maibelle, the woman responsible for his idealization of women, died of cancer on 10 June 1977 in the house at 166 W. Wesley where he grew up. His sister, Maibelle, wailed during the funeral, and when Dickey, who had been drinking, tried to comfort her, she continued to cry loudly and ultimately fainted. Overwhelmed by memories, he abruptly resolved to abandon alcohol. Because he refused to acknowledge his alcoholism, however, he dismissed all treatment for withdrawal, as he had following Maxine's death. Walking on Williams Street in Atlanta, he suffered a seizure, severely bit his tongue, and nearly bled to death. In the hospital he suffered another seizure and again bit his tongue.

Robert Lowell had died in a New York taxi on 12 September 1977. Dickey had spent years trying to best him but now sent Lowell's second wife, Elizabeth Hardwick (whom Lowell was visiting after leaving his third wife, Caroline Blackwood, in England), a telegram, saying, "All we can do for him is to love him forever." Despite their rivalry, Dickey in his classes referred to Lowell as "his oldest friend." In April 1974 Lowell read from his poetry at the University of South Carolina, having been invited to receive its Award for Distinction in Literature (other winners included Allen Tate, Robert Penn Warren, and Eudora Welty). The award was funded by student monies and presented on behalf of the students; students even coordinated the events. As Dickey approached the Business School Auditorium before the ceremony with Don Greiner, he said, "Don, tonight, it's as if Will Shakespeare and Ben Jonson were meeting at the Mermaid Tavern. And only time will tell which of us is Shakespeare." Before David Havird, who with Jim Mann had helped create the award, introduced Lowell, Dickey told the audience that "hearing Lowell read was like hearing Milton read" and asked for a standing ovation. "Will you do that for me, please?" (Keen Butterworth, Dickey's colleague in the department, later asked why he had compared Lowell to Milton. Dickey responded that he and Lowell had been sitting on his dock at Lake Katharine that morning when Lowell proceeded to tell him how he had written *Samson Agonistes*.) When Havird finished his introduction, Lowell rose slowly, moved to the lectern, and said that he was beginning his reading not with one of his own poems but with a poem written by another poet he much admired. He then read Dickey's "Adultery," citing it as a good example of the poet's prose style. When Lowell finished reading his own poems, Havird recalled, Dickey applauded with enthusiasm; Lowell "seemed entirely gratified." Although Greiner later stated that he discerned no antipathy between the two poets, who had indeed spent the afternoon talking on Dickey's dock, Butterworth believed differently: "I had the distinct impression I was watching New England and the South facing off against one another—Emerson and William Gilmore Simms revived from the dead."

On 9 February 1979, his early mentor Allen Tate died. Once more confronted with his inability to counter the inevitability of death, Dickey commented to a Columbia reporter on Tate's large presence. Tate, he declared, citing from Tate's poem "Aeneas in Washington," left "a mind imperishable / If time is." "Allen was the very last of his kind," he asserted, "the critic, essayist, the personal scholar, and finally the poet. He had a strong sense of values. He believed that the imagination, cultural cohesion, the sense of meaning something instead of nothing, are the qualities which define us. He was a marvelous, brilliant man" (Starr A15).

When Dickey was invited to deliver the fifth annual Ezra Pound lecture on 26 April 1979 at the University of Idaho, he accepted, partly for the attention he received, partly for the opportunity to honor Pound's originality, and partly because the recent deaths of family and friends had reinforced his growing sense of mortality and the need to do and say things of consequence. Since his years at North Fulton High School, he had always needed to confront whatever opposed him with a fierce counterthrust that would establish his own superiority, whether this meant hitting a fullback harder than he had been hit or writing a review that unflinchingly challenged poets he believed suspect. Now, however, he seemed unable to reconcile himself to death, with the result that he often dropped any public posing. Before the lecture, he talked to Ron McFarland, a local poet, about a variety of subjects, including his latest work, *The Zodiac*, and his public persona. His tone was honest and straightforward, at times even humble, admitting that he had been of only average ability in football and indifferent in advertising. When McFarland suggested that the "real James Dickey" might lie concealed by "a self-created and media-assisted mask," Dickey replied, "I suppose anybody would have a tendency to do that, would partially invent or would partially have invented for him a kind of persona. You don't know which the real one is. The person himself would be the least qualified to answer that." When McFarland inquired whether he had ever had his confidence shaken, Dickey answered, "I've never had it when it was not shaken. But if you let all that bother you, you just can't write, you won't try anything." McFarland also noted the sadness and terror of middle age in *Sorties*. Dickey responded, "It's even worse now that I've lived through it than I said it was." He believed that the only excuse for getting older was the achievement of a "mastery of something you would not without those years have been able to have in that degree." That experience, he declared, had made Ezra Pound an "oracle": "He had known all those people, he had done all those things, and had accumulated, maybe not wisdom, but a lot of things that were worth passing on" (Baughman, *Voiced Connections* 173–86).

Dickey knew his reputation was in decline. Astute to both publishing realities and literary politics, to the need for continual sales and awards as well as to public relations and gamesmanship that could bury worthy poets and elevate suspect ones, he attempted to dominate the air in which he flew. His sense of competition and his psychological need to win required him to achieve ever higher measures of success. He also needed to prove himself by continual experimentation in form and technique, a belief partly responsible for his efforts in fiction, screenplays, children's poetry, translation, and coffee-table books. Experimentation, however, entailed risk; winning formulas are just that—winning—but ultimately self-defeating. In the same interview with McFarland, he declared, "You should always be prepared to make a fool of yourself," and added, "I think the business of playing out there at the edge of consciousness where you're trying to push things out a bit beyond where they were before you made the attempt, that's the thing that interests me" (Baughman, *Voiced Connections* 173–86).

Increasingly, critics viewed Dickey's creative works as failures. No one, not even Dickey himself, viewed him as flying at "angels nine." In presenting himself as a football and track star, as a decorated combat pilot who had flown more than one hundred missions, as an expert archer, competent hunter, and guitar enthusiast, he had lost his poetic bearings. Alcohol had contributed. The lonely, self-watchful search for a unique subject matter and manner that had characterized his extended missions in the fifties and sixties—including his use of early notebooks to record and explore his literary reflections, his travels in Europe on *Sewanee Review* and Guggenheim Fellowships, and his years in business when "I was selling my soul to the devil all day and trying to buy it back at night" (*Self-Interviews* 44)—had, in the decade after *Deliverance*, yielded the rewards of literary success. Money and popular acclaim, however, had brought complacency. Sorties into new creative skies, such as translations and children's poetry, lacked the determined pursuit characteristic of his early motion. Other efforts, the screenplays and coffee-table books, seemed undertaken only for quick-and-easy financial gain, even as they generated a larger or different audience. He had, it appeared, abandoned his immaculateness of purpose.

Dickey had been upset when *The Zodiac* did not win the Pulitzer Prize for Poetry in 1976. In 1979 he asked Doubleday to move the scheduled 1980 publication date of his new collection, *The Strength of Fields*, to 1979, believing that the Pulitzer committee that year favored him. Richard Howard chaired the committee, and because Dickey had helped Howard win the prize in 1970, he anticipated Howard would return the favor. James Applewhite and Helen Vendler also sat on the committee, the former a poet whose values Dickey believed similar to his own and the latter a critic whom, though she had supported Lowell when she and Dickey both served on the 1977 Pulitzer committee (Dickey had favored Nemerov, who eventually won), he had flattered in a 14 July 1977 letter. Despite the political maneuvering, *The Strength of Fields* did not win; the prize was awarded to Donald Justice's *Selected Poems*. Neither the Pulitzer judges nor the critics were impressed with Dickey's collection, whose title evoked a softer resiliency than his earlier "virile" poems. Apart from the section of translations that Dickey labeled "Head-Deep in Strange Sounds: Free-Flight Improvisations from the UnEnglish," the volume contained only thirteen poems, all but one of which had been previously published. Two poems, moreover—"Root-Light, or the Lawyer's Daughter" and "Drums Where I Live"—had appeared in the *New Yorker* a full decade earlier. Calhoun and Hill concluded that the book was "mostly just a collection," one that was not "particularly fresh" and that constituted "a gathering of forces" (102).

What was not apparent in 1979 was the literary transformation that was already underway but which would not achieve distinct force for three more years. That force had tentatively manifested itself when Dickey published "Pine: Taste, Touch, and Sight" in the June 1969 issue of *Poetry* and when a two-part poem containing "Sound" and "Smell" appeared in the *New Yorker* the same month. The full poem, which he included (though without subtitles) in his 1970 collection, *The Eye-Beaters, Blood, Victory, Madness, Buckhead and Mercy*, was singled out for praise by reviewers who, as they would with *The Zodiac* and *The Strength of Fields*, generally disliked the volume, citing the feeble, clotted, or bathetic qualities of the remaining poems. Dickey, however, failed to pursue this distinctive new technique largely because he became involved first with the completion of *Deliverance* and then with its filming.

In 1982 *Puella* became the book in which Dickey finally accomplished his late poetic style, a motion that strove to synthesize or perhaps transcend two distinct types of poetry—on the one hand, "Magic Language," poems whose words play among themselves, illuminating one another, and, while referring to nature or existence, shimmer off the backdrop of the external world as a secondary necessity; on the other hand, "literal" poetry, which centers itself in ordinary reality not to invent or impose but to discover a real unity in the world (*Night Hurdling* 124–40). These later poems, which "Pine" first anticipates, were flights launched to reveal what new linguistic territory he might still explore and, if possible, claim; their mission, in effect, was to attack language itself in an effort to make it offer up correspondences, complicity, an extralinguistic kinship of the mind. Beginning with the appearance of "The Surround" in the July 1980 issue of *Atlantic*, they regularly saw print. Five poems appeared in the March 1981 issue of *Poetry* and won the Levinson Prize; "The Lyric Beasts" and "Tapestry and Sail" appeared later that year in *Paris Review* and *Lone Star Review*, respectively. After *The Eye-Beaters* and two derivative collections, volumes that he defined as his central motion and that critics generally condemned, Dickey's final attack on language, his progressive effort to apprehend existence from perspectives utterly outside himself, was decidedly underway.

CHAPTER 13

"SOMEWHERE ON
THE GENERAL BRINK"

James Dickey believed that great writers are more important than everybody else. Because he had chosen the profession of authorship relatively late in life, or so he felt, and because he wanted to be great, his commitment to literature was authentic and convincing. He did not begin to read poetry systematically until 1944, while stationed on Okinawa during his Pacific combat service. "I was not introduced to it," he recalled in *Self-Interviews*, "by anybody in my family or any teacher or acquaintance. That has its disadvantages, but it also has one enormous advantage. If you get into poetry this way, you come to look upon poetry as *your* possession, something that *you* discovered, that belongs to you in a way it could never have belonged to you if it had been forced upon you" (25). History, however, alters and informs the reception of a poet's work. Dickey's career provides an especially clear example of how changing cultural and social norms generated a widespread reversal of the enthusiastic reception of his early work.

As 1980 began, Dickey worked intently on *Alnilam*, though he continually asked for extensions from his editor, Stewart Richardson, delays necessitated in part by an intense schedule of readings and in part by uncertainty related to the novel's plot and the basic character of the protagonist. In the first five months of the year, he read at William Rainey Harper College, Emory University, the University of North Dakota, the Columbia Cultural Arts Center, and South Illinois University. The readings, he explained to Richardson in an unpublished letter dated 3 February, owed to his imminent poverty, an ironic statement because of his financial gains from *Deliverance* and his coffee-table books: "I have had to fill up a lot of time between now and May with reading and speaking dates, so that I won't go from the hospital to the alms-house.... But the novel is going fine, and now there comes the question of exactly in what stages you want to see it." He proposed sending sections of the work to Richardson every week or two and having the editor react to the narrative "as it unfolds bit by bit, as it would reveal itself to a reader, in his innocence, and—anticipation." Dickey had not yet clarified the motivations and goals of Joel Cahill's Alnilam plot.

Dickey was money-conscious throughout his life. Shaye Areheart had confided to Deborah that Dickey and Maxine had both worried about money during their marriage. To add to his concern, the Dickeys employed two full-time employees as well as an expensive certified public accountant. Commenting on her husband's financial concerns, Deborah declared, "He was always, always like this. My using expensive illegal drugs, and all of their equally expensive consequences, certainly did a lot of fiscal damage," adding however that "his obsessive fear of going broke far, far preceded that time. My struggles with addition exacerbated an already excessive worry of his going broke."

The framework for what he referred to as his "big novel about the air" first evidenced itself on page 46 of the fourth of Dickey's early notebooks, a bound ledger containing ninety-five handwritten pages. His dated the initial entry 29 September 1952, and other notations are dated the next day. The novel's original title was "The Romantic," and he intended that the story's three-day time frame possess archetypal significance. Conceived initially as a short story and then as a novella, "The Romantic" presents a father, a widowed automobile salesman now employed as a timekeeper in an aircraft factory, who arrives at a primary training base (Dickey planned to use his memories of the base at Camden, South Carolina, where he had been stationed) to interview various individuals about the death of his only son, Joel Mitchell, whom he has not known very well nor seen for some years. Like Joel Cahill in *Alnilam*, the protagonist in the novella has died in an unobserved plane crash, having inexplicably flown through the turbulence of a fire. Before his death, too, Joel had become obsessed with the poet James Thomson. Although Dickey changed their names, other principal characters in *Alnilam* are also recognizable. For example, the commanding officer becomes Colonel Hoccleve in the published novel, and the commander of cadets, Joe Riley, is Col. Malcolm Shears. Tactical Officer Bean is Lieutenant Spigner. Joel's flight instructor, Willis, becomes McClintock McCaig; his check rider, Broome, is Lieutenant Foy. Dickey does not name the woman with whom Joel Mitchell is having an affair; she becomes Hannah Pelham in *Alnilam*. However, he intended to base her on Mathilda Weller, the girl with whom James Thomson was obsessed and whose death at an early age aggravated his tendency toward melancholia and contributed to his imaginative visions. The narrative centers not so much on the use or abuse of power (the entries, for example, do not mention a plot to disrupt the military) as on the archetypal search of a father for his son and on that son's efforts to achieve individuality in the midst of training for a world war.

In a poem titled "Joel Cahill Dead," published in the summer 1958 issue of *Beloit Poetry Journal,* Dickey offered a poetic interpretation of the crucial scene—Joel's crash into a wildfire and the farmer's effort to rescue him:

> Like a man sent for, he ran,
> Waving his arms, and yelled through the sooty kerchief
> In a curving voice around
> The boy who stood, amazed, beside the plane,
> Exhaled in fire, his shirt at the shoulders smoking,
> Who got then down upon one ragged knee.

The farmer and his wife drag the burning boy to their house, which the fire also threatens, and lay him on "a peacock quilt," where he "dies," "remembering the Colonel, / To whom he must affirm / That he had less than no excuse to die / Alone." Early drafts of the poem also suggest Joel's rebellious nature, his decision to take the Stearman to "an unauthorized altitude of his own," and his imaginative daring:

> Many, the first time up alone,
> Sing wildly out, and cannot think of other
> Thing to do, become so free near death,
> It was the thing Joel Cahill chose to stretch:
>
> To hands and feet, the body of the air
> Came from the fire, and set him dancing wild
> Within the aircraft body he controlled.
> It was a new becoming, wholly from surprise.

Dickey's conception of the narrative during the fifties was slow to develop, largely because he was primarily focused on his poetic career. Two years later, Scribner's would publish *Into the Stone.*

By 1971, however, key scenes and characters in *Alnilam* had become established and the novel's focus had expanded, though Dickey remained uncertain about the character of Joel Cahill and the nature of the revolt he plans. In an effort to generate interest in the new work, Dickey included numerous entries in *Sorties* that centered on the novel, including notations that revealed his composition process. "The capacity to think up themes for stories, ideas, conceptions, and so on," he wrote, "depends very much on the *cultivation* of doing so. The more one sets his mind thinking, deliberately, along these lines, the more alert one becomes to possibilities of this sort" (111). Along with the theme of a father's search for his son (with the implications of Dickey's own relationships with his son Chris as well as his father, Eugene), the novel, now titled "Death's Baby Machine," attempted to present another concern—"the power of words in a certain order to move men to action" (129). Dickey had not yet worked out the details of Operation Freeze-Out, the plot his protagonist, now named Joel Cahill, was coordinating, or the nature of the new order Joel envisioned. That order, he postulated, might suggest that Joel has ideas of becoming "a very special kind of mystical fascist" (130). Although clearly excited in 1971 by the content of the new book, Dickey also expressed reservations about its success: "The basic problem of this novel is to create a character of potentially major dimensions who is never seen, but who is projected by means of his posthumous effect on other people, and whose implications, insofar as they may be known at all, come to rest in his blind father. This is a terribly difficult undertaking, and must be thought out slowly and in hundreds of details" (137–38).

In May 1980 Dickey and Deborah flew to Idaho, where Dickey accepted an honorary degree from the University of Idaho. They then traveled to Seattle, where he underwent major surgery to correct a hiatal hernia. For years he had had difficulty swallowing properly because his intestine was blocking his esophagus; now he was unable to eat solid food. The operation occurred on 20 May, two days after Mount St. Helen's spectacular explosion. In correspondence to Stewart Richardson and others, Dickey seemed to link the two events. In an unpublished missive dated 30 June to Jim Gaston, a friend at the US Air Force Academy who had recently inquired about writing an article on Dickey's formative years in the army air forces, Dickey declared that while under anesthesia,

> I was attempting to fly quite blind—under ether, without even eyesight or consciousness, much less instruments—through the stone snows of Mount St. Helen's.... It was all a very strange experience, like a dream of combat where you don't even know whom or what you're fighting, but must be the battlefield itself, either on the table or in some manner levitated, where the surgeons must go into action against the Dark Men, with only their short blades.

Because he viewed everything as warfare, Dickey described his ordeal as a death and resurrection. On 8 June he returned to Columbia, having been instructed to rest. By the end of the month he was eating enthusiastically and walking for exercise, praising the simple pleasures to friends in his correspondence.

A week later he applied himself to a new book of poems titled "Deborah Puella." The poems were originally intended as part of a limited edition entitled "Flowering," a collaborative effort with photographer Bookie Binkley, who had agreed in fall 1977 to pay Dickey $15,000 in two installments to write thirty poems that would accompany his thirty photographs. Early in their collaboration, Binkley would send four or five pictures to Dickey, who would then write poems that would accompany them, but because he composed so slowly, Dickey was relieved when Binkley decided to include only nineteen photographs. He wrote Sidney Stapleton, Binkley's business partner, on 22 September 1979, over a year past the agreed deadline, and in the unpublished letter reviewed his progress: "I have written out sketches of the settings, the activities, the attitudes and even the personality of each girl, and have written the poem to and around these conditions. In addition, I have made the poems sequential, and the presentation of the photographs progresses from dawn to night: from the girls running on the road to the girl asleep with the rose." Dickey was convinced that the limited printing of 2,500 copies would sell out quickly. A cover story on him in the November 1979 issue of *Reader's Digest*, titled "James Dickey—'Poet of Survival and Hope'"—as well as articles on "Flowering" that appeared in *Southern Living*, *Vogue*, *Harper's Bizarre*, and *Cosmopolitan*, would generate large interest. Binkley, however, who had invested large sums of money for studio expenses and materials and who was searching for a publisher to assist with printing and publicity, failed to acquire the necessary funding. When Dickey returned from Seattle following his hernia operation, he wrote Stewart Richardson that he doubted whether Binkley would find a commercial house to publish a book costing $250 a copy. "What I would really like," he declared in a letter of 17 June, "is eventually to get the 19 poems released to me so that I can then incorporate them into a new book with Doubleday, for they are surely the best sustained sequence anybody has done since Rilke's *Orpheus* sonnets." By the end of the summer, he was convinced that "Flowering" would not succeed.

Dickey contacted John O'Brien at Deerfield Press to inquire whether he wanted to select several of the *Puella* poems to publish as a chapbook, informing O'Brien that the original publisher, Golden Chalice Press, had "apparently" returned the nineteen poems to him to publish as a separate book without the photographs. He urged O'Brien to contact Golden Chalice Press and *Atlantic Monthly* (where one of the poems, "The Surround," had appeared) for permission to reprint the poems. On 28 June Dickey informed O'Brien that he had concluded all required arrangements not only with his agent but also with Golden Chalice Press and Doubleday for release of the poems and that O'Brien could now proceed. In December 1980 Deerfield Press published a limited edition titled *Scion*, despite warnings not to do so by Binkley and Sidney Stapleton to Theron Raines, Dickey's agent, and Kirkman Finley, Dickey's lawyer. Both Dickey and Findley knew that the contract was being violated but believed Dickey was not liable because he owned the poetry. Soon after *Puella* was published by Doubleday in 1982, Binkley's lawyer, James Humphrey, browsing in a New York bookstore, discovered a copy and contacted Binkley. Shocked, Binkley hired Vernon Glenn and Kendall Few in Winston-Salem to sue Dickey for breach of contract. In September 1983 the case went to trial; Dickey was eventually ordered to repay Binkley approximately $25,000.

Dickey again served on the Pulitzer Prize committee in 1980, this time as chairman; the other committee members were Nona Balakian, editor for the *New York Times Book Review*, and poet John Ashbery, whose poems Dickey had once described as "a kind of idling arbitrariness, offering their elements as a profound conjunction of secrecies one can't quite define or evaluate" (*Babel to Byzantium* 59). Disagreement immediately followed. Balakian, who had survived Turkey's massacre of Armenians, preferred the darker visions of Mark Strand, Galway Kinnell, and Louise Glück, while Ashbery, who favored avant-garde writing and abstract expressionism, voted to offer the prize to his friend James Schuyler for his collection *The Morning of the Poem*. Dickey preferred Brewster Ghiselin's *Windrose: Poems, 1929–1979*, but because he had listed Schuyler second, he effected a compromise and sided with Ashbery.

Dickey's service on the Pulitzer committee necessitated that he delay publication of *Puella*, which he had originally wanted Doubleday to publish in 1980. He wrote Stewart Richardson on 17 June 1980 that the only reason he had agreed to serve was because the committee included Ashbery, "a kind of clique writer up there, and I thought it best that the award not go to one of his friends." Dickey, however, understood the politics of such awards and committed himself insofar as possible to those whose poetry he himself liked and believed emotionally honest and valid. Because he also recognized that he needed to rehabilitate his reputation, he corresponded with those in the United States and England whose opinions influenced the literary landscape, including Helen Vendler, whom he had labeled "that dreadful woman 'critic'" in an unpublished 2 July 1982 letter to Stanley Burnshaw and whose antagonistic attitudes about his poetry he wished to mitigate, and Donald Davie, an important British poet and critic who was a member of The Movement and who had recently accepted a position at Vanderbilt. In his letter to Vendler, Dickey related that he had just read an article in *American Scholar* about her book on George Herbert, declaring that he admired the metaphysical poet and knew about the contemporary state of Herbert criticism. He had met Davie in late April 1968 when he had traveled to London, where he discussed the state of contemporary British and American poetry at an American Embassy conference that included M. L. Rosenthal and A. Alvarez. In a flattering letter to Davie dated 31 October 1980, Dickey wrote,

> I have been familiar with your work ever since Flannery O'Connor gave me a copy of your *Articulate Energy* on the front porch of her farm in Milledgeville, Georgia, and have since followed your writing as closely as I was able. In addition to your poetry, which I consider by far the best of the group you are conveniently...associated with, your work on Pound is the best that has yet been done, and despite the mountain of Pound interpretation that will be growing forever, probably, I don't see how your insights into him can easily be surpassed, on whatever mountain.

He added, "I hope the strongest warmth of which I am capable will come off this page." Despite such wording, Dickey rarely mentioned Davie in other letters when ranking England's best poets.

In September, Dickey traveled to England with Deborah for a five-day visit, the primary purpose of which was to participate, along with Auberon Waugh and Robin Maugham, in a series of telecasts by the British Broadcasting Company that William F. Buckley had organized. In witty and often contentious debates, the panel discussed such famous authors as D. H. Lawrence, Somerset Maugham, and Graham Greene. Dickey also visited famous places in London and made a trip to Sussex to see the grave of Malcolm Lowry, whose *Under the Volcano*, a moving portrayal of alcoholic hallucinations that had influenced Dickey's long poem *The Zodiac*, was one of his favorite novels.

By the end of 1980, Dickey had become involved in writing the screenplay for an epic movie about the Klondike Gold Rush. Jerome Hellman, who had produced *Midnight Cowboy* and *Coming Home*, would make the film. Interested in working with Dickey, Hellman had contacted Theron Raines to discuss his ideas for a gold rush film and a few months later visited Dickey in Columbia. They negotiated a contract with United Artists that would pay Dickey $50,000 for a treatment and $200,000 for a script based on the treatment. Dickey, however, was conscious of the precariousness of any Hollywood venture, and while he boasted of the project, he warned Raines not to expect completion. Success depended upon Michael Cimino's *Heaven's Gate*, which promised to be a financial disaster. It was, and Steven Bach, head of United Artists, was deposed because of the millions lost on the movie. When Paula Weinstein and Anthea Sylbert replaced Bach, the future of "Klondike" became precarious. No multi-million-dollar budget materialized, and no screenplay evolved past the treatment stage, though Dickey received $50,000 for his initial work. Even so, Dickey was slowly advancing on *Alnilam* and readying himself for the publication of *Puella*. Deborah, meanwhile, had informed him that she was pregnant with their first child.

Deborah would become a muse for Dickey, heightening his sensitivity to the physical world and quickening his intuitive responses. She revealed a self that Dickey had not previously discerned, offering him a feminine surround of intensity, mystery, and possibility. In his early notebooks, he had announced a poetic imperative: "It is the task of poetry to find and articulate the archetypal, individual (or possibly racial) vision, examine it, determine (or arrive at a tentative, or even assign one) its meaning, and make this meaning available" (*Striking In* 79). Early poems, such as "Into the Stone," "The Rib," "Mary Sheffield," "The Leap," and "The Scarred Girl," had presented this ideal. This attitude had not changed when, in his 1971 essay "Complicity," he quoted the poet Paul Claudel, "Woman is the promise that cannot be kept," and added, "If she is not the secret of the universe, then there is none" (*Night Hurdling* 217). Deborah suggested this ideality, and archetypal events from her life, poetically recreated, became the foundation for *Puella*. The book's pointed epigraph, T. Sturge Moore's lines, "I lived in thee, and dreamed, and waked / Twice what I had been," indicates Dickey's continuing belief in Woman as a source of life-enhancing possibilities. Pretty and resourceful, Maxine had embodied practicality and stability, necessary qualities for the wife of an aspiring young writer, but Dickey, now middle-aged and alcoholic, his career faltering, viewed Deborah as a new beginning. Taken together, the *Puella* poems trace her maturation and reveal her heightened conscious-ness of the world, including her kinship with the elements of fire, air, earth, and water and her growing knowledge of human relationships. The first-person perspective, in lyric poems that only in composite yield any real sense of "story," along with a technique that offers reality through sim-ultaneous, intuited images or associations, gives the collection a psycho-logical depth and richness not achieved with Dickey's previous narrative methods. In the collection's final poem, "The Surround," Deborah urges, "With delivery-room patience" a penetration into a power everywhere pre-sent, the achievement of "unparalleled rhythm" and "invention unending."

Nowhere were critics and reviewers in the eighties and nineties more deeply divided than over Dickey's depiction of and attitudes toward women. On the one hand, critics such as Robert Covel, Robert Kirschten, Richard Calhoun, Robert Hill, Ernest Suarez, and Joyce Pair mounted compelling defenses of Dickey's new work. Centering their analysis on such poems as "The Scarred Girl," "Cherrylog Road," "Falling," and "May Day Sermon," they variously argued that Dickey's poetry idealized women, citing "Complicity":

> From going to and fro in the earth, and from walking up and down in it—the real earth, and not just the enchanted fragment of it that blazes in the longing mind to furnish her setting—she becomes a hidden archetype to the beholder rendered god-like by her pres-ence: his possession and promise, soulless and soulful at the same time, receding, flashing up with terrible certainty at the most inop-portune times that she then makes opportune. (*Night Hurdling* 217)

In the literary warfare that erupted, Kirschten explicitly stated the ground on which defenders would stand: "Dickey's mythopoeic vision has been matriarchal and multi-cultural—even revolutionary feminist—for 25 years," a thematic concern that "has been continuous through [Dickey's] career" (1–25).

On the other hand, critics including Robert Bly, Jane Hill, Carolyn Heilbrun, and Sue Walker largely dismissed this analysis, suggesting that Dickey's work revealed a basic prejudice against women by treating them as objects or by denying them the transcendent experiences enjoyed by male personae. Jane Hill, for example, attacked what she labeled "the god-dess strain of feminism" and declared, "Dickey's women, as represented in the poems, do not, in general, overcome the obstacles that being female in the world as Dickey renders it presents. They do not, in general, find themselves living the fullest, most intense lives possible; they do not usually come close even to the level of pursuit of those goals that their male counterparts enjoy." Only in *Puella*, Hill asserts, does the poet grant the female character "her own voice and her own quest for the full realm of experience" (2–12). Yet even in this collection, Sue Walker argues, Dickey's presentation is, in effect, "an aggression":

> He has made us see what he sees. Only we see more. We see through our own eyes as well as his. We are neither dolls nor toys, playthings that can be manipulated. We see that the difficulty with the *Puella* poems, at least in part, is the fact that they reflect the poet's state. They [re]present where he is in his middle years, at age fifty-three, when he marries a woman less than half his age. The poems that seek to know Deborah, ferret out her identity as she comes into womanhood, mirror the poet's desires more than hers and attend to his need to have "things of this kind." (2–9)

Dickey's death in 1997 did little to effect a cessation of such hostilities; critical opinion remained entrenched.

The creativity promised by Deborah allowed for a second new muse, his daughter, Bronwen. Her birth on 17 May 1981 provided him with what he declared in an interview the following year to be "a wonderful renewal" (Baughman, *Voiced Connections* 187), and he celebrated her arrival with a new poem titled simply "Daughter," portraying her as life's true motion: "You are part / Of flowing stone," he wrote, "understand: you are part of the wave, / Of the glacier's irrevocable / Millennial inch." She confirmed for him the existence of a realm of intense mystery, of endless possibility. It is almost as if, in an Aristotelian world, she was proof of a Platonic ideal. In an unpublished letter to Stanley Burnshaw dated 24 September 1982, he proudly called Bronwen "my brand new little female superstar." At age eight, she began to compose poetry herself. In a 1982 interview, he declared of fathering Bronwen, "You feel like you're standing in the main cycle of time and nature, part of the great chain of being. You have to be 59 to appreciate how great it really is" (*Night Hurdling* 230–42).

That he should see her this way led him in 1986 to present his daughter in a book-length children's poem, *Bronwen, the Traw, and the Shape-Shifter*, in which a young girl is asked by the King of the Squirrels to defeat the forces of All-Dark. She does, entering nature with the ease that suggests her lack of differentiation from its rhythms and processes, an imaginative integration into it, so that as the flying squirrels return her to her bedroom, she thinks, "The whole land took over her memory, / And they were the same, just about." Random House and several other publishers rejected the book before Deborah urged her husband to approach Matthew Bruccoli, his colleague at USC, to publish it at Harcourt Brace Jovanovich, with whom he worked. The publisher offered a $5,000 advance and printing of twenty thousand copies. Sales were brisk. By 30 December 1986, ten thousand copies had sold but then slackened (Hart 669). Given Dickey's macho persona in the sixties and seventies, his portrayal of such a transformation in the mind of a little girl indicates that by the eighties he had acquired other visions. "Don't interfere at all, ideally," he asserted in a 1987 interview, "with the way children perceive nature. Don't impose too much explanation, scientific or otherwise, on what they see. Let it be to them what it is to them, right then" (Van Ness, "A Different Kind of Deliverance" 8–11). With Deborah and Bronwen, at least temporarily, Dickey achieved, if not a balance, at least the diminishment of the restless, un-stemming pursuit of the unattainable that characterized most of his personal and creative life. Until Deborah's descent into drugs and drug dealers undermined the situation at home, Dickey's voice seemed comfortable, as if he had accepted the limitations he felt everywhere.

In a letter dated 5 October 1981, film director John Boorman wrote Dickey asking him to assist Michael Ciment, a distinguished French critic who was writing a book on Boorman's movies. He added, "I am still haunted by 'Looking for the Buckhead Boys.' Why don't you write a film/book about that quest, a story that would flow back and forth between middle age and childhood?" Dickey responded on 22 October, assuring Boorman of his cooperation with Ciment but deferring on the proposal, stating that he would need to complete present projects "before I would ever be able to take the Boys out of mothballs and reexamine them." He hoped to make these film efforts good ones "and then return to the back pages of obscure poetry magazines, which is where I came from, and where I belonged all the time," a comment that suggests Dickey's own awareness of how far his reputation had declined and how much he had marginalized his poetry in pursuit of more lucrative projects. One project was "Klondike," the script to which Dickey returned in early 1982. The other involved Richard Roth, who had sent Dickey a screenplay based on Jon Hassler's 1981 novel *The Love Hunter* and asked Dickey to revise the script with Robert Redford. Redford, who had met Dickey in Columbia, believed that they could adapt a mediocre novel into something extraordinary; Dickey was not convinced and did not pursue the endeavor.

Despite informing Boorman that his work schedule was too heavy to involve himself in other films, he traveled to Beaufort, South Carolina, the following month to narrate a PBS documentary on the Depression. Entitled *One-Third of a Nation*, his colleague Bernie Dunlap had written the documentary; Dickey was paid $5,000 for his participation, his interest spurred partly because the subject intrigued him and partly because he was tempted by the money. Though in no sense financially strapped, he always sought more. He had lived through the Depression and, in the stories he fabricated for the personal mythology in which he centered himself, he had suffered from its effects. He was also conscious of James Agee's efforts to represent the era's hardships on the South in *Let Us Now Praise Famous Men*, one of his favorite books. Indeed, after learning while in Europe of Agee's death on 16 May 1955, he somberly wrote in his notebooks, "James Agee is dead. God keep him, in the depth and trembling of His open shadow," and he later composed an unpublished poem titled "In Memory of James Agee." It concluded:

> Great sorrow, continuing hope
> For the dead, the sun in the pines
> Changing the sea to light,
> Genius gone, and fewer left
> To remember it, with its amazing power
>
> To turn the face of the dead
> To light, and the sun
> To light, of the sea
> Walking between the pines to where you live.

However, his participation in the project as well as his continued interest in "Klondike" reflect his contradictory attitudes toward money, driving him toward and away from lucrative, but often distracting, movie contracts. On the one hand, Dickey early in his career had sought out Ezra Pound, with whose diatribes against capitalism and usury he sympathized, as he struggled to establish a financially successful career. In an unpublished letter dated 2 November 1981 to Dana Gioia, who was soliciting information for an essay titled "Poetry and Business," Dickey responded defensively regarding his years in advertising: "Myself and the others you mention are by no means the only ones of the Brethren who have worked in business, but if these are the ones you want to use, they should be good enough material." He was acutely conscious of the effects of wealth on those who have it, declaring in his 1979 essay "The Energized Man,"

> The enormous discomfort that settles on Americans as they grow older: the enormous discomfort that settles on them in the midst of all their Comforts, and we can spell that word with a capital, is that their lives—their real lives—seem somehow to have eluded them: to have been taken away from under their very noses. They feel— they *know* their real life, a life of vital concerns, of vivid interest in things, and above all, of consequence, was there, someplace: I just laid it down a minute ago...and so on. (Weigl, Hummer 163–65)

For Dickey, what mattered most was poetry. On the other hand, the success of *Deliverance* had enabled him to enjoy not only the previously unrealizable comforts of American life, including a second home on Pawleys Island, but also national recognition. In letters during the fifties, he bragged about the money advertising made him. In February 1982 he proudly announced to friends and family that his short essay "How to Enjoy Poetry," which was sponsored by the International Paper Company in its campaign to improve reading and writing skills, would reach eighty million people and was appearing simultaneously in *Newsweek*, *Time*, the *New York Times, Psychology Today*, and *Rolling Stone*. Dickey would have agreed with W. Somerset Maugham's contention that money was the sixth sense without which the other five senses cannot be properly enjoyed.

During summer 1982, Dickey worked diligently on *Alnilam* and then left for a week and a half on vacation with Deborah and Bronwen in Paris. Before leaving, however, he sent his new editor, Hugh O'Neill, another one hundred pages of the manuscript, which now totaled 474 pages, along with instructions as to how to proceed should he be killed. "In case our aircraft blows up or we are gunned down at a café by either Palestinians, Jews, Armenians, Turks, Greeks, or just criminals (*that* would be a relief, and understandable!)," he wrote in an unpublished letter dated 13 August, "publish what you have of the novel." He asked his editor to use his notes and "piece the thing out, as Edmund Wilson did with Fitzgerald's *The Last Tycoon*. The manuscript of *Alnilam* is three times longer than *Tycoon*, and if Fitzgerald-Wilson can edit and publish such a book, so can Dickey-O'Neill." In Paris, the Dickeys stayed at the Hotel du Louvre Concord and visited the Eiffel Tower, the Louvre, the Jeu de Paume, and the

Sorbonne as well as numerous bookstores. Dickey was particularly pleased to see his old friend Marcel Béalu at Le Pont Traversé and tried to visit French writers he admired, including Julien Green, whom he had written two days before his flight. In an unpublished letter dated 12 August, he declared, "I think I can truthfully say that your own writing and the example of your life I take from your *Journal* has had a great and good effect on my own work, and on my standards and values. I learned to read French by reading your *Journal*." While in Paris the Dickeys enjoyed a respite from the factiousness and discord of their domestic life together; they considered trying to conceive another child, whose name would be "Galen" if a girl and "Talbot" if a boy.

Deborah's growing addiction to drugs, including cocaine, and her increasing insecurities and lack of self-worth, led to verbal and physical confrontations with her husband. Dickey had expected her to assume the same household and financial responsibilities that Maxine routinely and successfully performed. Deborah, however, wished to continue her education (she earned a masters in arts in teaching in 1987) and exercise her creativity in theater. Her new husband's past womanizing mitigated her sense of trust. Emotional confrontations and shouting matches precluded domestic tranquility. "Those were days with lots of passion," Chris later stated, "lots and lots of drinking, lots of near-violence and threats of violence on Debbie's part. Those were the days when Bronnie, about five years old, would hide the kitchen knives." Real violence was rare, he remembered, although Deborah once cut Dickey with a broadhead arrow she was brandishing. The atmosphere was toxic.

When they returned to the United States, Dickey confronted the reviews of *Puella*, which had been published on 29 April; though he hoped the book would elevate his career, he prepared himself for critical attacks. The collection became a seminal work. Its involved technique is critical, for the images the persona conveys evoke an emotional complex inherent in certain narrative points in time that increasingly become timeless—that is to say, mythical—presenting the simultaneous penetration of worlds—male and female, present and past, transcendent and physical. Critics such as Peter Balakian, James Applewhite, Ronald Baughman, and Eugene Hollahan discerned in the work a positive advance over Dickey's "central motion." Balakian, for example, argued that the book provided another example of Dickey's search for Otherness whose form indicates a Whitmanesque affirmation and ambitiousness. The poems, he declared, constituted "a large monologue," not simply the outline of an entire mind but also "the pressures of the psyche, body, and spirit striving for transcendence," where the sexes finally unite in "a celebration of marriage" through the procreative powers of the feminine principle (135–46). Baughman believed the book's organizational structure displayed a pattern of imagery that involves the elements as well as images of sound, all of which evoke emotional response and promote reader participation. The thematic conclusion of the volume, he asserted, occurs in "The Surround," spoken to James Wright as he moves from life to death. In addition to depicting Deborah's final incarnation as the environment, the poem unites all the important images: the reflected echo of veer-sounds, the circles and rings that mirror the cycle of life and death, and the unity of fire, air, water, and earth. *Puella*, Baughman concluded, reveals "new voices and new tones" (*Understanding James Dickey*143). Poetry editor John Frederick Nims informed Dickey that the five *Puella* poems published in the March issue of *Poetry* had won the Levinson Prize. Past winners included Frost, Stevens, Cummings, and Dylan Thomas.

Other critics, however, met the volume with disdain. Dana Gioia, for example, strongly attacked the collection, labeling it "an unqualified disaster." Specifically, Gioia accused Dickey of meaningless linguistic frivolity—phrasing that consisted of "arbitrarily compounded words ('Afterglowing in the hang-time'), hopelessly vague description ('the wide-open collisionless color'), and clumsy wordplay ('All pores cold with cream')." Such strained effects, he asserted, obscured the general sense of many of the poems. "It takes a certain genius to write this badly," Goia sarcastically declared, and he concluded, "The more one scrutinizes the language of *Puella*, the more it seems improvised and approximate, nothing but pure, old-fashioned southern sound and fury" (190–93).

Although the poems only tangentially mirrored Deborah's childhood, reflecting instead more stereotypical moments in a girl's childhood and her maturation, they began as responses to Binkley's photographs of numerous girls whom Dickey had never seen. He had imaginatively unified them under his wife's name. In an unpublished letter to Shaye Areheart at Doubleday dated 23 April 1982, he endeavored to provide an extensive explanation of his sequence in hope that his commentary would assist the publisher in promoting the book. The letter suggests that within the lyric "moments" of Deborah's upbringing, he consciously presented a cyclical journey—the rites of passage of the mythic hero: "The whole book is intended to be cyclic, or at any rate semicyclic, beginning before dawn and running on through the following midnight. The nineteen poems touch on the various aspects of the female 'awakening' process, or at least as I have been able to imagine them." It opens, he wrote, "with a kind of ritual getting-rid-of-the-effects and environments of childhood" in a ceremonial burning of a doll and dollhouse, progresses through experiences in which the narrator "link[s] up with the enormous forces of the universe," and concludes with an invocation as well as "an affirmation of the imagination, of the mind's associational powers, so that literally the whole universe can result, or build up from, a single thought." In his biography of Dickey, Henry Hart asserts that *Puella*, in its presentation of a woman's coming of age, including menstruation and the growing awareness of temporal cycles, hypocritically "echoes" the poems of Anne Sexton and Sylvia Plath, both of whom Dickey denounced in *Babel to Byzantium* and *Sorties*. The portrait of Deborah, the "various snapshots, cut up and shuffled as they are," that present her as troubled and destabilized, is itself essentially confessional (646). Yet Dickey's poetic intent necessitated the treatment of such biological facts; unlike Sexton and Plath, his feminine vision in no way graphically presents a confessional, self-exposing, and psychologically vulnerable self.

Dickey instructed Shaye Areheart to send *Puella* to Richard Hugo, who was chairing the 1982 Pulitzer Prize committee. With his friend in charge, he hoped to win the coveted award, but he soon learned that Hugo had died. In an unpublished letter to Dave Smith dated 29 October, he declared that he wanted "to go up there to Montana and give a couple of benefit readings, and try to get a plaque or something put up in his memory." Then he expressed a melancholy despair: "Fat lot of good that'll do, though, death being what it is. But we go on, until we can't. Right now, you and I go on." He attempted to have Smith inducted into the National Institute of Arts and Letters, writing Robert Penn Warren on 15 September, "God help him, he did his PhD on my work, and has kept in touch all this time." "I do like his work," Dickey wrote, and with a football metaphor that suggested his abiding competitiveness, concluded, "I will be more than glad to back his play." He called Smith in an unpublished 22 November letter "my best, my old Pulling Guard." Again using football to help promote *Puella*, he urged his other supporters, including Richard Tillinghast and David Bottoms, to "knock 'em down," to continue the game he increasingly sensed he was losing but which he was determined to play. He wrote Tillinghast on 8 October that the *New York Times* might contact him to review *Puella*, stating that it would be good to have him "on the case." "The book is important," Dickey emphasized, "because it marks a shift in my way of going at things, concentrating more on the purely linguistic part of poetry—especially on the line—and less on the narrative or anecdotal." He also hoped Tillinghast would do an extensive review of his early work, as the latter had recently done on Charles Wright, informing him in an unpublished letter dated 14 December that "if the *Times* is willing for you to review Wright's old poems they should be twice as willing to do mine." He continued, "There would be a really interesting possibility, it seems to me of your doing some kind of retrospective, an assessment of some sort, using these books as a base, particularly, in view of the fact that a kind of new-wave movement, counter to Lowell's confessionalism, seems to be shaping up around the kind of thing that I have been trying to do over the years." Tillinghast, however, did not write such a review. Battered on several fronts, Dickey was nevertheless intent on maintaining new poetic directions, utilizing his friends for what he clearly understood was needed literary and political "lift." He also continued to be conscious of the physical debilitation of age. When Norman German, an English professor at Lamar University, wrote to both praise and ask questions about an early poem, "Looking for the Buckhead Boys," Dickey responded on 18 October, "Say hello to your class for me, and tell them I'm alive, though almost sixty. I'm going back to Buckhead next month, though, and I'll see if Charlie Gates...is still around, for I need gas."

In 1983, the year he turned sixty, Dickey was honored by the new governor of South Carolina, Richard Riley, who asked him to write a poem for his inauguration. In January, Dickey celebrated his state by reading "For a Time and Place" to assembled politicians and their families. As with his essay "The Starry Place between the Antlers," the poem celebrated both the abundant flora and fauna of South Carolina and its geographic diversity, everything arranged in a rich pattern of natural wealth:

> Where we best
> Are, and would be: our soil, our soul,
> Our sail, our black horizon simmering like a mainspring,
> Our rocky water falling like a mountain
> Ledge-to-ledge naturally headlong,
> Unstoppable, and our momentum
> In place, overcoming, coming over us
> And from us
> From now on out.

In 1989 he again championed the state's physical beauty in the forward he wrote for a coffee-table book entitled *South Carolina: The Natural Heritage.* "From the mountains of Oconee to the beaches of Pawleys Island," he stated,

> these kinds of original space exist any time we open ourselves to them, and merely *look* without thought of using.... We need to substitute instinct for reason, and merely to *behold* what is; and view with primal innocence those parts of creation that have nothing to do with us except to serve as material for contemplation and wonder, born into it as we were, living by means of its processes, part of a mystery, part of a whole scheme, a cosmos, the reason for which will never be known. (9–10)

Throughout his life, Dickey's attitude toward the natural world—South Carolina specifically and the South generally—was one of celebration and reverence at the inexplicable wonder and mystery of creation, a founding principle of the now well-established environmental movement.

Riley thanked Dickey in a letter dated 13 January 1983, stating that South Carolina was fortunate to have "someone of your talent who understands both the apparent and the hidden beauty of this great state and who has the capacity to capture this beauty in poetry." Dickey responded in an unpublished letter dated 19 January, declaring that the occasion "brought me closer to the things and people I live among, and that cannot be anything but good." He very much believed that being born a Southerner constituted the best circumstance that had happened to him, first as a man and then as a writer, and while Dickey never wished to indulge in regional chauvinism, he felt that the history of the South had imparted to him not only a set of values, particularly the sense of the nature of evil, but also a visionary sense of larger modes of existence. He requested the governor attend his literary birthday party, soon to be hosted for him by the University of South Carolina. Robert Penn Warren, Richard Howard, Norman Mailer, Saul Bellow, John Updike, Harold Bloom, R. W. B. Lewis, and Monroe Spears had been invited. Though not all could attend, including Updike, the gathering particularly delighted Dickey, whose troubled marriage and declining career threatened his self-identity. On 1 February, his colleague Bernie Dunlap discussed the film *Deliverance*; the following day, former students Franklin Ashley, Ben Greer, and Susan Ludvigson recounted his extraordinary teaching; and later in the afternoon Riley himself hosted a birthday gala at the Governor's Mansion. That night Bloom and Howard lectured on Dickey's poetry. On 4 February, the final day of the symposium, Monroe Spears, Dickey's professor at Vanderbilt, defended his former student's experiments in *The Zodiac* and *Puella*, which he viewed as advancing an exemplary career. Considering the maligned reception those volumes had received, Dickey was elated by their defense from so distinguished a scholar. The grand finale of the literary celebration was a banquet hosted by James Holderman, the university's president, who introduced Dickey's reading.

Financial worries engendered by Bookie Binkley's litigation soon caused Dickey to undertake another round of poetry readings. During the winter and spring, he again returned to "barnstorming for poetry," visiting Albright College, the University of North Texas, Savannah College of Art and Design, Fairleigh Dickinson University, New York's West Side YMCA, and the Guggenheim Museum. In March he also appeared at Clemson for a three-day conference where by chance he ran into his old football coach, Rock Norman, at a Holiday Inn restaurant. Dickey had written a tribute to his coaches in an early poem, "The Bee," first published in the June 1962 issue of *Harper's* magazine, declaring later that "the bad times they gave me come to seem like acts of faith, because they wouldn't have taken the time with me if they didn't think I was worth it" (*Self-Interviews* 171). Dickey, always needing to feel important, was pleased that Norman recognized and remembered him.

During summer 1983, Dickey focused on several older projects, among them another coffee-table book titled "The Wilderness of Heaven," whose deadline was in October. Shaye Areheart had mailed him reproductions of paintings by Hubert Shuptrine about which Dickey was supposed to write, but Dickey demurred. "I am proceeding in somewhat the same manner as I did for *Jericho*," he wrote Shuptrine in an unpublished letter dated 5 August, "for it seems to me that a kind of double vision of Appalachia—the artist's and the writer's—is better than having one of the interpreters comment on the work of the other, in effect." He informed the painter that he had divided the text into ten sections with two subsections in each. Dickey was more direct with Areheart, stating that Shuptrine's pictures did not afford him enough subject matter and declaring that it was better if he simply worked out his own interpretation of Appalachia. Because such an arrangement risked a fractured book, Shuptrine requested on 25 August that Dickey send him an outline of his narrative to guide his painting. Dickey finished the story quickly, sending a draft to Hugh O'Neill by the end of October and completing revisions in December.

He finished another book in late 1983. On 15 October, Bruccoli Clark published *Night Hurdling*, a collection of essays, poems, commencement addresses, interviews, and afterwords that projected the self-proclaimed and self-proclaiming threads of his identity, and that continued his exploration of the nature and intent of poetry. The readings Dickey offered presented a writer whose identity was eclectic if not contradictory. Dickey himself admitted as much to Stanley Burnshaw in an unpublished letter dated 28 July: "*Night Hurdling* is sure to be mighty controversial, because I say a lot of what I think in there, and, although some of it is self-contradictory—and therefore certain to displease *all* sides—I mean what I say when I say it, whenever it is." Essays such as "The Water-Bug's Mittens" and "The G.I. Can of Beets, the Fox in the Wave, and the Hammers Over Open Ground" constituted his most intense scrutiny of his own poetry as a means not only of examining himself but also of determining new poetic directions. Indeed, the images Dickey discusses in the latter, Jarrell's "G.I. can of beets," Dylan Thomas's "fox in the wave," and Michael Hamburger's translation of Paul Celan, "the hammers / will swing over open ground," a creative re-creation of the literal wording, "the hammers will swing free," offer a sense of his critical search for a new poetic ground where images are imaginatively delivered and built upon but held within the poet's imposed limits. That for Dickey involved not so much meter, rhyme, or any such traditional poetic conventions as "the right kind of arbitrariness," the language having the sense of possessing the world. His analyses of other writers, moreover, including Robert Penn Warren's angst, F. Scott Fitzgerald's poetry, Jack London's stylistic vices and narrative virtues, and Vachel Lindsay's suicidal decline, were incisive and convincing.

Dickey one again returned to his extensive reading tours in October and November 1983, visiting the Governor's School for the Arts in South Carolina, the Folger Shakespeare Library, George Mason University, Northern Virginia Community College, Colgate University, and the Alabama School of Fine Arts. Often he assumed the role of the drunken but brilliant bard, alternately offending and mesmerizing audiences with his conversations and readings, acting partly from frustration at the critical inattention his work was receiving and partly from a desire to shock and thereby assure audience attention.

As a respite from worries involving both his career and his domestic life, he began to participate in "power lunches" with close friends and colleagues in the English department of the University of South Carolina, a practice that he would continue twice a week until his death. Each Tuesday and Thursday midday, he would meet Ben Franklin and Don Greiner for lunch at the Faculty House. Because the tables there seated four people, a "mystery guest," whose identity was kept secret, was frequently invited, with Franklin serving as master of ceremonies. The mystery guest, Franklin remembers, could be anybody:

> Other faculty, students, people from the community. Anybody. We might see someone walking toward us on campus—let's say her name is Kim. We would say, "Kim, why don't you join us for lunch?" And then at the lunch I would begin by saying, "It's so nice to have you here, Kim. We try to find people we consider interesting, who might edify us or somehow amuse us, and we think you will. Now, we want you to feel at ease, no pressure, but really, we expect you to perform. And not only that, but at the end of this lunch, the three of us will get together, discuss how you did and decide whether to invite you back. So far, though, we have invited no one back." The guest always caught the humor, of course, and good conversation ensued. (Brandhorst 19)

Once, Henry Taylor joined the group and politely addressed Dickey with the gentle words "cher master." Novelist Frederick Busch, whom Dickey came to like personally and to respect professionally, was the mystery guest at least twice. The conversation was always brisk and high-spirited, with the guest expected to contribute to discussions of music, literature, sports, and movies. These gatherings, in addition to providing one of Dickey's few opportunities for friendly banter and private conversation, also enabled him to unburden himself about his marriage difficulties and private fears. "After a while I think Jim knew we weren't going to rush home to write an article about 'The Great Poet,'" Greiner recalled, "so he confided in us" (Brandhorst 24). With no mask to wear or role to perform and confident that neither colleague would repeat what he said, Dickey's essential voice was readily apparent. His retentive memory, acute critical analysis, and broad disciplinary knowledge as well as an obvious love of great writing all testified to who he was and the value he attributed to his craft. "What came through in the luncheon talk," Greiner stated, "were Jim's astonishing memory for literary matters and his eagerness to talk informally about such things." Matthew Bruccoli, who became his literary executor, agreed. After relating one of their afternoons together at his Columbia home, Bruccoli asserted, "His literary taste and critical judgment were impeccable. Jim was the best book-talker I have known. Anything he said about literature—drunk or sober—merited careful attention. He was not necessarily truthful about himself, but he was trustworthy on literature" (*Crux* xxi).

Once, as the three friends seated themselves (they always ate either at the same table inside the Faculty House or in the garden outside), Dickey asked Greiner what he had taught that morning; the latter responded that he was currently teaching Cooper's *The Last of the Mohicans* to a doctoral seminar. Dickey responded with genuine interest: "Do you recall the scene, late in the novel, when Cooper writes about the absolute confidence Natty and Chingachgook have in each other. How do you read that, Don?" The question led to a spirited, serious discussion on the male-bonding archetype that Cooper established in American literature, which led naturally to *Deliverance*. Similarly, when Dickey heard that Greiner had taught Wallace Stevens in a different seminar that morning, focusing on "The Snow Man," he murmured, "Another one of Stevens's innumerable conundrums." The comment sparked an hour-long exchange, with Greiner leading the defense of Stevens.

Franklin was more knowledgeable than Greiner about jazz, but the latter's expertise was in movies, so the conversation among the three men was always easy. With movies Dickey would frequently begin the conversation by mentioning a current film he had seen, such as *Platoon* or *The Remains of the Day* (he thought the title sounded "resonant"), but he would reminisce, recalling films he had admired in adolescence, such as *Dawn Patrol* and *Gunga Din*. Repeatedly he talked about the impact the original version of *The Four Feathers* had had on him, seeming to relive a moment from his youth. When Greiner inquired about *The Best Years of Our Lives*, Dickey suddenly became quiet. His favorite scene, he remembered, was the one when Dana Andrews, after the war, visits the "graveyard" of the bombers and climbs into the cockpit. He was less excited about the choices Greiner offered for discussion, including *Blow-Up* and *Claire's Knee*, although he liked such film noire classics as *The Big Sleep*, *The Maltese Falcon*, *Criss Cross*, and *Murder, My Sweet*.

When the conversation centered on music, Franklin took the lead. Greiner collected, listened to, and was conversant with "cool jazz" musicians such as Dave Brubeck and Gerry Mulligan, but Franklin knew all of jazz and could talk enthusiastically when Dickey turned the conversation to his own favorite, Bix Beiderbecke. Greiner remembers, "There was no one-up-manship during these lunch discussions, no showing off—just spirited talk among three friends who trusted one another and who thrived on these twice-a-week meetings." The conversations continued as Greiner and Franklin walked with Dickey from the Faculty House to the classroom where he would meet his two afternoon seminars.

Dickey's natural generosity came out during these lunches. He would often show up at the table with an inscribed copy of a newly released Dickey reprint, a new Dickey book, or a photocopy of a poem he was drafting. Not only did he offer his two friends bound, inscribed copies of the typescript of his novel *To the White Sea*, but he also gave them each inscribed copies of the typescript of "Breaking the Field," the poem he wrote about the Super Bowl for the NFL official program. Even more impressive, he wrote what he termed "a memorial poem" about the power lunches, a parody of eight-eenth-century heroic couplets. Ten lines in length and titled "Some Lines from Samuel Johnson, Slightly Re-written," it read:

> While still my steps the steady staff sustains,
> Tho' life still vig'rous revels in my veins,
> You grant, Kind Heaven, this indulgent place
> Where honesty and sense are no disgrace:
> These pleasing bricks where verdant osiers play,
> This peaceful vale with nature's paintings gay,
> Where Culture's harrass'd Heroes find repose,
> And safe in intellect defy our foes:
> This secret cell Your gracious Powers give,
> Let Don live here, for Don has learned to live.

"In one copy," Franklin said, "he inserted Don's name at the end, and in the other he inserted mine" (Brandhorst 19). Dickey signed both copies, "Samuel Johnson, Esq. J. Dickey, Scribe."

At these lunches, Dickey kept Franklin and Greiner informed on the progress of his projects, including *Alnilam*. He hoped that his friend George Plimpton would publish an excerpt from the novel in *Paris Review*. Plimpton did not. He had also sent Hugh O'Neill another portion of the novel with an unpublished letter dated 9 May 1983; most of this section of the manuscript centered on Frank Cahill and Joel's instructor, McCaig, their visit to the crash scene of Joel's aircraft, and the aftermath of the fire in which he went down. Dickey proposed that the material could be published either in *Playboy* or *Esquire* and suggested it be titled "The Black Farm." Now that spring semester was over, he declared, he could write with no distractions, citing his only commitment that summer as a two-week writers conference in Aspen. "I'll have the book in to you before I go," he asserted, "barring death or the transmigration of souls." In truth, the novel was nowhere near completion. On 17 December 1984 he signed another emended version of his 1971 contract, extending the deadline to 1 May 1985. Although Dickey made substantive progress on *Alnilam* in 1985, he again needed an extension, which promised the manuscript in August 1985. By mid-May, he had written twelve hundred pages. The August deadline passed, but in October he mailed all fifteen hundred pages to his editor. He variously blamed the delay on Maxine's death, his marriage to Deborah, and the birth of Bronwen and reminded those who inquired or interviewed him that throughout his career, poetry had remained his central focus. He asserted, moreover, that the novel would not have the popular appeal of *Deliverance*, telling William Starr, the book editor for *The State* newspaper, in a 1987 interview, "A writer has to go with his imagination. You're not really an artist if you try to give the people what they want. Because most of the time they don't know what they want until they get it" (Baughman, *Voiced Connections* 258–62). Nostalgic with memories of past success and piqued by the recent failures of "Flowering," "Klondike," and his other film treatments, he nevertheless hoped that it would become a best seller.

Despite the general critical decline in his reputation, Dickey's prestige remained high in some literary circles. Early in 1985 he was asked to serve on an international panel of nine judges for the Ritz Paris Hemingway Award, which Pierre Salinger had conceived and which had been formally established on 11 January. A prize of $50,000 honored the author of the best novel of the year in English or in English translation. Dickey flew to Paris to join Salinger, who presided over the judges, and cast his vote for Marguerite Duras's *The Lover*, which won. While there, Dickey reunited with his friend William Styron. Later that year Ted Koppel invited Dickey to participate in the Fourth of July edition of the ABC news show *Nightline*. Dickey was usually reticent to discuss political issues, but when now asked to discuss the significance of Independence Day, he did so from a sentimental perspective, remarking on America's good fortune to have had as its Founding Fathers such statesmen as Washington, Jefferson, Hamilton, Madison, and Adams. Despite these high-profile events, however, his appearances were more and more at small conferences or festivals and largely in the South, a measure of how regionalized the marketplace was to which he appealed. In March 1985, for example, he read at the Writers Workshop in Ashville, North Carolina, for $1,500, and in June he accepted $200 to read at the Association of Departments of English at the University of South Carolina. While he attended a 9 to 11 May conference on Eastern comparative literature at NYU, he received only $400 in payment and $200 for expenses. Indeed, Dickey's gross income from all his writings in 1986 totaled $27,563, a fraction of what his books had earned during the seventies when he commanded the literary air (Hart 661–62).

In 1986 Dickey determined to complete *Alnilam*. Because the novel centers on the crash of an airplane, he felt a grim coincidence when the *Challenger* space shuttle exploded on 28 January. Gus Combest, who worked with Dan Rather at CBS, remembered Dickey's accounts of the *Apollo* moon missions in *Life* and asked him to comment on the disaster. Rather read Dickey's eulogy at the end of his special late-night report, "Disaster in Space":

> Put them on the list of men and women who counted, these searchers and seekers, these astronauts and teachers who died today in what became the spaceship disaster; they died in the blue and silver furnaces of their space-suits. Think about them, who they were and the way they were dreamers, explorers, adventurers forcing themselves past the point of danger and deep fatigue, to expand our understanding of what is up there and out there. They may never have known the nature of the trouble that killed them. For them, no more cries of "Wow, what a view!"; no more jokes with Mission Control; no more thumbs up for cheering crowds; no more phone calls from the President. They will not see their parents and their wives or husbands and their children meeting them—gone with the rush of the engines and the exploding sky—gone, but theirs were lives that mattered.

The statement, reminiscent in tone of much of A. E. Housman's poetry, reflects Dickey's own desire for heroism, his psychological need for bravery and consequence on which he had first elaborated in his 1973 University of Virginia baccalaureate address titled "Upthrust and Its Men." That address had celebrated another astronaut, Ed White, the first American to walk in space, who was killed in a training accident. He recollected a photograph in *Life* of White in his space-walking suit, the gold-headed helmet off and a "fun grin" on his face. In the photograph and in the actions of the *Challenger* astronauts, Dickey perceived the bold daring that bespoke essential courage, a stringent and exuberant self-discipline that was not only what was most needed but also what most Americans lacked. "That is really my key word, the possible," he stated. "Possibility, and the openness to it, and the wit to recognize it and the daring to use it" (*Night Hurdling* 175–82). Ironically, perhaps, Dickey could write about such an ideal, could experience it through the illusion of language, but largely could not live it.

In late June 1986 South Carolina inducted Dickey into the Academy of Authors, the first living author to be so honored. The academy, founded several years earlier by Paul Talmadge, the vice president and academic dean of Anderson College, also honored Julia Peterkin and William Gilmore Simms. Speaking at an Anderson College banquet, Dickey declared, "My real wish is just to put down one word after another until I die." He continued, "Every writer is a failed writer. We're all amateurs at this. We don't live long enough to be anything else" (Hartung A1–2). The true writer, he suggested, was one who does what he is supposed to do—write—no matter what else is happening around him. With his dysfunctional domestic life, Dickey had difficulty working and soon developed headaches that he initially believed resulted from eyestrain. However, the headaches became more severe, and after he vomited at dinner, he went to the hospital the following day. Physicians at Richland Memorial Hospital administered a CAT scan of his brain and discovered a large blood clot under the skull whose cause was unknown; the subdural hematoma was so threatening they operated that day. He later told William Starr that, while under anesthesia, "I was consorting with the brothers Sleep and Death, and another fellow named Lazarus. I tried to bring him out with me, but he was waiting for someone else." Though the comment was lighthearted, Dickey had feared that he would die during the operation.

Much of the strength Dickey emotionally needed to recuperate fully from his successful surgery derived from his love for Bronwen and his concern for her psychological well-being should she lose her father. On 10 September 1986, he published *Bronwen, the Traw, and the Shape-Shifter*, presenting a highly idealized version of his daughter as a child of nature. As he did in his earlier works, he imposed on the narrative a mythic journey in which Bronwen leaves the warmth and safety of her home and undergoes an "otherworld" of trials as she experiences an initiation into a source of power before finally returning to her bedroom with lessons learned. Dickey contacted Richard Jesse Watson, whose illustrations accompanied the poetic text, about a sequel titled "Bronwen, the Cunicorn, and the Nomain." The fictional Bronwen, now living on the plains rather than on a cliff above a river, encounters the Cunicorn, a unicorn-like and equally mythological beast whose main characteristics are its highly stylized horn and its sad eyes. The animal cannot stay in the real world all the time and continually fades away, appearing again to Bronwen when no one else is awake. Dickey's notes state, "The Cunicorn, in other words, is like the unicorn in the poem by Rilke, which 'fed not on grain, but on the possibility of being.'" The only means by which the Cunicorn can remain in "full reality" is by retrieving and listening to the Lost Bell, which lies in Nomain, the land of no shadow. The project, however, never materialized.

As he always did, Dickey fervently promoted *Bronwen, the Traw, and the Shape-Shifter*, signing copies in Columbia and Charleston, South Carolina, and Atlanta, Georgia, and sending a copy to South Carolina's first lady. He also sent copies to Ted Koppel, Tom Brokaw, Barbara Walters, and Johnny Carson as well as most of the major newspapers, and he wrote Dan Rather in an unpublished letter dated 10 October 1986 that he would be in New York from 16–19 October if Rather would like him to appear on a network program where he might discuss the book. "It would be good to be on a program for your network," he stated, "and talk about something cheerful, and not the sad circumstances that had occurred before my other words, the ones about the shuttle explosion, went out over your waves." Rather, however, did not extend an invitation.

Reviews were primarily negative. The anonymous reviewer in the August 1986 issue of *Kirkus* complained of the "awkward" meter and "uneven" diction, occasionally simple and childlike and at other times extended into complex images (1289). Kathleen Whalin also criticized the book's style and substance in the October 1986 issue of *School Library Journal*, citing its "plodding language" and "dragging action." Intended as an epic, she declared, which should involve a quickened pace, the poem often remains stationary (173). David Macauley, in the *New York Times Book Review* issue of 8 March, concluded that the book was "an over-designed, ill-conceived, pretentious product" (31). Only Ann Sporborg in the fall 1987 issue of *James Dickey Newsletter* viewed the poem positively, noting its "powerful echoic verses" (25) and the changes in tone and cadence that reflect a deepening despair as Bronwen's "vision-quest" (26) becomes more threatening.

After finally sending *Alnilam* to Doubleday, Dickey worked diligently correcting proofs in the early weeks of 1987 so that he could return them by 25 February. After short visits to Clemson University to receive an award and to read at McNeese State in Louisiana, where his friend the poet Leon Stokesbury taught, he made a longer trip in March to Washington, DC, to attend the fortieth anniversary of the poetry consultantship and the inauguration of its replacement, the poet laureateship. He had written Robert Penn Warren to congratulate him on being named the first poet laureate and was disappointed that Warren could not attend because of throat surgery. Many of America's most distinguished poets attended the celebration, including Anthony Hecht, Richard Eberhart, Maxine Kumin, Stanley Kunitz, William Meredith, Howard Nemerov, Karl Shapiro, William Jay Smith, and William Stafford. Stephen Spender commented during the first evening of readings, "We will probably not meet again until we enter Purgatory," to which Dickey responded, "Or Parnassus," adding, "that's where good poets go." Asked what he would call such an august meeting, Dickey said, "I'd call it a Parnassus of poets." The *New York Times* printed his comments the following day (Robertson C13).

Doubleday finally published *Alnilam* on 5 June 1987 with a printing of 125,000 copies and a reported six-figure promotional budget. As with *Deliverance*, the novel's genesis lay in a single image, a superstition of World War II aviators, which Dickey later discussed in an essay titled "LIGHTNINGS, or *Visuals*":

> The novel is about the early days of World War II when the Air Force—in those days it was called the Army Air Corps—was desperately trying to prepare itself to fight a major war in the air. In fact, and probably because of these conditions, the air itself was full of myths and legends. One of those was that if you happen to look through a spinning propeller, on a flight line, say, and on the other side of it another propeller is turning and your look goes through both of them at the same time, the image of a man will be formed in the double-whirling metal, the blades. Whether true or not, that idea and that image appealed to me strongly; there was something about "the ghost in the machine" suggestion that sparked a part of my imagination.... As a result of the shadowy figure in the twin propellers, I began to feel that there might be some kind of spirit in the machines that men have made, and that this might be both indifferent and superior to them; in short, not so much a ghost in the machine but a God. (2–12)

Because of the book's massive length and its many layers of meaning, re- viewers variously identified its principal theme. Dickey, commenting on the book's composition in 1976, admitted that the conceptualization had grown: "The main thing I want to do with *Alnilam*, is write the ultimate. novel of fathers and sons; the mysteries, the frustrations, the revelations, and, at the end, the eventual renunciation and reconciliation." Along with this concern, however, he planned to exhibit both "the dangerousness— the sheer *dangerousness*—of ideas. Their applicability can result in the deaths and mutilations of many" and what he labeled "the concept of the *fabulous* death." He recognized that both *Alnilam* and its intended sequel, "Crux," endeavored to treat so many ideas that their full development and integration remained questionable. While his thematic concerns involved personal, military, artistic, and social relationships, as well as their impli- cations, he asserted, "I think the crux of the matter lies somewhere in the definition of what power does to a man and also charlatanry, and also love." "I mean to show here," he continued in his summary notes on the works in progress, "the fascination of power and personal mystery: mystiques. Mystiques, both in the absurdity and their grandeur, and their lending to the personal dramatic significance that human events and human beings so desperately need and respond to." He intended that the two novels "open out from a small incident at a primary training base into a vast Tol- stoyian vision of the Pacific air war" (Bruccoli 11–12, 14, 15).

Following the overwhelming critical and financial success of *Deliver- ance*, however, Dickey had declared in 1973 that he would never write a sequel and that his next novel would not achieve such success. "What I want to do now," he asserted, "as far as novels are concerned is to write a resounding and interesting failure. Which I think this [*Alnilam*] is going to be" (Baughman, *Voiced Connections* 107). In an unpublished letter dated 14 January 1974, he informed Stewart Richardson that the new novel would reach a thousand pages, warning, "It is very important that the *style* be right, for we are going a very long way, and the style *must* be right to sustain such a long narrative." Reviews were mixed. Expecting a work sim- ilar to his first novel, critics were baffled by the lack of action, the slow pacing, and the stylistic innovation of splitting particular pages into paral- lel columns to suggest the visible world as it is ordinarily perceived and as Frank Cahill, the blind protagonist, mentally envisions it. Reviewers also cited weak characterization and a poetic prose that occasionally yields to overwriting, flaws similar to those noted in *Deliverance*. Carolyn Blake- more, Dickey's latest editor at Doubleday, had expressed reservations in a seventeen-page letter dated 23 January 1986, not only about the length of the manuscript but also about the style. Dickey responded on 27 February with a missive of identical length, countering her proposed amendments both to his split-page technique and to his characterization of Frank Cahill, which Blakemore thought insufficiently developed. Dickey, however, assumed an *active* reader committed to his thematic concerns involving personal, military, artistic, and social relationships.

The novel on which Dickey had labored since the fifties sold reasonably well. By 31 October 1987, 52,453 copies had been returned by bookstores to the publisher (Hart 683). Jay Parini's response typified those criticizing the book. Writing in *USA Today*, he termed *Alnilam* disappointing, calling it a "melodrama" that was "windy, often incoherently organized, and—sometimes—downright bad" (70), particularly when Dickey split the narrative into vertical columns to reflect in the dark bold type Frank Cahill's subjective impressions. Robert Towers in the *New York Times Book Review*, while praising the novel as ambitious and overreaching, nevertheless asserted that it was alternately pretentious and hindered by windiness and slow pacing. The scrutiny required for the split columns of prose, he asserted, often brought some startling or original play of language, but when the narrative moved "like lava oozing from a fissure" in a work "Melvillean in its aspirations and scope," these sections seemed merely digressive. Because Dickey never clearly delineated the mystery of Alnilam, the secret group Joel created with plans to take over the military, the novel lacked, he concluded, "a white whale to pursue" (7). Gary Kerley and Ron Baughman, however, praised the novel. Kerley asserted that *Alnilam* becomes "essentially a labyrinth of questions about identity" (E5), while Baughman argued that the novel displays the many forms of power that radiate from and act on the individual and the need to rise above inconsequence. The danger of an "intensified life," he declared, is its lack of control, such that "its practitioner can become a monomaniac like Captain Ahab in *Moby-Dick* or Lewis Medlock in *Deliverance*" (S1, 8).

Ten years before Dickey published *Alnilam*, he talked about the novel with Christopher, on whom he had based his characterization of Joel Cahill, though he stated in interviews that his son was not as charismatic. Because Joel had died or perhaps only disappeared, Dickey believed that he needed to suggest some vision of the future that informs and motivates the actions of the mystical conspiracy. "The society would depend very heavily on *role-playing*, and on *lying*," he declared. "Joel believes that lying exercises the creative and imaginative faculties, and, when indulged in on either an individual or group basis, raises the consciousness of the party or parties concerned." In his reminiscence, Chris later related, "It was an idea that Jim Dickey tried to live, but he could never make it work in the novels, and in 1976 it started to fail him and everyone around him in his life." Chris blamed the novel's failure on his father's drinking and his consequent inability to impose discipline on or coherence to the technique of splitting the page into twin columns. "Jim Dickey wouldn't hear of changing them," Chris remembered, "James Dickey's voice was huge, the kind of a voice you don't find in American prose but about once in a generation" (*Summer of Deliverance* 226–27).

That was also the same voice as when he taught at Rice Institute and first conceived the idea for his big novel. It was a voice vulnerable to feelings of inadequacy and that countered real or perceived criticism by assuming a mask, playing whatever role would enable him to command attention. If the illusion he created was sublime enough, he might even believe himself a hero. Often the mask reflected an aspect of Dickey himself. Sometimes he invented one because he was curious about the perspective it offered; sometimes the mask simply seemed appropriate for the moment. It was a voice that wanted to save itself from inconsequence and to redeem society, which Dickey believed was sick, frustrated, and defeated. In a synopsis to "The Spell," he declared, "We live in a very affluent society, and we constantly have the feeling of dying of thirst, here at the fountain-side." As his brother, Tom, an expert on Civil War munitions, was dying of colon cancer, Dickey wrote Chris on 20 November and expressed the forlornness and inadequacy he felt: "It is a terrible thing, and the utter hopelessness is the worst of it. That, and the way the memory fills up with images of him when he was happy." When Tom died on 8 December 1987, Dickey eventually responded by re-creating the death-watch in a poem titled "Last Hours," published in the fall 1994 issue of *Southern Review*. In it, Tom is delivered from his fears of dying not by Stonewall Jackson and James Longstreet, the generals whose lives and actions in pursuit of the Southern cause had captivated him, but rather by Ted Bundy, whose serial murders of young women had intrigued Dickey in Seattle when he was preparing for his surgery.

Brother, take this: your blood kin's last word

Of love: follow not me
But the murderer. He will kill

The pain, in the one good act

Long after his execution. Follow. He is helping. Go with him,

Brother; he will cross you over.

Violence, personalized in the figure of Bundy, allows for an escape from the sterile hauntedness of the hospital room and offers a kind of salvation. With the reality of time and death again assaulting him, Dickey pursued new endeavors. From almost twenty years of classes, he gathered the poems of fifty of his former students and published them in an anthology titled *From the Green Horseshoe*. He also continued working on the poems he would include in his last collection, *The Eagle's Mile*. Most of his energy, however, went into the film treatment for *Alnilam*, for which Rockingham Productions on 4 August had paid him $10,000. Once again, he hoped the screenplay would generate a blockbuster movie.

Adding to Dickey's sense of optimism was his selection as the 1987 South Carolinian of the Year, an honor previously awarded to notables such as Gen. William C. Westmoreland, Sen. Strom Thurmond, Sen. Ernest "Fritz" Hollings, and Gov. Richard Riley. On 25 January 1988, he attended a luncheon at the Radisson Hotel in Columbia where Dixon Lovvorn, senior vice president and general manager of WIS Television, introduced him, celebrating Dickey's career and identifying "his contributions to the literary world and the recognition he has brought to our state." On 18 May, Dickey received even higher recognition, officially being inducted into the American Academy of Arts and Letters at a ceremony in New York. Also inducted were William Styron and, posthumously, Joseph Campbell. Onstage with Dickey and Styron were 126 distinguished fellows of the academy and its parent organization, the National Institute of Arts and Letters. The academy had been founded in 1904 to honor individuals of the highest distinction in literature, music, and the visual arts, and its first inductees included William Dean Howells, Henry James, and Mark Twain. The academy was limited to fifty lifetime members, each of whom since 1923 had been assigned a chair on the back of which was a brass plaque listing the names and dates of its previous occupants. Dickey's chair, #15, had been previously occupied by scholar William Cross, painter Raphael Soyer, and novelist John Steinbeck. In citing Dickey for this honor, Howard Nemerov stated, "James Dickey has done distinguished work in poetry for some 30 years. Original—sometimes to the point of eccentricity—his knowledge and regard for the tradition, as exemplified by his attentive and incisive criticism, of his own work and that of our contemporaries is, nevertheless, unquestionable" (Ashley A16). John Updike, the academy's chancellor, formally inducted Dickey.

Progress on the screenplay for *Alnilam* was slow. Dickey had sent the director, John Guillermin, whose World War I film *The Blue Max* he admired, a rough draft of act 1 on 16 November and another forty pages on 20 January 1988. Dickey was pleased to be working with Guillermin, who had achieved directorial fame for movies such as *King Kong, Tarzan's Greatest Adventure,* and *The Towering Inferno,* informing him, "My enthusiasm for the project grows, the more I write on it. If we do this film as you and I conceive it, people who watch it will understand that they have never really seen a movie before." Remembering his conflict with John Boorman during the seventies, he anticipated that the director would revise his script, though he urged Guillermin to consider seriously what he had done. Guillermin, however, was unable to acquire the necessary financial backing and abandoned the project by mid-1989. Disheartened after a long struggle to shape the material only to have his effort yield nothing tangible, Dickey nevertheless maintained a survivor's attitude and directed Theron Raines, his literary agent, to attempt to secure another Hollywood director.

On 15 May, Dickey flew to California to deliver the commencement address at Pitzer College, where he had made a similar address in 1965 when the college concluded its first year of operations. In the earlier talk, titled "Three Girls Outgoing," he celebrated those rare moments in life when the individual achieves a heightened sense of fulfillment. "Fragile and infinitely enduring," he declared, those moments "explain us and *are* us as we wish to be, as we exist at those times when we seem to ourselves to be existing as we were meant to." He cited passages from Antoine de Saint-Exupéry, W. N. P. Barbellion, and Alun Lewis and urged the graduates to "develop your private brinksmanship, your strategies, your ruses, your delightful and desperate games of inner survival" that would enable them "to live perpetually at the edge, but there very much on your own ground, and to live there with personal *style,* with dash and verve and a distinct and exhilarating sense of existing on your own terms as they develop, or as they become, with time, more and more what they have always been" (*Night Hurdling* 350–55). In the more than two decades that had passed, Dickey's career had soared, stalled, and then descended; friends and family had died; and literary efforts to push ahead had often failed to energize him or offer elevated moments of existence. Yet in this new address, he again stressed the individual's paramount importance. He now cited Saul Bellow's story "Seize the Day" as an indictment of Americans dying of alcohol, drugs, or boredom, and he inveighed against computers and other technologies that mitigated the imagination, emphasizing a single anecdote to these ills, a single imperative: "The solution to me is still wonder: amazement, mystery." He intended to pursue his own unique course, his address implied, and he advised the new graduates to do likewise.

The second commencement address was delivered shortly after Dickey and Deborah had flown for a ten-day visit to Japan, where he delivered an address at the University of Maryland in Tokyo. The talk centered on hope and peace and touched tangentially on his wartime experience in Japan and how it felt to return. The previous year he had conceived of another novel involving a tail-gunner shot down over the enemy's country during World War II, and he intended to familiarize himself with the land he had first visited in 1945. He needed to imagine not only the destruction of a firebombed Tokyo but also the peaceful countryside of terraced rice fields and contemplative peasants. "It was a good trip," Deborah Dickey recalled in 2019. "We ate a lot of wonderful Japanese cuisine. One place was over a hundred years old and had a water wheel. He used things like that in his last novel. He rescued a little lost girl in the Tokyo zoo. We lit a lot of incense (joss sticks) for his brother Tom. One of our hotels at the Air Force base where we stayed was nestled near Mt. Fuji, and we held hands and just stood in silent awe and worship." On 6 August 1987, he had sent Theron Raines a plot outline for a novel titled "Thalatta," a variant of *Thalassa*, the Greek word for sea, which derived from an account by the Greek general Xenophon in his war against the Persians. After fighting through Persian territory to the Black Sea, the Greeks triumphantly cried, "Thalatta!" Figuratively retracing the Greek journey, Dickey intended to depict the aviator's bloody trek from the fiery holocaust of Tokyo to the snowy island of Hokkaido in the northern Japanese archipelago. "In the case of my man," he stated to Raines, "Hokkaido signifies the protagonist's coming 'home' to the cold and desolation that are his true *patria*." The novel eventually became *To the White Sea*.

Because *Alnilam* had been a financial disappointment, Doubleday had little interest in publishing another novel, but Theron Raines had approached Marc Jaffe, an editor at Houghton Mifflin, who was attempting to attract writers and who viewed the proposal for "Thalatta" as an opportunity to lure Dickey back to the company. Unaffected by financial misgivings, Houghton offered Dickey a $500,000 advance. The sale of foreign rights added to the windfall. The novel also attracted advocates in Hollywood; Richard Roth agreed to produce the movie version for Universal Studios, though Dickey wanted the Coen Brothers. He also would have liked Houghton Mifflin to publish his poetry, but the company was hesitant. Dickey returned to Wesleyan in August 1988 after consulting Peter Davison, poetry editor for *Atlantic Monthly* and director of Atlantic Monthly Press.

Dickey completed another project in October when Oxmoor House printed 55,000 copies of his third coffee-table book, *Wayfarer: A Voice from the Southern Mountains*. The book's origin dated to the seventies when, following the success of *Jericho*, Dickey planned to collaborate again with Hubert Shuptrine for another book, whose proposed title was "The Wilderness of Heaven." The original publisher was to have been Doubleday, and the proposed publication date was 1982. However, the new coffee-table book was not a high priority for Dickey; he was working on *Puella* and *Alnilam* as well as various screenplays. He insisted, moreover, on presenting his own version of Appalachia; when Shuptrine received Dickey's text, he concluded that it was inappropriate because it did not cohere with his paintings. Shuptrine annulled the Doubleday contract by returning his $30,000 advance; when Doubleday insisted that Dickey's contract be cancelled and he repay his advance, Dickey resisted and obtained a new collaborator, William A. Bake, an acclaimed photographer with a doctorate from the University of Georgia who had published three other art books with Oxmoor House and whose work had appeared in such magazines as *Southern Living, Life*, and *Audubon*. Without deliberate synchronization, Bake's photographs naturally cohered with Dickey's prose, each portraying gritty, weathered Southerners living close to the rugged beauty inherent in the land. In his narrative Dickey returned to his father's heritage in North Georgia, dedicating the book "to the remainder of my father's family— Fannin County, Mineral Bluff, Georgia," and declaring on the inside dust jacket, "At age 63, I feel I have only arrived at the beginning."

As the book opens, the unnamed narrator greets a wayfarer he encounters. Superstitious and wise, the narrator has lived his life in the Appalachians. When the traveler becomes sick, the narrator uses mountain medicines to restore his health, taking the wayfarer on a figurative journey as he talks about food, geography, customs, handiwork, folklore, and music. He asserts, "We ain't got everything, but we got somethin'." The chance encounter presents a familiar Dickey concern—the confrontation between the individual and a force larger than himself that is part of the journey of the mythic hero. In *Wayfarer* that Other is the Southern mountains and people. While Dickey had poetically treated aspects of this subject before (for example, foxhunting and quilting in "Listening to Foxhounds" and "Chenille," respectively), the narrative framework of *Wayfarer* allows for a greater breadth of treatment to depict the larger natural inclusiveness Dickey perceived in the world. Consequently, when the speaker asserts, "It don't matter why it comes, but it does; it comes on through, and it's done been put in both of us, don't you see," Dickey moves beyond a discussion of family bloodlines not only into the connections that link all men to the land but also into the human impulse to create and re-create what one sees and hears. Unlike *Jericho* and *God's Images*, *Wayfarer* avoids inflated or poetic diction; instead, the voice of the main speaker exudes local color and a vitality that embodies a rich identification with the life around him. From late September through mid-December 1988, Dickey and Bake undertook an extensive promotional tour thorough the South, including visits to Columbia, South Carolina; Atlanta; Greensboro, North Carolina; Charleston, South Carolina; Nashville, Tennessee; Birmingham, Alabama; Charlotte, North Carolina; Miami; Jacksonville, Florida; Memphis, Tennessee; Lexington, Kentucky; and Louisville, Kentucky. Because the national economy was mired in a slump, the book sold only about one-fourth as many copies as *Jericho* had. Royalties for the financial year ending on 31 May 1989 totaled only $2,825 (Hart 695).

At the conclusion of the 1965 Pitzer commencement address, Dickey had looked at the three graduating young women and declared that when he had urged them to "live perpetually at the edge, but very much on their own ground," he had essentially desired that they "have something to give the world." What he meant, he said, was their "having a self to give" such that "one can say, when the time comes to say it, 'My life belongs to the world. I have done what I could'" (*Night Hurdling* 355). As the eighties closed, Dickey's career had critically declined for almost two decades. The afflatus and individual transcendence in his "early motion" had yielded to his socially conscious and violence-centered "central motion," as well as uninspiring coffee-table books, films, screenplays, and children's books whose lack of creativity and inspiration revealed the extent of Dickey's alcoholism. Reviewers and critics viewed his work indifferently, if at all. Endeavoring to counter what many viewed as literary free fall, he had attempted, poetically in *Puella* and fictionally in *Alnilam*, to be very much "at the edge, but very much on his own ground," his stylistic efforts so radically different in technique, so much an effort to create "new thresholds, new anatomies" that they stretched the limits of previous publications. Nothing, however, changed. Feelings of inadequacy and frustration during these years reside throughout *Puella*. For example, in "Ray Flowers II," whose epigraph reads, "Deborah as Winded Seed, Descending with Others," the persona finds herself "now resting / Somewhere on the general brink, / ... Total, seething and fronting / All the way to the hills, / The near hills, thinning with overreach."

CHAPTER 14

"SOMEWHERE IN ALL THOUGHT"

In the late eighties, offers of public appearances continued to arrive largely from the South, reinforcing misguided opinions that Dickey had only a regional audience. The USC's Ira and Nancy Kroger Center for the Arts, for example, requested his attendance at its 14 January 1989 opening, and Atlanta's Oglethorpe College awarded him an honorary degree in May. That October, Wilmington's Cape Fear Academy asked him to read and to teach some classes. Bright spots were infrequent. Birch Lane Press in New Jersey offered Dickey $75,000 that summer for a book of childhood reminiscences, though he declined (Hart 696). Indicative that editors typically perceived Dickey as a spokesman for Southern literature was the contract he signed on 7 July for $1,500 to write an article about the South Carolina "Low Country" for Condé Nast. Moreover, when Robert Penn Warren died on 15 September, the *Boston Globe* asked for Dickey's comments; he obliged, calling Warren a great writer whose personal roots lay in the frontier and in folk people, but who nevertheless combined primitive instinct with sophisticated intellect.

The most convincing argument that Dickey's influence remained national arrived in July from Yale, the university where Warren had taught. John Ryden, the director of Yale University Press, requested that Dickey judge its annual Younger Poets contest, a task that involved reading forty to fifty manuscripts culled from approximately seven hundred submissions, selecting a winner each year by 1 June, and then writing an introduction to each book. For his services, Dickey would receive $2,000 a year. In an unpublished letter to Ryden dated 26 July, he declared that "the Series is the best of all gateways to the slopes of Parnassus for new American poets, and has been so since its beginning. In other words, as a poet who struggled hard to get onto those slopes years ago, I realize the importance of what I am being asked to do, and can say in response that I will do the best I can, given my abilities and orientation." In becoming the series judge, Dickey joined a group of distinguished writers that included W. H. Auden, James Merrill, and Stanley Kunitz.

Despite a domestic life that continued to be unsettled by Deborah's drug problems, he worked on the new novel, informing Marc Jaffe, his editor at Houghton Mifflin, on 27 February 1990 that "I have been moving the book; moving Muldrow. I have another hundred pages, written mainly at night and just before dawn, but written. I have also revised the sequence of events, and now I have what I think will give us a straight run out to the end. This is something I value as a novelist: the knowing what happens next, and what that leads to." At age sixty-seven, he believed his creative energies strong enough to complete the new novel. In a 1981 essay, he had written of F. Scott Fitzgerald's poetic ability: "Beneath everything here, even the most trivial, there is the flicker of a fine unmistakable consciousness, and one could do worse" (*Night Hurdling* 56–60). Rather than a mere flicker, he felt his own talents to be a flame living within him, an extraordinary gift that was wasted if not utilized. His personality precluded a surrender to the situation. Like the aging protagonist in "False Youth: Spring: The Olympian," published in the summer 1982 issue of *Amicus Journal*, who races a former Olympic gold medalist on a makeshift home obstacle course, Dickey still found himself "ready for the Big One," the knockout literary punch that would restore him to the heralded heights he had known. The persona goes all-out in the race, "lagging lolloping hanging / In there with the best" and

> Getting the point
> At last, sighing like ghosts and like rubber, for fat
> And luck, all over the earth, where that day and any and every
> Day after it, devil hindmost and Goddamn it
>
> To glory, I lumbered for gold.

In his imagination, where fact and fiction, history and reminiscence and fantasy all melded, he determined such a victory possible.

He needed to believe it, for Deborah's medical, legal, and psychiatric bills threatened his sense, always tenuous, of financial security. Extensive reading tours were no longer possible because he lacked the physical stamina, and an extended absence from home was not advisable. Poems such as "Eagles" and "Moon Flock," published in the March/April 1987 and 1988 issues of *American Poetry Review*, respectively, reflect his feelings of frustration that alternated with desolation. "Eagles" insists on the inability of the individual ever to escape the world fully enough to gain an ideal or

Platonic understanding of it. While the effort remains doomed, the human need to strive above earthbound limitations is undeniable, necessary, and redemptive, as timeless as Icarus's failed attempt. The speaker imagines himself lifted by the feet of an eagle. The brief flight, which deposits him groveling on the ground among weeds, reveals a larger world, "the circular truth / Of the Void," one whose elements would satisfy any realm but the one where he lives and moves. Now, however, he asks only that the eagle leave "my unstretched weight" and "remember me in your feet." He understands that "the higher rock is / The more it lives," a recognition of human limitation and the need to transcend those restrictions. "Moon Flock" is Dickey's subsequent attempt to convey the strength of that impulse and his increased frustration at its failure, using the analogy of the moon's effort to create life. Here the imaginative ideal never begins to fulfill the world in which it finds itself. The speaker confesses that "nothing can be put / Up on a wind with no air," and he admonishes the reader not to inquire of his imaginative effort, for the moon remains merely "a wild white world" whose emptiness reflects his own. These poems as well as others on which he was working exposed his true feelings without the bravado that would have previously concealed them. Such poems would become part of his final collection, *The Eagle's Mile*, published in 1990.

In a 1987 interview Dickey commented on the poet's role: "I think a poet is trying, whether he would say this or not, to validate the individual viewpoint.... The vision and the true reaction of people to things, the true and if possible imaginative reaction to things, are threatened more and more" (Van Ness 23). In *The Eagle's Mile*, he undertook his final attempt to solidify the presence of the determining personality and in so doing his identity. In the midst of his marital discord, he assembled the poems that would compose *The Eagle's Mile*, which he dedicated to Deborah and his children and grandchildren. Its title derived from Blake's "Auguries of Innocence"—"The Emmet's Inch & Eagle's Mile / Make Lame Philosophy to smile. / He who Doubts from what he sees / Will ne'er believe, do what you please"—lines that emphasize the variety of approaches to experience. The collection presents two contrasting perspectives: the ideal, dispassionate, and inclusive gaze of the eagle in high flight and the restricted, anxious, and exclusive stare of a man walking on the ground. The speaker, both as he imaginatively rises with the bird in "Eagles," "receiving overlook," and as he stands on a beach in "Circuit," "foreseeing / Around a curve," recognizes these points of view as essential to knowing "the circular truth of the void." Each poem in the volume captures a singular experience or stance, an emotional and physical complex addressing one of the perspectives that reveals a moment of acceptance, celebration, or even transcendence. Each captures a still point in time, Frost's "momentary stay against confusion," that increasingly links each poem to others by patterns of imagery. Taken together, these poems and images reveal the principled physical relevance of things and the vital and redemptive role of the imagination in integrating them.

The series of opposite propositions or contraries become unified or reconciled in the volume's title poem, "The Eagle's Mile," dedicated to William Douglas, though Dickey mistakenly confused the chief justice with Ambassador Lewis Williams Douglas, who wore an eyepatch as a result of a fly fishing accident and who was the inspiration for the "man in the Hathaway shirt" ad which Dickey would have known from his years in advertising. Celebrating with Whitmanesque affirmation the godlike creative impulse, the speaker demands that Douglas, himself an avid outdoorsman, now "step out of grass-bed sleep" and possess the world anew, "drawing life / From growth / from flow." If he will "catch into this / With everything you have," Douglas can again enter into the multiplicity of physical reality, an endless and marvelously varied creation, because potential form once again becomes actual. Here Dickey suggests the interrelationship of all things, all natural forces, all individualities merging in their motions to render an eternal Idea—"The whole thing is worth." In a world of continual Becoming, the individual can "splinter uncontrollably whole" because death constitutes part of life's headlong, unstoppable momentum, part of the great hand of contraries dealt everyone. Life's circularity will bring death, actuality will become potentiality, but the process, enhanced here by the creative impulse, extends one into the many, which nevertheless always remains the One.

Dickey's persona intuits life, the dynamic and mysterious process of creation, as well as the immobility and anonymity of death, an intuition that provides a double vision. The earthbound speaker understands that the two perspectives, metaphorically rendered as the eagle's mile and the emmet's inch, encompass human truth and artistic impulse as manifested in physical reality. The book's poetic arrangement, moreover, reflects this larger comprehension of perspective; it traces the narrator's own physical and spiritual journey through his understanding of what he sees or intuits. In "Expanses," the collection's final poem, Dickey endeavors to establish the importance of the individual personality when the narrator figuratively becomes the eagle and now sees with the bird's sweeping gaze but without loss of the human perspective, a perspective that unites opposites. Ground-ing oneself only in and on the physical world, he suggests, limits the indi-vidual to an Aristotelian conception of reality that does not visualize the Platonic or ideal. As he views himself from the air walking on the beach, the persona experiences in his earthbound perceptions "all you want— / Joy like short grass," an image alluding to the cemetery but recognizing that life and death are both one and not one. The human voice will fail, Dickey understands, will finally lose its heat and become cold, but for an instant will break like lightning against the emptiness of space. When he declared in "For a Time and Place" that we "begin with ourselves / Under-foot and rising," he presents his philosophic awareness of the elemental human condition and the beginning of the imaginative process that vali-dates and resurrects the individual presence.

Technically and thematically, *The Eagle's Mile* constitutes a culmina-tion of Dickey's poetic journey, an extension of *Puella* in one sense and a return to poetic elements apparent in the early motion in another. In his essay "Metaphor as Pure Adventure," he had clearly stated the nature and function of poetry:

> I am against all marmoreal, closed, to-be-contemplated kinds of poems and conceive of the poem as a minute part of the Heraclitean flux, and of the object of the poem as not to slow or fix or limit at all but to try as it can to preserve and implement the "fluxness," the flow, and show this moving through the poem, coming in at the beginning and going back out, after the end, into the larger, non-verbal universe whence it came. (*Sorties* 173–74)

In this last collection before he died, Dickey searches for the basic human act and the proper net or form by which the poet allows experience to show itself. The making of this net, the use of metaphor and image to hold the experience and reveal its essential wonder, became a primary intent. In the process Dickey returned to elements present in earlier poems. The poems not so much offer a narrative situation reminiscent of his early work, alt-hough the action usually remains static, but they exhibit the spacings or interstices of the split-line technique. He utilizes the block format only in "The Olympian." Frequently the poems appear balanced on the page with the lines symmetrically branching off a central idea. Yet in *The Eagle's Mile*, he thematically relates the poems through a series of interconnected images that thread through the work. While *Puella* captures the individual moments in a girl's life as she matures, uniting the chronology and

emphasizing her elemental connections, *The Eagle's Mile* links many separate images, including those of grass or weeds; graves; footprints; rocks,
birds; the elements of air, water, and earth; curves or curving; and climatic
heat and cold. All life, Dickey implies, is fundamentally connected at all
times, continually changing. Poetry, therefore, should change, too. "There
are going to be people," he stated in a 1981 interview, "who want you to
do what they are familiar with. They inevitably say, 'He's slipping, he's not
as good as he used to be,' or 'His early work was much better,' and so on.
But I really don't care about being as good as, or not as good as, or better
than. That is not my primary consideration. My primary consideration is
to *change*." "I don't dare use the word *grow*," he added, "there may or may
not be growth involved, but to change. To still keep that openness, that
chance taking-ness as part of the work. Not to be afraid to make a mistake,
even if it's a long and costly mistake." Critical reception notwithstanding,
Dickey insisted, individual growth and transformation, qualities that reflected the universe itself, were imperatives. "That is what keeps poetry
exciting for me," he said. "Not only to do something that nobody else had
done before, but to do something which *I* haven't done before. There are
so many selves in everybody, and just to explore and exploit one is wrong,
dead wrong, for the creative person. He must get more selves to speak up
in different voices" (*Night Hurdling* 321).

Reviews of *The Eagle's Mile* were generally positive. Herbert Mitgang
and Fred Chappell, while admiring the collection, cited occasional problems with language. John Updike had contributed a dust jacket statement,
which declared, "James Dickey is the high flier of contemporary American
poets. In *The Eagle's Mile* he is flying higher than ever." Mitgang's review
in the 27 October 1990 issue of the *New York Times* saw the collection as
a continuation of Dickey's examination of man's connection with nature,
a relationship that included "many nuances about myth and machismo."
Mitgang, however, seemed to qualify his analysis by asserting that the language "meanders down the page in rivulets," although they finally merge
in "a rushing mainstream" that includes linked words and startling phrases
that, taken together, extend Dickey's vision (16). Chappell also praised the
volume in the 9 December 1990 issue of *The State* (Columbia, SC), citing
it as representative of an idiom he referred to as "the High Bardic, the
vatic, the transcendent—the Pindaric Grandiose, if you will," which he
then defined: "It is the poetic attitude that sets for itself heroic visionary
ambitions marching out to trample the limitations of ordinary poetic diction." Yet Chappell also asserted that in the "intoxicated grandeur" of these

tall flights, the collection suffered from a variety of flaws, including over-stated language, banality, bathos, slang, far-fetched tropes, disingenuous direct address, the overuse of certain words, and an insistence on gerunds. He concluded, however, that Dickey "has put everything on the line and has come off, on balance, a winner. He has suffered some pretty steep losses, but overall the book is a victory. If in some places he has not suc-ceeded, there are others in which he has advanced beyond what he has done before and has done so in a new and unexpected fashion" (F5).

In his biography of Dickey, Henry Hart notes that the book, not counting the section titled "Double-Tongue: Collaborations and Re-writes," offered only twenty-six poems, many short and written in the eighties (*Buckdancer's Choice*, which had won the National Book Award, contained twenty-one poems). Hart suggested that Dickey's "dependence" on translations and his use of older poems constituted "one sign of his struggle to find new inspiration" (706). Dickey, however, had used older poems in previous collections, and his interest in reworking poems written in other languages, what he variously referred to as rewrites, collaborations, or improvisations, dated back to *The Zodiac* and constituted part of his effort to enlarge his "voice." In an unpublished letter to the *Memphis State Review*, he insisted that his rewrites were not translations: "I don't want these poems to be presented as translations or adaptations of other trans-lations, which they are not. They are original poems—and much better than *the* originals, I can tell you." He had published several of these poems, including "Heads" (with Lucien Becker), "Attempted Departure" (with André du Bouchet), "Lakes of Varmland" (with André Frénaud), "Farm-ers" (with André Frénaud), and "Craters" (with Michel Leiris) in the March/April 1983 issue of *American Poetry Review*, and James Anderson of Breitenbush Publications had expressed interest in publishing a collec-tion of such poems to be entitled "Immortals." Dickey discussed his method of translation in an unpublished 19 January 1987 letter to Ben Belitt, declaring,

> The whole question of translation and the cross-pollinization of cultures by means of translation is very large and important, and will be more so. People are not only coming forth with more trans-lations, but with *theories* of translation, which is to say defenses of the kind they themselves practice. Since Pound at least, a new kind of curious form, which I try to experiment with myself, has come into existence. This is neither a translation or a completely original poem, but a kind of hybrid which for want of a better name I am

tempted to call "the rewrite." Such an approach may seem on the surface of it contemptible, but it is not, and I think more and more people, either those who don't know the foreign language or those who *do* know it well but want to do something *different* in English, will be the ones to watch.

Poets such as Robert Lowell and Robert Bly had also reworked poems in this form.

Work on *The Eagle's Mile* began in the early eighties, though it is doubtful that Dickey then had any organic sense either of the scope, the format, or even the focus of the volume. What would become the title poem had been published in the fall 1980 issue of *Hastings Constitutional Law Quarterly*. Other poems followed, but only a few, and slowly: "The Olympian," published as "False Spring: Youth: The Olympian" in the summer 1982 issue of *Amicus Journal*; "For a Time and Place," published as a broadside; and "To Be Done in Winter by Those Surviving Truman Capote," published in the *Dictionary of Literary Biography Yearbook 1984*. Dickey's primary interest during these years was *Alnilam*. Shortly after its publication on 5 June 1987, he was hired to write the screenplay for the movie, which he then began working on and which he completed in 1989. In 1983, however, he had published "Sand" in the spring issue of *Clockwatch Review*, a poem that derives from Vicente Aleixandre's "Always" ("Siempre") and that was included in Wallis Barnstone and David Garrison's *A Bird of Paper*, a book he held in his personal library. Published in 1982, it was an "en face" translation of Aleixandre's work. The tagline read "homage Vicente Aleixandre" and acknowledged the translations. "Sand" became Part I of Dickey's "Two Women," which he included in *The Eagle's Mile* while omitting the attribution. Part II derives from Aleixandre's "The Sun" ("El sol"). "Siempre," a reflection on the poet's relationship with nature as figuratively embodied in a woman, opens, "I am alone. Beach, hear me. / Out there dolphins or a sword. / The certainty of things, the no limits," and concludes, "Love, love, hold back your impure step." Dickey's rewrite establishes the same scene: "Alone here. Beach, drum out / What you want to say: a dolphin, / Sockets, sword-flats. Seething landscape of hilts, no limits are set / In you" and ends, "Hold back / A little, your printed pursuit, your unstemming impurity." However, whereas Aleixandre's imperative addresses sand, one aspect of the beach on which he walks but which nevertheless embodies the vacuity of his present relationship, Dickey directly addresses a woman: "Woman, because I don't love you, / Draw back."

Dickey's use of Aleixandre's "El sol" as the second part of "Two Women" is also obvious. While the former opens, "Light, almost weightless: / the sandal. Footsteps / with no flesh," Dickey begins: "Early light: light less / Than other light. Sandal without power / To mark sand." Aleixandre's sun is a "solitary goddess" who demands "walking space / for her body high / and solar"; Dickey's personification "walks here. Her foottouch / The place itself." Neither of Dickey's poems are translations as he conceived the term—he would have labeled them collaborations or rewrites—but both clearly resemble those of Aleixandre, and neither is acknowledged in *The Eagle's Mile*.

The following year, in the fall 1984 issue of *Kentucky Poetry Review*, Dickey published two rewrites from Aleixandre's "Immortals" ("Los inmortales"), a series of seven poems that the latter identified with aspects of nature, including "Rain" ("La iluvia"), "Sun" ("El sol"), "Word" ("La palabra"), "Earth" ("La tierra"), "Fire" ("El fuego"), "Air" ("El aire"), and "Sea" ("El mar"). Grouped under the title "Three Poems Improvised from Lines by Vicente Aleixandre (acknowledging the translation of Wallis Barnstone and David Garrison)," Dickey's versions included "Earth" and "Air" as well as a rewrite of Aleixandre's "World" ("Mundo inhumano"), which had appeared in *A Bird of Paper*. In *The Eagle's Mile*, Dickey presents his own group of poems titled "Immortals," which includes "Earth" and "Sea" as well as "Air," a rewrite first published in the 1985 issue of *Verse*. Again, Dickey failed to reference any of these Aleixandre poems.

During 1987 and 1988 Dickey published ten rewrites of Aleixandre's poems, none of which he acknowledged as derived from Aleixandre and all of which he included in *The Eagle's Mile*. It seems clear that Dickey was "building" the volume with Aleixandre's poems. These include "The One" ("Las una"), "The Three" ("Las tres"), "The Six" ("Las seis"), "Weeds" ("No estrella"), "Sleepers" ("Los dormidos"), "Expanses" ("Pájaros sin descenso"), "Eagles" ("Las águilas"), "The Little More" ("El nino y el hombre"), and "Tomb Stone" ("Epitafio"). In 1990, moreover, Dickey rewrote Aleixandre's "Circuit" ("Circuito") using the latter's *Poesias completes*. If in *The Eagle's Mile* Dickey sought a meditation on being, it was accomplished through Aleixandre's poetic efforts.

In a letter to Shaye Areheart dated 18 July 1984, Dickey notes that he had assembled a manuscript of "some strange off-the-wall poems I have been experimenting with. These take off from Spanish translations, after which I re-write them in Spanish for the sound-resonance and then translate them back into English." He added, "These are original poems, despite the take-off from Vicente Aleixandre's originals, which they do not in the final version resemble in the least" (Bruccoli, Baughman 437). Regardless of whether Dickey's rewrites are original—and the statement remains problematic—questions remain both as to why he used so many of Aleixandre's poems to structure *The Eagle's Mile* and why he failed to acknowledge his indebtedness, as he had previously done. Hart's assertion that age and alcoholism had diminished Dickey's own creativity and that, as he had earlier in his career, he turned to foreign poets for inspiration is, at best, speculative. Answers, it might be argued, lie more reasonably with a host of other factors. Alcoholism may indeed have lessened his muse but his major surgery in 1980 to correct a blocked esophagus, an operation that necessitated moving around his digestive organs and that resulted in his weight dropping from 250 pounds to 190 pounds, affected his writing abilities. Health concerns were reinforced by other family matters, including the birth of his only daughter, Bronwen, when he was almost sixty years old and his wife Deborah's subsequent problems with depression and drugs. Citing medical and legal expenses, he consequently undertook a series of reading tours, once more barnstorming for poetry but diminishing the time necessary to write. His creative efforts during the 1980s, however, were not insignificant. Not only did he complete *Alnilam* but he began his third novel, *To the White Sea*, and published a children's book, *Bronwen, the Traw, and the Shape-Shifter*, a collection of essays and miscellany, *Night Hurdling*; a coffee-table book, *Wayfarer*; and a volume of poetry, *Puella*. Additionally, there were film projects and screenplays. Dickey's use of Aleixandre's poems, therefore, seems more understandable within the context of these other factors, though his decision not to acknowledge his source is not. Given the breadth of that usage, reviewers and critics would have inevitably argued that such reliance indicated the loss of artistic abilities. With his reputation already in serious decline, he chose to believe that his creations, while "taking off" from Aleixandre, were indeed his own, new, and original poems that were in no sense translations.

"Basics," the final poem in the grouping of improvised poems in *The Eagle's Mile*, is not attributed to another poet, as are all the other rewrites. It is as if Dickey realized that this would likely be his final comment on the world as he knew it to be. The three parts of "Basics" all center on the human need for continuity and meaning, poems that both reaffirm and perhaps reconcile Aristotelian duality and Platonic idealism. In their hopeful tone and cadenced form and structure, both "Level" and "Simplex" resemble his own creative efforts in *The Eagle's Mile*. "Word," however, derives from Aleixandre's "Immortals."

> One day the word was
> Heat: a human lip.
> It was the light of young morning; more: lightning
> In this naked eternity. Someone
> Loved. With no before or after. And the logos
> Was born. Word alone and pure
> Forever—Love—in beautiful space!

Dickey expands Aleixandre's effort, which celebrates language as the center of love, and in lines typographically balanced sanctifies not only words themselves but also the human effort to communicate the world and one's place in it.

> Heat makes this, heat makes any
> Word: human lungs,
> Human lips. Not like eternity, which, naked, every time
> Will call on lightning
> To say it all: No after
> Or before. We try for that
>
> And fail. Our voice
> Fails, but for an instant
> Is like the other; breath alone
> That comes as though human panting
> From far back, in unspeakably beautiful
>
> Empty space
>
> And struck: at just this moment
> Found the word "golden."

In correspondence with me dated 11 March 2013, David Havird noted that "this poem concludes the whole of Dickey's 'motion'—after which, silence. But the motion itself gives shape to the poet's effort in poem after poem to call 'on lightning / To say it all: No after / Or before'—to create, in other words, a work of utter originality—all the while racking up many, many words, with any luck some of them golden, making great noise in the process, anything but silence." Dickey was always highly competitive, believing life to be warfare, and it is possible that in using Aleixandre so extensively, he was fighting his old battle with Robert Bly, who in 1977 had published with Lewis Hyde *Twenty Poems of Vicente Aleixandre* (Aleixandre had won the Nobel Prize that year). With his own death approaching, Dickey was obviously less concerned in this concluding poem with referencing Aleixandre than with making a point. For himself, as with all poets, every creative act resembled and re-created the original creative act; the "Let there be light" of Genesis not simply apes God but rather gives voice in an act of creative discovery, as though God himself were finding his own voice through poets, his secondary creators.

While Deborah's addictions remained a continual source of concern to Dickey, so too did his own medical ailments. He wrote Marc Jaffe on 18 June 1991 that he had a "semi-gangrenous situation" in his foot that would likely require partial amputation of his toe, a problem that resulted from a toenail fungus contracted during his combat in the Philippines. He also complained that he would likely require further surgery on his esophagus to improve his digestion. Both comments were overstatements. On 1 August he promised to complete the new novel, though he would not detail his present difficulties, "so disheartening, so endlessly complicated with legalities, with medical solutions that don't work, with lawyers, doctors, psychiatrists, policemen, judges, probation officers, and God knows who or what else, that to lay all this on you would be an extreme unkindness, so I won't." He apologized again on 18 December, this time citing the delay as resulting from the task of collecting his poems for *The Whole Motion*.

Other distractions, however, additionally complicated his creative efforts. On 30 July he had accepted an invitation from Cleanth Brooks to judge the Hanes Poetry Prize along with Fred Chappell, an award given by the Fellowship of Southern Writers. In October he published his fourth coffee-table book, *Southern Light*, which presented a circular journey that sectioned a day into dawn, morning, noon, afternoon, and evening and examined the world as light defined it during those times. Dickey's text was accompanied by 188 glossy photographs of Southern landscapes by Jim Valentine. Publication was followed by a two-month tour of book signings in Atlanta; Nashville, Tennessee; Birmingham, Alabama; Charlotte, North Carolina; and Columbia, South Carolina. Additionally, he spoke at the University of Arkansas in Monticello, Lee College in Texas, the Harbour Front in Toronto, DeKalb Community College in Atlanta, and the Book Fair in Miami. On 13 November he addressed the South Atlantic Modern Language Association in Atlanta; the paper, titled "LIGHTNINGS, or *Visuals*," described how images act to produce wonderfully involved stories.

In the introduction to *Southern Light*, Dickey urged the reader to understand the imaginative connection, a surrender similar to those critics had faulted in his other oversized books. "Enter light," Dickey demands, "as though you were part of it, as though you were pure spirit—or pure beholding human creature, which is the same thing—to become part of light in many places and intensities, to make it something like a dream of itself with you in it; that way you will be seeing by human light, as well as by the light shining since Genesis." In contrast to his previous mixed-media works, however, the prose text in *Southern Light* anticipates rather than complements Valentine's photographs. Their subtle textures and startling vibrancy demand confrontation, while Dickey's descriptions establish the uniqueness of the moments captured by the camera. When the dawn light, for example, causes the things of the world to emerge into themselves, Dickey invites participation by singling out what one might personally hold in perspective: "In all remoteness and closeness you have a hand; a quickening hand, as everything sharpens, attunes: sharpens *toward*. If you want more leaves, beckon, and they come." At evening, he asks how successful the encounters have been and reminds the reader of the special quality that the light makes possible: "Nothing like it ever given, except by means of Time. This time, this day." The artistic intent is to deliver a physical and emotional confrontation by having the words defer to the photographs and yet prepare one to experience them. Dickey establishes this collaborative dependency when, speaking of the creative impulse present throughout all human history, he states in the introduction, "The cave artist and the photographer, standing for all others, want to see not through but into: want you to stay with and *in* the work, and for it to stay with you, for it is in its very essence a form of ritual magic." When he guides the reader's journey through the twenty-four hours *Southern Light* captures in word and pictures, he paradoxically remains less tangible a presence than in *Wayfarer*, despite his use of the imperative and despite the latter's narrative, which often subsumes Dickey's voice. However, as in all his efforts, his principal concern is the sense of consequence derived from human connection with the world.

Throughout his career, Dickey always declared that poetry was the center of his creative wheel and that all other artistic efforts were secondary. In 1992 he published *The Whole Motion: Collected Poems, 1942–1992*. Wanting the poems to speak for themselves, he offered no introduction or preface that would establish his perspective on the half century of poems that he believed defined his career. "When you look at all of it gathered here," he told William Starr in a 12 July 1992 interview, "475 pages, almost 50 years, then you do have some trepidation. And when you open up the book, you know the blood in your stomach sinks. You think you're going to read those poems and say, 'You know, this is not as good as I thought.' Luckily, that didn't happen when I read through them again. I have to say in all honesty, this is better than I thought—sometimes a lot better." The collection underscored the diversity of techniques Dickey had attempted. "I've never forgotten the great lesson of Picasso," he declared, "which is that he never allowed himself to be trapped in a single style. When I start to explore some area of language or experience, I start with the question of 'What would happen if I did such and such,' and for me that invariably leads to, 'Well, let's try it and see what happens.'" He emphasized, however, that despite collecting his life's work, he was not finished. "I don't stop here," he asserted, "I try to explore new directions. I want to make each book I write different. I don't believe in repeating myself. I think the worst thing about so many American writers is that they're afraid to make a mistake. They're afraid one mistake, one book people don't like, will blow away everything else they've done" (F1).

Dickey hoped for a large critical response, but it never came. David Biespel in the *Washington Post Book World* typified the feelings of the critical community, praising the poems from Dickey's early motion and lamenting those published later: "By the 1970s Dickey's work had declined, and it's hard to find anyone who doesn't agree that his poetry is now uneven; the grace and control of that remarkable decade [1957–1967] reveal themselves only here and there in poems that retain, to paraphrase the poet, a one-drink-too-many tone and energy." He asserted that Dickey's best poems derive from the guilt and joy he experienced during the Second World War and his feelings of being a survivor, which resulted in a "unified vision" compromised by a quarter century of failed experiments (8). Reviews from Southern editors such as Starr, however, praised the book, referring to Dickey as a commanding poet of engulfing intelligence whose gigantic stature derived from his refusal to remain above the fight. Sales of *The Whole Motion* typified the critical conflict in which Dickey himself was mired. By 1994 Wesleyan had sold out of the hardback copies of the volume, but sales of the paperback had fallen off. Wesleyan had paid Dickey an advance of $4,500, a high figure for a university press, and decided not to reprint the hardback. The absence of critical attention and the failure of the book to win any awards revealed how low Dickey's literary flight had fallen. Although his voice remained loud, few were listening. Those who were, including students in his poetry courses, increasingly heard him talk about a poet's need to repudiate fame and fortune. What mattered, he emphasized, was writing poems that endured.

Determined at the beginning of 1993 to complete *To the White Sea*, he met with Marc Jaffe early in the summer in New York to go over revisions. Jaffe urged him to excise a scene in which Muldrow strangles a child he has entertained with string tricks as well as one in which he kills a young girl and sticks her head on a waterwheel. Dickey spared the child in the former and substituted an old woman for the decapitated girl. Houghton Mifflin published the novel in September amid a gala of publicity, and Dickey, who was on sabbatical, was optimistic about the book's marketability. He had simplified the heroic quest that had dominated his earlier novels, suggesting that Muldrow's journey returns him to his beginnings; he parachutes into Tokyo and travels to northern Japan, where the ice and snow parallel his childhood in northern Alaska. Dickey also abandoned the fictional technique that reviewers had so criticized in *Alnilam* in favor of the straightforward interior narrative of the protagonist. Central to the story is Dickey's conviction that life exemplifies Darwin's principle that the strongest endure. Muldrow, who has murdered a college girl from Kansas whom he met in Point Barrow, Alaska, has honed his survival skills; he is fascinated with disguise, priding himself on his ability to blend into a crowd or a landscape. Although he initially kills Japanese out of necessity, his killing quickly becomes pathological, satisfying sadistic whims. As he travels into the cold wasteland, he becomes his surroundings, embodying a naturalistic, amoral universe. In a 21 September 1993 interview with Alex Chadwick on National Public Radio's *Morning Edition*, Dickey declared that he wanted readers initially to ally themselves with Muldrow—he is, after all, an American airman in the enemy's country—but then slowly realize that his actions are barbarous and that "the American military has loosed on the Japanese civilian population the equivalent of Ted Bundy." Asked if he had ever known someone like Muldrow or whether the character was completely imagined, Dickey responded, "No, it's completely imaginary, but, like the characters of any author, there are certain parts of your own personality that come to the fore and you just maybe kind of exaggerate those. As the German poet

Goethe says, 'The strength of my own imagination as a poet and a novelist is the fact that I cannot imagine any crime of which I myself would not be capable.'" Creating the character of Muldrow, Dickey suggested, a figure whose brutality is so heinous and alien as to fascinate, was a creative exercise that explored self-identity and validated his imagination.

As Dickey anticipated, the reactions of reviewers depended on their attitudes toward Muldrow. John Skow in the 11 October 1993 issue of *Time* stated that Dickey had intentionally created "a strange airlessness to this brooding, mannered tale—part adventure story, part death chant," related in first-person meditation by a powerfully intuitive man. However, despite being a "primitive marvel," Muldrow remains incomplete, not fully human, because while he would be a sociopath in society, "out of it, for all his interior monologue, he is simply a doomed predator" (88). John Logue in the October 1993 issue of *Southern Living*, cited not only the originality of a point of view that compels reader involvement first for and then against Muldrow, but also Dickey's "great language," that "voice, the poet's instinctive voice [which] sings all the pages in *To the White Sea*" (78). In the 13 September issue of the *New York Times*, Christopher Lehmann-Haupt faulted the book's lack of dramatic tension, which he argued results from Muldrow's indiscriminate killings; unlike the horror of *Deliverance*, where circumstance forces four canoeists to commit and conceal murder, Muldrow kills "so mechanically that his acts lack any moral resonance" (C17). In one of the most negative reviews, Jonathan Yardley in the 29 August 1993 issue of *Washington Post Book World* asserted, "Since so little happens along the way, and since the wayfarer is in all respects unengaging...one is hard pressed to say anything more urgent than 'Who cares'" (3). Rather than scrutinize *To the White Sea* on its own merits, critics generally compared the novel to *Deliverance*, a tendency also evident when they reviewed Dickey's poetry after *Buckdancer's Choice*.

To the White Sea did not become a best seller in the US market, but German, French, and Japanese publishers paid large advances and secured healthy sales. Moreover, Dell paid Dickey a substantial fee for paperback rights, and Universal Studios, which had paid Dickey $500,000 for the movie rights, proceeded with its plan to film the novel. On 13 June 1993, Emory University confirmed its purchase of Dickey's personal papers for a sum in excess of $100,000. In addition to these monies, Dickey earned $5,000 from Audio Productions to tape-record *To the White Sea*, $9,000 from *Architectural Digest* to write an article on Shinto models, and substantial fees from several readings (Hart 721–22). Financially, Dickey was once again successful even if his critical reputation fell far short of its former heights.

On 17 December 1993 the University of South Carolina honored its Carolina Professor writer-in-residence with a lavish, three-day tribute that celebrated Dickey's seventieth year, his quarter century teaching at the university, and his publication that month of *To the White Sea*. The school announced that Dickey would now hold the honorary title of "distinguished professor." The tributes began with a dinner and reception at the Capital City Club; as master of ceremonies, George Plimpton delivered a humorous narration of Dickey's life. John Palms, the university's new president, hailed Dickey's intellect and passion. Other tributes followed, and the evening closed with Dickey reading from his new novel. On Saturday, a series of lectures and panels discussed Dickey's career. Richard Howard chaired the opening session on Dickey's criticism; Joyce Pair and I contributed. R. W. B. Lewis sat on a panel with Richard Calhoun and Robert Hill to explore Dickey's fiction, and on Sunday morning Robert Kirschten moderated a roundtable assessment of Dickey's career. That afternoon, Monroe Spears chaired a panel that discussed his former student's poetry and included Susan Ludvigson and Elizabeth Adams. As Spears reminisced in the Richland County Library auditorium about getting to know Dickey at Vanderbilt, Dickey, Deborah, and Bronwen listened in the front row.

In January 1994, Dickey's poem "Breaking the Field" appeared in the program for the Super Bowl. Several months earlier, an NFL representative had offered Dickey $3,000 to contribute a poem about returning a punted football. In his 4 December 1993 letter to Phil Barber, who had commissioned the poem, Dickey explained that he wanted "a sense of balanced chaos, which corresponds to the field in the last part of a punting situation.... What I have tried to do is give the essential fluidity and anarchy of the punt-return situation, as opposed to the rigidity, the straight-line formulations of the scrimmage, the rehearsed formations, and so on." The poem, however, also reflected Dickey's own literary situation. The persona sees "in the midst / One good block out of nowhere. Chaos field-breaking— / Closing jerseys, all wrong. Not many friends / But the right ones" and decides that importance lies in the "Green daylight.... Beyond friends and enemies." Dickey had long used football as a metaphor for life, beginning with the Hemingway-esque essay he had written in college, "Practice at Clemson," and later in such occasional poems as "In the Pocket" and "For the Death of Lombardi," written for money. "Breaking the Field" endeavored to depict the subjective impressions of a punt re-turner in a competitive sport, the coordinated and seamless fluidity, and in so doing became a means by which he acknowledged his present literary reputation.

Spring 1994 saw Dickey engaged in a variety of small duties. From 11–13 May he served in a Virginia Center for the Book Writing Life res-idency in Richmond, where he was honored at an authors' luncheon. His responsibilities included a public reading, during which he discussed the creative process and the writing craft; signing copies of his books at the Virginia State Library and Archives; and teaching a local high school class. "Teaching," he told a local reporter, Sibella Connor, "is an interchange and all that the human being has got is to interchange with other human be-ings. And the teacher and the learning experience is the height of it." His own writing process, he asserted, was not patterned.

> My whole house is booby-trapped with typewriters. If anybody wants to give me a Christmas present, a birthday present, a Father's Day present, just give me another cheap Japanese typewriter that runs on batteries. Six D batteries. So I can put another project in one. And in some weird way they all cross-pollinate with one an-other. It can be a screenplay, a poem, a children's book, a novel.
>
> I'm a very peripatetic person. The only thing I dislike about the writer's life is the sedentary aspect. I'm a restless person. I'm always moving around. And at any hour, if I move, I'm going to pass by a typewriter. I might start reading what's in it and think again, "I don't like this paragraph." I sit down and fool around with it until I get restless with it and move around and do something else. (G1, 4)

He also posed for a photo at the Poe Museum, sitting at a desk as if pen-ning a poem with a stuffed raven perched on his shoulder.

On 14 May, Dickey visited Appalachian State University in North Carolina, where he was awarded an honorary degree and gave the com-mencement address. Titled "The Eyes of the Egg," the lecture revealed agrarian influences and warned of the devastating effects that science had inflicted on the environment. Opening with references to the atomic de-vice exploded at Los Alamos, Dickey read a two-page account of the site by John Hay, which described the old, adobe Native American hut—which for Hay and Dickey represented the primitive, mysterious forces that had created the world—being obscured by modern houses and clipped lawns. The atomic blast, figuratively representing modern culture, had completely destroyed almost all signs of life's essential mystery. Deborah appeared in the address as an Indian earth mother tending the élan vital by the adobe hearth, and Bronwen became the thirteen-year-old girl who hung on the wall a copy of *The Egg* by the nineteenth-century French pre-surrealist Odilon Redon, whose symbolic works, often depicting a dream world, are related to those of writers such as Poe, Baudelaire, and Mallarmé. For Dickey, eggs were fertility symbols in the modern wasteland. The sterility of the modern condition demanded a deliberate, concerted response, and Dickey's voice clearly announced it: "We must take on faith, which is religious faith, that it will be given, for what we are attempting to connect with is nothing less than the Universe: something beyond those geometric premises, the tract houses, those quick-plotted human dwellings."

The seriousness of Dickey's medical problems became more evident late in October 1994 at one of his "power lunches" with Don Greiner and Ben Franklin, neither of whom suspected his deteriorating health. As they sat in the garden section by the fountain of the university's Faculty House and waited for Dickey, who was late, to arrive, they saw him hobbling across the shaded lawn. It took him five minutes to arrive, and when he did, he grasped the tables for support, his eyes yellow and sweat pouring off him in large droplets. He asked his colleagues for help. Once seated, however, he declined offers to drive him to the student health center or the hospital, declaring that the university paid him to teach and that was what he was going to do that afternoon. Later, Deborah drove her husband to Richland Hospital, where doctors discovered that his liver had stopped functioning, the result of years of alcoholism, and that he had a severe case of hepatitis. Bile had flooded his bloodstream, causing jaundice. Deborah called Christopher and left a message on his answering machine: "Chris, you better do something. Your father is in the hospital, and he's yellow, yellow, yellow—yellow as the Yangtze River." Thinking that Deborah was playing what he called "another of her fantasy games," Chris downplayed her communication. However, when Bronwen faxed a brief handwritten note that said simply, "Dad is in bad shape," he recognized the severity of the situation. "I knew it was bad," he later said (*Summer of Deliverance* 244–45). Dickey sufficiently recovered within ten days to return home, but by 14 November he had suffered a relapse and was readmitted to the hospital. Doctors in Columbia treated his hepatitis for another five days.

At home Deborah was unable to care for her husband properly; she lacked medical training and was taking methadone to cure her heroin addiction. Mayrie MacLamore, the housekeeper who had cooked, cleaned, and cared for the Dickey household since 1987, administered his medications—Duphalac, Colace, and Prilosec—and gently harassed him into eating vanilla pudding and drinking Ensure. Deeply devoted to Dickey, she had visited him daily in the hospital and now continually teased him to lighten his mood. When he had regained strength enough to play his guitar, he sang "The Cacklin' Head." "Oh, you don't like my Blues," he intoned, to which she would respond with feigned irritation, "Sing whatever you want to sing." Dickey continued to sing. She continued to needle.

On 28 November, however, he suffered another setback and was admitted to Providence Hospital; the effects of the hepatitis continued to assault him. He related to Henry Hart in a 5 August 1996 interview that the condition

> just depletes your system so much, it takes you years to recover from it. The main thing it did to me was take all the calcium out of my system, or almost all of it. I had enormous dental bills. It cost me ten thousand dollars to keep my teeth in my head. I lost fifty pounds in a week. I was supposed to die. In fact, I did die at Richland County Hospital, twice. I flat-lined on the monitor, watching the monitor with the doctor. The second time I went under, the last I heard was the doctor say, "We've lost him."

Dying, he later related, was not terrifying. "You have a sense of relief.... Everything just sort of goes, and that's it" (729–30). Finally sober, he now determined to set his life aright.

Earlier that fall, first-year student Stephanie Sonnenfeld Stinn had been a mystery guest at one of the power lunches that Dickey enjoyed with Don Greiner and Ben Franklin. She had heard about these repasts during a talk that Greiner, then vice provost and dean of undergraduate studies, had given to the Class of 1998 in which he spoke about the opportunities available to students and noted Dickey's presence at the university and about the "power lunches." After his presentation, she had approached Greiner and inquired how she could be a mystery guest. Greiner immediately invited her. They had met in late September, eating in the garden of the Faculty House. "The three men were all close friends," Stinn remembered, "each enjoying the others' company in the midst of greatness." She and Dickey discussed "Hunting Civil War Relics at Nimblewill Creek," a poem she liked, all the while overwhelmed and telling herself to "be quiet and soak it in." She was invited to lunch again during her junior year, when she found Dickey quieter, more frail, not loud or boisterous. He remembered their previous lunch and inquired what she was reading now and whose work she admired.

Later, in 1996, she would see him again. "I like to think the weather was cooler—fall or early winter—the last time I saw James Dickey," she stated in an interview.

> I remember only because anything outside of the blazing heat and humidity in Columbia, South Carolina, is something of note. He was sitting near Gambrell Hall, on a bench, across from the Humanities Building and near the Business School. In my memory, he's wearing a hat and coat. I knew it was him because I had seen him walking in a similar hat and coat a few times during my time at The University of South Carolina. What's key to this is the verb: walking. I always saw him walking. Walking and talking with colleagues, fellow professors and a graduate student from time-to-time. Smiling, joking, laughing. Always walking. On this day he sat.

> It looked like he was either resting or waiting—or maybe both. But not laughing. Not smiling or talking. Certainly not joking. All by himself. He looked smaller and older. He was just this, as he had been sick in those few years. It was a busy time of the day being that it was between classes. People were moving in all sorts of directions, but all uniformly walking at a quick pace. None of them noticed the man sitting there by the tree. They kept moving. But, he kept watching them. Observing. They didn't seem to notice one of the greatest poets of modern literature was over there, sitting. They stuck to their timetables and schedules. I could have gone over and said hello. We'd had lunch twice before. He'd dined with many students, so I suspected I wouldn't have stood out. Shyness aside, it was a moment where you know not to intrude. It was a time to just let things be.

> One of the most gifted writers of our time sat alone watching people move on with their lives as he was near the end of his. He was doing what good writers do: he was observing. I walked on to my next stop. He continued to sit. That was the last time I ever saw James Dickey.

In January 1995, however, Dickey's health had improved enough for him to teach one class of ten students at his home. They gathered together on the glassed-in porch that Dickey had added to his house several years previously from which they could see Lake Katharine. On 12–14 April he participated in a conference on World War II, "The Last Good War," organized by his university colleagues George Geckle and Bill Fox. Prominent writers, including Joseph Heller, William Styron, Paul Fussell, Mickey Spillane, and William Manchester spoke on topics such as "America, Then and Now" and "Revisionist History and World War II." On 13 April in the business school auditorium, Dickey read from *To the White Sea*, later commenting to Michael Sponhour, a *State* reporter, not only about his contempt for revisionists and his semester at Clemson, "which at that time meant the grueling discipline of a military school plus the demands of Coach Frank Howard," but also about the men killed in the war. "We felt like we were going to die," he declared. "We had seen so much, we had lost so many friends" (A1).

While his convalescence proceeded, Dickey usually sat in the large stuffed armchair in his living room where he read during the day and watched old movies at night. At the end of the summer, Deborah suffered another major relapse to heroin. With her addiction now seeming incurable and with his health failing, he signed his official last will and testament on 22 August 1995. He divided his personal property among his children, appointed NationsBank as his personal representative, and Matthew Bruccoli as his literary and personal representative with "full and complete authority" over his literary estate. Christopher and Kevin were named Bronwen's guardians. Despite the fact that Dickey still loved Deborah and wanted to keep the family together, he eliminated his wife from the estate and attempted to resolve the marital discord by proceeding with a divorce.

Emory University opened its James Dickey Archive on 11 October. An honorary banquet at the Houston Mill House featured William Chance, the president of Emory, as well as friends and family. Al Braselton, Lewis King, and Inman Mays, all former advertising colleagues, offered tributes to a friendship that began in the fifties; Tom Dickey Jr., Kevin, and Bronwen also spoke. (Chris, who worked for *Newsweek*, was on assignment in Bosnia.) Confined to a wheelchair, an exhausted but grateful Dickey made a few unrehearsed comments. Steve Ennis, head of special collections, and Joan Gotwals, the vice provost of Emory, then presented Dickey with an award. The following day Dickey talked informally to students gathered at Woodruff Library, asking his audience to identify the top poets of the twentieth century and chatting about the film version of *To the White Sea*. In the evening he read at Emory's Michael C. Carlos Museum and signed books in the special collections department.

That fall the English department at the University of South Carolina also honored Dickey, assigning *Deliverance* to all first-year students and showing the film several times at the university theater. On 3 November, he read from the novel to several hundred students assembled at the Koger Center. Wearing a sports coat and turtleneck, clearly frail and short of breath, he cautiously climbed the steps to the stage, greeted by whistles and shouts from the students, and answered questions about whether he could have written the novel without the strong language and the violence. "No, I don't think so," he said. He declared that the characters were derived from bits and pieces of individuals he knew in real life and that Lewis "is in many respects based on me." There have been few movies, he asserted, "which followed their source as closely as this one did," and added, to laughter from the students, "The book is better." The program closed with Dickey reading for fifteen minutes from the final whitewater journey in the last section of the novel, his voice growing stronger and more animated as he proceeded. Appreciative students applauded when he rose to leave. "I've enjoyed this," he said in closing, "Thank you," though Dickey quietly told Keen Butterworth and me, both of whom had made testimonial speeches, that the students merely felt sorry for him.

On 13 December he signed an agreement with the University of South Carolina Press that established a James Dickey poetry series. William Wadsworth, the director of the American Academy of American Poets, had assisted the press by suggesting possible editors for the series. Richard Howard agreed to serve as the series editor, and a grant of $9,000 a year from the academy enabled the series to begin the following spring. Since its inception, the James Dickey Contemporary Poetry Series has honored such poets as Robert Hahn, Maureen Bloomfield, Sarah Getty, and Michael Rosen.

On 18 December 1995, Dickey delivered the commencement address at the Carolina Coliseum. The night before, university officers and members of the board of trustees attended a dinner at the Faculty House. Matthew Bruccoli, Ward Briggs, Ben Franklin, and Don Greiner also were present. Dickey asked that he be placed next to the table where Greiner and his wife were to sit should he need to reach out and hold Greiner's arm for a few seconds. Anyone looking at Dickey would have realized he was ill. His face was drawn and gaunt, and he was using a wheelchair.

Nevertheless, he wore a friendly, calm smile. At commencement the following day, the large audience could not see the ramp placed at the back of the stage so that Dickey could be pushed up. Dark curtains were also placed on each side of the stage to block the view as Dickey was pushed to a specially constructed high chair for him to lean against as he stood at the podium.

In his commencement address, titled "The Weather of the Valley: Reflections on the Soul and Its Making," Dickey adopted Keats's definition of life as a "vale of soul-making" as he reflected on his career and his values. He had committed his life, he stated, to the works of the imagination and to the teaching of subjects related to them. He reminisced about how, while stationed on Okinawa, he had read the poems of Trumbull Stickney and discovered the line "his island shivered into flowers," which acted as an epiphany and determined his course to be a poet. His injunction to the graduates was clear and emphatic:

> We need the plural mind that the individual mind contains: the plural mind in the plural universe. We need to be occupied with the eternal problem of language, language expanding consciousness and then consciousness expanding language, in circular or spiral ascent, perhaps. This is exactly what makes the creative mind so inestimably precious, the one thing to which one must undeviatingly devote oneself, if only because in this one can fully realize that joyful dance, the delightful—and delighted—wisdom of being. Everything is included in the one expanding synthesis. (37)

"'The Weather of the Valley' was a brilliant speech," Greiner remembered. He continued,

> Anyone paying attention would understand that Jim had spent time drafting and then polishing the talk. It was one of the most intriguing commencement addresses of the many I've had to endure. It was an intellectual's speech, a speech delivered by a brilliant man to the most gifted, thinking people in the audience. It was a speech that had to be *listened to* to be comprehended, but, of course, most of the audience was too distracted by the specifics of the day: graduation, at last.

Although they were aware of Deborah's drug problems and the tumult they were causing at home, Don Greiner and Ben Franklin never seriously believed Dickey would follow through with a divorce; he remained stubbornly faithful to romantic ideals about marriage. On 18

January 1996, however, Dickey filed the requisite papers with the Richland County Court. An "Obligations of Each Party" agreement gave custody of Bronwen to Dickey, while Deborah would receive a $213 monthly payment as beneficiary of his retirement plan, $25,316 as her portion of the property, and $40,000 in death benefits from his life insurance. Additionally, she would receive 10 percent of future movie rights for *To the White Sea* and $8,333 in alimony payments each year. A financial declaration filed as part of the divorce estimated Dickey's assets at $800,000 and his income for the year at $187,000 (Hart 738). Legal maneuverings postponed the agreement on final terms until 8 November. By early January the divorce was ready to be finalized because Deborah had vacated the house for more than a year.

In his final months Dickey attempted to become closer to his children, opening himself to them as if needing the continuity they provided. He doted on Bronwen, who now attended Choate and was home on vacation, and conducted long taped interviews with Christopher, who had flown in from Paris to gather information for what would become his memoir, *Summer of Deliverance*. On 24 September he participated in a conference celebrating F. Scott Fitzgerald's one hundredth birthday, including a one-hour televised discussion with Joseph Heller. He wrote two tributes, a poem entitled "Entering Scott's Night," in which he imagined himself joining Fitzgerald in death—where "in the paper-lit garden / A dark-glowing field of folk, the dead, the celebrants / Making company as Scott would, / Who brought their time / Through time"—and an essay, written at the request of Matthew Bruccoli, entitled "The Slow Surprise and the Deepening of Art," which praised Fitzgerald's high aesthetic standards. After a sophisticated luncheon in the flower-filled backyard of university president John Palms's house, Frederick Busch spoke at the official opening of the F. Scott Fitzgerald collection in the rare-book room. Busch had been a mystery guest several years earlier at a power lunch when he gave a reading at the university. Dickey and Busch were comfortable together, so Greiner arranged for both men to sit together. They talked more or less privately throughout lunch; no one interfered in their conversation. At the conclusion of the event, Greiner recalled, Dickey hugged Busch: "I heard him say that this moment was likely the final time they would see one another. It was."

Dickey felt better in November when doctors took him off steroids, writing Marc Jaffe that he was proceeding with "Crux," the planned sequel to *Alnilam*, and had completed a section titled "Vines." Jaffe requested a proposal for the new novel. Although Dickey never complied, he did mail his editor the twenty-five-typed-page opening section of "Crux" at the end of the year. The pages open with Harbelis watching flying fish sail over the waves after he has embarked on a troopship for the Pacific, a scene that Dickey himself had experienced a half century previously on the USS *Anderson*. Henry Hart has asserted that the opening pages of the typescript "read like a thinly veiled memoir of Dickey's World War II experiences.... Unwilling to forget his failure to become a decorated war pilot, at the end of his life he was more prepared to write about it realistically" (743). Chris Dickey asserted in his memoir that "Harbelis is nothing but Intercept Office Jim Dickey" (47). It is possible to see in Harbelis's comments about pilots and radar observers, on the one hand, and his recollections about aerial gunnery school and P-61s, on the other, specific parallels with Dickey's training experiences. However, nothing in Dickey's early correspondence supports the contention that Dickey shared Harbelis's attitudes.

Dickey completed only twenty-nine pages of notes on "Crux," though he had fully elaborated his plans for the novel in 1976 when he detailed both *Alnilam* and its intended sequel, in which "the full diabolical scope of the Alnilam plot takes place, and culminates in a holocaust somewhere in the Pacific." At the conclusion of "Crux," Harbelis, who is "the decent guy and who always carries his E6B flight computer with him," has emerged from the war terribly burned. He is on rest leave in Japan, has played in a ping-pong tournament, and has visited a Japanese school where the children dance around him and give him American flags. He decides to decode Alnilam's final message, hidden on the inner strap of his goggles, which Joel had ordered never decoded unless Joel were dead or unless he gave the word. It is a single word—"nothing." Harbelis then goes out into the cold and with binoculars looks toward Mount Fuji, whose brightness blinds him. Swinging the binoculars toward the bottom of a tree, he moves up it, wanting it to be the right tree, the one whose beautiful and logical form complemented the mountain. The novel was then to read: "It drew what it needed from the earth, so the movement of life was in it." The last sentence of "Crux" was to be a statement of affirmation: "It was not impossible, like the mountain."

In notes dated 8 August 1994, however, Dickey altered the conclusion. Harbelis looks at Mount Fuji and decides he will let Alnilam go, will turn away and not look back: "This is the perfect mountain, the organization, the beautiful and logical form. Demented with rigidity and perfection, and he turned to the trees. The wind blew. They would die, but here they were alive, and they moved." Dickey did not believe he would finish the sequel, but the language, the voice of Harbelis, in the section that he did complete is among the strongest prose he ever wrote. Harbelis watches the flying fish as they leap free of the water:

> They broke; there just enough. Now he would add one thing to them, each time they rose. One thing. They flattened into their pattern, the sun catching everywhere on it, one spark to a fish. Or it could be a contest of some kind: not to get somewhere first but to go farthest, stay, hold out for more time in the air? Was the same one always in front? Yes, it must be, it must be that way, Harbelis thought. (Hart, *The James Dickey Reader* 212)

Dickey likewise had always wanted to go the farthest, to commit himself to the air at the front of the group, to fly point. Once he had done so, but now he was flying by words.

Despite his deteriorating health, labored breathing, and lack of stamina, Dickey remained determined to fulfill his teaching commitment. Like the high school geometry teacher in his 1965 poem "Mangham," who suffers a heart attack in class but continues to instruct his students in "Identities," in "those things that, once / Established, cannot be changed by angels, / Devils, lightning, ice or indifference," he was fiercely unwavering in his desire to reveal to his students the connections that poetry made possible. He had, however, informed the English department that he would take a sabbatical and a medical leave of absence for the 1997–1998 academic year and that the spring 1997 term would constitute his last. Realizing that his close friend was nearing death, Matthew Bruccoli arranged with instructional services to tape-record Dickey's final classes. On 14 January 1997, Dickey met his first group of students for the new term, coughing and retching for a few minutes until he was able to breathe. His lecture—too formal a term, really, for the personal tone, the climate of camaraderie that he always established with his students—ranged over a wide airspace of topics, including the poet's use of the unconscious, the necessity of imaginative lying, the nature of God, and the poet's role as secondary creator. The students listened as if hypnotized to a voice that was growing weaker. He informed them that, given his physical condition, this would undoubtedly be his last class.

The day after teaching his class, Dickey succumbed to feverish chills, shaking uncontrollably, and was rushed by ambulance to Providence

Hospital. Doctors diagnosed a chest infection they believed curable with antibiotics. Dickey, viewing his medical problems as warfare, remained unfazed, believing he would be home by Monday. Although he had trouble breathing Thursday night, the following morning brought renewed strength. Don Greiner visited, and together they recited Frost's "After Apple-Picking," Dickey's favorite Frost poem, a contemplation about approaching death and the uncertainty of what, if anything, followed, alternating lines until they reached the conclusion: "One can see what will trouble / This sleep of mine, whatever sleep it is. / Were he not gone, / The woodchuck could say whether it's like his / Long sleep, as I describe its coming on, / Or just some human sleep." The nurses did not interrupt. Moved by his favorite Frost poem, Dickey reached out and hugged his close friend and colleague, saying that he loved him. Other friends also visited. In the evening, however, Dickey weakened. He fought for breath and continued to lose weight. Notified of his decline, Christopher, Kevin, and Bronwen made arrangements to fly to Columbia.

On Sunday, Ben Franklin saw Kevin and Bronwen beside their father's bed and decided not to intrude. Matthew Bruccoli shortened his visit later, agonized by his friend's physical state. That night, Mayrie MacLamore attended him. She temporarily left the room when she received a call from one of her children who wanted to know how Dickey was doing, but returned around 11:00 P.M. He lay serene, as if sleeping, then suddenly gripped her hand. She said, "Mr. Dickey?" He gasped and said, "Don't leave me," afraid of being alone but not of dying. Then she watched him stop breathing. Almost a decade after telling me in conversation that he had dreamed of his death from a heart attack in the front foyer of his home on Lelia's Court, Dickey in 1997 had died of fibrosis of the lungs in the hospital.

The first announcements of his death summarized his life and career, noting his Rabelaisian lifestyle and the critical disputes surrounding his work. Almost all the articles linked him to *Deliverance*. The *Washington Post*, for example, observed, "He loved life and lived it with a macho swagger" (Pearson B5), and the *Richmond Times-Dispatch* declared that he "achieved his greatest fame for his novel and Oscar-nominated movie *Deliverance*" (B2). More personal tributes followed. Sibella Giorella in a 24 January article asserted, "The essential Dickey was pure poet. As a writer, he didn't so much pen his poems as wrestle the words until their meaning hit the ground; didn't so much employ phrases as bite them off of life, spit them onto the page.... Dickey steered away from inconsequence both in literary terms and real life, gravitating toward the edge. He lived hard, until his 6-foot-four-inch frame finally gave out." Describing the interview she had had with him, she remembered, "For several hours, we talked about books. He would reach into the paper tower and extract one level, read a portion aloud. Each piece was unlike the last. Poems, reminiscences, love stories. Yet each had the continuing thread of his own work—man against man, man against woman, man against nature, man against science" (C1, 3). The most moving statements came from Dickey's daughter, Bronwen, in *Newsweek*. Describing her father as he lay in the hospital, "nothing more than a pained skeleton" whose "chest heaved as though every breath was a last valiant effort" and whose "fingers were purple from lack of oxygen," she nevertheless remembered his greatness: "Not the greatness of the writer but the greatness of the father and the teacher." "My father was not physically recognizable," she wrote, "but his essence was still strong in the room. His books were strategically arranged nearby, and he still wore two watches, his Citizen Wingman and his Ironman Triathlon" (19). Against the onslaught of time and the prejudice of critics, Dickey pitted himself, armed with books and a poetic imagination and a fierce intellect and memory. In an extended defense of Dickey against the inadequacy of his critics, Jeffrey Meyers declared in *New Criterion*, "He knew the tears of things" ("What the Monsters Know"). Rodney Welch admitted Dickey's problem. "For most of his final years," he stated, "Dickey's life was in free fall. Professionally, his stock had dropped, the prices for books and readings fluctuated, and there was always the looming threat that his old lies would be exposed. That was the least of it. His home life was a nightmare; he was a hardened alcoholic and an incurable womanizer, and his much younger wife Deborah was a heroin addict who took out her rage on him." "Always at the forefront," he concluded, "was Dickey's expansive personality, easily eloquent on subjects both literary and domestic, his conversation peppered with brilliant judgments, well-remembered quotes, tall tales, and statements guaranteed to shock all but the most jaded" (25, 28–34). Even in death, Dickey remained controversial.

He was buried next to Maxine in the All Saints Waccamaw Church graveyard on Pawleys Island, South Carolina. The funeral was held on the afternoon of Friday, 24 January, the service limited to family and close friends. Ben Franklin, Matthew Bruccoli, Michael Allin, Don Greiner, Al Braselton, Lewis King, Ward Briggs, and Christopher's son were pallbearers. Dickey had instructed that his gravestone read, "James Dickey, 1923—, Poet, Father of Bronwen, Kevin, and Christopher." Additionally, his children decided to inscribe an eye like the one on the first edition dust jacket of *Deliverance* as well as the words, "I move at the heart of the world," from his 1961 poem, "In the Treehouse at Night." Chris, speaking from notes, addressed those at the funeral:

> My father—our father—died for the first time a little more than two years ago. He was in the hospital with hepatitis. His wife Deborah was with him, fierce and protective, the way he liked her. And the lines of the machine went flat. He was gone.
>
> But not for long. Maybe he thought there was unfinished business. Maybe there was just more he wanted to do. But he fought back with that tremendous will of his. And back to us.
>
> And what I want to say today is that for us, his children, these last two years have been the best life we ever had with him.

His father had reached out to family and beloved friends, Chris reminisced, to the people around him whose loyalty and love he got, and that he gave back in kind. "He was pulling us all to *him*," Chris said, "and *together*." Now his father knew the great secret of death.

On Monday the University of South Carolina held a memorial tribute on the green lawn of the Horseshoe near where Dickey, Don Greiner, and Ben Franklin had enjoyed the good conversation of so many power lunches. Despite the February date, the administration wanted the ceremony held on the Horseshoe because Dickey had loved the lovely, peaceful, tree-lined section of the campus. The morning was mild. An audience of around three hundred was expected; seven hundred people showed up. Grounds crew scurried to place additional chairs on the lawn. The Capital City Chorale sang "Sweet Chariot," "Amazing Grace," and "Shall We Gather at the River," all songs Dickey remembered from his childhood, and Julie Bloemeke, who had enrolled in his final class, read "The Heaven of Animals." Don Greiner, as interim vice president and provost, hosted the service because President Palms was out of town. Greiner wore a "boot" for a broken foot, limping to the podium, welcoming the crowd, acknowledging Mrs. Palms and the Dickey family, and commenting on the difficulty of speaking about his close friend. He named half a dozen poems that would, as Frost had memorably said, "be hard to get rid of." Ward Briggs and Matthew Bruccoli offered remarks. Pat Conroy, the principal speaker, told of Dickey's complicated life, opening his speech, "The biography of James Dickey will make that of Ernest Hemingway read like a biography of a florist in the Middle West" (24–25). The crowd laughed. Robert Newman, the English department chair, concluded the ceremony as "Dueling Banjoes" was played. Later, on 14 November 1998 at 11 A.M. in Thomas Cooper Library, the university would announce the dedication of the James Dickey Poetry Seminar Room and the acquisition of Dickey's 17,000-volume personal library. John Updike, who had given a talk the previous evening, attended.

In his last major interview before his death, Dickey had stressed the transformative power of language. He recalled Stickney's lines that had determined him to become a poet, and he intoned, "That's got it. That's for me. You see, everything is in there. You see some sort of magical transformation taking place, shaking with intensity. You see lots and lots of stuff. And, above all, you feel it.... I said, 'This is what I want to do. I've been piddling around with it before, writing these letters to girls, but now I'm going to go for it. This sets the sail on the course. *This* is going to be my life.' And it has been. And I've never been sorry" (Greiner, "Making the Truth" 26). In his 1983 essay "Starting from Buckhead: A Home Address," he reflected on the career he had embraced. "So if anybody asks you," he wrote,

> how Jim Dickey became a poet, tell him that the man fought in a war in airplanes, reading Plato between missions, that he got a desperate education at Vanderbilt, worked in some ad agencies, drank whiskey with Dave Sanders, hunted deer unsuccessfully with Lewis King, shot some rapids with Al Braselton, looked at pictures with Jarvin Parks, and watched Bess Finch dance, and that he published, in the end, some poems based on these things. (*Night Hurdling* 188)

"We have death, and the day's light," he once told me in conversation.

Following his death and the memorial service on the Horseshoe of the University of South Carolina, hundreds of cards, sympathy notes, letters of condolence, and even poems arrived, tributes to Dickey and the power of language. Dickey had told Don Greiner that he wanted a simple epitaph: "James Dickey: American Poet." Meredith Turner, an honors student in Greiner's seminar, wrote "American Poet," which she subtitled, "in memory of James Dickey." It concluded: "And when you die, / having lived so excessively within this dream / that there is still life to be had in waking, / we will gather on a lawn / on a mild day in January / in subconscious streams of folded chairs / and watch the sun tiptoe between the clouds / like the lone beggar at a feast / and there we will mourn the death of an American poet." Another student, Erin Bush, composed "In Memorium:

James Dickey," which ends, "I who never knew you / will remember you thus: / I will bite the ripest persimmon, / swallow the burning milk of stars, / and as this food devours me, / I will put one word in front of another." Such tributes by undergraduates, who responded to Dickey's death with poems honoring him, confirm what Dickey's presence on *their* campus meant to them.

Dickey's eyes could hold any person, eyes which opened onto a vast restless country, and his voice, the force of his words and the rhythms of its cadence, could transfix a listener. He had always been a man on fire with Time, and he knew that—a man who wanted to sit in the sun and feel both life and death outlined and waiting, a man who was always daring his skin to die. It had to die, and he knew that, too. He wanted Life, nothing less, wanted to know, as he wrote in an early poem, "the fires / Of the sun and the earth, / When they were one, burning plotless, unequalled, from the stone." In his poem "Daybreak," first published in the January 1987 issue of *Southern Magazine* and included in *The Eagle's Mile*, he countered the hopelessness and despair in poems such as "Moon Flock" with the essential afflatus and affirmation for which he always wanted to be known. As the persona stands at the jetty on Pawleys Island, he thinks:

> To those crests
> Dying hard, you have nothing to say:
> > You cannot help it
>
> If you emerge; it is not your fault. You show: you stare
>
> Into the cancelling gullies, saved only by dreaming a future
> > Of walking forward, in which you can always go flat
>
> In skylight, gradually cleaning, and you gaze straight into
>
> > The whole trembling forehead of yourself
> > Under you, and at your feet find your body
>
> > No different from cloud, among the other
> > > See-through images, as you are flawingly
> > > Thought of,
> > > > But purely, somewhere,
>
> > Somewhere in all thought.

Like his speaker, Dickey at the end of his life embraced the Ideal, recognizing the truth of continuity, even as he realistically understood, as he admits in "Sleepers," that "no one knows where his body will end." Like his speaker, too, he could not help it. It was who he was.

CHAPTER 15

DEBRIEFINGS

Jim Dickey once told his son Chris, "No true artist will tolerate for one minute the world as it is" (*Summer of Deliverance* 26). Dickey reimagined the world as he wanted it to be in an effort to enlarge and validate who he was and to impart to his life a sense of consequence he felt did not exist. The Pacific air campaign during World War II had confirmed an early need for such illusion. Adolescent insecurities, heightened sensitivities, and the perceived failure to satisfy parental and social expectations had led a young Dickey to imagine himself as such action heroes as Tarzan and Doc Savage. He wanted to be a superman who made himself superior to everyone else through sheer self-discipline and a stubbornness of will. The war's brutality provided the necessary impetus for him to escape into the literature he requested from his mother or that he himself procured on Okinawa. The grimness of the scene fractured the naïveté of a parochial childhood and worsened when he saw firsthand in the coral caves of Okinawa the blackened corpses of Japanese soldiers.

Such brutality encouraged a Romantic idealism that reviewers occasionally condemned as unbelievable and escapist in his poems. These critics resemble the officers during the war who manned ground control. In what Samuel Hynes, himself an aviator during the conflict, described as "a dark, cave-like room," they viewed the aerial combat from a distance: "This is where all the planes in the air over Okinawa and to the north were tracked, where enemy raids were first noted, and fighters sent against them." While the controller's job was "simply to see that his man wasn't shot down, he would watch the drama of fighter interception on the screen before him and follow the action on his earphones." It was vicarious participation, and Dickey himself wanted direct confrontation, not passivity. Ground control, which is to say the reviewers and critics, were what Hynes described as "the visual part of the show" (225), where operators watched the drama unfold apart from the real conflict. Refusing largely to cede any merit to Dickey's new literary directions, they continually condemned the experimentation of his central motion, insisting that such literary experiments were "a falling off." They simply ignored his late motion. As R. S. Gwynn wrote in a 1994 essay in *Sewanee Review*, "The mere mention of his name summon[ed] up sniffy dismissals" (155). Dickey felt that those whose roles dictated that they merely observe and evaluate writers did not understand what he was doing or his emphatic need to explore. It is not surprising then that he angrily declared to Dana Gioia in 1987 at the Library of Congress's fiftieth reunion of consultants, "You're all the same. I gotta grow, gotta try new things. All you want is the same damn thing" (Gioia, "How Nice to Meet You, Mr. Dickey" 83–88). Creatively and personally restless, unwilling to continue writing what had previously been successful, he determined to fly solo; he refused to be boxed in and he said so in a loud voice. In a letter to me, he wrote, "I was born for combat, for the struggle, and would be lost without it. He who ever strives upward, Goethe says: Ah! Him can we save."

As Matthew Bruccoli, his literary executor admitted, Dickey "deliberately promoted and exaggerated his various reputations—genius, drinker, woodsman, athlete—until the legends took over after *Deliverance*" (Bruccoli, Baughman xxii). Even Chris Dickey believed that his father's creative efforts diminished after the novel. "It seemed to me then," he wrote in his memoir, "and for a long time afterward that forces of self-indulgence and self-destruction, which were always there in my father but held in check, were now cut loose. And worse." *Deliverance*, he asserted, was "a line of demarcation," declaring that *Poems 1957–1967* remained "the single best and most consistent volume of his work" (*Summer of Deliverance* 14, 275). Dickey, nevertheless, dismissed all attacks directed at his current literary efforts even as he sought to counter them by having friends write favorable letters and reviews; it was warfare.

In his 1986 essay "Cosmic Deliverance," he reveled in what the universe had given him. "Toward where you are," he wrote, "the whole of it, alive with angles and exact, is pointing, and it will find you where you stand, and will—yet always with its wilderness arrogance—confirm you as surely as it does the lion and the comet, and bear you out, and on" (8–9). Yet Dickey's heightened sensitivity to the promises of life, to its wild and inexplicable wonder and possibility and mystery, necessitated that he re-create the past if for no other reason than that he wanted to be larger, better than he felt he was. He admitted in an interview four years later that because he was essentially fainthearted and lacked self-assurance, he deliberately embraced force and vigor, an "assumed personality" that he characterized as "big, strong, hard drinking, hard fighting." "Nothing could be less characteristic of the true James Dickey," he asserted, "who is a timid, cowardly person." Although the public perception was otherwise, Dickey said, "you can't fool yourself, so you spend your life fooling yourself. The self that you fool yourself into is the one that functions" (Suarez, "An Interview with James Dickey" 117–32). Dickey's personality then revealed this diversity, or contradiction, and his poetic voice often suggested it, which is the dilemma Peter Davison confronted when he examined Dickey's poetry in 1969.

Davison argued that the world for Dickey was not a classical structure that formulated a city governed by law, with anarchy, like a terrible ocean, ever nibbling at its shores. The world for Dickey had depth and dimension that demanded exploration by a sensibility that would penetrate ever more deeply into its guises of reality. His poetry, then, constituted, in a line from "Buckdancer's Choice," "the thousand variations of one song." From a linguistic standpoint, Dickey's problem became how to express his mystical intentions in concrete images—that is, how to discover a bridge between the flesh and the spirit, the Aristotelian and the Platonic—because his poetry was "a search, in a sense, for heaven on earth." Ironically, Davison asserted, the ultimate way of becoming more than the self is to die. Dickey's technique, however, still lagged behind his aspirations. Davison worried that in straining to reach the universal, Dickey would overstep the abilities of language, suggesting that such writing "requires a vast fire to keep the cauldron boiling. If he were to encounter a slight recession of energy, such as that which seems lately to have overtaken Robert Lowell, Dickey's value as a poet might easily enter into a decline just at the moment when his reputation, like Lowell's today, has reached its apogee" (116–21). It is possible to argue that with the financial success three years later of *Deliverance* and his ever-increasing use of alcohol to "keep the cauldron boiling," Dickey lost both the motivation and the creativity to explore reality more deeply. The public persona that he had created in the sixties (and that he continued largely to assume into the eighties) in order to promote himself specifically and poetry generally now seemed actively to work against him.

Despite proceedings to the contrary, Dickey's marriage to Deborah legally continued; the divorce was never officially finalized. Ill and at times uncertain as to whether he really wanted a divorce, he never signed the final papers. On 15 August 1997, all parties finally agreed to a settlement. Christopher, Kevin, and Bronwen became the beneficiaries of the estate, while Deborah received Dickey's retirement benefits, which totaled approximately $170,000.

In July 1998 the editorial board of Modern Library, which had been publishing classic English-language literature at affordable prices since 1917 and which was now a division of Random House, selected the top one hundred novels of the twentieth century. The board members making the selection included Christopher Cerf, Gore Vidal, Daniel J. Boorstin, Shelby Foote, Vartan Gregorian, A. S. Byatt, Edmund Morris, John Richardson, Arthur M. Schlesinger Jr., and William Styron. Heading the list was Joyce's *Ulysses*, followed by Fitzgerald's *The Great Gatsby* and Joyce's *A Portrait of the Artist as a Young Man*. Writers such as Flannery O'Connor and Nobel Laureate Toni Morrison were not included, nor were Eudora Welty, Thomas Pynchon, John Updike, and Doris Lessing. James Dickey's *Deliverance* was forty-second, a fact that would not have pleased Dickey; he would have viewed the entire selection process either as a fraud or as a marketing gimmick. The German publishing conglomerate Bertelsmann, which owned Random House, was then publishing fifty-nine of the one hundred novels, and nine of the ten board members were published by that group. Dickey, in any event, maintained until the end of his life that *Alnilam* was his best novel.

Following Dickey's death, Matthew Bruccoli published *Crux: The Letters of James Dickey* in 1994, a collection which documents his genius but more specifically reveals how he crafted his career. "Jim was unabashedly a careerist," Bruccoli wrote in his introduction. "He had a clear understanding of the odds against any poet, no matter how gifted, and he recognized that his poetry did not exist if it was not read" (xxii). The volume represented approximately 20 percent of Dickey's correspondence. "Try to get out at least three or four letters a day," Dickey wrote in *Sorties*. "Or five. Five would be better. There is no telling what that extra letter might bring into being" (17). I edited an enlarged sense of Dickey's personality in a two-volume collection of the correspondence, *The One Voice of James Dickey: His Letters and Life, 1942–1997*, published in 2003 and 2005, respectively. The volumes trace the development of a poetic mind; they document his growth from a callow teen who was interested primarily in sports to a mature poet who possessed genius and who deliberately advanced his poetry. In 2004, Don Greiner edited *James Dickey: Classes on Modern Poets and the Art of Poetry*, providing a close look at Dickey's lectures and teaching methodology. Joyce Pair, who founded the *James Dickey Newsletter* in 1984, provided a forum for information on the work, bibliography, and biography of Dickey. The newsletter offered a reliable and scholarly center for Dickey research late in his career. Finally, in 2013, Ward Briggs, a close friend and USC colleague of Dickey's, published *The Complete Poems*.

At his death, Dickey was working on a collection of poems entitled "Two Poems on the Survival of the Male Body." "My father said," Chris Dickey remembered, "with a touch of ironic humor and a kind of resignation, that he had worked on these poems for years, and that he thought they were the most important poems he had written. Certainly they were very important to him at that moment. And he asked me to finish them for him after he died." "My lines on the survival of the male body," Chris stated, "were stillborn. I closed the file, and did not reopen it" (*Death, and the Day's Light* x). With the permission of the Dickey estate, I proposed to complete the two long poems and to edit Dickey's final volume, which included poems that had previously been published but not collected. *Death, and the Day's Light* was published by Mercer University Press in 2015.

"Show Us the Sea," a long expansion of a poem Dickey had written years before, "Giving a Son to the Sea," concerns an aging father watching with binoculars his lifeguard son and other young men on the beach as they bodysurf and strike poses like weight lifters. The speaker, who is "invisible with sand," addresses what he calls "Real God," asking that the magnified physicality and male camaraderie be brought forward with him to witness. As "Kevin" poses and points to what his admirers ask him to reveal, he seems increasingly mythic, his body in its own "age / Of bronze" made of "Phidian stone" that is "burst up from sand but cast in no metal / From underground." Over the course of the poem, however, the focus shifts from Kevin to the speaker himself, whose silent requests for his son to show through his poses everything on or around the beach—the sea oats, the lighthouse, the lifeguard stand, the seagulls hovering above them, the conch shell, the school of mullet, the bowling alley over the pier, the graveyard, the three dolphins, the next wave—lead to his ultimate request to "show us the sea." If Dickey's "Giving a Son to the Sea" realized that in Kevin's love of the ocean he "must let you go, out of the gentle / Childhood into your own man suspended / In its body," he now comes to accept his own mortality and the connection he has to the world through his son: "I leave muscle / To you but go with you / For as long as sand will blow past / Me full of faint voices." What Kevin had given his father is the recognition, accepted finally, of "you and I and all / There is, all born and dying, forever, at once."

In "For Jules Bacon," who was Mr. America 1943, the persona affirms the human body in and of itself, its essential structure of muscles and blood, as a counterstatement against the destructiveness of combat, against death itself: "I rose. War, Jules, and nothing else / Jules, but death / But body. War. I rose. War, war, Jules, / War. War roared with life, and you saved me." If he can perfect his body, enter a mystique of perfection, the narrator believes, he will inexplicably achieve a state of invulnerability that time and circumstance cannot affect. At the conclusion of the poem, the speaker figuratively escapes his own death by uniting with the P-61 aircraft itself: "The runway opened / Slowly, with all its speed came forward / With the throttle, pouring / Into my mouth, Jules, / With no end to it, no end but life. Life! / War roared with life, and you saved me."

While "Show Us the Sea" and "For Jules Bacon," as concluding poems in *Death, and the Day's Light*, depict the inescapability of death, they also reveal the redemptive quality of that light just as they acknowledge the transience of its glory. Dickey believed in the reality of that redemptive transience, the prospect of imaginative re-creation, and while he believed, life was transformed magnificently enough. He was always aware he would die. Words, though, with luck might live on. It was possible. He had written as much in his 1962 poem "A Letter":

> But words light up in the head
> To take their strange place in the darkness,
>
> Beneath the huge blackness of time
> Which lies concealing, concealing
> What must gleam forth in the end,
> Glimpsed, unchanging, and gone
> When memory stands without sleep
> And gets its strange spark from the world.

CHRONOLOGY

1923   2 February: James Lafayette Dickey, the second son and third child of lawyer Eugene Dickey and Maibelle Swift Dickey, is born in Buckhead, a suburb of Atlanta, Georgia.

1941   Spring: graduates from North Fulton High School in Buckhead.

Fall: enrolls in Darlington School, Rome, Georgia, from which he receives a certificate in spring 1942; wins award from Society of Colonial Daughters for his "Essay on Patriotism."

1942   Fall: enrolls at Clemson A & M College, where he majors in civil engineering and plays on the freshman football team.

3 December: leaves Clemson and begins thirteen months as an aviation cadet in Army Air Corps pilot training: stationed successively at Miami Beach, Florida; High Point, North Carolina; Nashville, Tennessee; Maxwell Field, Alabama; and Camden, South Carolina, where he washes out as a pilot.

1944   7 January–11 December: trains as night fighter radar observer; stationed successively at Fort Myers and Boca Raton, Florida; and Hammer Field, Fresno, California.

1945   30 January: joins 418th Night Fighter Squadron in the Philippines; subsequently serves on Okinawa and in Japan; earns four medals, including the Asiatic-Pacific Medal with seven battle stars, as well as two combat ribbons, and is promoted to second lieutenant.

1946   1 March: separates from military service.

Summer: enrolls on the GI Bill at Vanderbilt University as an English major; between 1947 and 1949 publishes four poems in the Vanderbilt student literary magazine, *Gadfly*.

1948   4 November: marries Maxine Syerson; shortly thereafter his poem "The Shark at the Window" is accepted by *The Sewanee Review* (appears in April–June 1951 issue).

1949   Receives BA in English, magna cum laude, Phi Beta Kappa from Vanderbilt.

1950   Receives MA in English from Vanderbilt.

       September–December: instructor of English at Rice Institute, Houston, Texas, until he is recalled to service during Korean conflict.

1951   10 March–9 August 1952: stateside service in training command of army air force; stationed in Alabama, Mississippi, and Texas.

       31 August: son, Christopher, is born.

1952   Fall: returns to Rice where he teaches until summer 1954.

1954   August–June 1955: in Europe on *Sewanee Review* Fellowship; he and his family live primarily at Cap d'Antibes on the French Riviera.

1955   September: joins English faculty at the University of Florida, Gainesville.

1956   April: leaves University of Florida teaching position because of dispute over his reading of his poem "The Father's Body" and his dissatisfaction with his salary; takes job as advertising copywriter at McCann Erickson in New York. For the next five years he builds a successful advertising career in both New York and Atlanta advertising agencies.

1958   18 August: second son, Kevin, is born.

       September: wins Union League Civic and Arts Foundation Prize from Union League of Chicago for "Dover: Believing in Kings."

1959   Fall: wins Longview Foundation Award; also wins Vachel Lindsay Prize for eight poems published in the July issue of *Poetry*.

1960   23 August: publication of *Into the Stone and Other Poems*, in *Poets of Today VII* (New York: Scribners).

1961   10 July: leaves his advertising position; during his five years in business, he publishes ten reviews and more than sixty poems in magazines and literary journals.

1962   15 February: publication of *Drowning with Others* (Middletown, CT.: Wesleyan University Press).

February: travels with his family to Europe on a Guggenheim Fellowship; spends from 6 April to 20 June in Positano, Italy.

Fall: lives in Atlanta.

1963   January: becomes poet-in-residence at Reed College in Portland, Oregon, where he remains until May 1964.

1964   27 February: publication of *Helmets* (Middletown, CT: Wesleyan University Press).

10 July?: publication of *The Suspect in Poetry* (Madison, MN: Sixties Press).

September?: publication of *Two Poems of the Air* (Portland, OR: Centicore Press).

September: becomes poet-in-residence at San Fernando Valley College, Northridge, California, where he remains until June 1965.

1965   Summer: teaches at the University of Wisconsin, Milwaukee.

23 September: publication of *Buckdancer's Choice* (Middletown, CT: Wesleyan University Press).

Fall: "barnstorms" for poetry.

1966   January: receives Melville Cane Award from the Poetry Society of America for *Buckdancer's Choice*.

February–March: serves as poet-in-residence at the University of Wisconsin, Madison.

15 March: presented the National Book Award for *Buckdancer's Choice*.

May: receives grant of $2,500 for creative work in literature by the National Institute of Arts and Letters.

July: teaches at the University of Wisconsin, Milwaukee.

August: becomes Consultant in Poetry at the Library of Congress; serves two terms ending in June 1968.

1967   24 April: publication of *Poems 1957–1967* (Middletown, CT: Wesleyan University Press).

1968   9 February?: publication of *Spinning the Crystal Ball* (Washington, DC: Library of Congress, [dated 1967]).

1 May: publication of *Babel to Byzantium: Poets and Poetry Now* (New York: Farrar, Straus and Giroux).

Summer: publication of *Metaphor as Pure Adventure* (Washington, DC: Library of Congress).

Summer: named poet-in-residence and professor of English at the University of South Carolina; because of contractual obligations with other schools, he does not begin teaching at the university until January 1969 but then remains on staff there until his death in 1997.

1969   July: covers Apollo 11 liftoff for *Life*.

1970   13 February: publication of *The Eye-Beaters, Blood, Victory, Madness, Buckhead and Mercy* (Garden City, NY: Doubleday).

23 March: publication of *Deliverance* (Boston: Houghton Mifflin).

6 November: publication of *Self-Interviews* (Garden City, NY: Doubleday).

1971   January: named poetry editor for *Esquire*; fills position until August 1977.

May: production begins on the movie version of *Deliverance*, for which Dickey writes the screenplay and plays the role of Sheriff Bullard.

14 July: publication of *Exchanges* (Bloomfield Hills, MI: Bruccoli Clark).

November: *Deliverance* wins *Prix Medicis* for best foreign-language book published in France.

10 December: publication of *Sorties* (Garden City, NY: Doubleday).

1972   18 May: inducted into the National Institute of Arts and Letters.

1974   10 October?: publication of *Jericho: The South Beheld*, text by JD, illustrations by Hubert Shuptrine (Birmingham, AL: Oxmoor House).

1976   May: television broadcast of Jack London's *The Call of the Wild* from script by Dickey.

21 September: publication of limited edition of *The Zodiac* (Bloomfield Hills, MI, and Columbia, SC: Bruccoli Clark).

28 October: Maxine Dickey dies.

5 November: publication of trade edition of *The Zodiac* (Garden City, NY: Doubleday).

30 December: marries Deborah Dodson.

1977   19 January: reads his poem "The Strength of Fields" at President Jimmy Carter's inauguration celebration.

1 February: publication of *The Strength of Fields* (single poem) (Bloomfield Hills, MI, and Columbia, SC: Bruccoli Clark).

Spring: represents President Carter at the opening of the Franklin-Jefferson Exhibit in Mexico City.

15 October: publication of *God's Images: The Bible, A New Vision*, text by JD, etchings by Marvin Hayes (Birmingham, AL: Oxmoor House).

1978   27 May?: publication of *The Enemy from Eden*, text by JD, illustrations by Ron Sauter (Northridge, CA: Lord John Press).

11 October: publication of *Tucky the Hunter*, text by JD, illustrations by Marie Angel (New York: Crown).

16 October: publication of *Veteran Birth: The Gadfly Poems, 1947–1949*, text by JD, illustrations by Robert Dance (Winston-Salem, NC: Palaemon Press).

4 December: publication of *In Pursuit of the Grey Soul* (Bloomfield Hills, MI, and Columbia, SC: Bruccoli Clark).

1979   5 May: publication of *Head-Deep in Strange Sounds: Free-Flight Improvisations from the UnEnglish* (Winston-Salem, NC: Palaemon Press).

July: publication of *The Water-Bug's Mittens: Ezra Pound: What We Can Use* (Moscow: University of Idaho).

14 December: publication of *The Strength of Fields* (collection) (Garden City, NY: Doubleday).

1980   1 March: publication of limited edition of *The Water-Bug's Mittens: Ezra Pound: What We Can Use* (Bloomfield Hills, MI, and Columbia, SC: Bruccoli Clark).

December: publication of *Scion* (Deerfield, MA/Dublin, Ireland: Deerfield Press/Gallery Press).

1981   15 March: publication of *The Starry Place Between the Antlers: Why I Live in South Carolina* (Bloomfield Hills, MI, and Columbia, SC: Bruccoli Clark).

17 May: birth of daughter, Bronwen.

?: publication of *The Early Motion* (Middletown, CT: Wesleyan University Press).

?: publication of *Falling, May Day Sermon, and Other Poems* (Middletown, CT: Wesleyan University Press).

Fall: receives the Levinson Prize for five *Puella* poems that had appeared in *Poetry*.

1982   4 January: publication of *Deliverance*, the screenplay (Carbondale and Edwardsville: Southern Illinois University Press).

29 April: publication of *Puella* (Garden City, NY: Doubleday).

December: publication of *Värmland* (Winston-Salem, NC: Palaemon Press).

1983   March: publication of *False Youth: Four Seasons* (Dallas, TX: Pressworks).

?: publication of *The Central Motion: Poems, 1968–1979* (Middletown, CT: Wesleyan University Press).

15 October: publication of *Night Hurdling: Poems, Essays, Conversations, Commencements, and Afterwords* (Bloomfield Hills, MI, and Columbia, SC: Bruccoli Clark).

1985   October: publication of limited edition of *Puella* (Tempe, AZ: Pyracantha Press).

1986   10 September: publication of *Bronwen, the Traw, and the Shape-Shifter*, text by JD, illustrations by Richard Jesse Watson (San Diego, New York, and London: Bruccoli Clark/Harcourt Brace Jovanovich).

1987   5 June: publication of *Alnilam* (Garden City, NY: Doubleday).

1988   18 May: induction into the American Academy of Arts and Letters.

October: publication of *Wayfarer: A Voice from the Southern Mountains*, text by JD, photographs by William A. Bake (Birmingham, AL: Oxmoor House).

1989   28 July: accepts appointment as judge for Yale Series of Younger Poets competition; serves as judge through 1996.

November: publication of *The Voiced Connections of James Dickey: Interviews and Conversations*, edited by Ronald Baughman (Columbia: University of South Carolina Press).

1990   November: publication of *The Eagle's Mile* (Hanover, NH, and London: Wesleyan University Press/University Press of New England).

1991   ?: publication of *Southern Light*, text by JD, photographs by James Valentine (Birmingham, AL: Oxmoor House).

1992   July: publication of *The Whole Motion: Collected Poems, 1945–1992* (Hanover, NH, and London: Wesleyan University Press/University Press of New England).

1993   September: publication of *To the White Sea* (Boston and New York: Houghton Mifflin).

1994   October: hospitalized with acute hepatitis.

1996   ?: publication of *Striking In: The Early Notebooks of James Dickey*, edited by Gordon Van Ness (Columbia and London: University of Missouri Press).

Spring: afflicted with fibrosis of the lungs.

June: receives Harriet Monroe Prize for lifetime achievement in poetry.

1997   14 January: teaches last class for the University of South Carolina.

19 January: dies.

1999   ?: publication of *Crux: The Letters of James Dickey*, edited by Matthew J. Bruccoli and Judith S. Baughman (New York: Knopf).

2003   ?: publication of *The One Voice of James Dickey: His Letters and Life, 1942–1969*, edited by Gordon Van Ness (Columbia and London: University of Missouri Press).

2004   ?: publication of *James Dickey: Classes on Modern Poets and the Art of Poetry*, edited by Donald Greiner (Columbia: University of South Carolina Press).

2005   ?: publication of *The One Voice of James Dickey: His Letters and Life, 1970–1997*, edited by Gordon Van Ness (Columbia and London: University of Missouri Press).

2013   ?: publication of *The Complete Poems of James Dickey*, edited by Ward Briggs (Columbia: University of South Carolina Press).

2015   ?: publication of *Death, and the Day's Light: Poems*, edited by Gordon Van Ness (Macon, GA: Mercer University Press).

CRITICAL BIBLIOGRAPHY

Adams, Phoebe. "Potpourri." *Atlantic Monthly* CCXXI (May 1968): 114.

Anonymous. *American Literature* XL (November 1968): 436.

———. "Bookmarks." *Prairie Schooner* XXXIX (Summer 1965): 176.

———. "Bronwen, the Traw, and the Shape-Shifter." *Kirkus* 54 (15 August 1986): 1289–90.

———. "James Dickey Dies at 73," *Richmond* (VA) *Times-Dispatch* (21 January 1997): B5.

———. "*Tucky the Hunter.*" *Kirkus* 46 (15 August 1978): 917.

Ashley, Dottie. "Dickey Honored." *The State* (4 December 1987): A16.

Ashley, Franklin. "For Newly Widowed Poet James Dickey, Deliverance Is a Bride Named Debbie." *People* (17 January 1977): 28, 30.

———. "James Dickey: The Art of Poetry XX." *Paris Review* 17 (Spring 1976): 54–88.

Balakian, Peter. "Poets of Empathy." *Literary Review: An International Journal of Contemporary Writing* 27/1 (1983): 135–46.

Baro, Gene. "The Sound of Three Poetic Voices." *New York Herald Tribune Book Review* (30 October 1910): 10.

Baughman, Ronald. "In Dickey's Latest, Blindness Opens a Man's Eyes to Life." Review of *Alnilam*, by James Dickey. *Philadelphia Inquirer* (31 May 1987): S1, 8.

———. *Understanding James Dickey.* Columbia: University of South Carolina Press, 1985.

Bennett, Joseph. "A Man with a Voice." *New York Times Book Review* (6 February 1966): 10.

Berry, Wendell. "James Dickey's New Book." *Poetry* 105 (November 1964): 130–32.

Biespel, David. "Poetry: James Dickey." *Washington Post Book World.* 8 November 1992: 8.

Bly, Robert. "The Collapse of James Dickey." *The Sixties* (April 1967): 70–79.

Bowers, Neal. *James Dickey: The Poet as Pitchman.* Columbia: University of Missouri Press, 1985.

Brandhorst, Craig. "Big Man on Campus." *The Carolinian* (Fall 2018): 22–26.

———. "Power Lunch & Poetry." *USC Times* (Spring 2018): 16–21.

Bruccoli, Matthew J. *Pages: The World of Books, Writers, and Writing.* Detroit, MI: Gale Research, 1976.

Burnshaw, Stanley. *The Seamless Web.* New York: Braziller, 1991.

Calhoun, Richard and Robert Hill. *James Dickey.* Boston: Twayne Publishers, 1983.

Campbell, Joseph. *The Hero with a Thousand Faces*. Princeton, NJ: Princeton University Press, 1973.

Carey, Bill. *Chancellors, Commodores, and Coeds: A History of Vanderbilt University*. Nashville, TN: Clearbrooke Press, 2003.

Carroll, Paul. "The Poet as Critic." *Chicago Review* XX (November 1968): 82–87.

Cassity, Turner. "Double Dutch: *The Strength of Fields* and *The Zodiac*." *Parnassas: Poetry in Review* (Spring/Summer 1981): 177–93.

Chappell, Fred. "Vatic Poesy." *The State* (9 December 1991): F5.

Clabough, Casey. *Elements: The Novels of James Dickey*. Macon, GA: Mercer University Press, 2002.

Conkin, Paul K. *Gone with the Ivy: A Biography of Vanderbilt University*. Knoxville: University of Tennessee Press, 1985.

Connell, Evan S. "*Deliverance*." *New York Times Book Review* (22 March 1970): 1, 23.

Conner, Sibella. "James Dickey: Riding the Flood Tide." *Richmond Times-Dispatch* (8 May 1994): G1, 4.

Conroy, Pat. "'It's All Real within the Dream.'" *The Carolinian* (April 1997): 24–25.

Critical Essays on James Dickey. Edited by Robert Kirschten. New York: G. K. Hall, 1994.

Crux: The Letters of James Dickey. Edited by Matthew J. Bruccoli and Judith Baughman. New York: Knopf, 1994.

Davidson, Donald. *The Attack on Leviathan*. London and New York: Routledge, 2017.

Davidson, Donald, John Gould Fletcher, Henry Blue Kline, Lyle H. Lanier, Andrew Nelson Lytle, Herman Clarence Nixon, Frank Lawrence Owsley, John Crowe Ransom, Allen Tate, John Donald Wade, Robert Penn Warren, and Stark Young. *I'll Take My Stand: The South and the Agrarian Tradition*. Baton Rouge and London: Louisiana State University Press, 1977.

Davison, Peter. "The Difficulties of Being Major: The Poetry of Robert Lowell and James Dickey." *Atlantic Monthly* 220 (October 1967): 116–21.

DeCandido, GraceAnne. "*God's Images: The Bible—A New Vision*." *Library Journal* 103 (15 January 1987): 154.

DeMott, Benjamin. "The 'More Life' School and James Dickey." *Saturday Review* (28 March 1970): 25–26, 38.

Dickey, Bronwen. "He Caught the Dream." *Newsweek* (24 March 1997): 19.

Dickey, Christopher. "Foreword." *Death, and the Day's Light*. Macon, GA: Mercer University Press, 2015: ix–xi.

———. "Poems and Memories of James Dickey." *Here and Now* (12 April 2013). https://www.wbur.org/hereandnow/2013/04/12/james-dickey-poems (accessed February 2020).

———. *Summer of Deliverance: A Memoir of Father and Son.* New York: Simon & Schuster, 1998.

———. "23 Years after My Father's Death: A Poet's Family Album." *James Dickey: Deep Deliverance* (blog), 19 January 2020. http://jamesdickey.blog-spot.com/2020/01/22-years-after-my-fathers-death.html (accessed February 2020).

Donoghue, Denis. "The Good Old Complex Fate." *Hudson Review* 17 (Summer 1964): 267–77.

Dupee, F. W. "The Muse as House Guest." *Partisan Review* 25/3 (Summer 1958): 454–60.

Egerton, John. *Speak Now Against the Day: The Generation before the Civil Rights Movement in the South.* New York: Knopf, 1994.

Evans, Eli. "The South the South Sees: *Jericho.*" *New York Times Book Review* (9 February 1975): 4–5.

Fields, Kenneth. "Strategies of Criticism." *Southern Review* II (Autumn 1966): 967–75.

Flint, R. W. "Poetry Chronicle." *Partisan Review* XXIX (Spring 1962): 290–92.

Francis, H. E. "Dickey Shows New Growth in Meaning Chant." *Atlanta Journal-Constitution.* Review of *Drowning with Others*, by James Dickey (25 February 1962): D6.

Gioia, Dana. *Can Poetry Matter?* St. Paul, MN: Graywolf Press, 1992.

———. "'How Nice to Meet You, Mr. Dickey.'" *The American Scholar* (Winter 2002): 83–88.

Giorella, Sibella. "Seeking His Deliverance." *Richmond Times-Dispatch* (24 January 1997): C1, 3.

Goodman, Paul. *Growing Up Absurd: Problems of Youth in a Disorganized Society.* New York: Vintage, 1960.

Greiner, Donald. "Making the Truth: James Dickey's Last Major Interview." *James Dickey Newsletter* 23/1 (Fall 2006): 1–25.

Gwynn, R. S. "Runaway Cannons: At War with Dickey and Bly." *The Sewanee Review* CII/I (Winter 1994): 152–60.

Hart, Henry. *James Dickey: The World as a Lie.* New York: Picador, 2000.

Hartung, Anne. "Dickey Plays 'Metaphysical Scrabble Game.'" *Anderson Independent-Mail* (29 June 1986): A1–2.

Havird, David. "A 'Clamorous Amassment' Beyond-Speech Golden: *The Complete Poems of James Dickey.*" *James Dickey Newsletter.* Web. 27.2 (2013).

———"In and Out of Class with James Dickey." *Virginia Quarterly Review* 76 (Summer 2000): 455–469. Rpt. In *Weathering: Poems and Recollection.* Macon, GA: Mercer UP, 2020: 57-72.

Hill, Jane. "Relinquishing Power and Light: Dickey's Legacy and the Woman Question." *James Dickey Newsletter* 15/2 (Spring 1999): 2–12.

Hyman, Stanley Edgar. "Myth, Ritual, and Nonsense." *Kenyon Review* (Summer 1949): 455–75.

Hynes, Samuel. *Flights of Passage: Reflections of a World War II Aviator.* New York and Annapolis: Frederic C. Beil and Naval Institute Press, 1988.

The Imagination as Glory: The Poetry of James Dickey. Edited by Bruce Weigl and
    T. R. Hummer. Urbanna and Chicago: University of Illinois Press, 1984.
James Dickey: Classes on Modern Poets and the Art of Poetry. Edited by Donald
    Greiner. Columbia: University of South Carolina Press, 2004.
"James Dickey Dies at 73." *Richmond* (VA) *Times-Dispatch* (21 January 1997): B2.
The James Dickey Reader. Edited by Henry Hart. New York: Simon and Schuster,
    1999.
Jarrell, Randall. "The Obscurity of the Poet." *Partisan Review* 18/1 (January/Febru-
    ary 1951): 66–81.
Kalstone, David. *"Sorties."* *New York Times Book Review* (23 January 1972): 6, 24.
Kaye, Howard. "Why Review Poetry." *New Republic* CLVIII (29 June 1968): 28–29.
Kennedy, X. J. "Joys, Griefs, and 'All Things Innocent, Hapless, Forsaken.'" *New
    York Times Book Review* (23 August 1964): 5.
Kerley, Gary. "Dickey Delivers Second Novel." Review of *Alnilam,* by James Dickey.
    Gainesville (GA) *Times* (19 July 1987): E5.
Kierkegaard, Soren. *Fear and Trembling and the Sickness unto Death.* Princeton and
    Oxford: Princeton University Press, 2013.
Lask, Thomas. "Serene and Star-Crazed." Review of *The Zodiac,* by James Dickey.
    New York Times (22 January 1977): 19.
———. "Writer Turned Reader." Review of *Babel to Byzantium,* by James Dickey.
    New York Times (10 May 1968): M45.
Lehmann-Haupt, Christopher. "From Man to Beast of Prey." *New York Times* (13
    September 1993): C17.
Leibowitz, Herbert. "The Moiling of Secret Forces: The Eye-Beaters, Blood, Vic-
    tory, Madness, Buckhead and Mercy." *New York Times Book Review* (8 No-
    vember 1970): 20, 22.
Lieberman, Laurence. "The Worldly Mystic." *Hudson Review* 20 (Autumn 1967):
    513–20.
Loercher, Diana. "Georgia Poet Who Cast Carter as a Mythical Hero." *Christian
    Science Monitor* (5 October 1977): 19.
Logue, John. "Books about the South." *Southern Living* 9 (January 1979): 68.
———. "Books about the South." *Southern Living* (October 1993): 78.
Macaulay, David. "Bronwen, the Traw, and the Shape-Shifter." *New York Times
    Book Review* (8 March 1987): 31.
Martz, Louis. "Recent Poetry: The Elegiac Mode." *Yale Review* LIV (December
    1964): 285–98.
McGill, Ralph. *The South and the Southerner.* Boston: Little Brown and Company,
    1964.
Meyers, Jeffrey. "What the Monsters Know." *New Criterion* 18/9 (May 2000): 69–
    74.
Miller, Douglas and Marion Nowak. *The Fifties: The Way We Really Were.* Gar-
    den City, NY: Doubleday, 1977.

Mills, Ralph. "Brilliant Essays on Contemporary Poets." Review of *Babel to Byzantium*, by James Dickey. *Chicago Sun Times*. Book Week (5 May 1968): 4.

Mitgang, Herbert. "Man, Nature, and Everyday Activities in Verse." *New York Times* (27 October 1990): 16.

Monagham, Charles. "*Buckdancer's Choice*." *Commonweal* LXXXIV (15 April 1966): 120–22.

Morris, Christopher. "Dark Night of the Flesh: The Apotheosis of the Bestial in James Dickey's *The Zodiac*." *Contemporary Poetry* 4/4 (1982): 31–47.

New Poets of England and America. Edited by Donald Hall, Robert Pack, and Louis Simpson. New York: Meridian Books, 1957.

Norton, John. "Ego-Tripping with James Dickey." *Osceola* (23 May 1972): 10–11.

Oates, Joyce Carol. "Out of Stone into Flesh: The Imagination of James Dickey." *Modern Poetry Studies* 5/2 (1974): 97–144.

Parini, Jay. "James Dickey's Massive and Mystifying *Alnilam*." *USA Today* (29 May 1987): 70.

Pearson, Richard. "James Dickey Dies: Author of *Deliverance*." *Washington Post* (21 January 1997): B5.

Price, Reynolds. "James Dickey, XL." *New York Times Book Review* (23 March 1997): 31.

Priestley, J. B. *Man & Time*. New York: Crescent Books, 1989.

Redman, George. "A New Beast Slouches toward Bethlehem." *Portfolio* (November 1980): 10–14.

Robertson, Nan. "Parnassus-on-Potomac: Poets Celebrate English." *New York Times* (31 March 1987): C13.

Sante, Luc. "Corporate Culture: Gotham Book Mart & Gallery Inc." *Manhattan, inc.* (May 1985): np.

Schwartz, Delmore. "The Isolation of Modern Poetry." *Kenyon Review* 3 (Spring 1941): 209–20.

———. "The Literary Dictatorship of T. S. Eliot." *Partisan Review* 16/2 (February/March 1949): 119–37.

———. "The Present State of Poetry." *American Poetry at Mid-Century*. Edited by Delmore Schwartz, John Crowe Ransom, and John Hall Wheelock. Washington, DC: Library of Congress, 1958: 15–31.

"Shantif, Shantif, Shantif: Has the Reader Any Rights before the Bar of Literature." Review of *The Wasteland*, by T. S. Eliot. *Time* (3 March 1920): 12.

Shaw, Robert B. "Poets in Midstream." *Poetry* 118 (July 1971): 228–33.

Siddons, Anne Rivers. *Peachtree Road*. New York: Harper & Row, 1988.

Simon, John. "More Brass Than Enduring." *Hudson Review* XV (Autumn 1962): 455–68.

Skipp, Francis. "James Dickey's *The Zodiac*: The Heart of the Matter." *Concerning Poetry* 14/1 (1981): 1–10.

Skow, John. "Alone and on the Run." *Time* (11 October 1993): 88.

Smith, Dave. "Afterword." *Death, and the Day's Light*. Edited by Gordon Van Ness. Macon, GA: Mercer University Press, 2015: 79–88.

———. "The Strength of James Dickey." *Poetry* 137 (March 1981): 349–58.

Spears, Monroe. "James Dickey's Poetry." *The Southern Review* 30/4 (Fall 1994): 751.

Sponhour, Michael. "Literary Veterans of World War II Revile Revisionists." *The State* (14 April 1995): A1.

Sporburg, Anne. "Bronwen, the Traw, and the Shape-Shifter." James Dickey Newsletter 4 (Fall 1987): 25–38.

Starr, William. "American Poet Ezra Pound Dies." *The State* (2 November 1972): A1, 7.

———. "James Dickey." *The State* (12 July 1992): F1.

———. "Literary Giant Allen Tate Dies." *The State* (10 February 1979): A15.

Stearns, Harold. *Civilization in the United States: An Inquiry by Thirty Americans*. New York: Harcourt Brace and Company, 1922.

Striking In: The Early Notebooks of James Dickey. Edited by Gordon Van Ness. Columbia and London: University of Missouri Press, 1996.

Suarez, Ernest. "An Interview with James Dickey." *Contemporary Literature* 31/2 (1990): 117–32.

———. *James Dickey and the Politics of Canon: Assessing the Savage Ideal*. Columbia and London: University of Missouri Press, 1993.

Thompson, John. "A Catalogue of Poets." *Hudson Review* XIII (Winter 1960–1961): 618–25.

Tiejens, Eunice. "The End of Ezra Pound." *Poetry* (April 1942): 38–40.

Tillich, Paul. *The Courage to Be*. New Haven and London: Yale University Press, 1952.

Towers, Robert. "Prometheus Blind." Review of *Alnilam*, by James Dickey. *New York Times Book Review* (21 June 1987): 7.

Trueheart, Charles. "The Author, Turning to Flight, and Philosophy, in His Novel *Alnilam*." Review of *Alnilam*, by James Dickey. *The Washington Post* (24 May 1987): F6.

Van Ness, Gordon. "A Different Kind of Deliverance." *State Magazine* (25 January 1987): 8–11.

———. "Living beyond Recall." *James Dickey Newsletter* 3 (Spring 1987): 17–26.

———. *The One Voice of James Dickey: His Letters and Life, 1942–1969*. Vol. I. Columbia and London: University of Missouri Press, 2003.

———. *The One Voice of James Dickey: His Letters and Life, 1970–1997*. Vol. II. Columbia and London: University of Missouri Press, 2005.

———. Personal interview with James Dickey, 13 September 1990.

———. Personal interview with James Dickey, 20 March 1987.

The Voiced Connections of James Dickey: Interviews and Conversations. Edited by Ronald Baughman. Columbia: University of South Carolina Press, 1989.

Walker, Sue. "Playing with Dolls: Girls Male-Imagined in James Dickey's *Puella.*" *James Dickey Newsletter* 15/1 (Fall 1998): 2–9.

Warren, Robert Penn. "A Poem about the Ambition of Poetry: *The Zodiac.*" *New York Times Book Review* (14 November 1976): 8.

Watson, Robert. "Two Books of Criticism." *Poetry* CVII (February 1966): 332–33.

Weatherby, H. L. "The Way of Exchange in James Dickey's Poetry." *The Sewanee Review* 74 (Summer 1966): 669–80.

Welch, Rodney. "The Haggard Heroes Recall Their Lost Pal." *Free Times* (19–25 April 2000): 25, 28–34.

Weldon Kees and the Midcentury Generation: Letters, 1935–1955. Edited by Robert E. Knoll. Lincoln and London: University of Nebraska Press, 1986.

Whalen, Kathleen. "Bronwen, the Traw, and the Shape-Shifter." *School Library Journal* 33 (October 1986): 173.

Wilson, Edmund. *The Fifties: From the Notebooks and Diaries of the Period.* Edited by Leon Edel. New York: Farrar, Straus and Giroux, 1986.

Wimsatt, Margaret. "*Self-Interviews.*" *Commonweal* 93 (19 February 1971): 501–503.

Wright, James. "Shelf of New Poets." *Poetry* (December 1961): 178–83.

Yardley, Jonathan. "The Great Escape." *Washington Post Book World* (29 August 1993): 3.

PRIMARY BIBLIOGRAPHY

WORKS BY JAMES DICKEY

Alnilam. Garden City, NY: Doubleday, 1987.

Babel to Byzantium: Poets & Poetry Now. New York: Farrar, Straus and Giroux, 1968.

Bronwen, the Traw, and the Shape-Shifter. San Diego, New York, and London: Bruccoli Clark and Harcourt Brace Jovanovich, 1986.

Buckdancer's Choice. Middletown, CT: Wesleyan University Press, 1965.

The Central Motion: Poems, 1968–1979. Middletown, CT: Wesleyan University Press, 1983.

"Clarksville Man Competent Stylist," Review of *The Last Husband and Other Stories*, by ed. William Humphrey. *The Houston Post* (12 April 1953): Sec. 7, p. 7.

"Collection Includes Aiken's Early Work," Review of *Collected Poems*, by ed. Conrad Aiken, *The Houston Post* (18 October 1953): Sec.6, p. 5.

The Complete Poems of James Dickey. Edited by Ward Briggs. Columbia: University of South Carolina Press, 2013.

"Cosmic Deliverance." *Halley's Comet*. Commemorative Issue. Prestige Publications, 1986: 8–9.

Death, and the Day's Light. Edited by Gordon Van Ness. Macon, GA: Mercer University Press, 2015.

Deliverance. Boston: Houghton Mifflin, 1970.

Drowning with Others. Middletown, CT: Wesleyan University Press, 1962.

The Eagle's Mile. Hanover and London: Wesleyan University Press and University Press of New England, 1990.

The Early Motion: Drowning with Others and Helmets. Middletown, CT: Wesleyan University Press, 1981.

The Enemy from Eden. Northridge, CA: Lord Jim Press, 1978.

The Entrance to the Honeycomb. Irvin Department of Rare Books and Special Collections. Ernest F. Hollings Library. University of South Carolina. Typescript.

The Eye-Beaters, Blood, Victory, Madness, Buckhead and Mercy. Garden City, NY: Doubleday, 1970.

"Foreword." *South Carolina: The Natural History*. Columbia: University of South Carolina Press, 1989: 9–10.

From the Green Horseshoe. Columbia: University of South Carolina Press, 1987.

God's Images: The Bible—A New Vision. Birmingham, AL: Oxmoor House, 1977.

Head-Deep in Strange Sounds. Charlotte, NC: Palaemon Press, 1969.
Helmets. Middletown, CT: Wesleyan University Press, 1964.
History of the 418th Night Fighter Squadron. Irvin Department of Rare Books and
	Special Collections. Ernest F. Hollings Library. University of South Caro-
	lina. Typescript.
How to Enjoy Poetry. Broadside. International Paper Company, 1982.
In Pursuit of the Grey Soul. Columbia, SC, and Bloomfield Hills, MI: Bruccoli
	Clark, 1978.
"International Magazine Presents Good Cross Section." Review of *Botteghe Os-
	cure XII*. *The Houston Post* (14 February 1954): Sec. 7, p.7.
"In the Presence of Anthologies." *The Sewanee Review* 66 (April–June 1958):
	294–314.
Into the Stone and Other Poems, in *Poems of Today VII*. Edited by John Hall
	Wheelock. New York: Scribner's, 1960.
"Jean Stafford's Inventive Stories." Review of *Children Are Bored on Sunday*, by
	Jean Stafford. *The Houston Post* (17 May 1953): Sec. 7, p.7.
Jericho: The South Beheld. Birmingham, AL: Oxmoor House, 1974.
"LIGHTNINGS, or *Visuals*." *James Dickey Newsletter* 8/2 (Spring 1992): 2–12.
Night Hurdling: Poems, Essays, Conversations, Commencements, and Afterwords.
	Columbia, SC, and Bloomfield Hills, MI: Bruccoli Clark, 1983.
The Owl King. New York: Red Angel Press, 1977.
Poems 1957–1967. Middletown, CT: Wesleyan University Press, 1967.
"Poetical Remains." Rose Manuscript, Archives, and Rare Book Library. Emory
	University. Typescript.
"Prospectus for 'The Spell.'" Rose Manuscript, Archives, and Rare Book Li-
	brary. Emory University. Typescript.
Puella. Garden City, NY: Doubleday, 1982.
Scion. Deerfield, MA: Deerfield Press, 1980.
Self-Interviews. Garden City, NY: Doubleday, 1970.
Sorties. Garden City, NY: Doubleday, 1971.
Southern Light. Birmingham, AL: Oxmoor House, 1991.
The Starry Place between the Antlers. Columbia, SC: Bruccoli Clark, 1981.
The Strength of Fields. Garden City, NY: Doubleday, 1979.
The Suspect in Poetry. Madison, MN: Sixties, 1964.
"Symbol and Imagery in the Shorter Poems of Herman Melville." MA thesis,
	Vanderbilt University, Nashville, 1950.
"Synopsis for Projected Movie to Be Called 'The Spell.'" Rose Manuscript, Ar-
	chives, and Rare Book Library. Emory University. Typescript.
"The Total Act." *The Seamless Web*, by Stanley Burnshaw. New York: Braziller,
	1991: vii–x.
To the White Sea. Boston and New York: Houghton Mifflin, 1993.
Tucky the Hunter. New York: Crown, 1978.
Two Poems of the Air. Portland, OR: Centimore Press, 1964.

Veteran Birth: The Gadfly Poems, 1947–1949. Charlotte, NC: Palaemon Press, 1978.

Wayfarer: A Voice from the Southern Mountains. Birmingham, AL: Oxmoor House, 1988.

The Weather of the Valley: Reflections on the Soul and Its Making. Columbia: University of South Carolina Press, 1998.

The Whole Motion. Hanover and London: Wesleyan University Press and University Press of New England, 1992.

The Zodiac. Garden City, NY: Doubleday, 1976.

INDEX

Index

Index

Index

Index

Index

Index

Index

Index

Index